T0360602

Theory and Programming of
Computable General Equilibrium (CGE) Models

A Textbook for Beginners

Theory and Programming of
Computable General Equilibrium (CGE) Models
A Textbook for Beginners

Gene H Chang

 **World Scientific**

NEW JERSEY · LONDON · SINGAPORE · BEIJING · SHANGHAI · HONG KONG · TAIPEI · CHENNAI · TOKYO

Published by

World Scientific Publishing Co. Pte. Ltd.

5 Toh Tuck Link, Singapore 596224

USA office: 27 Warren Street, Suite 401-402, Hackensack, NJ 07601

UK office: 57 Shelton Street, Covent Garden, London WC2H 9HE

Library of Congress Cataloging-in-Publication Data
Names: Chang, Gene H., author.
Title: Theory and programming of computable general equilibrium (CGE) models :
      a textbook for beginners / Gene H. Chang.
Description: New Jersey : World Scientific, [2022] | Includes bibliographical references and index.
Identifiers: LCCN 2021035001 | ISBN 9789811238970 (hardcover) |
      ISBN 9789811238987 (ebook for institutions) | ISBN 9789811238994 (ebook for individuals)
Subjects: LCSH: Computable general equilibrium models--Textbooks.
Classification: LCC HB141.3.C66 C43 2022 | DDC 330.01/5195--dc23
LC record available at https://lccn.loc.gov/2021035001

British Library Cataloguing-in-Publication Data
A catalogue record for this book is available from the British Library.

For any available supplementary material, please visit
https://www.worldscientific.com/worldscibooks/10.1142/12335#t=suppl

Desk Editors: Balamurugan Rajendran/Sylvia Koh

Typeset by Stallion Press
Email: enquiries@stallionpress.com

Printed in Singapore

To my mother Huang Jiahui and my family

Preface

This book is a true textbook for beginners on the theory and programming of Computable General Equilibrium models, rather than a byproduct of a CGE research monograph. It has been completely rewritten in English from an earlier book I published in Chinese, which has become the most popular CGE textbook among graduate students and scholars in China.

A decade ago, as a part of international exchange programs supported by the Ford Foundation, I taught CGE modeling to a group of economics students in China. They were interested in using CGE models for their research on the national economy including fiscal and public policies, but had no background at all in the subject. The group was a mix of undergraduate and graduate students with typically three semesters of calculus and linear algebra. They had taken intermediate microeconomics and macroeconomics; and most had one semester of advanced microeconomics. None had training in computer programming. Their background is similar to the students in a typical American Master's program in economics.

How to teach these beginners in CGE modeling? The most effective way is to follow the standard format of an introductory course, including giving lectures, distributing study notes, illustrating the theory by giving examples and diagrams, demonstrating and practicing the computer program GAMS in class, and assigning after-class exercises and homework. Based on student feedback, I repeatedly revised the lecture notes and other course materials, and eventually drew on this experience to write the first edition of a CGE textbook in Chinese. The book was well received among university students and policy researchers — it sold out quickly. The second edition was published in 2017 and also sold out; the Chinese publisher is currently reprinting the book. Meanwhile, World Scientific Publishing invited me to write a CGE textbook in English. Due to personal reasons, it took a long time to complete, but the additional feedback during these years from readers of the Chinese version and teaching CGE courses means this English book reflects the cumulative improvements in the CGE teaching materials. In addition, the content and examples in the book have been substantially changed to reflect real-world cases in the U.S. and other countries to meet the demand of global students.

My thanks go to a long list of people who helped me prepare and improve this book although they are not all named here. They include everyone I acknowledged in the Chinese books, plus many readers and students who wrote to me indicating errors and making suggestions (address: studycge@gmail.com). In preparing this English version, I particularly thank Sherman Robinson and Zhi Wang for their help and communication on modeling, Ye Chen for helpful discussions on various related issues, and Elaine Chang for proofreading. I also thank the publisher for their professional enthusiasm and patience. Without all these people, this book would not exist.

About the Author

 **Gene Chang** is Professor Emeritus of Economics at the University of Toledo, USA. He received a B.A. from Fudan University, China; M.A. from UC Berkeley; and Ph.D. in Economics from the University of Michigan. He was the Co-Editor of *China Economic Review* and held research, visiting, teaching and honorary positions at the World Bank, Harvard University, the Chinese University of Hong Kong, Fudan University, Shanghai University of Finance and Economics, University of International Business and Economics, China, and the University of Warsaw in Poland.

Contents

Chapter 13.   Activities, Trade and Transport Margins   237

Chapter 14.   CGE Models in Open Economies   263

Chapter 15.   Complexities in Data and Modeling   293

Chapter 1

Introduction

Computable General Equilibrium (CGE) models, also referred to as Applied General Equilibrium (AGE) Models, are important quantitative research instruments for economic and public policy issues. CGE models simulate the interdependent relationships among various sectors and national accounts in the whole economy and analyze the impacts of external factors, such as policy changes, on economic variables in the system. CGE models are widely used in the areas of macroeconomics, international trade, agriculture, environment, fiscal expenditure and taxation, and public affairs.

Empirical research in economics and public affairs heavily relies on quantitative approaches, which have the benefits of providing numerical details of the economy and quantitative analysis of possible changes. Referring to empirical research in economics, many people would think of an econometric model with regressions or other statistical techniques. However, CGE is different from a typical econometric model, in terms of the subject, scope, basic model structure and technique used. The subjects of most econometric empirical researches may be grouped into three dimensions. The first group, including dynamic models and time series analyzes, studies changes in economic variables over time. The second group, including spatial models in econometrics and economic geography, studies changes in variables across spaces and geographic locations. The third group, including panel analysis models, studies the differences in variables across sections or individuals. Econometric research can be quite microeconomics-scoped, for instance, a study on the influence of temperature changes in the ice cream market. The data for an econometric study must have many observations for each variable to run regression so statistical inferences can be drawn.

Differing from the above econometric models, CGE models study the interrelationships among all sectors and national accounts in the entire economy. Structurally, a CGE model is a simultaneous non-linear equation system that describes these multiple sectors and national accounts. Similar research models in this group include some macroeconomic models and input–output models. A CGE model can easily have thousands of equations and variables, which is huge compared to most econometric or macroeconomic models. Because the system is so big, no datasets have the number of observations to give enough degrees of freedom to draw statistical inferences for each variable in a CGE model. Instead, a CGE model uses a data table of national accounts, called SAM table, as the database; constructs the model by assumptions and other techniques; and simulates the economy and analyzes the changes in these accounts from external shocks by using computer optimization programs.

The interdependence of sectors and accounts in the economy has been long recognized in economics. For instance, suppose Detroit increases automobile production for export. Then the economy needs more steel as inputs, and, to produce more steel, it needs more coal. To produce more coal, it needs to expand highways to reduce traffic congestion. Then it needs more cement and steel for construction, more transportation trucks, and so on. Changes in the commodity outputs would also affect the financial accounts. Importing iron ore requires foreign exchange. Constructing highways needs government funding. Changes in income affect consumption and employment, as well as the government's fiscal revenue, resulting in changes in commodity demands. These changes in the supplies and demands of commodities would affect prices, interest rates, exchange rates and so on. All these variables are interdependent in the economy-wide network.

The direct relationship of the activities between two sectors or accounts is called "linkage". An activity in one account causes changes in other accounts, which are called "spillover effects". When a spillover effect to another account later impacts the original account, it is a "feedback". The complex and multiple spillovers and feedbacks among all the accounts are the interdependence features of the national economy and CGE models.

Compared with a standard macroeconomic model, a CGE model typically has many more details in the national accounts. On the expenditure side, instead of aggregate consumption or aggregate investment, a CGE model may have breakdown information for consumption and investment from various groups of households and enterprises. It may have various sub-accounts of government expenditure, exports and imports. On the production side, instead of a single production with factors in typical macroeconomic models, a CGE model has not only labor, capital and other factors, but also intermediate inputs, in a nested structure of production functions.

The early research on multi-sectoral interdependent relationships is the input–output model, also known as the Leontief model. An input–output model assumes fixed proportions among the quantities of inputs and outputs in all sectors. It has a simultaneous linear equation system to characterize production in the entire economy. The application of the input–output model is to solve this linear equation system based on input–output table data and simulate changes. Because of the fixed proportion setup, input–output models do not allow for substitution effects among the inputs in production, even if the input prices change. A CGE model can have the same details of the inputs in production as an input–output model. In addition, a CGE model can simulate complex and flexible non-linear relationships of inputs and outputs, such as substitution among the inputs as their relative prices change, while an input–output model cannot.

The most important deficiency of input–output models is that they only address the production side, but not the complete chart of all flows in the economy. An input–output model does not cover the relationships from factor supply to income, from income to demand, etc. In other words, an input–output model is only of a partial equilibrium in the production process, while a CGE model is of the general equilibrium in the whole economy. A CGE model includes supplies and demands in both commodity and factor markets. It includes other national accounts. Prices in CGE are variables rather than constants. More important, as a general equilibrium model, CGE must address all flows of the entire economy, not only from inputs to outputs in the production process, but also from income to spending in the consumption process by households. A more comprehensive CGE model also includes the government, foreign sectors and other institutions in the economy.

The data foundation of a CGE model is the Social Accounting Matrix (SAM) table. A SAM table includes the data from national accounts. It includes input–output data in production, data about households, businesses, governments, external sector accounts such as current and capital accounts, taxation, fiscal expenditures, transfer payments, savings and investment, etc. The United Nations (2008) has set up a standard for these accounts in its publication System of National Accounts (SNA). A SAM table should follow the SNA standard but modifications are allowed in constructing SAM tables so long as they are justified in economics. Based on the SAM table, a CGE model uses modern general equilibrium theory to establish a system of simultaneous non-linear equations to describe the economy.

The first CGE modeling work was published by Norwegian economist Leif Johansen (Johansen, 1960). Since then, the field has grown rapidly, with thousands of economists and policy researchers all over the world now working on CGE modeling. CGE models are widely used in economics and public administration. They are applied in macroeconomic accounts balancing, as well as policy research in international trade, employment, tax reform and impact, industrial policy, energy and natural resources, social security, environment, sustainable economic development, public expenditure and health issues. For example, Shoven and Whalley (1973, 1984) use a CGE model to study tax policy issues in the United States and other countries. Wang *et al.* (2004) apply a CGE model to examine the social security issue in China. Recently, much CGE research has been done in the environmental area, on topics such as carbon taxes, water resource, etc. One example is the SAGE model by the Environmental Protection Agency (2019) in the U.S. A handbook edited by Dixon and Jorgenson (2013) collects the surveys of CGE modeling with definitive sources and references in various subjects.

This book adopts a typical textbook approach and format for CGE beginners to learn and master the subject. It explains the economics theory behind the CGE model structure. The learning proceeds from basic economic theories to advanced topics, from simple to more comprehensive CGE structures, step by step. Each chapter reviews relevant economic theories; illustrates new material with examples, diagrams and exercises; and provides the mathematical models along with the GAMS computer programming codes. At the end of a chapter, exercises are assigned for practice and enhancing understanding. After completing this book, students shall understand a standard CGE model structure represented in the IFPRI[1] model by Lofgren *et al.* (2002) and master the basics of CGE modeling and programming. They are expected to be able to design a standard CGE model, write GAMS

---

[1]IFPRI stands for International Food Policy Research Institute.

program for simulation, and analyze policy impacts for their research topics. With this background, they can continue to more advanced topics in CGE research.

Based on my teaching experiences on the subject in the U.S. and China, I found that it was easier for students to start with input–output models due to the similarities between the input–output models and CGE in dealing with matrix data and simultaneous equation systems. Therefore, in this book, we start with an input–output model to familiarize ourselves with the multi-sectoral model structure, basic GAMS program language, and the SAM. Next we review the general equilibrium theory so we can explain the theory behind the CGE model structure. Concluding this training, we move to CGE modeling.

While the book is an introduction to CGE modeling, it still expects the readers to have adequate background in economics and mathematics — the equivalent to and above the junior year level of undergraduate economics, plus solid training in calculus and linear algebra. It would be very helpful if the readers have also taken advanced microeconomics. Economics background is needed to understand the setup of the CGE structure and macro closures. Advanced microeconomics background will help students understand various forms of equations in the CGE literature. Some mathematics students taking my CGE classes had no problems with the technical side of mathematics and computer programming, but their lack of understanding of economics caused their CGE models to fail in late stages. If you do not have advanced microeconomics training, you will have to make up the deficiency in economics in due course as you study this book.

One difficulty with learning CGE modeling is the various styles and forms used by different individual scholars in the past. There are countless publications in CGE literature, yet these publications often do not provide the entire set of models and computer program codes (mostly due to length) unless the readers request them from the authors. Even if a reader is lucky enough to obtain the computer program of the model, it is still very difficult for a beginner to understand the setup. Different authors often use different expressions, styles, and functional forms for the same mathematical nature, but a beginner will often mistake them for different contents in nature. For example, as illustrated in Section 7.4, for the production module, some scholars use explicit conditional input demand functions, while others use a production function plus the first-order condition of optimal factor uses. They appear quite different although they are the same in nature and can be derived from each other. Use of different notations by different scholars for the same variables often confuses readers, too. This book will explain these typical mathematical variants in CGE literature and show to the readers they are actually the same. This book adopts commonly used symbols and notations for variables in the economics textbooks, and, commonly used variable names for CGE models in the GAMS program (such as in the IFPRI model). This makes readers easier to recognize them and remember.

CGE models have two major styles (schools): the American style and the Australian style. While in theory they are the same, the mathematical forms of these two styles are structurally different. The American genre is a direct copy of mathematical models from the economics theory. The functions in the computer programs are the same as those mathematical functions in the economic models. They are standard, intuitive and concise, easily interpretable and convenient to learn. Searching the numerical solutions of a model is performed by available computer programs. Nowadays, a number of software (such as GAMS) with optimization algorithms are capable of doing these jobs. It is easier to use the American style to write a complete new CGE model with any special macroeconomic closure to fit the particular research needs.

The Australian genre was originated from the Johansen model. It needs to transform the original functions in the model by linearization and taking percentage terms. The mathematical expressions especially for complex functions are not intuitive for beginners to match them to the original mathematical models. The Australian style uses the GEMPACK programming language. The advantage of the Australian style model is that it does not require powerful computer software to solve a large set of non-linear equation systems, which was important for Johansen in his time. Another advantage, as is often said but not verified, is running the Australian model is easier to converge to the solution. Both advantages are not obvious today as computers and solver programs are powerful enough for the American style models. However, many existing CGE models in the GTAP, a global network for CGE researchers on international policy issues, use the Australian genre and the GEMPACK program. They are called GTAP models. They are quite comprehensive and are extensively used globally. Therefore, for convenience and communication, many scholars use the ready-made GEMPACK CGE models to study trade, environment and other issues.

This book adopts the American style to take advantage of the ease and intuitiveness in learning the theory, as well as advantage of the flexibility to adapt to different real-world cases. After finishing this book, if the reader needs to learn the Australian style models and write a GEMPACK program, the background gained here will be very helpful in studying the GEMPACK CGE programs. A helpful manual for readers of this book to learn GEMPACK is *Introduction to GEMPACK for GAMS Users* by Kohlhaas and Person (2002).

Ideally, we wish a CGE model can be explained first by the mathematical equations, then the corresponding GAMS program. This would help the readers understand the structure of the model before they get familiar with the GAMS language. In this book, we will do our best to present our discussion in this way. When a new topic is presented in mathematics in a chapter, the corresponding GAMS program is provided afterward with an explanation of the GAMS language codes. The readers can learn GAMS by first copying the attached GAMS programs, then running the program successfully (often after correcting errors). With this experience, the readers can do the assigned exercise at the end of each chapter to practice. To assist the readers in learning and programming, most GAMS programs in this book are available online in digital form at GAMS model library https://worldscientific. com/worldscibooks/10.1142/12335#t=suppl. These programs are text files that can be run directly with the GAMS software. The electronic files have an additional learning benefit: printed text in the book often does not distinguish obviously between letter l and number 1, letter O and number 0. Comparing to the electronic files can help readers to distinguish letters or numbers that appear in the print copy of the book. GAMS language is not difficult, but it takes time and patience to get skillful to write and run a CGE program successfully.

Chapter 2

Input–Output Models and Tables

2.1 An Input–Output Model and Table

An input–output (IO) model, also called a Leontief model, describes the interdependent relationships among inputs and outputs in various sectors in the economy. For example, products of three sectors of steel, machinery and coal are interdependent in an economy. Steel production requires coal as input, coal production requires machinery as input, and machinery production requires steel as input. IO models link these IO interdependencies with a linear equation system. It is straightforward to handle such an equation system by linear algebra.

In an IO model, the relationships among inputs and outputs are assumed to be in fixed proportions. In economics, this is called fixed proportion technology, or, Leontief technology. For instance, it requires 0.5 tons of coal to produce 1 ton of steel. This 1:2 IO ratio is fixed regardless of how many tons of steel are produced. Because of the fixed proportion assumption, the IO model does not allow substitution between the inputs in production of the output. For instance, it does not allow substitution of labor with machinery in producing cars when the labor cost increases. An IO model depicts only a picture for the production block rather than a chart of all transaction flows in the entire economy. This is the limitation of an IO model. However, its multi-sector characteristic with a simultaneous equations system is similar to a CGE model. Because the linear structure is simpler, it would be good to have the IO model as the background, before learning CGEs. Besides, the IO matrix is often a component of a CGE model, thus being familiar with the IO model would also help modeling in future.

The IO model uses the input–output table (hereafter also called the IO table) as the database. The Bureau of Economic Analysis (BEA) in the U.S. compiles benchmark IO tables every five years and updates some data each year during the intervals (www.bea.gov). The IO tables for other countries can be found from various sources such as the World Input–Output Database (WIOD) online (www.wiod.org). All these agencies first collect the data then make the tables through similar mathematical methods.

How to measure the amounts of inputs and resulting output in a sector in an IO table? There are two options: by using physical units or monetary units. Take the auto industry as an example. Suppose the output is 8 million cars, the input steel used is 2 million tons, and the input electricity used is 500 million kWh. These physical units of "cars", "tons" and "kWh" are used in the table. Measuring output in physical units looks intuitive. Their prices are also intuitive as observed in daily life by the currency unit, say, the price of a car is $30,000 and the price of electricity is $0.10 a kWh. Hence, the physical unit data in the IO table look straightforward.

But using physical units poses problems in practice, especially, in aggregation. For example, steel products are not homogeneous. They have different alloy compositions, different qualities and different specifications. They should not be simply added up by their weights. Cars are even more heterogeneous. Compact sedans and limousines are very different in terms of performance and configuration, and their prices can be many times different. When combining different commodities to an aggregate product in an industry, say, textiles, it is more troublesome. How do you aggregate suits and fabrics by using physical units? These two products use different physical units. The former uses countable unit of "suits" and the latter uses the physical unit "square meters".

Modern IO tables use the monetary (currency) unit to solve the problem. Different types of products can be summed up by their monetary values, say, dollar, euro or yuan. This is called a monetary-unit type IO table, or in short, monetary IO table. The advantage is that we can aggregate all kinds of commodities and services simply by their monetary values, without worrying about their various physical units or various physical natures. For the above example about output in the textile sector, suppose the fabric output is 3 billion dollars worth and the suit output is 7 billion dollars worth, and the industry has only these two products, then the total textile output is 10 billion dollars. Table 2.1.1 presents a 6-sector IO table of China in 2000. The monetary unit in the table is the Chinese currency yuan. Most IO tables are much larger, and consist of many more sectors. The WIOD tables consist of 56 sectors. The larger U.S. IO tables provided by BEA have 405 sectors. Any of them is too big for the page size of this book to illustrate, but the basic structure of these IO tables is the same as the 6-sector table of Table 2.1.1.

For illustration purposes, Table 2.1.2 is an IO table for a hypothetical economy, Country A, in the year 2000. Country A has only three sectors: agriculture, industry and service. All products require labor and capital inputs to produce. Labor and capital are primary factor inputs, or simply called "factor inputs". Primary factors cannot be produced by other industries within the current time period. They include labor, capital and land. Total labor input is determined by the current labor force. Capital input is determined by the accumulation of the past production. Land input is normally fixed because the land area is determined by nature.

To simplify the IO table for illustration, in Table 2.1.2, we omit the subtotals including intermediate inputs, total value-added, total intermediate use and the total final demand. In the table header, "final demand" is the amount of commodity consumed by the final users, which consists of consumption by households and investment by enterprises. "Final demand" may be alternatively labeled as "final use", "final expenditure" or "final purchase" by some other IO tables. In the first column, we have the information about the "factor input" used in each sector. It is alternatively labeled as "value-added" in other IO tables. "Value-added"

Table 2.1.1. China's IO table (6 sectors) in 2000 (Unit: billion yuan).

	Agriculture	Industry	Construction industry	Transportation and Telecommunication	Food services	Other services	Total intermediate demand	Consumption	Capital formation	Export	Total final demand	Import	other	Total output
Agriculture	40.4	87.1	0.9	0.1	9.1	2.3	139.8	109.6	11.1	5.8	126.5	−5.4	3.6	264.6
Industry	54.2	857.5	120.2	36.6	46.7	70.3	1185.5	211.9	87.6	192.4	491.9	−181	11.7	1508.1
Construction industry	0.6	1.5	0.1	2.1	0.7	8.6	13.6	0	216.9	0.2	217.1	−0.4	−8.8	221.6
Transportation and Telecommunications	3.7	36.7	15.4	4.1	5.3	20.1	85.4	16.5	0.8	7.6	24.9	−1.6	−3	105.7
Food services	5.0	61.2	14.4	2.1	14.6	12.1	109.5	34.7	3.7	15	53.4	−0.7	7.2	169.3
Other services	7.7	39	11.1	6.2	19.3	34.9	118.3	188.1	5.0	10.9	204	−7.7	−8.2	306.3
Total intermediate inputs	111.5	1083	162.1	51.2	95.8	148.3	1652.1	560.8	325	232	1117.8	−196.8	2.5	2575.5
Fixed capital depreciation	6	81.5	4.5	19.9	5.4	28.7	146.1							
Worker compensation	134.4	169.6	39.1	22.6	40.2	93.4	499.2							
Net production tax	4.2	83.4	5.5	3.4	18.5	19.2	134.1							
Operating surplus	8.4	90.6	10.4	8.6	9.4	16.7	144.1							
Total value-added	153	425.1	59.4	54.5	73.5	158	923.5							
Total input	264.5	1508.1	221.6	105.7	169.3	306.3	2575.5							

Source: National Bureau of Statistics of China.

Table 2.1.2.   IO table of Country A in 2000 (Unit: billion dollars).

		Intermediate demand			Final demand		Total outputs
		Agriculture	Industry	Service	Households	Enterprises	
Intermediate input	Agriculture	200	300	150	280	70	1000
	Industry	80	400	250	550	320	1600
	Service	30	420	240	350	110	1150
Factor input/ Value-added	Labor	500	250	330			
	Capital	190	230	180			
Total inputs		1000	1600	1150			

is defined as the total value of the product minus intermediate input values. It is called value-added because only the factor inputs add "true value" to GDP and intermediate inputs just transfer values from factor inputs in other sectors. Country A's GDP is 1680 billion dollars. This GDP value is calculated by adding up the amounts of all final demands or adding up all values-added in the economy.

Total output value of Country A is 3750 billion dollars, which is the sum of all total outputs, or, all the total inputs. The total output value is greater than GDP because the figure double counts the intermediate input values.

Each row of the IO table indicates how the product of this sector is distributed to users and demanders of various sectors. Take the first row, the agricultural sector, as an example. The total output of the agricultural sector is 1000 billion dollars. This amount is distributed as follows: The agricultural sector demands 200 billion dollars of its own products as the inputs, such as using feed to raise livestock. The industrial sector demands 300 billion dollars of agricultural products as inputs, such as using cotton to make fabric. The service sector demands 150 billion dollars of agricultural products as inputs (such as restaurant service). These are intermediate demands for production rather than for the ultimate consumption. In the block of final demand, we see in the IO table: as ultimate users, households demand 280 billion dollars of agricultural products for consumption, and enterprises demand 70 billion dollars of agricultural products to form fixed capital goods and inventory. Fixed capital goods are used for primary inputs in the future periods, such as machinery. In economics, this is called "investment". However, the term "investment" can mean different things in different situations. To avoid confusion, it is formally termed "fixed capital formation" by the System of National Accounts of United Nations (SNA). These demands from intermediate users and final users add up to 1000 billion dollars of total demands. The last column is labeled "total output".

Each column in the table indicates how much of the various inputs are used in producing the products of a sector. Take the first column, the agricultural sector, as an example. It indicates that, to produce 1000 billion dollars of the agricultural product, it requires inputs of

200 billion dollars worth of agricultural products (such as feed for chickens), 80 billion dollars worth of industrial products (such as fertilizer), and 30 billion dollars worth of services (such as agricultural machinery maintenance, agricultural technology service, etc.). These are intermediate inputs. In addition, the agricultural sector needs factor inputs: 500 billion dollars worth of labor and 190 billion dollars worth of fixed capital such as machinery. The use of fixed capital for the production purpose is formally termed "capital consumption" by the SNA standard. In most IO tables, this figure is obtained from the data of fixed capital deprecation during the current period. Depreciation of fixed capital is considered as the amount of fixed capital "being consumed" in production, such as wear and tear of the machinery being used during the period. The "households" and "enterprises" columns to the right of the table can be thought of in a similar manner. When the column sectors purchase goods from the row sectors, we can also say that the row sectors supply goods to the column sectors.

The IO table can be divided into four sub-blocks, as that in Table 2.1.3, which is similar to the four quadrants of a graph. The upper left part, Quadrant II, is for the intermediate input and demand. The lower left part, Quadrant III, is for value-added components, mostly, factor inputs. The upper right part, Quadrant I, is for the final demand. Quadrant IV is generally left blank in the IO table. It is for the flows from factor supply to income, then from income to demands, which are omitted in the standard IO model. In later chapters, in the SAM table for CGE models, we have to fill data in Quadrant IV.

The value-added block has factor inputs including labor, capital, land, etc. Production taxes are also in this block. In the BEA IO table, the amount of labor input is termed "compensation of employees". The amount of capital inputs, termed "capital consumption" by SNA, is labeled as "depreciation of fixed capital" in the IO table in Table 2.1.1. In the BEA IO table, it is termed "gross operating surplus", which includes both fixed capital depreciation and other operating surplus (such as profits). There are some minor differences in terms and details among various IO tables, but one can recognize the same underlying principles.

The IO table shows the balanced relationship between the various sectors of the industry. In particular, the main balance relationships are as follows:

Row balance relationship:

$$\text{Intermediate demands} + \text{Final demands} = \text{Total output} \tag{2.1.1}$$

Column balance relationship:

$$\text{Intermediate inputs} + \text{Factor inputs} = \text{Total input} \tag{2.1.2}$$

Table 2.1.3.   Quadrants of the IO table.

Quadrant II: Intermediate demand	Quadrant I: Final demand
Quadrant III: Value-added components	Quadrant IV: Blank in the IO table

Table 2.1.4.   IO table of Country A.

Input \ output		Intermediate demand			Final demand		Total output
		Sector 1	Sector i	Sector n	House-hold	Enter-prise	
Intermediate input	Sector 1	q_{11} $\cdots$	q_{1j} $\cdots$	q_{1n}	H_1	I_1	q_1
		$\cdots$ $\cdots$	$\cdots$ $\cdots$	$\cdots$	$\cdots$	$\cdots$	$\cdots$
	Sector i	q_{i1} $\cdots$	q_{ij} $\cdots$	q_{in}	H_i	I_i	q_i
		$\cdots$ $\cdots$	$\cdots$ $\cdots$	$\cdots$	$\cdots$	$\cdots$	$\cdots$
	Sector n	q_{n1} $\cdots$	q_{nj} $\cdots$	q_{nn}	H_n	I_n	q_n
Factor input/ Value-added	Labor	L_1 $\cdots$	L_j $\cdots$	L_n			
	Capital	K_1 $\cdots$	K_j $\cdots$	K_n			
Total input		q_1 $\cdots$	q_j $\cdots$	q_n			

Total balance relationship:

Total input of each sector = Total output of the sector   (2.1.3)

Aggregate total intermediate input = Aggregate total intermediate demand   (2.1.4)

Aggregate total input = Aggregate total output   (2.1.5)

GDP = Aggregate final demand = Aggregate value-added   (2.1.6)

It can be seen from Table 2.1.2, in the agricultural sector, the total output is 1000 billion dollars, and the total input is also 1000 billion dollars. The same goes for each sector. Adding up all final demands including consumption by consumers and capital formation by enterprises, the gross national product (GDP) is 1680 billion dollars. The same GDP figure can be obtained from the sum of the values of the value-added.

Below we use mathematical symbols to represent the numbers in IO tables,

q_j is the quantity of commodity produced in sector j

q_{ij} is sector i's input needed to produce q_j

L_j is labor factor needed to produce q_j

K_j is capital factor needed to produce q_j

H_i is the final consumption of commodity i by households

I_i is the final consumption (capital formation) of commodity i by enterprises

Suppose the economy of Country A has n sectors, we can convert the format of Table 2.1.2 to a generalized one with the above variable symbols as shown in Table 2.1.4.

2.2 Structure of an IO Model

An input-output model (also called the IO model) is based on the data from the IO table. The IO model assumes that the ratios between inputs and outputs in each sector always remain constant. For example, in the IO table of Table 2.1.2, to produce 1000 billion dollars of agricultural product requires 80 billion dollars of industrial product as input. Then it can be calculated that, to produce one dollar's worth of agricultural product, it requires $80/1000 = 0.08$ dollars worth of industrial product. Similarly, to produce one dollar of agricultural good, we need $30/1000 = 0.03$ dollar of service, and $500/1000 = 0.5$ dollar of labor. The same principle applies to other sectors. This IO ratio is called "input coefficient". It is also called "direct input coefficient" or "input–output coefficient" in some literature. The input coefficient is conventionally denoted by a_{ij}. It is defined as how many dollars' worth of commodity i is needed to produce a dollar's worth of commodity j.

Suppose the output in sector j is q_j. To produce q_j, we need certain amount of commodity i as the input. This amount of commodity i is denoted by q_{ij}. Then the input coefficient a_{ij} is

$$a_{ij} = \frac{q_{ij}}{q_j} \tag{2.2.1}$$

It can be seen that the IO relationship here corresponds to a fixed-proportion production function, which is also called the "Leontief production function". The mathematical expression for the production function is, for commodity j:

$$q_j = \min\{a_{1j}^{-1}q_{1j},\ a_{2j}^{-1}q_{2j},\ \cdots,\ a_{nj}^{-1}q_{nj}\} \tag{2.2.2}$$

where the economy has n sectors. The corresponding conditional input demand function is

$$q_{ij} = a_{ij}q_j \qquad i = 1,\ldots,n \tag{2.2.3}$$

In other words, to produce the quantity of q_j, the quantity required of sector i's input is $q_{ij} = a_{ij}q_j$. Table 2.2.1 converts the numbers in Table 2.1.2 to corresponding input coefficients.

The standard Leontief IO model is a "row" model, which is based on the balance of the supply and demand in each sector in the rows in quadrants I and II in the IO table (Equation (2.1.1)). Supposing there are n commodity sectors in the economy, the model is a simultaneous linear equation system with n equations. The commodity quantities q_i are endogenous variables in the system. The numbers of the final demand in the Leontief model are given externally, which are called exogenous variables in economics but are called

Table 2.2.1. Input coefficients of Country A in 2000.

Input \ output		Intermediate demands		
		Sector 1	Sector 2	Sector 3
Intermediate inputs	Sector 1	0.20	0.19	0.13
	Sector 2	0.08	0.25	0.22
	Sector 3	0.03	0.26	0.21
Factor inputs/ Value-added	Labor	0.50	0.16	0.29
	Capital	0.19	0.14	0.16
Total input		1.00	1.00	1.00

"parameters" in the GAMS program. In the mathematical form, the IO model based on the Table 2.1.4 data is as follows:

$$q_{11} + \cdots + q_{1j} + \cdots + q_{1n} + H_1 + I_1 = q_1$$

$$\ldots$$

$$q_{i1} + \cdots + q_{ij} + \cdots + q_{in} + H_i + I_i = q_i \qquad (2.2.4)$$

$$\ldots$$

$$q_{n1} + \cdots + q_{nj} + \cdots + q_{nn} + H_n + I_n = q_n$$

Using input coefficients $q_{ij} = a_{ij}q_j$, system (2.2.4) can be written as

$$a_{11}q_1 + \cdots + a_{1j}q_j + \cdots + a_{1n}q_n + H_1 + I_1 = q_1$$

$$\ldots$$

$$a_{i1}q_1 + \cdots + a_{ij}q_j + \cdots + a_{in}q_n + H_i + I_i = q_i \qquad (2.2.5)$$

$$\ldots$$

$$a_{n1}q_1 + \cdots + a_{nj}q_j + \cdots + a_{nn}q_n + H_n + I_n = q_n$$

The input coefficients for intermediate inputs can be expressed by the following IO matrix:

$$\mathbf{A} = \begin{bmatrix} a_{11} & \cdots & a_{1n} \\ \vdots & a_{ij} & \vdots \\ a_{n1} & \cdots & a_{nn} \end{bmatrix} \qquad (2.2.6)$$

The vectors for the final demands $\mathbf{d}$ and for quantities produced in the n sectors $\mathbf{q}$ are expressed, respectively, by

$$\mathbf{d} = \begin{bmatrix} H_1 + I_1 \\ \vdots \\ H_i + I_i \\ \vdots \\ H_n + I_n \end{bmatrix} \qquad \mathbf{q} = \begin{bmatrix} q_1 \\ \vdots \\ q_i \\ \vdots \\ q_n \end{bmatrix} \qquad (2.2.7)$$

The IO model (2.2.5) can be expressed by the matrix form as follows:

$$\mathbf{Aq} + \mathbf{d} = \mathbf{q} \qquad (2.2.8)$$

The above matrix equation represents the balances of supplies and demands in all sectors. We may combine the terms with $\mathbf{q}$ to have

$$\mathbf{d} = \mathbf{q} - \mathbf{Aq} = (\mathbf{I} - \mathbf{A})\mathbf{q} \qquad (2.2.9)$$

Matrix $(\mathbf{I\text{-}A})$ is useful in the IO analysis. Note its main diagonal is $1 - a_{ii}$, but other elements are $-a_{ij}$:

$$\mathbf{I} - \mathbf{A} = \begin{bmatrix} 1 - a_{11} & \cdots & -a_{1n} \\ \vdots & 1 - a_{ii} & \vdots \\ -a_{n1} & \cdots & 1 - a_{nn} \end{bmatrix} \qquad (2.2.10)$$

Often, we wish to solve the following problem: given the amount of final demands, such as consumption and capital investment (which is capital formation in the IO tables), how much needs to be produced in each sector? In other words, $\mathbf{d}$ are exogenous variables (determined from outside), $\mathbf{q}$ are endogenous variables to be solved. $\mathbf{q}$ can be solved by

$$\mathbf{q} = (\mathbf{I} - \mathbf{A})^{-1}\mathbf{d} \qquad (2.2.11)$$

$(\mathbf{I} - \mathbf{A})^{-1}$ is the inverse of matrix of $(\mathbf{I\text{-}A})$. It can be seen in the equation, demand $\mathbf{d}$ determines the quantity $\mathbf{q}$. Hence, this standard IO model, also called the Leontief model, is a demand-driven open model.

Sometimes, we are just interested in finding how much changes in $\mathbf{q}$ would be in response to a change in $\mathbf{d}$. Let the Greek letter Δ denote "change in", then we have

$$\Delta\mathbf{q} = (\mathbf{I} - \mathbf{A})^{-1}\Delta\mathbf{d} \qquad (2.2.12)$$

Example 2.2.1 Country B has two sectors, sectors 1 and 2, and one factor input, labor. Its IO table is Table 2.2.2.

(a) Write down the Leontief "row" model in the matrix form, including all elements.
(b) If the final demand in sector 2 increases by 100, solve for the resulting changes in outputs in the two sectors by hand or by using Excel.

Solution: We use the spreadsheet software of Microsoft Excel to do the calculation. To answer question (a), first we calculate the corresponding input coefficients. The results are shown in Table 2.2.3.

Therefore, the matrix form is

$$\mathbf{A} = \begin{bmatrix} 0.333 & 0.3 \\ 0.25 & 0.32 \end{bmatrix} \quad \mathbf{d} = \begin{bmatrix} 100 \\ 530 \end{bmatrix} \quad \mathbf{q} = \begin{bmatrix} 600 \\ 1000 \end{bmatrix} \qquad (2.2.13)$$

Table 2.2.2.   IO table of Country B.

	Sector 1 Intermediate demand	Sector 2 Intermediate demand	Final demand	Total output
Sector 1	200	300	100	600
Sector 2	150	320	530	1000
Labor	250	380		
Total input	600	1000		

Table 2.2.3.   Input coefficients of Country B.

	Sector 1 Intermediate demand	Sector 2 Intermediate demand
Sector 1	0.333	0.300
Sector 2	0.250	0.320
Labor	0.417	0.380
Total input	1.000	1.000

The IO model is

$$\begin{bmatrix} 0.333 & 0.3 \\ 0.25 & 0.32 \end{bmatrix} \begin{bmatrix} 600 \\ 1000 \end{bmatrix} + \begin{bmatrix} 100 \\ 530 \end{bmatrix} = \begin{bmatrix} 600 \\ 1000 \end{bmatrix} \qquad (2.2.14)$$

It can be expressed as

$$\begin{bmatrix} 0.667 & -0.3 \\ -0.25 & 0.68 \end{bmatrix} \begin{bmatrix} 600 \\ 1000 \end{bmatrix} = \begin{bmatrix} 100 \\ 530 \end{bmatrix} \qquad (2.2.15)$$

To answer question (b), note that the output in sector 2 increases by 100, but the output in sector 1 remains unchanged, thus it can be expressed in vector form as follows:

$$\begin{bmatrix} \Delta D_1 \\ \Delta D_2 \end{bmatrix} = \begin{bmatrix} 0 \\ 100 \end{bmatrix}$$

Substitute it into Equation (2.1.12), solve it by using the matrix algebra, and we have

$$\begin{bmatrix} \Delta Q_1 \\ \Delta Q_2 \end{bmatrix} = \begin{bmatrix} 0.667 & -0.3 \\ -0.25 & 0.68 \end{bmatrix}^{-1} \begin{bmatrix} \Delta D_1 \\ \Delta D_2 \end{bmatrix} = \begin{bmatrix} 0.667 & -0.3 \\ -0.25 & 0.68 \end{bmatrix}^{-1} \begin{bmatrix} 0 \\ 100 \end{bmatrix}$$

$$= \begin{bmatrix} 1.80 & 0.79 \\ 0.66 & 1.76 \end{bmatrix} \begin{bmatrix} 0 \\ 100 \end{bmatrix} = \begin{bmatrix} 79 \\ 176 \end{bmatrix} \qquad (2.2.16)$$

2.3 GAMS Language Program

The above numerical example in Section 2.3 can be solved by Excel or even by hand. When the problems get bigger, especially for those real-world problems that may involve hundreds of sectors, we have to use special computer programs to do the job. GAMS is a very popular software used to handle multi-sectoral models and solve for the optimal solutions. Hereafter, we will teach readers GAMS programming, step by step, as we proceed with our teaching in the CGE theory and models.

GAMS is a high-level modeling system for mathematical planning and optimization. Its full name is General Algebraic Modeling System. It consists of the computer language program and many integrated solvers. In this book, we mostly use the MCP solver. The MCP (mixed complementarity problems) solver is capable of finding the optimal solutions for large linear and non-linear equation systems with constraints, such as the IO and CGE models.

To use GAMS, you need to first install the GAMS software in your computer. The software is provided in their website www.gams.com. Select and download the version for your operating system (platform), whether MS Windows, Mac OS or Linux. In order to run the program, you need a license. A demo version of GAMS is free, but it has restriction on the numbers of variables and constraints you can have in your model. The free demo version includes the solvers needed in this book, and is powerful enough for learning and practicing the examples and exercises in this book. If you just need the demo version, you can fill and submit the request for a demo license in the GAMS website. GAMS will email you a demo license (currently consisting of six text lines). Use Notepad or any text editor to make a file with filename gamslice.txt. Paste the license text in the file and save the file on the desktop. Then you install the program. By the end of the installation process it will ask you to copy the license file. Follow the instruction and copy gamslice.txt. After successfully completing the installation, you should find "gamside" on your app list, and click to open it.

In the future, when you need to work on large models exceeding 1000 variables, you should purchase a license for GAMS and the necessary solvers. The purchase URL is http://www.gams.com/sales/sales.htm, and price discounts are offered for academic and educational uses. When you purchase solvers, select one having MCP and NLP functions, such as the PATH solver. There are also other MCP solvers such as MILES. While there are some minor variations in performance among different MCP solvers, their general capacities and functions are similar.

A GAMS program consists of a series of statements (sentences). As a high-level program language, the input statements in GAMS are close to our natural language in English. There are some format and syntax rules we need to understand and follow. You will gradually study the command keywords, syntax, verbs and functions of the GAMS language from illustrations provided in this book. When you run into problems or you want to learn more, you may query GAMS manuals, reference books and examples. Most of these documents are available online, free of charge.

GAMS is flexible with capitalization or blanks. That is, GAMS inputs are not case or space sensitive. You can feel free to add spaces or capitalize a letter in a sentence. From time to time, for the purposes of explanation or remarks, we need to insert comments in the program but do not want GAMS to take these comments as command inputs. In the GAMS program, when a line starts with an asterisk, "*", the following text is treated as a comment. If the comment is very long, you may place the entire comment block between codes $ontext and $offtext. In the following Example 2.3.1, we insert the explanations as comments in the program.

In a GAMS program, you need to distinguish between two different kinds of values, "parameters" and "variables". These terms have their specific definitions in GAMS, which may be different from the definitions in economics or other fields. In the GAMS language, "parameters" are those values given externally, such as constants, data and scalars. "Variables" are the endogenous variables which are to be solved by the system internally. For economics students, it can be distinguished as follows: "parameters" in GAMS refer to the exogenous variables, data or parameters in economics, while "variables" in GAMS refer only to endogenous variables in economics. In order to avoid possible confusion that may rise in later part of the discussion, in this book we follow the GAMS definition for "variables". When we say "variable", it only refers to an endogenous variable. In the case we talk about exogenous variables, we will use the full term "exogenous variable".

In what follows, we illustrate the GAMS program language through concrete GAMS programs (Examples 2.3.1, 2.3.2 and 2.3.3). The GAMS statements/inputs are between the double lines. The explanation for these statements is in a comment format (either starting with * in the line or being placed between $ontext and $offtext). The following program can be run directly by GAMS. You may simply copy the text and paste it in the GAMS program window to execute it. Section 2.4 will further explain how to use the GAMS software to run a program.

Example 2.3.1 Use GAMS to calculate the input coefficients of the IO model of Example 2.2.1. Write a GAMS program to set up the IO model for Country B. Run the GAMS program successfully and check if the displayed outputs replicate the original values. This last step to replicate the initial (base) state of the model is called "replication".

Solution: For clarity, we use the Consolas font for the GAMS programs in this book, which helps us to distinguish between 0 and O. The following is the GAMS program. It runs successfully. After inspection in the output file, we find that the results solved by the model exactly replicate the original data in the IO table.

```
*=======================================================
$title   Example 2.3.1  Input-Output Model
*=======================================================
*$title is used for a title text or a head on a new page.
*In a line starting with *, the text followed is a comment. It is not
processed as a command.
*Texts between directives $ontext and $offtext are comments. See the
following example:
$ontext
        In this program we use GAMS to estimate the input coefficients
of the input-output model, set up the base model and simulate the
external policy changes. We will explain the GAMS model structure,
syntax and commands.
        We first need to name symbols and tell GAMS the classifications
of the symbols. This is done by declaration, followed by definition
or assignment. See the following example.
        Let us use "ac" to name the set for the accounts (sectors) in
the input-output table.
        The first sentence below declares "ac" as a set, then defines
the elements of the set by placing the elements between two slashes,
"/". In the same sentence, using commas to separate elements.
```

The second sentence declares a subset "i" of set ac.
Similarly, define the elements of set i by placing them between "/"
Terminating each statement by a semicolon ";".
$offtext

```
* ===== ================================================
set ac / sec1, sec2, labor, finaldemand, total /;
set i (ac) / sec1, sec2 /;
* ======================================================
```

*Use the alias command to give another name for the set. This is
useful when we need to work on interactions of the same set in
operation without confusing the GAMS program. For instance, working
on the rows i and columns j of an input-output table.

```
* ======================================================
alias (i, j);
* ======================================================
```

* In what follows, we input the data.
* First declare that the dataset is a table. Name the table as IO.
The parentheses include two variable elements, row and column. Align
the data vertically along columns. If a table cell is left empty
without data, GAMS treats its value as 0.

```
* ======================================================
table IO(*,*)
            sec1    sec2    finaldemand   Total
sec1        200     300     100           600
sec2        150     320     530           1000
labor       250     380
Total       600     1000
;
* ======================================================
```

$ontext

Next we declare and define "parameter". In GAMS, parameter is
defined as a number whose value is fixed and given exogenously. That
includes constants, parameters, scalar number and exogenous
variables.

Start with "parameter" to declare the following symbols are
parameters. Then list one parameter per line. The parameter symbol
is a combination of letters and numbers, but it must begin with a
letter and can be followed by a letter or number, such as B, Ta, q3, etc.

Each line begins with defining a parameter symbol. After a few spaces, you can comment on the parameters (although this comment is optional, but it is helpful for understanding the parameters later).

In the two-dimensional table data, as int(i,j) shown below, the first element in the parentheses refers to the row, the second element refers to the column.

Conventionally, to name a parameter with the initial value, we put "0" at the end of the symbol, to recognize this is the initial value. For instance, q0 represents the initial value of the total output.

Finally, use semicolon to end the parameter declaration and definition environment.

```
$offtext
* =======================================================
parameter
int(i,j)               intermediate input (intermediate demand)
use(i)                 final demand in sector i
lab(i)                 factor input (labor input) in sector i
a(i,j)                 input coefficients
q0(i)                  initial total output in sector i
;
* =======================================================
$ontext
```

Next we need to assign the values for the defined parameters. Sometimes the values may be read directly from inputted data. For example, the first line below "int(i,j) = IO(i,j)". Sometimes the parameters values need to be calculated from the existing data. For instance, the 5th line below the double dashed lines calculates input coefficients, a(i,j) = int(i,j)/q0(j). This calculation for the parameter values is called "calibration" in CGE modeling.

The value assignment uses an equation sign "=". The parameter values on the right-hand side must be provided already in the previous statements. Then the value of the parameter on the left-hand side is derived or assigned.

A semicolon terminates each assignment equation.

At the end, to verify if the values are correct, it is suggested to use command "display" to print the values in the output file.

```
$offtext
*=======================================================
```

```
int(i,j) = IO(i,j);
use(i) = IO(i, "finaldemand");
lab(i) = IO("labor", i);
q0(i) = IO("total", i);
a(i,j) = int(i,j) / q0(j);
display int, use, lab, q0, a;
*=======================================================
$ontext
```

Here we declare and define variables. In GAMS, "variable" only
refer to the variables to be solved in the system or model. In
economics, they are called "endogenous variables".

Start with "variable" to declare the following symbols are
variables. Each line begins with a variable symbol or name. Like
parameters, a variable symbol begins with a letter and can be followed by
letters or numbers. A few spaces after the symbol, you can describe
the variable. Finally, use a semicolon to terminate the variable
declaration and the definition environment.

```
$offtext
*=======================================================
variable
q(i) total output variable;
*=======================================================
$ontext
```

In what follows, we set up the equation(s). The whole section
forms the equation system to be solved numerically.

First, use keyword "equation" or "equations" to declare the
equation environment.

Then name all equations and end with a semicolon. For
instance, the equation here is named "commodityequi", which is the
equilibrium of supply and demand in the commodity market. In this
model, we only have one equation.

```
$offtext
*=======================================================
equation
commodityequi(i);
*=======================================================
$ontext
```

Now we define each equation in the system. First, repeat the
equation name and end with ".."

Then start a new line and write down the mathematical expressions of the
equation by GAMS syntax as follows (GAMS uses the standard arithmetic

operation symbols in programming languages):

    Add: +, subtract: -, multiply: *, divide: /, power: **.

    Use the following symbols to relate two expressions in an equation between LHS (left-hand side) and RHS (right-hand side).

    =e=: equality of lhs and rhs

    =g=: lhs is greater than rhs

    =l=: lhs is smaller than rhs

    Terminate the equation by a semicolon.

    Finally, following the syntax, write down all equations of the model.

$offtext

*This IO model is simple. It has only one equation group as follows:

*==

commodityequi(i)..

sum(j,a(i,j)*q(j)) + use(i) =e= q(i);

*==

*Note the above syntax of "sum" for the summation operation. It sums the indexed variables a(i,j)*q(j) by index "j".

$ontext

    Assigning initial values to variables:

    Before the program is executed, each variable should have an initial value. You should assign initial values to all variables. If a variable does not have an assigned value, GAMS internally would set its initial value to be zero. When a solver searches for the final results of the variables, the process starts with these initial values.

    For most CGE models, the initial values assigned are based on the available data or calculated values based on the theory.

    In order to distinguish between the initial value and the changeable value of a variable in the system, the changeable value should add a suffix ".L", such as q.L(i) in the equation below. q.L(i) is placed on the left-hand side of the equation. On the right-hand side of the equation is the assigned initial value, which uses the current total output value q0(i).

    q.L can be written by the lowercase letter "l", as q.l, because GAMS does not distinguish between uppercase and lowercase letters. The problem is that lowercase letter "l" is often visually indistinguishable from number "1" and it is easy to mess up between them in reading and writing. If you mess up between letter "l" and number "1", the program won't work properly. Therefore, we use uppercase L in this case.

If suffix ".L" is replaced by ".fx", the variable's value is fixed at the value given on RHS. In such a case, the variable is forced to be a parameter. For instance, if instead we write q.fx(i)=q0(i), then the total output value is fixed at the initial value of q0(i) in the solving process. Suffix ".fx" can be useful in some situations, which will be discussed later.
$offtext

```
*=====================================================
q.L(i)=q0(i);
*=====================================================
```

$ontext

The following section is to tell the computer to execute and solve the model.

First, use the keyword "model" to declare the model. Then name the model (here we make a name "IOmodel"). In the same line, define the model system by listing the equation names to be included between two slashes "/" . When all previously declared equations are to be included in the model, you may simply use /all/, as in the following example.

Then use command "run" to tell GAMS to execute the model. You need to give the model name, and the solver to be used. For the following example, "using mcp" is telling GAMS to use the MCP solver.
$offtext

```
*=====================================================
model IOmodel /all/;
solve IOmodel using mcp;
*=====================================================
```

```
* Finally, display the results of the solution by using command
"display".  Check if the results replicate the base state in the SAM
table.
*=====================================================
display q.L
*=====================================================
```

Sometimes, we wish to check the quality of the replication. If we perturb the initial values in the same model and the solved final results still replicate the base state, we would say the model and the results are robust.

Example 2.3.2 Following the above Example 2.3.1, write the GAMS program to replicate the base state by perturbing the initial values.

Solution: The following is the GAMS program for Example 2.3.2. The program needs to be attached to the previous program for Example 2.3.1 to execute. The results exactly replicate the base state so the model and replication results are robust.

```
*=======================================================
$title Replication by perturbing the initial values
*=======================================================
$ontext
        Keep the original model structure and parameters, but perturb
the initial values of variables, and check if the optimized results
still replicate the base state.  The range of disturbance can be from
small to large to check how robust the solutions are.
        In what follows, we perturb the initial values of variable
q(i).  The initial values of q(i) now are arbitrarily set at 300 and
500, rather than the original 600 and 1000.  The new set of the
initial values is named repq0(i).  Because repq0(i) is a new
parameter, we need first to declare it by using "parameter":
$offtext
*=======================================================
parameter
repq0(i)  the  perturbed initial values of total output of sector i
        / sec1 300
          sec2 500 /;
*=======================================================
$ontext
        Then we set the initial values of q(i) at repq0(i).  When we
assign a new value to the same variable, GAMS discards the old value
and takes the new value. To double check if the q.L values are truly
the new initial values 300 and 500, use the command "display":
$offtext
*=======================================================
q.L(i)=repq0(i);
display q.L;
*=======================================================
$ontext
        Give a new name to the model "repIOmodel".  We still run the
same model (only with different initial values) with the same system
equations.  Hence, just use /all/ to include all previous equations.
        Instruct GAMS to solve the model and display the new results.
To help interpreting the output, we can use single quotes " ' " to
display a description for the variable. If the solved output values
q.L(i) are 600 and 1000, which are the original values, we know the
model and results are robust.
$offtext
*=========================================================
```

```
model repIOmodel /all/
solve repIOmodel using mcp;

display q.L, 'Check if they are consistent with the original values
of the total output';
* ==========================================================
```

Example 2.3.3 Following the above IO model in Example 2.3.1, simulate the external change that the final demand in sector 2 increases by 100. This is the question asked by 2(b) in Example 2.2.1. Find the resulting changes in the total output.

Solution: This is simulation. The following is the GAMS program for Example 2.3.3. The program needs to be attached to the previous program for Example 2.3.1 to execute. The simulation results after execution are the same as those in Equation (2.2.16).

```
*==========================================================
$title Simulation: Final demand in sector 2 increases by 100
*==========================================================
$ontext
This section is a simulation.  Simulation is to see how the values of
variables change in response to some external changes.  In this case,
the external change is that the final demand in sector 2 increases by 100,
but there are no changes in sector 1.  In what follows, we specify
the changes in the final demand:
$offtext
*==========================================================
parameter
simuse(i) changes in the final demand
        / sec1 0
          sec2 100 /;
*==========================================================
$ontext
     Give a new name for the equation, "simcommodityequi".  Again,
this model consists of only this equation group.
     Give a new name for the simulation model "simIOmodel", which
means simulation.
     Instruct GAMS to run and solve the model with the new equation
"simcommodityequi" in the model.
     The same variable name q.L can still be used.  For variables,
GAMS replaces the new values with the previous values. Variable q.L
will display the most recent value solved by the previous program
execution.
```

```
     Then display the simulation results and remark "End of the
program".
$offtext
*=============================================================
equation
simcommodityequi(i);

simcommodityequi(i)..
sum(j, a(i, j)*q(j)) + simuse(i) =e= q(i);

model simIOmodel / simcommodityequi /
solve simIOmodel using mcp;

display q.L, 'q.L , the simulation results';

*End of the program
*=============================================================
```

2.4 Executing GAMS Program and Reading Results

GAMS programs can be written and edited directly in a text editor software such as Notepad, giving a file name with the suffix ".gms". You use GAMS software to open and execute the file. Another option is use GAMS IDE, a very convenient interface for writing and editing GAMS programs. You can also execute and check the programs in the same interface. GAMS IDE can be downloaded at www.gams.com and installed, as explained previously. Figure 2.4.1 shows a screenshot of GAMS IDE interface with the above program of Example 2.3.1.

After writing the program, press F9 or hit the red right arrow key on top, to run the program. If the model is solvable without syntax errors, the operation will continue until it shows "solution found" in a new window with the label "no active process". GAMS IDE will also pop up a window to show a report file with the same file name but a different suffix ".1st". This file is a detailed report of the execution process. If there are problems in the program, GAMS stops running in the middle and points out the problems in red in a window. You click the first red part, which would direct you to the first problem in the program. Locate the problem which may be caused by syntax or other errors, make corrections and run the program again. Repeat the process until all problems are solved and the program runs smoothly till the end. Note, although the program runs smoothly to the end, it does not mean that the results are correct. You need to check the results and analyze them based on the theory. Replication and simulation are commonly used approaches to check if the results are correct and robust. The following is part of the report file (the report file name has suffix .1st) for the simulation part of Example 2.3.1. The external change (also called "shock") is that the final demand in sector 2 increases by 100. It can be seen in the report

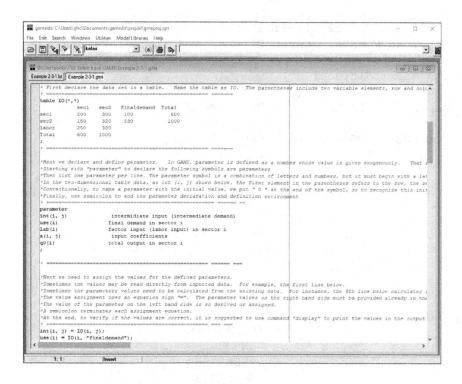

Figure 2.4.1. GAMS IDE with a program.

that we need to increase total output in sectors 1 and 2 by 79.295 and 176.211, respectively. These numbers are consistent with the results we calculated by Excel in Section 2.2.

(Some less important report details about the execution process are omitted below)

```
              S O L V E      S U M M A R Y

      MODEL    simIOmodel
      TYPE     MCP
      SOLVER   PATH              FROM LINE   212


****  SOLVER STATUS     1 NORMAL COMPLETION
****  MODEL STATUS      1 OPTIMAL


  RESOURCE USAGE, LIMIT        0.002     1000.000
  ITERATION COUNT, LIMIT       0         10000
  EVALUATION ERRORS            0         0

PATH          Feb 14, 2009 23.0.2 WIN 6185.9411 VIS x86/MS Windows

2 row/cols, 4 non—zeros, 100.00% dense.
```

Path 4.7.01 (Thu Feb 12 11:29:53 2009)
Written by Todd Munson, Steven Dirkse, and Michael Ferris

———— EQU simcommodityequi

	LOWER	LEVEL	UPPER	MARGINAL
sec1	.	.	.	79.295
sec2	−100.000	−100.000	−100.000	176.211

———— VAR q total output variable

	LOWER	LEVEL	UPPER	MARGINAL
sec1	−INF	79.295	+INF	.
sec2	−INF	176.211	+INF	.

**** REPORT SUMMARY: 0   NONOPT
                            0 INFEASIBLE
                            0   UNBOUNDED
                            0   REDEFINED
                            0   ERRORS

GAMS Rev 230 WEX—VIS 23.0.2 x86/MS Windows   02/24/20
22:07:03 Page 20
Simulation: The following section is simulation for external changes
E x e c u t i o n

————   214 VARIABLE q.L total output variable

sec1 79.295,   sec2 176.211

————   214 q.L , the result of the solution

EXECUTION TIME   =   0.000 SECONDS

Exercises

2E.1 Based on the available data, replace the question marks with numbers in the following IO Table 2E.1.1.

2E.2 An economy has three sectors, agriculture, industry and services. It has two primary factors, labor and capital. Its IO table is as follows.

Table 2E.1.1. Fill the cells in the IO table below with correct numbers.

	Agriculture	Industry	Total intermediate demand	Final demand	Total output
Agriculture	160	210	?	?	750
Industry	140	?	?	630	1090
Total intermediate demand	?	?			
Value-added	?	?	GDP=	?	
Total input	?	?			

(a) Write down the IO row model by the matrix form, including the elements in the matrices.

(b) Suppose the final demand in the industry sector increases by 200, while final demands in other sectors remain unchanged. Write a GAMS program for the IO model, simulate this "shock", and, analyze changes in total outputs in the three sectors. Read the report file and review the printed results in the file.

	Agriculture	Industry	Service	Final demand	Total output
Agriculture	160	150	90	480	880
Industry	140	320	170	900	1530
Service	80	150	250	590	1070
Labor	320	350	410		
Capital	180	560	150		
Total inputs	880	1530	1070		

Appendix: Review of Microeconomics

2A.1 Leontief production function

In what follows, q is the output quantity, x is the input quantity, p is the output price and w is the factor price, lowercase a are parameters, subscripts are indexes for sectors. The Leontief production function is

$$q = \min\{a_1 x_1, \ldots, a_n x_n\} \tag{2A.1.1}$$

Production optimization requires that inputs be used by fixed proportions with the output q.

$$q = a_1 x_1 = a_2 x_2 =, \ldots, = a_n x_n, \tag{2A.1.2}$$

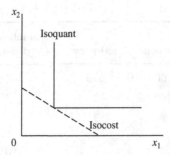

Figure 2A.1.1. Leontief production function.

It can be seen that the input coefficient for input i is $1/a_i$. If the amount of an input exceeds the required proportion, this input becomes a slack variable whose marginal productivity is zero, because the excessive input amount does not contribute to output.

Because the optimal input use is at the right angle point of the isoquant (Figure 2A.1.1), where the isoquant is not differentiable, we cannot use the differentiation approach to derive the input demand functions as we do for a Cobb–Douglas production function. Instead, the input demand functions can be directly obtained from equations as that in (2A.1.2).

Example 2A.1.1 The Leontief production function is $q = \min\{a_1 x_1, a_2 x_2\}$. Solve for the conditional input demand and cost functions.

From the above production function, we directly have the conditional input demand for x_1 and x_2:

$$x_1^c = \frac{q}{a_1} \quad x_2^c = \frac{q}{a_2} \tag{2A.1.3}$$

This function form is different from a standard conditional input demand function $x_i^c(q, \mathbf{w})$, as the function does not have the element of inputs price $\mathbf{w}$. This is because the optimal inputs uses are of fixed proportions, thus independent of inputs price changes. The cost function is

$$c(q, \mathbf{w}) = w_1 x_1^c + w_2 x_2^c = w_1 \frac{q}{a_1} + w_2 \frac{q}{a_2} = (\frac{w_1}{a_1} + \frac{w_2}{a_2})q \tag{2A.1.4}$$

This cost function is constant returns to scale. The marginal cost $c_q \equiv \frac{\partial c}{\partial q} = \frac{w_1}{a_1} + \frac{w_2}{a_2}$ is also the unit cost, which is independent of the amount of output q. If the price of the commodity (which is marginal revenue) p *is* less than c_q, in order to avoid loss, the firm's quantity supplied would be zero. If p is greater than c_q, to maximize profit, the firm would continue to increase output to infinity. If p is exactly equal to c_q, regardless of what quantity is produced, the firm is always in a breakeven state with zero economic profit. In this case, its quantity supplied q could be any non-negative real number.

This conclusion can be extended to any production function with constant returns to scale. If the commodity price p is greater than average cost (unit cost) c_q, the firm would continue expanding its production to infinity, therefore the equilibrium from the supply side does not exist. If the quantity supplied is defined at a positive real number, then price p must be equal to the unit cost c_q.

2A.2 Constant, increasing and decreasing returns to scale of a production function

If all inputs increase by the same proportion, which leads to a same proportional increase in the output, we say this production function $f(x_1, \ldots, x_n)$ exhibits the property of constant returns to scale. Mathematically, it is

$$tf(x_1, \cdots, x_n) = f(tx_1, \cdots, tx_n) \quad t > 0 \tag{2A.2.1}$$

Similarly, increasing returns to scale is that increases in all inputs by the same ratio lead to a more proportional increase in the output,

$$tf(x_1, \ldots, x_n) < f(tx_1, \ldots, tx_n) \quad t > 1 \tag{2A.2.2}$$

And, decreasing returns to scale is

$$tf(x_1, \ldots, x_n) > f(tx_1, \ldots, tx_n) \quad t > 1 \tag{2A.2.3}$$

Chapter 3

Prices in Input–Output Tables and Models

3.1 Prices in a Monetary Input–Output Table

As discussed in Chapter 2, the modern input–output (IO) tables and SAM tables usually use the monetary (currency) unit, say dollar, to measure the quantities of commodities. For instance, Table 2.1.1 is China's IO table measured in billions of the Chinese currency yuan. In the second row, the number 54.2 (billion yuan) means that, to produce 264.5 billion yuan of agricultural product, it requires 54.2 billion yuan of industrial commodity as input. In the previous chapter, these numbers are interpreted as quantities produced or used. However, if the commodity quantities are measured in the currency unit, then what unit should we use for the price of the commodity?

The prices used in a monetary IO table are the price indexes. It is similar to that we use a price index to measure the price level of national output GDP, but here a price index is for a commodity, say, the price index of steel or the price index of the agricultural product. For convenience, we usually just call it "price". Conventionally, the price index in the base period is set to 1, which serves as the benchmark. Changes in the price level because of inflation or other factors would be measured against this benchmark level.

Now we need to refine our understanding of the monetary IO table. The numbers in the table should be understood as the nominal values of the commodities. That is, the number in an entry of the table is the value obtained from multiplying the quantity of commodity by its price: "Nominal Value = Price × Quantity". The measurement unit of the quantity is still a monetary unit, but with a label "real", such as "real dollar". The quantity of a commodity is equivalent to its real value. If in the monetary IO table the steel output is recorded as 200 billion dollars, this should be interpreted as the nominal value of the steel, i.e., a product of multiplication of quantity of 200 by price of 1. Below is the concrete example for the above steel output case, suppose the base period is 2007.

$$\text{Steel price in 2007} \times \text{quantity of steel produced (billion dollars) in 2007} \qquad (3.1.1)$$

$$= 1 \times 200$$

$$= 200 \text{ (billion dollars, nominal output of steel in 2007)}$$

Using variable symbols, it is

$$p_i \times q_i = Q_i \qquad (3.1.2)$$

33

where p_i and q_i are the price and quantity of commodity i. Uppercase Q_i denotes the nominal output in sector i in the current year. Now we should say that, in a monetary IO table, the numbers are always interpreted as the nominal values of outputs and inputs, and they are the products of multiplication of prices and quantities.

In the base period when prices are set to 1, on the surface whether multiplying by 1 or not would make no difference in the numbers in the IO tables, because nominal and real outputs are the same. Yet in modeling and programming of CGE or IO models, the implied prices should never be omitted. When the price variables are omitted, the model may appear fine without obvious errors in the base period, but in simulation the outcomes will not be correct because the prices often change to values other than 1 in response to the external shocks. In some other cases, if the prices are omitted, the model would simply crash in execution.

This can be illustrated as follows. Using the above example, suppose in the following year 2008, the steel output remains the same but the steel price increases by 20%. Hence, the steel price index is 1.2. Thus, we have

$$\text{Steel price index in 2008} \times \text{steel real output in 2008 (at 2007 price)} \qquad (3.1.3)$$

$$= 1.2 \times 200$$

$$= 240 \text{ (nominal output at 2008 price)}$$

It can be seen that the quantity (real output) of steel in 2008 remains at 200 billion dollars (at 2007 price). Yet the nominal value of steel output in 2008 increases to 240 billion dollars, which is caused by the inflation in the steel price during the period. Changes in prices are common in simulation of the real-world changes. Hence, in modeling, one should never forget to include the prices for output values in the IO or SAM tables.

Sometimes, for research purposes, we need to find the inputs or outputs measured in physical units, in these cases we use some approaches to convert the quantities in a monetary table to the physical units. This is often done by dividing the value by the price or similar factor to obtain the quantity in physical unit. For example, we may need to calculate the number of workers employed in the steel sector. We can divide the total wage bill or total labor cost by the average wage in the steel sector to obtain the number of workers. Other approaches can be used, too. An example is using an environmental CGE model to estimate changes in the amount of a greenhouse gas emission under certain policies. The researcher may first conduct the simulation to find the resulting percentage changes in the greenhouse-gas-related industrial outputs, then use the conversion ratios to calculate the industrial greenhouse gas changes in physical units, finally sum these changes to derive the aggregate change in the greenhouse gas emission.

3.2 Computing Quantities and Input Coefficients in Monetary IO Tables

Based on the above discussion, we refine our understanding of the monetary IO table. Table 3.2.1 replicates Table 2.1.2, but the interpretation of the numbers inside is different. Now they should be understood as the nominal values of outputs or inputs, that is, the products of multiplication of the real quantities and prices.

Table 3.2.1.   Input–output table of Country A in 2000 (Unit: billion dollar).

		Intermediate demand			Final demand		Total outputs
		Agriculture	Industry	Service	Households	Enterprises	
Intermediate inputs	Agriculture	200	300	150	280	70	1000
	Industry	80	400	250	550	320	1600
	Service	30	420	240	350	110	1150
Factor inputs/ Value-added	Labor	500	250	330			
	Capital	190	230	180			
Total inputs		1000	1600	1150			

Table 3.2.2.   Monetary input–output of Country A.

Input \ output		Intermediate demands			Final demands		Total outputs
		Sector 1	Sector j	Sector n	Households	Enterprises	
Intermediate Inputs	Sector 1	$p_1 q_{11}$	$\cdots$ $p_1 q_{1j}$ $\cdots$	$p_1 q_{1n}$	$p_1 H_1$	$p_1 I_1$	$p_1 q_1$
		$\cdots$	$\cdots$ $\cdots$ $\cdots$	$\cdots$	$\cdots$	$\cdots$	$\cdots$
	Sector i	$p_i q_{i1}$	$\cdots$ $p_i q_{ij}$ $\cdots$	$p_i q_{in}$	$p_i H_i$	$p_i I_i$	$p_i q_i$
		$\cdots$	$\cdots$ $\cdots$ $\cdots$	$\cdots$	$\cdots$	$\cdots$	$\cdots$
	Sector n	$p_n q_{n1}$	$\cdots$ $p_n q_{nj}$ $\cdots$	$p_n q_{nn}$	$p_n H_n$	$p_n I_n$	$p_n q_n$
Factor inputs/ Value-added	Labor	$w_l L_1$	$\cdots$ $w_l L_j$ $\cdots$	$w_l L_n$			
	Capital	$w_k K_1$	$\cdots$ $w_k K_j$ $\cdots$	$w_k K_n$			
Total input		$p_1 q_1$	$\cdots$ $p_j q_j$ $\cdots$	$p_n q_n$			

We use uppercase Q to denote the monetary value (nominal value) and lowercase q for the quantity (real output), accordingly, we have $Q_{ij} = p_i q_{ij}$ and $Q_i = p_i q_i$. Hence, we change Table 2.1.4 by adding the price factors. The mathematical expression is presented in Table 3.2.2 where p_i is the price of sector i and w_x is the price of factor input x.

The nominal values of the supply and demand of each sector (the monetary "row" IO model) should be balanced:

$$p_i q_{i1} + \cdots + p_i q_{ij} + \cdots + p_i q_{in} + p_i H_i + p_i I_i = p_i q_i \quad i = 1, \cdots, n \qquad (3.2.1)$$

Dividing both sides by price p_i, we have the real quantity balance equation

$$q_{i1} + \cdots + q_{ij} + \cdots + q_{in} + H_i + I_i = q_i \quad i = 1, \cdots, n \qquad (3.2.2)$$

This is the same as the row model in physical units in Chapter 2.

In calculating the input coefficients, we follow the principle of using the real quantities, i.e., $a_{ij} = q_{ij}/q_j$. This is because the production function is the relationship between real quantities of inputs and the output. Hence, to calculate input coefficients, we need first to derive the real quantities from the data in the monetary IO tables. This is done by dividing the values in the table cells by prices. For instance, if the value in the table cell ij is Q_{ij}, then dividing the value Q_{ij} by p_i we obtain real quantity q_{ij}. The quantities of final demand d_i are derived similarly:

$$q_{ij} = Q_{ij}/p_i \qquad q_i = Q_i/p_i \qquad d_i = D_i/p_i \tag{3.2.3}$$

Because in a monetary IO table the numbers for factor inputs "X_j" are also nominal values, they should be divided by factor prices w_x to obtain the real quantities of factor inputs:

$$x_j = X_j/w_x \tag{3.2.4}$$

Then the input coefficients including factor coefficients are calculated as follows:

$$a_{ij} = \frac{q_{ij}}{q_j} = \frac{Q_{ij}/p_i}{Q_j/p_j} \qquad a_{xj} = \frac{x_j}{q_j} = \frac{X_j/w_x}{Q_j/p_j} \tag{3.2.5}$$

Again, it should be reminded that in calculating the input coefficients from monetary IO tables, prices p and w should not be omitted in the setup of modeling and GAMS programs. That is, you should not directly write $a_{ij} = \frac{Q_{ij}}{Q_j}$! Using this equation you may still obtain the same numbers for a_{ij} when the prices are set to 1, however conceptually this setup is wrong. In some cases the initial prices are not set to 1, for instance for the purchasers' prices in more complicated CGE models in later chapters, missing the step of dividing prices would cause errors in the early stage of modeling.

From the derived input coefficients above, we construct the following IO matrix $\mathbf{A}$ of Equation (3.2.6). This is the same matrix of Equation (2.2.6), because the derived Leontief production function should be the same.

$$\mathbf{A} = \begin{bmatrix} a_{11} & \cdots & a_{1n} \\ \vdots & a_{ij} & \vdots \\ a_{n1} & \cdots & a_{nn} \end{bmatrix} \tag{3.2.6}$$

Similar to the discussion in Section 2.2, the real output and final demand vectors are denoted by $\mathbf{q}$ and $\mathbf{d}$, respectively. In addition, we introduce a price matrix $\mathbf{P}$. They are listed as follows:

$$\mathbf{q} = \begin{bmatrix} q_1 \\ \vdots \\ q_i \\ \vdots \\ q_n \end{bmatrix} \qquad \mathbf{d} = \begin{bmatrix} d_1 \\ \vdots \\ d_i \\ \vdots \\ d_n \end{bmatrix} \qquad \mathbf{P} = \begin{bmatrix} p_1 & 0 & \cdots & & 0 \\ 0 & \ddots & & & 0 \\ \vdots & & p_i & & \vdots \\ 0 & & & \ddots & 0 \\ 0 & & \cdots & 0 & p_n \end{bmatrix} \tag{3.2.7}$$

Based on the production function, which is the relationship between real inputs and real output, we derived the IO row model (in Section 2.2) as follows:

$$\mathbf{Aq} + \mathbf{d} = \mathbf{q} \qquad \text{or} \qquad \mathbf{q} = (\mathbf{I} - \mathbf{A})^{-1}\mathbf{d} \tag{3.2.8}$$

Now we need to extend the model beyond the production. In equilibrium, the nominal values of supply and demand should also be balanced in each sector. Hence, the IO row model is refined in value terms as follows:

$$\mathbf{PAq} + \mathbf{Pd} = \mathbf{Pq} \qquad \text{or} \qquad \mathbf{Pq} = \mathbf{P(I - A)}^{-1}\mathbf{d} \qquad (3.2.9)$$

While the above equation is mathematically equivalent to Equation (3.2.8), conceptually is not. It says that the *value* of total demands including intermediate and final demands equals the *value* of total outputs.

3.3 Input–Output Price Models

The standard IO row model is characterized by the balance of quantities supplied and demanded in each sector. In the row model, except the final demands are given externally, other quantities are endogenous variables. The prices are implicitly assumed to be fixed, hence we may not even see the price "variables" in the standard IO row models, for instance, if the prices in Equation (3.2.9) are cancelled out in a simplified form of an IO model.

The IO price model studies the commodity price changes in the framework of IO models. It is characterized by the balance of the total revenue and total cost in production of the commodity in each sector. In the IO price model, the commodity prices are endogenous variables in the system while the factor prices are given externally. In addition, quantities (or the ratios among the quantities) are assumed to be fixed, and do not directly appear in the model except for calculating the input coefficients. Because the price balance is a balance of the values along a column of a monetary IO table, thus it is also called an "input–output price column model".

The balance in a column of a monetary IO table is determined as follows:

Value of total inputs = the aggregate value of intermediate inputs and factor inputs (value-added).

For instance, the first column is

$$p_1 q_1 = p_1 q_{11} + \cdots + p_i q_{i1} + \cdots + p_n q_{n1} + w_l L_1 + w_k K_1 \qquad (3.3.1)$$

This column balance relationship applies to all sectors, hence we have the following IO price column model:

$$p_j q_j = p_1 q_{1j} + \cdots + p_i q_{ij} + \cdots + p_n q_{nj} + w_l L_j + w_k K_j \qquad j = 1, \cdots, n \qquad (3.3.2)$$

From the above equation, dividing by the quantity, it shows how the commodity price is formed. Take commodity 1 as an example, i.e., $j = 1$. Dividing both sides of Equation (3.3.2) by q_1, we have

$$\begin{aligned} p_1 &= p_1 \frac{q_{11}}{q_1} + \cdots + p_i \frac{q_{i1}}{q_1} + \cdots + p_n \frac{q_{n1}}{q_1} + w_l \frac{L_1}{q_1} + w_k \frac{K_1}{q_1} \\ &= p_1 a_{11} + \cdots + p_i a_{i1} + \cdots + p_n a_{n1} + w_l a_{l1} + w_k a_{k1} \end{aligned} \qquad (3.3.3)$$

where a_{i1} is input coefficient, a_{l1} and a_{k1} are factor coefficients of labor and capital, respectively, to produce one unit of real output q_1. This equation can be extended to all n sectors in the economy:

$$p_j = p_1 a_{1j} + \cdots + p_i a_{ij} + \cdots + p_n a_{nj} + w_l a_{lj} + w_k a_{kj} \qquad j = 1, \cdots, n \qquad (3.3.4)$$

Equation (3.3.4) is called an IO price model. Its matrix form is

$$\mathbf{p} = \mathbf{A}'\mathbf{p} + \mathbf{A}_l w_l + \mathbf{A}_k w_k \qquad (3.3.5)$$

where
$$\mathbf{p} = \begin{bmatrix} p_1 \\ \vdots \\ p_i \\ \vdots \\ p_n \end{bmatrix} \qquad \mathbf{A}_l = \begin{bmatrix} a_{l1} \\ a_{l2} \\ \cdots \\ a_{ln} \end{bmatrix} \qquad \mathbf{A}_k = \begin{bmatrix} a_{k1} \\ a_{k2} \\ \cdots \\ a_{kn} \end{bmatrix}$$

To simplify, we aggregate the factors in the block of factors or value-added $\mathbf{A}_l w_l + \mathbf{A}_k w_k = \mathbf{A}_x w_x$, then we have

$$(\mathbf{I} - \mathbf{A}')\mathbf{p} = \mathbf{A}_l w_l + \mathbf{A}_k w_k \equiv \mathbf{A}_x w_x \qquad (3.3.6)$$

The commodity price vector is expressed as follows:

$$\mathbf{p} = (\mathbf{I} - \mathbf{A}')^{-1} \mathbf{A}_x w_x \qquad (3.3.7)$$

A factor price change would cause changes in commodity prices. Let factor price change be denoted by Δw_x, commodity price change denoted by $\mathbf{\Delta P}$, thus,

$$\mathbf{\Delta p} = (\mathbf{I} - \mathbf{A}')^{-1} \mathbf{A}_x \Delta w_x \qquad (3.3.8)$$

In application of the above model, one should (1) make a monetary IO table based on available data, (2) set all prices to one, including commodity and factor prices, (3) estimate input and factor coefficients accordingly, and, (4) establish a benchmark IO price model which uses the base state prices. Then one could use the model to estimate the changes in the commodity prices over the base state level, in response to outside shocks, say, labor cost increases.

Example 3.3.1 Based on the data provided by the IO table in Table 3.2.1, set up an IO price column model by using an Excel spreadsheet. Replicate and verify the results.

Solution: First we calculate the input coefficients $a_{ij} = \frac{q_{ij}}{q_j}$. Note p_i and p_j are set to 1. For instance, a_{13} is derived as $a_{13} = \frac{Q_{13}/p_1}{Q_3/p_3} = \frac{q_{13}}{q_3} = \frac{150}{1150} = 0.13$. The calculated input coefficients are the same as those in Table 2.2.1. The IO price column model therefore is as follows:

$$\begin{cases} p_1 = 0.2p_1 + 0.08p_2 + 0.03p_3 + 0.5w_l + 0.19w_k \\ p_2 = 0.19p_1 + 0.25p_2 + 0.26p_3 + 0.16w_l + 0.14w_k \\ p_3 = 0.13p_1 + 0.22p_2 + 0.21p_3 + 0.29w_l + 0.16w_k \end{cases} \qquad (3.3.9)$$

The matrix form corresponding to Equation (3.3.7) is as follows:

$$\begin{bmatrix} p_1 \\ p_2 \\ p_3 \end{bmatrix} = \begin{bmatrix} 1-0.2 & -0.08 & -0.03 \\ -0.19 & 1-0.25 & -0.26 \\ -0.13 & -0.22 & 1-0.21 \end{bmatrix}^{-1} \begin{bmatrix} 0.5w_l + 0.19w_k \\ 0.16w_l + 0.14w_k \\ 0.29w_l + 0.16w_k \end{bmatrix}. \quad (3.3.10)$$

To replicate, we first set the factor prices to 1. Note factor prices are exogenous. Then we execute the model and check if the commodity prices, which are endogenous and to be solved by the model, would return to 1. By using Excel, the calculated results are as follows. One can see that the so calculated commodity prices are 1, as we expect:

$$\begin{bmatrix} p_1 \\ p_2 \\ p_3 \end{bmatrix} = \begin{bmatrix} 1.307 & 0.445 & 0.338 \\ 0.170 & 1.533 & 0.449 \\ 0.106 & 0.525 & 1.426 \end{bmatrix} \begin{bmatrix} 0.5 \times 1 + 0.19 \times 1 \\ 0.16 \times 1 + 0.14 \times 1 \\ 0.29 \times 1 + 0.16 \times 1 \end{bmatrix} = \begin{bmatrix} 1 \\ 1 \\ 1 \end{bmatrix} \quad (3.3.11)$$

Example 3.3.2 Continue working on the above price model. Suppose there is an outside shock whereby the labor cost increases by 20%. Estimate how commodity prices change as a result.

Solution: Using the above inverse matrix data, we obtain the following results by Excel:

$$\begin{bmatrix} \Delta p_1 \\ \Delta p_2 \\ \Delta p_3 \end{bmatrix} = \begin{bmatrix} 1.307 & 0.445 & 0.338 \\ 0.170 & 1.533 & 0.449 \\ 0.106 & 0.525 & 1.426 \end{bmatrix} \begin{bmatrix} 0.5 \times 0.20 \\ 0.16 \times 0.20 \\ 0.29 \times 0.20 \end{bmatrix} = \begin{bmatrix} 0.142 \\ 0.123 \\ 0.130 \end{bmatrix} \quad (3.3.12)$$

The prices of commodities 1, 2 and 3 would increase by 14.2%, 12.3% and 13%, respectively.

Similar to the above two examples, a CGE research project normally consists of two steps. The first step is setting up a CGE model, treating the SAM table data as the initial equilibrium state (also called the base state) and replicating this state. The second step is to simulate external shocks, solve for the new equilibrium state (also called the counterfactual state) and analyze the changes from the base state. The analysis of changes between the two equilibrium states is called "comparative statics" in economics.

3.4 Exogenous Price Cases

Sometimes we need to study how changes in some commodity prices would affect prices of other commodities, for instance, if the government decides to raise the controlled price of water. Another example is the change in the oil price, which is affected by the world market. In these cases, changes occur in some commodity price **p** rather than in factor price **w**. Since commodity prices are previously treated as endogenous variables, we need to make some structural modification in the model setting.

Suppose in an economy with n sectors, the government now controls the price in sector s and plans to adjust the price. In this case, price p_s becomes exogenously given — it is no longer an endogenous variable. The model originally has n price variables, because p_s drops out, the model now has only $n-1$ endogenous price variables to be solved by the system. According to the linear algebra theory, the equation system must have exactly $n-1$ linearly independent equations in order to solve the $n-1$ prices. This is called the condition of "squareness" of the equation system. Hence, we must delete one equation from the original system. Because price in sector s now is determined exogenously, this price is no longer determined by the balance relationship as described by the model. Hence, we should delete in the system the following price balance equation for sector s:

$$p_s = p_1 a_{1s} + \cdots + p_i a_{is} + \cdots + p_n a_{ns} + w_l a_{ls} + w_k a_{ks} \qquad (3.4.1)$$

After deleting the above equation, the $n-1$ equation system to be solved is

$$p_j = p_1 a_{1j} + \cdots + p_i a_{ij} + \cdots + p_n a_{nj} + w_l a_{lj} + w_k a_{kj} \qquad j = 1, .., s-1, \ s+1, .., n \quad (3.4.2)$$

The n-1 variables to be solved are: $p_1, \cdots, p_{s-1}, p_{s+1}, \cdots, p_n$. The following parameters need to be given externally: w_l, w_k, p_s.

The same principle can be applied to the case of price control over multiple commodities. Suppose the government would adjust prices of the m commodities. For instance, the government would lower the price of natural gas but raise the price of electricity. These m prices now are set to be parameters or exogenous variables. Then the price balance equations of the m sectors need to be deleted. As a result, only $n - m$ equations and endogenous price variables are left in the system. Then we solve this equation system for the endogenous price variables.

In modeling, one can manually delete the m equations in the model and construct a new model accordingly. If one already has a GAMS program model for the entire economy with all n sectors but now wishes to study the impacts from several scenarios of adjusting prices, it can be done by modifying the GAMS program by selecting a subset of equations to do the simulation.

Similar issues would occur in later CGE modeling and solving. The GAMS solvers also require that the numbers of equations and variables must be equal — the squareness condition — to solve the equation system. If some of the variables (like the m prices in the above case) become parameters, which means that their values are now fixed, then the model structure needs to be modified accordingly by deleting the same amount of equations, or by adding the same amount of other variables, to make the numbers of equations and variables equal again. Otherwise the model is not correct and the program won't work.

After the price adjustment, the price balance relationship only holds in the remaining $n - m$ sectors. In the m sectors where the prices are externally adjusted, the price equations $p_j = p_1 a_{1j} + \cdots + p_i a_{ij} + \cdots + p_n a_{nj} + w_l a_{lj} + w_k a_{kj}$ no longer hold with the new prices. Hence, a monetary IO table based on the new set of prices after adjustment is no longer globally balanced. This is because the prices in the m sectors are externally controlled, thus out of balance. To deal with this problem, we need some additional explanations for the price discrepancies in the m sectors. In what follows, we use an example to illustrate a model with exogenous adjustment of some commodity prices. Then the resulting balance issue is discussed.

Example 3.4.1 Based on Table 3.2.1 and the IO model of Example 3.3.1, suppose the price in commodity 2 is raised by 10% by some external forces, while the factor prices remain unchanged, find the impacts on the prices of other commodities.

Solution: Deleting the price equation of sector 2, we have the following equation system for the economy:

$$\begin{cases} p_1 = 0.2p_1 + 0.08p_2 + 0.03p_3 + 0.5w_l + 0.19w_k \\ p_3 = 0.13p_1 + 0.217p_2 + 0.209p_3 + 0.287w_l + 0.157w_k \end{cases} \tag{3.4.3}$$

Now the price of commodity 2 is a parameter. Only prices of commodities 1 and 3 are endogenous variables in the system. Set the parameters for price 2 and factor prices as $p_2 = 1.1$, $w_l = 1$, $w_k = 1$, respectively. Rearrange the above equation system (3.4.3) to have

$$(1 - 0.2)p_1 - 0.03p_3 = 0.08p_2 + 0.5w_l + 0.19w_k$$
$$-0.13p_1 + (1 - 0.209)p_3 = 0.217p_2 + 0.287w_l + 0.157w_k \tag{3.4.4}$$

Transform it to the form for the incremental changes, note there are no changes in factor prices, $\Delta w_l = 0$ and $\Delta w_k = 0$:

$$0.8\Delta p_1 - 0.03\Delta p_3 = 0.08\Delta p_2 = 0.08 \times 0.1$$
$$-0.13\Delta p_1 + 0.791\Delta p_3 = 0.217\Delta p_2 = 0.217 \times 0.1 \tag{3.4.5}$$

Solving it by matrix,

$$\begin{bmatrix} \Delta p_1 \\ \Delta p_3 \end{bmatrix} = \begin{bmatrix} 0.8 & -0.03 \\ -0.13 & 0.791 \end{bmatrix}^{-1} \begin{bmatrix} 0.008 \\ 0.0217 \end{bmatrix} = \begin{bmatrix} 0.011 \\ 0.030 \end{bmatrix} \tag{3.4.6}$$

So, the price of commodities 1 and 3 increase by 1.1% and 3.0%, respectively.

By using the new prices, the price balance relationship of Equation (3.3.9) holds for sectors 1 and 3, but not for sector 2. To illustrate, let us first collect and rearrange terms in the three equations in Equation (3.3.9) (In the equation of p3, here we use three decimals for the input coefficients to reduce rounding errors), then fill in the new prices of each sector and check for consistency. For sectors 1 or 3, after we replace the new prices in other sectors, the derived own price is consistent with its changes:

$$p_1 = \frac{1}{1 - 0.2}[0.08p_2 + 0.03p_3 + 0.5w_l + 0.19w_k] \tag{3.4.7}$$

$$= 1.25[0.08(1.1) + 0.03(1 + 0.030) + 0.5(1) + 0.19(1)] = 1.011$$

$$p_3 = \frac{1}{1 - 0.209}[0.13p_1 + 0.217p_2 + 0.287w_l + 0.157w_k]$$

$$= 1.264[0.13(1.011) + 0.217(1.1) + 0.287(1) + 0.157(1)] = 1.03$$

However, after replacing the prices of other sectors, in sector 2, the derived price change is 1.035, which is inconsistent with $p_2 = 1.1$, the supposed value after 10% increase change:

$$p_2 = \frac{1}{1 - 0.25}(0.19p_1 + 0.26p_3 + 0.16w_l + 0.14w_k)$$
$$= 3/4[0.19(1 + 0.011) + 0.26(1 + 0.030) + 0.16(1) + 0.14(1)] \qquad (3.4.8)$$
$$= 1.035$$

This inconsistency is caused by changing the previous endogenous variables to parameters, and consequently, changing the original model structure. It is a disequilibrium case caused by external constraints on the prices. The discrepancy has to be explained by some additional stories out of the model. For instance, suppose the government administratively raises the price in sector 2. The discrepancy of $10\% - 3.5\% = 6.5\%$ between the final price and the costs may be explained by a new sales tax in commodity 2 collected by the government. In summary, when a previous endogenous variable becomes a parameter, the structures of the original IO table and IO model have changed. Some structural modification has to be made to reconcile the discrepancy and to restore the global balance of the model.

3.5 GAMS Programming

In what follows, we use GAMS to solve the problems in Examples 3.3.1, 3.3.2 and 3.4.1. Readers can compare the above mathematical expressions to the GAMS language in the program, to understand the GAMS syntax. Chapter 2 has already explained some basic codes, keywords and syntax, which will not be repeated here.

Example 3.5.1 Write the GAMS program for the IO price model example.

Solution: The GAMS program is as follows.

```
$title Input-output price model of Chapter 3, Example 3.5.1

* The words to the right of the set names are comments.  They are not GAMS
commands. Note the syntax to define three subsets i, x and s.

set ac     all accounts /sec1,sec2,sec3,labor,capital,consumption,investment,total/;
set i(ac)  commodity subset   /sec1,sec2,sec3/;
set x(ac)  factor subset      /labor,capital/;
set s(ac)  subset excluding sector 2 for simulation   /sec1,sec3/;

alias (i,j);
alias (s,ss);

*Read the IO table
table IO(*,*)
        sec1    sec2    sec3    consumption  investment  Total
sec1    200     300     150     280          70          1000
sec2    80      400     250     550          320         1600
sec3    30      420     240     350          110         1150
labor   500     250     330
```

```
capital 190      230      180
Total   1000     1600     1150
;


parameter

realq(i,j) real quantities of the IO table
realf(x,j) real quantities of factor
q0(i)      initial quantity (value of real total output)
a(i,j)     input coefficients
b(x,j)     factor coefficients
p0(i)      initial commodity prices
w0(x)      initial factor prices
con(i)     consumption
inv(i)     capital formation (investment)
lab(j)     labor input
cap(j)     capital input
;


$ontext
    In what follows, we assign parameter values or calculate their values. To
calculate the values of parameters from the existing data is called "calibration"
in the CGE terminology.
    Note, to calibrate the initial quantities of real outputs or real inputs from
a monetary IO table, we need to divide the values in the IO table by the initial prices,
such as p0 and w0 below.  All numbers in the monetary IO table are the monetary values;
hence, we need to divide the nominal values by prices to obtain real quantities.
    The input or factor coefficients must be derived from real quantities. When
the initial price values are 1, missing the initial price won't affect the numbers
of the input coefficients; however, it is conceptually wrong. This error may cause
problems later in the model.
$offtext

p0(i)=1;
w0(x)=1;
realq(i,j)=IO(i,j)/p0(i);
realf(x,j)=IO(x,j)/w0(x);
q0(i)=IO("total",i)/p0(i);
a(i,j)=realq(i,j)/q0(j);
b(x,j)=realf(x,j)/q0(j);
con(i)=IO(i,"consumption")/p0(i);
inv(i)=IO(i,"investment")/p0(i);
lab(j)=IO("labor",j)/w0("labor");
cap(j)=IO("capital",j)/w0("capital");

*declare and define variables

variable
p(i)            price of commodities
```

```
w(x)            price of factors
q(i)            total real output
;

display realq,realf,Q0,a,b,p0,w0,con,inv,lab,cap;

*declare and set up the equations
equation
priceequ(j);

priceequ(j)..
sum(i,a(i,j)*p(i))+sum(x,b(x,j)*w(x))=e=p(j);

*Assign initial values to variables
p.L(i)=p0(i);
w.fx(x)=w0(x);

*Declare the model and issue the execution instruction
model IOPricemodel  /all/;
solve IOPricemodel using mcp
;

*Display the result
display p.L,  w.L;

*==================================================
*Simulation for increase in wages by 20%
*==================================================

*Set up new parameter and assign values
parameter
wl1         labor price
wk1         capital cost
;

wl1=1.2;
wk1=1;

display wl1, wk1;

*equation part
equation
Sim1priceequ(j);

Sim1priceequ(j)..
sum(i,a(i,j)*p(i))+b("capital",j)*wk1+b("labor",j)*wl1=e=p(j);

*Assign initial values
```

```
p.L(i)=p0(i);

*Model and execution part
model SimPricemodel  /Sim1priceequ/;
solve SimPricemodel using mcp
;

*Solve for the percentage increases in the commodity prices parameter
Pincrease(j)   increase in price in various sectors
;

Pincrease(j)=(p.L(j)-1)/p.L(j);

*Display results
display p.L,  Pincrease;

*==================================================================
*Simulation: Price of commodity 2 increases by 20%
*==================================================================
*Note in this case the model structure changes. There are only two equations in the
system, price equations 1 and 3.  "S" stands for the subset for sec1 and sec3

parameter
PS0(s)        price of sec1 and sec3
P2fx(ss)      price of sector 2
aS(s,ss)      direct input-output coefficients for sec1 and sec3
aS2(ss)       direct input-output coefficients for sec2
bS(x,ss)      factor-input-output coefficients for sec1 and sec3
;

PS0(s)=1;
P2fx(ss)=1.1;
aS(s,ss)=IO(s,ss)/IO("total",ss);
aS2(ss)=IO("sec2",ss)/IO("total",ss);
bS(x,ss)=IO(x,ss)/IO("total",ss);

display aS, bS, P2fx;

variable
PS(s);

equation
Sim2priceequ(ss);

Sim2priceequ(ss)..
sum(s,aS(s,ss)*PS(s))+aS2(ss)*P2fx(ss)+sum(x,bS(x,ss)*w(x))=e=PS(ss);

PS.L(s)=PS0(s);
```

```
model Sim2Pricemodel  /Sim2priceequ/;
solve Sim2Pricemodel using mcp
;

parameter
Pincrease2(ss)   increase in price in various sectors
;

Pincrease2(ss)=PS.L(ss)-1

display PS.L,  Pincrease2;

*the end
```

Exercises

3E.1 The following is the IO table of Country Leonland. Based on its data, write an IO price column model in the mathematical form. If the capital price increases by 10%, what happens to the prices of other commodities? Write a GAMS program to answer the above questions.

	Agriculture	Industry	Service	Final demand	Total outputs
Agriculture	160	150	90	480	880
Industry	140	320	170	900	1530
Service	80	150	250	590	1070
Labor	320	350	410		
Capital	180	560	150		
Total inputs	880	1530	1070		

3E.2 Because of the political pressure from the farmers, the government of Leonland now administratively controls the agricultural prices. If they raise the price of agricultural products by 15%, while labor and capital prices remain at the initial values at 1, what happens to the prices of industry and service products? Write a corresponding GAMS program to solve this problem.

Appendix: Review of Mathematics

3A.1 Linear equation system

A linear equation system of m equations and n variables has the following form:

$$\begin{cases} a_{11}x_1 + \cdots + a_{1j}x_j + \cdots + a_{1n}x_n = d_1 \\ \cdots \\ a_{i1}x_1 + \cdots + a_{ij}x_j + \cdots + a_{in}x_{ni} = d_i \\ \cdots \\ a_{m1}x_1 + \cdots + a_{mj}x_j + \cdots + a_{mn}x_n = d_m \end{cases} \qquad (3A.1.1)$$

In matrix form, it is as follows:

$$\begin{bmatrix} a_{11} & \cdots & a_{1n} \\ \vdots & \cdots & \vdots \\ a_{m1} & \cdots & a_{mn} \end{bmatrix} \begin{bmatrix} x_1 \\ \vdots \\ x_m \end{bmatrix} = \begin{bmatrix} d_1 \\ \vdots \\ d_m \end{bmatrix} \qquad (3A.1.2)$$

Or by matrix notation

$$\mathbf{Ax} = \mathbf{d} \qquad (3A.1.3)$$

The sufficient condition for $\mathbf{x}$ to have a unique solution is that matrix $\mathbf{A}$ is non-singular (the determinant of $\mathbf{A}$ is non-zero). Alternatively, we use these conditions: (1) $m = n$ (numbers of equations and variables are equal, which is also called "square"), and (2) all m equations are linearly independent.

A linear equation system does not have a solution if inconsistency exists. Here is an example of inconsistency:

$$\begin{cases} 5x_1 + 3x_2 = 6 \\ 10x_1 + 6x_2 = 10 \end{cases} \qquad (3A.1.4)$$

The system may have an infinite number of solutions if $m < n$; or $m = n$, but the equations are linearly dependent.

Let $\mathbf{a}_i$ be the ith row of $\mathbf{A}$. Linear dependence means that rows of matrix $\mathbf{A}$ can be expressed in the following way:

$$\sum_i k_i \mathbf{a}_i = 0 \qquad (3A.1.5)$$

where $k_1, \cdots, k_n$ are not all zeros.

Walras's law is an example of linear dependence of the excess demand functions in an economy.

Chapter 4

SAM (Social Accounting Matrix) Table

4.1 Structure of a SAM Table

The previous chapters have discussed the input–output (IO) table. The scope of an IO table is limited: it depicts only the IO flows among the sectors in the production processes. The IO table does not cover the comprehensive relationships among various national accounts in the economy, such as the financial flows among the institutions, factor income and households' expenditure, government revenue and expenditure, etc.

To describe the relationships among the flows of national accounts, scholars have developed the Social Accounting Matrix, in short, the SAM table. The SAM table describes not only the balance of flows of the supply and demand of commodities and factors in each sector, but also the balance of financial flows between income and expenditure in each account as described in the System of National Accounts (SNA). SNA is a standard set by the United Nations for national economic and other social accounts. A SAM table is the data foundation of the CGE model.

The structure of a SAM table is similar to a monetary IO table but is more complete. It is a two-dimensional square matrix with rows and columns for sectors as well as for other national accounts. Values in the table cells are the transaction flows between supply and demand or between income and expenditure of the related accounts, measured in currency units. A standard IO table does not have the fourth quadrant (the lower right block of the table), but a SAM table does. The fourth quadrant provides the information of monetary flows from factor income (such as households' wage income) to expenditure (such as consumption), which is missing in the IO table. Hence, we say the SAM table data is competed/closed because it provides data of completed circular flows of the economy, while a typical IO table does not.

A national account can be an economic sector or an institutional account such as households, governments, firms, the rest of the world, etc. Each account is represented by a row and a column. The number in a cell of the table is the monetary value of transactions between corresponding row and column. Similar to the idea in the IO table, the column accounts are the demanders or buyers. The row accounts are the suppliers or sellers. The value in a cell is the payment made by the column account to the row account. Because the row account is the supplier, the total value of the row is the total income of this account.

Because the column account is the buyer, the total value of the column is the total expenditure of this account. Total income must equal total expenditure in each account.

Table 4.1.1 is a description of a "standard" SAM table. There are eight main grouped accounts: Activities, Commodities, Factors, Households, Enterprises, Government, Rest of the World (ROW) and Savings–Investment accounts.

In the table there are two account groups, "activities" and "commodities". An activity refers to the production activity in a sector. It is also called an "industry". A commodity refers to the commodity produced in the sector. In a typical IO table as shown in the previous chapters, production activity in one sector produces exactly one commodity, so the IO table has only commodity accounts in which the production activities are integrated. In a more complex economy, activities and commodities are not the same. An activity may produce several commodities such as the activity in the coal sector produces chemical, electricity and construction commodities. A commodity may be produced by different activities such as fuel gas is produced by petroleum, coal and agricultural sectors. In order to investigate some other issues, we may also need to separate accounts of activities and commodities. For instance, to study the coffee production in some developing countries, we need to separate the production activities by large-scale farms and by small household farmers. To study the productivities of various ownership enterprises in transitional economies, we need to separate state-owned enterprises and private enterprises in producing the same commodities.

In general, the value of activities are calculated by the suppliers' prices. The value of commodities are calculated by market prices (purchasers' prices). This separation gives a convenience in the case of an open economy when we need to distinguish between two "kinds" of commodities — one for export and the other for domestic consumption — produced by the same activity. The former is shipped overseas and paid by foreign buyers, and the latter will go through the wholesale, retail and delivery process to reach the domestic consumers. They are subject to different marketing services, taxes, and purchasers' prices.

Factors are the primary factors, including labor, capital, land, technology, etc. There are four economic agent groups (or institutions), including households, enterprises, the government, and ROW. These terms are consistent with the concepts in macroeconomics, which is straightforward for understanding and economic analysis.

ROW account is the balance of earnings and outlays of the foreign exchange. The column of the ROW account lists foreign exchange earnings from exports and transfer payments from overseas to the country. On the row of the ROW account are items of foreign exchange outlays, which include imports, domestic transfer payment to overseas recipients, and so on. $IM - X$ in the savings–investment identity is the trade or current account deficit. Assuming the country does not allow capital flows crossing border, $IM - X$ reflects the country's position in borrowing money from overseas to finance the deficit. That is why $IM - X$ is also termed "net foreign savings".

The last account is the savings–investment account, which helps analyze the accounts of savings and investment in the economy. In macroeconomics, the savings–investment identity can be derived from the two national income identities:

$$C + I + G + X - IM = Y$$
$$C + S + T = Y$$

(4.1.1)

Table 4.1.1. Description of a typical SAM table.

	1 Activities	2 Commodities	3 Factors	4 Households	5 Enterprises	6 Government	7 ROW	8 Savings–Investment	Total incomes
1 Activities		Domestically marketed outputs							Output
2 Commodities	Intermediate inputs	Wholesale and retail trade margins		Household consumption		Government expenditure	Exports	Investment	Demand
3 Factors	Value-added						Factor income from ROW		Factor income
4 Households			Households factor income	Transfer among households	Enterprise transfer to households	Government transfer to households	Transfer to households from ROW		Household income
5 Enterprises			Enterprise factor income			Government transfer to enterprises	Transfer to enterprises from ROW		Enterprise income
6 Government	VAT tax*, Employment tax, production tax	VAT tax*, Sales tax, tariffs, export tax	Factor taxes as income tax to government	Income tax, direct tax	Enterprise direct tax to government		Transfer to government from ROW		Government income
7 ROW		Imports	Factor income to ROW		Enterprise surplus to ROW	Government transfers to ROW			Foreign exchange outflow
8 Savings-Investment				Household savings	Enterprise savings	Government savings	Foreign savings		Savings
Total expenditures	Activity	Supply	Factor expenditures	Household expenditures	Enterprises expenditures	Government expenditures	Foreign exchange inflow	Investment	

Note: *See explanation in Chapter 15.

where C is consumption, I is investment, G is government spending, X is exports, IM is imports, S is savings, T is tax. These are conventional notations used in macroeconomics. Combining the two equations, we have

$$I = S + (T - G) + (IM - X) \qquad (4.1.2)$$

On the left hand side, I is investment. It includes new physical capital formation, such as a new machinery or plant. It also includes changes in inventory and new residential housing. On the right hand side, S is household savings, $T - G$ is net government savings. $IM - X$ is net foreign savings (assuming the foreign reserve remains unchanged). Adding the terms on right hand side together, we get the total savings. The savings–investment account includes important variables in macroeconomics.

The eight accounts in Table 4.1.1 are highly integrated. Indeed, most of the time, each of them is a group of more detailed subaccounts. In practice, we would have to add, segment and merge the accounts in the SAM table according to our research needs. In many cases, the activities and commodities accounts can be merged. In other cases, the capital formation (investment) account can be segmented into fixed capital, inventory and residential housing, to investigate the details of the changes in investment. A broad account can include many detailed subaccounts. A cell in Table 4.1.1 can also be a submatrix, which can be quite big sometimes. For instance, the cell located in the first column and second row is "intermediate inputs", which is the IO matrix and can be very sizeable.

In views of the monetary flows of transactions, each row account of the SAM table represents the incomes it receives from column accounts, and each column account represents the expenditures it spends on row accounts. The text in each cell of the table explains the details of the transaction. For instance, in Table 4.1.1, the second row shows the income received by the commodity account from its sales to other accounts. The cell of the fourth row and third column is the households' incomes from the supplies of their owned factors, such as wage and rent. The same cell can also be interpreted another way around, as the payment of the factors account to the households for using factors. In the bottom right block — the fourth quadrant of the table, there are various transfer payments, as well as capital flows between savings and investment. These are not presented in a typical IO table.

Table 4.1.2 is a SAM table for a hypothetical Country C. It is a "real" SAM table with the quantitative data in the cells, while it is in the same structure as that of Table 4.1.1. The number in each cell is the transaction value as explained in Table 4.1.1. For instance, the 53,000 million dollars in row 4 and column 3 is the income that households receive from their factor inputs, including wages and rent.

4.2 National Accounts and Designing a SAM Table

Various issues may emerge in making a SAM table from data for research. The first problems to encounter are designing the structure of the table and data availability. The data in the SAM table should be collected and filled in accordance with the definitions and specification of SNA. In the real world, as data sources, availability and definitions vary from country to country, some adjustments may have to be made to compromise.

Table 4.1.2. A hypothetical SAM table for Country C. (million dollars)

		1	2	3	4	5	6	7	8	Total incomes
		Activities	Commodities	Factors	Households	Enterprises	Government	ROW	Savings–Investment	
1	Activities		189800					12730		202530
2	Commodities	135150	19000		51000		12000		10650	227800
3	Factors	63380						300		63680
4	Households			53000		5000	8000	3000		69000
5	Enterprises			8200						8200
6	Government	4000	3000	180	10000	1700		790		19670
7	ROW		16000	2300			170			18470
8	Savings–Investment				8000	1500	−500	1650		10650
	Total expenditures	202530	227800	63680	69000	8200	19670	18470	10650	

The SAM table structure should be designed according to the research project needs and data availability. Some accounts need to be segmented to more specific and detailed subaccounts, while others can be merged to simplify. Take one example, if we plan to study the impacts of the taxes on the income distribution, we need to separate the households to various income groups. Take another example. Suppose that the U.S. government plans to change the current tax system to a value-added tax (VAT) system, and the U.S. government wants to compare various types of VAT taxes such as an equal VAT tax rate for all factor inputs, or a VAT tax with exemption for fixed capital consumption. Currently, the U.S. does not have VAT taxes, hence the U.S. SAM table does not have a VAT tax account; but to simulate this policy change, we need to add a VAT tax account in the U.S. SAM table. Further, we may have to separate VAT tax into several subaccounts according to the non-deductible VAT burdens: one is levied on capital consumption, one is levied on other factor inputs, one is levied on ultimate consumers. By doing so, we can study the impacts of various VAT types on the economy.

Technical issues can also be involved in making a SAM table. According to economics theories or in a real-world situation, negative transaction values in some cells are realistic and legitimate. For instances, Earned Income Credit in the U.S. is a negative income tax, and the government savings are negative if the government is running a budget deficit. In Table 4.1.2, the government budget deficit would be a negative number in the cell of row 8 and column 6. This cell is denoted by the address cell (8, 6), where the first and second numbers refer to row and column numbers, respectively. There is nothing wrong with a negative value in cell (8, 6) in economics theory or in mathematics; however, the negative value may pose a technical problem in using some approaches like using the entropy method in balancing the SAM table. In some other cases, a negative entry value may cause problems in running a CGE model successfully to find solutions. These issues will be discussed in later chapters.

In practice, some techniques are used to work around with negative values in a SAM table. For instance, in balancing a SAM table by using the entropy method, because the values in table cells must be positive, a "relocating value" approach can be used. We relocate a negative value to the opposite cell address and change its sign to positive. After the SAM table is balanced, we move the adjusted value back to the original cell and change its sign back.

Occasionally, for some reasons we need to relocate the values in the SAM table but still need to preserve the integrity of the original SAM data. An example is the treatment of the export subsidies discussed in Chapter 15. This can be done by moving the value in the cell to the opposite cell address and changing the sign of the value. For instance, to relocate the value of 700 in cell (i, j), we deduct 700 from cell (i, j) and add 700 in cell (j, i) which is located in the opposite position in the table. While this method would change the total values in rows and columns of i and j, the information and accuracy of the data, and the balance properties in the SAM table, are still preserved. Often we can have the same interpretation for the relocated value. For example, in Table 4.1.2, cell (8,6) has the negative number of −500, which is interpreted as negative government savings of 500. To move this number in the SAM table, we change the value in cell (8, 6) to zero and add 500 in cell (6, 8). This "relocated value" of 500 in cell (6, 8) can be interpreted as a positive government budget deficit, or the government's borrowing from the other institutions' savings in the economy. They still mean the same thing. Let us take another example: cell (4, 7) of 3000 is interpreted as a positive net transfer payment by the rest of the world to the domestic households. If instead we relocate the value to the opposite address cell (7, 4) and flip its sign to −3000, the economic interpretation is the same. It still says that, in net, the rest of the world pays 3000 to the domestic households.

It should also be noted that in some situations the value relocation by the above method may not have a meaningful interpretation. For instance, in Table 4.1.1, the value in cell (factors, activities) is interpreted as adding values by factor inputs in production. If we relocate this value to cell (activities, factors) with a negative sign, there is no meaningful economic interpretation.

The appendix of this chapter provides an example of designing a SAM structure according to the research need and data availability. The format of this SAM table is slightly different from that of Table 4.1.1, but the principles are the same. The SAM Table 4A.1.1 is made by Li *et al.* (1997) for China during the reform period. Table 4A.1.1 in the appendix is descriptive, the real table with data is available in GTAP or online. Because of limited data availability, capital consumption is based on the statistics of fixed capital depreciation. In order to capture the special structure of the government revenue in China, their SAM table has three subaccounts in the government group: government subsidy, extra-budgetary income and government. To study the very large inventory changes in the capital formation in China, the SAM table adds one subaccount of "inventory" in the savings–investment group. Comparing to Table 4.1.1, this SAM table has switched the positions of the activity and commodity accounts. Both arrangements are common in the CGE literature. The arrangement is chosen by personal preference but won't change the data and the computation outcomes. Mathematically, interchanging two rows and then interchanging two corresponding columns in a matrix won't change the computation results, except the indexes of the two accounts would be interchanged.

A typical SAM format used by SNA is illustrated in Table 16.5.1. This format directly combines the supply and use tables in the SNA system. The supply table is a data table giving the information about the resources of commodities. The use table is a data table giving the information about the uses of commodities and the cost structure of activities. Statistical authorities for national accounts in many developed countries, such as the Bureau of Economic Analysis in the U.S., regularly publish the supply and use tables. These tables are quite convenient for CGE researchers to construct the accounts and fill in entry data in quadrants I, II and III in a SAM table. At this stage of learning, we do not go to details about the supply and use tables. However, as you learn more about the structure and term definitions of the national accounts discussed in this book, by Chapter 16, it would be quite easy and straightforward to understand the supply and use tables, and, how they are organized and combined in the SAM table. You will find that, the supply table consists of the commodity column accounts in Table 16.5.1; and the use table consists of the commodity row accounts and activity column accounts in Table 16.5.1. From these two tables you already have the raw data for the first three quadrants of the SAM table, although more work still needs to be done such as filling in the data in quadrant IV, refining the raw data, or even restructuring the SAM table format for research needs.

Exercises

4E.1 Design a SAM table, set up corresponding accounts, and place the following variables in the appropriate cells of a descriptive SAM table: Commodity sales on the market, foreign factor income, households factor income, transfer payments among households, enterprise-to-household transfer payment, government-to-household transfer payment, factor income of enterprises, households home consumed outputs, intermediate inputs, transaction costs, household consumption of commodities on market, government consumption, investment, value-added, production tax, VAT, sales tax, customs duties, export tax, government factor income, personal direct tax, income tax, direct corporate tax, enterprises profit remittance to the government, transfer payment from foreign government, household savings, enterprise savings, government savings, net foreign savings, government transfer payment to enterprises, overseas transfer payment to domestic enterprises, exports, imports, payments to foreign factor inputs, companies' remittance of profits to overseas owners, domestic government transfer payments to overseas and foreign transfer payments to households.

Appendix

Table 4A.1.1. Descriptive SAM table of China, 1997.

	1 Commodity	2 Activity	3 Labor	4 Capital	5 Households	6 Enterprises	7 Government subsidies
1 Commodity		Intermediate input			Household consumption		
2 Activity	Gross domestic output						
3 Labor		Worker compensation					
4 Capital		Return on capital					
5 Households			Labor income	Capital income		Enterprise transfer	Government subsidies
6 Enterprises				Capital income			
7 Government subsidies		Production subsidy					
8 Extra-budgetary		Extra-budgetary charges					
9 Government	Income tax	Production tax			Direct tax	Direct tax	
10 ROW	Imports			Foreign investment income			
11 Capital account					Household savings	Corporate savings	
12 Inventory changes							
Total	Total supply	Total inputs	Labor expenditure	Capital expenditure	Household expenditure	Business expenditure	Government subsidies

Table 4A.1.1. (Continued)

	8 Extra-budgetary	9 Government	10 ROW	11 Capital account	12 Inventory changes	Total
1 Commodity	Public self-funded consumption	Government consumption	Exports	Fixed capital formation	Net changes in inventory	Total demand
2 Activity						Total output
3 Labor						Labor income
4 Capital						Capital income
5 Households		Government transfers	Foreign income			Gross resident income
6 Enterprises						Enterprise income
7 Government subsidies		Expenditure due to subsidy				Government subsidies
8 Extra-budgetary						Extra-budgetary income
9 Government			Income from overseas	Income from Government debt		Total government revenue
10 ROW		Payments to abroad				Foreign exchange outlays
11 Capital account	Extra-budgetary account savings	Government savings	Net foreign savings			Total savings
12 Inventory changes				Inventory changes		Net changes in inventory
Total	Extra-budgetary expenditure	Government spending	Foreign exchange earnings	Total investment	Net changes in inventory	

Note: Li *et al.* (1997), Development Research Center of the State Council, China, "Social Accounting Matrix of China's Economy, 1997".

Chapter 5

Balancing SAM Tables

5.1 Consistency Principle in a SAM table

In building a SAM table from raw data, one often encounters some inconsistency problems. Because individual raw data may come from various sources and with different technical issues involved, the sum of a row usually does not equal the sum of the column of the same account. Some other inconsistencies may also arise, for instance, the raw data recorded do not obey the national accounting identities required by the economics theory. This chapter discusses these inconsistency problems and the approaches to balance the SAM table.

Suppose a SAM table has n accounts. Mathematically, this is a $n \times n$ square matrix. Let Q_{ij} denote the element of row i and column j of the matrix. Q_{ij} also refers to the value of the corresponding cell in the SAM table. Let $\overline{Q}_{ij}$ denote the original number filled in the SAM table before we do any balancing. So the original matrix is

$$\overline{\mathbf{Q}} = \left[\overline{Q}_{ij}\right] \qquad i = 1, \cdots n \quad j = 1, \cdots, n \tag{5.1.1}$$

As the input–output (IO) table, the SAM table must follow the balance principle of national accounting. The sum of a row should equal the sum of the column of the same account. For instance, in Table 4.1.2, the second row and the second column are for the same account "commodity". Therefore, the sums of the row and column are equally 227,800. This balance principle is mathematically expressed as follows. For each account k, we have

$$\sum_i^n Q_{ik} = \sum_j^n Q_{kj} \qquad k = 1, \cdots, n \tag{5.1.2}$$

In practice, to start building a SAM table from raw data, the initial results are not balanced. Disaggregated data for the SAM table often come from different sources, such as different surveys or statistical agencies. Estimates are used for missing data. For instance, IO tables are published every five years so estimates are used for those years between the reporting years. Data can contain other legitimate deviation errors. All these technical issues would contribute to inconsistencies in balancing SAM tables. Hence, in building a SAM table, initially the sum of a row and the sum of the column of the same account are not equal:

$$\sum_i^n \overline{Q}_{ik} \neq \sum_j^n \overline{Q}_{kj} \qquad k = 1, \cdots, n \tag{5.1.3}$$

Therefore, we need to adjust the values in the SAM table so their corresponding rows and columns have the same total numbers. This adjustment process is called balancing SAM tables.

There are different methods to balance SAM tables. In addition to the mathematical approaches, one should also utilize all available information, knowledge, experience and judgement, solidly based on economics theories. In what follows, we introduce some popular balancing methods, along with the corresponding GAMS programs.

5.2 Least Squares Method

The idea of the least squares method is the same as that in statistical regression. Let the values in cells to be adjusted in the adjustment process be Q_{ij}, the least squares method is to minimize the sum of the squared differences, where the objective function is z:

$$\min_{Q_{ij}} z = \sum_i^n \sum_j^n (Q_{ij} - \overline{Q}_{ij})^2 \tag{5.2.1}$$

and subject to the following constraint:

$$s.t. \quad \sum_i^n Q_{ik} = \sum_j^n Q_{kj} \qquad k = 1, \cdots, n \tag{5.2.2}$$

In the case where the scale differences among the data are hugely different, to avoid some large scale data taking too much weight in minimization, we should normalize the data by changing the objective function z and minimize the following:

$$\min_{Q_{ij}} z = \sum_i^n \sum_j^n (Q_{ij}/\overline{Q}_{ij} - 1)^2 \tag{5.2.3}$$

subject to the same constraint (5.2.2).

In what follows, we use an example to illustrate. Suppose the initial SAM table of Country A is the following Table 5.2.1. We can see the inconsistency problem: the row totals and column totals of the same accounts are not equal.

Table 5.2.1. The unbalanced initial SAM table of Country A.

	Commodity 1/ Activity 1	Commodity 2/ Activity 2	Factor/ labor	Households	Row total
Commodity 1/ Activity 1	52	45		150	247
Commodity 2/ Activity 2	95	48		90	233
Factor/labor	120	89			209
Households			192		192
Column total	267	182	192	240	

Table 5.2.2. Balanced results by the least squares method for Country A's SAM table.

	Commodity 1/ Activity 1	Commodity 2/ Activity 2	Factor/ labor	Households	Row total
Commodity 1/ Activity 1	52	57		140	249
Commodity 2/ Activity 2	83	48		68	199
Factor/labor	114	94			208
Households			208		208
Column total	249	199	208	208	

Applying the least squares method to the above SAM table data, we solve the following problem:

$$\min z = (Q_{11} - 52)^2 + (Q_{12} - 45)^2 + (Q_{14} - 150)^2 + (Q_{21} - 95)^2 + (Q_{22} - 48)^2$$
$$+ (Q_{24} - 90)^2 + (Q_{31} - 120)^2 + (Q_{32} - 89)^2 + (Q_{43} - 192)^2 \qquad (5.2.4)$$

$$\text{s.t.} \quad \sum_i^4 Q_{i1} = \sum_j^4 Q_{1j} \quad \sum_i^4 Q_{i2} = \sum_j^4 Q_{2j} \quad \sum_i^4 Q_{i3} = \sum_j^4 Q_{3j} \quad \sum_i^4 Q_{i4} = \sum_j^4 Q_{4j}$$

$$Q_{ij} \geq 0, i = 1, \cdots, 4, j = 1, \cdots, 4$$

In what follows, we use GAMS program to solve the above example question. The obtained results are in Table 5.2.2.

Example 5.2.1 Write the GAMS program to use the least squares method to balance the SAM table of Table 5.2.1. Based on the prior knowledge from economics, those blank cells without data values are correct. Hence, you should keep these cells blank in the final results.

Solution: The GAMS program is as follows.

```
$title Example 5.2.1  Least squares  balance method
*Declare and define set i
   set i   /sec1,sec2,lab,hh/;
   alias  (i,j);


*=========== SAM ===============
   table SAM(*,*)
          sec1   sec2   lab   hh    total
   sec1   52     45           150   247
   sec2   95     48           90    233
   lab    120    89                 209
   hh                   192         192
   total  267    182    192   240
   ;


*Declare parameters and assign their values
parameters
   Q0(i,j)          initial values;
   Q0(i,j)=sam(i,j);


*Declare and define variables and functions
variables
   Q(i,j) Values to be adjusted in the SAM table
   z  value of the objective function to be minimized;


*Values of each individual variable should be non-negative. Otherwise it might
cause problems for GAMS to reach solutions
positive variable Q(i,j);


equations
    sumsquare          Objective function z
    balance            Constraints to equalize same account totals;
```

*In GAMS program, "$" is often used as a condition operator. In what follows, we use "$" operator in the equation, which means "under condition of ⬚ this equation is valid".
*The $ operator is placed immediately after the index in the following example. This condition operator $(SAM(i,j) means: the equation would only be executed under the condition that cell(i,j) in the SAM table has a non-zero value. Hence, we keep the blank cells unchanged.

```
    sumsquare..
    z =e= sum((i,j)$sam(i,j),sqr(Q(i,j)-sam(i,j)));


$ontext
```
    "sqr" is the function symbol for square of the number, meaning x*x. Note if sqr(Q(i,j) is changed to (Q(i,j)**2?although mathematically it is equivalent to x2, the MCP solvers would treat them differently in computation, therefore, it can encounter technical problems in optimization. So, avoid using Q(i,j)**2.

The following format shows how to handle the indexed variables. Equation balance(i) means there are i=1,..n of the indexed equations.

Note how the summation code "sum" operates. It sums the indexed variables by the particular index as instructed. In the following example, the index instructed is "j". Inside the parentheses of the variable Q, the first number in the parentheses refers to the row, and the second number refers to the column. The indexes of (i,j switch positions between the left-hand side (LHS) and the right-hand side (RHS) of the equation sign, so on LHS is the row sum and on RHS is the column sum of account i.
$offtext

```
    balance(i)..
    sum(j$sam(i,j),Q(i,j)) =e= sum(j,Q(j,i));

*Assign initial values for the variables
    Q.L(i,j)=Q0(i,j);

*In this case we use GAMS model type NLP instead of MCP to solve
model sambal  /all/;
solve sambal using nlp minimizing z;

*Printing outcomes
display Q.L,z.L;

*end
```

5.3 Inconsistency Problems and Adding Constraints in Balancing

In balancing SAM tables, it would be more efficient and accurate to take advantage of the available information and make judgments based on the economics theory and the real-world situation.

Suppose we have information obtained from other sources that some data values in the SAM table are very reliable. For example, we know that the data of external trade, tariff and consumer expenditures are mostly reliable, but the depreciation data and household income are generally more error-prone. Hence, when using the least squares method to balance SAM tables, we may assign greater weights to those more reliable values and smaller weights for the less reliable values. Concretely, we can multiply each square difference term in Equation (5.2.3) by a positive weight, δ_{ij}:

$$\min_{Q_{ij}} z = \sum_i^n \sum_j^n \delta_{ij}(Q_{ij}/\overline{Q}_{ij} - 1)^2 \tag{5.3.1}$$

Let the benchmark value of the weight δ_{ij} be 1. For the reliable data, the weight should be greater than 1. The more reliable the data is, the larger the coefficient would be. If you know some data in the SAM table are extremely reliable or should remain unchanged, you can set up a constraint to fix this value. For instance, in Table 5.2.1, if the prior information reveals that the value 45 of Q_{12} is a reliable number, you can add a constraint of $Q_{12} = \overline{Q}_{12} = 45$ in the minimization problem of Equation (5.2.4).

We should also obey the accounting identities by adding corresponding constraints. The national accounting system requires that value-added from each factor should equal the factor income of the owners. For example, in the simple economy as described in Table 5.2.1, the sum of payment from commodity sectors to the labor input should be equal to the labor income of households. In the original SAM table, the total payment from the commodity sectors to labor is $120 + 89 = 209$, but the factor income of households from labor is 192, which is not equal. Therefore, an equality restriction should be added in least squares minimization, i.e., $Q_{31} + Q_{32} = Q_{43}$.

The national accounting system also requires that GDP measured by the expenditure approach should be equal to the GDP measured by the income approach. That is, nationwide the total income and total expenditure of all economic agents/institutions should be equal. In the economy of Table 5.2.1, there is only one economic institution — household. The total income of institutions therefore is the household income 192, but the total expenditure is 240, which is not equal. So we should add a constraint to make sure the values of the two concepts are equal in the final balanced SAM table. What is the final result? Should it be equal to 192 or 240, or some number in between? This requires some judgment based on economic theory and experience. Suppose we are working with a developing economy or transitional economy, in which unreported gray income is rampant in practice, then the number from the expenditure 240 is more reliable.

When inconsistencies arise from the initial data in the SAM table, we should deal with it seriously, utilizing the available information, as well as the knowledge about economics theory, the country's system, economic environment, social practices and the national statistical system. As mentioned earlier, in transitional economies like China and Russia, households' aggregate spending often is much greater than their aggregate income recorded by national statistics. It is common in these economies, because of the underdeveloped tax system, that much of the household incomes are not reported, illegally, illegitimately or legitimately. Yet such a problem is not uncommon in developed economies either. In some OECD (Organization for Economic Co-operation and Development) countries like Italy, underground and informal economies are very active, the revealed value of the total expenditure is substantially greater than that from recorded total income. In these cases, the numbers from the expenditure is more reliable. Hence, we should discount the numbers from value-added from the income side, such as Q_{31} and Q_{32} in Table 5.2.1. Instead, we can take more seriously the numbers of households' expenditure in each sector, by setting $Q_{43} = 150 + 90 = 240$ as a constraint and letting the numbers in the value-added part adjust in the balancing process.

5.4 Manual Balancing

In the case where the inconsistencies between the row and column sums are not significant, the SAM table may be balanced by manual adjustment. The advantages of manual adjustment are simplicity and flexibility in utilizing the available additional information.

Table 5.4.1. Excel worksheet for Country A's SAM table.

	Commodity 1/ Activity 1	Commodity 2/ Activity 2	Factor/ labor	Households	Row total	Differences between row & col
Commodity 1/ Activity 1	52	45		150	247	−20
Commodity 2/ Activity 2	95	48		90	233	51
Factor/labor	120	89			209	17
Households			192		192	−48
Column total	267	182	192	240		

The disadvantage is lack of an objective standard. Everyone may have a different final balanced SAM table from his subjective judgment. Therefore, the conditions for using the manual adjustment method are: First, the difference between the sums of each pair of row and column is small — a rule of thumb is that the percentage difference (in absolute value) of the two numbers is less than 5%. Secondly, the researcher should be quite knowledgeable about the reliability of each individual data collected. Take an example of the SAM table in Table 5.2.1. The percentage difference of sector 2 is $(233 − 182)/[(233 + 182)/2] = −24.6\%$. The absolute value is 24.6%, which is too big. Therefore, the approach of manually balancing SAM is not suggested. However, for the purpose of illustration, in what follows we still use Table 5.2.1 as an example to show how to manually adjust a SAM table.

We use the Excel spreadsheet to make manual adjustments. First, record the original SAM data Q_{ij} in the Excel sheet, as that in Table 5.4.1. Then use the Excel summation function to generate the sums of rows and columns. In particular, in the cells of the second column from the right, enter the Excel formula to calculate the row total values, $Y_k^r = \sum_{j}^{n} Q_{kj}$. In the cells of the bottom row for column totals, enter the Excel formula to calculate the column total values, $Y_k^c = \sum_{i}^{n} Q_{ik}$. The last column on the right is the differences of the row total and column total values. In the cells of the last column, enter the Excel formula to calculate $Y_k^r - Y_k^c$. Our purpose is to adjust Q_{ij} values so finally the differences $Y_k^r - Y_k^c$ in the last column disappear and the numbers converge to zeros.

The most efficient way is to start the adjustment from the larger gaps. From the last column, it can be seen account 2 (Commodity 2) and account 4 (households) have the two largest gaps, with +51 and −48, respectively. To decrease +51 and increase −48, we have two options: one is to reduce the value of Q_{24}, another is raise the value of Q_{42}. Yet there is no economic justification for having a value in Q_{42} in this SAM table. Hence, we can only adjust Q_{24}. So we reduce Q_{24} by 48, the smaller of the magnitudes of the two numbers +51 and −48. The result is in Table 5.4.2. Account 4 is balanced, partially, at this stage.

After the first adjustment, the two largest gaps occur in account 1 (Commodity 1) and account 3 (labor), with −20 and +17, respectively. We can either raise the value of Q_{13} or

Table 5.4.2.   Country A's SAM table — Excel worksheet after the first adjustment.

	Commodity 1/ Activity 1	Commodity 2/ Activity 2	Factor/ labor	Households	Row total	Differences between row & col
Commodity 1/ Activity 1	52	45		150	247	−20
Commodity 2/ Activity 2	95	48		42	185	3
Factor/labor	120	89			209	17
Households			192		192	0
Column total	267	182	192	192		

Table 5.4.3.   Country A's SAM table — Excel worksheet after the second adjustment.

	Commodity 1/ Activity 1	Commodity 2/ Activity 2	Factor/ labor	Households	Row total	Differences between row & col
Commodity 1/ Activity 1	52	45		150	247	−3
Commodity 2/ Activity 2	95	48		42	185	3
Factor/labor	103	89			192	0
Households			192		192	0
Column total	250	182	192	192		

reduce the value of Q_{31}. Similar to the previous case, there is no economic justification for having data in Q_{13}, so we can only adjust Q_{31}. Hence, we reduce Q_{31} by 17. The result of this second adjustment is in Table 5.4.3.

After the second adjustment, only account 1 and account 2 are not balanced. We can either raise the value of Q_{12} by 3 or reduce the value of Q_{21} by 3 to finish the balancing job. If we have no knowledge about which data is more reliable, we can make a partial adjustment of 1.5 for both variables. The result after this third adjustment is in Table 5.4.4.

The above manual adjustment method is efficient in terms of mathematical operations. In practice, we should always utilize the available information about the reliability of individual data, knowledge about economics and statistical theories, and experience, to avoid unreasonable adjustments. If prior information reveals that the data of Q_{24}, households' spending on Commodity 2, is reliable, then we can keep this number fixed in the adjustment process. Suppose Country A is a developing economy in which the household spending data and intermediate input data are more reliable, but labor income Q_{31} and Q_{32} and transfer payment are error-prone thus not reliable, then we should adjust the values of Q_{31} and Q_{32} first. The following is an illustration of how to take into account this prior information in balancing the SAM table of 5.4.1:

(1) Based on the accounting identity theory, households' total spending should be equal to their total income. We observe the two numbers are not equal in the SAM table. This would be caused by the unreported income in the deficient statistical system in a developing economy. Hence, we take the household total spending 240 as the reliable data. Accordingly, we adjust households' income from labor, $Q_{43} = 240$.

(2) After the above adjustment, the two largest gaps occur in accounts 2 and 3, with $+51$ and -31, respectively. Hence, increase the value of Q_{32} by 31.

(3) Now only account 1 and 2 are unbalanced, with -20 and $+20$, respectively. We need to adjust Q_{12} and Q_{21}. But both data are considered to be relatively reliable, and we do not have additional information about the two individual data. Hence, we divide the adjustment task evenly between the two accounts. That is, raise Q_{12} by 10 and deduct Q_{21} by 10.

Table 5.4.5 shows the final balanced SAM table by using the above process. Note the final results are different from Table 5.4.4.

It can be seen from the above procedures, using manual adjustment may involve subjective judgment. From the same raw data, the final results of the balanced SAM table may be quite different from different individual researchers. Hence, one can use manual adjustment

Table 5.4.4. Country A's SAM table — Excel worksheet after the third adjustment.

	Commodity 1/ Activity 1	Commodity 2/ Activity 2	Factor/ labor	Households	Row total	Differences between row & col
Commodity 1/ Activity 1	52	46.5		150	248.5	0
Commodity 2/ Activity 2	93.5	48		42	183.5	0
Factor/labor	103	89			192	0
Households			192		192	0
Column total	248.5	183.5	192	192		

Table 5.4.5. County A's balanced SAM table based on economics judgement.

	Commodity 1/ Activity 1	Commodity 2/ Activity 2	Factor/ labor	Households	Row total	Differences between row & col
Commodity 1/Activity 1	52	55		150	257	0
Commodity 2/Activity 2	85	48		90	223	0
Factor/labor	120	120			240	0
Households			240		240	0
Column total	257	223	240	240		

but with great caution, if manual balancing is justified and makes more sense based on economics theory because of some obvious problems with other methods. Researchers should still check the above described conditions for manual adjustment before proceeding. That is, the magnitudes of the deviations in the original SAM table are small, and the researchers have a lot of additional information about the data.

Note the property of the linear dependence of the equations implied in the SAM table. Because the sum of all row totals in the SAM table is equal to the sum of all column totals, as they are the aggregate value of all elements Q_{ij} in the matrix

$$\sum_i^n \sum_j^n Q_{ij} = \sum_j^n \sum_i^n Q_{ij} \tag{5.4.1}$$

therefore, in balancing the SAM table, as long as $n-1$ rows are balanced, the remaining row is automatically balanced. The same property also applies to the columns. As long as $n-1$ columns are balanced, the remaining column is automatically balanced.

5.5 RAS Method

Quite often, the job of balancing a SAM table for a researcher is to update the previous SAM table. When new information becomes available about the changes in the sectoral sums such as the total outputs, we need to update the SAM table with these new total values, but keeping the previous structural information about the inter-sectoral flows. RAS is a popular method to update the SAM table with the new targeted sectoral total values. The idea of the RAS method is proportionally adjusting the existing element values to fit the new sectoral sums, from column sums to row sums, then from row sums to column sums, through an iterative process, finally converging to the target (updated) new sums. The following is an illustration of the RAS method through examples.

Suppose the initial SAM table has the values as in the previous Table 5.2.1. Now we obtain some updated sectoral total values. These new data are listed in the last column and the bottom row of Table 5.5.1, termed as row total target and column total target values. Our purpose is to adjust the individual flow values (the numbers in the table cells) so the row and column sums of the SAM table are updated to the target values. Let us denote the target values with the superscript "*", thus the row total target is Q_i^* and the column total target is Q_j^*.

The first step is to multiply each original element value of a column Q_{ij}^0 of the matrix by a common factor, so the new column sum is equal to the target column sum. For column j, the common factor is $Q_j^* / \sum_i Q_{ij}^0$, where superscript "0" denotes the initial period, and superscript "1" denotes the state after the first adjustment. The new element value Q_{ij}^1 after this first step adjustment is as follows:

$$Q_{ij}^1 = Q_{ij}^0 \frac{Q_j^*}{\sum_i Q_{ij}^0} \tag{5.5.1}$$

Table 5.5.1. County A's SAM table — with existing and targeted sectoral total values.

	Commodity 1/ Activity 1	Commodity 2/ Activity 2	Factor/ labor	Households	Row total	Row total target
Commodity 1/ Activity 1	52	45		150	247	270
Commodity 2/ Activity 2	95	48		90	233	233
Factor/labor	120	89			209	210
Households			192		192	210
Column total	267	182	192	240		
Column total target	270	233	210	210		

Table 5.5.2. County A's SAM table — after the first step of adjustment.

	Commodity 1/ Activity 1	Commodity 2/ Activity 2	Factor/ labor	Households	Row total	Row total target
Commodity 1/ Activity 1	52.6	57.6		131.3	241.4	270
Commodity 2/ Activity 2	96.1	61.5		78.8	236.3	233
Factor/labor	121.3	113.9			235.3	210
Households			210.0		210.0	210
Column total	270.0	233.0	210.0	210.0	923.0	
Column total target	270	233	210	210		

For elements in column 1, $Q_{i1}^1 = Q_{i1}^0 \frac{270}{267}$. After this adjustment, the first matrix element (1,1) is $52 \div 267 \times 270 = 52.6$. It can be seen that after all elements of the first column are adjusted, the column sum is the targeted value of 270. Similarly, each element in the second column is adjusted by $Q_{i2}^1 = Q_{i2}^0 \frac{233}{182}$; and each element of the third column is adjusted by $Q_{i3}^1 = Q_{i3}^0 \frac{210}{192}$. After adjusting elements of all columns in the table, the column sums are adjusted to the targeted values, as that in Table 5.5.2. Note the row sums are changed from the initial values.

The second step is working on the rows. We adjust element values of each row to approach the targeted row sum with the same technique as the first step. For each element of row i, multiplying a common factor:

$$Q_{ij}^2 = Q_{ij}^1 \frac{Q_i^*}{\sum_j Q_{ij}} \qquad (5.5.2)$$

For instance, each element of the first row is calculated by $Q_{1j}^2 = Q_{1j}^1 \frac{270}{241.4}$. After elements of all rows are adjusted accordingly, we have Table 5.5.3. The row sums are now adjusted to the target values.

After this adjustment, the column sums deviate away from the target values but by smaller magnitudes on average than those in Table 5.5.2. Then in the third step we repeat the method of the first step of adjustment to make the column sums consistent. Then in the fourth step we repeat the second step method of adjustment to make the row sums consistent. $\cdots$. Repeating these steps, through an iterative process, finally the row sums and column sums converge to the targeted values (or with tiny errors within the allowable range), as shown in Table 5.5.4.

The RAS method can be expressed by the matrix system as follows. The first step of Equation (5.5.1) and second step of Equation (5.5.2) are combined and written as

$$\mathbf{Q}^2 = r_1 \mathbf{Q}^0 s_0 = \begin{bmatrix} \frac{270}{241.4} & \cdots & \cdots & 0 \\ \vdots & \ddots & & \vdots \\ \vdots & 0 & \frac{Q_i^*}{\sum_j Q_{ij}^1} & 0 \\ 0 & \cdots & 0 & \frac{Q_{i=n}^*}{\sum_j Q_{nj}^1} \end{bmatrix} \mathbf{Q}^0 \begin{bmatrix} \frac{210}{267} & \cdots & \cdots & 0 \\ \vdots & \ddots & & \vdots \\ \vdots & 0 & \frac{Q_j^*}{\sum_i Q_{ij}^0} & 0 \\ 0 & \cdots & 0 & \frac{Q_{j=n}^*}{\sum_i Q_{in}^0} \end{bmatrix}$$

(5.5.3)

where $\mathbf{Q}^t$ is the $n \times n$ SAM matrix in the adjustment process in the tth step. We repeat this work through the iterative process, until the values in $\mathbf{Q}^t$ converge to the targeted sums. Table 5.5.4 is the finally balanced SAM table for the above example.

The advantage of the RAS method is that the proportional structure of the element values is maintained in the adjustment process.[1] The RAS method can also be used in a

Table 5.5.3.   County A's SAM table — after the second step of adjustment.

	Commodity 1/ Activity 1	Commodity 2/ Activity 2	Factor/ labor	Households	Row total	Row total target
Commodity 1/ Activity 1	58.8	64.4		146.8	270.0	270
Commodity 2/ Activity 2	94.7	60.6		77.7	233.0	233
Factor/labor	108.3	101.7			210.0	210
Households			210.0		210.0	210
Column total	261.8	226.7	210.0	224.4	923.0	
Column total target	270	233	210	210		

---

[1]The original ratio values are changed somewhat during the adjustment process when the process switches back and forth in balancing between columns-to-rows then rows-to-columns.

Table 5.5.4.   Country A's SAM table — final RAS results from the above GAMS program.

	Commodity 1/ Activity 1	Commodity 2/ Activity 2	Factor/labor	Households	Row total
Commodity 1/ Activity 1	62.8	68.6		138.6	270.0
Commodity 2/ Activity 2	98.7	62.9		71.4	233.0
Factor/labor	108.5	101.5			210.0
Households			210.0		210.0
Column total	270.0	233.0	210.0	210.0	

non-square matrix. The disadvantage of the RAS method is the targeted sum values must be fixed. It also lacks flexibility to adjust individual values away from the ratios of the original elements, if we have additional individual data information that can be utilized. The cross-entropy method introduced in Section 5.7 would keep the advantage of the RAS in recognizing the implied ratio coefficients but add flexibilities to process individual data or sums according to other prior information.

Example 5.5.1 Write a GAMS program to balance SAM Table 5.2.1 by the RAS method. Execute the program and fill in the final results in the SAM table.

Solution: The GAMS program is as follows.

```
$title Example 5.5.1  The RAS balancing method
*Define sets
   set i        /sec1,sec2,lab,hh/;
   alias(i,j);

*tartot is targeted total values
table SAM(*,*) the social accounting matrix
         sec1 sec2 lab  hh  total  tartot
   sec1   52   45        150  247   270
   sec2   95   48        90   233   233
   lab    120  89             209   210
   hh          192            192   210
   total  267  182  192  240
   tartot 270  233  210  210
   ;

parameter
   rowdis(i)      Difference in row sums from the targeted sums
   condis(j)      Difference in column sums from the targeted sums
   maxdis         Maximum error between sums and targets in this calculation
   iter           Number of iterative calculations;

$ontext
```

"while(condition, statement)" is a loop code for doing iterative calculations. In the parentheses, the first part describes the condition to continue to loop. The following statement says that if the number of iterative calculations is less than 5000 and the error term maxdis is greater than 1e-10, the loop calculation continues. Otherwise stop. In the parentheses, the second part describes the iterative calculation.

First assign the starting value of the loop: iter=1
$offtext

```
    maxdis=0.1;
    iter=1;

    while( iter < 5000 and maxdis > 1e-10,

*Adjusting element values to match the targeted column sums (called R adjustment)
    SAM('total',j)=sum(i,SAM(i,j));
    SAM(i,j)=SAM(i,j)*SAM('tartot',j)/SAM('total',j);

*Adjusting the element values to match the targeted row sums (called S adjustment)
    SAM(i,'total')=sum(j,SAM(i,j)) ;
    SAM(i,j)=SAM(i,j)*SAM(i,'tartot')/SAM(i,'total');

*Check the maximum error after this loop of calculation
*First, calculate the absolute values of the row and column differences
    condis(j)=abs(sum(i,SAM(i,j))-SAM('tartot',j));
    rowdis(i)=abs(sum(j,SAM(i,j))-SAM(i,'tartot'));
*Find the maximum value among these differences
*function smax means the maximum value of the indexed values
    maxdis=max{smax{i,rowdis(i)},smax{j,condis(j)}};

*If the loop conditions are satisfied, repeat the calculation
    iter=iter+1;
    );

display SAM,maxdis,iter;

*end
```

5.6 Direct Cross-Entropy

Cross-entropy is a modern technique for balancing SAM tables. It is developed from the properties of the cross-entropy functions, which are used in many fields including information theory, economics and statistics. Information theory uses cross-entropy to measure the intensity of information brought by a new message. Suppose we consider a priori that the probability distribution of an event is $\mathbf{p} = (p_1, \cdots, p_n)$. After a new message arrives, the posterior probability distribution of the event becomes $\mathbf{s} = (s_1, \cdots, s_n)$. Then the intensity of the information from the message is indicated by the following expected cross-entropy

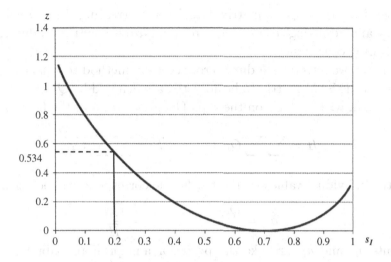

Figure 5.6.1. Expected cross-entropy value z at various s.

value z:

$$z = \sum_{i}^{n} s_i \log \frac{s_i}{p_i} \quad \left(0 \le p_i \le 1, 0 \le s_i \le 1; \sum p_i = 1, \sum s_i = 1 \right) \quad (5.6.1)$$

The above function form is called relative entropy or the Kullbak–Leibler divergence in the information theory. The base of the log can be natural base or 2. z measures the intensity of the information the new message has brought. If each pair of the prior probability p_i and posterior probability s_i are exactly the same, then z is zero, which indicates that the new message brings no new information. It is easy to verify that, the greater the difference between p_i and s_i is, the greater the z is. Figure 5.6.1 shows that in the case of $n = 2$, the expected entropy value z is obtained by different values of s_1 and s_2, with the prior probabilities of $p_1 = 0.7$ and $p_2 = 0.3$. When the prior and posterior probabilities are the same, $p_1 = s_1 = 0.7$ (therefore $p_2 = s_2 = 0.3$), the function reaches its minimum, z is zero. The greater the gap between p_i and s_i is, the greater the expected cross-entropy value z would be.

In other fields of social sciences, the property of the expected cross-entropy function is utilized to measure the inequality of distribution between two indicators corresponding to p_i and s_i. For example, let p_i be the share of a group in the population and s_i be the share of the income this group receives in the economy, then z measures the inequality of income distribution in the population. This is called the Theil index. A nice property of the Theil index is that it is additively decomposable, while the more popular indicator Gini index is not.

If an additional constraint is imposed on s, say, s is restricted in the interval $[0, 0.2]$, then z is minimized at $s_1 = 0.2$ (Figure 5.6.1) This is where s_1 is closest to the prior probability $p_1 = 0.7$, subject to the constraint. Using this property, similar to the idea of the least squares method, we search for the new adjusted SAM flow values by minimizing their differences from the original matrix data. That is, treating the original set of the SAM matrix set as p and adjusting set as s so as to minimize the entropy value z, subject to the constraints of SAM consistency.

In what follows, we introduce a direct cross-entropy method to balance SAM. As before, the flow values in the SAM matrix to be adjusted are denoted by Q_{ij}, the original flow data are denoted by $\overline{Q}_{ij}$, with a "bar" on the top. The grand total of the flows, respectively, are

$$H = \sum_{i}^{n}\sum_{j}^{n} Q_{ij} \qquad\qquad \overline{H} = \sum_{i}^{n}\sum_{j}^{n} \overline{Q}_{ij_j} \tag{5.6.2}$$

Dividing the individual values by the totals, the corresponding coefficients are

$$a_{ij} = \frac{Q_{ij}}{H} \qquad\qquad \overline{a}_{ij} = \frac{\overline{Q}_{ij}}{\overline{H}} \tag{5.6.3}$$

The coefficients a_{ij} and $\overline{a}_{ij}$ are like the posterior and prior probabilities s and p in the cross-entropy function as we discussed above. The cross-entropy function is

$$
\begin{aligned}
z &= \sum_{j}^{n}\sum_{i}^{n} a_{ij} \log \frac{a_{ij}}{\overline{a}_{ij}} \\
&= \sum_{j}^{n}\sum_{i}^{n} \frac{Q_{ij}}{H} \log \left(\frac{Q_{ij}}{H} \Big/ \frac{\overline{Q}_{ij}}{\overline{H}} \right) = \frac{1}{H}\sum_{j}^{n}\sum_{i}^{n} Q_{ij} \left(\log \frac{Q_{ij}}{\overline{Q}_{ij}} - \log \frac{H}{\overline{H}} \right) \\
&= \frac{1}{H}\sum_{j}^{n}\sum_{i}^{n} Q_{ij} \log \frac{Q_{ij}}{\overline{Q}_{ij}} - \frac{1}{H}\sum_{j}^{n}\sum_{i}^{n} Q_{ij} \log \frac{H}{\overline{H}} \\
&= \frac{1}{H}\sum_{j}^{n}\sum_{i}^{n} Q_{ij} \log \frac{Q_{ij}}{\overline{Q}_{ij}} - \log \frac{H}{\overline{H}} \left(\frac{1}{H}\sum_{j}^{n}\sum_{i}^{n} Q_{ij} \right) \\
&= \frac{1}{H}\sum_{j}^{n}\sum_{i}^{n} Q_{ij} \log \frac{Q_{ij}}{\overline{Q}_{ij}} - \log \frac{H}{\overline{H}}
\end{aligned} \tag{5.6.4}
$$

The direct cross-entropy method is to minimize z by adjusting the flow values of Q_{ij}, subject to the constraints of (1) sectoral sum balance and (2) positive Q_{ij} values. That is:

$$\min_{Q_{ij}} z = \frac{1}{H}\sum_{j}^{n}\sum_{i}^{n} Q_{ij} \log \frac{Q_{ij}}{\overline{Q}_{ij}} - \log \frac{H}{\overline{H}} \tag{5.6.5}$$

$$s.t. \quad \sum_{i}^{n} Q_{ik} = \sum_{j}^{n} Q_{kj} \quad k = 1, \ldots, n \quad \text{(sectoral balance condition)}$$

$$Q_{ij} > 0 \quad i = 1, \ldots, n; \quad j = 1, \ldots, n$$

$$H = \sum_{i}^{n}\sum_{j}^{n} Q_{ij} \qquad \overline{H} = \sum_{i}^{n}\sum_{j}^{n} \overline{Q}_{ij_j}$$

Table 5.6.1. Country A's SAM table — balanced values by the direct cross-entropy method.

	Commodity 1/ Activity 1	Commodity 2/ Activity 2	Factor/labor	Households	Row total
Commodity 1/ Activity 1	52.2	53.2		142.2	247.6
Commodity 2/ Activity 2	80.9	48.2		72.4	201.5
Factor/labor	114.5	100.1			214.6
Households			214.6		214.6
Column total	247.6	201.5	214.6	214.6	

In objective function z, $\log \bar{H}$ is a constant, which would not affect the optimal choice for Q_{ij}. Q_{ij} are the choice variables. H is a function of Q_{ij}, therefore it is a variable, too. While the above problem seems to be theoretically correct, it would encounter a computational problem by GAMS solvers. The z function in Equation (5.6.4) has an extra variable H, which is restricted to be a positive-value, and H is linearly dependent on Q_{ij}. In the process of minimizing z, H would approach positive infinity, so the first term of function z in Equation (5.6.5) approaches zero and the last term approaches negative infinity, thus z explodes to negative infinity, leaving Problem 5.6.5 without a meaningful solution. Hence, we should limit the range of H in the computation process. From the theory, we know that the adjusted values of Q_{ij} should not deviate too much from the original SAM data $\bar{Q}_{ij}$. Hence, the grand total H should not deviate too much from $\bar{H}$. Accordingly, we restrict the ratio of the adjusted grand total to the original total $\frac{H}{\bar{H}}$ to be within the interval of $[0.5, 2]$. It means that the total adjusted value is no less than one half and no greater than twice as much as that from the original data. This is a very generous tolerance for the range of adjustment. In general, we expect the ratio from the computation should be just in the neighborhood of 1.

The following is the GAMS program for using direct cross-entropy to balance the SAM table in Table 5.2.1. The final balanced results are shown in Table 5.6.1.[2] Readers can see the adjusted values are close to those by the least squares method, although not identical. The final adjusted values are denoted by Q_{ij}^* and H^*, respectively, adding superscript "*". The ratio $\frac{H^*}{\bar{H}} = 0.997$. It is very close to 1, with a deviation from the original total by only 0.3%.

Example 5.6.1 Use the direct cross-entropy method to balance the previous sample SAM table by a GAMS program.

Solution: The GAMS program is as follows.

---

[2]The solver we use is PATH. Some readers reported that they reach different results by using other solvers.

```
$title Example 5.6.1 using direct cross-entropy to balance SAM
*Define set
    set ac              /sec1,sec2,lab,hh,total/;
    set i(ac)           /sec1,sec2,lab,hh/;

alias (ac,acp);
alias (i,j);

table sam(*,*)
          sec1    sec2    lab    hh     total
sec1      52      45             150    247
sec2      95      48             90     233
lab       120     89                    209
hh                        192           192
total     267     182     192    240
;

parameters
    Q0(i,j)     initial value
    H0          sum of all transaction flows;

*Assignment for parameters
    Q0(i,j)=sam(i,j);
    H0=sum((i,j),sam(i,j));

display H0,sam;

Variables
    Q(i,j)      Values to be adjusted in SAM
    H           Grand total of flows in SA
    Hratio      Ratio of two total H numbers
    z           Cross-entropy objective function value;

*Q should be positive
Positive variable Q(i,j);

equations
    totalsum        Aggregating all flow values
    directentropy   Direct cross-entropy function
    balance         Sectoral balance constraint
    Hratiodef       Ratio of H;
```

```
totalsum..      H =e= sum((i,j),Q(i,j));
directentropy.. z=e=sum((i,j)$sam(i,j),(1/H)*Q(i,j)*log(Q(i,j)/
                    sam(i,j)))-log(Hratio);
balance(i)..    sum(j$sam(i,j),Q(i,j)) =e= sum(j,Q(j,i)));
Hratiodef..     Hratio =e= H/H0;

*Assign initial values to variableso
*Below the Hratio range is restricted to the interval 0.5 to 2
    Q.L(i,j)=Q0(i,j);
    H.L=H0;
Hratio.Lo=0.5;
Hratio.up=2;

model sambal  /all/;
solve sambal using nlp minimizing z;

display Q.L,H.L,Hratio.L;
*end
```

5.7 Coefficient Cross-Entropy with Prior Information

In practice, we often need to update and adjust the existing SAM tables by including the new data and information which become available. The RAS method in Section 5.5 is a method to update SAM with the new sectoral total data. In the case of the RAS method, the only new information obtained is the row and column sums, which serve as the target numbers for the adjustment to reach. In the real world, however, we often find the sectoral sums are not strictly reliable because of conflicts between different data sources, deficiency in data collection and calculations, and other technical problems. In addition, we may have some other prior information, such as information of some individual transaction data that can be used for updating SAM. Robinson *et al.* (2001) proposed a (coefficient) cross-entropy balancing method with flexibility that allows various prior information to be used in updating SAM. In what follows, we illustrate the basic structure of this method.

Let us first consider a case similar to that under the RAS method. Suppose we have a balanced SAM table with n sectors from previous years. Now the new data about the sums of several sectors and accounts are released. We need to update all individual flow values in the SAM table so the new row and column sums are consistent with the updated sectoral sum values.

Denote the variables of individual flows by Q_{ij}. Denote the variable of the row sum by Y_i^r with a superscript "r". Denote the variable of the column sum by Y_j^c with a superscript "c". The original values from the existing SAM table including row sums, column sums and individual flows are denoted by $\bar{Y}_i^r$, $\bar{Y}_j^c$ and $\bar{Q}_{ij}$, respectively, with a hat bar "-". Note they are fixed numbers. The values after adjustment are denoted by Y_i^{r*}, Y_j^{c*} and Q_{ij}^* with asterisk "*" superscripts. We have the following relationship,

$$Y_i^r = \sum_j^n Q_{ij} \qquad \bar{Y}_i^r = \sum_j^n \bar{Q}_{ij} \qquad Y_i^{r*} = \sum_j^n Q_{ij}^*$$

$$Y_j^c = \sum_i^n Q_{ij} \qquad \bar{Y}_j^c = \sum_i^n \bar{Q}_{ij} \qquad Y_j^{c*} = \sum_i^n Q_{ij}^* \qquad (5.7.1)$$

Dividing the flow values by their column sums gives the coefficients of the SAM table, similar to the input coefficients in the IO table. They are:

$$\bar{A}_{ij} = \frac{\bar{Q}_{ij}}{\bar{Y}_j^c} \qquad A_{ij} = \frac{Q_{ij}}{Y_j^c} \qquad (5.7.2)$$

The following information is known: Values of $\bar{Y}_i^r$, $\bar{Y}_j^c$ and $\bar{Q}_{ij}$ are given in the original SAM table data. The values of $\bar{A}_{ij}$ are thus calculated and assigned. Further, the original SAM table is balanced, row sum equals to the corresponding column sum, $\bar{Y}_j^r = \bar{Y}_j^c$, $j = 1, \ldots, n$. The newly obtained information includes a set of updated sectoral sum data Y_j^{c*}, which are considered to be reliable. Therefore, Y_j^{c*} is set as the targeted sum values to be reached through adjustment. Each pair of row and column sums are equal: $Y_j^{r*} = Y_j^{c*}$.

The problem to be solved is to minimize z in the following cross entropy function by choosing the variable coefficient A_{ij}, subject to the constraints that the corresponding row and column sums are equal to Y_i^{c*} and some other constraints as follows:

$$\min_{A_{ij}} \quad z = \sum_i^n \sum_j^n A_{ij} \log \frac{A_{ij}}{\bar{A}_{ij}} \qquad (5.7.3)$$

$$\text{s.t.} \quad Y_i^{r*} = Y_i^{c*} \qquad i = 1, \ldots, n$$

$$\sum_j^n A_{ij} Y_j^{c*} = Y_i^{r*} \qquad i = 1, \ldots, n$$

$$\sum_i^n A_{ij} = 1 \qquad j = 1, \ldots, n$$

$$0 \le A_{ij} \le 1 \qquad \forall i, \forall j$$

When the optimal values A_{ij}^* are found, the updated flow values of the SAM table can be calculated by $Q_{ij}^* = A_{ij}^* Y_j^{c*}$.

Now we consider the case that the original SAM is not balanced in sectoral totals. The row sums do not equal corresponding column sums, $\bar{Y}_j^r \ne \bar{Y}_j^c$, for some or all accounts. This may be caused by including some updated individual flow data $\bar{Q}_{ij}$ or updated sectoral sums in the SAM table. Now we want to balance the SAM table. We do not know the true sectoral sum Y_j^{c*} for certain. It can be $\bar{Y}_j^r$, $\bar{Y}_j^c$, or some value between them. But we have some information about the distribution of Y_j^{c*} in the interval. In this case, a refined coefficient cross-entropy method is set as follows. Let Y_j^c in column j be the sum of the original data $\bar{Y}_j^c$ plus an error term e_j:

$$Y_j^c = \bar{Y}_j^c + e_j \tag{5.7.4}$$

The error terms would take account of the additional information mentioned. They are to be adjusted, so are Y_j^c, in the balancing process. Finally, the sectoral sums are balanced:

$$Y_j^r = Y_j^c \qquad j = 1, \cdots, n \tag{5.7.5}$$

Because $\bar{Y}_j^c$ is given, it can be seen that the final value of the sectoral sum Y_j^{c*} would also be determined by the value of error term e_j. How is the value of e_j determined? As it is assumed that we have some prior knowledge about its distribution in an interval, let error term e_j be a weighted average of a set of numbers $\bar{v}_{jk}$:

$$e_j = \sum_k^m w_{jk} \bar{v}_{jk} \tag{5.7.6}$$

Weights w_{jk} have the following properties:

$$\sum_k^m w_{jk} = 1 \quad w_{jk} \geq 0 \qquad j = 1, \cdots, n \tag{5.7.7}$$

The above setup for e_j is similar to the form of the expected value of random variables in statistics, with "random numbers" $\bar{v}_{jk}$ and associated "probabilities" w_{jk}. Numbers $\bar{v}_{jk}$ and weights w_{jk} would characterize the distribution of e_j. Let $\tilde{w}_{jk}$ be the weights assigned based on our prior knowledge. Both $\bar{v}_{jk}$ and $\tilde{w}_{jk}$ are determined a priori by the researcher from the available information, experience and economics theory. Then $\tilde{e}_j = \sum_k^m \tilde{w}_{jk} \bar{v}_{jk}$, and, $\tilde{Y}_j^c$ (which equals $\bar{Y}_j^c + \tilde{e}_j$) is the prior expected sectoral sum before the balancing process. The distribution of $\tilde{e}_j$, depending on the information available to the researcher, can have various forms, say, uniform, normal, skewed or a function of measure errors of related flow and sum values.

Here we give an example to illustrate. Suppose we are going to balance the SAM table of Table 5.2.1. In sector 2, the column sum $\bar{Y}_j^c = 182$ and row sum $\bar{Y}_j^r = 233$. While we do not know for certain the true sum of sector 2, we have some knowledge about its distribution in the interval of [182,233] so we can assign the possible values and associated probabilities. The hypothetical distribution of this example is shown in Table 5.7.1.

The prior distribution of the error term e_2 in Table 5.7.1 is skewed a little to the column sum $\bar{Y}_j^c = 182$ based on prior knowledge. It implies that before balancing, based on the

Table 5.7.1. A hypothetical prior distribution of the error term e_2.

k	1	2	3	4	5	6	7
$Y_2^c = 182 + \bar{v}_{2k}$	182	192	202	212	222	232	233
$\bar{v}_{2k}$	0	10	20	30	40	50	51
$\tilde{w}_{2k}$	0.1	0.2	0.45	0.15	0.09	0.01	0

prior information, the expected value of the error term is $\tilde{e}_2 = \sum_k^m \tilde{w}_{2k} \bar{v}_{2k} = 19.6$. And the expected value of the sectoral sum is $\tilde{Y}_2^c = 182 + 19.6 = 201.6$. Y_2^c is a variable and it would be adjusted in the balancing process.

In the real world, we are unlikely to have the information luxury to assign detailed prior distributions for error terms. If little prior information is in hand, for simplicity, we can have just two terminal $\bar{v}_{jk}$: $\bar{v}_{j1} = 0$ and $\bar{v}_{j2} = \bar{Y}_j^r - \bar{Y}_j^c$, together with two weights:

$$e_j = \tilde{w}_{j1} \bar{v}_{j1} + \tilde{w}_{j2} \bar{v}_{j2} = \tilde{w}_{j1} \times 0 + \tilde{w}_{j2}(\bar{Y}_j^r - \bar{Y}_j^c) \tag{5.7.8}$$

The weights are assigned to reflect our belief as to which side, column sum or row sum, is more likely to be true. If there is no preference, a uniform distribution can be assumed so each weight $\tilde{w}_{jk}$ is 0.5. Take Table 5.2.1 as an example, note $w_{j1} + w_{j2} = 1$, we have
For sector 1: $e_1 = \tilde{w}_{11} \times 0 + (1 - \tilde{w}_{11}) \times (247 - 267) = \tilde{w}_{11} \times 0 + \tilde{w}_{12} \times (247 - 267)$;
For sector 2, $e_2 = \tilde{w}_{21} \times 0 + \tilde{w}_{22} \times (233 - 182)$;
For account 3 of factor or labor: $e_3 = \tilde{w}_{31} \times 0 + \tilde{w}_{32} \times (209 - 192)$;
For account 4 of households: $e_4 = \tilde{w}_{41} \times 0 + \tilde{w}_{42} \times (192 - 240)$.
The corresponding cross-entropy function for finding the posterior weights is

$$u_j = \sum_k^m w_{jk} \log \frac{w_{jk}}{\tilde{w}_{jk}} = w_{j1} \log \frac{w_{j1}}{\tilde{w}_{j1}} + w_{j2} \log \frac{w_{j2}}{\tilde{w}_{j2}} \tag{5.7.9}$$

Take an example for sector 2. Suppose we assume a uniform distribution in the interval of the row sum and column sum, then cross-entropy u_2 is

$$u_2 = (1 - w_{22}) \log \frac{1 - w_{22}}{0.5} + w_{22} \log \frac{w_{22}}{0.5} \tag{5.7.10}$$

The posterior weight w_{22}^* would be solved in the cross-entropy minimization process. The error term e_2 is simplified to the following form:

$$e_2 = w_{21} \bar{v}_{21} + w_{22} \bar{v}_{22} = w_{21} \times 0 + w_{22}(\bar{Y}_2^r - \bar{Y}_2^c) = w_{22}(233 - 182) = w_{22} \cdot 51 \tag{5.7.11}$$

After optimization, the solved weight value is w_{22}^*. Then the error term is $e_2^* = w_{22}^* \cdot 51$.

Suppose Country A is a developing economy in which income is often underreported. Hence, the prior information reveals that the row sum $\bar{Y}_2^r$, which is based on expenditure, is more reliable, and a greater weight should be placed for $\tilde{w}_{22}$. Say, we a priori consider that the row sum 233 has 90% probability to be true, then $\tilde{w}_{21} = 0.1$ $\tilde{w}_{22} = 0.9$. Then solved e_2^* tends to be bigger, closer to the row sum 233. If the prior information reveals that the true row sum is in a smaller interval [210, 233], we can set $\bar{v}_{21} = 18$ and $\bar{v}_{22} = 51$, to have $e_2 = w_{21} \times 18 + w_{22} \times 51$. Then we decide the weight $\tilde{w}_{2k}$ based on the prior information on distribution, as discussed above.

The balancing process requires that we also minimize the cross-entropy z by choosing A_{ij}. That is, we should minimize both entropies z and u by adjusting SAM coefficients A_{ij} and error term weights w_{jk}. The objective function is thus a weighted average of the two cross entropies:

$$\min_{A_{ij},w_{jk}} \quad I(A_{ij}, w_{jk}) = \delta_z z + \delta_u u = \delta_z \sum_i^n \sum_j^n A_{ij} \log \frac{A_{ij}}{\bar{A}_{ij}} + \delta_u \sum_j^n \sum_k^m w_{jk} \log \frac{w_{jk}}{\tilde{w}_{jk}}$$

$$(5.7.12)$$

where δ_z and δ_u are weights assigned by the researcher. For simplicity, they can just be 1, which means giving equal weights for both terms. To summarize, the coefficient cross-entropy method is to minimize Equation (5.7.12) subject to the following constraints:

$$A_{ij} = Q_{ij}/Y_j^c \qquad \text{SAM coefficient} \qquad (5.7.13)$$

$$\sum_j^n Q_{ij} = Y_i^r \qquad \text{Row sum} \qquad (5.7.14)$$

$$\sum_i^n Q_{ij} = Y_j^c \qquad \text{Column sum} \qquad (5.7.15)$$

$$Y_j^c = \bar{Y}_j^c + e_j \qquad \text{Variables, error term and the column sum} \qquad (5.7.16)$$

$$Y_j^r = Y_j^c \quad j = 1, \cdots, n \quad \text{Sectoral balancing condition} \qquad (5.7.17)$$

$$e_j = \sum_k^m w_{jk} \bar{v}_{jk} \qquad \text{Error term is a sum of numbers with weights} \qquad (5.7.18)$$

$$\sum_i^n A_{ij} = 1 \quad j = 1, \cdots, n; \qquad 0 < A_{ij} < 1 \quad \forall i, \forall j \qquad (5.7.19)$$

$$\sum_k^m w_{jk} = 1 \quad 0 < w_{jk} < 1 \qquad j = 1, \cdots, n \qquad (5.7.20)$$

The above system from (5.7.12) to (5.7.20) is the coefficient cross-entropy method for balancing the SAM. It will solve the new values for the individual flow variables and balanced sectoral sums. The parameters (i.e., whose values are given exogenously) are: $\bar{Y}_j^c$, $\bar{Q}_{ij}$, $\bar{A}_{ij}$ (derived by $\bar{A}_{ij} = \bar{Q}_{ij}/\bar{Y}_j^c$), $\tilde{w}_{jk}$ and $\bar{v}_{jk}$. $\bar{Y}_j^c$ and $\bar{Q}_{ij}$ are directly obtained from the original SAM table. $\bar{A}_{ij}$ is calculated accordingly. $\bar{v}_{jk}$ and $\tilde{w}_{jk}$ must be set exogenously by the researcher based on prior information, theory and experience. The variables in the system to be solved include $A_{ij}, w_{jk}, Q_{ij}, e_j, Y_i^r, Y_j^c$. The form is quite flexible in terms of utilizing all the information available to shape the final outcomes. One may also add more constraints to influence the final values after balancing. The GAMS program for this cross-entropy method is available by Robinson and El-Said (2000). Readers who are interested in the GAMS codes are referred to that article.

Table 5E.1.1. Country A's preliminary SAM table.

	Agriculture	Industry	Service	Labor	Capital	Households	Row total
Agriculture	160	150	90			540	940
Industry	140	320	170			910	1540
Service	80	150	250			610	1090
Labor	320	360	400				1080
Capital	170	550	150				870
Households				1050	860		1910
Column total	870	1530	1060	1050	860	2060	

Table 5E.1.2. Updated sectoral total values.

Accounts	Agriculture	Industry	Service	Labor	Capital	Households
Sectoral total	920	1540	2000	2000	900	2900

Exercises

5E.1 Country A has a preliminary SAM table as shown in Table 5E.1.1, which needs to be balanced.

(a) Write the GAMS program for the least squares method to balance the SAM table. Read and check the results.

(b) Write the GAMS program for the least squares method to balance the SAM table, but now assuming the data of household expenditure is reliable and must be fixed.

(c) Use Microsoft Excel to manually balance the SAM table, again, assuming household expenditure data is reliable and must be fixed.

(d) Country Mileland recently has updated total values of each account in the previous SAM to those in Table 5E.1.2. We need to update the SAM table with the new account total values. Write the GAMS program for using RAS to update the SAM table accordingly.

(e) Write the GAMS program to balance the SAM Table 5E.1.1 by the direct cross-entropy method.

Chapter 6

General Equilibrium Theory and Its Application

General equilibrium theory forms the core of advanced economics, in both microeconomics and macroeconomics. The CGE model is the practical application of the general equilibrium theory to the real-world cases. To fully understand CGE modeling and be able to independently design the structure of CGE models, it is important to understand the general equilibrium theory. A new graduate student in economics may think the general equilibrium theory challenging and difficult. In fact, the idea of general equilibrium theory is not complicated. The difficult part for new students is to prove the existence, uniqueness, stability, welfare implication and other properties of the general equilibrium by using topology and advanced mathematical concepts. Fortunately, the theoretical proof details are not needed in CGE modeling. CGE modeling is the application of the established general equilibrium theory. The conventional structure and the functions commonly used in the CGE models ensure the existence of the equilibrium. For most conventional models, the equilibrium point is unique in a fairly large neighborhood range, so the same solution often can be reached from various initial points.

While CGE modeling does not require the theoretical proofs of general equilibrium, the researchers should still have solid understanding of the conditions and conclusions stated in the theory. It would turn out to be quite useful in the work, in particular, in designing a new CGE model structure. For instance, the general equilibrium theory concludes that equilibrium does not exist if the production function is increasing returns to scale, because profit-maximizing firms keep expanding production. Hence, a CGE model should avoid using production functions of increasing returns to scale, unless other constraints are set up to limit the firms' production.

In this chapter, we review the core concepts of the general equilibrium theory that are relevant to CGE modeling. For our practical purpose of CGE modeling, we omit the details of the pure theory. Instead, we use simplified examples to illustrate the idea and to give the insight of the general equilibrium theory. We discuss the important conclusions implied in the theory, which are useful for CGE modeling. Throughout this book, we use conventional function forms rather than topological concepts to describe the general equilibrium theory and the conditions for its existence, so the discussions in this book would be easy to follow. The theoretical knowledge provided by this chapter should be sufficient for general works in CGE modeling and policy research. Readers are referred to advanced microeconomics textbooks and literature if they want to look for more theoretical details.

6.1 Partial Equilibrium

Market equilibrium in microeconomics usually refers to the balance of the supply and demand reached in a single market, which is only a "partial equilibrium". Suppose in commodity market i, the supply function is $q_i^s = f_i(p_i)$ and the demand function is $q_i^d = g_i(p_i)$, then the market equilibrium is where quantity supplied equals quantity demanded:

$$q_i^s = q_i^d \tag{6.1.1}$$

This equilibrium is reached at a particular price level:

$$f_i(p_i) = g_i(p_i) \tag{6.1.2}$$

Solving the above equation we have the equilibrium price p_i^* and equilibrium quantity q_i^*. This is a partial equilibrium, because it is the balance reached only in market i and we assume the prices and quantities in other markets remain unchanged during the process of adjustment in p_i and q_i in market i. This partial equilibrium and its condition are expressed as follows:

$$q_i^s = f_i(p_i, \bar{p}_{-i}) \qquad \text{Supply function} \tag{6.1.3}$$
$$q_i^d = g_i(p_i, \bar{p}_{-i}) \qquad \text{Demand function}$$
$$q_i^s = q_i^d \qquad \text{Equilibrium condition}$$

where $-i$ means all markets other than market i. p_{-i} denotes the prices of other markets. Notation bar "−" on the top of the variable symbol $\bar{p}_{-i}$ means its value is kept fixed. Figure 6.1.1 illustrates this partial equilibrium state.

6.2 General Equilibrium

The assumption for partial equilibrium, "assuming the prices and quantities of other markets remain unchanged by the changes in market i", is problematic in a large economic framework

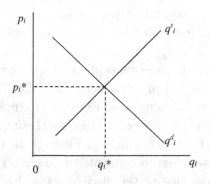

Figure 6.1.1.   Partial equilibrium in a single market.

in which markets and sectors are interdependent. An adjustment in one market would affect other markets, impacting on their supply and demand functions, thus the market prices p_{-i} and quantities q_{-i}. This is called "spillover effect". As illustrated in Figure 6.2.1, when the adjustment in price and quantities occur in market i in the left panel, it would shift the supply and demand curves in other market $-i$, which would disturb the equilibrium state in other market $-i$ (as shown in the right panel).

When we consider a larger economic framework including multiple interdependent markets, we have to consider the spillover and feedback effects, and the linkages among all markets. General equilibrium is the state wherein all markets in the economy reach equilibrium at the same time. Its original idea is not complicated, it is just an extension of the partial equilibrium in a single market to all markets of the economy. While the structure for a system of multiple markets is more complex, we have a mathematical technique — system of multiple equations — to handle the problem. The following is the mathematical expression for the general equilibrium.

Suppose an economy has n sectors, each sector produces one commodity and trades in one market. The price of commodity i is p_i. All prices are expressed by vector $\mathbf{p} = (p_1, \cdots, p_n)$. The supply function of commodity i by all firms in sector i is $q_i^s(\mathbf{p})$. The demand for commodity i by all households is $q_i^d(\mathbf{p})$. Strongly speaking, the general equilibrium is a state in which the quantities supplied equal the quantities demanded in all n markets at a particular price vector

$$q_i^s(\mathbf{p}^*) = q_i^d(\mathbf{p}^*) \qquad i = 1, \cdots, n \qquad (6.2.1)$$

In the Arrow–Debreu theory, under certain conditions, the above equality may not hold and surplus can exist in some markets in the equilibrium state. However, in these markets the commodity prices must be zeros. This implies that the consumers are satisfied with the current quantities of these goods. Consuming beyond the current amounts would only bring negative utility. In these markets, the demand sides determine the actual transaction amounts. Formally, the Arrow–Debreu general equilibrium is defined as follows. For all markets $i = 1, \cdots, n$, under fairly weak conditions, there exists a price vector $\mathbf{p}^* = (p_1^*, \cdots, p_n^*)$,

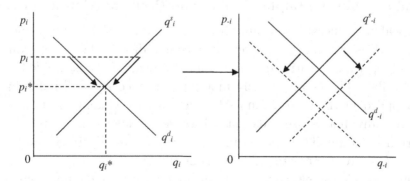

Figure 6.2.1. Spillover effects to other markets.

at which

$$q_i^s(\mathbf{p}^*) = q_i^d(\mathbf{p}^*) \qquad \text{if } p_i > 0 \qquad\qquad (6.2.2)$$
$$q_i^s(\mathbf{p}^*) \geq q_i^d(\mathbf{p}^*) \qquad \text{if } p_i = 0$$

The above balance situation is called market clearing. In general, however, we assume that all commodities are desirable for consumers, which means that more consumption will yield a higher utility for consumers. Hence, we only need the simple market balance condition as that in Equation (6.2.1). This would greatly simplify the computation in economic models without loss of generality for real-world cases. Hence, in CGE modeling, by default we assume the strict positive prices and strict balance equations as Equation (6.2.1).

Definition. General Equilibrium is a set of price and quantity vectors $(\mathbf{p}^*, \mathbf{q}^*)$ that clear all markets.

In economics classes, the exercise to find a general equilibrium state is to solve the equilibrium prices and quantities that satisfy the definition. The Arrow–Debreu theory proves the existence of the general equilibrium state under fairly weak conditions. In a theoretical or ideal textbook case, we can solve for the general equilibrium. The equilibrium under the ideal state is also called the Walrasian equilibrium. The Arrow–Debreu theory, regardless of how beautiful it is, is far away from being an applied model to simulate the real-world cases. Much more simplification and modification needs to be made to construct an applied model. The CGE model is the application of the Arrow–Debreu model to real-world cases. Hence, the CGE model is also called the Applied General Equilibrium (AGE) model.

When you start learning CGE from the background of input–output (IO) models, you may consider CGE models are a giant step forward in evolution from the IO models. An IO model is just a multiple-sector model addressing the production process, while CGE models extend the multiple-sector productions to a general equilibrium state that involves not only the production sides but also demand sides from consumers, and clear all markets at to-be-solved particular prices.

6.3 General Equilibrium Implies Utility and Profit Maximization

Intuitively speaking, general equilibrium is the intersection of the supply and demand functions in all markets. Quantity supplied of a commodity is decided by an enterprise to maximize profits, while quantity demanded for the commodity is decided by a household to maximize utility. The market supply function is formed from all individual enterprises' quantities supplied in the sector. Similarly, the market demand function is formed from the sum of all individual households' quantities demanded in the sector. Hence, the general equilibrium state implies that consumers have maximized utility and enterprises have maximized profits, given the external conditions they face.

A market economic system consists of multiple markets, including commodity markets and factor markets. It also consists of various agents, including households, enterprises,

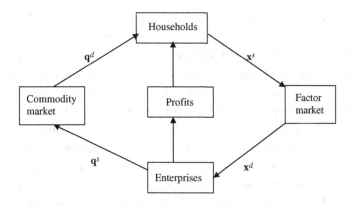

Figure 6.3.1. A completed/closed economy.

government, etc. The "agents" are called "institutions" in the CGE literature. These agents interact in the markets as demanders (buyers) or suppliers (sellers). In addition, there are other financial transactions among the agents, such as taxes or transfer payments between the government and households. Figure 6.3.1 illustrates a very simple but complete economy consisting of four basic blocks. There are two agent groups, households and enterprises. There are two markets, commodity market and factor market. The two agent groups interact in the two markets. In the commodity market, households are buyers and enterprises are sellers. In the factor market, their roles are reversed. Enterprises buy factors for production, households as the factor owners sell factors such as labor or capital. Enterprises remit profits to households who are the owners of the enterprises. Figure 6.3.1 shows this financial flow of profits from enterprises to the households. This is a small simple economy but a completed system. In CGE terms, the "completed"[1] system means that the economic activities and goods and financial flows are circular and self-sustained within the system. When the quantities of supplied equals demanded in both commodity and factor markets in this economy, it is in a state of general equilibrium.

To allow more sectors, let the economy have n commodities and m factors. Let the commodity quantity be denoted by q and factor quantity by x. Superscripts d and s denote demand and supply, respectively. The vector of commodity quantities is $\mathbf{q} = (q_1, \cdots, q_n)$ and vector of factor quantities is $\mathbf{x} = (x_1, \cdots, x_m)$. General equilibrium implies all quantities supplied equal quantities demanded: $\mathbf{q}^s = \mathbf{q}^d$ and $\mathbf{x}^s = \mathbf{x}^d$.

Households maximize their utility, subject to their budget constraints. Their budget constraints are in turn determined by their factor endowments. This behavior forms the commodity demand functions and factor supply functions. For simplicity, hereafter in this chapter we treat all households as one single group, and refer to the group as one individual household in the discussion. Suppose this household (who actually is a group) buys

---

[1] A "completed" system is also called a "closed" system. But "closed" in economics commonly refers to the autarky state of an economy without international trade. To avoid confusion, we avoid using the term "closed" in these contexts.

commodity, say, food. At the same time, he sells his factor in the factor market, say, providing labor service. Given the prices in the market and his factor endowment, he attempts to maximize his utility. His utility function is $u(\cdots)$ and his factor endowment is $\mathbf{e} = (e_1, \cdots, e_m)$. The existence of general equilibrium requires that the endowment $\mathbf{e}$ must be positive. Let $\mathbf{w} = (w_1, \cdots, w_m)$ be the factor price vector. The household's factor income is $\mathbf{w} \cdot \mathbf{e}$ (hereafter we drop the dot for dot product). Let π be the profit remitted from enterprises to the household. So the household total income is $Y = \mathbf{w}\mathbf{e} + \pi$.

The household utility level is determined by the transacted quantities of commodities and factors. Consuming more commodities is pleasant for the household thus brings him positive utility. Providing more factors brings negative utility. For instance, people normally prefer leisure to working. Working means the household is spending his labor endowment. Thus his utility function is $u(\mathbf{q}, \mathbf{e} - \mathbf{x})$. The household provides factors in order to derive an income, which is used to purchase commodities. There is a trade-off between commodity consumption and leisure, thus the household needs to make an optimal choice between them. Economics theory requires that the utility function is quasi-concave, hence the household preference is convex, so the derived commodity demand function and factor supply function are continuous. The continuity property of the functions is important for the existence of the equilibrium. The Constant Elasticity of Substitution (CES) or Linear Expenditure System (LES) utility functions used in CGE modeling are all quasi-concave functions, so in general we do not need to worry about the issue of continuity of the commodity demand and factor supply functions.

The household behavior is to maximize his utility subject to his budget constraint, as follows:

$$\max_{\mathbf{q},\mathbf{x}} u(\mathbf{q}, \mathbf{e} - \mathbf{x}) \qquad s.t. \quad \mathbf{p}\mathbf{q} + \mathbf{w}(\mathbf{e} - \mathbf{x}) \leq Y \qquad (6.3.1)$$

We assume that all commodities are desirable so the household would continue to expand his consumption until exhausting his budget.

In what follows, we use a concrete numerical example to illustrate the household utility maximization behavior. Let a household factor endowment, labor, be 16 hours a day (24 hours minus sleeping time), which is denoted by $\bar{L}$. Let the variable of labor supply be L^s. Subtracting labor supply from labor endowment, it is leisure $l = \bar{L} - L^s$. Leisure is desirable, thus brings positive utility. The budget constraint is that the household spends his labor income on purchasing the commodity:

$$\mathbf{p}\mathbf{q}_i^d = wL^s = w(\bar{L} - l) \qquad (6.3.2)$$

where w is wage. Rewrite Equation (6.3.2) to

$$\mathbf{p}\mathbf{q}_i^d + wl = w\bar{L} \qquad (6.3.3)$$

Equation (6.3.3) can be interpreted as follows: On the right-hand side is the household wealth which is the product of his labor endowment times wage rate. On the left-hand side is how he allocates this wealth between purchasing commodity and leisure.

The commodities demand function $\mathbf{q}^d(\mathbf{p})$ and factor supply function $\mathbf{x}^s(\mathbf{p})$ of the household are derived from his utility maximization problem. When the utility function $u(q, l)$ is specified, solving the utility maximization problem for optimal choices of q and l leads to the two functions. In what follows, we use examples to illustrate.

Example 6.3.1 Suppose the household utility function is a Cobb–Douglas function $U = \alpha \ln q + (1 - \alpha) \ln l$. His factor (labor) endowment is $\bar{L}$. The household receives labor income plus profit π transferred from enterprises. Solve for his commodity demand and factor supply functions.

Solution: The household maximizes his utility subject to the budget constraint which includes monetary income π:

$$\max_{q,l} U = \alpha \ln q + (1 - \alpha) \ln l \qquad s.t. \quad pq + wl = w\bar{L} + \pi \qquad (6.3.4)$$

The Lagrange function is

$$\max_{q,l,\lambda} L = \alpha \ln q + (1 - \alpha) \ln l - \lambda(pq + wl - w\bar{L} - \pi) \qquad (6.3.5)$$

Solve the above maximization problem for choice variables q, l and Lagrange multiplier λ, note $L^s = \bar{L} - l$, we have the following commodity demand function:

$$q^d = \frac{\alpha}{p}(w\bar{L} + \pi) \qquad (6.3.6)$$

and factor supply function

$$L^s = \bar{L} - l = \bar{L} - \frac{1 - \alpha}{w}(w\bar{L} + \pi) = \alpha\bar{L} - \frac{1 - \alpha}{w}\pi \qquad (6.3.7)$$

Now let us examine the enterprises side and derive the commodity supply and input demand functions. The behavior of an enterprise is to maximize profits given the available technology. In advanced economics, technology is described by a production set. The existence of the general equilibrium requires the production set to be convex. For simplicity, here we use the production function form rather than the set concepts to describe the technology. Let each commodity be produced by only one production activity. In intermediate economics, the production function has only primary factor inputs but not intermediate inputs, such as, the production function of commodity i is $q_i = f_i(K, L)$, where capital K and labor L are the factor inputs contributing to the production. In the general equilibrium framework, the production process involves not only factors but also intermediate inputs. The intermediate inputs are commodities produced by other sectors, such as steel, coal, IC chips, etc. This production relationship is expressed by production sets and netputs in advanced theory. Here we use the function form to illustrate. The production function of commodity i is:

$$q_i = f_i(g(q_i), \mathbf{q}_{-i}, \mathbf{x}) \qquad (6.3.8)$$

where q_i is the gross output of commodity i, $\mathbf{x}$ is the vector of factor inputs used in production, $g(q_i)$ is sector i's own product used as an intermediate input in the production, and $\mathbf{q}_{-i}$ are the other commodities that are used as intermediate inputs.

The existence of general equilibrium requires that the production function is weakly concave, or it exhibits constant or decreasing returns to scale. A production function with increasing returns to scale would violate the conditions for the existence of equilibrium. This is because, if the production function is increasing returns to scale, it would induce the enterprises to expand production for more profits without limit; hence, the equilibrium of supply and demand would not exist.

Given the production function, the enterprise attempts to maximize profits at the market prices by choosing the optimal use of factors and intermediate inputs:

$$\max_{\mathbf{q},\mathbf{x}} \pi_i = p f_i(g(q_i), \mathbf{q}_{-i}, \mathbf{x}) - p_i g(q_i) - \mathbf{p}_{-i}\mathbf{q}_{-i} - \mathbf{wx} \tag{6.3.9}$$

Solving the above problem, we can derive the commodity supply and input demand functions.

When enterprises make profits, the profits are finally transferred to the household who is the enterprise owner. Summing profits remitted from all sectors $\pi = \sum_i \pi_i$, it is the total transfer payment received by the household from enterprises.

Example 6.3.2 Let the enterprise's production function be $y = \sqrt{L}$, solve for the commodity supply function, input demand function and realized profit π^*.

Solution: The enterprise maximizes the profit, revenue over cost, by choosing labor input

$$\max_{L} \pi = p\sqrt{L} - wL \tag{6.3.10}$$

Differentiate the above profit function with respect to L, get the first-order condition, and obtain

$$L^d = \left(\frac{p}{2w}\right)^2, \quad q^s = \frac{p}{2w}, \quad \pi^* = \frac{p^2}{4w} \tag{6.3.11}$$

The state of the general equilibrium requires that all markets clear, including commodities and factors markets. If all commodities are desirable and all factors are productive, then, in all commodity and factor markets, the quantities supplied should strictly equal the quantities demanded. The combination of the price and quantity vectors that meet these conditions is the general equilibrium.

Example 6.3.3 Suppose the household utility function and enterprise's production function are as those in Examples 6.3.1 and 6.3.2, respectively. Suppose the entire economy has only one commodity q and one factor L. Solve for the general equilibrium prices (p^*, w^*) and quantities (q^*, L^*).

Solution: The previous examples have already given the supply and demand functions in both markets. We just need to equate quantity supplied to quantity demanded to solve for the equilibrium price and quantity in each market. Note the enterprises make positive profits and households receive the profits as their additional income. The commodity market clearing is $q^s = q^d$, which is

$$\frac{p}{2w} = \frac{\alpha}{p}\left(w\bar{L} + \pi\right) = \frac{\alpha}{p}\left(w\bar{L} + \frac{p^2}{4w}\right) \tag{6.3.12}$$

The solved equilibrium prices and quantities from the above commodity market clearing equation are

$$\frac{p}{w} = \sqrt{\frac{4\alpha \bar{L}}{2 - \alpha}} \qquad q^* = \frac{1}{2}\sqrt{\frac{4\alpha \bar{L}}{2 - \alpha}} \qquad L^* = \frac{\alpha \bar{L}}{2 - \alpha} \qquad (6.3.13)$$

The factor market clearing $L^d = L^s$ is

$$\left(\frac{p}{2w}\right)^2 = \alpha \bar{L} - \frac{1 - \alpha}{w}\pi, \qquad (6.3.14)$$

The solved equilibrium prices and quantities from the above factor market clearing equation are

$$\frac{p}{w} = \sqrt{\frac{4\alpha \bar{L}}{2 - \alpha}} \qquad q^* = \frac{1}{2}\sqrt{\frac{4\alpha \bar{L}}{2 - \alpha}} \qquad L^* = \frac{\alpha \bar{L}}{2 - \alpha} \qquad (6.3.15)$$

Note that the obtained results of (6.3.15) from factor market clearing are exactly the same results of (6.3.13) from the commodity market clearing. At the price ratio $\frac{p}{w} = \sqrt{\frac{4\alpha \bar{L}}{2-\alpha}}$, both commodity and factor markets clear. Further, the equilibrium prices solved are just the ratio of two prices, $\frac{p}{w}$, rather than two individual price levels p and w. This phenomenon is a major conclusion from Walras' law, which will be discussed in the following section.

6.4 Walras' Law

Walras' law is an important principle in the general equilibrium theory. It says that the sum of all excess demands in an economy equals zero. Let the economy have m commodities and n factors. So it has total $m + n$ markets including commodity and factor markets. Let the vector of excess demands in the commodity markets be $\mathbf{z_q}(\mathbf{p}) = \mathbf{q}^d - \mathbf{q}^s$. Let the vector of excess demands in the factor markets be $\mathbf{z_x}(\mathbf{w}) = \mathbf{x}^d - \mathbf{x}^s$. Walras' law claims that

$$\mathbf{p z_q} + \mathbf{w z_x} = 0 \qquad (6.4.1)$$

Or, is expressed by the following function form:

$$\sum_{i}^{n} p_i(q_i^d - q_i^s) + \sum_{k}^{m} w_k(x_k^d - x_k^s) = 0 \qquad (6.4.2)$$

Walras' law is a natural result from households' behavior of exhausting their budget constraints. Walras' law is broadly valid. Even if the economy is not in the general equilibrium state, as long as households are maximizing their utilities and enterprises are maximizing their profits, and households are exhausting their budgets, then Walras' law holds.

An important conclusion from Walras' law is that, because of Equation (6.4.2), the excess demand functions in the $m+n$ markets are linearly dependent. When we construct a system of $m+n$ excess demand equations for $m+n$ markets, there are only $m+n-1$ independent equations, with one equation redundant. In other words, if $m+n-1$ clear, the remaining market automatically clears. Let the remaining market be denoted by j, and suppose j is a commodity market. Rewriting from Equation (6.4.2), we have

$$p_j(q_j^d - q_j^s) = -\sum_{i=1}^{j-1} p_i(q_i^d - q_i^s) - \sum_{i=j+1}^{n} p_i(q_i^d - q_i^s) - \sum_{k}^{m} w_k(x_k^d - x_k^s). \qquad (6.4.3)$$

If the $m + n - 1$ markets on the right-hand side clear, i.e., $p_i(q_i^d - q_i^s) = 0$ for $(i \neq j)$ and $w_k(x_k^d - x_k^s) = 0$, then the remaining market j on left-hand side must be $p_j(q_j^d - q_j^s) = 0$. Because as assumed the commodity is desirable, then $p_j > 0$. Hence, $q_j^d - q_j^s = 0$, market j must clear. The same argument applies if the remaining market is a factor market.

For an economy with $m + n$ markets, only $m + n - 1$ excess demand functions are independent, but we have $m + n$ variables of prices p_i and w_j in the system. The number of variables exceeds the number of independent equations in the system, thus we do not have a unique solution set for the price variables. In fact, we would have infinite possible solution sets for the prices. Mathematically, for $m + n - 1$ independent excess demand equations, we can only determine $m + n - 1$ unique values for variables. This can be seen from Example 6.3.3. with two markets. By Walras' law, there can be only one independent excess demand function. When the commodity market clears, the remaining factor market automatically clears, and vice versa. Further, we can only determine one value for the price variables. That is why we only have the price ratio $\frac{p}{w}$ but not the unique individual price levels of p and w. Any pair values of p and w satisfying $\frac{p}{w} = \sqrt{\frac{4\alpha\bar{L}}{2-\alpha}}$ are qualified for the equilibrium prices.

To generalize, for $m + n$ markets, we can only determine $m + n - 1$ price ratios. If all commodity and factor prices change by the same proportion, so long as they satisfy these ratios, the equilibrium state is maintained with the same equilibrium quantities in all markets. In order to determine a unique set of equilibrium price, we can choose a numeraire price which serves as the benchmark for other prices. For instance, we may choose labor as the numeraire. Then the labor price is fixed at 1. Other $m + n - 1$ prices can be uniquely determined from their ratios to the numeraire. In addition to labor, one may use a weighted price index as the numeraire price. All these approaches would reduce the degree of freedom so the other prices can be uniquely determined. Walras' law and the dependence property of the equation system in CGE models are important for issues that will be discussed later in this book.

6.5 From the General Equilibrium Theory to CGE Models

How can the general equilibrium theory be transformed into an applicable model to quantitatively simulate the real-world economy with interdependent relationship of economic variables? For instance, what are the specific supply and demand functions $\mathbf{q^d, q^s, x^d, x^s}$? A CGE model is an application of the general equilibrium theory to the real-world cases. In order to be practical, it is necessary to make some simplifications and some assumptions, but keeping them theoretically sound based on economics and the general equilibrium theory.

The development of CGE models in the economics literature can be viewed as a mutual movement from two directions. One is the attempt to construct applicable models for the general equilibrium theory, and the other is the evolution of the IO model from the open system which only addresses the production process to a completed/closed framework which includes the link of the demand-side transaction. We can still see that modern CGE models inherit the basic features from both directions. A modern CGE model is multi-sectoral. The intermediate input block has an IO model. The production functions and demand functions are in general non-linear, such as CES or LES, which are used often in economics. Finally, the equations representing economic relationships are set up under the general equilibrium framework, which is called *closure* in the CGE terminology.

In what follows, we describe a framework for a simple CGE model, from which readers can see how a CGE model is constructed in line with the general equilibrium theory and the theoretical examples in Section 6.3.

There are two agent groups, enterprises and households. Enterprises maximize profits, which derives the supply functions of i commodities, the demand functions of k factors, and the profit function π:

$$q_i^s = q_i^s(p_1, \cdots, p_n, w_1, \cdots, w_m) \qquad i = 1, \cdots, n \qquad (6.5.1)$$

$$x_k^d = x_k^d(p_1, \cdots, p_n, w_1, \cdots, w_m) \qquad k = 1, \cdots, m \qquad (6.5.2)$$

$$\pi = \pi(p_1, \cdots, p_n, w_1, \cdots, w_m) \qquad (6.5.3)$$

Households have factor endowment e, from which they receive factor incomes. They also receive profit π transferred from the enterprises. Adding together is their income Y. Again, here households are treated as a group for simplicity, so Y is the income of the whole group.

$$Y = \sum_k^m w_k e_k + \pi \qquad (6.5.4)$$

Households maximize utility, which leads to the commodity supply function:

$$q_i^d = q_i^d(p_1, \cdots, p_n, Y) \qquad i = 1, \cdots, n \qquad (6.5.5)$$

Households supply factors. For simplicity, adopting the neoclassical assumption, factors are fully employed. Hence, the quantities of factor supplied equal the endowments.

$$x_k^s = e_k^s \qquad k = 1, \cdots, m \qquad (6.5.6)$$

The market clearing conditions are

$$q_i^s(p_1, \cdots, p_n, w_1, \cdots, w_m) = q_i^d(p_1, \cdots, p_n, Y) \qquad i = 1, \cdots, n \qquad (6.5.7)$$

$$x_k^d(p_1, \cdots, p_n, w_1, \cdots, w_m) = x_k^s \qquad k = 1, \cdots, m \qquad (6.5.8)$$

The above seven Equations from (6.5.1) to (6.5.8) constitute this CGE model. It can be seen that it is different from the IO model. The CGE model has to explain how the households get income from providing factors and receiving transfer payments, then use the income to purchase commodities to maximum utility, which forms the demands for commodities. This link is missing in the IO model. Adding this link completes the economic closure, which is a basic property of a general equilibrium model.

A CGE models must have its closure. There can be different closures based on different macroeconomic hypotheses, such as neoclassical closure, Keynesian closure, Lewis closure, and so on. The term "closure" is used so broadly and loosely in the CGE literature that its exact definition is dependent on the particular context. The issue of closures will be discussed later.

To be applicable, in CGE models the demand and supply functions must be specified. The input demand and commodity supply functions of the enterprises are derived from the production function and their production decision. The production functions can be Leontief, Cobb–Douglas, CES or others. The commodity demand and factor supply functions by household are derived from utility functions such as Cobb–Douglas, CES or Stony–Geary utility functions. We will discuss these functions and derivations later in the book. The following section provides a specific CGE example and corresponding GAMS program.

6.6 A Very Simple but Completed CGE Model

Here we present a very simple CGE model. It is probably the simplest but still has the essential feature of a CGE model. Figure 6.6.1 that follows is a schematic diagram of this completed and closed economy. The economy has two agents, one enterprise and one resident. It has no government and no foreign sector. This economy is similar to that in Figure 6.3.1, except that we would specify all functions and their relationships.

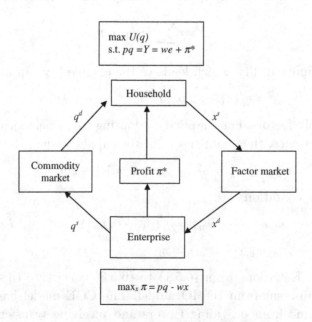

Figure 6.6.1. A simple but completed economy.

It has two commodity markets, sector 1 and sector 2, and one factor, labor. The production function is Leontief type, which uses intermediate and factor inputs by fixed input coefficients. Differing from an IO model, here we add the transaction link from the household side, which provides factors, receives income, and forms commodity final demands. So the system is completed with the closure.

Table 6.6.1 is the descriptive SAM table for this economy. w and p are prices of labor and commodity, respectively. q, h, x, e are the real quantities of a commodity, final demand by households, labor input and labor endowment, respectively. Y is the household monetary income. Table 6.6.2 is a "real" SAM table for this model economy with hypothetical data.

We construct a CGE model for this economy, using the above SAM table as the data. The production function is Leontief, which has input coefficients $a_{11}, a_{12}, a_{21}, a_{22}$ in the intermediate input block and factor coefficients a_{n1}, a_{n2} in the value-added block. The price equations from the Leontief production are

$$p_1 = p_1 a_{11} + p_2 a_{21} + w a_{n1} \qquad (6.6.1)$$

$$p_2 = p_1 a_{12} + p_2 a_{22} + w a_{n2} \qquad (6.6.2)$$

The above price equations serve as the supply functions in the Leontief case, which implies profit has been maximized at these prices. Quantities supplied q_1 and q_2 are not explicitly shown in the equations, which mean that at these prices enterprises are willing to supply any quantities of q_1 and q_2. To see the point, take sector 1 as an example, multiplying both sides of the price equation by q_1, we have

$$p_1 q_1 = p_1 a_{11} q_1 + p_2 a_{21} q_1 + w a_{n1} q_1 \qquad (6.6.3)$$

Table 6.6.1. Descriptive SAM table for the model economy.

	Commodity 1	Commodity 2	Labor	Household	Total
Commodity 1	$p_1 q_{11}$	$p_1 q_{12}$		$p_1 h_1$	$p_1 q_1$
Commodity 2	$p_2 q_{21}$	$p_2 q_{22}$		$p_2 h_2$	$p_2 q_2$
Labor	$w x_1$	$w x_2$			$w \cdot e$
Household			$w \cdot e$		Y
Total	$p_1 q_1$	$p_2 q_2$	$w \cdot e$	Y	

Table 6.6.2. The "real" SAM table for the model economy.

	Commodity 1	Commodity 2	Labor	Household	Total
Commodity 1	4	3		3	10
Commodity 2	2	5		6	13
Labor	4	5			9
Household			9		9
Total	10	13	9	9	

The left-hand side is the total revenue, the right-hand side is the total cost. The equation is the "breakeven" condition for the firm. Profit is defined by total revenue minus total cost:

$$\pi_1 = p_1 q_1 - (p_1 a_{11} q_1 + p_2 a_{21} q_1 + w a_{n1} q_1) = (p_1 - p_1 a_{11} - p_2 a_{21} - w a_{n1}) q_1 \qquad (6.6.4)$$

Let v_1 denote the expression in the last parentheses above, i.e.

$$v_1 \equiv p_1 - p_1 a_{11} - p_2 a_{21} - w a_{n1} \qquad (6.6.5)$$

When the enterprise attempts to maximize profits, from Equation (6.6.3) we can see its choice: If $v_1 > 0$, the more q_1 is produced, the larger the profit would be. Then the quantity supplied by the enterprise would approach infinity, and equilibrium does not exist. If $v_1 < 0$, the enterprise would incur loss if it produces any positive amount. Hence, the enterprise stops production and the quantity supplied is $q_1 = 0$. If $v_1 = 0$, the economic profit is zero, the enterprise is at "breakeven". It is willing to supply any amount if demand is defined. The quantity supplied is $q_1^s = [0, \infty)$. Hence, the price equation of Equations (6.6.1) or (6.6.2) is actually the supply function if the technology is constant returns to scale. Breakeven condition like Equation (6.6.3) is a variant of price equation, thus can be substituted for the price equation in the production module.

The labor input demand functions derived from the Leontief production function are

$$a_{n1} q_1 = x_1 \qquad (6.6.6)$$

$$a_{n2} q_2 = x_2 \qquad (6.6.7)$$

The household's labor endowment is e. Assuming full employment, labor supply is also e. The household's income includes that from labor supply and profit remittance π from the enterprise:

$$Y = w \cdot e + \pi \qquad (6.6.8)$$

where w is the wage rate. Because the production exhibits constant returns to scale, $\pi = 0$. Hence, the above income equation is simply

$$Y = w \cdot e \qquad (6.6.8')$$

The household's utility function is a Cobb–Douglas function, as shown in Example 6.3.1 and in the appendix of this chapter, and the commodity demand functions derived are

$$p_1 h_1 = \alpha Y \qquad (6.6.9)$$

$$p_2 h_2 = (1 - \alpha) Y \qquad (6.6.10)$$

where h_i are the commodity quantities demanded by the household for Commodity i.

The commodity market clearing condition is *intermediate inputs + final demands = total output*:

$$a_{11} q_1 + a_{12} q_2 + h_1 = q_1 \qquad (6.6.11)$$

$$a_{21} q_1 + a_{22} q_2 + h_2 = q_2 \qquad (6.6.12)$$

The factor market clearing condition is

$$x_1 + x_2 = e \tag{6.6.13}$$

Thus, we have completed the CGE model. Let us summarize the model as follows:

$$p_1 = p_1 a_{11} + p_2 a_{21} + w a_{n1} \tag{6.6.14}$$

$$p_2 = p_1 a_{12} + p_2 a_{22} + w a_{n2} \tag{6.6.15}$$

$$a_{n1} q_1 = x_1 \tag{6.6.16}$$

$$a_{n2} q_2 = x_2 \tag{6.6.17}$$

$$Y = w \cdot e \tag{6.6.18}$$

$$p_1 h_1 = \alpha Y \tag{6.6.19}$$

$$p_2 h_2 = (1 - \alpha) Y \tag{6.6.20}$$

$$a_{11} q_1 + a_{12} q_2 + h_1 = q_1 \tag{6.6.21}$$

$$a_{21} q_1 + a_{22} q_2 + h_2 = q_2 \tag{6.6.22}$$

$$x_1 + x_2 = e \tag{6.6.23}$$

The model has 10 Equations, from (6.6.14) to (6.6.23), and 10 variables $q_1, q_2,$ $h_1, h_2, x_1, x_2, Y, p_1, p_2, w$. The exogenous variable is labor endowment e, which determines the scale of the economy. Other parameters are $a_{11}, a_{12}, a_{21}, a_{22}, a_{n1}, a_{n2}, \alpha$. It is a simple but completed CGE model, beyond the IO model structure. This is because the model has a macroeconomic closure. It addresses the entire circular flow of the economy. The household provides labor and receives labor income $w(a_{n1} q_1 + a_{n2} q_2) = Y = we$. Under utility maximization and budget constraint, the household forms commodity demands $p_1 h_1 = \alpha Y$ and $p_2 h_2 = (1 - \alpha) Y$. Finally, all commodity and factor markets clear:

$$a_{11} q_1 + a_{12} q_2 + h_1 = q_1 \qquad a_{21} q_1 + a_{22} q_2 + h_2 = q_2 \qquad x_1 + x_2 = e \tag{6.6.24}$$

Therefore, the model has equations representing all links and flows of an economy as shown by the circular flow chart in Figure 6.3.1, which is laid out based on the general equilibrium theory. CGE models, regardless of what variations there are, must have such a general equilibrium closure.

As expected, Walras' law applies. There are totally three markets, two commodities and one labor. Hence, if any two markets clear, the remaining one automatically clears. We will also have to determine a numeraire price. As a remark, the production functions in the above CGE model are the Leontief technology. Hence, all the prices are fixed by proportions, and thus are not flexible. One cannot study how changes in the prices would affect the real quantities in this model. In later discussion, we will use other non-linear production functions for the CGE models, so the relative prices can change and influence the quantities.

The following is the corresponding GAMS program for the above model. Readers can compare the GAMS program to the above equations to help understand the GAMS codes for a CGE model.

Example 6.6.1 Write the GAMS program for the above CGE model in this section. Use the data of the SAM table in Table 6.6.2. Check the results and show the original SAM table is successfully replicated. Do the following simulation: if the factor endowment e increases by 10%, what are the resulting changes in the variables in the model?

Solution: The GAMS program is as follows. The simulation results show that, after the labor endowment increases by 10%, all quantities and the monetary income increase by 10%, as expected. Prices remain at the original levels of one.

```
$title Example 6.6.1: A very simple CGE model

*define sets: ac for all accounts, i for commodities, x for factors
set ac      /sec1,sec2,lab,hh,total/
    i(ac)   /sec1,sec2/
;

alias (ac,acp), (i,j);

*read the SAM data
    table sam(ac,acp)
          sec1  sec2  lab  hh   total
    sec1   4     3          3    10
    sec2   2     5          6    13
    lab    4     5               9
    hh                 9         9
    total  10    13    9    9
;

*Declare parameters
parameters
    a(i,j)      Input coefficients
    ax(i)       Factor coefficients
    q0(i)       initial value for the quantity of commodity i
    p0(i)       initial value for the price of commodity i
    x0(i)       initial value of labor demand in sector i
    xe0         labor endowment and supply
    w0          initial value of labor price (wage)
    Y0          initial value of household's monetary income
    h0(i)       initial value of demand for commodity i by household
    alpha(i)    share of household's incomes spending on i
;

*Calibrating and assigning parameter values
*Reminder: dividing values by prices to obtain quantities
```

```
      p0(i)=1;
      w0=1;
      q0(i)=sam('total',i)/p0(i);
      x0(i)=sam('lab',i)/w0;
      xe0=sam('lab','total')/w0;
      Y0=w0*xe0;
      h0(i)=SAM(i,'hh')/p0(i);

*Calibrating input coefficients
      a(i,j)=(sam(i,j)/p0(i))/(sam('total',j)/p0(j));
      ax(j)=(sam('lab',j)/w0)/(sam('total',j)/p0(j));

*Calibrating income share spending on commodity i
      alpha(i)=p0(i)*h0(i)/Y0;

*Display parameter values to check if they are right
      display  a,ax,q0,x0,xe0,Y0,h0;

*Declare variables
variable
      p(i),q(i),x(i),h(i),Y,w;

*Start the equation part
equation
      Priceeq(i),factoreq(i),IncomeYeq,Hdemand(i),Qmarket(i),Xmarket;

*The equations are the same equations of the mathematical model in this section.
Operator sum works like the sigma notation for summation in equations.
      Priceeq(i)..
      p(i)=e=sum(j, p(j)*a(j,i))+w*ax(i);

      Factoreq(i)..
      ax(i)*q(i)=e=x(i);

      IncomeYeq..
      Y=e=w*xe0;

      Hdemand(i)..
      p(i)*h(i)=e=alpha(i)*Y;

      Qmarket(i)..
      sum(j,a(i,j)*q(j))+h(i)=e=q(i);

      Xmarket..
      sum(i,x(i))=e=xe0;

*Assign initial values to variables
       p.L(i)=p0(i);
```

```
     q.L(i)=q0(i);
     x.L(i)=x0(i);
     h.L(i)=h0(i);
     Y.L=Y0;
     w.L=w0;

*Define the model and run the optimization process
     model cge   /all/;
     solve cge using mcp;

$ontext
     When the above process finishes, check the results displayed in the report
file (the file name has suffix .1st) generated by GAMS.  The numerical results of
variables should be consistent with the SAM table data.  Otherwise, the model is
not successfully replicated.
$offtext

*The following is the simulation for labor endowment increases by 10%
*Assign new value for xe0.  When a new value is assigned to the same parameter in
GAMS, the previous value is replaced with the new value.
     xe0=1.1*sam('lab','total')/w0;

*Run optimization program
     model simulation  /all/;
     solve simulation using mcp;

*end of the program.
```

6.7 Existence of General Equilibrium and CGE Models

As stated at the beginning of this chapter, understanding of the basics about the existence of general equilibrium is important for independently constructing CGE models, although the pure theoretical details are not required. A CGE model uses a balanced SAM table data as its initial equilibrium state. So at least this initial equilibrium exists. Yet another practical issue of our CGE modeling rises: will a new equilibrium exist after introducing an external policy shock? We need to ensure the new equilibrium state exists in the situation of simulation.

The Arrow–Debreu theory, roughly speaking, demonstrates that if the production and consumption sets are convex, then the derived supply and demand functions in markets are continuous. Hence, in the proper range general equilibrium exists. If an external shock does not change these properties, a new equilibrium exists. This conclusion is helpful for us to choose production functions and utility functions in modeling. A general requirement is that the production functions are weakly convex and the utility functions should be quasi-concave. The following chapters will discuss the various functions and their properties. All these commonly used functions in CGE modeling satisfy the convexity property as required.

Exercises

6E.1 Suppose a simple model economy has only one commodity q and one factor L. The household group has utility function $U = q^\alpha l^{1-\alpha}$, where l is leisure. Households' labor endowment is 1. The enterprise production function is $q = cL$ where c is a constant and L is labor input. Solve for the general equilibrium prices (p^*, w^*) and quantities (y^*, L^*).

6E.2 Prove Walras' law. (You may use advanced microeconomics textbooks for reference).

Appendix: Review of Microeconomics

Review how to derive the commodity demand functions $q = q^d(\text{p}, Y)$ from the Cobb–Douglas utility function. A Cobb–Douglas utility function is

$$u = Aq_1^\alpha q_2^{1-\alpha} \tag{6A.1}$$

where u is the utility level, q_1, q_2 are commodities 1 and 2. Households (consumers) maximize utility subject to the following constraint:

$$\max \ u = Aq_1^\alpha q_2^{1-\alpha} \tag{6A.2}$$

$$\text{s.t.} \ \ p_1 q_1 + p_2 q_2 = Y$$

The Lagrange function is as follows, with choice variables q_1, q_2 and λ. Maximize L,

$$\max_{q_1, q_1, \lambda} L = Aq_1^\alpha q_2^{1-\alpha} - \lambda(p_1 q_1 + p_2 q_2 - Y) \tag{6A.3}$$

Solve the above problem and obtain

$$q_1 = \alpha \frac{Y}{p_1} \qquad q_2 = (1-\alpha)\frac{Y}{p_2} \tag{6A.4}$$

The log form of the above Cobb–Douglas utility function is

$$u = \log A + \alpha \log q_1 + (1 - \alpha) \log q_2 \tag{6A.5}$$

which is frequently used in economics. The log form of Cobb–Douglas utility function yields the same demand functions, because a monotonic transformation of the utility function does not change optimal choices of the consumption bundle.

Chapter 7

Supply and Demand Functions of Enterprises

Chapter 6 has outlined the basic structure of CGE models. General equilibrium is the state in which quantities supplied equal quantities demanded in all markets. Now we will examine the details of supplies and demands, in particular, how the supply and demand functions are formed and specified in CGE models. This chapter will discuss the production side by enterprises: how the enterprises form the commodity supply functions and input demand functions.

In our previous discussion on the input–output (IO) model, we have introduced the Leontief production function. The Leontief production function is convenient but has a shortcoming: the ratios among inputs used are fixed in production, regardless of changes in the relative input prices. This is not quite realistic in the real economy. The input composition normally changes in response to changes in input prices, especially in the long run, when the enterprises can adjust or replace the technology they use. For example, if wages and other compensation to labor rise faster than the capital price, enterprises will shift to automation or other capital-intensive technology for production. However, adopting the Leontief production function in CGE models cannot simulate this kind of adjustment, as the ratio between labor and capital is always fixed. To allow the composition of inputs to change, non-linear production functions need to be adopted.

The most popular non-linear production function used in CGE modeling is the Constant Elasticity of Substitution (CES) production function. The advantage of the CES function is it has the combination of flexibility and simplicity. It is flexible as it allows different elasticities of substitution among inputs, whether they are substitutes or complements. It is relatively simple as the only information needed to be given from outside sources is the elasticity of substitution, other parameters of the function can be calculated (also called "calibrated") from the data in the SAM table.

In addition to the production function, the CES function form is also used for other functions in CGE models, for instance, the CES utility function. Another variant is the Constant Elasticity of Transformation (CET) function, which is used to simulate the combination of various outputs in a production possibility frontier, such as between domestic sale and exports of a domestically produced product in CGE trade models. Therefore, it is important to be familiar with CES functions, including their various mathematical expressions, first-order optimization conditions and other properties.

7.1 CES Production Function and Its Properties

In CGE models, a CES production function usually consists of only two inputs. If more inputs in production need to be included for the research purpose, we combine several CES production functions together in a nested structure. The reasons for the nested structure will be discussed later. The standard form of the CES production function is

$$q = f(x_1, x_2) = A(\delta_1 x_1^\rho + \delta_2 x_2^\rho)^{1/\rho} \qquad (7.1.1)$$

where q is output, x_1 and x_2 are inputs. Output q depends on the two inputs. Parameter A is a scale factor, which is also referred to as "total factor productivity" (or TFP) in economics. Exponent ρ is related to the elasticity of substitution, which is discussed in what follows.

 Parameters δ_1 and δ_2 are the shares of output q contributed by x_1 and x_2 inputs. Because all shares add up to 1, so $\delta_1 + \delta_2 = 1$. Hence, the CES production function in CGE models is often directly written as

$$q = f(x_1, x_2) = A[\delta_1 x_1^\rho + (1 - \delta_1)x_2^\rho]^{1/\rho} \qquad (7.1.2)$$

 The interesting and important property of the CES function is its elasticity of substitution ε. ε is a constant in the CES function, whose value can range from 0 to infinity.[1] Different values of the elasticity of substitution represent different relationships among two inputs, from complements to substitutes. When ε equals 1, the CES function becomes the familiar Cobb–Douglas function.

 This property of CES functions can be illustrated by an isoquant–isocost diagram in economics. The slope of the isoquant (in absolute value) is called "*technical rate of substitution* (TRS)". (Hereafter, referring to the slopes of isoquants and isocosts, we may omit the word "in absolute value" in the discussion). The TRS of the CES function is

$$
\begin{aligned}
TRS &= -\frac{dx_2}{dx_1}\bigg|_{y=y_0} = \frac{\partial f/\partial x_1}{\partial f/\partial x_2} = \frac{A\frac{1}{\rho}(\delta_1 x_1^\rho + \delta_2 x_2^\rho)^{\frac{1}{\rho}-1} \cdot \delta_1 \cdot \rho x_1^{\rho-1}}{A\frac{1}{\rho}(\delta_1 x_1^\rho + \delta_2 x_2^\rho)^{\frac{1}{\rho}-1} \cdot \delta_2 \cdot \rho x_2^{\rho-1}} \\
&= \frac{\delta_1}{\delta_2}\left(\frac{x_1}{x_2}\right)^{\rho-1} \qquad\qquad (7.1.3) \\
&= \frac{\delta_1}{\delta_2}\left(\frac{x_2}{x_1}\right)^{1-\rho}
\end{aligned}
$$

 The equation of the isocost line is $c = w_1 x_1 + w_2 x_2$. w_1 and w_2 are input prices. The slope of the isocost line in absolute value is w_1/w_2. The optimal use of inputs is at the point

---

[1]In the case of a CET function, the elasticity of substitution can take a negative value.

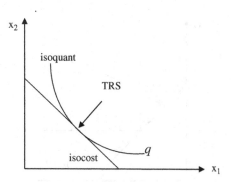

Figure 7.1.1. Optimal use of inputs.

where the isocost line is tangent to the isoquant curve, as shown in Figure 7.1.1. That is, their slopes are equal at the tangent point, $w_1/w_2 = TRS$:

$$\frac{w_1}{w_2} = TRS = -\frac{dx_2}{dx_1} = \frac{\delta_1}{\delta_2}\left(\frac{x_2}{x_1}\right)^{1-\rho} \tag{7.1.4}$$

Elasticity of substitution ε characterizes the curvature of the isoquant curve. It is defined as the percentage change in the ratio of input combination x_2/x_1 when the isoquant slope TRS increases by one percent:

$$\varepsilon \equiv \frac{\dfrac{d(x_2/x_1)}{x_2/x_1}}{\dfrac{d(TRS)}{TRS}} = \frac{d\ln\left(\dfrac{x_2}{x_1}\right)}{d\ln(TRS)} = \frac{\dfrac{d(x_2/x_1)}{x_2/x_1}}{\dfrac{d(w_1/w_2)}{w_1/w_2}} \tag{7.1.5}$$

The TRS of a CES function is Equation (7.1.3): $TRS = \frac{\delta_1}{\delta_2}\left(\frac{x_2}{x_1}\right)^{1-\rho}$. Take the log of both sides, then differentiate the two log terms:

$$\ln TRS = \ln\frac{\delta_1}{\delta_2} + (1-\rho)\ln\left(\frac{x_2}{x_1}\right) \tag{7.1.6}$$

$$d\ln TRS = (1-\rho)d\ln\left(\frac{x_2}{x_1}\right) \tag{7.1.7}$$

The elasticity of substitution of a CES function is

$$\varepsilon = \frac{d\ln\left(\dfrac{x_2}{x_1}\right)}{d\ln TRS} = \frac{\dfrac{d(x_2/x_1)}{x_2/x_1}}{d(TRS)/TRS} = \frac{1}{1-\rho} \tag{7.1.8}$$

In CGE modeling, often the opposite situation occurs: the value of elasticity of substitution ε is obtained, then we need to calculate (calibrate) the value ρ for the CES function. This is calculated by

$$\rho = 1 - \frac{1}{\varepsilon} \tag{7.1.9}$$

What happens to the CES function as the value of ρ changes?

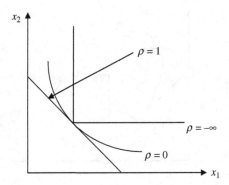

Figure 7.1.2.   Isoquants with different ρ values.

(a) If $\rho = 1$, elasticity of substitution ε approaches infinity. The CES production function becomes a linear function:

$$f(x_1, x_2) = (\delta_1 x_1^\rho + \delta_2 x_2^\rho)^{1/\rho} = \delta_1 x_1 + \delta_2 x_2 \qquad (7.1.10)$$

The isoquant is a line as shown in Figure 7.1.2. The two inputs are perfect substitutes.

(b) If $\rho = -\infty$, then elasticity of substitution ε is infinitesimal, the isoquant becomes a right-angled line as that in Figure 7.1.2. The two inputs are perfect complements. The CES production function becomes the Leontief function:

$$f(x_1, x_2) = (\delta_1 x_1^\rho + \delta_2 x_2^\rho)^{\frac{1}{\rho}} = \min\{x_1, x_2\} \qquad (7.1.11)$$

This can intuitively be seen from TRS, the slope of the isoquant of the CES function. When $\rho = -\infty$, TRS is

$$TRS = -\frac{dx_2}{dx_1} = \frac{\delta_1}{\delta_2}\left(\frac{x_2}{x_1}\right)^{1-\rho} = \frac{\delta_1}{\delta_2}\left(\frac{x_2}{x_1}\right)^\infty \qquad (7.1.12)$$

If $x_2 > x_1$, TRS approaches infinity, then the segment of the isoquant is vertical. If $x_1 > x_2$, TRS approaches 0, the segment of the isoquant is horizontal. Hence, the isoquant is a right-angle L-shape as that in Figure 7.1.2. This kind of isoquants are those coming from the Leontief production function.

(c) If $\rho = 0$, the CES production function is the Cobb–Douglas production function:

$$f(x_1, x_2) = (\delta_1 x_1^\rho + \delta_2 x_2^\rho)^{\frac{1}{\rho}} = A x_1^{\delta_1} x_2^{\delta_2} \qquad (7.1.13)$$

This can be seen from the TRS of the CES function. When $\rho = 0$, the TRS of the CES function is

$$TRS = -\frac{dx_2}{dx_1} = \frac{\delta_1}{\delta_2}\left(\frac{x_2}{x_1}\right)^{1-\rho} = \frac{\delta_1}{\delta_2}\frac{x_2}{x_1} \qquad (7.1.14)$$

This is the TRS of a Cobb–Douglas function. Formal proofs can be found in any advanced microeconomics book.

To summarize, if $-\infty < \rho < 0$, the inputs are complements; if $0 < \rho < 1$, they are substitutes. If $\rho = 0$, they are neither.

In some economics books, the CES function is in a more general form, as

$$q = f(x_1, x_2) = A[\delta_1(a_1x_1)^\rho + \delta_2(a_2x_2)^\rho]^{\frac{1}{\rho}} \tag{7.1.15}$$

It has coefficients a_1 and a_2, associated with the two input variables x_1 and x_2. In CGE modeling, we normalize the units of inputs and use the standard function form of Equation (7.1.1). By unit normalization, we scale up and down the units of x_1 and x_2, so the coefficients a_1 and a_2 equal 1, thus dropping out. This unit normalization simplifies the equation form and saves parameter data work, without sacrificing research quality because the simulation results are expressed in terms of percentage changes.

The CES function of Equation (7.1.1) exhibits constant returns to scale. In case a CGE model needs a CES function exhibiting decreasing returns to scale, it can be done by monotonic transformation as follows:

$$q = g[f(x_1, x_2)] \tag{7.1.16}$$

where $f(x_1, x_2)$ is the standard CES function (7.1.1), $g[..]$ is a monotonically decreasing function, $g' < 0$, for instance, $g[..] = [..]^{2/3}$.

7.2 Deriving Input Demand and Cost Functions

Economics theory assumes that a private enterprise optimizes the use of inputs to minimize its cost. Given the quantity of output q and input prices w_1 and w_2, an enterprise minimizes cost c as follows:

$$\min \quad c = w_1x_1 + w_2x_2 \tag{7.2.1}$$

$$\text{s.t.} \quad f(x_1, x_2) = A(\delta_1x_1^\rho + \delta_2x_2^\rho)^{1/\rho} = q$$

How much of each input should be used? Set up the Lagrange equation to solve as follows:

$$\min_{x_1, x_2, \lambda} \quad L = w_1x_1 + w_2x_2 - \lambda[A(\delta_1x_1^\rho + \delta_2x_2^\rho)^{1/\rho} - q] \tag{7.2.2}$$

Differentiating it with respect to the input variables and the Lagrange multiplier, we have the following three first-order conditions of optimization:

$$\partial L/\partial x_1 = w_1 - \lambda A\frac{1}{\rho}(\delta_1x_1^\rho + \delta_2x_2^\rho)^{\frac{1}{\rho}-1} \cdot \delta_1 \cdot \rho x_1^{\rho-1} = 0 \tag{7.2.3}$$

$$\partial L/\partial x_2 = w_2 - \lambda A\frac{1}{\rho}(\delta_1x_1^\rho + \delta_2x_2^\rho)^{\frac{1}{\rho}-1} \cdot \delta_2 \cdot \rho x_2^{\rho-1} = 0 \tag{7.2.4}$$

$$A(\delta_1x_1^\rho + \delta_2x_2^\rho)^{\frac{1}{\rho}} - q = 0 \tag{7.2.5}$$

Combining Equations (7.2.3) and (7.2.4), rearrange,

$$\frac{w_1}{w_2} = \frac{A\frac{1}{\rho}(\cdots)^{\frac{1}{\rho}-1} \cdot \delta_1 \cdot \rho x_1^{\rho-1}}{A\frac{1}{\rho}(\cdots)^{\frac{1}{\rho}-1} \cdot \delta_2 \cdot \rho x_2^{\rho-1}} = \frac{\delta_1}{\delta_2}\left(\frac{x_1}{x_2}\right)^{\rho-1} \tag{7.2.6}$$

Because $\delta_1 + \delta_2 = 1$, it can be written as

$$\frac{w_1}{w_2} = \frac{\delta_1}{(1 - \delta_1)} \left(\frac{x_1}{x_2}\right)^{\rho-1} \tag{7.2.7}$$

Equation (7.2.7) is the optimal condition for cost minimization. The term on the right-hand side (RHS) of the equation is TRS, the slope of isoquant. The term on the left-hand side (LHS) of the equation is the slope of the isocost line, which can be derived from the cost line equation $c = w_1 x_1 + w_2 x_2$. Intuitively, this just says that the optimal use of inputs is at the point where the isocost line is tangent to the isoquant (Figure 7.1.1). Combining (7.2.7) with the production function (7.2.5) solves for the optimal uses of inputs given output q. The solution leads to two important functions in economics:

(1) Conditional input demand function. It means the input demand is conditional upon the given amount of output q. In economics, an alternative term is "conditional factor demand". (Hereafter, we use the two terms "factor demand" and "input demand" interchangeably depending on the context, because the inputs in a production function can be either primary factors or intermediate inputs.) The general expression of conditional input demand function is $x_i^c(\mathbf{w}, q)$. If there are only two inputs involved in production, it is $x_i^c(w_1, w_2, q)$.
(2) Cost function. Its general expression is $c(\mathbf{w}, q)$. If only two inputs are involved in production, it is $c(w_1, w_2, q) = w_1 x_1^c + w_2 x_2^c$.

Example 7.2.1 Derive the conditional input demand function and cost function from the CES function with two inputs.

Solution: Combine the first-order condition (7.2.7) and production function (7.1.1), to form the following simultaneous equation system to be solved:

$$\begin{cases} \frac{w_1}{w_2} = \frac{\delta_1}{\delta_2} \left(\frac{x_1}{x_2}\right)^{\rho-1} \\ q = A(\delta_1 x_1^\rho + \delta_2 x_2^\rho)^{1/\rho} \end{cases} \tag{7.2.8}$$

To solve, rearrange (7.2.7),

$$x_2 = \left(\frac{w_1}{w_2} \cdot \frac{\delta_2}{\delta_1}\right)^{\frac{1}{1-\rho}} x_1 \tag{7.2.9}$$

Substituting it for x_2 in the production function,

$$q = A\left[\delta_1 x_1^\rho + \delta_2 \left(\frac{w_1}{w_2} \cdot \frac{\delta_2}{\delta_1}\right)^{\frac{\rho}{1-\rho}} x_1^\rho\right]^{\frac{1}{\rho}} = x_1 A \left[\delta_1 + \delta_2 \left(\frac{w_1}{w_2} \cdot \frac{\delta_2}{\delta_1}\right)^{\frac{\rho}{1-\rho}}\right]^{\frac{1}{\rho}} \tag{7.2.10}$$

Rearrange and obtain the conditional input demand function for x_1:

$$x_1^c = \frac{1}{A} \left[\delta_1 + \delta_2 \left(\frac{w_1}{w_2} \cdot \frac{\delta_2}{\delta_1}\right)^{\frac{\rho}{1-\rho}}\right]^{-\frac{1}{\rho}} \cdot q \tag{7.2.11}$$

This conditional input demand function has another popular form in CGE models using the elasticity of substitution ε rather than the exponent ρ. Rearrange (7.2.11),

$$x_1^c = \frac{1}{A} \left(\frac{\delta_1}{w_1} \right)^{\frac{1}{1-\rho}} \left[\delta_1^{\frac{1}{1-\rho}} w_1^{\frac{-\rho}{1-\rho}} + \delta_2^{\frac{1}{1-\rho}} w_2^{\frac{-\rho}{1-\rho}} \right]^{-\frac{1}{\rho}} \cdot q \tag{7.2.12}$$

Recall $\rho = 1 - \frac{1}{\varepsilon}$ in the previous section. Replace ρ in the equation to obtain the conditional input demand

$$x_1^c = \frac{1}{A} \left(\frac{\delta_1}{w_1} \right)^{\varepsilon} \left[\delta_1^{\varepsilon} w_1^{1-\varepsilon} + \delta_2^{\varepsilon} w_2^{1-\varepsilon} \right]^{\frac{\varepsilon}{1-\varepsilon}} \cdot q \tag{7.2.13}$$

which is easier to memorize.

Here are some properties with this conditional input demand function. First, demand for input x_1^c is a function of input prices w_1 and w_2. Quantity demanded of x_1 would change in response to changes in input prices. Secondly, quantity q is explicitly independent in the equation on RHS. This means that input use x_1^c is proportional to quantity q. In other words, the conditional input demand function (7.2.13) is linearly homogeneous with respect to output q. This gives a lot of convenience in CGE modeling and computation. Definition of homogenous functions and the important properties of linearly homogeneous functions are reviewed in the appendix of this chapter.

Take an example to see some convenience with this function form. What does the conditional input demand function (7.2.13) mean if $q = 1$?

$$x_1^c(w_1, w_2, q = 1) = \frac{1}{A} \left(\frac{\delta_1}{w_1} \right)^{\varepsilon} \left[\delta_1^{\varepsilon} w_1^{1-\varepsilon} + \delta_2^{\varepsilon} w_2^{1-\varepsilon} \right]^{\frac{\varepsilon}{1-\varepsilon}} \tag{7.2.14}$$

It is actually the input coefficient $a_{1j}(w_1, w_2)$ as in the Leontief model, i.e., how much of x_1 is needed to produce one unit of output q_j. Differing from the input coefficients in the Leontief model, here $a_{1j}(w_1, w_2)$ is not a constant, but can be affected by input prices.

Similarly, the conditional input demand for x_2 is

$$x_2^c = \frac{1}{A} \left(\frac{\delta_2}{w_2} \right)^{\varepsilon} \left[\delta_1^{\varepsilon} w_1^{1-\varepsilon} + \delta_2^{\varepsilon} w_2^{1-\varepsilon} \right]^{\frac{\varepsilon}{1-\varepsilon}} \cdot q \tag{7.2.15}$$

Note that the input demand function in the market clearing equation $x^s(p, \mathbf{w}) = x^d(p, \mathbf{w})$ is the *ordinary* input demand function, not the above conditional input demand function. An ordinary input demand function is a function of factor prices and *output price* $x^d(p, \mathbf{w})$, while a conditional input demand is a function of input prices and *output quantity* $x^c(q, \mathbf{w})$. We can convert conditional input demand to ordinary input demand function by substituting q with the commodity supply $q^s(p, \mathbf{w})$ as

$$x^d(p, \mathbf{w}) = x^c(q^s(p, \mathbf{w}), \mathbf{w}) \tag{7.2.16}$$

The commodity supply and ordinary input demand in CGE modeling will be discussed in the following two sections.

The cost function can be derived from conditional input demands

$$c(w_1, w_2, q) = w_1 x_1^c(w_1, w_2, q) + w_2 x_2^c(w_1, w_2, q)$$

$$= w_1 \frac{1}{A} \left(\frac{\delta_1}{w_1} \right)^\varepsilon \left[\delta_1^\varepsilon w_1^{1-\varepsilon} + \delta_2^\varepsilon w_2^{1-\varepsilon} \right]^{\frac{\varepsilon}{1-\varepsilon}} \cdot q$$

$$+ w_2 \frac{1}{A} \left(\frac{\delta_2}{w_2} \right)^\varepsilon \left[\delta_1^\varepsilon w_1^{1-\varepsilon} + \delta_2^\varepsilon w_2^{1-\varepsilon} \right]^{\frac{\varepsilon}{1-\varepsilon}} \cdot q \qquad (7.2.17)$$

$$= \frac{1}{A} \left[\delta_1^\varepsilon w_1^{1-\varepsilon} + \delta_2^\varepsilon w_2^{1-\varepsilon} \right] \left[\delta_1^\varepsilon w_1^{1-\varepsilon} + \delta_2^\varepsilon w_2^{1-\varepsilon} \right]^{\frac{\varepsilon}{1-\varepsilon}} \cdot q$$

$$= \frac{1}{A} \left[\delta_1^\varepsilon w_1^{1-\varepsilon} + \delta_2^\varepsilon w_2^{1-\varepsilon} \right]^{\frac{1}{1-\varepsilon}} \cdot q$$

The unit cost function is defined as the cost to produce one unit of output, i.e., $q = 1$:

$$c(w_1, w_2, 1) = \frac{1}{A} \left[\delta_1^\varepsilon w_1^{1-\varepsilon} + \delta_2^\varepsilon w_2^{1-\varepsilon} \right]^{\frac{1}{1-\varepsilon}} \qquad (7.2.18)$$

The unit cost function is quite useful in CGE modeling.

7.3 Commodity Supply Functions in CGE Models

In the general equilibrium framework as presented in Chapter 6, the commodity supply function $q_i^s = q_i^s(p_1, \ldots, p_n, w_1, \ldots, w_m)$ explicitly shows the quantity supplied as a function of the commodity and factor prices. This is the standard form of the commodity supply function in economics textbooks. In most CGE models and their computer programs, we do not observe this textbook standard form of commodity supply functions. As discussed in Section 6.6, because of the constant-returns-to-scale property of the production function, the price function in CGE models implies the optimal quantity supplied; thus, the price function serves as the commodity supply function.

If the production function is decreasing returns to scale, the derived commodity supply function will have the textbook standard form. The following is an example to derive the supply function in this situation.

Example 7.3.1 The production function is a Cobb–Douglas one $q = x_1^{1/3} x_2^{1/2}$. The commodity and factor prices are p, w_1 and w_2, respectively. Solve for the conditional input demand function, the cost function, and the commodity supply function.

Solution: Note the production function is decreasing returns to scale. By the same approach in Section 7.2, set up the cost-minimization problem of the enterprise, to obtain the conditional input demand functions:

$$x_1^c = (2/3)^{3/5} w_1^{-3/5} w_2^{3/5} q^{6/5} \qquad\qquad x_2^c = (2/3)^{-2/5} w_1^{2/5} w_2^{-2/5} q^{6/5} \qquad (7.3.1)$$

By $c(w_1, w_2, q) = w_1 x_1^c + w_2 x_2^c$, the cost function is

$$c(w_1, w_2, q) = (5 \cdot 3^{-3/5} \cdot 2^{-2/5}) w_1^{2/5} w_2^{3/5} q^{6/5} \qquad (7.3.2)$$

To derive the commodity supply function, set up the profit maximization problem for the enterprise as follows:

$$\max_{q} \pi = pq - c(w_1, w_2, q) = pq - (5 \cdot 3^{-3/5} \cdot 2^{-2/5})w_1^{2/5}w_2^{3/5}q^{6/5} \qquad (7.3.3)$$

The first-order condition of the above problem is that the commodity price equals the marginal cost — the optimal output condition stated in economics textbooks:

$$p = \frac{\partial c}{\partial y}(w_1, w_2, q) = \frac{5}{6}(5 \cdot 3^{-3/5} \cdot 2^{-2/5})w_1^{2/5}w_2^{3/5}q^{1/5} \qquad (7.3.4)$$

Differentiating and rearranging, we have the commodity supply function

$$q^s(p, w_1, w_2) = (1/72)w_1^{-1/2}w_2^{-1/3}p^5 \qquad (7.3.5)$$

Equation (7.3.5) conforms the standard form of the supply function. Quantity q is the dependent variable explicitly shown on the LHS. Explanatory variables p, w_1 and w_2 are explicitly shown on RHS. Note this is because the original production function $q = x_1^{1/3}x_2^{1/2}$ is decreasing returns to scale. If the production function is constant returns to scale, the derived supply function would be different.

Example 7.3.2 Change the production function in the above example to $q = x_1^{1/3}x_2^{2/3}$, which exhibits constant returns to scale. Solve for the conditional input demand function, the cost function and the commodity supply function.

Solution: Using the same approach, the conditional input demand functions are

$$x_1^c = (1/2)^{2/3}w_1^{-2/3}w_2^{2/3}q \qquad\qquad x_2^c = (1/2)^{-1/3}w_1^{1/3}w_2^{-1/3}q \qquad (7.3.6)$$

The cost function is

$$c(w_1, w_2, q) = (2^{-2/3} + 2^{1/3})w_1^{1/3}w_2^{2/3}q \qquad (7.3.7)$$

The profit maximization leads to the first-order condition of "output-price-equals-marginal-cost":

$$p = \frac{\partial c}{\partial y}(w_1, w_2, q) = (2^{-2/3} + 2^{1/3})w_1^{1/3}w_2^{2/3} \qquad (7.3.8)$$

While both Equation (7.3.4) and Equation (7.3.8) are the first-order conditions of profit maximization from the Cobb–Douglas functions, because the latter is constant returns to scale, it does not have quantity q shown on RHS. That is, when the commodity price satisfies the price Equation (7.3.8), the firm has optimized its profit and would supply any non-negative amount of quantity q as demanded. The price equation is the horizontal commodity supply function. It normally takes the form of $p(q^s)$, the inverted form of the conventional supply function $q^s(p)$. Because $p(q^s)$ is horizontal, infinite numbers of q^s satisfy the equation at the optimal price, hence q is not explicitly shown in Equation (7.3.8).

This is illustrated in Figure 7.3.1. p^* denotes the particular price satisfying price Equation (7.3.8), which equals the unit cost. If the market price is lower than p^*, the quantity supplied is zero. If price is higher than p^*, the quantity supplied goes to infinity, thus there

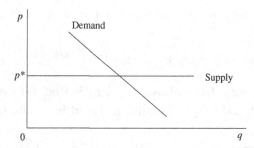

Figure 7.3.1.   Horizontal supply function and its functional form.

is no equilibrium. If quantity supplied q is a positive number, the market price must be p^*. The exact quantity supplied would be determined by the intersection with the demand side. Figure 7.3.1 shows an example with a hypothetical demand curve. The intersection is the market equilibrium.

The same property applies to the CES production function of $q = A(\delta_1 x_1^\rho + \delta_2 x_2^\rho)^{1/\rho}$. Following the same approach, the enterprise maximizes profit, from the first-order condition to derive the following price function:

$$p = \frac{\partial c}{\partial y}(w_1, w_2, q) = \frac{1}{A}\left[w_1^{1-\varepsilon}\delta_1^\varepsilon + w_2^{1-\varepsilon}\delta_2^\varepsilon\right]^{\frac{1}{1-\varepsilon}} \qquad (7.3.9)$$

This price function is the supply function of the CES production function. It is a horizontal line as in Figure 7.3.1. and the quantity q is not explicitly shown.

In many CGE models, the price equation often takes the breakeven condition form. Multiplying both sides of Equation (7.3.9) by quantity q:

$$pq = \frac{1}{A}\left[w_1^{1-\varepsilon}\delta_1^\varepsilon + w_2^{1-\varepsilon}\delta_2^\varepsilon\right]^{\frac{1}{1-\varepsilon}} q = c(w_1, w_2, q) = w_1 x_1^c(w_1, w_2, q) + w_2 x_2^c(w_1, w_2, q)$$

$$(7.3.10)$$

On LHS, it is total revenue. On RHS, it is total cost. It means the enterprise has maximized its profit when it breaks even. On the surface it seems that the quantity q is explicitly shown in Equation (7.3.10), but in fact it is not. Note the conditional input demands are

$$x_i^c = \frac{1}{A}\left(\frac{\delta_i}{w_i}\right)^\varepsilon \left[\delta_1^\varepsilon w_1^{1-\varepsilon} + \delta_2^\varepsilon w_2^{1-\varepsilon}\right]^{\frac{\varepsilon}{1-\varepsilon}} \cdot q \qquad (7.3.11)$$

Replacing the two conditional input demand functions into Equation (7.3.9), we will cancel out q from both sides, thus q disappears again. To summarize, it is important to know that the price equation is actually the horizontal supply function when the production function is constant returns to scale.

7.4   Alternative Forms in the CGE Production Module

In textbooks, general equilibrium is expressed mathematically by the balance of supply and demand equations in all commodity and factor markets, $q_i^s(\mathbf{p}, \mathbf{w}) = q_i^d(\mathbf{p}, \mathbf{w})$ and $x_i^s(\mathbf{p}, \mathbf{w}) = x_i^d(\mathbf{p}, \mathbf{w})$. From the profit-maximization behavior of enterprises, when the production function is specified, we can derive the commodity supply function and input/-factor demand function. In CGE modeling, there is a set of equations, we call it "production function module", or in short, "production module", which specifies the commodity supply and input demands from the enterprise side.

In economics theory, these functions are expressed explicitly like $q_i^s(\mathbf{p}, \mathbf{w})$ and $x_i^d(\mathbf{p}, \mathbf{w})$. In the practice of CGE modeling, we can take advantage of the computer solving process, instead of presenting the explicit commodity supply function or input demand function, we can simply write down a system of equations of the enterprises' optimization decision. When GAMS is solving the system, it automatically generates the optimized quantity supplied and input demanded, thus implying the commodity supply function $q_i^s(\mathbf{p}, \mathbf{w})$ and input demand function $x_i^d(\mathbf{p}, \mathbf{w})$.

In what follows, we introduce three alternative forms (or expressions) of the equation system in the CGE production module, which forms the commodity supply and input demand functions from the standard CES function. The forms or the expressions look different, but they represent the same mathematical content, and can be derived from each other.

Form 1 uses the explicit conditional input demand function, which will be referred to as *input demand form* in later discussions in the book. This form is used in Shoven and Whalley (1984) and others:

$$\begin{cases} x_i^c = \frac{1}{A}\left(\frac{\delta_i}{w_i}\right)^\varepsilon \left[\delta_1^\varepsilon w_1^{1-\varepsilon} + \delta_2^\varepsilon w_2^{1-\varepsilon}\right]^{\frac{\varepsilon}{1-\varepsilon}} \cdot q & i = 1, 2 \\ pq = w_1 x_1 + w_2 x_2 \end{cases} \tag{7.4.1}$$

There are actually three individual equations in the system. The top one has indexed two individual conditional input demand functions for the two inputs. The bottom one is the breakeven condition — a variant of the price equation, which is actually the commodity supply function. As discussed in Equation (7.2.16), the conditional input demand becomes the ordinary demand function when the output level q is defined by the supply equation. Thus, the above simultaneous equation system implies the (ordinary) input demand function $x_i^d(p, w_1, w_2)$ and output supply functions $q_i^s(p, w_1, w_2)$ in the market.

Form 2 is implicit but a neat expression. It uses the first-order condition (FOC) for optimal input use $\frac{w_1}{w_2} = \frac{\delta_1}{\delta_2}(\frac{x_1}{x_2})^{\rho-1}$, thus it is referred to as *FOC form* in later discussions. The form is used in the IFPRI model and others:

$$\begin{cases} q = A(\delta_1 x_1^\rho + \delta_2 x_2^\rho)^{\frac{1}{\rho}} \\ \frac{w_1}{w_2} = \frac{\delta_1}{\delta_2}\left(\frac{x_1}{x_2}\right)^{\rho-1} \\ pq = w_1 x_1 + w_2 x_2 \end{cases} \tag{7.4.2}$$

The first equation is the production function itself. The second one is the first-order condition for optimal use of inputs: factor price ratio equals TRS. The two equations determine conditional input demands. The bottom one is the breakeven condition, which implies the supply function. Together the ordinary input demand function is also defined.

Form 3 is neat but more implicit. It uses the unit cost function, thus will be referred to as *unit cost form* in later discussions. This form is used in Robinson *et al.* (2002):

$$\begin{cases} x_i^c(w_1, w_2, q) = A^{\varepsilon-1} \left[\delta_i \dfrac{p}{w_i} \right]^\varepsilon \cdot q \quad i = 1, 2 \\[2ex] p = \dfrac{1}{A} \left[\delta_1^\varepsilon w_1^{1-\varepsilon} + \delta_2^\varepsilon w_2^{1-\varepsilon} \right]^{\frac{1}{1-\varepsilon}} \end{cases} \tag{7.4.3}$$

Form 3 utilizes the following unit cost function (Equation (7.2.18)) $c(w_1, w_2, 1) = \frac{1}{A}[\delta_1^\varepsilon w_1^{1-\varepsilon} + \delta_2^\varepsilon w_2^{1-\varepsilon}]^{\frac{1}{1-\varepsilon}}$. The unit cost is also marginal cost when the production function is constant returns to scale. The bottom equation is actually the price equation $p = \partial c(w_1, w_2, q)/\partial q = c(w_1, w_2, 1)$, because on LHS is the price and on RHS is the marginal cost. The top set is conditional input demand function. It can be derived from the cost function by Shephard's lemma $x_i^c = \partial c/\partial w_i$, then substituting the same term inside the equation with p to yield the current form.

Each of the above forms has its own advantages and disadvantages. Form 1 is closest to the mathematical expression in economics textbooks. This helps us to interpret the corresponding GAMS codes. Form 2 is neat and the three equations are quite easy to remember. This helps writing the CGE program by reducing errors. We will use this form more often in this book. The disadvantage of Form 2 is that, if a CES function has more than two inputs, this form does not utilize the convenience of the indexed expression as compared with other forms. Form 3 is neat, but because each equation has more than one parameter to be calibrated, we have to use different equations to calibrate the parameters.

Mathematically, the three forms are equivalent. They can be derived from each other. When the GAMS program solves any of the three, the process finds quantity supplied of the commodity and quantities demanded of the inputs, implicitly generates the commodity supply functions $q_i^s(\mathbf{p}, \mathbf{w})$ and input demand functions $x_i^d(\mathbf{p}, \mathbf{w})$. Combined with the demands for commodities and supplies of factors specified from the households' side in the CGE model, the equilibrium quantities and prices of markets are determined.

7.5 Calibrating CES Function Parameters from SAM Table Data

Most parameters of functions in the CGE model can be computed from the SAM table data. It is called *calibration* of parameters in CGE modeling. Calibrating parameter values from the SAM table implies the assumption that the SAM table data are the results of a general equilibrium state. In what follows, we illustrate how to calibrate the parameters of the CES function from the SAM data.

Let the production function be $q = A(\delta_1 x_1^\rho + \delta_2 x_2^\rho)^{\frac{1}{\rho}}$. Shares add up to one, so $\delta_1 + \delta_2 = 1$. Exponent ρ is related to elasticity of substitution, which is given externally. The values of q, x_1, x_2 are provided directly in the SAM table. Shares of δ_1 and δ_2, and total factor productivity A can be calibrated from the SAM table data.

Example 7.5.1 The production function in the service sector is $q = A(\delta_1 x_1^\rho + \delta_2 x_2^\rho)^{\frac{1}{\rho}}$. The data from the SAM table show that in the service sector, $w_1 x_1 = 26$, $w_2 x_2 = 39$ and $pq = 65$. From external sources we know the elasticity of substitution $\varepsilon = 0.5$. Calibrate the parameters of A, δ_1 and δ_2.

Solution: First we normalize all prices to 1, i.e., $w_1 = 1, w_2 = 1, p = 1$, thus quantities are $x_1 = 26$, $x_2 = 39$ and $pq = 65$. The exponent of the CES function is

$$\rho = 1 - \frac{1}{\varepsilon} = 1 - 2 = -1 \tag{7.5.1}$$

The first-order condition for optimizing input use is

$$\frac{w_1}{w_2} = \frac{\delta_1}{1 - \delta_1} \left(\frac{x_1}{x_2} \right)^{\rho - 1} \tag{7.5.2}$$

Rearrange and get the formula for calibrating share δ_1 as follows:

$$\delta_1 = \frac{w_1 x_1^{1-\rho}}{w_1 x_1^{1-\rho} + w_2 x_2^{1-\rho}} \tag{7.5.3}$$

Using the formula to calibrate the shares from the SAM data,

$$\delta_1 = \frac{4}{13}, \qquad \delta_2 = 1 - \delta_1 = \frac{9}{13} \tag{7.5.4}$$

The formula to calibrate the scale factor A is

$$A = q/(\delta_1 x_1^\rho + \delta_2 x_2^\rho)^{\frac{1}{\rho}} \tag{7.5.5}$$

Substitute the data into the formula and obtain

$$A = 65/ \left(\frac{4}{13} \cdot 26^{-1} + \frac{9}{13} \cdot 39^{-1} \right)^{-1} = 1.923077 \tag{7.5.6}$$

Example 7.5.2 After calibrating the above parameters, verify the calibrated parameter values by replication.

Solution: The approach to verify the parameter values in this case is replacing the parameters with the calibrated values in the production function, then using GAMS or other programs to check the consistency of variable values. In particular, substitute 26 and 39 with x_1 and x_2 into the production function and solve for the output value q:

$$q = 1.923077 \left(\frac{4}{13} \cdot 26^{-1} + \frac{9}{13} \cdot 39^{-1} \right)^{-1} = 65 \tag{7.5.7}$$

The calculated value is $q = 65$, which is consistent with the original data. Therefore, we approve the calibrated values for the parameters.

Example 7.5.3 Given the same production function, suppose input price w_1 increases by 10%. The output level in the service sector q remains at 65. What are the changes in input demands for x_1 and x_2?

Solution: This is a simulation problem to test the conditional input demand functions. Use the conditional input demand function (7.2.12) to find

$$x_1^c = \frac{1}{A} \left(\frac{\delta_1}{w_1} \right)^\varepsilon [\delta_1^\varepsilon w_1^{1-\varepsilon} + \delta_2^\varepsilon w_2^{1-\varepsilon}]^{\frac{\varepsilon}{1-\varepsilon}} \cdot q \tag{7.5.8}$$

$$= \frac{1}{1.923} \left(\frac{4/13}{1.1} \right)^{0.5} [(4/13)^{0.5} 1.1^{0.5} + (9/13)^{0.5} 1^{0.5}]^{\frac{0.5}{0.5}} \cdot 65 = 25.274$$

$$x_2^c = \frac{1}{A} \left(\frac{\delta_2}{w_2} \right)^\varepsilon [\delta_1^\varepsilon w_1^{1-\varepsilon} + \delta_2^\varepsilon w_2^{1-\varepsilon}]^{\frac{\varepsilon}{1-\varepsilon}} \cdot q \tag{7.5.9}$$

$$= \frac{1}{1.923} \left(\frac{9/13}{1} \right)^{0.5} [(4/13)^{0.5} 1.1^{0.5} + (9/13)^{0.5} 1^{0.5}]^{\frac{0.5}{0.5}} \cdot 65 = 39.761$$

It can be seen that as w_1 increases, the enterprise would demand less x_1 but more x_2, which is the substitution effect in input combination in response to the factor price changes.

Here, we introduce another method to solve the problem by using a computer optimization software, say, a solver in Excel or GAMS. The equation forms are neat. It solves a simultaneous equation system for the enterprise input decision:

$$\begin{cases} 65 = 1.923077 \left(\frac{4}{13} x_1^{-1} + \frac{9}{13} x_2^{-1} \right)^{-1} \\ \frac{1.1}{1} = \frac{4/13}{9/13} \left(\frac{x_1}{x_2} \right)^{\rho-1} \end{cases} \tag{7.5.10}$$

In the above system, the top is the production function and the bottom is the first-order condition for optimal use of inputs. Output level q is fixed at the given value. Input price w_1 is the exogenous variable in which we introduce an external "shock" of $w_1 = 1 \times (1+10\%) = 1.1$; hence, on LHS of the first-order condition, we have $w_1/w_2 = 1.1/1$. The endogenous variables are inputs x_1 and x_2.

We can use either Excel or GAMS to solve this system. Indeed, some economists use Excel instead of GAMS to solve real CGE models. If you use Excel, you need to first install and enable the add-in program "Solver" (which is included in Microsoft Office) or other similar third-party add-in programs. Before executing the program, you have to assign initial values to the variables, for instance, just use the original data in SAM, such as 26 and 39 for x_1 and x_2 as the initial values. The simulation results solved by Excel for the above problem are $x_1 = 25.27$ and $x_2 = 39.76$. The method of using the computer software to solve a system is advantageous when the explicit mathematical expression is too cumbersome or simply does not exist.

7.6 GAMS Program

The following is the GAMS program for the above three examples in Section 7.5, including parameter calibration, replication of the original state and simulation for a 10% increase in factor price w_1. In the simulation case, we would check the resulting changes in the output price p. Hence, the price equation is added in the model. The GAMS simulation confirms the numerical results in Section 7.5. In addition, the simulation shows that output price p increases by 3.9%, which is consistent with the expectation. Remarks in the following GAMS program are additional explanations.

```
$title Section 7.6 Demonstration for working on a CES function


*=====================================================
*calibration
*=====================================================
parameter
        elas            elasticity
        rho             CES function exponent rho
        delta1          share of input x1
        delta2          share of input x2
        scaleA          CES function scale factor A
        x10             initial value of input x1
        x20             initial value of input x2
        q0              initial value of output q
        w10             initial value of price of input 1
        w20             initial value of price of input 2
        p0              initial value of price of q;

* Assign parameter values which are directly provided by SAM or other information
        elas =0.5;
        w10=1;
        w20=1;
        p0=1;
        x10=26;
        x20=39;
        q0=65;

*Calibrate the parameters which are not directly obtained
        rho=1-1/elas;
        delta1=w10*x10**(1-rho)/(w10*x10**(1-rho)+w20*x20**(1-rho));
        delta2=1-delta1;
        scaleA=q0/(delta1*x10**rho+delta2*x20**rho)**(1/rho);

*display parameter values for checking
        display  rho ,delta1,delta2 ,scaleA, x10,x20,q0,w10,w20,p0;


*=============
*Replication
*=============
*Check if the production function with the calibrated parameters can replicate the
original state.

*Declare and define variables
```

```
variable
        x1          Quantity of input 1
        x2          Quantity of input 2
        q           Quantity of output q
        w1          input 1 price
        w2          Input 2 price
        p           Output price
;
```

```
*Declare and define equations
equation
        Prodfn          production function
        FOCeq           first-order condition for cost minimization
        PRICEeq         commodity price equals the unit total cost
;
```

```
        Prodfn..
        q=e=scaleA*(delta1*x1**rho+delta2*x2**rho)**(1/rho) ;
*In the above production function, we use exponent rho rather than elasticity,
for visual convenience.
```

```
        FOCeq..
        w1/w2=e=(delta1/delta2)*(x1/x2)**(rho-1);
```

```
        PRICEeq..
        p*q=e=w1*x1+w2*x2;
*Above is the price equation, which is used to find the equilibrium output price
level.
```

```
*Assign initial values to the variables
        p.L=p0;
        x1.L=x10;
        x2.L=x20;
```

```
*q, w1, w2 are constants, so use fx to fix their values. In fact, now they become
parameters in nature.
        q.fx=q0;
        w1.fx=w10;
        w2.fx=w20;
```

```
*Execute  the model and replicate the data values of the original SAM.
```

```
model CES  /all/;
solve CES using mcp;
```

```
*Display replicated values, note the syntax of repbase('input x1')
parameter  repbase;
      repbase('input x1')=x1.L;
      repbase('input x2')=x2.L;
      repbase('q price p0')=p.L;
display repbase;


*===================================================
*Simulation for price of x1 increases by 10%
*===================================================
*The outside shock is w1 increases by 10%.
*Set up a new price w1.fx=1.1*w10.  GAMS takes this new price for w1.

w1.fx=1.1*w10;
solve CES using mcp;

*Display the simulation results
parameter  simoutput ;
      simoutput('input x1')=x1.L ;
      simoutput('input x2')=x2.L ;
      simoutput('q price p')=p.L ;
display  simoutput;

*end
```

Exercises

7E.1 Shepard's Lemma is $\frac{\partial}{\partial w_i} c(w_1, w_2, q) = x_i^c(w_1, w_2, q)$. Use Shepard's lemma to derive the conditional input demand from the cost function in Section 7.1. Check the result.

7E.2 The production function is $f(x_1, x_2, x_2) = A(\delta_1 x_1^\rho + \delta_2 x_2^\rho + \delta_3 x_3^\rho)^{\frac{1}{\rho}} = q$. The prices of commodity and factors are p, w_1, w_2, w_3, respectively. Solve for conditional input demand, cost and commodity supply functions.

7E.3 The production function is $f(x_1, x_2, x_2) = A(\delta_1 x_1^\rho + \delta_2 x_2^\rho + \delta_3 x_3^\rho)^{\frac{1}{\rho}} = q$. All prices p, w_1, w_2, w_3 equal 1. Elasticity of substitution $\varepsilon = 2$. Relevant data from the SAM table are: $w_1 x_1 = 130$, $w_2 x_2 = 195$, $w_3 x_3 = 90$, $pq = 415$. Write a GAMS program to calibrate the values of A, δ_1, δ_2 and δ_3.

7E.4 Use the above production function and calibrated parameter values for A, δ_1, δ_2 and δ_3. Elasticity of substitution $\varepsilon = 2$. All prices p, w_1, w_2, w_3 equal 1. Output level $q = 415$. x_1, x_2, x_3 are endogenous variables whose quantities are unknown. Using the three forms provided in Section 7.4, write a GAMS program, solve for the quantities of inputs x_1, x_2, x_3.

Appendix: Review of Microeconomics

7A.1 Profit maximization and input choice

A firm (enterprise) chooses inputs $\mathbf{x}$ to maximize profits

$$\max_{\mathbf{x}} \pi = pf(\mathbf{x}) - \mathbf{wx} \qquad (7\text{A}.1.1)$$

where $\mathbf{x}$ and $\mathbf{w}$ are input and vector vectors. The first-order condition is

$$p\frac{\partial f(\mathbf{x})}{\partial x_i} = w_i \qquad i = 1, \ldots, n \qquad (7\text{A}.1.2)$$

The optimal condition thus is, for each input i, its marginal revenue product $p \cdot \partial f(\mathbf{x})/\partial x_i$ equals its price w_i.

7A.2 Homogeneous function

If function $f(\mathbf{x})$ has the property

$$f(t\mathbf{x}) = t^k f(\mathbf{x}) \qquad \forall t > 0 \qquad (7\text{A}.2.1)$$

this function is called homogeneous function of degree k. If $k = 1$, it is called a linearly homogeneous function. The production function with constant-returns-to-scale property is mathematically a linearly homogeneous function because $tq = f(t\mathbf{x}) \quad \forall t > 0$.

Some properties of linearly homogeneous functions are very useful in economic models. According to Euler's Law,

$$f(\mathbf{x}) = \sum_i \frac{\partial f(\mathbf{x})}{\partial x_i} x_i \qquad \forall t > 0 \qquad (7\text{A}.2.2)$$

Hence, for production function $q = f(K, L)$, we have $q = f_k K + f_L L$. Because of the optimal condition $w_x = pf_x$, we have $pq = w_k K + w_L L$, total revenue equals total cost, which is the breakeven condition. Dividing both sides by q, we have the price equation. This repeats the statement that when the production function is linearly homogenous, the breakeven condition or the price equation in CGE models implies enterprises' optimization decision.

The proof of Euler's law is as follows. Because $f(t\mathbf{x}) \equiv t^k f(\mathbf{x})$ is an identity and is valid for any positive real number t, differentiating both sides of $f(t\mathbf{x}) \equiv t^k f(\mathbf{x})$ with respect to t, we have

$$\sum_i \frac{\partial f(t\mathbf{x})}{\partial(tx_i)} x_i = t^{k-1} f(\mathbf{x}) \qquad (7\text{A}.2.3)$$

Then set $t = 1$, it proves Euler's law.

Chapter 8

CGE Models with Non-Linear Production Functions

Section 6.6 presents a simple but completed CGE model with the Leontief production function. It is a linear function which requires that all inputs be used in fixed proportions, therefore no input substitution is allowed in production. This does not describe much of the real-world situation. In this chapter, we will use the CES production functions discussed in Chapter 7 to set up CGE models. The non-linear property of the CES functions would allow the input substitution when their relative price ratios change.

8.1 A Simple CGE Model in Input Demand Form

This section presents a simple CGE model with a CES production function. It has two commodity sectors and two factors, labor and capital. Each commodity needs two factor inputs but no intermediate inputs to produce. The SAM table for this model economy is Table 8.1.1.

The production function in each sector of this model economy is a standard CES function $q_i = A_i[\delta_i L_i^{\rho_i} + (1 - \delta_i)K_i^{\rho_i}]^{1/\rho_i}$. To solve for input demand and commodity supply functions, we adopt the first solving form, "input demand form", presented in Section 7.4.

Table 8.1.1. SAM table of the model economy.

	Commodity 1	Commodity 2	Labor	Capital	Household	Total
Commodity 1					12	12
Commodity 2					21	21
Labor	9	7				16
Capital	3	14				17
Household			16	17		33
Total	12	21	16	17	33	

The conditional input demand functions are

$$L_i^d = \frac{1}{A_i} \left(\frac{\delta_1}{w_l} \right)^{\varepsilon_i} \left[\delta_i^{\varepsilon_i} w_l^{1-\varepsilon_i} + (1-\delta_i)^{\varepsilon_i} w_k^{1-\varepsilon_i} \right]^{\varepsilon_i/(1-\varepsilon_i)} \cdot q_i \qquad i = 1, 2 \qquad (8.1.1)$$

$$K_i^d = \frac{1}{A_i} \left(\frac{\delta_i}{w_k} \right)^{\varepsilon_i} \left[\delta_i^{\varepsilon_i} w_l^{1-\varepsilon_i} + (1-\delta_i)^{\varepsilon_i} w_k^{1-\varepsilon_i} \right]^{\varepsilon_i/(1-\varepsilon_i)} \cdot q_i \qquad i = 1, 2 \qquad (8.1.2)$$

q_i and p_i denote the quantity and price of commodity i, respectively. w_j denotes the factor price of factor j. The breakeven condition in each sector, which implies the supply function from the enterprise's profit maximization, is the following equation:

$$p_1 q_1 = w_l L_1 + w_k K_1 \qquad (8.1.3)$$

$$p_2 q_2 = w_l L_2 + w_k K_2 \qquad (8.1.4)$$

Households' factor endowment are L^s and K^s, which are also the total factor supplies. Their income Y is

$$Y = w_l L^s + w_k K^s \qquad (8.1.5)$$

The households' utility function is the Cobb–Douglas function with exponent α. The corresponding commodity demand functions are

$$p_1 q_1^h = \alpha Y \qquad (8.1.6)$$

$$p_2 q_2^h = (1-\alpha) Y \qquad (8.1.7)$$

q_i^h is the quantity demanded for commodity i by households for consumption. The market clearing equations are

$$q_1^h = q_1 \qquad (8.1.8)$$

$$q_2^h = q_2 \qquad (8.1.9)$$

The factor market clearing conditions are

$$L_1^d + L_2^d = L^s \qquad (8.1.10)$$

$$K_1^d + K_2^d = K^s \qquad (8.1.11)$$

Note that (8.1.1) and (8.1.2) are equation groups, with two equations in each group. Hence, there are a total of 13 Equations from (8.1.1) through (8.1.11), which constitute this CGE model. There are also 13 endogenous variables: $q_1, q_2, q_1^h, q_2^h, L_1, L_2, K_1, K_2, Y, P_1, P_2, W_l, W_k$, to be solved in the system. Exogenous variables are the factor endowment L^s, K^s. Elasticities of substitution ε_1 and ε_2 are given externally. They are used to calibrate exponents ρ_1 and ρ_2 in the conditional input demand functions. Other parameters that can be calibrated from the SAM table are $\delta_1, \delta_2, A_1, A_2, \alpha_1, \alpha_2$. The above form for the production module, Equations (8.1.1)–(8.1.4), is explicitly clear and understandable, which has been used in many CGE models.

8.2 CGE Models with CES Production Functions and Model Squareness

Starting now, our CGE models would include more commodities, factors and other national accounts. To help modeling and analysis, we need to sort and organize the accounts into groups and update the notations. In a GAMS program, these groups are treated and denoted by sets. For instance, a CGE model often has tens or even hundreds of commodity sectors. These sectors can be grouped into a big commodity set and we name it C. Suppose there are n commodities. The elements in set C can be denoted by index $i = 1, \ldots, n$, or we use lowercase letter c for the index symbol, $c = 1, \ldots, n$, which helps recognize that the index is for commodity sectors. More conveniently, we use $c \in C$ to indicate these elements belong to commodity set C. Similarly, factors can be grouped into a factor set F. Its elements are denoted by $f = l, k, \ldots$ where l is labor, k is capital, etc. Alternatively, it is denoted by $f \in F$. In mathematical expression, the indices are commonly denoted by subscripts, indicating which sets the elements belong to. For instance, the CES production functions of all commodity sectors can be expressed as

$$A_c[\delta_c L_c^{\rho_c} + (1 - \delta_c) K_c^{\rho_c}]^{1/\rho_c} = q_c \qquad c \in C \qquad (8.2.1)$$

Alternatively, it can be expressed as

$$A_c \left[\sum_f \delta_{cf} F_f^{\rho_c} \right]^{1/\rho_c} = q_c \qquad c \in C, \quad f \in F, \quad \sum_f \delta_{if} = 1 \qquad (8.2.2)$$

This expression format is convenient if there are many factors in each production function. GAMS program treats the indexed variables and equations in a similar manner. Instead of using subscripts, GAMS program uses parentheses for indices, "Variablename(c)". For instance, household demand for commodity c is mathematically written as q_c^h, while in GAMS program we write it as QH(c). This GAMS index notation will be demonstrated in more detail in Example 8.2.1.

In Section 8.1, we used "input demand form" for the production module. Here we use the FOC form (Equation (7.4.2)) for the production module, which is neat and easy to remember. The following is the CGE model for the same model economy described by SAM Table 8.1.1.

The production module includes three equations: production function, first-order condition for optimal inputs use, and the price equation (breakeven condition):

$$A_c[\delta_c L_c^{\rho_c} + (1 - \delta_c) K_c^{\rho_c}]^{1/\rho_c} = q_c \qquad c \in C \qquad (8.2.3)$$

$$\frac{w_l}{w_k} = \frac{\delta_c}{(1 - \delta_c)} \left(\frac{L_c}{K_c} \right)^{\rho_c - 1} \qquad c \in C \qquad (8.2.4)$$

$$p_c q_c = w_l L_c + w_k K_c \qquad c \in C \qquad (8.2.5)$$

Households' income is from their factor supplies

$$w_l L^s + w_k K^s = Y \tag{8.2.6}$$

Because their utility function is a Cobb–Douglas function with exponent α, their consumption demands for commodities are

$$p_c q_c^h = \alpha_c Y \qquad c \in C \tag{8.2.7}$$

The commodity market clearing conditions are

$$q_c^h = q_c \qquad c \in C \tag{8.2.8}$$

The factor market clearing conditions are

$$\sum_c K_c = K^s \tag{8.2.9}$$

$$\sum_c L_c = L^s \tag{8.2.10}$$

The model consists of a total of eight groups of equations. Among them, five groups indicated with $c \in C$ have two equations ($n = 2$) in each group. Hence, there are a total of $(8 - 5) + 5n = 13$ equations in this model. The endogenous variables in the system are Y, w_l, w_k; plus five groups of variables $q_c, q_c^h, L_c, K_c, p_c$, each group has $n = 2$ variables. Thus there are a total of $3 + 5n = 13$ endogenous variables. When the equation system has the same numbers of equations and variables, the system is "square". If the system is square, in general the model is solvable (although it is not automatically guaranteed when equation inconsistency or other problems occur). The equality of the numbers of equations and variables, called the "squareness condition", is the basic requirement for CGE models. If squareness is not met, GAMS solvers would stop execution and display an error message. Hence, it is always important to check the equality between the numbers of equations and variables in CGE modeling and GAMS programming.

Because of Walras' law, the above system is linearly dependent. There are a total of four markets, including two commodity markets and two factor markets; but only $2 + 2 - 1 = 3$ markets are independent. We can only determine 3 instead 4 price levels. GAMS optimization solvers can continue to run without problems if linear dependence is present in the system, as long as the system is square and equations are consistent, but the solved results of the model may not be unique.

Parameters $\delta_1, \delta_2, A_1, A_2, \alpha_1, \alpha_2$ need to be calibrated from the SAM data. Elasticities of substitution should be given externally. The total amounts of labor and capital supply, L^s and K^s, can be obtained from the SAM table data. Example 8.2.1 that follows is the GAMS program of the model.

Because exogenous variables are likely to be changed later in simulation or optional model structures, for convenience, we can first declare them as variables but later use suffix .fx to fix their values. In Example 8.2.1, we use this approach to treat L^s and K^s

as exogenous variables. In the program, we first declare them as variables. At this stage, GAMS would consider the model has $13 + 2 = 15$ variables. Later in the program, we use the following sentences to fix their values:

```
LS.fx=LS0;
KS.fx=KS0;
```

When the values of the variables are fixed, GAMS would treat them as parameters. Then the number of variables in the model reduces to 13. The squareness condition is met.

This technique may cause some confusion in reading the messages in the GAMS report. In the report file with suffix .1st, after using MCP to solve the model, GAMS would report the numbers of rows and columns in the model as follows:

```
--- Example 8-2-1.gms(125) 6 Mb
---     13 rows 15 columns 47 non-zeroes
```

In the above message, rows means the individual equations, columns mean the individual variables. L^s and K^s are initially declared as variables, GAMS takes these initial numbers of equations and variables in the above report, so the numbers of rows and columns are 13 and 15, respectively. They do not look equal and this message can be a warning sign. Yet we do not worry in this case, because we know in the program later the number of variables would be reduced when the values of L^s and K^s are fixed. After the solver reads the later instruction of fixing values of the two variables, it would recount the numbers of equations and variables. If GAMS no longer complains and runs smoothly to the end, it means the squareness condition is met.

Example 8.2.1 The economy is described as Equations (8.2.3)–(8.2.10). Its SAM table is Table 8.1.1. Elasticities of substitution are 2.5 and 2 for sectors 1 and 2, respectively. It is a classical economic world: so all factor endowments are fully employed, and all prices of commodities and factors are flexible. The initial prices in the base state are 1. Write the GAMS program for the model. Display the replication results. Analyze the impacts on the variables in the economy if the labor force increases by 10%.

Solution: The GAMS program is as follows. The simulation results are in Table 8.2.1.

Table 8.2.1. Percentage changes after 10% increase in labor supply.

	Commodity 1	Commodity 2
Commodity price	1.012	1.032
Labor price	1	1
Capital price	1.05	1.05
Commodity output	12.737	21.844
Labor supply	9.838	7.762
Capital supply	2.906	14.094

```
$title Example 8.2.1, A basic CGE model with CES production function

*Define sets AC and C with indices symbols ac and c
*Index ac stands for account, index c stands for commodities

set ac    /sec1,sec2,lab,cap,hh,total/
    c(ac)  /sec1,sec2/;

alias (ac,acp);

*Input SAM table data
    table sam(ac,acp)
           sec1   sec2   lab   cap   hh    total
    sec1                              12    12
    sec2                              21    21
    lab      9      7                       16
    cap      3     14                       17
    hh                    16    17          33
    total   12     21     16    17    33
;

*Input elasticity of substitution data, note the syntax
Parameter elas(c)          /sec1=2.5, sec2=2/

*Define parameters
parameters
        Q0(c)         Initial quantity of commodity c
        P0(c)         Initial price of commodity c
        LD0(c)        Initial labor demand in commodity sector c
        KD0(c)        Initial capital demand in commodity sector c
        LS0           Labor endowment or total labor supply
        KS0           Capital endowment or total capital supply
        WL0           Initial labor price
        WK0           Initial capital price
        Y0            Initial household income
        QH0(c)        Initial consumption demand for c by households
        scaleA(c)     Scale factor of the CES production function of c
        delta(c)      Share parameter of the CES production function of c
        rho(c)        Exponent of the CES production function of c
        alphah(c)     Share of households income spent on c;

*Calibrating parameters
        rho(c)=1-1/elas(c);
        P0(c) =1;
        WL0=1;
        WK0=1;
        Q0(c)=sam('total',c)/P0(c);
        LD0(c)=sam('lab',c)/WL0;
```

```
      KD0(c)=sam('cap',c)/WK0;
      LS0=sum(c,LD0(c));
      KS0=sum(c,KD0(c));
      Y0=WL0*LS0+WK0*KS0;
      QH0(c)=SAM(c,'hh')/P0(c);
```

*Calibrating the CES production function parameters
```
      delta(c)=WL0*LD0(c)**(1-rho(c))/( WL0*LD0(c)**(1-rho(c))+WK0*KD0(c)**(1-
rho(c)));
      scaleA(c)=Q0(c)/(delta(c)*LD0(c)**rho(c)+(1-
delta(c))*KD0(c)**rho(c))**(1/rho(c));
```

*Calibrating share of income spent on commodities
```
      alphah(c)=P0(c)*QH0(c)/Y0;
```

*Display calibrated parameters for checking
```
      display   rho,delta,scaleA,Q0,LD0,KD0,LS0,KS0,Y0,QH0;
```

*Define variables
```
variable
      P(c),WK,WL,Q(c),LD(c),KD(c),Y,QH(c),LS,KS;
```

```
$ontext
```
     In the economics theory, in general, total labor supply LS and capital
supply KS are variables. In an overwhelming number of CGE models, factors are
assumed to be fully employed so their numbers are fixed at the amounts of
endowments. Hence, in GAMS programs they are parameters in nature.
     Instead of defining them as parameters at the beginning, alternatively, we
declare them as variables first, but adding suffix .fx to these variables to fix
their values later and change the nature back to parameters. This approach is more
convenient in simulation when we have to frequently change the values of exogenous
variables in the GAMS program.
     In the case that we need to convert them back to variables, we just replace
their suffix .fx with .L.
```
$offtext
```

*Define equations
```
equation
```

```
      Qeq(c),FOCeq(c),PRICEeq(c),IncomeYeq,QHeq(c),Qbal(c),Leq,Keq;
```

```
      Qeq(c)..
      Q(c)=e=scaleA(c)*(delta(c)*LD(c)**rho(c)+(1-
delta(c))*KD(c)**rho(c))**(1/rho(c));
```

```
      FOCeq(c)..
      WL/WK=e=delta(c)/(1-delta(c))*(LD(c)/KD(c))**(rho(c)-1);
```

```
    PRICEeq(c)..
    WL*LD(c)+WK*KD(c)=e=P(c)*Q(c);

    IncomeYeq..
    WL*LS+WK*KS=e=Y;

    QHeq(c)..
    P(c)*QH(c)=e=alphah(c)*Y;

    Qbal(c)..
    QH(c)=e=Q(c);

    Leq..
    Sum(c,LD(c))=e=LS;

    Keq..
    Sum(c,KD(c))=e=KS;

*Assign initial values to the variables
    P.L(c)=P0(c);
    WL.L=WL0;
    WK.L=WK0;
    Q.L(c)= Q0(c);
    LD.L(c)= LD0(c);
    KD.L(c)=KD0(c);
    LS.L=LS0;
    KS.L=KS0;
    Y.L=Y0;
    QH.L(c)=QH0(c);

*Fixed total values of labor and capital supplies by using suffix .fx
    LS.fx=LS0;
    KS.fx=KS0;

*Executing the program
model cge  /all/;
solve cge using mcp;

*Replication
*By perturbing to a different initial value but expecting the model to converge to
the original values
WL.L=1.1;
model replic /all/;
solve replic using mcp;
display P.L, WL.L, WK.L, Q.L, LD.L, KD.L,LS.L, KS.L;

*Simulation
*If total labor endowment and supply increases by 10%
```

```
WL.L=1;
LS.fx=1.1*LS0;
model sim /all/;
solve sim using mcp;
display P.L, WL.L, WK.L, Q.L, LD.L, KD.L,LS.L, KS.L

*end
```

8.3 Multiple Inputs and Nested Functions

A production process often involves more than two inputs. In theory, a CES function can include three or more than three inputs:

$$q = f(x_1, x_2, \cdots\cdots, x_n) = A(\delta_1 x_1^\rho + \delta_2 x_2^\rho +, \cdots\cdots, +\delta_n x_n^\rho)^{1/\rho} \qquad \sum_c^n \delta_c = 1 \qquad (8.3.1)$$

The problem of this CES function is that the elasticity of substitution between any pair of inputs has to be the same. Suppose this production has three inputs: intermediate input M, labor L and capital K:

$$q = A(\delta_1 M^\rho + \delta_2 L^\rho + \delta_3 K^\rho)^{1/\rho} \qquad \sum_c^n \delta_c = 1 \qquad (8.3.2)$$

Then the elasticities of substitution ε between intermediate input and labor, or between labor and capital, etc., must have the same value, because they all share the same exponent ρ. If the elasticity of substitution ε between intermediate input and labor is 0.5, then the elasticity of substitution between labor and capital is also 0.5. This is apparently not true in most cases.

To avoid this problem, we use a nested structure to combine two CES functions with different ρ values, thus they can have different elasticities. The two CES functions are

$$q = A_q[\delta_q V^\rho + (1 - \delta_q)M^\rho]^{1/\rho} \qquad (8.3.3)$$

$$V = A_v[\delta_v L^{\rho_v} + (1 - \delta_v)K^{\rho_v}]^{1/\rho_v} \qquad (8.3.4)$$

There are two aggregate terms. V is aggregate value-added for the primary factor inputs and M is the aggregate intermediate input. They have different exponents, ρ and ρ_v. Combining them in a nested structure, it is

$$q = A_q\{\delta_q[A_v(\delta_v L^{\rho_v} + (1 - \delta_v)K^{\rho_v})^{1/\rho_v}]^\rho + (1 - \delta_q)M^\rho\}^{1/\rho} \qquad (8.3.5)$$

Figure 8.3.1 shows the nested function structure for the inputs and functions.

When the production function is nested in the production function module in a CGE model, the price equation and the optimal input-use condition are also nested, in order to be consistent with the nested structure. For the nested production function system consisting of Equations (8.3.3) and (8.3.4), the corresponding price equations (in the "breakeven

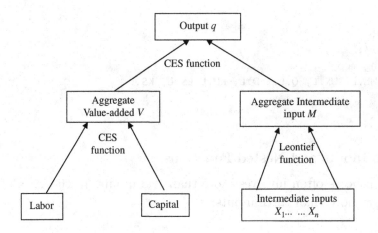

Figure 8.3.1.　Example of a nested function structure.

equation" form) in the production module are

$$p_q q = p_v V + p_M M \tag{8.3.6}$$

$$p_v V = w_l L + w_k K \tag{8.3.7}$$

The two aggregates V and M have their own prices P_v and P_M. Dividing both sides of the above by the quantity of the aggregate quantity terms, we see the following two weighted price equations:

$$p_q = p_v \frac{V}{q} + p_M \frac{M}{q} \tag{8.3.8}$$

$$p_v = w_l \frac{L}{V} + w_k \frac{K}{V} \tag{8.3.9}$$

It can be seen that the price at a higher level in the nested structure is weighted prices at the lower level. As discussed before, these price equations imply the enterprises' optimal output decision thus the supply function of q.

To complete the production block, we need to further add the first-order conditions of optimal input uses at the two levels of the nested structure:

$$\frac{P_v}{P_M} = \frac{\delta_q}{1 - \delta_q} \left(\frac{V}{M} \right)^{\rho - 1} \tag{8.3.10}$$

$$\frac{W_l}{W_k} = \frac{\delta_v}{1 - \delta_v} \left(\frac{L}{K} \right)^{\rho_v - 1} \tag{8.3.11}$$

Combining these equations, we have two levels of production function modules with the FOC form. The top level module consists of Equations (8.3.3), (8.3.6) and (8.3.10). The lower level module for value-added consists of Equations (8.3.4), (8.3.7) and (8.3.11). Each group forms the input demands and output supply in their corresponding modules.

What about the intermediate input module at the second level? Most CGE models use the Leontief production function for the intermediate inputs for the reasons of simplicity and data availability. Its setup is similar to our early discussion in the input–output (IO) model. The module includes the Leontief production function and the price equation. The inputs are used in fixed proportions to the aggregate intermediate input M. Let X_{ij} be the use of input i in sector j. Let a_{ij} be the input coefficient, so

$$X_{ij} = a_{ij} M_j \qquad i \in C \quad j \in C \qquad (8.3.12)$$

Note the input coefficient a_{ij} is different from the previous IO models. Here the input coefficient a_{ij} is the input required to produce the aggregate *intermediate* input M_j. In the previous IO model, the input coefficients a_{ij} are the inputs required to produce the *final* output j. The price equation in the module is

$$p_{M_j} M_j = \sum_i p_i X_{ij} \qquad j \in C \qquad (8.3.13)$$

If the above function form does not look like the price function, just dividing both sides by M_j, the nature of the price equation becomes obvious:

$$p_{M_j} = \sum_i p_i a_{ij} \qquad j \in C \qquad (8.3.13')$$

For the intermediate input module, the above two Equations (8.3.12) and (8.3.13′) have implied the optimal use of intermediate inputs and optimal quantity supplied of the aggregate intermediate input M_j.

Many CGE models have more complex nested structures in the production block with multiple levels and many modules. Yet the basic principle in modeling is the same as discussed earlier. The structure needs to specify the levels, the modules at each level, and individual functions in the modules. In each module, whichever production function and whichever module form is used, it must include the optimal use of inputs and optimal quantity supplied, together with the associated prices. The individual production function in each module can be any legitimate functions, such as Leontief, Cobb–Douglas and other CES functions, depending on the research needs and data available.

8.4 A CGE Model with Nested Production Function

In what follows, we demonstrate a CGE model with a nested production function. The model economy is represented by the SAM Table 8.4.1. It has three commodity sectors and two primary factors. The nested structure of the production function is shown in Figure 8.3.1. The top level for the final output is a CES function consisting of two inputs, aggregate value-added and aggregate intermediate input. At the bottom level, the value-added production module is a CES function with two inputs, labor and capital. The intermediate input production module has a Leontief function with commodity inputs. The household utility function is a Cobb–Douglas function.

As the CGE model is getting more and more complicated in our discussion, we need to further upgrade the variable notation, because there are not enough English or Greek letters for all variables if we rely only on a single letter symbol for each variable. In addition, it is

Table 8.4.1.   SAM table of a model economy.

	Agriculture	Industry	Service	Labor	Capital	Household	Total
Agriculture	260	320	150			635	1365
Industry	345	390	390			600	1725
Service	400	365	320			385	1470
Labor	200	250	400				850
Capital	160	400	210				770
Household				850	770		1620
Total	1365	1725	1470	850	770	1620	

not easy to memorize the variable definition represented by a particular symbol when there are too many variables and symbols. From now on we adopt the notations used in the IFPRI model and others in the CGE literature. These notations are used both in the mathematical models and GAMS programs in later chapters. Some minor modifications of the variable names or their definitions may be made to adapt to the special needs in this book. This new notation set has the advantages of the capability to handle many variables and the convenience of recognizing the variable definitions. The following are the basic principles for the notation and names of variables and parameters.

Parameters are named by a string of lowercase letters or a greek letter. Variable names are represented by a string of several uppercase Latin letters, instead of just one single letter. The first letter of a variable name has the following meaning: Q stands for quantity; P for commodity price; W for factor price; Y for monetary income (income in the currency unit), E for monetary expenditure; etc. The following letters in a variable name have the specified meaning: C for commodity, VA for value-added, H for household, G for the government, etc. For instance, YH is household income, and EG is the government expenditure. The names can be further compounded. For instance, $INTA$ stands for intermediate input and aggregate; PVA stands for the price of aggregate value-added input.

The following is the list of the variables in this notational format for this model. A Latin letter used as a subscript is the index (of the index set) to the variable, such as: $PINTA_c$ is the price of the aggregate intermediate input in sector c.

QC: quantity of the commodity
PC: price of the commodity
QVA: quantity of aggregate value-added input
PVA: price of aggregate value-added input
$QINTA$: quantity of aggregate intermediate input. Here A stands for aggregate.
$PINTA$: price of aggregate intermediate input
$QINT$:   quantity of intermediate input, which is X_{ij} in Section 8.3.
QLD: quantity of labor demand
QKD: quantity of capital demand

C: set of all commodities

F: set of all factors

α^q: scale factor parameter of the output CES production function of QC

α^{va}:   scale factor parameter of the value-added CES production function of QVA

ρ: exponent of the output CES production function of QC

ρ^{va}:   exponent of the value-added CES function of QVA

δ^q: share parameter of the output CES production function of QC

δ^{va}:   share parameter of the value-added CES function of QVA

$ia_{cc'}$:   input coefficient of using c to produce one unit of $QINTA_{c'}$.

The production block of the mathematical model is similar to that in the previous section but with this upgraded notation. The top level production module consists of the three following equations:

$$QC_c = \alpha_c^q [\delta_c^q QVA_c^{\rho_c} + (1 - \delta_c^q) QINTA_c^{\rho_c}]^{1/\rho_c} \qquad c \in C \qquad (8.4.1)$$

$$\frac{PVA_c}{PINTA_c} = \frac{\delta_c^q}{(1 - \delta_c^q)} \left(\frac{QVA_c}{QINTA_c} \right)^{\rho_c - 1} \qquad c \in C \qquad (8.4.2)$$

$$PC_c \cdot QC_c = PVA_c \cdot QVA_c + PINTA_c \cdot QINTA_c \qquad c \in C \qquad (8.4.3)$$

The bottom level has two production modules. The value-added module consists of

$$QVA_c = \alpha_c^{va} [\delta_c^{va} QLD_c^{\rho_c^{va}} + (1 - \delta_c^{va}) QKD_c^{\rho_c^{va}}]^{1/\rho_c^{va}} \qquad c \in C \qquad (8.4.4)$$

$$\frac{WL}{WK} = \frac{\delta_c^{va}}{(1 - \delta_c^{va})} \left(\frac{QLD_c}{QKD_c} \right)^{\rho_c^{va} - 1} \qquad c \in C \qquad (8.4.5)$$

$$PVA_c \cdot QVA_c = WL \cdot QLD_c + WK \cdot QKD_c \qquad c \in C \qquad (8.4.6)$$

The intermediate input module consists of two equations:

$$QINT_{cc'} = ia_{cc'} \cdot QINTA_{c'} \qquad c \in C, \quad c' \in C \qquad (8.4.7)$$

$$PINTA_{c'} \cdot QINTA_{c'} = \sum_{c \in C} PC_c \cdot QINT_{cc'} \qquad c' \in C \qquad (8.4.8)$$

The last Equation (8.4.8) is the price equation, which can alternatively take the direct form

$$PINTA_{c'} = \sum_{c \in C} ia_{cc'} \cdot PC_c \qquad c' \in C \qquad (8.4.8')$$

The aggregate intermediate input quantity $QINTA$ is the sum of intermediate input $QINT$ in each sector. Lowercase $ia_{cc'}$ are input coefficients. As discussed, here input coefficient $ia_{cc'}$ is the input required to produce the aggregate intermediate input $QINTA_{c'}$, not the final output $QC_{c'}$. Take an example of SAM Table 8.4.1. All prices are set to 1, the input coefficient a_{11} defined in the previous IO models would be $a_{11} = 260/1365 = 0.19$. Yet the input coefficient $ia_{11'}$ is $ia_{11} = 260/(260 + 345 + 460) = 260/1005 = 0.26$. The difference is that the denominator used in the former is the total final output QC, but in the latter it is aggregate intermediate input $QINTA$. Hence, to calibrate the input coefficients here, one should first calibrate the aggregate intermediate inputs $QINTA$.

The set of above eight equations constitute the production block of the model, which forms the commodity supply production function and input demand function by enterprises in each commodity sector c. Next we set up the commodity demand functions from households' utility maximization. Households' incomes are from their factor supplies (because enterprises' profit is zero, hence no profit remittance takes place):

$$YH = WL \cdot QLS + WK \cdot QKS \qquad (8.4.9)$$

where

    QLS: quantity of total labor supply
    QKS: quantity of total capital supply
    YH: monetary income of households

Households' utility function is a Cobb–Douglas function, hence their monetary spending on commodity c is a fixed share $shareh_c$ of their income, regardless of the price level. The derived consumption demand by households for commodity c is

$$QH_c = \frac{shareh_c}{PC_c} \cdot YH \qquad c \in C \qquad (8.4.10)$$

The commodity market clearing equation is

$$\sum_{c' \in C} QINT_{cc'} + QH_c = QC_c \qquad (8.4.11)$$

This economy is assumed to be in a classical world where all factors are fully employed. Hence, factor demands equal supplies:

$$\sum_{c \in C} QLD_c = QLS \qquad (8.4.12)$$

$$\sum_{c \in C} QKD_c = QKS \qquad (8.4.13)$$

The model has a total of 13 groups of Equations, from (8.4.1)–(8.4.13). It has 15 groups of endogenous variables: QC_c, QVA_c, $QINTA_c$, $QINT_{cc'}$ QLD_c, QKD_c, QLS_c, QKS_c, YH, QH_c PC_c, PVA_c, $PINTA_c$, WL, WK. There are two more variables than the number of equations. We need to add two more constraints for the variables to fix their values, in order to reduce the number of endogenous variables to 13 groups. Because of the full employment assumption, factor supplies equal factor endowments, which are determined exogenously. Let notation "bar" denote exogenous variables (whose values are determined outside the model), so $\overline{QLS}$ and $\overline{QKS}$ denote the labor and capital endowments, respectively. Note in GAMS program exogenous variables are treated as parameters. We add two more constraint equations in the model as follows:

$$QL = \overline{QLS} \qquad (8.4.14)$$

$$QKS = \overline{QKS} \qquad (8.4.15)$$

The above two Equations (8.4.14) and (8.4.15) are constraints that fix the values of QLS and QKS. Note in nature they are different from other 13 equations of the model which are the model's system equations. Let us repeat the important GAMS syntax rules in CGE models. In GAMS programming, to assign values to parameters or to fix variable values by constraints, the syntax of the equation equality is "=". The system equations of the CGE model for the GAMS solver to search for the optimal values of variables have the equality sign of "= e =".

In GAMS program, there are several ways to assign fixed values to variables, which actually change the nature of these variables to parameters. One way is adding constraint equations to assign values, such as the above Equations (8.4.14) and (8.4.15). The second way is adding suffix .fx to the variable names so the assigned values are fixed, as discussed in Sections 2.3 and 8.2. The third way is directly declaring them as parameters in the model, then assigning values.

After adding the two constraints, now the model has 13 variables, which equal the 13 equations from (8.4.1) through (8.4.13), thus meeting the squareness condition and being solvable. Parameters that need to be calibrated from the SAM table data are α_c^q, α_c^{va}, δ_c^q, δ_c^{va}, $ia_{cc'}$ and $shareh_c$. Parameter values that need to be given from outside sources are exponents ρ_c and ρ_c^{va}. The following is the GAMS program for this model. Some further setup details are explained in the program.

8.5 GAMS Program of the CGE Model with Nested Production Function

Example 8.5.1 The model economy is described in the above section with the SAM Table 8.4.1. In addition, we have the information about exponents of the individual CES functions in the table.

Values of exponent ρ of	Agriculture	Industry	Service
Top level CES function	0.2	0.3	0.1
CES function for the value-added module at the bottom level	0.25	0.5	0.8

Write the GAMS program for the CGE model. Calibrate the parameters and replicate the results. Then, assuming the labor force increases by 8%, do the simulation and display the resulting changes in economic variables.

Solution: The production block of this model is more complicated than the previous model in Section 8.2. This model has a multilevel nested structure, and has intermediate inputs involved in production. The following is the GAMS program for the mathematical model in Section 8.4. Readers can compare it to the mathematical model to learn more about GAMS language.

```
$title Example 8.5.1 CGE model with nested CES functions

*Set definition. all accounts: ac  commodities: c  factors: f
*Sector names are: agriculture: agri; industry: indu; service: serv
set ac    /agri,indu,serv,lab,cap,hh,total/;
set c(ac)  /agri,indu,serv/;
set f(ac)  /lab,cap/;

alias (ac,acp),(c,cp),(f,fp);

table sam(ac,acp)
         agri   indu   serv  lab   cap   hh     total
agri     260    320    150               635    1365
indu     345    390    390               600    1725
serv     400    365    320               385    1470
lab      200    250    400                      850
cap      160    400    210                      770
hh                           850   770          1620
total    1365   1725   1470  850   770   1620
;

*Read the exponent data
parameter  rhoq(c)    /agri =  0.2,   indu = 0.3,   serv = 0.1 /
           rhoVA(c)   /agri    0.25,  indu   0.5,   serv   0.8 /;

parameters
*Variable name followed by 0 denotes the corresponding variable fixed at its
initial level

scaleAq(c)        Scale factor of top level CES function
deltaq(c)         Share parameter of top level CES function
scaleAVA(c)       Scale factor of value-added CES function
deltaVA(c)        Share parameter of value-added CES function
ia(c,cp)          Input coefficient of intermediate inputs
shareh(c)         Households' income share spent on commodity c
PC0(c)            Price of c
QC0(c)            Quantity of c
PVA0(c)           Price of aggregate value-added
QVA0(c)           Quantity of aggregate value-added
PINTA0(c)         Price of aggregate intermediate input
QINTA0(c)         Quantity of aggregate intermediate input
QINT0(c,cp)       Quantity of intermediate input c used in cp
QLD0(c)           Labor demand
QKD0(c)           Capital demand
```

```
QLS0                    Labor supply
QKS0                    Capital supply
WL0                     Labor price
WK0                     Capital price
YH0                     Household income in dollars (monetary unit)
QH0(c)                  Consumption demand for c by households
;

*Calibration of parameters.  All initial prices are set to 1.
PC0(c)=1;
PVA0(c)=1;
PINTA0(c)=1;
WK0=1;
WL0=1;
QC0(c)=sam('total',c)/PC0(c);
QVA0(c)=SUM(f,Sam(f,c));
QINT0(c,cp)=sam(c,cp)/PC0(c);
QINTA0(c)=SUM(cp,QINT0(cp,c));
ia(c,cp)=QINT0(c,cp)/QINTA0(cp);
QLS0=sum(c,sam('lab',c))/WL0;
QKS0=sum(c,sam('cap',c))/WK0;
QLD0(c)=sam('lab',c)/WL0;
QKD0(c)=sam('cap',c)/WK0;
deltaq(c)=PVA0(c)*QVA0(c)**(1-rhoq(c))/(PVA0(c)*QVA0(c)**(1-
rhoq(c))+PINTA0(c)*QINTA0(c)**(1-rhoq(c)));
scaleAq(c)=QC0(c)/(deltaq(c)*QVA0(c)**rhoq(c)+(1-
deltaq(c))*QINTA0(c)**rhoq(c))**(1/rhoq(c));
deltaVA(c)=WL0*QLD0(c)**(1-rhoVA(c))/(WL0*QLD0(c)**(1-rhoVA(c))+WK0*QKD0(c)**(1-
rhoVA(c)));
scaleAVA(c)=QVA0(c)/(deltaVA(c)*QLD0(c)**rhoVA(c)+(1-
deltaVA(c))*QKD0(c)**rhoVA(c))**(1/rhoVA(c));
YH0=WL0*QLS0+WK0*QKS0;
QH0(c)=SAM(c,'hh')/PC0(c);
shareh(c)=(PC0(c)*QH0(c))/sum(cp,sam(cp,'hh'));

*display and check data inputs and calibrate parameters
display
PC0,PVA0,PINTA0,QC0,QVA0,QINTA0,QINT0,rhoq,rhoVA,scaleAq,deltaq,scaleAVA,deltaVA,i
a,shareh,QLD0,QKD0,QLS0,QKS0,WL0,WK0,YH0,QH0;

variable
PC(c),PVA(c),PINTA(c),WL,WK,QC(c),QVA(c),QINTA(c),QINT(c,cp),QLD(c),QKD(c),QLS,QKS
,YH,QH(c);

equation
QCfn(c),QCFOCeq(c),PCeq(c),QVAfn(c),QVAFOC(c),PVAeq(c),QINTfn(c,cp),PINTAeq(cp),YH
eq,QHeq(c),ComEqui(c),Leq,Keq;
```

```
QCfn(c)..
QC(c)=e=scaleAq(c)*(deltaq(c)*QVA(c)**rhoq(c)+(1-
deltaq(c))*QINTA(c)**rhoq(c))**(1/rhoq(c));

*The optimal input use condition.  "FOC" stands for first-order condition
QCFOCeq(c)..
PVA(c)/PINTA(c)=e=(deltaq(c)/(1-deltaq(c)))*(QVA(c)/QINTA(c))**(rhoq(c)-1);

PCeq(c)..
PC(c)*QC(c)=e=PVA(c)*QVA(c)+PINTA(c)*QINTA(c);

QVAfn(c)..
QVA(c)=e=scaleAVA(c)*(deltaVA(c)*QLD(c)**rhoVA(c)+(1-
deltaVA(c))*QKD(c)**rhoVA(c))**(1/rhoVA(c));

QVAFOC(c)..
WL/WK=e=(deltaVA(c)/(1-deltaVA(c)))*(QLD(c)/QKD(c))**(rhoVA(c)-1);

PVAeq(c)..
PVA(c)*QVA(c)=e=WL*QLD(c)+WK*QKD(c);

QINTfn(c,cp)..
QINT(c,cp)=e=ia(c,cp)*QINTA(cp);

PINTAeq(cp)..
PINTA(cp)=e=SUM(c,ia(c,cp)*PC(c));

YHeq..
YH=e=WL*QLS+WK*QKS;

QHeq(c)..
PC(c)*QH(c)=e=shareh(c)*YH;

ComEqui(c)..
QC(c)=e=sum(cp,QINT(c,cp))+QH(c);

Leq..
Sum(c,QLD(c))=e=QLS;

Keq..
Sum(c,QKD(c))=e=QKS;


*Assign initial values
PC.L(c)=PC0(c);
PVA.L(c)=PVA0(c);
PINTA.L(c)=PINTA0(c);
QC.L(c)=QC0(c);
```

```
QVA.L(c)=QVA0(c);
QINTA.L(c)=QINTA0(c);
QINT.L(c,cp)=QINT0(c,cp);
QLD.L(c)=QLD0(c);
QKD.L(c)=QKD0(c);
WK.L=1;
WL.L=1;
YH.L=YH0;
QH.L(c)=QH0(c);

*Fix values of QLS and QKS.  They become parameters in nature.
QLS.fx=QLS0;
QKS.fx=QKS0;

*Run the program
model cge  /all/;
solve cge using mcp;

*Simulation for 8 percent increase in labor force
QLS.fx=QLS0*1.08;
model sim1  /all/;
solve sim1 using mcp;

*End
```

8.6 Complex Production Structure

The nested structure in the production block can be quite complex for some research needs. One example is the SAGE model by EPA (2019) for the analysis of environmental policies. Another example is the GTAP-E model, which has been used to study energy and environmental issues. Figure 8.6.1 is the structure diagram of the original GTAP-E model (Burniaux and Truong, 2002). There have been many variants of these models in literature in the past 20 years.

The production block has eight levels with a number of production function modules. The technique to set up equations for each production function module is the same as discussed in the previous section. One variant here from the standard CES function is a CES function with more than two inputs. This multiple inputs situation occurs in four modules in the GTAP-E model. For instance, the CES function in the value-added-and-energy composite module has four inputs: natural resources, labor, land and capital-energy composite. Another case is in the foreign import module, for instance, petroleum product import. The production function treats the same petroleum imports from several foreign countries as several different inputs. In any of these cases, it implies that the elasticities of substitution between any pair of inputs in the same production function are the same. For the same imported input from different countries for production, we can agree this assumption is reasonable. For instance, the same petroleum product from various

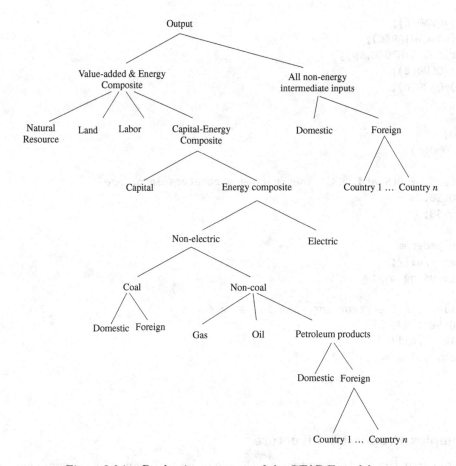

Figure 8.6.1.   Production structure of the GTAP-E model.

countries should be quite the same, thus the elasticities of substitution among them are the same.

Let n be the number of inputs in input set X, for convenience here we use input indexes i and j $(i \in X, j \in X)$, we have the following multiple-input CES function:

$$q = f(x_1, x_2, \cdots\cdots, x_n) = A(\delta_1 x_1^\rho + \delta_2 x_2^\rho +, \cdots\cdots, +\delta_n x_n^\rho)^{1/\rho} \qquad \sum_i^n \delta_i = 1 \qquad (8.6.1)$$

The technical rate of substitution TRS between any pair of inputs i and j is the same as before:

$$\mathrm{TRS} = \frac{\partial f/\partial x_i}{\partial f/\partial x_j} = \frac{A\frac{1}{\rho}(\delta_1 x_1^\rho + \cdots + \delta_n x_n^\rho)^{\frac{1}{\rho}-1} \cdot \delta_i \cdot \rho x_i^{\rho-1}}{A\frac{1}{\rho}(\delta_1 x_1^\rho + \delta_2 x_2^\rho)^{\frac{1}{\rho}-1} \cdot \delta_j \cdot \rho x_j^{\rho-1}} = \frac{\delta_i}{\delta_j}\left(\frac{x_i}{x_j}\right)^{\rho-1} \quad i \in X, \ j \in X, \ i \neq j$$

$$(8.6.2)$$

The first-order conditions for input uses are the same:

$$\frac{w_i}{w_j} = \frac{\delta_i}{\delta_j}\left(\frac{x_i}{x_j}\right)^{\rho-1} \qquad i \in X, \quad j \in X, \quad i \neq j \tag{8.6.3}$$

The relationship between exponent ρ and elasticity of substitution ε is the same:

$$\varepsilon = \frac{1}{1-\rho} \qquad \text{and} \qquad \rho = 1 - \frac{1}{\varepsilon} \tag{8.6.4}$$

where the values of exponents ρ or ε are given externally.

Using n-1 first-order conditions $\frac{w_i}{w_j} = \frac{\delta_i}{\delta_j}(\frac{x_j}{x_i})^{1-\rho}$ $i = 2, \ldots, n$, after some messy but straightforward substitutions and rearrangements, we have the following equations for calibrating the parameters:

$$\delta_j = \frac{w_j x_j^{1-\rho}}{w_1 x_1^{1-\rho} + \cdots + w_i x_i^{1-\rho} + \cdots + w_n x_n^{1-\rho}} = \frac{w_j x_j^{1-\rho}}{\sum_{i \in X} w_i x_i^{1-\rho}} \qquad j \in X \tag{8.6.5}$$

$$A = q/(\delta_1 x_1^\rho +, \ldots, +\delta_n x_n^\rho)^{1/\rho} \tag{8.6.6}$$

The equations in the production module, following the "FOC form", include production function, first-order conditions and price equation:

$$\begin{cases} q = A(\delta_1 x_1^\rho + \delta_2 x_2^\rho +, \cdots \cdots, +\delta_n x_n^\rho)^{1/\rho} \quad \sum_i^n \delta_i = 1 \\ \frac{w_i}{w_1} = \frac{\delta_i}{\delta_1}\left(\frac{x_i}{x_1}\right)^{\rho-1} \qquad i = 2, \ldots, n \\ pq = w_1 x_1 +, \cdots \cdots, +w_n x_n \end{cases} \tag{8.6.7}$$

The system has three groups of equations. Each of the first and third groups has only a single equation. The second group consists of $n-1$ equations, which are first-order conditions for all possible pairs of inputs. Here we let input 1 serve as the common denominator input to calculate elasticities with other denominator inputs, but this is just an arbitrary choice — any other input can serve as the common denominator input. In total, there are $1 + (n-1) + 1 = n + 1$ equations in the production module.

Because the second equation group is only for $i = 2, \ldots, n$ equations, in writing a GAMS program for Equation (8.6.7), we need to define a subset of X for index $i = 2, \ldots, n$ to exclude sector 1. While some GAMS codes can be used to handle this problem, it is not as convenient as using the other forms.

If using the "input-demand form", the module has two equation groups:

$$\begin{cases} x_i^c = \frac{q}{A}\left(\frac{\delta_i}{w_i}\right)^\varepsilon [\delta_1^\varepsilon w_1^{1-\varepsilon} + \cdots + \delta_n^\varepsilon w_n^{1-\varepsilon}]^{\frac{\varepsilon}{1-\varepsilon}} \qquad i = 1, \ldots, n \quad \text{or} \quad i \in C \\ pq = w_1 x_1 + \cdots + w_n x_n \end{cases} \tag{8.6.8}$$

The first equation group can simply use the already defined set C, thus the GAMS codes are simple.

If using the "unit-cost form", it has the following two equation groups. It is also neat:

$$\begin{cases} x_i^c = A^{\varepsilon-1} \left[p \frac{\delta_i}{w_i} \right]^\varepsilon \cdot q & i = 1, \ldots, n \\ p = \frac{1}{A} \left[\delta_1^\varepsilon w_1^{1-\varepsilon} + \cdots + \delta_n^\varepsilon w_n^{1-\varepsilon} \right]^{1/(1-\varepsilon)} \end{cases} \tag{8.6.9}$$

Another form in literature is to utilize the optimal condition in microeconomics textbooks: input price equals marginal-revenue product of that input. In equation form, it is $w_i = p \cdot \partial f / \partial x_i$. Then it adds the production function to complete the system in the production module:

$$\begin{cases} w_i = pq(\delta_1 x_1^\rho + \delta_2 x_2^\rho +, \cdots \cdots, + \delta_n x_n^\rho)^{-1} \delta_i x_i^{\rho-1} & i = 1, \ldots, n \\ q = A(\delta_1 x_1^\rho + \delta_2 x_2^\rho +, \cdots \cdots, + \delta_n x_n^\rho)^{1/\rho} \end{cases} \tag{8.6.10}$$

This form is used occasionally for input demands in the IFPRI model. We may name it *marginal-revenue-product form*. When inputs are subject to taxes, the price markup varies across individual inputs, so using this form is convenient.

In general, if the CES function has more than two inputs, for convenience in GAMS coding, it is preferred to use the bottom three forms for the production modules in the GAMS program. This is particularly true to treat import inputs from many countries/ regions because there are many inputs within the same CES production function.

When the production structure gets more complex, we may ask a legitimate question: will the complex nested structure cause the problem so the CGE model cannot converge to equilibrium in simulation? This is essentially the problem of existence of equilibrium and the answer is behind the general equilibrium theory. The condition from the Arrow–Debreu theory requires the production set to be convex. The production sets of the CES $(-\infty < \rho < 1)$ and Leontief production functions are convex. Intersection of convex sets is still convex, so the nested CES and Leontief production functions preserve the convexity property. As long as we follow the principles of the above structure and modules, the production set of the production block is convex, thus the existence condition is met.

Some setups in production functions would violate the convexity property, thus should be avoided. One warning is avoiding "increasing-returns-to-scale" functions. Another caution for CES functions is, exponent ρ should not be greater than unity. In case a CGE model really needs these setups, other constraints should be added to make the model converge to an equilibrium.

8.7 Variable Input Coefficient Structure

In a standard IO model with the Leontief technology, the input coefficients are constants. In Section 7.2, we have shown that the unit-conditional-input-demand $x_i^c(w_1, \ldots, w_n, q_j = 1)$ of Equation (7.2.14) actually is the input coefficient that input i is required to produce one unit of commodity j. Further, it is variable — its value can change in response to changes in factor prices. It can be denoted by $a_{ij}(w_1, \ldots, w_n)$.

Ginsburge and Keyzer (2002) present a CGE model structure by using variable input coefficients in the production block. Assume the economy has $c \in C$ commodities, $f \in F$ factors and multiple households $h \in H$. The variable notations are as follows:

$\mathbf{e}_h$ factor endowment vector of household h

$\mathbf{q}$ commodity output vector

$\mathbf{D}_h$ commodity demand vector by household h

$\mathbf{F}_h^d$ factor demand vector by household h

$\mathbf{p}$ commodity price vector

$\mathbf{w}$ factor price vector

Y_h monetary income of household h

The production functions of commodities are CES functions. The unit-conditional-input-demand function for f is derived and denoted by $a_{fc}(\mathbf{p}, \mathbf{w})$, which is the input coefficient. Similarly, for intermediate inputs, the input coefficient is $a_{cc}(\mathbf{p}, \mathbf{w})$.

Suppose there are n commodities in set C and m factors in set F. The IO matrix for intermediate inputs is

$$\mathbf{A}_C(\mathbf{p}, \mathbf{w}) = \begin{pmatrix} a_{11}(\mathbf{p}, \mathbf{w}) & \cdots & \\ \cdots & a_{cc}(\mathbf{p}, \mathbf{w}) & \cdots \\ \cdots & \cdots & a_{nn}(\mathbf{p}, \mathbf{w}) \end{pmatrix} \tag{8.7.1}$$

The factor input demand matrix is

$$\mathbf{A}_F(\mathbf{p}, \mathbf{w}) = \begin{pmatrix} a_{f1}(\mathbf{p}, \mathbf{w}) & \cdots & \\ \cdots & a_{ff}(\mathbf{p}, \mathbf{w}) & \cdots \\ \cdots & \cdots & a_{fm}(\mathbf{p}, \mathbf{w}) \end{pmatrix} \tag{8.7.2}$$

The two matrices establish conditional input demands. The price equation is

$$\mathbf{p}' = \mathbf{p}' \mathbf{A}_C(\mathbf{p}, \mathbf{w}) + \mathbf{w}' \mathbf{A}_F(\mathbf{p}, \mathbf{w}) \tag{8.7.3}$$

which serves as the commodity supply function. The three Equations (8.7.1)–(8.7.3) establish the commodity supplies and input demands in the production block.

Household h's income comes from his factor endowment:

$$Y_h = \mathbf{w} \cdot \mathbf{e}_h \tag{8.7.4}$$

The consumption demand of household h is derived from his utility maximization:

$$\mathbf{D}_h(\mathbf{p}, \mathbf{w}, Y_h) = \mathbf{D}_h \tag{8.7.5}$$

In this model, the households also demand factors from their endowment. For instance, when households spend time to enjoy leisure, it can be viewed as their consumption of their labor time endowment. Household h's demand for factor input is

$$\mathbf{F}_h^d = \mathbf{F}_h(\mathbf{p}, \mathbf{w}, Y_h) \tag{8.7.6}$$

Factor demand by all households is $\sum_h \mathbf{F}_h^d(\mathbf{p}, \mathbf{w}, Y_h)$. Demand factor by enterprises is $\mathbf{A}_F(\mathbf{p}, \mathbf{w})\mathbf{q}$. Hence, the total demand factor in the economy is

$$\mathbf{F^d} = \sum_h \mathbf{F}_h^d(\mathbf{p}, \mathbf{w}, Y_h) + \mathbf{A}_F(\mathbf{p}, \mathbf{w})\mathbf{q} \tag{8.7.7}$$

Commodity market clearing condition is

$$\sum_h \mathbf{D}_h(\mathbf{p}, \mathbf{w}, Y_h) + \mathbf{A}_C(\mathbf{p}, \mathbf{w})\mathbf{q} = \mathbf{q} \tag{8.7.8}$$

Factor market clearing condition is

$$\mathbf{F^d} = \sum_h \mathbf{e}_h \tag{8.7.9}$$

Equations (8.7.3)–(8.7.9), a total of seven equation groups, establish the CGE model. There are seven variable groups: $\mathbf{p}, \mathbf{w}, \mathbf{D}_h, \mathbf{F}_h^d, \mathbf{F}^d, \mathbf{q}, Y_h$. Endowment $\mathbf{e}_h$ is given, which is exogenous. The structure of the production block resembles the IO model, with the IO matrix and factor input matrix. Yet the input coefficients inside the matrices are unit-conditional-input-demand functions, rather than constants.

This model is conceptually interesting but practically has limitations. If the CES production function in each sector has only two inputs, or it has multiple inputs with the same elasticity of substitution like Equation (8.6.1), we can derive a unit input demand in the explicit form without too big problems:

$$x_{ij}^c = \frac{1}{A_j} \left(\frac{\delta_{ij}}{p_i} \right)^{\varepsilon_j} \left[\delta_{1j}^{\varepsilon_j} p_1^{1-\varepsilon_j} + \cdots + \delta_n^{\varepsilon_j} p_n^{1-\varepsilon_j} \right]^{\frac{\varepsilon_j}{1-\varepsilon_j}} \tag{8.7.10}$$

for the intermediate input coefficients $a_{ij}(\mathbf{p}, \mathbf{w})$. Similarly, we can get the factor input coefficients. If the inputs in the production function have different elasticities of substitution among them, the explicit expression for a unit input coefficient would get very complex, if available. If relying on GAMS to write a block program to solve the non-linear input coefficients first, it would be very lengthy. Overall, using non-linear input coefficients in the matrix form does not provide advantages or convenience over the conventional nested production function form.

Exercises

8E.1 The model economy has the SAM Table 8E.1.1. Its production block has a CES production function. Households have a Cobb–Douglas utility function. Develop a CGE model in the mathematical form. Then write the GAMS program for the model. Calibrate parameters of the CES function and households' share of income spent on the two commodities. Run the program and replicate. Verify the outcomes.

8E.2 An economy has the SAM Table 8E.2.1. You are asked to set up a CGE model for this economy. The production block has a nested structure with two levels. The first level is a Leontief production function with two inputs, the value-added composite and the intermediate input composite. The second level has two production modules.

Table 8E.1.1. SAM table of the model economy.

	Good 1	Good 2	Labor	Capital	Households	Total
Good 1					325	325
Good 2					340	340
Labor	200	130				330
Capital	125	210				335
Households			330	335		675
Total	325	340	330	335	675	

Table 8E.2.1. SAM table of the economy.

	Agriculture	Industry	Service	Labor	Capital	Household	Total
Agriculture	300	240	185			835	1560
Industry	285	380	290			1015	1970
Service	375	315	355			465	1510
Labor	450	495	450				1395
Capital	150	540	230				920
Household				1395	920		2315
Total	1560	1970	1510	1395	920	2315	

In the value-added module, it is a CES production function. In the intermediate input module, it is a Leontief production function. The utility function of the household is Cobb–Douglas. All factors and inputs are fully employed. Prices are flexible.

(a) First, write down the model in the form of mathematical equations. Secondly, write the corresponding GAMS program.

(b) Assume capital endowment increases by 10% in the second year. Do a simulation and display the changes in other variables.

Appendix: Review of Mathematics

8A.1 Non-linear equation system

A non-linear equation system can be expressed in the following form:

$$\begin{cases} f^1(x_1, \ldots, x_n; \mathbf{b}) = 0 \\ \ldots \\ f^m(x_1, \ldots, x_n; \mathbf{b}) = 0 \end{cases} \tag{8A.1.1}$$

where f^i denotes the ith function, not raising to ith power. $\mathbf{b}$ is a parameter vector.

In the appendix of Chapter 3, we discussed the conditions for existence of a unique solution for the linear equation system. The issue of existence of solutions for the non-linear equation system is more complicated, but some principles are similar:

(1) If inconsistency exists among functions, the system has no solution;

(2) In general, for existence of a unique solution, the *squareness* condition $m = n$, number of equations equal to number of variables, should be met. If $m < n$, there can be infinite solutions.

(3) In general, for existence of a unique or finite number of solutions, the functions should be functionally independent. The way to check the independence is that the Jacobian determinant (8A.1.2) is non-zero for all values of x:

$$\begin{vmatrix} \partial f^1/\partial x_1 & \cdots & \partial f^1/\partial x_n \\ \cdots & \cdots & \cdots \\ \partial f^m/\partial x_1 & \cdots & \partial f^m/\partial x_n \end{vmatrix} \neq 0 \qquad (8A.1.2)$$

Even if both (2) and (3) conditions are met, they are not sufficient to guarantee the existence of a solution. The fixed-point theorem provides the sufficient conditions for the existence of the equilibrium (which is the solution) of a system of equations (the excess demand functions in an economy). Interested readers are referred to advanced microeconomics and mathematics books.

Chapter 9

Utility Function and Households' Demand

The last two chapters discuss the commodity supply and input demand functions formed from the enterprise side. This chapter will discuss the commodity demand and factor supply functions formed from the households' side. Example 6.3.1 shows how a household forms the commodity demand and labor supply from utility maximization, given the labor endowments he has. For simplicity, in this chapter we assume full employment of factors, hence, factor supplies equal factor endowments. Thus we can focus on the commodity demand functions in the markets. This assumption can be relaxed later as needed. In what follows, we discuss various commodity demand functions derived from utility functions.

9.1 Utility Maximization and the Cobb–Douglas Utility Function

A household maximizes his utility function, subject to his budget constraint. Suppose there are n commodities in the household's consumption basket. Let q_i be the quantity of commodity i, and p_i be its price. The household's monetary income is Y. The household's behavior is expressed by

$$\max \ u(q_1, \ldots, q_n)$$
$$s.t. \quad p_1 q_1 + \cdots + p_n q_n = Y \tag{9.1.1}$$

Or in a compact form:

$$\max \left\{ u(q_1, \ldots, q_n) \mid \sum_i p_i q_i = Y \right\} \tag{9.1.2}$$

where $u(q_1, \ldots, q_n)$ is the utility function and $\sum_i p_i q_i = Y$ is the budget constraint. Solving this system, we obtain the quantity demanded for each commodity.

The Cobb–Douglas utility function is very simple but remains popular in CGE modeling. Its standard form is

$$u(q_1, \ldots, q_n) = A q_1^{\alpha_1} \ldots q_n^{\alpha_n} = A \prod_i^n q_i^{\alpha_i} \qquad \sum_i \alpha_i = 1 \tag{9.1.3}$$

A monotonic transformation of the utility function does not change the shape of its indifference curves, thus it won't change the optimal consumption bundle. Therefore, to

147

simplify the solving process, we can normalize the Cobb–Douglas utility function by dividing it by A, then transforming it to the following log form:

$$u(q_1, \ldots, q_n) = \log\left[\left(A\prod_i^n q_i^{\alpha_i}\right)/A\right] = \sum_i \alpha_i \log q_i \qquad \sum_i \alpha_i = 1 \qquad (9.1.4)$$

The log form of Equation (9.1.4) will lead to the same demand functions as the general form 9.1.3. Set the Lagrange function with choice variables q_i and λ. Maximize L,

$$\max_{q_1, \ldots, q_n, \lambda} L = \sum_i \alpha_i \log q_i - \lambda\left(\sum_i p_i q_i - Y\right) \qquad (9.1.5)$$

Solve it and obtain the demands for commodities as follows:

$$q_i = \alpha_i \frac{Y}{p_i} \qquad (9.1.6)$$

This commodity demand $q_i = f(p_1, \ldots, p_n, Y)$ is also call *ordinary demand* or *Marshallian demand* in economics.

The demand function derived from the Cobb–Douglas utility function has some advantages. It does not need the information of elasticity of substitution (it assumes the elasticity of substitution equals one). Spending on each commodity i is a fixed-share α_i of the total income Y. Share α_i can be calibrated from the SAM table directly by dividing spending on each commodity by the total income. In the case there is a lack of data for estimating the demand functions and the fixed-spending-share assumption is acceptable, using the Cobb–Douglas utility function is convenient and efficient.

9.2 CES Utility Function

The elasticity of substitution between two commodities in the Cobb–Douglas function equals one. When the elasticity of substitution does not equal one, say, the two commodities are substitutes or complements, then the more general form, the CES utility function, can be used. Similar to the previous discussion in the production block, the standard form of the CES utility function includes two commodities. For multiple commodities, if the substitution elasticities are the same among all commodities, we can include all these commodities in one CES equation. If not, a nested structure to include several CES utility functions is used.

The standard CES utility function is

$$u(q_1, q_2) = [\alpha q_1^\rho + (1-\alpha)q_2^\rho]^{1/\rho} \qquad (9.2.1)$$

Similar to the CES production function, the elasticity of substitution between the two commodities is defined as

$$\varepsilon \equiv \frac{d(q_2/q_1)}{q_2/q_1} \bigg/ \frac{d(p_1/p_2)}{p_1/p_2} \qquad (9.2.2)$$

The relationship between ε and the exponent ρ is

$$\varepsilon = \frac{1}{1-\rho} \qquad \text{or} \qquad \rho = 1 - \frac{1}{\varepsilon} \qquad (9.2.3)$$

Table 9.2.1. Elasticity of substitution and characteristics of the commodities.

$\rho =$	$-\infty$	0	1
Elasticity of substitution ε	0	1	∞
The two commodities are:	Perfect complements	Cobb–Douglas	Perfect substitutes

The relationship between the two commodities is described in Table 9.2.1. It can be seen that the Cobb–Douglas function is just a special case in the CES function family.

In deriving the demand functions, for convenience we monotonically transform the standard CES utility function by raising it to exponent ρ:

$$u(q_1, q_2) = [(\alpha q_1^\rho + (1 - \alpha)q_2^\rho)^{1/\rho}]^\rho = \alpha q_1^\rho + (1 - \alpha)q_2^\rho \tag{9.2.4}$$

The Lagrange function for utility maximization is

$$\max_{q_1, q_1, \lambda} L = \alpha q_1^\rho + (1 - \alpha)q_2^\rho - \lambda(p_1 q_1 + p_2 q_2 - Y) \tag{9.2.5}$$

Differentiating L with respect to the choice variables, the first-order condition leads to the optimal consumption combination:

$$\frac{p_1}{p_2} = \frac{\alpha}{(1 - \alpha)} \left(\frac{q_1}{q_2}\right)^{\rho - 1} \tag{9.2.6}$$

Substituting Equation (9.2.6) into the budget constraint $p_1 q_1 + p_2 q_2 - Y$, rearrange and have the Marshallian demand function for the commodities:

$$q_i = \left(\frac{\alpha_i}{p_i}\right)^\varepsilon \frac{Y}{\alpha^\varepsilon p_1^{1-\varepsilon} + (1 - \alpha)^\varepsilon p_2^{1-\varepsilon}} \qquad (\alpha_1 = \alpha \quad \alpha_2 = 1 - \alpha) \tag{9.2.7}$$

Substituting the Marshallian demands into the utility function, we have the indirect utility function as follows:

$$V(p_1, p_2, Y) = [\alpha^\varepsilon p_1^{1-\varepsilon} + (1 - \alpha)^\varepsilon p_2^{1-\varepsilon}]^{\frac{1}{\varepsilon-1}} Y \tag{9.2.8}$$

The expenditure function is derived by converting indirect utility V to direct utility u, and income Y to expenditure e:

$$e(p_1, p_2, u) = [\alpha^\varepsilon p_1^{1-\varepsilon} + (1 - \alpha)^\varepsilon p_2^{1-\varepsilon}]^{\frac{1}{1-\varepsilon}} u \tag{9.2.9}$$

By Shepard's lemma, the Hicksian demand is

$$h_i(p_1, p_2, u) = \frac{\partial}{\partial p_i} e(p_1, p_2, u) = \left(\frac{\alpha_i}{p_i}\right)^\varepsilon [\alpha^\varepsilon p_1^{1-\varepsilon} + (1 - \alpha)^\varepsilon p_2^{1-\varepsilon}]^{\frac{\varepsilon}{1-\varepsilon}} u \tag{9.2.10}$$

$(\alpha_1 = \alpha \quad \alpha_2 = 1 - \alpha)$

The indirect utility, expenditure and Hicksian demand functions are useful in quantitatively evaluating the policies in CGE modeling.

If multiple consumption commodities share the same elasticity of substitution among them, the corresponding CES utility function is

$$u(q_1, \ldots, q_n) = \sum_i \alpha_i q_i^\rho \qquad \sum_i \alpha_i = 1 \qquad (9.2.11)$$

The derived Marshallian demand function for commodity i is

$$q_i = \left(\frac{\alpha_i}{p_i}\right)^\varepsilon \left(\sum_i \alpha_i^\varepsilon p_i^{1-\varepsilon}\right)^{-1} Y \qquad (9.2.12)$$

The indirect utility, expenditure and Hicksian demand functions of the multiple commodity CES function can be obtained easily by substituting $[\alpha^\varepsilon p_1^{1-\varepsilon} + (1-\alpha)^\varepsilon p_2^{1-\varepsilon}]$ with $\sum_i \alpha_i^\varepsilon p_i^{1-\varepsilon}$ into Equations (9.2.8)–(9.2.10).

The advantages of the CES family functions include (1) freely using various levels of the elasticity of substitution to characterize the relationships among commodities; and (2) requiring only the information about elasticity of substitution from external sources (other parameter values can be calibrated from the SAM table), which are readily available in existing literature like the GTAP publications.

9.3 Linear Expenditure System (LES)

A CES utility function is a homothetic function. Its elasticity of substitution remains constant regardless of the income levels. This property of homothetic functions is shown in Figure 9.3.1 along the ray labeled by "CES", which intersects all indifference curves at the same slope. So long as the commodity prices remain unchanged, the households would spend the same share of their income on each good, even if their income level increases. When income increases by one percent, the spending on each commodity increases exactly by one percent. In other words, the income elasticity of demand of each commodity equals one. This characteristic becomes a problem when we need to study the Engel curve effect, which hypothesizes that the proportions spent on commodities vary with income, for instance, the share of households' total expenditure spent on food is supposed to decline as income increases (Figure 9.3.1).

The linear expenditure system, abbreviated to LES, is a popular form used in econometrics and CGE modeling for demand functions. It can include many commodities in one single equation and can simulate the Engel curve effect. As its name implies, expenditure on commodity is in a linear relationship with prices and income:

$$p_i q_i = \beta_0 + \beta_1 p_1 + \beta_2 p_2 + \cdots + \beta_n p_n + \beta_{n+1} Y \qquad (9.3.1)$$

where β_i are parameters of positive real numbers.

LES system is derived from the Stone–Geary utility function. The original Stone–Geary utility function form is

$$u(\mathbf{q}) = \prod_{i=1}^n (q_i - \gamma_i)^{\beta_i} \qquad \beta_i > 0, \qquad q_i - \gamma_i > 0, \qquad \sum_{i=1}^n \beta_i = 1 \qquad (9.3.2)$$

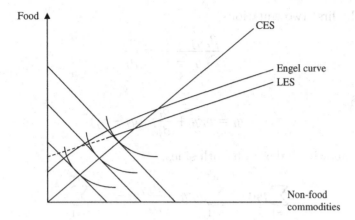

Figure 9.3.1. Share of income spend on various items under different demand functions.

Many people use its log form after a monotonic transformation:

$$u(\mathbf{q}) = \sum_{i=1}^{n} \beta_i \ln(q_i - \gamma_i) \qquad \beta_i > 0, \qquad q_i - \gamma_i > 0, \qquad \sum_{i=1}^{n} \beta_i = 1 \qquad (9.3.3)$$

It can be seen how the Stone–Geary function evolves from the Cobb–Douglas function. When $\gamma_i = 0$, it is the Cobb–Douglas function. The coefficient β_i is the budget share parameter, similar to α_i in the Cobb–Douglas utility function. The sum of the shares equals 1, $\sum_{i=1}^{n} \beta_i = 1$.

The difference is that the Stone–Geary utility function has added a fixed subsistence consumption level γ_i for every commodity i. This subsistence level γ_i can be thought as the minimum consumption required for survival. Consumption below the subsistence level is not sustainable for survival, hence no utility is defined. Only consumption beyond this subsistence level $q_i - \gamma_i$ generates utility. In Figure 9.3.1, this subsistence level "shifts up" the "LES" line of the food expenditure as the percentage of income, hence the new line, is flatter than a ray from the origin. It thus approximates the Engel curve shown in the figure. The following is the derivation of the LES function from the Stone–Geary utility function.

The household utility maximization problem is

$$\max \quad u(\mathbf{q}) = \sum_{i=1}^{n} \beta_i \ln(q_i - \gamma_i) \qquad \text{s.t.} \quad \sum_{i=1}^{n} p_i q_i = Y \qquad (9.3.4)$$

From the Lagrange function $L = \sum_{i}^{n} \beta_i \ln(q_i - \gamma_i) - \lambda(\sum p_i q_i - Y)$, we have the following first-order conditions:

$$\begin{cases} \dfrac{\partial L}{\partial q_i} = \beta_i \frac{1}{q_i - \gamma_i} - \lambda p_i = 0 \\[2mm] \dfrac{\partial L}{\partial q_j} = \beta_j \frac{1}{q_j - \gamma_j} - \lambda p_j = 0 \\[2mm] \displaystyle\sum_{i=1}^{n} p_i q_i = Y \end{cases} \qquad (9.3.5)$$

Combining the first two equations,

$$\frac{\beta_i}{\beta_j}\frac{q_j - \gamma_j}{q_i - \gamma_i} = \frac{p_i}{p_j} \tag{9.3.6}$$

Rearrange

$$p_i q_i = p_i \gamma_i + \frac{\beta_i}{\beta_j} p_j (q_j - \gamma_j) \tag{9.3.7}$$

summing the terms with index i on both sides,

$$\sum_{i=1}^{n} p_i q_i = \sum_{i=1}^{n} p_i \gamma_i + \frac{p_j}{\beta_j}(q_j - \gamma_j)\sum_{i=1}^{n}\beta_i \tag{9.3.8}$$

Because $\sum_{i=1}^{n}\beta_i = 1$ and $\sum_{i=1}^{n}p_i q_i = Y$, we have

$$Y = \sum_{i=1}^{n} p_i \gamma_i + \frac{p_j}{\beta_j}(q_j - \gamma_j) \tag{9.3.9}$$

This leads to the function for expenditure on commodity j,

$$p_j q_j = \beta_j Y - \beta_j \sum_i p_i \gamma_i + p_j \gamma_j = p_j \gamma_j + \beta_j \left(Y - \underbrace{\sum_i p_i \gamma_i}_{\text{Spending on subsistence}} \right) \tag{9.3.10}$$

"Supernumerary" income

The Marshallian demand function for j is

$$q_j = \gamma_j + \frac{\beta_j}{p_j}\left(Y - \sum_i p_i \gamma_i \right) = \gamma_j - \frac{\beta_j}{p_j}\sum_i p_i \gamma_i + \frac{\beta_j}{p_j}Y \tag{9.3.11}$$

The parameters of the LES have the following interpretations:

β_j : is the marginal budget share spent on commodity j.
γ_j : is the subsistence consumption level of commodity j.

$Y - \sum_i p_i b_i$ is the discretionary budget after spending on subsistence amounts of commodities. It is called "discretionary income" or "supernumerary income"

$p_j q_j = (p_j \gamma_j - \beta_j \sum_i p_i \gamma_i) + \beta_i Y$ is actually an Engel curve. Its intercept[1] is $p_j \gamma_j - \beta_j \sum_i p_i \gamma_i$. Its slope is β_j — that is why β_j is called "marginal budget share", or "marginal expenditure/consumption share", which is interpreted as the incremental spending on j if income Y increases by one unit.

---

[1]The "intercept" used here is imaginary. Because any commodity quantity below the subsistence level is not defined in the Stone–Geary utility function, so it cannot have a real intercept on an axis.

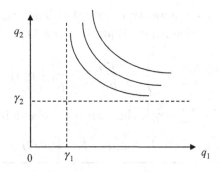

Figure 9.3.2. The indifference curve map of the Stone-Geary utility function.

Figure 9.3.2 shows the Stone-Geary indifference curve map for the LES function. The dashed lines are the subsistence amounts of commodities γ_1 and γ_2. Below the dash lines, the utility is not defined so there are no indifference curves. In the region to the northeast of the dashed lines, the shape of the indifference curves resemble those under the Cobb–Douglas function.

To derive the indirect utility V, we use the original utility form of Equation (9.3.2), and substituting the Marshallian demand q_i:

$$V(\mathbf{q}) = \prod_{j=1}^{n} (q_j - \gamma_j)^{\beta_j} = \prod_{j=1}^{n} \left[\frac{\beta_j}{p_j} \left(Y - \sum_i p_i \gamma_i \right) \right]^{\beta_j} \tag{9.3.12}$$

$$= \prod_{j=1}^{n} \left(\frac{\beta_j}{p_j} \right)^{\beta_j} \left[\prod_j^n (Y - \sum_i p_i \gamma_i)^{\beta_j} \right]$$

Because $\sum_j \beta_j = 1$, the last product term in square brackets is simplified to $(Y - \sum_i p_i \gamma_i)$. Then the indirect utility for the LES function is

$$V(\mathbf{q}) = \prod_{j=1}^{n} \left(\frac{\beta_j}{p_j} \right)^{\beta_j} \left(Y - \sum_i p_i \gamma_i \right) \tag{9.3.13}$$

Replacing V with u and Y with e, we have the following expenditure function. It is useful for policy assessment in CGE modeling.

$$e(\mathbf{p}, u) = \sum_i p_i \gamma_i + u \prod_j [p_j / \beta_j]^{\beta_j} \tag{9.3.14}$$

9.4 Properties of the LES Demand Function and Calibrating Parameters

The LES has some advantages over the CES family function. It can simulate the Engel curve. It can include many commodity variables in one equation. The function form is linear and simple. Yet it has some limitations which one needs to be aware of in application.

First, all commodities in the LES function must be "normal goods". None of them can be an inferior good. This is because $\beta_i > 0$, hence $dq_i / dY > 0$.

Secondly, demand for any commodity is inelastic. That is, price elasticity of demand is restricted to be less than 1. Differentiate Equation (9.3.11) with respect to its own price:

$$\frac{dq_j}{dp_j} = -\frac{\beta_j}{p_j^2}\left(Y - \sum_i p_i\gamma_i\right) - \frac{\beta_j\gamma_j}{p_j} = -\frac{\beta_j}{p_j^2}\left(p_j\gamma_j + \left(Y - \sum_i p_i\gamma_i\right)\right) \qquad (9.4.1)$$

Because $p_jq_j = p_j\gamma_j + \beta_j(Y - \sum_i p_i\gamma_i)$, the own price elasticity of demand e_{jj} is

$$e_{jj} = -\frac{dq_j}{dp_j}\frac{p_j}{q_j} = \frac{\beta_j(p_j\gamma_j + Y - \sum_i p_i\gamma_i)}{p_jq_j} = \frac{\beta_jp_j\gamma_j + \beta_j(Y - \sum_i p_i\gamma_i)}{p_j\gamma_j + \beta_j(Y - \sum_i p_i\gamma_i)} < 1 \qquad (9.4.2)$$

This is not desirable for study on a commodity whose demand is price elastic, such as the tourism sector.

Thirdly, any commodity must be a complement of other commodities, because the cross-price elasticity among any pair of the commodities in the LES system is always negative:

$$\frac{\partial q_j}{\partial p_i}\frac{p_i}{q_j} = -\frac{\beta_j\gamma_i}{p_j}\frac{p_i}{q_j} < 0 \qquad \forall i; \forall j \qquad (9.4.3)$$

Hence, by definition of microeconomics, commodities j and i are complements. Thus, in CGE modeling when a substitute case is important for research, the LES function is not a proper candidate for the demand function.

To calibrate the parameters of the LES function, we need some external information in addition to the SAM table data. From the SAM table, we calculate the average budget share spent on commodity j, denoted by s_j as follows:

$$s_j = \frac{p_jq_j}{Y} \qquad (9.4.4)$$

From Equation (9.3.10), the marginal budget share β_j is

$$\beta_j = d(p_jq_j)/dY \qquad (9.4.5)$$

The income elasticity of expenditure of the Engel curve e_j is defined as

$$e_j \equiv \frac{d(p_jq_j)}{p_jq_j} \Big/ \frac{dY}{Y} = \frac{d(p_jq_j)}{dY}\frac{Y}{p_jq_j} = \beta_j/s_j \qquad (9.4.6)$$

If the income elasticity of expenditure e_j is known, the marginal budget share can be calibrated as follows:

$$\beta_j = e_js_j \qquad (9.4.7)$$

The information of income elasticity of expenditure e_j is widely available in economics literature. In CGE modeling, most researchers obtain this information from existing data or references. Yet we will often encounter one problem. Individual values of e_j are often obtained from difference sources. After we calculate the β_j according to Equation (9.4.7), the sum of β_j normally does not meet the theoretical constraint $\sum_j \beta_j = 1$. To deal with the problem, we adopt various approaches to adjust (or "balance") the β_j values. One approach is treating some elasticities as residuals to be freely adjusted. Another approach is to scale up or down the whole set of β_j values by the same proportion to make the sum be unity. These methods will be further discussed later.

Data about the subsistence consumption level in each commodity γ_j is not readily available. Instead, in CGE modeling, scholars use "Frisch parameter" to derive γ_j. The original Frisch coefficient is "income elasticity of marginal utility", yet the popular definition for Frisch parameter in CGE literature is a variation with a negative sign. This Frisch parameter is defined as $\varphi \equiv -\frac{dV/V}{dY/Y}$. The Frisch parameter for the LES function can be derived from indirect utility function of Equation (9.3.13):

$$\varphi = -\frac{dV}{dY}\frac{Y}{V} = -\frac{Y}{Y - \sum_i p_i \gamma_i} \tag{9.4.8}$$

which simply is the ratio of total income to supernumerary income, plus a negative sign. This form is not easily interpretable, as compared with an alternative concept by using its reciprocal and removing the negative sign:

$$\tilde{\varphi} = \frac{Y - \sum_i p_i \gamma_i}{Y} \tag{9.4.9}$$

It is simply the supernumerary portion of the total income, which is a straightforward concept in theoretical discussion. In this book, we follow the popular definition of Equation (9.4.8), but readers may use the alternative concept to help interpretation.

It can be seen that the value of the Frisch parameter φ should be in the range of $(-\infty, -1)$. In an economy, for the richer households who have more supernumerary income for discretionary spending, their Frisch parameter would be smaller in magnitude. For the poorer households, as they have to spend a larger portion of income on necessities, the magnitude of the Frisch parameter would be larger. Suppose the 90% of the rich group income is supernumerary, then we can infer their Frisch number is $\varphi = -1/0.9 = -1.1$. If the very poor group spends 90% of their income on necessities (subsistence level), their supernumerary income accounts only 10% of their total income. Then their Frisch number is $\varphi = -1/(1 - 0.9) = -10$. There are numerous Frisch parameter estimates available in literature, which can be searched and used for research. Table 9.4.1 is the rough numbers collected online. The very original sources cannot be identified, they are provided here only for illustration purposes.

With the Frisch parameter, the subsistence consumption γ_j can be calibrated. From Equation (9.4.8), we have $Y - \sum_i p_i \gamma_i = -Y/\varphi$. Substituting it into the Marshallian demand function (9.3.11), γ_j can be derived by the following formula:

$$\gamma_j = q_j - \frac{\beta_j}{p_j}\left(Y - \sum_i p_i \gamma_i\right) = q_j + \frac{\beta_j}{p_j}\frac{Y}{\varphi} \tag{9.4.10}$$

In calibrating parameters of the LES function, the condition of $\sum_j \beta_j = 1$ needs to be checked. Based on the theory, all marginal budget shares should add up to unity, so

Table 9.4.1.   Frisch parameter values for different income groups.

Household income level	Frisch parameter φ value
Very poor	−10
Low income	−4
Middle income	−2
Upper middle income	−1.5
Rich	−1.2

$\sum_j \beta_j = 1$. Yet in practice, because the data of income elasticities of expenditure of various commodities often come from various sources with various definitions, they in general would not add to 1. Hence, the raw parameter values need to be adjusted to satisfy the theoretical requirement. If some commodities have no elasticity data and the values of their elasticities are not sensitive to our main research interests, we can treat their elasticity as the residual. To illustrate, say commodity k has no elasticity information thus no β_k value can be directly calibrated, we take the elasticity of commodity k as the residual, by using the following formula to determine β_k:

$$\beta_k = 1 - \sum_{j,j \neq k}^{n-1} \beta_j \qquad (9.4.11)$$

If all commodities have their elasticity data, we can scale up and down their values by the same proportion so the new values sum to 1. Suppose we have commodities $j = 1, \ldots, n$. Let the raw data of income elasticity of expenditure be denoted by e_j^0. Then $\beta_j^0 = e_j^0 \cdot s_j$. If $\sum_j^n \beta_j^0 \neq 1$, we use the following scale-up formula to adjust:

$$\beta_j^1 = \beta_j^0 \Big/ \sum_i^n \beta_i^0 = (e_j^0 \cdot s_j) \Big/ \left(\sum_i^n e_i^0 \cdot s_i \right) \qquad (9.4.12)$$

the new beta values are normalized to $\sum_j \beta_j^1 = 1$.

9.5 Translog Functions

When the research interest of a CGE model has to be related to the substitutability among commodities, the LES function is not appropriate because it requires that all commodities must be complements. We need to use some functions with flexibility in the substitutability. In addition to the CES functions, the translog family functions are good candidates to accomplish the job.

There are other flexible demand functions, including AIDS, CDE, etc., in empirical studies; in theory they can also be candidates for researches on commodity substitutabilities. Yet there is a tradeoff. When a demand function form becomes more complicated, it would need more external information for the parameters, and need more work to calibrate and balance the parameters. Further, when the function structure becomes more complicated and non-linear, in general the solved outcomes are more sensitive to data errors, thus are not robust. After all, there are no perfect utility or demand functions that can capture all details of human preferences and behaviors. Hence, unless necessary for the research, we should adopt a simpler function form.

The translog functions, abbreviated as the TL functions, are used in empirical studies and CGE modeling. The advantages of translog functions are flexible and relatively simple for handling multi-commodities under one equation. Different pairs of the commodities can have different cross-price elasticities. The basic form in this family is the homothetic translog function, or HTL function (Pollack and Wales, 1992). The HTL indirect utility function is

$$V(\mathbf{p}, Y) = \ln Y - \sum_i \beta_i \ln p_i - \frac{1}{2} \sum_j \sum_i \lambda_{ij} \ln p_i \ln p_j \qquad (9.5.1)$$

$$\text{s.t.} \quad \lambda_{ij} = \lambda_{ji} \quad \forall i, j; \quad \sum_i \lambda_{ij} = 0; \quad \sum_\iota \beta_i = 1$$

The constraints in the above system are set up to satisfy the theoretical requirement: $\lambda_{ij} = \lambda_{ji}$ because the cross-price elasticities are symmetric; $\sum_i \lambda_{ij} = 0$ so the function is homogeneous of degree 0 in price vector $\mathbf{p}$ and monetary income Y; and $\sum_i \beta_i = 1$, because the shares of spending in all commodities should sum to one.

By Roy's identity, the Marshallian demand for commodity i is:

$$q_i = -\frac{\partial V / \partial p_i}{\partial V / \partial Y} = \underbrace{\frac{\beta_i Y}{p_i}}_{\text{Cobb--Douglas part}} + \frac{Y}{p_i} \sum_j \lambda_{ij} \ln p_j \qquad (9.5.2)$$

Then, the average budget share of income spent on commodity i is

$$s_i \equiv \frac{p_i q_i}{Y} = \beta_i + \sum_j \lambda_{ij} \ln p_j \qquad (9.5.3)$$

When prices are normalized to one, the last term of the above equation drops to zero, so $\beta_i = p_i q_i / Y$. Hence parameter β_i is the income share spent on commodity i. It can be calibrated from the SAM data directly.

It can be seen that the first part of the above Marshallian demand Equation (9.5.2) is the Cobb–Douglas part, which is independent of other commodity prices. The second part adds the impacts from other prices on the demand for commodity i. If $\lambda_{ij} > 0$, commodity j is a substitute of commodity i. If $\lambda_{ij} < 0$, commodities j and i are complements. λ_{ij} can be interpreted as the cross-price elasticity of expenditure share spent on i:

$$\frac{d(p_i q_i) / Y}{d p_j / p_j} = \frac{d(p_i q_i / Y)}{d \ln p_j} = \lambda_{ij} \qquad (9.5.4)$$

Intuitively, it is the percentage change in the income share spent on commodity i if the price of commodity j increases by one percent. The λ_{ij} values must be provided externally for CGE modeling. They may be collected from available data or be estimated from some sampling data or other sources. If some λ_{ij} values are not directly available and based on theory we consider that the corresponding cross-prices do not impact the demand that much, these λ_{ij} can be set to zero. This is a practical simplification when the number of commodities is getting very large and many λ_{ij} values are trivial.

After the raw data for the parameters are obtained, we need to adjust their values by using Excel or writing a separate GAMS program to satisfy the theoretical requirement: $\lambda_{ij} = \lambda_{ji} \forall i, j; \sum_i \lambda_{ij} = 0; \sum_i \beta_i = 1$. The balancing can be done by the least squares approach, or other techniques similar to those of balancing the SAM table in Chapter 5.

The expenditure function is directly derived from the HTL indirect utility function:

$$\ln e = \ln u + \sum_i \beta_i \ln p_i + \frac{1}{2} \sum_j \sum_i \lambda_{ij} \ln p_i \ln p_j \tag{9.5.5}$$

9.6 Linear TL Function

The limitation of the above homothetic translog (HTL) function is that the consumption share on each commodity is independent of income level, hence the HTL function cannot capture the Engel effect. A variation in the TL function family called the linear translog function, abbreviated as the LTL function, can simulate the Engel curve effect. The LTL function is a combination of the HTL function and the LES function. Its indirect utility function is

$$V(\mathbf{p}, Y) = \ln(Y - \sum p_i \gamma_i) - \sum \beta_i \ln p_i - \frac{1}{2} \sum_i \sum_j \lambda_{ij} \ln p_i \ln p_j \tag{9.6.1}$$

$$s.t. \quad \lambda_{ij} = \lambda_{ji} \qquad \sum_i \lambda_{ij} = 0 \qquad \sum \beta_i = 1$$

where parameters β_i and λ_{ij} are the same concepts as those in the HTL function. Parameter γ_i is the subsistence consumption level of commodity i, the same concept in the LES function. Its mathematical role in the function is the same: it adds a "vertical intercept" of the consumption expansion path in the indifference curve map, so as to approximate the Engel curve. The Marshallian demand for commodity i is

$$q_i(\mathbf{p}, Y) = \underbrace{\gamma_i}_{\text{Subsistence}} + \underbrace{\frac{1}{p_i}[\beta_i + \sum_j \lambda_{ij} \ln p_j]}_{\text{Similar to HTL}} \underbrace{[Y - \sum_j p_j \gamma_j]}_{\text{Supernumerary income}} \tag{9.6.2}$$

This demand function includes some typical demand functions as its components. When $\lambda_{ij} = 0$, it is the LES function:

$$q_i(\mathbf{p}, Y) = \gamma_i + \frac{1}{p_i}\left[\beta_i + \sum_j \lambda_{ij} \ln p_j\right]\left[Y - \sum_j p_j \gamma_j\right] = \gamma_i + \frac{\beta_i}{p_i}\left(Y - \sum_j p_j \gamma_j\right) \tag{9.6.3}$$

If further $\gamma_i = 0$, it is an HTL function. If both $\gamma_i = 0$ and $\lambda_{ij} = 0$, it is a Cobb–Douglas function: $q_i(\mathbf{p}, Y) = \frac{\beta_i}{p_i} Y$.

The expenditure share of i (the income share spent on i) of the LTL function is

$$s_i \equiv \frac{p_i q_i}{Y} = \frac{p_i \gamma_i}{Y} + \left[\beta_i + \sum_j \lambda_{ij} \ln p_j\right]\left[1 - \frac{1}{Y}\sum_j p_j \gamma_j\right] \qquad (9.6.4)$$

In CGE models, the Marshallian demand Equation (9.6.2) or the expenditure share Equation (9.6.4) can be used for commodity demand functions. The LTL function is flexible and powerful, but it has more parameters which need external data and additional calibration work. In what follows, we discuss this issue. Note the following Equation (9.6.5) includes simplifications. It is used only for parameter calibration but not for the system equations in the model.

In calibration, for simplicity, the Frisch parameter φ is assumed to be a constant, thus the supernumerary income share $[1 - \frac{1}{Y}\sum_j p_j \gamma_j]$ is fixed. We differentiate the share Equation (9.6.4) only with respect to $\ln(p_k)$ and have the cross-price elasticity of expenditure:

$$e_{ik} \equiv \frac{d(p_i q_i)/Y}{dp_k/p_k} = \frac{d(p_i q_i/Y)}{d \ln p_k} = \lambda_{ik}\left[1 - \frac{1}{Y}\sum_j p_j \gamma_j\right] \qquad (9.6.5)$$

To calibrate the λ_{ik} values, in practice we often first obtain the data for e_{ik} and Frisch parameter φ, by relationship $Y - \sum_i p_i \gamma_i = -Y/\varphi$, λ_{ik} then can be calibrated by

$$\lambda_{ik} = -e_{ik}\varphi \qquad (9.6.6)$$

Equation (9.6.2) can be rearranged to

$$p_i q_i = p_i \gamma_i - \left[\beta_i + \sum_j \lambda_{ij} \ln p_j\right]\frac{Y}{\varphi} \qquad (9.6.7)$$

In calibration of parameters, because the prices are normalized to one, the last term in brackets in the above equation drops out, thus the above equation is simplified to

$$p_i q_i = p_i \gamma_i - \beta_i \frac{Y}{\varphi} \qquad (9.6.8)$$

To calibrate parameter β_j, in practice we first obtain the income elasticity of expenditure e_j, which is defined and computed as

$$e_j \equiv \frac{d(p_j q_j)}{p_j q_j}\Big/\frac{dY}{Y} = \frac{d(p_j q_j)}{dY}\frac{Y}{p_j q_j} = -\frac{\beta_j}{\varphi}\frac{1}{s_j} \qquad (9.6.9)$$

Then marginal budget share β_j is calibrated by

$$\beta_j = -e_j s_j \varphi \qquad (9.6.10)$$

The subsistence consumption level can be calibrated by

$$\gamma_i = q_i + \frac{\beta_i}{p_i}\frac{Y}{\varphi} \qquad (9.6.11)$$

In addition, we need to adjust and balance the parameters according to the following theoretical constraints before using them in the CGE model execution.

$$\lambda_{ij} = \lambda_{ji} \qquad \sum_i \lambda_{ij} = 0 \qquad \sum \beta_i = 1 \qquad (9.6.12)$$

If the above conditions are not met, the results from the CGE model, in particular, the simulation results, would not be consistent with the predictions based on economics theory. For instance, demands for commodities are no longer homogenous of degree 0 in prices and income, which violates the theoretical expectation.

9.7 Using Various Demand Functions in CGE Models

The CGE model examples in Chapter 8 use the fixed-share demand functions derived from the Cobb–Douglas utility function. We can replace it with other demand functions in the model for research needs. In general, changes to more flexible demand functions such as LES or LTL functions do not involve a lot of work in the system equations in CGE models, but it can add many additional works in parameter calibration and balancing. Many researchers set up independent programs to first calibrate and balance the parameters, then let the CGE model input the calibrated parameter values.

The following is a CGE model example. It is the same model as in Section 8.2, except the household demand function is replaced by an LTL function.

$$A_c[\delta_c L_c^{\rho_c} + (1 - \delta_c) K_c^{\rho_c}]^{1/\rho_c} = q_c \qquad c \in C \qquad (9.7.1)$$

$$\frac{w_l}{w_k} = \frac{\delta_c}{(1 - \delta_c)} \left(\frac{L_c}{K_c}\right)^{\rho_c - 1} \qquad c \in C \qquad (9.7.2)$$

$$p_c q_c = w_l L_c + w_k K_c \qquad c \in C \qquad (9.7.3)$$

$$w_l L^s + w_k K^s = Y \qquad (9.7.4)$$

The original fixed-share demand function is replaced by the Marshallian demand from the LTL function:

$$p_c q_c^h = p_c \gamma_c + \left[\beta_c + \sum_{c'} \lambda_{cc'} \ln p_{c'}\right]\left[Y - \sum_{c'} p_{c'} \gamma_{c'}\right] \qquad c \in C; \quad c' \in C \qquad (9.7.5)$$

The market clearing equations are still the same:

$$q_c^h = q_c \qquad c \in C \qquad (9.7.6)$$

$$\sum_c K_c = K^s \qquad (9.7.7)$$

$$\sum_c L_c = L^s \qquad (9.7.8)$$

Comparing it with the model in Section 8.2, the only equation changed is Equation (9.7.5).

9.8 GAMS Program with the LES Demand Function

Here we use the LES system for the household demand function to set up a CGE model, and write the corresponding GAMS program.

Example 9.8.1 A model economy has only three commodity sectors: agriculture, industry and service. Households spend all their income on commodity consumption. Household demand function is characterized by the LES. From the SAM table, the expenditure on each commodity respectively is as follows: $p_1q_1 = 500$, $p_2q_2 = 450$, $p_3q_3 = 350$. From external data sources we obtain the following parameter values: Frisch parameter $\varphi = -2$, income elasticity of expenditure e_j are 0.5, 1.0 and 1.2 for agriculture, industry and service commodities, respectively.

1. Write the GAMS program to calibrate the parameters of the LES system. Check the calibrated values by replication.
2. Suppose the household income increases by 20%, find the changes in the demands by simulation.
3. Suppose further all commodity prices increase by 20%. Because the demand function is homogeneous of degree zero in prices and income, we expect the quantities demanded should return to the original levels. Display the results and see if they are consistent with the prediction.

Solution: The GAMS program is presented in what follows. Readers can compare the program sentences to the equations of Section 9.4, in particular, the equations of calibrating the β_i values and adjusting β_i values by a scale factor to satisfy the constraint for the sum value.

```
$title   Example 9.8.1 LES parameter calibration and verification

*Three commodity sectors
set C  /agri,manu,serv/;
set inst  institution which is households     /hh/;

alias (c,cp);

table sam(c,inst)     Household expenditure on commodities
          hh
agri      500
manu      450
serv      350
;

*Input LES elasticity and Frisch parameters
parameter  LESelas(c)  /agri  0.5,     manu  1.0,     serv  1.2 /
           Frisch      /-2/;
```

```
parameters
PC0(c)          Price of commodity c
QH0(c)          Quantity demanded for c by households
EH0             Total expenditure by households
bgtshare(c)     Average budget share on c in the LES function
bgtsharechk1    Check if average budget share sum is 1
LESbeta(c)      Marginal budget share of LES
LESbetachk1     Check if the marginal budget share beta sum is 1
LESsub(c)       Subsistence consumption level of c of LES
;

PC0(c)=1;
QH0(c)=sam(c,'hh')/PC0(c);
EH0=sum(c,PC0(c)*QH0(c));
bgtshare(c)=SAM(c,'hh')/EH0;
bgtsharechk1=sum(c,bgtshare(c));
*Below calibrating marginal expenditure beta parameter of LES and scaling up beta
value to satisfy sum equal 1 condition
LESbeta(c)=LESelas(c)*bgtshare(c)/(sum(cp,LESelas(cp)*bgtshare(cp)));
LESbetachk1=sum(c,LESbeta(c));
*Below calibrating the subsistence levels
LESsub(c)=sam(c,'hh')+(LESbeta(c)/PC0(c))*(EH0/Frisch);

display
frisch,PC0,QH0,EH0,bgtshare,bgtsharechk1,LESbeta,LESbetachk1,LESsub,LESelas;

variable
PC(c),QH(c),EH;

equation
QHeq(c);

QHeq(c)..
PC(c)*QH(c)=e=PC(c)*LESsub(c)+LESbeta(c)*(EH-sum(cp,PC(cp)*LESsub(cp)));

PC.fx(c)=PC0(c);
QH.L(c)=QH0(c);
EH.fx=EH0;

model LES  /all/;
solve LES using mcp;

*Display outcome for checking
display PC.L,QH.L,EH.L;

*Simulation for 20% increase in income EH
EH.fx=EH0*1.2;
```

```
model sim1  /all/;
solve sim1 using mcp;
display PC.L,QH.L,EH.L;

*Simulation for 20% increase in prices
*If the results are the same as the original one, it means that the function is
homogeneous of degree 0 in income and prices
PC.fx(c)=PC0(c)*1.2;

model sim2  /all/;
solve sim2 using mcp;
display PC.L,QH.L,EH.L;

*End
```

Exercises

9E.1 A model economy has three commodity sectors: agriculture, industry and service. The commodity consumption data from the SAM table are $p_1 q_1 = 500$, $p_2 q_2 = 550$, $p_3 q_3 = 450$ where index 1, 2 and 3 denote agriculture, industry and service sectors, respectively. Households spend all their income on the commodity consumption. The utility function is a CES function with a common elasticity of substitution of 0.3 between any pair of commodities. Write a GAMS program to calibrate the other parameters of the CES utility function.

9E.2 Unlike the case of the CES production function in Chapter 7, the above Question 9.1 does not need to calibrate the scale factor A value in the CES production function. Why?

9E.3 Suppose a model economy has three commodity sectors: agriculture, industry and service. The commodity consumption data from the SAM table are $p_1 q_1 = 500$, $p_2 q_2 = 550$, $p_3 q_3 = 450$ where index 1, 2 and 3 refer to agriculture, industry and service sectors, respectively. Households spend all their income on commodities. Their demand for commodities is characterized by an LES demand function. We also know that the Frisch parameter is -3, and the income elasticities e_j are 0.4, 1.2 and 1.5 for commodities 1, 2 and 3. Write a GAMS program to calibrate the parameters of the LES function. Check the parameters and conform if they sum to one. Further, assume the household income increases by 10%, find the impacts on the demands for the commodities.

Appendix: Review of Microeconomics

9A.1 Deriving the expenditure function from the Stoney–Geary utility function

Using the original Stone–Geary utility function form

$$u(\mathbf{q}) = \prod_{i=1}^{n} (q_i - \gamma_i)^{\beta_i}. \tag{9A.1.1}$$

The Lagrange function to minimize expenditure subject to the utility level of u is

$$L = \sum_i p_i q_i - \lambda \left[\prod_j (q_j - \gamma_j)^{\beta_j} - u \right] \tag{9A.1.2}$$

Obtain the first-order conditions, then substitute into u:

$$p_i - \lambda \beta_i (q_i - \gamma_i)^{-1} \prod_j (q_j - \gamma_j)^{\beta_j} = p_i - \lambda \beta_i (q_i - \gamma_i)^{-1} u = 0 \quad i = 1, \dots, n \tag{9A.1.3}$$

So we have,

$$\lambda u = \frac{p_i}{\beta_i} (q_i - \gamma_i) \qquad i = 1, \dots, n \tag{9A.1.4}$$

Because λu is independent of i,

$$q_j - \gamma_j = \frac{p_i}{\beta_i} (q_i - \gamma_i) \frac{\beta_j}{p_j} \qquad j = 1, \dots, n \tag{9A.1.5}$$

Substitute to the utility function 9.A.1:

$$u = \prod_j (q_j - \gamma_j)^{\beta_j} = \prod_j \left[\frac{p_i}{\beta_i} (q_i - \gamma_i) \frac{\beta_j}{p_j} \right]^{\beta_j} = \prod_j \left[\frac{p_i}{\beta_i} (q_i - \gamma_i) \right]^{\beta_j} \prod_j \left[\frac{\beta_j}{p_j} \right]^{\beta_j}$$

$$= \frac{p_i}{\beta_i} (q_i - \gamma_i) \prod_j \left[\frac{\beta_j}{p_j} \right]^{\beta_j} \tag{9A.1.6}$$

The last step of the above equation is due to the fact that $\sum_j \beta_j = 1$. This gives

$$p_i q_i = p_i \gamma_i + u \beta_i \prod_j [p_j / \beta_j]^{\beta_j} \tag{9A.1.7}$$

Summing the above equation, we have the expenditure function:

$$e(\mathbf{p}, u) = \sum_i p_i q_i = \sum_i p_i \gamma_i + u \prod_j [p_j / \beta_j]^{\beta_j} \tag{9A.1.8}$$

Chapter 10

Price Numeraire and Macro Closures

10.1 Price Numeraire

As discussed in Section 6.4, the equilibrium quantities in the Walrasian equilibrium models are homogenous of degree zero in prices. That is, if we change all prices — factor prices and commodity prices — by the same proportion, the model is still balanced and the equilibrium quantities remain unchanged. Further, because of Walras's law, the market clearing equations in an economy are linearly dependent. If the economy has n markets, we have only $n-1$ independent equations. We cannot uniquely determine the values of all n prices but can only determine $n-1$ price ratios. The equilibrium prices we solved in the previous CGE models in this book are not unique. It is only one of an infinite number of possible price solution sets. This could cause problems when we need to study the individual price levels by an external shock in CGE models.

To deal with this problem, we can set up a price numeraire which would be used as the benchmark for other prices in the economy. Then all other prices would have their own unique values as compared with the benchmark price. Theoretically, we may arbitrarily choose the price of any factor or commodity as the numeraire. In the practice of CGE modeling, however, we often choose the price of a basic and broadly used factor or input such as labor as the numeraire.

The numeraire price is a constant. It is commonly set to 1 in simple CGE models, although it can be other positive numbers. In GAMS programming, the numeraire is a parameter. Alternatively, if the would-be numeraire is previously defined as a variable in the GAMS program, we can add a suffix ".fx" to the variable name to fix its value, thus practically converting the price variable to a parameter. For instance, if the labor price was a variable with variable name and suffix WL.L in the GAMS program, now we choose labor to be the numeraire, we can write "WL.fx=1" in the program to fix the labor price to 1.

After converting the numeraire price from a variable to a constant, the total number of variables is reduced to $n-1$, but we still have n equations in the model system. GAMS solvers such as MCP (mixed complementarity problems) require the system to be square, which means that the numbers of variables and equations are equal. If the condition is violated, the solvers would stop execution and issue an error message. There are several approaches to deal with this problem.

Supposing in a model with n equations, we choose labor price as numeraire, so $WL = 1$. The first approach is deleting a market clearing equation. It can be any market clearing equation, but it would be convenient to pick up the equation that directly involves the numeraire factor/commodity in the model. For instance, if labor price is chosen as the numeraire, we can delete the labor market clearing equation $QLD = QLS$. Then the number of equations reduces to $n - 1$. So there are $n - 1$ independent equations left with $n - 1$ variables, thus the system is square. This is a straightforward and simple way to solve the problem. To avoid possible confusion rising later on, in the GAMS program you should make a remark indicating which original equation is deleted and include in the remark the text of the original equation. In case in future for other research purposes you need to restore the equation, you can just copy it and paste.

The second approach is adding a dummy variable in a market clearing equation in the system. This dummy variable is named $WALRAS$ in many CGE models. For convenience, this dummy variable can be added in a market clearing equation that is related to the numeraire factor or commodity in the model. For instance, if labor is the numeraire, we add $WALRAS$ in the original labor market clearing equation $QLD = QLS$, so it becomes:

$$QLD = QLS + WALRAS \qquad (10.1.1)$$

Because of adding this dummy variable, the model has n variables again. With n equations and n variables, the system is square and GAMS solvers would not complain in searching for the optimal solution. As the search finally converges to the solution, the value of $WALRAS$ should be 0 or some value very close to zero, such as 1.2×10^{-10}. This verifies the expectation that the $WALRAS$ variable is actually "redundant" in terms of solved other quantities in the model. If, after running the model, the $WALRAS$ value is not zero, it indicates that the CGE model does not converge to the equilibrium solution and the outcomes are incorrect. The model needs to be fixed.

The third approach is using an NLP (non-linear programming) solver to do the job. The idea is to design an objective function to minimize the excess demands in markets in order to reach the equilibrium solution. Because all markets are related in the model system, we need to pick up only one market to minimize its excess demand, keeping other market clearing equations as constraints, to search for the model solution. Suppose labor is the numeraire, we can convert its market clearing equation to an objective function with an excess demand variable z. Our goal is to use the NLP command to minimize this excess demand z:

$$z = QLD - QLS \qquad (10.1.2)$$

subject to the constraints which are other equations in the model. After the solution is found, the value of z needs to be checked. This value should be close to zero. If not, the model has problems and needs to be fixed.

In general, the results from any of the above approaches are the same, or with small deviations if different solvers are used. In what follows, we use the CGE model of Example 8.2.1 to illustrate how to apply these alternative approaches.

First, we decide a numeraire. Suppose we choose the labor price as the numeraire. Then, in the GAMS program, we just change the suffix of the labor price variable from `WL.L` to `WL.fx`, to fix its value. That is, to change the code sentence from `WL.L=WL0` to `WL.fx=1`.

Next, we decide how to make the system square again. If using the first approach, we need to functionally delete the labor market clearing equation in the program: `Sum(c,LD(c))=e=LS`. In practice, we may just change this equation in the GAMS program to a text remark in the program by placing an "*" at the front. Note in the equation defining part, equation name "Leq" also needs to be deleted.

If using the second approach, we add a dummy variable *WALRAS* in the labor market equation, changing it to `Sum(c,QLD(c))=e=QLS+WALRAS`. By the end of the program, we add "`display WALRAS`" to check if the value of *WALRAS* is close to zero.

If using the third approach, in the program we first add a new variable z, then we convert the labor market equation to the objective function `z=e=Sum(c,QLD(c))-QLS`. Finally, we change the model solving execution command to: "`solve cge using nlp minimizing z`".

The exercise questions at the end of this chapter let readers practice the three alternative approaches to the GAMS model of Example 8.2.1. Readers can follow the above instructions to change the codes in the model and compare the outcomes.

10.2 Price Index as Numeraire

In the real world, economists use various price indices as economy-wide price indicators. A commonly used price indicator for the entire economy is GDP price index, or GDP deflator. In CGE models, we can also use the GDP price index as the numeraire. GDP price index is the quantity-weighted price of all final products produced in the economy. Let the quantities of final products (intermediate products are not included) be $QCFD_c$ where FD stands for "final demand". Let their prices be PC_c. From the SAM table the final product of each commodity $QCFD_c$ can be obtained by adding the numbers of final demands from households, enterprises, the government and the foreign sector. Then the quantity weights $gdpwt$ are

$$gdpwt_c = \frac{QCFD_c}{\sum\limits_{c' \in C} QCFD_{c'}} \tag{10.2.1}$$

The calculated $gdpwt$ weights are constants in the model. The GDP price index, denoted by $PGDP$, is a weighted price index calculated by

$$PGDP = \sum_{c \in C} PC_c \cdot gdpwt_c \tag{10.2.2}$$

The above calculated $PGDP$ can be used as the numeraire in the CGE model. In our simple model, for convenience $PGDP$ in the base state is set to 1:

$$PGDP = 1 \tag{10.2.3}$$

Then all other prices have their unique values determined against this benchmark *PGDP*. Note setting value to 1 is just for convenience, the value of *PGDP* can be exogenously changed. Because a CGE model is homogenous of degree 0 in prices, a change in the value of numeraire $PGDP$ leads to changes in all prices by the same proportion. A change in $PGDP$ is a change in the economy-wide price level, which is inflation or deflation in the economy. By using the GDP price index or other economy-wide price indices in CGE models, we can better simulate the real-world situation in measuring an external impact on the average price level. For instance, if there is a 30% increase in the oil price, we can inspect the resulting change in $PGDP$ to infer what the economy-wide inflation rate is, and to find the magnitude of the oil price increase against the general price level.

Because Equations (10.2.2) and (10.2.3) add one more constraint for the prices, the number of independent prices drops by 1. Then the system is no longer square. We can adopt one of the above three approaches to fix the squareness problem so the GAMS solver can search for the solution.

Another commonly used price indicator in the real world is Consumer Price Index (CPI). The weights of CPI are different from the GDP price index. CPI uses the consumption basket of a typical urban household as the weight. For ordinary households, CPI is a more relevant price index than the GDP price index. Changes in CPI impact directly on households' purchasing power. Many transfer payments to households, for instance social security payments, are indexed or partially indexed by CPI. Hence, many CGE models use CPI as the price index to study policy impacts on households' welfare.

Using CPI as the numeraire in the CGE model is similar to using the GDP price index. Let the amount of each commodity consumed by households be QH_c and price be PC_c. QH_c data can be obtained from the SAM table. Denote the CPI weights by *cpiwt* which is calculated by

$$cpiwt_c = \frac{QH_c}{\sum\limits_{c' \in C} QH_{c'}} \tag{10.2.4}$$

where QH_c must be fixed at the base period values. Then CPI is

$$CPI = \sum_{c \in C} PC_c \cdot cpiwt_c \tag{10.2.5}$$

Once Equation (10.2.5) is set up in the model, it reduces the independent prices to $n-1$. While all prices now can have unique values against CPI, we have to use one of the above three approaches to deal with the squareness issue to make the GAMS solver work.

10.3 Money and Neutrality

Money neutrality refers to the hypothesis that a change in money supply affects only nominal economic variables like prices and monetary income, with no effects on real variables such as quantities of commodities and factors, quantities supplied and demanded, in the economy. This hypothesis is consistent with the zero-degree homogeneity property in prices of a general equilibrium model.

Money in CGE models only serves as a medium of exchange and a unit of account. Apart from the monetary income received from economic activities directly and indirectly, monetary stock by itself is not a part of wealth of rational households or other economic agents/institutions in our CGE models. In this classical world, price numeraire serves both as the monetary unit and the proxy of the money stock. If we want to study how 30% increase in the money supply would affect the economy, we can simply raise the numeraire price by 30% in the CGE model and find the results.

To see why the numeraire can represent money stock in CGE models, we should understand the underlying assumptions in the classical economics world. Here money velocity V is assumed to be fixed. The real GDP output Y in the full employment state is not affected by changes in money supply. Then, by equation of exchange $MV = PY$, where M is the money stock and P is the numeraire, say the GDP price index, we have

$$P = \frac{V}{Y}M = vM \tag{10.3.1}$$

where v is a constant. Then a percentage change in price P is completely equal to that in money stock M. Because in CGE models we only measure the percentage changes in simulation, the numeraire price change can represent the money stock change in research. In addition, Equation (10.3.1) is consistent with the money neutrality hypothesis.

Some economists would argue that money neutrality may not hold, especially in the short-run because of various factors such as money illusion, paper money is viewed as wealth by households, households' consumption and saving pattern can change because of inflation, etc. Normally these factors are not important in CGE projects because scholars using CGE models are more interested in the real quantity changes in various national accounts through their inter-sectoral relationships. Yet if for some reasons these issues are important for a CGE project, they can still be included in the model by revising the specification of the household demand functions.

Strict money neutrality may not hold in CGE models, especially in a complicated model structure. In simulation of the real-world situation in those models, some nominal variables like prices, transfer payments and taxes may not change by the same proportion as the numeraire changes. Examples include: pension payment is not 100% indexed by inflation; parcel tax is a fixed tax; some transfer payment such as government's special subsidy to business is lump-sum; exchange rate is fixed in many countries thus the prices of the imports are rigid, etc. But these deviations do not carry big weights in the total national account transactions. If these cases are included in the CGE models, when we change the value of numeraire to test, we do not have the strict money neutrality, but we should still observe that resulting changes in nominal variables are close to the money-neutrality prediction. The small deviation does not alter our general conclusion about the money neutrality or homogeneity property of CGE models: in a CGE model with the classical economics environment (which is called "macroeconomic closure" in CGE literature), the homogeneity and money-neutrality properties largely should hold.

It is always useful to check the homogeneity property of the CGE models even though the GAMS program runs smoothly and finds the solution. A simple way to check is increasing the numeraire value by certain proportion such as 30%. When the results are not consistent with the prediction, such as, (1) the real quantities have changed rather than stay the same; or (2) the values of the nominal variables do not change by the same proportion, we should take a further look at the model. Normally, for a large and complicated CGE model with transfer payments, taxes and foreign trades, small deviations are possible because of the issues mentioned above. If instead the inconsistencies are substantial, the model is likely to have errors.

10.4 Macroeconomic Closures

The economic system, structure and environment in the real economic world vary across countries and time periods. They differ between developed and developing economies, differ between economic expansion and recession. The same economic variables can behave and perform substantially differently in different economic environments and structures. That is why we have different macroeconomic models including classical, Keynesian and neoclassical models, to simulate different situations. When we construct a CGE model to study the real-world issues, it is important to set up a right model structure that fits the situation. This model structure is termed "macroeconomic closure".

Initially, closure refers to the setup that the CGE model is completed and "closed" in terms of the circular flows of the economy, as discussed in Section 6.3. Now it is broadly used in the CGE literature to refer to the various environmental settings of CGE models including micro- or macro-economic environment, savings and investment relationship, exchange rate regimes, etc. In this chapter, "closure" refers to the macroeconomic closures, which is the fundamental setting between supply-driven classical and demand-driven Keynesian economics.

The structure to complete the circular flows of the economy can be different due to various environments, hence there can be different closures. Technically in CGE models, different closures mean different choices of endogenous and exogenous variables, and different system equations. The closure difference can be a modification within the same model, rather than rewriting the entire model. Sometimes a CGE model program may include several closure options for researchers to choose from and to compare. The outcomes from various closures in the same CGE model can be quite different. This is exactly what is observed in the real world: while the overall economic structure of the US has remained basically the same in the past 30 years, the macroeconomic environments and associated economic indicators like GDP and unemployment rates are quite different in the booming period of 1990s and the recessional period of 2008–2010.

In what follows, we use examples to illustrate major macroeconomic closures and their typical settings in CGE models. The classical or neoclassical macroeconomic closure is the most popular one used in CGE models. Our previous CGE models like those in Chapter 8 have the neoclassical closure. The neoclassical closure is based on the Walrasian equilibrium setting. Its basic characteristics are: factor and commodity prices are fully flexible and endogenously determined by the model system. Factors are fully employed. Factor endowments are exogenously determined.

Let us take a look at the CGE model in Section 8.4 and examine the setting of the neoclassical closure. In the model, commodity prices are all endogenous variables and flexible. The same is true for factors. Labor and capital prices, WL and WK, are endogenous variables and determined by the factor markets:

$$QLD(WL, WK, \mathbf{P}) = QLS(WL, WK, \mathbf{P}) \tag{10.4.1}$$

$$QKD(WL, WK, \mathbf{P}) = QKS(WL, WK, \mathbf{P}) \tag{10.4.2}$$

The above equations are the same as Equations (8.4.12) and (8.4.13). The full employment setup is represented by the equation that labor and capital supplies equal their endowments:

$$QLS(WL, WK, \mathbf{P}) = \overline{QLS} \tag{10.4.3}$$

$$QKS(WL, WK, \mathbf{P}) = \overline{QKS} \tag{10.4.4}$$

where $\overline{QLS}$ and $\overline{QKS}$ denote the corresponding factor endowments. These are Equations (8.4.14) and (8.4.15).

In addition, as discussed in Section 10.1, we need to set up the numeraire to improve the model. In theory, we can choose any commodity or factor price as numeraire, say, choose price of Commodity 1, adding the constraint of $PC_1 = 1$. Here let us use labor price as the numeraire, thus adding the following constraint:

$$WL = \overline{WL} = 1 \tag{10.4.5}$$

where bar "-" denotes a constant. Note the purpose of this equation is setting up a numeraire rather than fixing the labor price for economic reasons. After using the labor price as numeraire, the number of variables has reduced by 1. Hence, we need to use one of the three approaches to restore the squareness of the model. Let us use the approach of adding a dummy variable $WALRAS$:

$$QLS(WL, WK, \mathbf{P}) = \overline{QLS} + WALRAS \tag{10.4.6}$$

This equation represents the basic setting of the neoclassical macroeconomic closure. Additional equations can be added to adapt to the real-world situations for the research needs, but the above basic principle for the neoclassical closure is the same.

While the neoclassical closure is popular in CGE models, it has limitations. The real-world economy is often not a Walrasian type, hence the neoclassical closure may not be the right structure to simulate the economy. For instance, in economic recession, the economy may be in the Keynesian equilibrium state with high unemployment of factors. In a developing country with a dual sector structure, or in a transitional economy where the market price system is not fully developed, the assumptions of flexible prices and full factor employment of the neoclassical closure are not right. With the full employment assumption in the neoclassical closure, one cannot study changes in the nation-wide unemployment rate because the number of labor employed is already fixed. The only allowed changes in the labor market are the labor movement among the sectors rather than changes in the overall number.

10.5 The Keynesian Closure

If the economy to be studied in the CGE model is in recession as described by Keynes, then the neoclassical closure should not be used. Suppose we want to study which fiscal stimulus policy can increase employment in the labor market characterized by high unemployment, the full factor employment setting of the neoclassical closure would prevent us from doing any meaningful study. In the literature there are few CGE models having the Keynesian closure, but in reality the Keynesian recession is common. Hence, the Keynesian closure is useful and we will discuss its setting and programming.

According to the Keynesian theory, in economic recession many workers are unemployed and considerable amount of capital sits idle. Factor supplies are not constrained: quantities of factors effectively employed are variables determined by the demand side.

Further, factor prices, in particular the wage rate, are rigid downwards. These important features would characterize the Keynesian closure in the model. In a more comprehensive CGE model framework, additional details from the Keynesian model can be added, including the consumers' saving behavior, wealth effect, and business investment decision, etc.

To better illustrate, in what follows we present a general CGE model with various macroeconomic closure options. By changing the constraints in the model, we can have classical, Keynesian or other macroeconomic closures. This would help readers compare different closures by watching the changes in the constraint equations. This general CGE model is formed by the following system of Equations (10.5.1)–(10.5.14).

$$QC_c = \alpha_c^q [\delta_c^q QVA_c^{\rho_c} + (1 - \delta_c^q) QINTA_c^{\rho_c}]^{1/\rho_c} \qquad c \in C \qquad (10.5.1)$$

$$\frac{PVA_c}{PINTA_c} = \frac{\delta_c^q}{(1 - \delta_c^q)} \left(\frac{QVA_c}{QINTA_c} \right)^{\rho_c - 1} \qquad c \in C \qquad (10.5.2)$$

$$PC_c \cdot QC_c = PVA_c \cdot QVA_c + PINTA_c \cdot QINTA_c \qquad c \in C \qquad (10.5.3)$$

$$QVA_c = \alpha_c^{va} [\delta_c^{va} QLD_c^{\rho_c^{va}} + (1 - \delta_c^{va}) QKD_c^{\rho_c^{va}}]^{1/\rho_c^{va}} \qquad c \in C \qquad (10.5.4)$$

$$\frac{WL}{WK} = \frac{\delta_c^{va}}{(1 - \delta_c^{va})} \left(\frac{QLD_c}{QKD_c} \right)^{\rho_c^{va} - 1} \qquad c \in C \qquad (10.5.5)$$

$$PVA_c \cdot QVA_c = WL \cdot QLD_c + WK \cdot QKD_c \qquad c \in C \qquad (10.5.6)$$

$$QINT_{cc'} = ia_{cc'} \cdot QINTA_{c'} \qquad c \in C \quad c' \in C \qquad (10.5.7)$$

$$PINTA_{c'} = \sum_{c \in C} ia_{cc'} \cdot PC_c \qquad c' \in C \qquad (10.5.8)$$

$$YH = WL \cdot QLS + WK \cdot QKS \qquad (10.5.9)$$

$$PC_c \cdot QH_c = PC_c \cdot \gamma_c + \beta_c \left(YH - \sum_{c' \in C} PC_{c'} \cdot \gamma_{c'} \right) \qquad c \in C \qquad (10.5.10)$$

$$QC_c = \sum_{c' \in C} QINT_{cc'} + QH_c + WALRAS \qquad c \in C \qquad (10.5.11)$$

$$\sum_{c \in C} QLD_c = QLS \qquad (10.5.12)$$

$$\sum_{c \in C} QKD_c = QKS \qquad (10.5.13)$$

$$CPI = \sum_{c \in C} PC_c \cdot cpiwt_c \qquad (10.5.14)$$

It can be seen that the above model is similar to the previous CGE model of Equations (8.4.1)–(8.4.13). The variations include: (1) the household demand function changes from the fixed share function to the LES system; (2) dummy variable *WALRAS* is added in all commodity clearing equations rather than adding in the labor market clearing equation. The reason will be explained later; and (3) using CPI as the numeraire. *cpiwt* is a parameter which can be calibrated from the SAM data. In this simple model, only households are the final product users, so in fact households' total consumption is GDP, and CPI is equivalent to *PGDP*. *cpiwt* values are calibrated as follows:

$$cpiwt_c = \frac{QH_c^0}{\sum_{c'} QH_{c'}^0} \qquad c \in C \qquad (10.5.15)$$

where superscripts 0 denote the data values from the SAM table. *cpiwt* are parameters and they remain fixed in the model.

The model consists of (10.5.1)–(10.5.14), a total of 14 equation groups. It has 17 variable groups. The variables are: QC_c, QVA_c, $QINTA_c$, $QINT_{cc'}$, QLD_c, QKD_c, QLS, QKS, YH, QH_c, PC_c, PVA_c, $PINTA_c$, WL, WK, CPI, $WALRAS$. We need to add three additional constraints on the variable groups to convert them to parameters, so we can satisfy the system squareness condition.

If a neoclassical closure is chosen, we would add the following three additional constraints, where $\overline{QLS}$ and $\overline{QKS}$ are corresponding factor endowments, exogenously determined:

$$QLS = \overline{QLS} \qquad (10.5.16)$$

$$QKS = \overline{QKS} \qquad (10.5.17)$$

$$CPI = \overline{CPI} = 1 \qquad (10.5.18)$$

If a Keynesian closure is chosen, what would be the constraints? In the Keynesian state, there exists unemployment of labor and capital, therefore, the effective supplies of factors fall below factor endowment. The full employment setting for the neoclassical closure Equations (10.5.16) and (10.5.17) is not proper in this state. Instead, the factor quantities demanded and supplied, QLD, QLS, QKD, QKS, are endogenously determined by effective demand in the Keynesian closure.

The Keynesian theory maintains that factor prices are rigid. Accordingly, the prices of labor and capital in the closure should be fixed. Thus we change variables WL and WK to constants, denoted by $\overline{WL}$ and $\overline{WK}$.

In addition, we need an exogenous variable to determine the overall size of the economy. In the neoclassical model, the size of the economy is determined by the factor endowment. In the Keynesian model, the size of the economy is determined by the effective aggregate demand. In the current simple model, only households form the demand for final products. The aggregate demand of the economy equals the total household consumption. In turn, the household consumption equals the total household monetary income YH, because households have no savings in this simple model. Let income YH be determined by an exogenous income level $\overline{YH}$. $\overline{YH}$ represents the effective aggregate demand, which determines the size of the economy. Based on the above arguments, we add these three constraints for the Keynesian closure:

$$WL = \overline{WL} = 1 \tag{10.5.19}$$

$$WK = \overline{WK} \tag{10.5.20}$$

$$YH = \overline{YH} \tag{10.5.21}$$

After adding the above three constraints on variables, the model has 14 equation groups and 14 variable groups, thus satisfying the squareness condition. The GAMS program for this model with the Keynesian closure is provided in Section 10.7.

In the neoclassical closure, we use a price index as the numeraire (e.g., Equation (10.5.18)) because all other prices are variables. In the Keynesian closure, the situation is different. Note that factor prices are fixed. When labor price WL is fixed, $WL = \overline{WL} = 1$, it also functions as the numeraire in the model, because other prices can have unique values against the labor price. When we add three constraints, Equations (10.5.19)–(10.5.21), the system is already square, so we cannot add one more constraint on the price, otherwise the model would be overdetermined. In this case, CPI should be an endogenously determined variable, which could be used to study the general price level of the economy, but its value cannot be fixed.

An alternative setup would be fixing the labor price WL and commodity price CPI, but letting capital price WK be a variable:

$$WL = \overline{WL} \tag{10.5.22}$$

$$CPI = \overline{CPI} = 1 \tag{10.5.23}$$

$$YH = \overline{YH} \tag{10.5.24}$$

An economic justification for this setup is as follows: In the Keynesian state, both the wage rate and commodity prices are said to be rigid. The real wage of workers (after correcting for inflation), which equals the nominal wage WL divided by the price CPI, is also fixed. This rigidity in the real-wage rate sustains the high unemployment in economic recessions. Because the model already has three constraints, capital price in this case cannot be fixed and has to be a variable. Regarding the price numeraire issue, either the labor price or GDP price index can be interpreted as the numeraire here. The other commodity prices in the model are uniquely determined against the numeraire.

In the model, the dummy variable $WALRAS$ is added in the commodity market clearing equations. It cannot be added in the labor market clearing condition, as it did in the past. This is because in the past we were working with the neoclassical closure, where labor is fully employed and the supply-and-demand balance equation in the labor market has no slackness. But in the Keynesian closure, the labor market is not cleared and the market balance equation is left open. QLS is solely to be determined by labor demand QLD. If we add another variable, $WALRAS$ in the equation, it becomes $\sum_{a \in A} QLD_a = QLS + WALRAS$, then both QLS and $WALRAS$ solely rely on QLD to determine their values, which causes $WALRAS$ to be underdetermined, and it cannot be used to check the model convergence.

In the past, we added $WALRAS$ in only one commodity market clearing equation. In Equation (10.5.11), we add $WALRAS$ in all commodity market clearing equations. This arrangement is made simply for convenience in the GAMS program. Otherwise, we have to write additional program sentences to separate one market equation from the rest, then adding $WALRAS$ only in that separated market equation. The model program would look less neat. As adding $WALRAS$ in all equations won't affect the solvers to search and find the same final solution, we prefer this more convenient setup. Exercise 10.6 of this chapter provides examples of the program codes for separating a particular market from others, in case a programmer needs it for particular purposes.

Here are some comments on the Keynesian closure. In the Keynesian closure, in general, using the LES system for the consumption function is preferred. This is because the LES function has the subsistence level of consumption, which is similar to the constant term in the consumption function of the Keynesian model.

While the above closure has rightly captured the feature of the demand side determination, it has not specified the household saving behavior, which is also important in Keynesian theory. In the current simple model, households spend all income in consumption and have no savings. Yet an important argument by the Keynesian theory is that the recession is caused by the imbalance between households' savings and the economy's total investment. Without specifying the households' saving behavior, the model cannot simulate the entire process of an economic downturn and the multiplier effect. In Chapter 12, we will introduce the factors of saving and saving rate, so we can better simulate the real world economy in recession.

10.6 The Lewis Closure

Nobel laureate Arthur Lewis has described a typical situation of a developing economy. This economy is characterized by a dual-sector structure. There is an industrial sector where the production is determined by the existing capital stock. There is a traditional and subsistence sector with huge surplus labor living at the subsistence level. The subsistence sector provides an unlimited labor supply to the industrial sector at the subsistence wage. The capitalists in the industrial sector make profits and reinvest in the sector. The investment expands the capital stock in the industrial sector and promotes the overall economic growth. The above theory about a developing economy is referred to as the Lewis model.

Accordingly, the Lewis closure setup is as follows. Labor price WL is exogenously fixed by $\overline{WL}$. Labor supply QLS is unconstrained, endogenously determined. Capital QKS is scarce, so it equals its current endowment $\overline{QKS}$. Capital price is flexible, hence a variable. In a sense, in the labor market it is similar to the Keynesian closure, but in the capital market it is similar to the classical closure. The size of the economy is determined by the capital stock $\overline{QKS}$. Therefore, we have the following three constraints for the Lewis closure, to be added in the general model of Equations (10.5.1)–(10.5.14):

$$WL = \overline{WL} \qquad \text{Nominal wage rate is fixed} \qquad (10.6.1)$$

$$CPI = \overline{CPI} = 1 \quad \text{Commodity prices are fixed} \qquad (10.6.2)$$

$$QKS = \overline{QKS} \qquad \text{Capital stock is constrained by current endowment} \qquad (10.6.3)$$

Equations (10.6.1) and (10.6.2) have fixed the nominal wage rate and the consumer price index. Together the real wage rate is also fixed and the Lewis model maintains that this real wage rate is the subsistence level. Either of these two prices, WL or CPI, can be used as the numeraire, because their ratio is fixed thus mutually substitutable for being the benchmark price level. All other prices can be uniquely determined against the numeraire. Equation (10.6.3) refers to the scarcity of the capital stock, which is the determinant of the size of the economy.

The Lewis model implies that labor and capital are not substitutable, or the elasticity of substitution is very low. Otherwise we won't observe the scarcity of capital and the unlimited supply of labor. Hence, in the value-added module of the production block, the elasticity of substitution between capital and labor should be set very low if a CES production function is used. Alternatively, we can use the Leontief production function in the value-added module, which means that labor and capital are perfect complements.

10.7 GAMS Program of a CGE Model with the Keynesian Closure

Example 10.7.1 The data of the model economy are provided by SAM Table 8.4.1. The data for the exponents of the CES production functions are provided in the following table. In the value-added module, the exponents take negative values, which implies labor and capital are complements in production in these sectors. The households' commodity demand functions are LES. We have the following information for the LES function parameters: Frisch parameter $\varphi = -2$, income elasticity of expenditure e_j are 0.5, 1.0 and 1.2 for agriculture, industry and service commodities, respectively.

CES function exponent ρ value	Agriculture	Industry	Service
Top level CES production function	0.2	0.3	0.1
CES function for the value-added module at the bottom level	−1	−2	−1.5

1. Write the GAMS program for the model of Section 10.5. Using CPI as the numeraire and using dummy variable *WALRAS* to meet the squareness of the system.
2. Run the program and check if *WALRAS* is zero after the model finds the solution. Replicate the model and check consistency.
3. Finally, in line with Keynesian theory, suppose the final demand increases by 20%, find the corresponding increases in employment of labor and capital.

Solution: The corresponding GAMS program is as follows. After successfully executing the program, we found that *WALRAS* equals zero, indicating that the model converges successfully. The simulation parts show that, if the final demand increases by 20%, it would increase labor employment from 850 to 1020, and capital employment from 770 to 924.

```
$title  Example 10.7.1 CGE Model of Keynesian closure with CPI numeraire

$ontext
Keynesian closure:
Labor and capital quantities endogenously determined. Households' total income YH
exogenously determined.
Labor price and consumer price index CPI are fixed.
CPI is considered to be the numeraire.
$offtext

set ac accounts  /agri,indu,serv,lab,cap,hh,total/;
set c(ac) commodities  /agri,indu,serv/;
set f(ac) factors /lab,cap/;

alias (ac,acp),(c,cp),(f,fp);

table sam(ac,acp)
        agri   indu   serv  lab   cap   hh     total
agri    260    320    150               635    1365
indu    345    390    390               600    1725
serv    400    365    320               385    1470
lab     200    250    400                      850
cap     160    400    210                      770
hh                          850   770          1620
total   1365   1725   1470  850   770   1620
;

parameter   rhoq(c)    /agri =   0.2,   indu = 0.3,   serv =  0.1 /
            rhoVA(c)   /agri     -1,    indu    -2,   serv   -1.5 /
            LESelas(c) /agri    0.5,    indu   1.0,   serv    1.2 /;


Parameters
*Variable name followed by 0 denotes the corresponding parameters fixed at its
initial level
```

```
scaleAq(c)          Scale parameter A of top level CES function
deltaq(c)           Share parameter of top level CES function
scaleAVA(c)         Scale factor of value-added CES function
deltaVA(c)          Share parameter of value-added CES function
ia(c,cp)            Input coefficient of intermediate inputs
PC0(c)              Price of c
QC0(c)              Quantity of c
PVA0(c)             Price of aggregate value-added
QVA0(c)             Quantity of aggregate value-added
PINTA0(c)           Price of aggregate intermediate input
QINTA0(c)           Quantity of aggregate intermediate input
QINT0(c,cp)         Quantity of intermediate input c used in cp
QLD0(c)             Labor demand
QKD0(c)             Capital demand
QLS0                Labor supply
QKS0                Capital supply
WL0                 Labor price
WK0                 Capital price
cpiwt(c)            Weights used for calculating CPI
CPI0                CPI at the base year
YH0                 Household income but also aggregate demand in $s
QH0(c)              Consumption demand for c by households
bgtshare(c)         Average budget share on c in the LES function
bgtsharechk1        Check if average budget share sum is 1
LESbeta(c)          Marginal budget share of LES
LESbetachk1         Check if the marginal budget share beta sum is 1
LESsub(c)           Subsistence consumption level of c of LES
Frisch              Frisch parameter
;

*Calibration of parameters and exogenous variables
Frisch=-2;
PC0(c)=1;
PVA0(c)=1;
PINTA0(c)=1;
WK0=1;
WL0=1;
QC0(c)=sam('total',c)/PC0(c);
QVA0(c)=SUM(f,sam(f,c));
QINT0(c,cp)=sam(c,cp)/PC0(c);
QINTA0(c)=SUM(cp,QINT0(cp,c));
ia(c,cp)=QINT0(c,cp)/QINTA0(cp);
QLS0=sum(c,sam('lab',c))/WL0;
QKS0=sum(c,sam('cap',c))/WK0;
QLD0(c)=sam('lab',c)/WL0;
QKD0(c)=sam('cap',c)/WK0;
deltaq(c)=PVA0(c)*QVA0(c)**(1-rhoq(c))/(PVA0(c)*QVA0(c)**(1-
```

```
rhoq(c))+PINTA0(c)*QINTA0(c)**(1-rhoq(c)));
scaleAq(c)=QC0(c)/(deltaq(c)*QVA0(c)**rhoq(c)+(1-
deltaq(c))*QINTA0(c)**rhoq(c))**(1/rhoq(c));
deltaVA(c)=WL0*QLD0(c)**(1-rhoVA(c))/(WL0*QLD0(c)**(1-rhoVA(c))+WK0*QKD0(c)**(1-
rhoVA(c)));
scaleAVA(c)=QVA0(c)/(deltaVA(c)*QLD0(c)**rhoVA(c)+(1-
deltaVA(c))*QKD0(c)**rhoVA(c))**(1/rhoVA(c));
YH0=WL0*QLS0+WK0*QKS0;
QH0(c)=SAM(c,'hh')/PC0(c);
cpiwt(c)=QH0(c)/sum(cp,QH0(cp));
CPI0=sum(c,PC0(c)*cpiwt(c));
*Below is the LES system block
bgtshare(c)=SAM(c,'hh')/YH0;
bgtsharechk1=sum(c,bgtshare(c));
LESbeta(c)=LESelas(c)*bgtshare(c)/(sum(cp,LESelas(cp)*bgtshare(cp)));
LESbetachk1=sum(c,LESbeta(c));
LESsub(c)=sam(c,'hh')+(LESbeta(c)/PC0(c))*(YH0/frisch);

display
PC0,PVA0,PINTA0,QC0,QVA0,QINTA0,QINT0,rhoq,rhoVA,scaleAq,deltaq,scaleAVA,deltaVA,i
a,frisch,
QLD0,QKD0,QLS0,QKS0,WL0,WK0,YH0,QH0,cpiwt,bgtsharechk1,LESbetachk1,LESsub;

variable
PA(c),PVA(c),PINTA(c),WL,WK,QA(c),QVA(c),QINTA(c),QINT(c,cp),QLD(c),QKD(c),QLS,QKS,
YH,QH(c),
*Add CPI and Walras
CPI,WALRAS
;

equation
QAfn(c),QAFOCeq(c),PAeq(c),QVAfn(c),QVAFOC(c),PVAeq(c),QINTfn(c,cp),PINTAeq(cp),YH
eq,QHeq(c),ComEqui(c),Leq,Keq,CPIeq;

QAfn(c)..
QA(c)=e=scaleAq(c)*(deltaq(c)*QVA(c)**rhoq(c)+(1-
deltaq(c))*QINTA(c)**rhoq(c))**(1/rhoq(c));

QAFOCeq(c)..
PVA(c)/PINTA(c)=e=(deltaq(c)/(1-deltaq(c)))*(QINTA(c)/QVA(c))**(1-rhoq(c));

PAeq(c)..
PA(c)*QA(c)=e=PVA(c)*QVA(c)+PINTA(c)*QINTA(c);

QVAfn(c)..
QVA(c)=e=scaleAVA(c)*(deltaVA(c)*QLD(c)**rhoVA(c)+(1-
deltaVA(c))*QKD(c)**rhoVA(c))**(1/rhoVA(c));
```

```
QVAFOC(c)..
WL/WK=e=(deltaVA(c)/(1-deltaVA(c)))*(QKD(c)/QLD(c))**(1-rhoVA(c));

PVAeq(c)..
PVA(c)*QVA(c)=e=WL*QLD(c)+WK*QKD(c);

QINTfn(c,cp)..
QINT(c,cp)=e=ia(c,cp)*QINTA(cp);

PINTAeq(cp)..
PINTA(cp)=e=SUM(c,ia(c,cp)*PA(c));

YHeq..
YH=e=WL*QLS+WK*QKS;

QHeq(c)..
PA(c)*QH(c)=e=PA(c)*LESsub(c)+LESbeta(c)*(YH-sum(cp,PA(cp)*LESsub(cp)));

*Add WALRAS here
ComEqui(c)..
QA(c)=e=sum(cp,QINT(c,cp))+QH(c)+WALRAS;

Leq..
Sum(c,QLD(c))=e=QLS;

Keq..
Sum(c,QKD(c))=e=QKS;

CPIeq..
CPI=e=sum(c,PA(c)*cpiwt(c));

*Assign initial values

PA.L(c)=PC0(c);
PVA.L(c)=PVA0(c);
PINTA.L(c)=PINTA0(c);
QA.L(c)=QC0(c);
QVA.L(c)=QVA0(c);
QINTA.L(c)=QINTA0(c);
QINT.L(c,cp)=QINT0(c,cp);
QLD.L(c)=QLD0(c);
QKD.L(c)=QKD0(c);
YH.L=YH0;
QH.L(c)=QH0(c);
QLS.L=QLS0;
QKS.L=QKS0;
WK.L=1;
WALRAS.L=0;
```

```
*Keynesian closure constraints
WL.fx=1;
CPI.fx=CPI0;
YH.fx=YH0;

*Executing the model
model cgeKeynes  /all/;
solve cgeKeynes using mcp;
*Check if WALRAS is zero
display WALRAS.L,QLS.L,QKS.L;

*Simulation when aggregate demand increases by 20 percent
YH.fx=YH0*1.2;
model checkKeynesYHup  /all/;
solve checkKEYnesYHup using mcp;
*Check if WALRAS is zero
display WALRAS.L,QLS.L,QKS.L;

*End
```

Exercises

10E.1 Practice different methods of setting up a price numeraire in CGE models. First, revise the GAMS program of Example (10.7.1) by (1) using labor price as the numeraire; and (2) using the classical closure. Then try three methods to restore the squareness of the model system: (1) deleting the labor market clearing equation; (2) adding a dummy variable *WALRAS*; or (3) using non-linear-programming solver NLP to minimize the excess demand in the labor market. Compare the differences in the replication results of the three methods.

10E.2 Examine the properties of homogeneity of degree 1 in nominal variables (and money neutrality) of a CGE model. In your model for Exercise 10E.1, increase the level of numeraire by 20%, i.e., $WL.fx = 1.2$. Let other prices still have the same initial values (initial prices = 1). After running the model program, check if all prices increase by 20%.

10E.3 In your model of Exercise 10E.1, change the numeraire to the GDP price index, and use dummy variable *WALRAS* to make the model system square. First, you increase the GDP price index by 10%, then check the results to see if the nominal terms have changed homogenously as predicted? Second, in this model, can you simulate a situation where you raise labor price by 10% instead?

10E.4 In Example 10.7.1, the model simulates an external shock that the total final demand represented by *YH* has increased by 20%. Check the resulting changes in other real variables, such as commodity outputs, factor employment, etc. Expenditure multiplier in the Keynesian model is defined as the ratio of increase in GDP to an autonomous increase in expenditure. What is the multiplier here? Why is the multiplier here not as big as those predicted by macroeconomics theory?

10E.5 Revise the model of Example 10.7.1: change the macroeconomic closure to the Lewis closure. The Lewis model maintains that the economic growth and absorption of surplus labor are determined by the expansion of the capital stock. Assuming the capital stock increases by 10%, what are the corresponding changes in labor employment?

10E.6 In the model of Exercise 10E.1, use the neoclassical closure with the labor price as the numeraire. Yet this time we add the *WALRAS* dummy variable only in the agricultural sector (agri), and leave the original market clearing equations in industry and service as they are. Write the corresponding GAMS program.

Hint: To separate the agriculture sector from other sectors, make a subset of commodities for agriculture, and make another subset for commodities of other sectors. Then write two different market clearing equation groups:

$$QC_c = \sum_{c' \in C} QINT_{cc'} + QH_c + WALRAS \qquad c = \text{`agri'}$$

$$QC_c = \sum_{c' \in C} QINT_{cc'} + QH_c \qquad c = \text{`indu', `serv'}$$

If the rest of the commodity group consists of many sectors, it would be awkward to list all the sectors. Instead, we can use the following GAMS codes. Note the syntax `Nagr('agri')=No` means subset `Nagr` only excludes the agriculture sector.

```
set agr(c) "the subset only for agriculture" /agri/ ;
set Nagr(c) "All commodity sectors except agriculture";
Nagr(c)=YES; Nagr('agri')=NO;
```

Chapter 11

Government, Taxes, and Prices

11.1 Government's Role in the Economy

The CGE models in previous chapters have only two economic agents/institutions: households and enterprises. In this chapter we would add the third institution — the government — in the CGE model. Government plays an indispensable role in the modern economy. It provides public goods and service such as defense and weather forecast; corrects market failures such as regulating production causing environmental hazard. Government collects taxes from the private sector and makes transfer payments to them. Government buys commodities and makes public investment such as infrastructure.

In recent centuries, the role of the government in the economy, measured by its expenditure as percentage of GDP, has steadily increased to a very significant level. Take the U.S. as an example, during the past decade the U.S. government spending on the final goods accounts for 17% of GDP, which is roughly the same size of the investment made by private enterprises. If including transfer payments such as Social Security, the government's total spending accounts for more than 33% of GDP, which is far larger than the private investment.

Figure 11.1.1 shows the government's role in the national economic flow chart. The government's purchase of commodities on the markets, denoted by QG in the follow chart, includes the commodity consumption and public capital formation by the government. In the flow chat, the final demand for commodities is the sum of demands from households QH, from enterprises $QINV$, and from the government QG. In CGE models, the total demand for commodity in each sector includes intermediate input $QINT$ is:

$$QC_c = \sum_{c' \in C} QINT_{cc'} + QINV_c + QH_c + QG_c \qquad c \in C \quad c' \in C \qquad (11.1.1)$$

The sum of final demands is the GDP of the economy. In macroeconomics, it is expressed by:

$$\text{GDP}(Y) = \text{Consumption } (C) + \text{Investment } (I) + \text{Government spending } (G) \qquad (11.1.2)$$

The differences between Equations (11.1.1) and (11.1.2) are that (1) the GDP equation includes only the final products thus has no intermediate input demands; and (2) the GDP equation is in the aggregate term rather than breaking down into individual sectors.

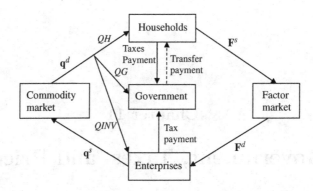

Figure 11.1.1.   The government's role in the national economic flow chart.

In addition to consuming commodities, government also makes monetary transfer payments to households and enterprises. It includes Social Security, Medicare, unemployment insurance, etc. The sum of the transfer payment is roughly the same size of consumption of final goods in the U.S. government budget.

To finance its expenditure, government collects taxes from households, which include income tax, sales tax, property tax, etc. Government collects taxes from enterprises, which include value-added tax, corporate income tax, employment tax, excise tax, etc. Government collects tariff, export tax, and many other fees from the foreign sectors. Government also provides subsidies such as export subsidies to producers. Subsidies can be considered as negative taxes in most cases. SAM Table 4.1.1 lists a series of taxes collected in the government row account.

The difference between government's revenue YG and expenditure EG is the fiscal budget balance, commonly referred to as fiscal deficit or surplus. In economics and CGE models, fiscal balance is also called "public savings" or "government savings", denoted by $SAVEG$:

$$SAVEG = YG - EG \qquad\qquad (11.1.3)$$

A positive government savings $SAVEG$ means fiscal budget surplus; a negative one means fiscal deficit. When government savings is not balanced, the gap must be financed by savings from other agent groups in the economy. This subject will be discussed in Chapter 12.

CGE models are widely used to study fiscal policies of the government and to evaluate their impacts on the economy. In summary, the government's fiscal policies consist of two components: taxation and government spending. Here we discuss the government's behavior functions and fiscal component variables in CGE models.

11.2 Government Expenditure

Let us take a look at the government's expenditure side in CGE models. The government expenditure includes its consumption of goods and transfer of payments to other institutions such as households or enterprises. Government's consumption of goods includes compensation of public employees, use of goods and services, etc. Let EG denote the total government expenditure in nominal term. The government's consumption of commodity c in real terms is QG_c. The transfer payment made by the government to households is cost-of-living adjusted by price index CPI; hence, it is $transfer_{hg} \cdot CPI$. Transfer payment to enterprises $transfer_{eg}$ is a lump-sum dollar amount. Then we have:

$$\sum_c PC_c \cdot QG_c + transfer_{hg} \cdot CPI + transfer_{eg} = EG \qquad (11.2.1)$$

A CGE model needs to specify how EG is determined, which in turn is related to the government's fiscal behavior. Let us first consider an ideal case. Suppose this government is very fiscally disciplined. It sets up a strict budget balance target so $SAVEG = 0$. Thus the total amount of money EG depends on the fiscal revenue. This behavior may be motivated by various political and economic reasons. Transfer payments to households and enterprises $transfer_{hg} \cdot CPI$ and $transfer_{eg}$ often are mandatory, which were set up in the previous period. Further, the government follows a prior consumption rule to spend on each commodity c. In this case, once EG is endogenously determined from the fiscal revenue by the system, and the government consumption rule on c is specified, the model automatically solves the government purchase amount on each commodity QG_c.

The government's consumption rule can be derived from its utility function, which should be specified first. This is similar to the household's case. Suppose the government has a Cobb–Douglas utility function and it faces a hard budget constraint. By maximizing its utility subject to the budget constraints, we can derive the government demand on commodity c. Similar to the household's case, the derived demand is a fixed proportion $shareg_c$ of its total expenditure net of transfer payments:

$$PC_c \cdot QG_c = shareg_c(EG - transfer_{hg} \cdot CPI - transfer_{eg}) \qquad (11.2.2)$$

Other demand functions such as the LES function can also be used for the government's demand for commodities, just like the case for the household's consumption demands.

The above disciplined fiscal rule may be too idealistic. Government often has other priorities over the principle of following a strict budget balance target. Some reasons are legitimate, for instance, to stimulate the economy in recession; other reasons are simply political or for group interests. In most real world cases, a large portion of the government expenditure is exogenously or discretionarily determined, albeit through some legislative processes. The discretionary spending can be very sizeable in economic recession, when there is an economic justification for the government to stimulate the economy with less concern over the diminished tax revenue. In these cases, total government expenditure EG is exogenously determined. It is denoted by $\overline{EG}$ where the overline indicates it is an exogenous variable.

If $\overline{EG}$ is exogenously given, the budget balance $SAVEG$ should be a variable and endogenously determined, which allows government spending $\overline{EG}$ to exceed its revenue YG. When the government raises $\overline{EG}$, if it still follows the consumption rule of Equation (11.2.2), it would increase spending on each commodity by the same proportion. In this case, QG_c are still endogenously determined in the model.

In the real world, however, that is normally not the case. When a government determines its budget spending, in general the budget can be very detailed, often to each commodity category. The government budget would specify the amount of transfer payment to each institutional group, and the amount to be spend on each commodity. In this case, the demand for a particular commodity c is exogenously determined. Let it be denoted by $\overline{QG_c}$. When $\overline{QG_c}$ become exogenous variables, EG cannot be exogenous. Otherwise we would have an over-determination problem. This is explained by the following relationship:

$$\sum_c PC_c \cdot \overline{QG_c} \neq \overline{EG} - transfer_{hg} \cdot CPI - transfer_{eg} \tag{11.2.3}$$

The two transfer payments are the parameters whose values are fixed. Supposing prices PC and CPI are also rigid, then in the equation the LHS does not equal RHS except by coincidence. Hence, when individual commodity spending $\overline{QG_c}$ are exogenous, EG needs to be an endogenous variable whose value is solved by the model.

To summarize, we have three optional settings for the government spending module. The first one is a rule-following government which has no discretionary power. Its equation set is:

$$SAVEG = YG - EG = 0 \tag{11.2.4}$$

$$PC_c \cdot QG_c = shareg_c(EG - transfer_{hg} \cdot CPI - transfer_{eg}) \tag{11.2.5}$$

where Equation (11.2.5) can be replaced by other demand functions, similar to the household consumption functions. Equation (11.2.4) is the balance budget constraint.

The second government spending option is a hybrid type. It discretionally determines the total spending, so $\overline{EG}$ is exogenous but the government follows the fixed-share consumption rule for QG_c.

$$SAVEG = YG - \overline{EG} \tag{11.2.6}$$

$$PC_c \cdot QG_c = shareg_c(\overline{EG} - transfer_{hg} \cdot CPI - transfer_{eg}) \tag{11.2.7}$$

The third government spending option is completely discretionary. It determines the consumption in each sector $\overline{QG_c}$:

$$SAVEG = YG - EG \tag{11.2.8}$$

$$\sum_c PC_c \cdot \overline{QG_c} = EG - transfer_{hg} \cdot CPI - transfer_{eg} \tag{11.2.9}$$

For the rule-following types, all spending variables are endogenous. For the hybrid or discretionary spending types, there is one exogenous variable $\overline{EG}$ or $\overline{QG_c}$ but other variables are endogenous. The rule-following type may be academically interesting but the discretionary spending type is observed more frequently in the real world.

Depending on the macroeconomic situation and the research topic of the CGE model, we may set up different equations for the government spending behavior. The principle of modeling is to simulate the real world situation with allowable simplifications. Take an example of the U.S. The U.S. federal government budget is detailed. It consists of two major parts, mandatory and discretionary. The mandatory part includes payments of Social Security,

Medicare, interest, unemployment compensation, etc., which accounts roughly for 60% of the total expenditure. These are commitments made before thus cannot really change in the current fiscal year budget. The discretionary part consists of military, education, science and health research, transportation, etc., which can be negotiated among all political groups for adjustment. In general, the historical number of spending in each category is served as the basis for negotiation, so changes are still limited in this sense. But in a special situation such as a need of fiscal stimulus in recession, the scale of the spending change can be very sizeable. Even under a normal economic situation, the U.S. budget is not very disciplined. The government budget deficit continues to balloon and spending ceiling has been lifted repeatedly. Hence the U.S. government spending in a CGE model sometimes is treated as the discretionary type, in which $\overline{QG_c}$ are exogenously given. Suppose the research interest is to find the impacts on various sectors by a 300 billion dollar spending increase in infrastructure spending, the shock in the simulation would be an increase in $\overline{QG_c}$ where c refers to the infrastructure commodity.

11.3 Households and Income Taxes

Government's revenue comes mainly from taxes. Direct taxes are the taxes paid directly to the government by taxpayers by the reason of ownership, for instances, individual or corporate income taxes, property tax, etc., More than 50% of the U.S. federal revenue comes from individual's income taxes. Enterprises also pay income taxes, but the amount is much smaller in size. Corporate income taxes account for only 6% of the U.S. federal tax revenue.

The amount of income tax paid by a household is its income multiplied by income tax rate ti_h. In a flat tax rate system, ti_h is a constant. Most countries adopt a progressive income tax rate system, ti_h increases as the household's income increases. To simulate a progressive income tax rate system in CGE models, the households are separated into income groups. Each income group is subject to a different income tax rate. For a simple CGE model with only one household group, we can use the average income tax rate for ti_h. Here we use an example to illustrate.

Suppose a model economy is described by the SAM table of Table 11.3.1. This SAM table has a government account. Enterprises produce commodities in the current period and they do not invest. Their uses of factors and their payments to the households are recorded in the labor and capital accounts. The government has no transfer payment to the enterprises. Hence an enterprise account is not explicitly needed in the table. Household's monetary income before tax is $YH = 360$, which is the sum of (1) factor income $190 + 165 = 355$, and (2) transfer payment from the government $transfer_{hg} = 5$. In the SAM table (Table 11.3.1), we can find the income tax paid by households to the government is 36. The income tax rate thus is calibrated by $ti_h = $ (income tax)/income $= 36/360 = 10\%$. Households pay income tax $ti_h \cdot YH$. Their after tax disposable income $YDISPH$ is:

$$YDISPH = (1 - ti_h)\,YH. \tag{11.3.1}$$

$YDISPH = (1 - ti_h)\,YH = (1 - 10\%) \cdot 360 = 324$. Disposable income can be used to purchase commodities.

Table 11.3.1.   SAM table of the model economy with government.

	Commodity 1	Commodity 2	Labor	Capital	Households	Government	Total
Commodity 1					152	11	163
Commodity 2					172	20	192
Labor	110	80					190
Capital	53	112					165
Households			190	165		5	360
Government					36		36
Total	163	192	190	165	360	36	

In this economy, the government's revenue YG comes entirely from household's income tax,

$$YG = ti_h \cdot YH \tag{11.3.2}$$

The fiscal system is the rule-following type and budget balance is mandatory in this economy, $SAVEG = 0$. We have:

$$EG = YG \tag{11.3.3}$$

The economy has a CES production function. Production only needs primary inputs but no intermediate inputs. Households have a Cobb–Douglas utility function. Following is the CGE model for this economy. Commodity set is C. The production block is the same equation set as previous models:

$$QC_c = \alpha_c^q [\delta_c^q QLD_c^{\rho_c} + (1 - \delta_c^q) QKD_c^{\rho_c}]^{1/\rho_c} \qquad c \in C \tag{11.3.4}$$

$$\frac{WL}{WK} = \frac{\delta_c^q}{(1 - \delta_c^q)} \left(\frac{QLD_c}{QKD_c} \right)^{\rho_c - 1} \qquad c \in C \tag{11.3.5}$$

$$PC_c \cdot QC_c = WL \cdot QLD_c + WK \cdot QKD_c \qquad c \in C \tag{11.3.6}$$

Household's income includes the government transfer payment:

$$YH = WL \cdot QLS + WK \cdot QKS + transfer_{hg} \cdot CPI \tag{11.3.7}$$

After paying the income tax, households use all disposable income to purchase commodities. Their spending on commodity QH_c is a fixed share $shareh_c$ of their disposable income, which is derived from the Cobb–Douglas utility function:

$$PC_c \cdot QH_c = shareh_c \cdot (1 - ti_h) \cdot YH \qquad c \in C \tag{11.3.8}$$

The government revenue comes from income tax paid by households:

$$YG = ti_h \cdot YH \tag{11.3.9}$$

The government adheres to the principle of budget balance, so

$$EG = YG \tag{11.3.10}$$

The government's spending follows rules and has no discretionary part. Transfer payment to households was set up in the previous periods, so it is given. Similar to the household's behavior, the government's expenditure on each commodity is a fixed share *shareg$_c$* of its total spending budget after transfer payment:

$$PC_c \cdot QG_c = shareg_c \cdot (EG - transfer_{hg} \cdot CPI) \qquad c \in C \tag{11.3.11}$$

The market clearing equations are:

$$QC_c = QH_c + QG_c \qquad c \in C \tag{11.3.12}$$

$$\sum_{c \in C} QLD_c = QLS \qquad c \in C \tag{11.3.13}$$

$$\sum_{c \in C} QKD_c = QKS \qquad c \in C \tag{11.3.14}$$

The consumer price index CPI is used for the government to adjust transfer payments, which is:

$$CPI = \sum_{c \in C} PC_c \cdot cpiwt_c \tag{11.3.15}$$

Equations (11.3.4)–(11.3.15) form the CGE model. Parameters α_c^q, *transfer$_{hg}$*, ti_h, *shareh*, *shareg*, *cpiwt$_c$* can be calibrated from the SAM table data. There are total 12 equation groups and 14 variable groups. The variables are: QC_c, QLD_c, QKD_c, QLS, QKS, YH, QH_c, QG_c, YG, EG, PC_c, WL, WK, CPI.

The number of variables exceeds the number of equations, thus the squareness condition is not met. We need to add constraints to reduce the number of variables. Suppose the macroeconomic closure is neoclassical. Then we have full factor employment and flexible prices. The factor supplies equal their endowments:

$$QLS = \overline{QLS} \tag{11.3.16}$$

$$QKS = \overline{QKS} \tag{11.3.17}$$

By adding above two constraints, QLS and QKS become parameters because their values are fixed. The model has 12 groups of variables. It is square and solvable.

Next, we would like to add the price numeraire. We can use labor price WL as numeraire by setting up $WL = 1$ or we use Price index CPI as the numeraire:

$$CPI = 1 \tag{11.3.18}$$

After we fix the numeraire value by Equation (11.3.18), the number of variable groups reduces to 11, the system is not square. So we add dummy variable $WALRAS$ in the labor market clearing equation, Equation (11.3.13) is changed to the following one:

$$\sum_{a \in A} QLD_a = QLS + WALRAS \tag{11.3.19}$$

Now we have 12 variable groups including *WALRAS* and 12 equation groups. The model system is square and solvable.

11.4 Sales Taxes, Basic Prices and Purchasers' Prices

Indirect taxes are those collected by intermediaries (such as suppliers or retail stores) for the government from buyers upon transactions. Indirect taxes include sales tax, excise tax, value-added tax (VAT), goods and services tax (GST), etc.

The U.S. and many other countries in the world have sales taxes. A sales tax is charged to the buyers by the sellers for the government, typically taking place in the retail sector selling the commodities to the consumers. Most sales taxes are ad valorem taxes, which are proportional to the value of the sales by the sales tax rate. Excise taxes such as the gasoline tax are also collected upon the final stage of sales, but are included in the list prices and paid by the sellers. A sales tax paid by the buyers or paid by the sellers would be recorded differently in enterprise bookkeeping and national accounts. In economics a sales tax (or an excise tax) is a wedge inserted between the price paid by the buyers and the price received by sellers. Whether buyers or sellers nominally pay the tax does not matter, the final cost to each side is the same. Further, the true tax burden (i.e., tax incidence) falls more on the side who is less elastic to adjust his quantity. For instance, if supply is less elastic than demand, then the sellers eventually bear more the sales tax burden, although buyers (consumers) nominally pay the taxes. This economic theorem applies to other indirect taxes such as excise taxes or VAT. It can also be seen from the algebra of CGE models.

Let the buyer's price be denoted by PQ_c. In national accounting, it is referred to as "purchaser's price", which includes the sales tax and is the actual cost for the purchaser to get the commodity. Purchaser's price is an important concept and variable in national accounting and in more complicated CGE models. Let the seller's price be denoted by PC_c. It is referred to as "basic price", which is the unit cost to produce the commodity by the enterprise, and net of the sales tax.[1] Let $tsale_c$ be the sales tax rate. We have

$$PQ_c = (1 + tsale_c) \cdot PC_c \qquad (11.4.1)$$

Before having the sales tax, PC_c and PQ_c were equal. Now there is a sales tax wedge between them. In CGE models, the nominal values of the same quantity of a commodity can be different, depending on which price is used.

To illustrate, suppose in the same model economy in previous chapters, the government now levies a sales tax. The new economy is described by the SAM table (Table 11.4.1) with some numbers modified to reflect adding the sales tax. The SAM table has a sales tax account. The government uses the tax revenue to purchase commodities. It is important to note that we now have two prices for the same commodity. One is the before-tax "basic price" and the other is the after-tax "purchaser's price". Sales tax raises the basic price to purchaser's price but sales tax does not change the quantity of the commodity.

---

[1]There are more details about the definitions of "basic price", "producer's price", and "purchaser's price" in national accounting, but we will leave these details to late discussion.

Table 11.4.1. SAM table with a sales tax.

	Commodity 1	Commodity 2	Labor	Capital	Households	Government	Sales tax	Total
Commodity 1					150	26.04		176.04
Commodity 2					190	28		218
Labor	110	70						180
Capital	53	130						183
Households			180	183		11		374
Government						34	31.04	65.04
Sales tax	13.04	18						31.04
Total	176.04	218	180	183	374	65.04	31.04	

In the model economy of Table 11.4.1, because there is no intermediate inputs in production, the total cost to produce, thus the total output value of commodity 1 is $110 + 53 = 163$. If we use "basic price" as the *base price* so $PC_1 = 1$, the quantity of the commodity 1 is

$$QC_1 = 163/PC_1 = 163 \tag{11.4.2}$$

where *base price* is defined as the particular price whose value is set at 1. This term is useful in CGE modeling.

The sales tax rate *tsale* is calibrated by

$$tsale_1 = \text{"sales tax"}/\text{"output value at basic price"} = 13.04/163 = 8\%. \tag{11.4.3}$$

It can be verified that the sales tax rate in sector 2 is also 8%.

The market value of commodity 1 after 8% sales tax is $163 + 13.04 = 176.04$. Because it includes the sales tax, 176.04 is in the purchaser's price. This is the buyer's cost. At base price $PC_1 = 1$, the purchaser's price is calibrated as $PQ_1 = (1 + 8\%) \cdot PC_1 = 1.08$. For the same quantity 163 of commodity 1, the total value is different, depending on the price used:

$$PC_1 \times QC_1 = 1 \times 163 = 163 \tag{11.4.4}$$

$$PQ_1 \times QC_1 = 1.08 \times 163 = 176.04 \tag{11.4.5}$$

In SAM tables the final user accounts are valued at purchaser's prices, such as consumptions by households and the government. It is based on the assumption these final users buy the commodities at the purchaser's prices. When sales taxes present, thus the purchasers' prices are greater than the basic prices, to calculate the real quantity of the commodity, we need to divide the nominal values by the purchaser's prices. In the above example, it is:

$$QC_1 = (\text{Value of output 1})/PQ_1 = 176.04/(1 + tsale_1) = 176.04/1.08 = 163 \tag{11.4.6}$$

The final users' values in the commodity row accounts are all valued at purchaser's prices $PQ_c = 1.08$. Their quantities can be obtained by the same method. For instance, the household consumption of commodity 1 in basic price is

$$QH_1 = 150/PQ_1 = 150/1.08 = 138.9 \tag{11.4.7}$$

The difference in the monetary values between 138.9 and 150 is the sales tax paid by the household.

To adapt to the situation with sales taxes, we need to make following changes in equations from the previous CGE model. In the production block, the price equation including the sales tax is changed to:

$$PQ_c \cdot QC_c = (1 + tsale_c) \cdot PC_c \cdot QC_c$$
$$= (1 + tsale_c) \cdot (WL \cdot QLD_c + WK \cdot QKD_c) \quad c \in C \qquad (11.4.8)$$

Note the price has changed to purchaser's price PQ on LHS. The government revenue includes those from sales tax:

$$YG = ti_h \cdot YH + \sum_c tsale_c \cdot PC_c \cdot QC_c \qquad (11.4.9)$$

The consumptions by households and the government are at the purchaser's prices:

$$PQ_c \cdot QH_c = shareh_c \cdot (1 - ti_h) \cdot YH \qquad c \in C \qquad (11.4.10)$$

$$PQ_c \cdot QG_c = shareg_c \cdot (EG - transfer_{hg} \cdot CPI) \qquad c \in C \qquad (11.4.11)$$

Here we briefly discuss the price terms used in System of National Accounts (SNA). The definitions are important when you check data from published IO or SAM tables or you collect data to make your own SAM tables. There are three prices used in calculating output values: basic price, producer's price and purchaser's price. The relationships of the three prices are summarized in Table 11.4.2.

In CGE modeling, the choice of the base price can vary according to the needs or for convenience. If a different base price is chosen, given the same value in a cell of the SAM table, the unit of quantity and the derived quantity would change accordingly. However, as long as you consistently use the same set of the prices with their mathematical relationships correctly specified, the new set of quantities are inherently consistent throughout the model; therefore, the simulation results are the same.

Take an example. In the same economy of SAM table (Table 11.4.1). Suppose now we instead use the purchaser price as the base price, so $PQ_1 = 1$, thus the unit of commodity 1 has changed. The total output value is still 176.04. But the quantity of the total output:

$$QC_1 = 176.04/PQ_1 = 176.04/1 = 176.04 \qquad (11.4.12)$$

The quantity of QC_1 changes to 176.04 instead of 163 before. This is because the unit of the quantity of commodity 1 has changed when we use a different base price. What is

Table 11.4.2.   Relationships among the basic, producer's and purchaser's prices.

Basic price = production cost + some taxes on production such as employment taxes paid by employers
Producer's price = Basic price + product taxes (such as excise tax)
Purchaser's price = Producer's price + non-deductible VAT + transport and trade costs

Note: From SNA (2008). Readers can find more detailed classifications, definitions and explanations about the three prices from the original document.

the basic price now? It can be calculated by discounting the sales tax from the purchaser's price. For instance, the basic price PC_1 is calibrated by:

$$PC_1 = \frac{1}{1 + tsale} PQ_1 = \frac{1}{1 + 8\%} PC_1 = \frac{1}{1.08} \times 1 = 0.926 \qquad (11.4.13)$$

Basic prices are used for the values before the sales taxes. The output value in sector 1 before sales tax is $110 + 53 = 163$. Dividing the basic price we can get the same output quantity of commodity 1:

$$QC_1 = 163/PC_1 = 163/0.926 = 176.04 \qquad (11.4.14)$$

which is consistent with the quantity in Equation (11.4.11).

To summarize, after a change in the base price, the unit of quantity has changed, so the quantity looks different from the previous case. As long as we consistently use the same base price and the "new" units throughout the model, it won't affect simulation results. Using purchase price PQ as the base price has some convenience, as all final uses like consumption and government purchases are valued at purchasers' prices in the SAM table. This issue will be discussed further in Chapter 13.

An excise tax has the same tax wedge effect as a sales tax, but it is paid by the enterprises directly and included in the listed price. An excise tax can be based on unit or value. Let us denote "producer's price" by PP, which includes the excise tax. After imposing an excise tax rate of *texcise*, the relationship between producer price PP and basic price PC is

$$(1 - texcise)PP_c = PC_c \qquad (11.4.15)$$

The price equation used in production block is revised to:

$$(1 - texcise)PP_c \cdot QC_c = PC_c \cdot QC_c = WL \cdot QLD_c + WK \cdot QKD_c \qquad (11.4.16)$$

The above form is often used in CGE models for excise taxes, and, sometimes for sales taxes as well. After all, the economics inferences and economic impacts of an excise tax are the same as a sales tax, although nominally they are paid by different sides.

Mathematically, the only difference between equation for a sales tax (11.4.1) and that for an excise tax (11.4.14) (if $PP_c = PQ_c$) is a numerical difference caused by the different bases of the denominator. If the two tax rates would have same impacts on the economy, they need to satisfy the equation:

$$1 - texcise = 1/(1 + tsale) \qquad (11.4.17)$$

To satisfy Equation (11.4.16), *texcise* and *tsale* would not be exact the same number but their difference is marginal.

11.5 Value-Added Taxes (VAT)

The major indirect tax adopted in most countries in the world is VAT, stands for value-added taxes. It is also called Good and Service Tax (GST) in some countries. The U.S. does not have VAT. VAT has some advantages including: simple to administer, neutrally imposed on all business types, creating a large tax base, and reducing tax evasion. It is recommended by the United Nations and the World Bank for developing countries where the tax administrative system is not well developed.

VAT is charged by sellers to the buyers upon transaction. By the SNA convention, VAT is included in purchaser's price but not in producer's price. In practice, at each stage of the supply chain, from production to the point of sale, a seller charges VAT from the buyer for the government but claims VAT tax refund from what he has paid to previous intermediate input suppliers. The full tax amount is ultimately passed to the final buyers. The process sounds complicated but the nature of the original type of VAT is pretty straightforward. The tax base of VAT is the value added in the production process of an enterprise, which is its revenue minus the cost of intermediate inputs. In the real world, because of refunds for intermediate input uses and various other exemptions, treating VAT in CGE models is somewhat complex, which will be further discussed in Chapter 15. We keep the model simple in this chapter as we have no intermediate inputs nor their VAT refunds.

Suppose in an economy with only labor and capital as factor inputs, the total value added is the sum of factor income from labor and capital inputs. Let *tvat* be the VAT tax rate. Then the amount of the VAT tax is:

$$\text{VAT} = tvat \cdot \sum_c (WL \cdot QLD_c + WK \cdot QKD_c) \tag{11.5.1}$$

There are three types of VAT: production-type, income-type, and consumption-type. The production-type VAT levies the tax on all value-added part in the production as that in Equation (11.5.1). This is the original idea of the VAT tax. The income-type VAT allows enterprises to deduct depreciation of fixed capital. The consumption-type VAT allows enterprises to deduct the entire amount of the expense on fixed capital during the year of purchase. In either of the latter two cases, by nature no VAT tax is levied on the capital use. Hence the VAT tax paid by the enterprises is

$$VAT = tvat \cdot \sum_c WL \cdot QLD_c \tag{11.5.2}$$

In theory, the production-type VAT equally treats all factor inputs so it is neutral. The income-type and consumption-type VAT taxes encourage use of capital but discourage employment of labor. However some scholars challenge the neutrality property by arguing capital inputs should be treated like intermediate inputs.

To illustrate the setup for VAT in CGE models, suppose the model economy has the SAM table as Table 11.5.1. We have two VAT accounts in this table, VAT on labor and VAT on capital. In their column accounts, the numbers are the VAT taxes paid by enterprises to the government. In the row accounts, the numbers represent the taxes would be added by producers in sale and charge to buyers. When a part of the VAT on the factor use is not deductible, this part of tax burden falls directly on the enterprise. It can be calibrated that the VAT tax rate is 10% for both labor and capital inputs. For instance, in the sector of commodity 1, the VAT tax rate for labor *tvat* is (VAT on labor)/(labor cost) = 11/110 = 10%. The same rate applies to capital and labor in other commodity sectors. Because all factor uses are equally taxed, this is a production-type VAT.

Table 11.5.1. Model economy with VAT taxes.

	Commodity 1	Commodity 2	Labor	Capital	Households	Government	VAT on labor	VAT on capital	Total
Commodity 1					150	29.3			179.3
Commodity 2		70			190	30			220
Labor	110	70							180
Capital	53	130							183
Households			180	183		11			374
Government					34		18	18.3	70.3
VAT on labor	11	7							18
VAT on capital	5.3	13							18.3
Total	179.3	220	180	183	374	70.3	18	18.3	

In setting up CGE models with VAT, we modify the previous model in Section 11.3 as follows. In the production block, the production function remains unchanged. When a VAT is imposed, the costs of using factors increase. In economics, this is true regardless whether VAT is nominally paid by buyers or not. The labor employment cost now is $(1 + tvat) \cdot WL$, a 10% increase, so is the capital cost. The FOC for optimal input combination is:

$$\frac{(1 + tvat) \cdot WL}{(1 + tvat) \cdot WK} = \frac{\delta_c^q}{(1 - \delta_c^q)} \left(\frac{QLD_c}{QKD_c} \right)^{\rho_c - 1} \qquad c \in C \qquad (11.5.3)$$

Under the production-type VAT, however, when labor and capital face the same VAT rate, because cancelling a common factor, the first order condition (FOC) remains unchanged as shown above. But the price equation is to be adjusted. Using the purchaser's price PQ, it is:

$$PQ_c \cdot QC_c = (1 + tvat)(WL \cdot QLD_c + WK \cdot QKD_c) \qquad c \in C \qquad (11.5.4)$$

It can be seen that VAT has an impact on the purchaser's price.

In the government block, its revenue now has the VAT components. The government revenue Equation (11.3.9) is changed to:

$$YG = ti_h \cdot YH + tvat \cdot \sum_c (WL \cdot QLD_c + WK \cdot QKD_c) \qquad (11.5.5)$$

The consumptions by households and the government are at the purchaser's prices. CPI is also based on the purchaser's prices. These equations are changed to:

$$PQ_c \cdot QH_c = shareh_c \cdot (1 - ti_h) \cdot YH \qquad c \in C \qquad (11.5.6)$$

$$PQ_c \cdot QG_c = shareg_c \cdot (EG - transfer_{hg} \cdot CPI) \qquad c \in C \qquad (11.5.7)$$

$$CPI = \sum_{c \in C} PQ_c \cdot cpiwt_c \qquad (11.5.8)$$

The market clearing and other equations are in real quantities so they have no changes. In this model only the purchaser's price is explicitly shown. The basic price is not explicitly shown although it can be computed by Equation (11.5.4). Because the production-type VAT does not change the first-order-condition of optimal factor use (Equation (11.5.3)), and the optimal input bundle remains the same, in this sense the production-type VAT is neutral for all factor inputs.

Most countries in the world now adopt consumption-type VAT system based on the argument for stimulating technology investment, because the consumption-type VAT exempts taxes on capital inputs thus provides an incentive to replace labor with capital. By doing so, the exempted VAT taxes on capital and others in the value-added part eventually pass to the final consumers. This issue will be further discussed in Chapter 15.

Here we list all equations in the CGE model with production-type VAT, for the economy described by Table 11.5.1. The macroeconomic closure is neoclassical. Hence, factors are fully employed and prices are flexible. The government adheres to fiscal budget balance and is a rule-follower. *tvatl* and *tvatk* are VAT rates for labor and capital inputs respectively. PQ is the purchaser's price and used as the base price.

$$QC_c = \alpha_c^q [\delta_c^q QLD_c^{\rho_c} + (1 - \delta_c^q) QKD_c^{\rho_c}]^{1/\rho_c} \qquad c \in C \tag{11.5.9}$$

$$\frac{(1 + tvatl) \cdot WL}{(1 + tvatk) \cdot WK} = \frac{\delta_c^q}{(1 - \delta_c^q)} \left(\frac{QLD_c}{QKD_c} \right)^{\rho_c - 1} \qquad c \in C \tag{11.5.10}$$

$$PQ_c \cdot QC_c = (1 + tvatl) \cdot WL \cdot QLD_c + (1 + tvatk) \cdot WK \cdot QKD_c \quad c \in C \tag{11.5.11}$$

$$YH = WL \cdot QLS + WK \cdot QKS + transfer_{hg} \cdot CPI \tag{11.5.12}$$

$$YDISPH = (1 - ti_h) YH \tag{11.5.13}$$

$$PQ_c \cdot QH_c = shareh_c \cdot YDISPH \qquad c \in C \tag{11.5.14}$$

$$YG = ti_h \cdot YH + tvatl_c \cdot WL \cdot \sum_c QLD_c + tvatk_c \cdot WK \cdot \sum_c QKD_c \tag{11.5.15}$$

$$YG - EG = 0 \tag{11.5.16}$$

$$PQ_c \cdot QG_c = shareg_c \cdot (EG - transfer_{hg} \cdot CPI) \qquad c \in C \tag{11.5.17}$$

$$QC_c = QH_c + QG_c \qquad c \in C \tag{11.5.18}$$

$$\sum_{c \in C} QLD_c = QLS \tag{11.5.19}$$

$$\sum_{c \in C} QKD_c = QKS \tag{11.5.20}$$

$$QLS = \overline{QLS} \tag{11.5.21}$$

$$QKS = \overline{QKS} \tag{11.5.22}$$

$$CPI = \sum_{c \in C} PQ_c \cdot cpiwt_c \tag{11.5.23}$$

The model consists of 15 equation groups. CPI is computed in the system and used for cost-of-living adjustment for transfer payments to households. From the SAM table, we can calibrate parameters α_c^q, δ_c^q, $transfer_{hg}$, ti_h, $tvatl_c$, $tvatk_c$, $shareh_c$, $shareg_c$, $cpiwt_c$. Exponents ρ_c need to be obtained from external information. The equations used to calibrate parameters are similar to the system equations. For instances, $shareh_c$ and $shareg_c$ are calibrated by equation forms like Equations (11.5.14) and (11.5.17) from the SAM table data.

There are 15 variable groups in the system: QC_c, QLD_c, QKD_c, QLS, QKS, YH, $YDISPH$, QH_c, QG_c, YG, EG, PQ_c, WL, WK, CPI. But we need a numeraire. Suppose we choose labor price WL as the numeraire:

$$WL = \overline{WL} = 1 \tag{11.5.24}$$

Hence the variable groups reduces to 14. To restore the system squareness, we can add a dummy variable $WALRAS$ in the system or delete one equation in the system. Suppose this time we choose the latter method and delete the market clearing equation of commodity sector 1. So Equation (11.5.18) is replaced by (11.5.18′), whose commodity index is restrict to only sector 2 ($c = 2$ rather than $c = 1, 2$):

$$QC_c = QH_c + QG_c \qquad\qquad c = 2 \qquad\qquad (11.5.18')$$

After deleting one commodity market clearing equation, the system is square and solvable. Section 11.7 provides the GAMS program for the above model. It can be tested that the outcomes from deleting one equation are the same as adding $WALRAS$ dummy variable in the system.

As a note here, PQ is the purchaser's price which includes the VAT taxes. If instead we wish to computer the basic price PC, which is net of VAT, we can include the following price equation given in the model:

$$PC_c \cdot QC_c = WL \cdot QLD_c + WK \cdot QKD_c \qquad\qquad c \in C \qquad\qquad (11.5.25)$$

11.6 Payroll Tax and Enterprise Income Tax

In addition to individual income taxes, sales taxes, and VAT, governments in the world levy numerous other taxes in their economies. A country's tax structure like that in the U.S. can be quite complicated. In constructing CGE models for tax issues, a researcher should focus on the major taxes related to the research subject and make simplifications for other taxes. Some taxes may need to break down to details to analyze, others need to be combined for simplification.

Take an example of the U.S. The U.S. does not have VAT but the federal and local governments levy many other taxes. In addition to the individual income taxes, the second major federal tax revenue comes from payroll taxes, which roughly account for 35% of the total revenue. The payroll taxes are based on the enterprise's wage bills and shared between employers and employees. They include taxes of Social Security, Medicare, unemployment insurance, etc. Some of these "payroll taxes" in business accounting may be classified differently in the SNA system. For instance, social security paid by employers is classified as "compensation of employees" rather than "taxes" in SNA. These differences in terms won't change the following economic analysis because they constitute the same increase in the labor cost for the employers.

The U.S. payroll taxes consist of many component taxes. These component taxes in the payroll tax group need to be regrouped according to their natures before setting up their equations in CGE models. Suppose the enterprises as employers pay 9% of the wage bill for payroll taxes for their workers. Let *tpayent* be the payroll tax rate paid by the enterprises, this employer-part-of-payroll-taxes is

$$\text{Payroll-taxes-paid-by-employers} = tpayent \cdot WL \cdot \sum_c QLD_c \qquad\qquad (11.6.1)$$

Payroll taxes paid by employers are additional costs on labor employment, which would impact on the enterprise production decision; hence the production block needs to be updated accordingly. In the CGE model of Section 11.5, if the VAT tax system is replaced by the employer-part-of-payroll-taxes, Equations (11.5.14), (11.5.15), and (11.5.19) would be revised to the following equations:

$$\frac{(1 + tpayent) \cdot WL}{WK} = \frac{\delta_c^q}{(1 - \delta_c^q)} \left(\frac{QLD_c}{QKD_c}\right)^{\rho_c - 1} \qquad c \in C \qquad (11.6.2)$$

$$PC_c \cdot QC_c = (1 + tpayent) WL \cdot QLD_c + WK \cdot QKD_c \qquad c \in C \qquad (11.6.3)$$

$$YG = ti_h \cdot YH + tpayent \cdot \sum_c WL \cdot QLD_c \qquad (11.6.4)$$

Note in Equation (11.6.3), the price is basic price, because the payroll tax paid by employers is included in the basic price. If the model economy has sales taxes, we need to further add sales taxes to reach purchaser's price PQ by equation $PQ_c = (1 + tsale_c) \cdot PC_c$:

$$PQ_c \cdot QC_c = (1 + tsale_c)[(1 + tpayent) WL \cdot QLD_c + WK \cdot QKD_c] \qquad c \in C \qquad (11.6.5)$$

then we also include the sales tax amount in the government revenue.

Now let us examine the part of payroll taxes paid by employees. Suppose among the payroll taxes, the employees pay 8% of their wage earnings (which is also the enterprise wage bill) for Social Security and Medicare taxes to the government. This employee-part-payroll-taxes by nature are similar to the individual income taxes. In the SAM table, the figure is placed in cell of the household's column account paying to the government row account. Let *tpayhh* be the payroll tax rate 8% paid by households from their labor earnings, this employee-part-of-payroll-taxes is

$$\text{Payroll-taxes-paid-by-employees} = tpayhh \cdot WL \cdot \sum_c QLD_c \qquad (11.6.6)$$

Because this part of payroll tax functions as individual income taxes, it does not change the relative factor prices in enterprise's decision on production, and does not change equations in the production block. It reduces household's disposable income and increases the government's tax revenue. If the employee-part-of-payroll-taxes is not deductible from the household's income tax (such as the Social Security tax in the U.S.), the household's disposable income *YISPH* in Equation (11.5.17) is reduced by this amount:

$$YDISPH = (1 - ti_h) YH - tpayhh \cdot WL \cdot \sum_c QLD_c \qquad (11.6.7)$$

The government revenue in Equation (11.6.4) increases by this amount:

$$YG = ti_h \cdot YH + tpayent \cdot WL \cdot \sum_c QLD_c + tpayhh \cdot WL \cdot \sum_c QLD_c \qquad (11.6.8)$$

If this payroll tax is fully deductible from household's income taxes, then the household's total tax bill and the government received is still $ti_h \cdot YH$, no net changes in the model equations. If it is partially deductible, then we have to further break down to percentage details and set up accordingly.

In most countries, enterprises also pay business income taxes, which are levied on the profits recorded in their books. Business income tax is a direct tax. CGE models assume that in a commodity sector, on average economic profit is zero, although individual firms may earn positive accounting profits. The accounting profits in the SNA system are recorded as "net operating surplus", a component of gross income from capital, in the SNA system. In our previous simple CGE models, capital income is all transferred to households. Now we should revise the model so part of the capital income of $WK \cdot QKS$ is retained by the enterprises. Let $shareif_{hk}$ be the share of the capital income being transferred to the households. Parameter $shareif$ stands for the share of factor "f" income going to institution "i". So the household's income YH includes their share of capital income of:

$$shareif_{hk} \cdot WK \cdot QKS \qquad (11.6.9)$$

Let $shareif_{ent\,k}$ be the share of the capital income retained by the enterprises. So the enterprises' retained own income is

$$shareif_{ent\,k} \cdot WK \cdot QKS \qquad (11.6.10)$$

Let ti_{ent} be the business income tax rate. Then the business income tax amount from the retained own capital income is

$$ti_{ent} \cdot shareif_{ent\,k} \cdot WK \cdot QKS \qquad (11.6.11)$$

In CGE models, this tax amount needs to be added to the government tax revenue YG. As a direct tax, it does not affect the relative factor prices hence does not change equations in the production block.

In recent years it has been argued that a cut of business income tax would encourage enterprises to use fixed capital thus inducing more investment. The underlying assumptions are that (1) the saved direct business tax would be reinvested in the enterprises, and (2) the tax cut would lower the cost of capital consumption. To simulate this theory, in addition to the tax payment to the government, the production block equations need to be revised to reflect the changes in the enterprises' behavior. Following the argument that corporate income tax is an additional tax burden on the capital use, which has raised the unit capital cost to $(1 + ti_{ent} \cdot shareif_{ent\,k}) \cdot WK$, the original FOC of the input use is revised to:

$$\frac{WL}{(1 + ti_{ent} \cdot shareif_{ent\,k}) \cdot WK} = \frac{\delta_c^q}{(1 - \delta_c^q)} \left(\frac{QLD_c}{QKD_c} \right)^{\rho_c - 1} \qquad c \in C \qquad (11.6.12)$$

Hence a cut in business income tax would reduce ti_{ent}, thus the capital cost. In turn, it encourages the use of capital.

This argument is subject to academic controversy. Business income tax is levied on enterprise profits after subtracting labor and fixed capital costs (depreciation), so this tax should be neutral to labor and fixed capital uses. Cut in the business income tax rate should not only benefit capital use: enterprises may use the saved tax money to benefit labor use, such as to improve management, hire better engineers or give bonus to workers to raise their productivity. A cut in the business income tax is not lowering the fixed capital price but is providing the incentive for the overall growth of the enterprise.

To compromise different views, we can consider the following setup. Many SAM tables distinguish between depreciation (fixed capital consumption) and net operating surplus accounts. As said the latter can be the proxy for enterprise accounting profits. In the production function of constant returns to scale, to specify the contributing source for net operating surplus, we can add a primary factor of "efficiency", in addition to the existing primary factors of labor and capital. This efficiency factor has various names in economics models: technology, entrepreneurship, total factor productivity (TFP), Solow residual, etc. Net operating surplus can be set as the contribution to the output from the efficiency factor input. The production function in the value-added module can be in a nested structure for the three factor inputs. Then a cut in business income tax can be set as reducing the cost of the efficiency factor thus improving management, efficiency or technology used in enterprises.

The above discussion serves as an example of studying a controversial topic. Often we have to specify new behavior functions and have to change the model structure. Yet all the changes must be theoretically justified and be consistent with the basic national accounting concepts.

11.7 GAMS Program of a CGE Model with Government

In this section we provide the GAM program for the CGE model with production-type VAT and income taxes in Section 11.5. Because only the purchaser's price PQ is explicitly present in the model for commodities, it is chosen as the base price, so $PQ_c = 1$. Basic price PC is not explicitly shown in the model and is not needed to solve the model. It can be computed by the following equation added in the model if we wish to know the markup from basic price PC_c to purchaser's price PQ_c:

$$PC_c = (WL \cdot QLD_c + WK \cdot QKD_c)/QC_c \qquad c \in C \qquad (11.7.1)$$

Example 11.7.1. The model economy is described as the SAM table of Table 11.5.1. It is in a neoclassical world with full employment of factors. Write a GAMS program for the CGE model in Section 11.5. The production function is a CES function with exponent $\rho = 0.6$. Using labor price WL as the numeraire. Instead of using dummy variable $WALRAS$, delete market clearing equation of commodity 1 to satisfy the squareness of the model system. Replicate the initial equilibrium. (1) Check the homogeneity property of the model by raising numeraire value (labor price) by 10% and verify all real quantities remain unchanged. (2) Simulating a 10% increase in the capital supply. What happens to the capital price? (3) What is the capital multiplier if it is defined as the increase in GDP due to one percent increase in capital stock?

Solution: The GAMS program is given as follows. In order to calculate the change in GDP, the program adds the variable of GDP and an equation to calculate GDP. GDP is the sum of all final commodities consumed by households and government. The simulation results are:

(1) After the numeraire value increases by 10%, all prices increase by the same proportion, and all real quantities remain the same. So the model is homogenous of degree 1 in prices.

Remark: If in the model that the government's transfer payment to households is not CPI indexed, then the homogeneity property will not hold.

(2) After the capital supply increases by 10%, the capital price decreases by 4%, and GDP increases by 5%. The capital stock multiplier is therefore computed as $5\%/10\% = 0.5$.

```
$title Example 11.7.1 CGE model with government and fiscal policy

*Define accounts
set ac /sec1,sec2,lab,cap,gov,hh,vatl,vatk,total/;
set c(ac) /sec1,sec2/;

alias (ac,acp),(c,cp);

table sam(ac,acp)
```

	sec1	sec2	lab	cap	hh	gov	vatl	vatk	total
sec1					150	29.3			179.3
sec2					190	30			220
lab	110	70							180
cap	53	130							183
hh			180	183		11			374
gov					34		18	18.3	70.3
vatl	11	7							18
vatk	5.3	13							18.3
total	179.3	220	180	183	374	70.3	18	18.3	

```
Parameter
*Variable name followed by 0 denotes the corresponding parameter at the
initial level of the variable

PQ0(c)          Purchaser's price of commodity c
WL0             Labor price
WK0             Capital price
QC0(c)          Real quantity of c
QLD0(c)         Labor demand
QKD0(c)         Capital demand
QLS0            Labor supply
QKS0            Capital supply
QH0(c)          Households consumption of commodity c
YH0             Households income in dollars
YDISPH0         Household disposable income
EG0             Government expenditure
```

```
YG0                     Government revenue
QG0(c)                  Government consumption of commodity c
rho(c)                  CES production function exponent
delta(c)                Share parameter of the CES production function
scaleA(c)               Scale parameter of the CES production function
shareh(c)               Share of households income spending on consumption c
shareg(c)               Share of government income spending on consumption c
tih                     Households income tax rate
tvatl(c)                VAT tax rate on labor inputs
tvatk(c)                VAT tax rate on capital inputs
transferhg0             Government transfer payments to households
CPI0                    Consumer price index
cpiwt(c)                CPI weights
GDP0                    GDP
;

*Calibration and assigning numbers
PQ0(c)=1;
WK0=1;
WL0=1;
QC0(c)=sam('total',c)/PQ0(c);
QLD0(c)=(sam('lab',c))/WL0;
QKD0(c)=sam('cap',c)/wk0;
QLS0=sum(c,sam('lab',c))/WL0;
QKS0=sum(c,sam('cap',c))/WK0;
QH0(c) =SAM(c,'hh')/PQ0(c);
transferhg0=sam('hh','gov');
cpiwt(c)=QH0(c)/sum(cp,QH0(cp));
CPI0=sum(c,PQ0(c)*cpiwt(c));
YH0=WL0*QLS0+WK0*QKS0+transferhg0*CPI0;
tih=sam('gov','hh')/YH0;
YDISPH0=(1-tih)*YH0;
YG0=tih*YH0+sam('gov','vatl')+sam('gov','vatk');
EG0=YG0;
QG0(c) =SAM(c,'GOV')/PQ0(c);
rho(c)=0.6;
delta(c)=WL0*QLD0(c)**(1-rho(c))/(WL0*QLD0(c)**(1-rho(c))+WK0*QKD0(c)**(1-
rho(c)));
scaleA(c)=QC0(c)/(delta(c)*QLD0(c)**rho(c)+(1-
delta(c))*QKD0(c)**rho(c))**(1/rho(c));
shareh(c)=PQ0(c)*QH0(c)/((1-tih)*YH0);
```

```
shareg(c)=PQ0(c)*QG0(c)/(YG0-transferhg0*CPI0);
tvatl(c)=sam('vatl',c)/sam('lab',c);
tvatk(c)=sam('vatk',c)/sam('cap',c);
GDP0=sum(c,(sam(c,'hh')+sam(c,'gov'))/PQ0(c));

display
PQ0,WK0,WL0,QC0,QLD0,QKD0,QLS0,QKS0,QH0,transferhg0,YH0,tih,YDISPH0,YG0,QG0,
shareh,shareg,tvatl,tvatk,GDP0,cpiwt;

Variable
QC(c),QLD(c),QKD(c),YH,YDISPH,QH(c),QG(c),YG,EG,GDP,PQ(c),WL,WK,CPI
*The following variables would be converted to parameters by .fx late
QLS,QKS
;

Equation
QCeq(c),FOCQCeq(c),PQeq(c),YHeq,YDISPHeq,QHeq(c),YGeq,QGeq(c),EGeq,
ComEqui2,Leq,Keq,GDPeq,CPIeq
;

QCeq(c)..
QC(c)=e=scaleA(c)*(delta(c)*QLD(c)**rho(c)+(1-
delta(c))*QKD(c)**rho(c))**(1/rho(c));

FOCQCeq(c)..
((1+tvatl(c))*WL)/((1+tvatk(c))*WK)=e=delta(c)/(1-delta(c))*(QKD(c)/QLD(c))
**(1-rho(c));

PQeq(c)..
PQ(c)*QC(c)=e=(1+tvatl(c))*WL*QLD(c)+(1+tvatk(c))*WK*QKD(c);

YHeq..
YH=e=WL*QLS+WK*QKS+transferhg0*CPI;

YDISPHeq..
YDISPH=e=(1-tih)*YH;

QHeq(c)..
PQ(c)*QH(c)=e=shareh(c)*YDISPH;
```

```
YGeq..
YG=e=tih*YH+sum(c,tvatl(c)*WL*QLD(c))+sum(c,tvatk(c)*WK*QKD(c));

QGeq(c)..
PQ(c)*QG(c)=e=shareg(c)*(EG-transferhg0*CPI);

EGeq..
YG=e=EG;
```

*After WL is used for numeraire, we delete the market clearing equation of
sector 1 to reduce the number of equations, to satisfy system squareness.
Hence, only sector 2 market clearing equation ComEqui2 is kept:

```
ComEqui2..
QC('sec2')=e=QH('sec2')+QG('sec2');

Leq..
Sum(c,QLD(c))=e=QLS;

Keq..
Sum(c,QKD(c))=e=QKS;
```

*Below is the equation to compute GDP
```
GDPeq..
GDP=e=sum(c,QH(c)+QG(c));

CPIeq..
CPI=e=sum(c,PQ(c)*cpiwt(c));
```

*Assign initial values
```
QC.L(c)=QC0(c);
QLD.L(c)=QLD0(c);
QKD.L(c)=QKD0(c);
YH.L=YH0;
QH.L(c)=QH0(c);
QG.L(c)=QG0(c);
YG.L=YG0;
EG.L=EG0;
GDP.L=GDP0;
PQ.L(c)=PQ0(c);
WL.L=WL0;
```

```
WK.L=WK0;
CPI.L=CPI0;
QLS.fx=QLS0;
QKS.fx=QKS0;
WL.fx=1;

*Executing model
model cge /all/;
solve cge using mcp;

display PQ.L,WK.L,WL.L,QC.L,QLD.L,QKD.L,QLS.L,QKS.L,QH.L,transferhg0,
YH.L,YDISPH.L,tih,YG.L,EG.L,QG.L,shareh,shareg,tvatl,tvatk,GDP.L;

$title Simulation for changing the numeraire value by 10%
*WL increases by 10%
WL.fx=1.1

model sim1 /all/;
solve sim1 using mcp;

display PQ.L,WK.L,WL.L,QC.L,QLD.L,QKD.L,QLS.L,QKS.L,QH.L,transferhg0,
        YH.L,tih,YG.L,EG.L,QG.L,shareh,shareg,tvatl,tvatk,GDP.L,CPI.L;

$title Simulation for increasing capital stock by 10%

*Capital stock increase by 10%
QKS.fx=QKS0*1.1;

*Restore numeraire to 1
WL.fx=1;

parameter
GDPold Save the initial GDP value;
GDPold=GDP.L;

model sim2 /all/;
solve sim2 using mcp;

display
PQ.L,WK.L,WL.L,QC.L,QLD.L,QKD.L,QLS.L,QKS.L,QH.L,transferhg0,YH.L,tih,YG.L,
EG.L,QG.L,shareh,shareg,tvatl,tvatk,GDP.L,CPI.L;
```

```
Parameter
Multiplier;
Multiplier=(GDP.L-GDPold)/GDPold;

display Multiplier;

*End
```

Exercises

11E.1 The model economy has the following SAM table (Table 11E.1.1). Use GAMS to calibrate the income tax rate, and the shares spending on commodities out of the budgets of the households and the government.

Table 11E.1.1. Model economy SAM table.

	Commodity 1	Commodity 2	Labor	Capital	Households	Government	Total
Commodity 1					280	45	325
Commodity 2					250	90	340
Labor	200	130					330
Capital	125	210					335
Households			330	335		10	675
Government					145		145
Total	325	340	330	335	675	145	

11E.2 In the GAMS program of the CGE model in Section 11.7, suppose the VAT rates change to $tvatl = 0.9$ and $tvatk = 0.3$ for both commodities. Add basic price variable PC_c and corresponding equations to compute PC_c and the price markup $PQ_c/PC_c - 1$. Review the outcomes.

11E.3 In our above model, there is no private savings. That is, households spend all their budget on consumption. In this environment, why does the government have to balance its fiscal budget, that is, $YG = EG$?

Chapter 12

Savings and Investment

In previous chapters, we work on simple economies. Households and the government spend all their budgets on consumption of commodities. Enterprises transfer all their capital incomes to households and do not make capital investment. The real-world is not that simple. Consumers save out of their disposable income for various reasons. The government may spend more or less than its revenue. Enterprises borrow money in the financial market to fund their investment. In a real economy, some institutions (agent groups) save, some other institutions borrow and overspend. The financial deficiency gap of some institutions must be filled by other institutions who underspend their budgets. This balance relationship of savings and dissavings must be true in the real economy as well as in the national accounts. In this chapter, we will include the important real-world economic variables savings, investment, and their related functions in the framework of the computable general equilibrium (CGE) models.

12.1 Personal Savings

Why do households save? Saving means that they consume less than their disposable income. Economics explanations are that people save for future consumption because of retirement, precaution for uncertainty, bequests to children, etc. Households allocate their budget between consumption and savings. In macroeconomics textbooks, this is written as

$$C + S = Y - T \qquad (12.1.1)$$

where C, S, Y, T stand for consumption, savings, national income and tax, respectively. $Y - T$ is disposable income. Savings is the difference after subtracting consumption from disposable income. In our CGE model notation, $S = Y - T - C$ is

$$SAVEH = YDISPH - EH \qquad (12.1.2)$$

where $SAVEH$ is household savings and EH is the total consumption expenditure of households. Changes in savings are the sums of changes in consumption and in disposable income.

During macroeconomic cycles, consumption is relatively stable because it is more difficult for households to adjust their basic needs and life style in the short run. The major determinant for consumption is disposable income. Other determinants including interest rate (r), wealth (A) and price (P) may also have influences. Thus a general consumption function is

$$C = C(Y - T, r, A, P) \tag{12.1.3}$$

A simple regression for the past 18 years since 2002 in the U.S. shows that disposable income alone explains 91% of changes in consumption, revealed by R-square. Hence, households' consumption is often specified as just a function of disposable income. Let mpc be the rate of marginal-propensity-to-consume, in macroeconomics symbols, the consumption function is:

$$C = C_0 + mpc \cdot (Y - T) \tag{12.1.4}$$

where C_0 is the constant term. It is "the subsistence level of consumption", so must be positive. The saving function is

$$S = (Y - T) - [C_0 + mpc \cdot (Y - T)] = -C_0 + (1 - mpc) \cdot (Y - T)$$
$$= -C_0 + mps \cdot (Y - T) \tag{12.1.5}$$

The saving function is a mirror image of the consumption function. Its slope is marginal-propensity-to-save mps. It is a mirror image of mpc: $mps = 1 - mpc$. Its constant term is $-C_0$, which means that households have to dissave to buy necessities when they have no disposable income. Savings are more volatile than consumption in economic cycles, as they serve as the buffering mechanism for households to cope with income volatility.

Following the above discussion, in our CGE model notation, the consumption function is

$$EH = eho + mpc \cdot YDISPH \tag{12.1.6}$$

eho is the constant term. o is lowercase letter O, which means that the constant term is at the "origin". Readers should always distinguish between letter o and number 0 in variable names as they look similar. Households then spend EH on consumption of various commodities.

The saving function in a CGE model can be either in the form of Equation (12.1.2) or the direct form as follows:

$$SAVEH = -eho + (1 - mpc) \cdot YDISPH = -eho + mps \cdot YDISPH \tag{12.1.7}$$

The intercept of the saving function $-eho$ is negative, which is the amount of dissavings at zero disposable income.

In principle macroeconomics, eho and mpc are constants. Accordingly, in CGE models they can be set as parameters whose values are obtained externally or calibrated from the data. In some CGE macro closures, however, mpc or mps are treated as endogenous variables to be determined by the model system, or, as a function of interest rate, wealth position, or a consumer confidence indicator. In some CGE models, for simplicity eho is set to zero. Then mps equals average-propensity-to-save, which can be easily derived from dividing savings by disposable income.

When a CGE research project requires that households be disaggregated into several income groups, each household group may have its own consumption and saving functions with different parameters. The CGE model would have EH_h and $SAVH_h$ where subscript h denotes the group index. In this case, mpc_h and mps_h are group-specific. Indeed, it is well known in economics that mpc and mps vary substantially across income groups.

12.2 Private Investment

Investment is the spending by enterprises on new physical capitals. In national accounts, it is termed "gross capital formation", which refers to the fixed-capital investment by the private sector. The capital formation by the government, such as building highways, is included in the government spending.

Private investment includes enterprises' spending on new equipment, structures, residential houses, intellectual property products (which are usually intangible), plus changes in inventory. Gross capital formation accounts for 21% of the U.S. GDP in 2018. The same figure is much higher in East Asian countries. For instance, gross capital formation accounts for 43% of GDP in China in 2018. Investment accounts for a smaller share in GDP than consumption; but investment changes are much more volatile than consumption in economic cycles.

Enterprises make investment because they want more profits. The dominant determinant for their investment decision is the prospect of sales and profits in future. Another determinant for investment is the interest rate, which is the cost of borrowing money for investment. Enterprises may fund their investment from their net operating surplus, which in nature is from enterprises' own savings. Mostly, enterprises raise funds through the financial market to finance their investment as their own savings are often insufficient. Enterprises can either raise funds by selling companies' equities or by borrowing money from banks and other creditors. This money must come from savings of other institutions in the economy.

In specifying the investment function in empirical studies, because it is difficult to quantify enterprises' confidence and their vision about future profitability, various other measurable proxy variables are used. An investment function can include these explanatory variables: (1) current capital stock size; (2) depreciation of the existing capital stock; (3) size of the investment in the previous period; (4) GDP growth rate in the previous period (a proxy of growth momentum); (5) GDP growth rate in the current period; (6) business confidence index; (7) interest rate (which is the cost of loans). The information about the determinants of (1)–(4) are historical, which are available in constructing the CGE model. The latter three determinants can be included in the investment function if needed. In practice, however, we should keep the investment function form simple to avoid unnecessary complications.

Let the investment amount in sector c be $QINV_C$. The investment function is

$$QINV_c = \overline{QINVO_c} \cdot INVADJ_c \qquad (12.2.1)$$

where $\overline{QINVO_c}$ is the capital formation in the current period in the social accounting matrix (SAM) table. $INVADJ_C$ is an adjustment factor, which can be a variable, a parameter, or a function of other variables. Its initial value is 1.

Suppose our research project is to simulate an external shock from an increase in investment by optimistic business owners. We can first conduct an independent study to estimate possible scenarios of the increases in investment. Then we convert these increases to the changes in the values of $INVADJ_C$. Then we run the CGE model to simulate these shocks. In this example, $INVADJ_C$ is treated as an exogenous variable (or parameter in GAMS).

Suppose in another research, the external shock is from other third parties, say, a stock market crash. The economy is in downturn. We are concerned with the impacts of the volatility of investment. In the research project, we postulate that the economic downturn would hurt investment, and the proposed government's cut in the interest rate would encourage investment. In this case, $QINV_C$ must be a function of related variables. In turn, $INVADJ_c$ is endogenously determined by the model. We may specify $INVADJ_C$ as follows:

$$INVADJ_c = 1 + para1_c \cdot (\overline{INTRATE} - INTRATE0)$$
$$+ para2_c \cdot (\log QC_c - \log QC0_c) \tag{12.2.2}$$

where *para1* and *para2* are coefficients, whose values are obtained externally by independent estimations. $INTRATE$ is the interest rate. "0" stands for the base (which is the current) period rate, and $\overline{INTRATE}$ is the proposed new rate. Without changes in the interest rate and the output QC_C level, $INVADJ_C$ equals 1, which means the investment level $QINV_C$ maintains the current level. In simulation of the government's cut of the interest rate, the exogenous variable $\overline{INTRATE}$ would change from the initial value. Meanwhile, the growth of the sectoral output QC_C would affect business confidence, thus $INVADJ_C$, too. Both factors would affect investment $QINV_C$ through the adjustment factor $INVADJ_C$.

Investment $QINV_C$ is the enterprises' demand for the final product c. In CGE models, we need to add this new component of spending on commodities. The commodity market clearing equation including $QINV_C$ is

$$QC_c = \sum_{c' \in C} QINT_{cc'} + QH_c + QINV_c + QG_c \qquad c \in C \tag{12.2.3}$$

12.3 Aggregate Expenditure and the Keynesian Equilibrium

When two separate groups make their own independent decisions — households decide how much to save and enterprises decide how much to invest — we would have a problem. Can the market system coordinate and harmonize savings and investment? According to Keynes, the answer is no. This theoretical issue also poses a problem in CGE modeling.

Recall that the proof of existence of the general equilibrium needs to use Walras' law. An important condition for Walras' law is that all households exhaust their budgets. When households save, which means they do not exhaust their budgets, Walras' law would not hold, then the economy may not reach the Walras equilibrium. An early response in economics to this question is that the households' savings would be channeled through the financial market to enterprises for capital investment. The interest rate functions as the price in the financial market to balance savings and investment. Then the economy returns to equilibrium.

The Keynesian theory maintains that the interest rate plays a limited and unreliable role in clearing the financial market between savings and investment, especially in an economic downturn. The main determinant of savings is households' disposable income, plus wealth and expectation of future income. The main determinant for enterprises' investment is the outlook of sales and profits. In an economic downturn, enterprises cut their investment out of pessimism, households cut consumption and increase precautionary savings out of pessimism. This causes savings to exceed investment. In the commodity market, a large amount of commodities produced cannot be sold. The interest rate provides no help in clearing the market, even if it drops to zero. Because of the insufficient demand, the economy plunges into recession.

Let us use the variable symbols in macroeconomics textbooks to address this theory. For simplicity, suppose the economy is closed without international trade. Then the income–expenditure equation is

$$Y = C + I + G \qquad (12.3.1)$$

where Y is aggregate output. C, I and G are consumption, investment and government spending, respectively.

Equation (12.3.1) may represent different concepts, depending on the context and definition of I. It can be used as the national income identity in national accounts. On the left-hand side (LHS), Y is GDP or national income; and the right-hand side (RHS) is the sum of expenditures of final products by households, enterprises and the government. Investment I is *actual investment* amount recorded in the national accounts. As an accounting identity, it always holds either in the real economy or in SAM tables and CGE models.

In a different context and by a different definition of investment I, Equation (12.3.1) stands for the Keynesian income–expenditure equilibrium condition. Here, LHS is national income and RHS is *planned* aggregate expenditure. The key difference from the accounting identity is that here I is *planned investment*. Actual investment is the sum of planned and unplanned investment. Actual investment often does not equal planned investment. Recall that investment includes changes in the inventory. In an economic downturn, there is unplanned inventory accumulation. The unplanned inventory is recorded on book and is physically stored in the enterprise warehouse, but it is not planned. So the enterprise will reduce the inventory level by cutting output in the next production cycle. This process would continue until the actual inventory falls to the planned level, which is the Keynesian equilibrium state.

The important message here is that, the economy relies on the fall in output Y to reach the new equilibrium, rather than relying on price adjustment as described in classical economics. This is shown in the typical income–expenditure diagram in macroeconomics as in Figure 12.3.1. AE stands for aggregate expenditure:

$$AE = C(Y - T) + I(Y) + G \qquad (12.3.2)$$

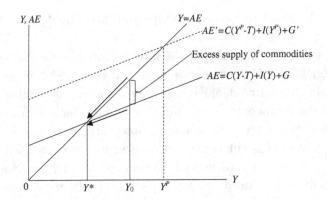

Figure 12.3.1.   Relying on adjustment in output Y rather than prices to reach equilibrium.

For simplicity, tax is lump-sum tax so T is a constant. C is a function of disposable income $Y - T$. I is a function of Y. Y_0 is the current state characterized by unplanned inventory accumulation and excess supply of commodities. The cut of output by enterprises causes the output Y to fall and in the diagram it moves leftwards. Eventually the economy reaches the Keynesian equilibrium Y^*, where the actual inventory is at the planned level and commodity surplus disappears, although output Y is at a lower level. Accordingly, the Keynesian equilibrium condition is defined as the state where output Y equals the planned total expenditure, $Y = AE$.

What about the savings and investment? As income Y falls, households reduce their savings but less proportionally than the fall in income. Eventually, the falling savings converge to the investment level at the Keynesian equilibrium Y^*. Y^* is below potential GDP Y^P, which implies it suffers from high unemployment and economic recession. Because Y^* is an equilibrium state, it won't change further unless being disturbed by external forces. The economy thus is trapped in a prolonged recession. That is why the Keynesian theory suggests increasing government spending as an external force to stimulate the economy.

When we set up CGE models in accordance with the above theory, we need to specify macroeconomic closure correctly. As demonstrated above, aggregate output Y is endogenously determined by aggregate expenditure AE. In the diagram, solved Y must be at the intersection of the AE line and the 45 degree line $AE = Y$. Accordingly, factor employment in the economy is also endogenously determined, which can fall below the full employment level. If the macro closure of a CGE model is a Keynesian closure, this is not a problem, because we do not require full employment of factors.

The classical or neoclassical closure assumes full factor employment. That is, the equilibrium output should be at potential GDP, $Y^* = Y^p$. Intuitively, this means that the AE line in the diagram should be shifted to the dashed AE' position, so the new intersection with the 45 degree line is at potential GDP. The closure must have a mechanism in the CGE model to automatically increase aggregate expenditure AE to the level of the dashed line. Economists propose various macro closures to solve this problem. Mathematically, all these suggested closures are workable, but none of them is convincingly justified by economics theory or reality.

To explain, let us take a look at the aggregate expenditure and its components: $AE = C(Y - T) + I + G$. We have the following four options to increase aggregate expenditure AE to reach the potential GDP:

1. Increasing government spending G. G is set as an endogenous variable, determined by the model system at the full employment state.
2. Reducing tax T. T is set as an endogenous variable in the model.
3. Increasing private investment I. I is set as an endogenous variable in the model.
4. Increasing autonomous consumption C, which means reducing autonomous savings.[1] In the consumption equation, this can be done by increasing the value of component *eho* or *mpc*. So we need to make either *eho* or *mpc* an endogenous variable.

The first two solutions mean that the government automatically increases spending or cuts the tax to maintain full employment. Hence, government savings $SAVEG$ is endogenous and its fiscal budget cannot be forced to balance. In this case, we need to assume a very effective Keynesian government who can always implement its fiscal policies. Solution 3 assumes that the private enterprises would automatically increase investment during economic downturn, which counters the Keynesian theory and the real-world observation. Solution 4 assumes that consumers would automatically increase consumption and reduce savings even in an economic downturn. This saving-driven closure rule is termed the "Johansen closure", which was set up by Johansen (1960). The Johansen closure may be remotely explained by a positive wealth effect on consumption due to a fall in the commodity prices, or the fall in the interest rate to discourage savings, as some neoclassical models suggest. Yet these hypotheses are exactly what Keynes critiqued and are not backed by the evidence in economic recession.

In summary, the above closure rules would mathematically solve the problem to ensure full employment of factors in a CGE model, but the economics justifications for them are often questionable.

12.4 The Savings–Investment Equation

The Keynesian equilibrium condition can also be expressed by the savings–investment equation, which is a mirror image of the income–expenditure function form. Indeed, the savings–investment equation is often included in CGE models for a more direct and explicit observation of the Keynesian equilibrium condition in CGE models.

From the perspective of how national income is used, we have another national accounting identity

$$Y = C + S + T \tag{12.4.1}$$

---

[1]In macroeconomics, "autonomous" spending is defined as the spending that does not vary with the income level Y. An autonomous change in consumption will vertically shift the AE line in Figure 12.3.1. An autonomous change in savings will vertically shift the national savings line in Figure 12.4.1.

It means that after households receive income Y, they pay taxes T, save S and spend C. Combining national income identity of Equation (12.3.1), we have

$$I + G = S + T \qquad\qquad (12.4.2)$$

$$I = S + (T - G) \qquad\qquad (12.4.2')$$

Equation (12.4.2′) is the "savings–investment equation", abbreviated to the S-I equation in literature. The LHS is private investment by enterprises, the RHS is national savings which consist of private savings S and government savings (or public savings) $SAVEG = T - G$. The equation says that investment must equal national savings in the economy:

$$\text{Investment} = \text{private savings} + \text{government savings} \qquad (12.4.3)$$

Because $I = S + (T - G)$ is the alternative form of the same equation $Y = C + I + G$, depending on the context, the savings–investment equation is also (1) a national accounting identity; or (2) the Keynesian equilibrium condition. As the national account identity, I stands for *actual* investment. The equation must always hold implicitly or explicitly in a CGE model. As the Keynesian equilibrium condition, I stands for *planned* investment. It is only reached after we successfully solved the CGE model.

The Keynesian model can be expressed by the savings–investment equation as follows:

$$I(Y) = S(Y - T) + T - G \qquad\qquad (12.4.4)$$

Savings is directly related to income Y by marginal-propensity-to-save *mps*.

We can explain the Keynesian model by Equation (12.4.4). Figure 12.4.1 is a mirror image of Figure 12.3.1. In an economic downturn at Y_0, households become more pessimistic. They take precaution so they increase autonomous saving and cut consumption, which shifts the national saving function $S(Y - T) + T - G$ upwards. On the other hand, enterprises are pessimistic so they cut investment I so this function I shifts downward. This causes investment I to be smaller than national savings at Y_0. Enterprises cut inventory and output, income Y falls. When Y falls, households' actual savings fall, too. Eventually, savings are so low that they equal planned investment at Y^*, where the savings and investment lines intersect. This is the Keynesian equilibrium state.

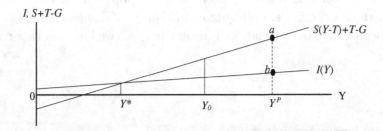

Figure 12.4.1. Keynesian model explained by the investment–savings equation.

Converting Equation (12.4.4) to our CGE notation, the Keynesian equilibrium condition in the savings–investment form is

$$\sum_c QINV_c = SAVEH + SAVEG \qquad (12.4.5)$$

where $SAVEG$ is government savings $T - G$. When working on the classical or neoclassical full employment condition for CGE models, the four optional closures discussed in the previous section would be intuitively explained as follows. In Figure 12.4.1, we need the investment and savings lines to intersect at the potential GDP level, represented by the dashed line at Y^P. The four optional ways to do so are as follows:

1. Increasing government spending G, which shifts the national savings line downward to point b. G is set to be endogenous in the model.
2. Reducing tax T and shifting national savings line downward to point b. T is endogenous in the model.
3. Increasing private investment I and shifting investment line upward to point a. I is endogenous in the model.
4. Reducing autonomous savings, so the national saving line shifts downward to point b. Savings are set endogenous in the model. This is done by changing eho or mpc (which is the mirror image of mps) from a parameter to a variable in the model.

The savings–investment equation for the Keynesian equilibrium condition provides convenience in CGE modeling and analysis. It allows us to directly check if the Keynesian condition holds, and directly observe and discuss the relationships of investment, private savings and government savings in a CGE model. For instance, when we want to observe the Keynesian equilibrium condition in the form of the income–expenditure equation $Y = C + I + G$, there is no such reduced form shown explicitly in a CGE model. Equation (12.2.3) is close but is not the income–expenditure equation. It has a component of intermediate inputs and it is not in the aggregate form. In addition, it has no tax explicitly shown so we cannot directly observe the behaviors of the government and private savings. Because of these reasons, in CGE research, the S-I equation and the concepts of savings and investment are more popularly used to discuss the Keynesian equilibrium condition, rather than using the income–expenditure framework concepts.

As shown above, in macroeconomics the S-I equation is derived from the income–expenditure equation. It is also true that the S-I equation of Equation (12.4.5) can be derived from the other equations of a CGE model. In the appendix of this chapter, we provide an example to demonstrate how the S-I equation can be derived from other equations of a CGE model. In other words, the S-I equation is functionally dependent on other equations of the CGE model. It is mathematically "redundant" except it provides the convenience as discussed in the previous paragraph. Without the S-I equation, the model still works and provides the right outcomes. Indeed, some CGE models do not have the S-I equation. When we include the S-I equation in a CGE model, we need to add a dummy variable in order to meet the squareness requirement of the GAMS solvers. Because of the dependency property, the value of this dummy variable should be zero when the model converges.

In previous CGE models, without households' savings we add a dummy variable *WALRAS* because the equations of a CGE model are linearly dependent due to Walras' law. Once households start to save and do not exhaust their budgets, Walras' law is invalid and the CGE model equations are no longer linearly dependent. When the S-I equation is added, because it is functionally dependent, we need to add one dummy variable again. The dummy variable is commonly added to the S-I equation, but in general it can also be added in other system equations in the model.

In many CGE models including the IFPRI model, this dummy variable is still named *WALRAS*. Theoretically, the name is conceptually misleading. The functional dependence of the S-I equation is not because of Walras' law, but because of the mirror image relationship between income–expenditure and savings–investment equations. They are the same equation of the Keynesian equilibrium condition but in different algebra forms.

In addition, suppose we construct a perfectly forward-looking neoclassical model, in which households' savings are their demand for future commodities' consumption, and enterprises investment is their optimal choice to supply future commodities. They trade these future commodities freely in the markets and the markets are cleared by the prices of the future commodities. Thus, Walras' law is restored because institutions/agents optimize their supply and demand by exhausting their budgets. Then we need a *WALRAS* dummy variable for this dependence caused by Walras' law, plus another dummy variable for dependence by the S-I equation. We would have a conflict in naming the two dummy variables. Hence, to make the new dummy variable conceptually distinguishable, in this book, we use a name *DUMMYSI* for the dummy variable for dependence caused by adding the S-I equation.

$$\sum_c QINV_c = SAVEH + SAVEG + DUMMYSI \tag{12.4.6}$$

12.5 A CGE Model with Savings and Investment

In what follows, we set up a CGE model with savings and investment. The economy is described by the SAM Table 12.5.1. It is a closed economy without trade. The model has the standard aggregate consumption function. The government collects individual income tax of 162 from households and business income tax of 40 from enterprises. It also collects sales taxes. The government spends a fixed share of its budget on each commodity. The savings–investment account is placed as the last account in the SAM table.

The production block has a nested structure. The top level is a constant elasticity of substitution (CES) function with aggregate value-added and aggregate intermediate input. At the bottom level, the value-added production module is a CES function with two inputs, labor and capital. The intermediate input production module is a Leontief function with commodity inputs.

The production block is similar to the model in Chapter 8, except there is a sales tax here. Commodity prices PQ are purchasers' prices. Basic prices are not explicitly shown but

Table 12.5.1. SAM table of model economy with savings and investment.

	Agriculture	Industry	Service	Labor	Capital	Household	Enterprise	Government	Sales tax	Savings–Investment	Total
Agriculture	260	320	150			500		71		155	1456
Industry	345	390	390			450		65		150	1790
Service	400	365	320			350		48		48	1531
Labor	200	250	400								850
Capital	210	400	210								820
Household				850	770			17			1637
Enterprise					50			40			90
Government						162	40		167		369
Sales tax	41	65	61								167
Savings–Investment						175	50	128			353
Total	1456	1790	1531	850	820	1637	90	369	167	353	8896

can be computed from the model.

$$QC_c = \alpha_c^q [\delta_c^q QVA_c^{\rho_c} + (1 - \delta_c^q) QINTA_c^{\rho_c}]^{1/\rho_c} \qquad c \in C \qquad (12.5.1)$$

$$\frac{PVA_c}{PINTA_c} = \frac{\delta_c^q}{(1 - \delta_c^q)} \left(\frac{QVA_c}{QINTA_c} \right)^{\rho_c - 1} \qquad c \in C \qquad (12.5.2)$$

$$PQ_c \cdot QC_c = (1 + tsale_c)(PVA_c \cdot QVA_c + PINTA_c \cdot QINTA_c) \qquad c \in C \qquad (12.5.3)$$

$$QVA_c = \alpha_c^{va} [\delta_c^{va} QLD_c^{\rho_c^{va}} + (1 - \delta_c^{va}) QKD_c^{\rho_c^{va}}]^{1/\rho_c^{va}} \qquad c \in C \qquad (12.5.4)$$

$$\frac{WL}{WK} = \frac{\delta_c^{va}}{(1 - \delta_c^{va})} \left(\frac{QLD_c}{QKD_c} \right)^{\rho_c^{va} - 1} \qquad c \in C \qquad (12.5.5)$$

$$PVA_c \cdot QVA_c = WL \cdot QLD_c + WK \cdot QKD_c \qquad c \in C \qquad (12.5.6)$$

$$QINT_{cc'} = ia_{cc'} \cdot QINTA_{c'} \qquad c \in C \quad c' \in C \qquad (12.5.7)$$

$$PINTA_{c'} = \sum_{c \in C} ia_{cc'} \cdot PC_c \qquad c' \in C \qquad (12.5.8)$$

The household income includes labor income and capital income transferred from enterprises, plus consumer price index (CPI) adjusted government transfer payment:

$$YH = WL \cdot QLS + shareif_{hk} \cdot WK \cdot QKS + transfer_{h\,gov} \cdot CPI \qquad (12.5.9)$$

The household demand function is an linear expenditure system (LES) function:

$$PQ_c \cdot QH_c = PQ_c \cdot \gamma_c + \beta_c (EH - \sum_{c' \in C} PQ_c \cdot \gamma_{c'}) \qquad c \in C \qquad (12.5.10)$$

The key upgrading from the previous models is including a consumption function here, which implies households do not exhaust their budgets in consumption — they also save. The Walrasian equilibrium condition no longer holds; so we use the concept of the Keynesian equilibrium condition to complete a CGE model.

$$EH = eho \cdot cpi + mpc \cdot (1 - ti_h) \cdot YH \qquad (12.5.11)$$

The constant terms *eho*cpi* are calibrated from the subsistence consumption $\gamma * PQ$ of the LES system in the base period. Marginal propensity to consume *mpc* is calibrated accordingly. The calibration formulas will be provided later.

The enterprise income *YENT* includes the retained earnings of enterprises, which is the share of the capital income kept internally: $shareif_{ent\,k} WK \cdot QKS$. It also includes government transfer payment $transfer_{ent\,gov}$. Parameter *shareif* stands for the share of factor f income which goes to the i institution (agent group). The subscript denotes the direction.[2]

---

[2]This notation is used in the IFPRI model (2002). This notation can be extended to other situations for the *f*factor income to be distributed to the *i* institution (agent group).

Government's subsidy to enterprises $transfer_{ent\,gov}$ is a lump-sum transfer, not adjusted by price changes. Therefore:

$$YENT = shareif_{ent\,k}\,WK \cdot QKS + transfer_{ent\,gov} \tag{12.5.12}$$

Enterprises pay business income tax to the government at the tax rate of ti_{ENT}. The remaining balance of enterprise savings $SAVEENT$ is

$$SAVEENT = YENT - ti_{ENT} \cdot YENT = (1 - ti_{ENT})YENT \tag{12.5.13}$$

Investment (fixed capital formation) $QINVc$ is exogenously determined by enterprises. Enterprises adjust the investment level by factor $INVADJ$ based on their forecast of future sales. The investment in the base period $\overline{QINV}_c$ is calibrated from the SAM table. The adjustment factor $INVADJ$ in the base period equals 1.

$$QINV_c = \overline{QINV}_c \cdot INVADJ \tag{12.5.14}$$

The government's income equation includes indirect taxes and direct taxes:

$$YG = \sum_c (tsale_c/(1 + tsale_c) \cdot PQ_c \cdot QC_c) + ti_h \cdot YH + ti_{ent} \cdot YENT \tag{12.5.15}$$

The government savings function is

$$EG = YG - SAVEG \tag{12.5.16}$$

The government follows the fixed share spending rule on commodities, after subtracting transfer payments:

$$PQ_c \cdot QG_c = shareg_c \cdot (EG - transfer_{h\,g} \cdot CPI - transfer_{ent\,g}) \qquad c \in C \tag{12.5.17}$$

Commodity markets clearing conditions are

$$QC_c = \sum_{c'} QINT_{cc'} + QH_c + QINV_c + QG_c \qquad c \in C \tag{12.5.18}$$

Factor market equations are as follows. The factor supplies are *actual* supplies, which may not equal factor endowments. That means, it may not be at full employment if the economy is in recession. Hence, we can simulate the Keynesian world.

$$\sum_c QLD_c = QLS \tag{12.5.19}$$

$$\sum_c QKD_c = QKS \tag{12.5.20}$$

Consumer price index CPI:

$$CPI = \sum_{c \in C} PC_c \cdot cpiwt_c \tag{12.5.21}$$

To obtain the figure of the real GDP produced in the economy:

$$GDP = \sum_{c \in C} (QH_c + QINV_c + QG_c) \tag{12.5.22}$$

The savings–investment equation is as follows:

$$\sum_c PQ_c \cdot \overline{QINV}_c \cdot INVADJ = -eho \cdot cpi + (1 - mpc) \cdot (1 - tih) \cdot YH$$

$$+ SAVEENT + SAVEG + DUMMYSI \qquad (12.5.23)$$

On LHS, it is the total investment value. On RHS, there are savings from various institutions. Households' savings are the sum of the first two items $-eho \cdot cpi + (1 - mpc) \cdot (1 - tih) \cdot YH$. The other two components are enterprises and government savings. Because this equation is functionally dependent on the system, we add dummy variable $DUMMYSI$.

The above model has a total of 23 equation groups. It has 27 variable groups: PQ_c, PVA_c, $PINTA_c$, WL, WK, QC_c, QVA_c, $QINTA_c$, $QINT_{cc'}$, QLD_c, QKD_c, QLS, QKS, YH, EH, QH_c, $YENT$, $QINV_c$, $INVADJ$, $SAVEENT$, YG, EG, QG_c, $SAVEG$, CP, GDP, $DUMMYSI$. We need to add four constraints to reduce the variable numbers to 23 to meet the squareness requirement. If the model has the Keynesian closure, we fix two prices (one of them also serves as the price numeraire):

$$WL = \overline{WL} = 1 \qquad (12.5.24)$$

$$WK = \overline{WK} = 1 \qquad (12.5.25)$$

In addition, investment and government spending must be exogenously determined:

$$INVADJ = 1 \qquad (12.5.26)$$

$$EG = \overline{EG} \qquad (12.5.27)$$

The aggregate expenditure function $AE = C(Y - T) + I + G$ needs to be solidly determined in the system so to control the size of the economy. Intuitively, this means that in Figure 12.3.1, the position of the AE line should be fixed to determine the intersection with the 45 degree line. Accordingly, all components of the AE function, C, I and G, should be determined. If we leave a component in AE undetermined, then the position of the AE line is underdetermined, consequently the model will not work. In the above model, the consumption function is already determined by Equation (12.5.10). Equation (12.5.26) fixes the value of investment adjustment factor so investment levels are determined by $\overline{QINV}_c \cdot INVADJ = \overline{QINV}_c \cdot 1$. The government spending is determined by Equation (12.5.27). Alternatively, the government spending can be determined by fixing $SAVEG$. After all components are determined, the aggregate expenditure function AE is determined and the equilibrium of the model can be determined. The exogenous variable controlling the economic size in this Keynesian closure is government spending $\overline{EG}$. It in turn determines aggregate effective demand AE. Finally, output Y is determined by Keynesian condition $AE = Y$.

By the above constraints, values of WL, WK, $QINV$ and EG are fixed. Thus, we reduce the number of variable groups to 23. The system is square and solvable.

The parameters of consumption function (12.5.11) are calibrated as follows. The constant term eho is the subsistence consumption of the LES function:

$$eho \cdot cpi = \sum_{c' \in C} PQ_c \cdot \gamma 0_{c'} \qquad (12.5.28)$$

where "0" denotes those values already calibrated. After *eho* and *tih* values are calibrated, marginal propensity to consume *mpc* is calibrated by

$$mpc = (EH0 - eho \cdot cpi)/[(1 - ti_h) \cdot YH0] \tag{12.5.29}$$

Note in this Keynesian closure model, GDP, or aggregate output Y, is endogenously determined by aggregate expenditure AE. In what follows, we write a GAMS program for the above model. The GAMS program includes the list of the above variable names with their definitions.

12.6 GAMS Program for CGE Model with Savings and Investment

Example 12.6.1. A model economy has the SAM Table 12.5.1. In addition, we have the parameter information as described in Table 12.6.1. Write a GAMS program for the CGE model in Section 12.5 with the Keynesian macro closure. (1) Replicate the model and find the vales for *eho* and *mpc*. (2) Show that the savings–investment equation is functionally dependent on the system. (3) Run simulation by increasing the government spending, then find the government expenditure multiplier which is defined as the increase in GDP due to one more unit increase in government spending.

Solution: The GAMS program is provided in what follows. To show that the S-I equation is functionally dependent, we first run the model without the S-I equation, then add the S-I equation with dummy variable *DUMMYSI*. If the results of the former and latter are the same, and *DUMMYSI* converges to zero, it means the model has the same results with or without the S-I equation. This proves that the S-I is functionally dependent on other equations in the system.

To construct a CGE model in this case, it is more convenient to set purchasers' prices PQ to 1, so the commodity quantities are equal to their value numbers in the SAM table. The basic price PC can be computed by $PC_c \cdot QC_c = (PVA_c \cdot QVA_c + PINTA_c \cdot QINTA_c)$ or $PC_c = (1/(1 + tsale_c))PQ_c$ if needed. The commodity values at basic prices in the three commodity row accounts are $PC_c \cdot QC_c$, $PC_c \cdot QH_c$, etc. Apparently, these values would be smaller than those values at purchasers' prices in the SAM table. For instance, the computed basic prices of industry $PC_2 = 0.964$, the total value of the industry sector at basic price is $PC_2 \cdot QC_2 = 1725$, while it is 1790 at purchaser's price in the SAM table.

The program runs successfully. The results confirm that the S-I is dependent. The constant term of the consumption function *eho* is 650. The marginal propensity to consume *mpc* is 0.441. The government expenditure multiplier is 1.539.

Table 12.6.1.   Parameter values of the model economy.

Parameters	Agriculture	Industry	Service
Top level CES function exponent	0.2	0.3	0.1
CES function for the value-added module at the bottom level	0.25	0.5	0.8
LES system elasticity	0.5	1.0	1.2
Frisch parameter		-2	

```
$title Example 12.6.1 CGE model with savings and investment,
Keynesian closure

* Define accounts ac, commodities c, and factors f
set ac /agri,indu,serv,lab,cap,hh,ent,gov,saltx,invsav,total/;
set c(ac) /agri,indu,serv/;
set f(ac) /lab,cap/;

alias (ac,acp),(c,cp),(f,fp);

table sam(ac,acp)
```

	agri	indu	serv	lab	cap	hh	ent	gov	saltx	invsav	total
agri	260	320	150			500		71		155	1456
indu	345	390	390			450		65		150	1790
serv	400	365	320			350		48		48	1531
lab	200	250	400								850
cap	210	400	210								820
hh				850	770			17			1637
ent					50			40			90
gov						162	40		167		369
saltx	41	65	61								167
invsav						175	50	128			353
total	1456	1790	1531	850	820	1637	90	369	167	353	

```
;

*Input parameter values given externally
parameter  rhoq(c)    /agri =   0.2,   indu = 0.3,   serv = 0.1 /
           rhoVA(c)   /agri    0.25,  indu 0.5,     serv 0.8 /
           LESelas(c) /agri    0.5,   indu 1.0,     serv 1.2 /
           Frisch     /-2/;

parameters
scaleAq(c)    Scale factor of top level CES function
deltaq(c)     Value-added share parameter in top level CES function
scaleAVA(c)   Scale factor of value added CES function
deltaVA(c)    Labor share parameter in value-added CES function
ia(c,cp)      Input coefficient of intermediate inputs
shareg(c)     Share of government income spending on c
tih           Households income tax rate
tiEnt         Business income tax rate
```

tsale(c)	Sales tax rate on commodity c
transferHG0	Government transfer payment to households
transferEntG0	Government transfer payment (subsidies) to enterprises
shareifhk	Households share of capital income of enterprises
shareifentk	Share of capital income retained by enterprises
eho	Consumption function constant
mpc	Marginal propensity to consume
bgtshare(c)	Average budget share on c in the LES function
bhtsharechk1	Check if average budget share sum is 1
LESbeta(c)	Marginal budget share of LES
Lesbetachk1	Check if the marginal budget share beta sum is 1
LESsub(c)	Subsistence consumption level of c of LES
cpiwt(c)	CPI weights

*Variable name followed by 0 denotes the corresponding parameter at its initial level

PQ0(c)	Price of commodity c
QC0(c)	Quantity of commodity c
PVA0(c)	Price of aggregate value-added
QVA0(c)	Quantity of aggregate value-added
PINTA0(c)	Price of aggregate intermediate input
QINTA0(c)	Quantity of aggregate intermediate input
QINT0(c,cp)	Quantity of intermediate input c used in cp
QLD0(c)	Labor demand
QKD0(c)	Capital demand
WL0	Labor price
WK0	Capital price
QLS0	Labor supply
QKS0	Capital supply
YH0	Household income
EH0	Total consumption expenditure of households
QH0(c)	Quantity demanded for c by households
YENT0	Enterprise income
QINV0(c)	Investment (fixed capital consumption) of c by enterprises
SAVEENT0	Enterprise savings
YG0	Government total revenue
EG0	Government total expenditure
QG0(c)	Government consumption on c
SAVEG0	Government savings, fiscal budget balance
CPI0	Consumer price index
GDP0	Real GDP

;

```
*Parameter calibration
PQ0(c)=1;
PINTA0(c)=1;
WK0=1;
WL0=1;
CPI0=1;
tsale(c)=sam('saltx',c)/(sum(cp,sam(cp,c))+sum(fp,sam(fp,c)));
QLD0(c)=sam('lab',c)/WL0;
QKD0(c)=sam('cap',c)/WK0;
QVA0(c)=SUM(f,Sam(f,c));
PVA0(c)=(WL0*QLD0(c)+WK0*QKD0(c))/QVA0(c);
QC0(c)=sam('total',c)/PQ0(c);
QINT0(c,cp)=sam(c,cp)/PQ0(c);
QINTA0(c)=SUM(cp,QINT0(cp,c));
ia(c,cp)=QINT0(c,cp)/QINTA0(cp);
QLS0=sum(c,sam('lab',c))/WL0;
QKS0=sum(c,sam('cap',c))/WK0;
deltaq(c)=PVA0(c)*QVA0(c)**(1-rhoq(c))/(PVA0(c)*QVA0(c)**(1-
rhoq(c))+PINTA0(c)*QINTA0(c)**(1-rhoq(c)));
scaleAq(c)=QC0(c)/(deltaq(c)*QVA0(c)**rhoq(c)+(1-
deltaq(c))*QINTA0(c)**rhoq(c))**(1/rhoq(c));
deltaVA(c)=WL0*QLD0(c)**(1-rhoVA(c))/(WL0*QLD0(c)**(1-rhoVA(c))+WK0*QKD0(c)
**(1-rhoVA(c)));
scaleAVA(c)=QVA0(c)/(deltaVA(c)*QLD0(c)**rhoVA(c)+(1-
deltaVA(c))*QKD0(c)**rhoVA(c))**(1/rhoVA(c));
transferHG0=sam('hh','gov');
transferEntG0=sam('ent','gov');
shareifhk=sam('hh','cap')/(sam('hh','cap')+sam('ent','cap'));
shareifentk=sam('ent','cap')/(sam('hh','cap')+sam('ent','cap'));
YH0=WL0*QLS0+shareifhk*WK0*QKS0+transferHG0*CPI0;
tih=sam('gov','hh')/YH0;
EH0=sum(c,sam(c,'hh'));
QH0(c)=SAM(c,'hh')/PQ0(c);
*Below is the LES function block, the LES marginal share coefficient is
scaled to satisfy the constraint.
bgtshare(c)=SAM(c,'hh')/EH0;
bhtsharechk1=sum(c,bgtshare(c));
LESbeta(c)=LESelas(c)*bgtshare(c)/(sum(cp,LESelas(cp)*bgtshare(cp)));
Lesbetachk1=sum(c,LESbeta(c));
LESsub(c)=sam(c,'hh')/PQ0(c)+(LESbeta(c)/PQ0(c))*(EH0/frisch);
cpiwt(c)=QH0(c)/sum(cp,QH0(cp));
```

```
CPI0=sum(c,PQ0(c)*cpiwt(c));
eho=sum(c,PQ0(c)*LESsub(c))/cpi0;
mpc=(EH0-eho*cpi0)/((1-tih)*YH0);
YENT0=shareifentk*WK0*QKS0+transferEntG0;
QINV0(c)=sam(c,'invsav')/PQ0(c);
tiEnt=sam('gov','ent')/YEnt0;
SAVEENT0=(1-tiEnt)*YENT0;
YG0=tih*YH0+tiEnt*YENT0+sam('gov','saltx');
EG0=sum(c,sam(c,'gov'))+transferHG0*CPI0+transferEntG0;
SAVEG0=YG0-EG0;
QG0(c)=sam(c,'gov')/PQ0(c);
shareg(c)=PQ0(c)*QG0(c)/(EG0-transferHG0*CPI0-transferEntG0);
GDP0=sum(c,(QH0(c)+QINV0(c)+QG0(c)));

display
LESbeta,LESsub,LESelas,rhoq,rhoVA,bhtsharechk1,Lesbetachk1,PQ0,WK0,WL0,QC0,
QLD0,QKD0,QLS0,QKS0,QH0,eho,mpc,EH0,transferhg0,YH0,tih,tient,shareifhk,
shareifentk,YG0,QG0,shareg,tsale,cpiwt,CPI0;

variable
PQ(c),PVA(c),PINTA(c),WL,WK,QC(c),QVA(c),QINTA(c),QINT(c,cp),QLD(c),QKD(c),
QLS,QKS,YH,EH,QH(c),YENT,QINV(c),INVADJ,SAVEENT,YG,EG,QG(c),SAVEG,CPI,GDP;

equation
QCfn(c),QCFOCeq(c),PQeq(c),QVAfn(c),QVAFOC(c),PVAeq(c),QINTfn(c,cp),PINTAeq
(cp),YHeq,EHeq,QHeq(c),YENTeq,QINVeq(c),SAVEENTeq,YGeq,EGeq,QGeq(c),ComEqui
(c),Leq,Keq,CPIeq,GDPeq;

QCfn(c)..
QC(c)=e=scaleAq(c)*(deltaq(c)*QVA(c)**rhoq(c)+(1-
deltaq(c))*QINTA(c)**rhoq(c))**(1/rhoq(c));

QCFOCeq(c)..
PVA(c)/PINTA(c)=e=(deltaq(c)/(1-deltaq(c)))*(QINTA(c)/QVA(c))**(1-rhoq(c));

PQeq(c)..
PQ(c)*QC(c)=e=(1+tsale(c))*(PVA(c)*QVA(c)+PINTA(c)*QINTA(c));

QVAfn(c)..
QVA(c)=e=scaleAVA(c)*(deltaVA(c)*QLD(c)**rhoVA(c)+(1-
deltaVA(c))*QKD(c)**rhoVA(c))**(1/rhoVA(c));
```

```
QVAFOC(c)..
WL/WK=e=(deltaVA(c)/(1-deltaVA(c)))*(QKD(c)/QLD(c))**(1-rhoVA(c));

PVAeq(c)..
PVA(c)*QVA(c)=e=WL*QLD(c)+WK*QKD(c);

QINTfn(c,cp)..
QINT(c,cp)=e=ia(c,cp)*QINTA(cp);

PINTAeq(cp)..
PINTA(cp)=e=SUM(c,ia(c,cp)*PQ(c));

YHeq..
YH=e=WL*QLS+shareifhk*WK*QKS+transferHG0*CPI;

QHeq(c)..
PQ(c)*QH(c)=e=PQ(c)*LESsub(c)+LESbeta(c)*(EH-sum(cp,PQ(cp)*LESsub(cp)));

EHeq..
EH=e=eho*cpi+mpc*(1-tih)*YH;

YENTeq..
YENT=e=shareifentk*WK*QKS+transferentg0;

SAVEENTeq..
SAVEENT=e=(1-tiEnt)*YENT;

QINVeq(c)..
QINV(c)=e=QINV0(c)*INVADJ;

YGeq..
YG=e=sum(c,PQ(c)*QC(c)*tsale(c)/(1+tsale(c)))+tih*YH+tiEnt*YENT;

EGeq..
EG=e=YG-SAVEG;

QGeq(c)..
PQ(c)*QG(c)=e=shareg(c)*(EG-transferHG0*CPI-transferEntG0);

ComEqui(c)..
QC(c)=e=sum(cp,QINT(c,cp))+QH(c)+QINV(c)+QG(c);
```

```
Leq..
Sum(c,QLD(c))=e=QLS;

Keq..
Sum(c,QKD(c))=e=QKS;

CPIeq..
CPI=e=sum(c,PQ(c)*cpiwt(c));

GDPeq..
GDP=e=sum(c,(QH(c)+QINV(c)+QG(c)));

*Assign initial values of variables
PQ.L(c)=PQ0(c);
PVA.L(c)=PVA0(c);
PINTA.L(c)=PINTA0(c);
QC.L(c)=QC0(c);
QVA.L(c)=QVA0(c);
QINTA.L(c)=QINTA0(c);
QINT.L(c,cp)=QINT0(c,cp);
QLD.L(c)=QLD0(c);
QKD.L(c)=QKD0(c);
QLS.L=QLS0;
QKS.L=QKS0;
YH.L=YH0;
EH.L=EH0;
QH.L(c)=QH0(c);
YENT.L=YENT0;
QINV.L(c)=QINV0(c);
INVADJ.L=1;
SAVEENT.L=SAVEENT0;
YG.L=YG0;
EG.L=EG0;
QG.L(c)=QG0(c);
QLS.L=QLS0;
QKS.L=QKS0;
WL.L=1;
WK.L=1;
CPI.L=CPI0;
GDP.L=GDP0;
```

```
*Keynesian closure constraints
WL.fx=1;
WK.fx=1;
INVADJ.fx=1;
EG.fx=EG0;

*Executing the model (without the S-I equation)
model cge /all/;
solve cge using mcp;

*Adding the S-I equation check if the results are the same as above

variable
DUMMYSI;
equations
SIeq;
SIeq..
sum(c,PQ(c)*QINV(c))=e=-eho*cpi+(1-mpc)*(1-tih)*YH+SAVEENT+SAVEG+DUMMYSI;

model cgewithSI /all/;
solve cgewithSI using mcp;
display DUMMYSI.L;

*Simulation of government expenditure increase and calculating multiplier
EG.fx=EG0+1;

*Executing the model
model sim1 /all/;
solve sim1 using mcp;

Parameter
Multiplier government expenditure multiplier;
Multiplier=(GDP.L-GDP0)/1;
display GDP0,GDP.L,Multiplier;

*end
```

12.7 The Government Spending Closure

The above model can describe the Keynesian equilibrium state in an economic recession. Most CGE models, however, follow the classical or neoclassical hypothesis to assume full employment. What economic mechanism in a CGE model can automatically adjust the aggregate expenditure level to reach potential GDP? One mechanism is the government spending closure which assumes that the government automatically adjusts its spending to ensure full employment. Accordingly, we would have a different set of constraints in the model.

In the mathematical model of Section 12.5, for this government spending closure, we delete the set of constraints of (12.5.24)–(12.5.27) and replace them with the following four constraints. Assuming the initial state of the economy is of full employment, $QLS0$ and $QKS0$ equal factor endowments. Factor are always fully employed:

$$QLS = QLS0 \tag{12.7.1}$$

$$QKS = QKS0 \tag{12.7.2}$$

Private investment is fixed:

$$INVADJ = 1 \tag{12.7.3}$$

Let CPI be the price numeraire:

$$CPI = 1 \tag{12.7.4}$$

In the model, government spending EG is the endogenous variable to be solved by the system to ensure the full employment conditions of Equations (12.7.1) and (12.7.2).

Example 12.7.1. Revise the GAMS program in Section 12.6 to the government spending closure. The economy is always at full employment. Suppose the private investment falls by 20%, run simulation and find the resulting changes in GDP, government spending and private investment.

Solution: The following are the major new statements of the GAMS program in response to the question. Other part of the program repeats the codes in Section 12.6. Readers can work as an exercise to complete the entire model. The simulation results are in Table 12.7.1. It can be seen that the government spending automatically fills in the gap of aggregate demand caused by the fall in private investment. Therefore, the real GDP output remains unchanged.

The new constraints are

```
QLS.fx=QLS0;
QKS.fx=QKS0;
CPI.fx=CPI0;
INVADJ.fx=1;
```

The simulation part of the program is

```
*Simulation if investment falls by 20%
INVADJ.fx=0.8;
*Executing the model
model simfallinvest /all/;
solve simfallinvest using mcp;
display  GDP0,GDP.L,EG0,EG.L,QINV0
```

Table 12.7.1.　Simulation of a fall in investment.

	Real GDP	EG	QINV agriculture	QINV industry	QINV service
Initial state	1837.000	241.000	155	150	48
After investment falls by 20%	1836.998	311.592	124	120	38.4

12.8　The Johansen Closure

Instead of adjusting the government spending, the Johansen closure lets savings be flexible to ensure full employment. Intuitively, in Figure 12.4.1, the savings line automatically shifts to intersect the investment line at the full employment level. Or, in Figure 12.3.1, the consumption function shifts the AE line to intersect the 45 degree line at the potential GDP level. This implies that in an economic downturn, households would automatically cut their autonomous savings and increase autonomous consumption, so the economy returns to full employment. This kind of households' behavior does not sound plausible, but some neoclassical models develop a mechanism through adjustments in prices and the interest rate to show that may be possible. In the case of an overheated economy, the hypothesis by the Johansen closure is more plausible, as households may cut their consumption under the inflationary pressure.

To let savings automatically adjust to full employment, we can change parameter mpc ($mpc = 1 - mps$) to a variable in the above CGE model. Hence, changing mpc would change the consumption function thus shifting the AE line in Figure 12.3.1 to the full employment GDP level. In the CGE model of Section 12.5, we make the following changes for the Johansen closure. It is similar to the above government spending closure, except the new variable is mpc instead of government spending EG.

Delete the three constraints from (12.5.24)–(12.5.26) and replace them with following four constraints.

$$QLS = QLS0 \tag{12.8.1}$$

$$QKS = QKS0 \tag{12.8.2}$$

$$INVADJ = 1 \tag{12.8.3}$$

$$CPI = 1 \tag{12.8.4}$$

Then change mpc from a parameter to an endogenous variable to be solved by the model system.

Example 12.8.1. Revise the GAMS program in Section 12.6 for the Johansen closure. Suppose the government increases spending EG by 50%, run simulation and find the changes in GDP, mpc, government spending EG, and households consumption EH. Confirm that the government spending crowds out household consumption.

Table 12.8.1. Simulation results with the Johansen closure.

	Real GDP	mpc	EG	EH
Initial state	1837.000	0.441	241	1300
After government spending increases by 50%	1837.001	0.359	361.5	1179.5

Solution: To answer this question, most part of the new GAMS program would repeat that in Section 12.6. The new constraint parts include five equations:

```
QLS.fx=QLS0;
QKS.fx=QKS0;
CPI.fx=CPI0;
INVADJ.fx=1;
EG.fx=EG0;
```

In addition, the status of *mpc* should be changed from a parameter to a variable in the program. The codes for simulation of the government spending increase are as follows:

```
EG.fx=EG0*1.5;
model sim2 /all/;
solve sim2 using mcp;
```

The simulation results are shown in Table 12.8.1. Household consumption is indeed reduced by the increase in government spending.

12.9 Homogeneity Property and Simulation of Changes in Money Supply

The Keynesian equilibrium model in Section 12.6 is not strictly homogenous in prices, because some transactions in the model are lump-sums, that is, they are not price indexed. For instance, government's transfer payment to enterprises is a lump-sum payment. This setup is to simulate the real-world situation: while the government's transfer payments to households like social security payment are adjusted by CPI, the subsidy to private business is not. These lump-sum transaction terms would invalidate the homogeneity property of the model.

Accordingly, we expect that change in the price numeraire may cause the real quantities to change. The quantity changes should not be substantial, because the lump-sum transactions account for a small fraction of overall transactions in the model. As discussed previously, price numeraire in CGE models can serve as the proxy for money supply. Hence, we can study the impacts of money supply on real quantities by changing the numeraire in the model.

For instance, we use the government spending closure model, let numeraire CPI increase by 20%, the model converges successfully. All prices increase by 20%, but real quantities have moderate changes, as expected. Table 12.9.1 shows selected resulting quantity changes. Nominal values *SAVEG*, *EH* and *YENT* have been deflated by the factor of 1.2 to obtain the real values in the base prices. The real GDP is the same because of the full employment

Table 12.9.1.   Impacts on real quantities by changing price numeraire.

	Real GDP	SAVEG (base price)	EH (base price)	YENT (base price)	QH service
Initial state	1837.000	128	1300	90	350
After price numeraire increased by 20%	1837.001	131.7	1300	83.33	350

output. Households' spending and consumption remain unchanged because their income is fully price indexed and the consumption function is homogenous in prices and income. In real terms the government savings increase, but enterprises' income decreases. This is because the transfer payment from the government to enterprises is fixed in the nominal value. We can infer that changes in money supply can cause redistribution among the government and enterprises through inflation.

Exercises

12E.1 Example 12.7.1 does not provide the entire GAMS program. Use the same information as provided in Section 12.6, write the GAMS program for the model with the government spending closure, and simulate the situation that the enterprises' investment falls by 20%. Find and verify the outcomes. Explain the changes in transactions by using your economics insight.

12E.2 Example 12.8.1 does not provide the entire GAMS program. Use the same information as provided in Section 12.6, rewrite the GAMS program for the model with the Johansen closure, and simulate the situation that the government spending increases by 50%. Find and verify the outcomes. Explain the changes in transactions by using your economics insight.

12E.3 Section 12.9 suggests that changing the numeraire can be used as a proxy for changes in money supply. Using the model with the government spending closure, simulate the case of raising numeraire CPI by 20%. What are the changes in real quantities? How do you explain these changes, such as that in government spending, household spending, and various savings terms?

12E.4 Changes in taxes can also change the aggregate expenditure. Revise the GAMS program in Section 12.6, let households' income tax rate *tih* be the endogenous variable to ensure full employment. Assume the private investment falls by 10%. By how much should the income tax rate be cut to resume full employment?

Appendix: S-I Equation is a Mirror Image of the Income–Expenditure Equation

Because a CGE model includes a lot of equations, it is not easy to see how the aggregate income–expenditure equation of a standard macroeconomic model is implied in the CGE model system. A related question is: can the S-I equation be derived from other equations in the model system? In what follows, we use a completed CGE model to demonstrate that the S-I equation is just a mirror image of the income–expenditure condition.

The following CGE model has one commodity Q and two inputs L and K. Their prices are PQ, WL, WK. Aggregate commodity supply is QS. Aggregate commodity demand is QD. Quantities demanded and supplied of labor are QLD and QKD. Factor endowments are $\overline{QLS}$ and $\overline{QKS}$. The following production block provides the commodity supply and factor demand functions:

$$QS = \alpha[\delta \cdot QLD^{\rho} + (1 - \delta)QKD^{\rho}]^{1/\rho} \tag{12.A.1}$$

$$\frac{WL}{WK} = \frac{\delta}{(1 - \delta)}\left(\frac{QLD}{QKD}\right)^{\rho} \tag{12.A.2}$$

$$PQ \cdot QS = WL \cdot QLD + WK \cdot QKD \tag{12.A.3}$$

Households' income is

$$YH = WL \cdot QLD + WK \cdot QKD \tag{12.A.4}$$

Households pay income tax at rate *tih*. Households' consumption is QH:

$$QH = \frac{1}{PQ} \cdot mpc \cdot (1 - tih) \cdot YH \tag{12.A.5}$$

Enterprises' investment $QINV$ and government consumption QG are exogenous. The aggregate demand is QD:

$$QD = \overline{QINV} + QH + \overline{QG} \tag{12.A.6}$$

Factor endowments are $\overline{QLS}$ and $\overline{QKS}$. Assuming full employment, the commodity and factor markets clearing equations are as follows:

$$QS = QD \tag{12.A.7}$$

$$QLD = \overline{QLS} \tag{12.A.8}$$

$$QKD = \overline{QKS} \tag{12.A.9}$$

Equations (12.A.1)–(12.A.9) is a completed CGE model with 9 equations and 9 variables: $PQ, WL, WK, QLD, QKD, QS, QD, YH, QH$. The exogenous variables and parameters are: $\overline{QLS}, \overline{QKS}, \overline{QINV}, \overline{QG}, mpc$ and *tih*. Combining Equations (12.A.6) and (12.A.7):

$$QS = \overline{QINV} + QH + \overline{QG} \tag{12.A.10}$$

The above equation is the aggregate income–expenditure equation, i.e., $Y = C + I + G$. The S-I equation should be

$$\overline{QINV} = \frac{1}{PQ} \cdot (1 - mpc) \cdot (1 - tih) \cdot YH + \frac{1}{PQ} \cdot tih \cdot YH - \overline{QG} \qquad (12.A.11)$$

The LHS is investment. On RHS, the first term is household savings, the second term is the government revenue, and the third term is the government spending. Hence, it is the S-I equation $I = S + (T - G)$. In what follows, we prove that (12.A.11) can be derived from the model system (12.A.1)–(12.A.9). Because both income–expenditure Equation (12.A.10) and the S-I equation can be derived from the same system, they are just different reduced forms of the same equation system.

Proof. Combine Equations (12.A.5) and (12.A.6). Rearrange,

$$\overline{QINV} = QD - QH - \overline{QG} = QD - \frac{1}{PQ} \cdot mpc \cdot (1 - tih) \cdot YH - \overline{QG} \qquad (12.A.12)$$

Because $PQ \cdot QD = PQ \cdot QS = WL \cdot \overline{QLS} + WK \cdot \overline{QKS} = YH$, we have $\frac{1}{PQ} YH = QD$. Substituting into 12.A.12, we have

$$\overline{QINV} = QD - \frac{1}{PQ} \cdot mpc \cdot (1 - tih) \cdot YH - \overline{QG}$$

$$= \frac{1}{PQ} YH - \frac{1}{PQ} \cdot mpc \cdot (1 - tih) \cdot YH - \overline{QG}$$

$$= \frac{1}{PQ} YH[1 - mpc + mpc \cdot tih)] - \overline{QG}$$

$$= \frac{1}{PQ}(1 - mpc) YH + \frac{1}{PQ} \cdot mpc \cdot tih \cdot YH - \frac{1}{PQ} \cdot tih \cdot YH + \frac{1}{PQ} tih \cdot YH - \overline{QG}$$

$$= \frac{1}{PQ}(1 - mpc) YH - \frac{1}{PQ} \cdot (1 - mpc) \cdot tih \cdot YH + \frac{1}{PQ} \cdot tih \cdot YH - \overline{QG}$$

$$= \frac{1}{PQ}(1 - mpc) \cdot (1 - tih) \cdot YH + \frac{1}{PQ} \cdot tih \cdot YH - \overline{QG} \qquad (12.A.13)$$

The mathematical expression of the last step is exactly the S-I equation of (12.A.11). $\quad\square$

Chapter 13

Activities, Trade and Transport Margins

13.1 Activities and Commodities

As our computable general equilibrium (CGE) models become more complicated, we need to investigate in more detail the process from production to distribution of the commodities in each sector. To better handle these issues in CGE modeling, the system of national accounts (SNA) convention separates the production activities from the commodity accounts. Now we have two sets of sectoral accounts in a social accounting matrix (SAM) table: activities and commodities. Activity accounts are the sectors engaged in the production process. Commodity accounts are the sectors engaged in transportation, distribution and sales of the commodities in the process from receiving the commodities from activity accounts to delivering them to the final purchasers. Table 13.1.1 is a descriptive SAM table for this structure. Account group 1 are activities. Account group 2 are commodities. Table 13.1.2 is an example of a "real" SAM table for a model economy with data filled in the entries.

In Chapter 4, we have briefly discussed some reasons to distinguish between activities and commodities. A production activity may produce several commodities, e.g., the coal sector production activity produces chemical, electricity and construction commodities. Or, a commodity may be produced by different activities, e.g., fuel gas is produced by petroleum, coal and agricultural sectors. To record these situations, we need separate activities and commodities. If one activity produces exactly one commodity in the economy, then the total volume/quantity of an activity and the corresponding commodity would be equal. Otherwise, they may not be equal. There are other advantages to separate activities and commodities in handling wholesale, retailing and transport costs; product taxes; etc., which will be discussed in this chapter.

Let us take a look at Table 13.1.1, these entries in their accounts look familiar: The activity column accounts record transactions in production activities, from the value-added block to the intermediate input block. The commodity row accounts record the commodities purchased by enterprises as intermediate inputs and investment goods, and by households and government as final goods.

Let us update the notations of the variables. The group of activities now is denoted by set A. An activity in set A is indexed by a. QA_a and PA_a are quantity and price of the

Table 13.1.1.   Descriptive SAM table for a closed economy.

	1 Activities	2 Commodities	3 Factors	4 Households	5 Enterprises	6 Government	7 Savings–Investment	Total incomes
1 Activities		Activity products to commodities $QA * PA = QQ * PQS$						Output $QA * PA$
2 Commodities	Intermediate inputs $QINT * PQ$	Trade and transport margins		Household consumption $QH * PQ$		Government expenditure $QG * PQ$	Investment $QINV * PQ$	Demand $QQ * PQ$
3 Factors	Value-added							Factor income
4 Households			Households factor income	Transfer among households	Enterprise transfer to households	Government transfer to households		Household income
5 Enterprises			Enterprise factor income			Government transfer to enterprises		Enterprise income
6 Government	Employment tax, production tax	Sales tax	Factor taxes as income tax to government	Income tax, direct tax	Enterprise direct tax to government			Government income
7 Savings–Investment				Household savings	Enterprise savings	Government savings		
Total expenditures	Activity $QA * PA$	Supply $QQ * PQ$	Factor expenditures	Household expenditures	Enterprises expenditures	Government expenditures	Investment	

Table 13.1.2. SAM table of a model economy with trade and transport margins.

	Act1	Act2	Act3	Com1	Com2	Com3	Transp	Wholes	Retail	Lab	Cap	HH	Ent	Gov	sales tax	Investment	Total
Act1 (agriculture)				1897													1897
Act2 (industry)					2900												2900
Act3 (service)						2355											2355
Com1 (agriculture)	280	420	270									834		178		143	2125
Com2 (industry)	377	520	380									1450		230		273	3230
Com3 (service)	220	260	250				130	112	145			983		250		200	2550
Transport				60	50	20											130
Wholesale				30	60	22											112
Retail				40	80	25											145
Labor	650	700	800														2150
Capital	370	1000	655														2025
Households										2150	1725			293			4168
Enterprises											300						300
Government												515	100		366		981
Sales tax				98	140	128											366
Savings												386	200	30			616
Total	1897	2900	2355	2125	3230	2550	130	112	145	2150	2025	4168	300	981	366	616	

product produced by activity A, respectively. PA_a is basic price. Basic price is defined by SNA as the price received by the producer before product taxes such as sales taxes.

The group of commodities in the market is still denoted by set C. A commodity in set C is still indexed by lowercase c. In the commodity markets, QQ_c is the total quantity of the commodity c. PQS_c is the supplier's price of commodity c. PQ_c is the purchaser's price of commodity c. The difference between them is that PQ_c includes the sales tax, VAT tax, trade and transportation costs in the passing process from the supplier to the purchaser, while PQS_c does not. Along the commodity row accounts, there are consumers of households, the government, and enterprises, who purchase the commodities; hence the entries are values at purchasers' prices. For instance, the consumption value by households is $PQ_c \times QH_c$.

13.2 Mapping from Activities to Commodities

The relationship between activities and commodities can also be illustrated by a transaction flow chart in Figure 13.2.1.

In the above chart, the first issue to deal with is moving from the top block of activities to the second block of commodities. In writing the GAMS program, the variables of PA and QA have the domain of activities A; while the variables of PQS and QQ have the domain of commodities C. Their domains are different. To relate them, we need to map from activities to commodities. That is, we need to map from QA_a to QQ_c and from PA_a to PQS_c. For simplicity, let us assume one activity produces only one commodity. So there is a one-to-one corresponding relationship between an activity and a commodity. The prices and quantities

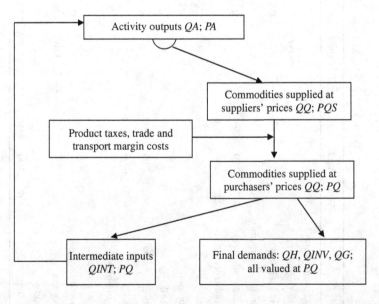

Figure 13.2.1.   Flows of activities and commodities.

of the corresponding a and c are exactly the same:

$$QA(\text{activity}\,1) = QQ(\text{commodity}\,1) \quad PA(\text{activity}\,1) = PQS(\text{commodity}\,1)$$
$$QA(\text{activity}\,2) = QQ(\text{commodity}\,2) \quad PA(\text{activity}\,2) = PQS(\text{commodity}\,2)$$
$$QA(\text{activity}\,3) = QQ(\text{commodity}\,3) \quad PA(\text{activity}\,3) = PQS(\text{commodity}\,3)$$

$$\ldots \qquad\qquad \ldots \qquad\qquad (13.2.1)$$

Or it can be written as

$$QA_a = QQ_c \qquad \forall a = c$$
$$PA_a = PQS_c \qquad \forall a = c \qquad\qquad (13.2.2)$$

The mathematical operation for the mapping relationship uses identity matrix $\mathbf{I}$:

$$\mathbf{QQ(c)} = \mathbf{I} \times \mathbf{QA(a)} \qquad \mathbf{PQS(c)} = \mathbf{I} \times \mathbf{PA(a)} \qquad (13.2.3)$$

where $\mathbf{QQ}$, $\mathbf{QA}$, $\mathbf{PA}$, and $\mathbf{PQS}$ are the vectors with n elements. The identity matrix $\mathbf{I}$ is an $n \times n$ matrix:

$$\mathbf{I} = \begin{bmatrix} 1 & 0 & & 0 \\ 0 & 1 & & 0 \\ & & \ldots & \\ 0 & 0 & & 1 \end{bmatrix} \qquad (13.2.4)$$

Let an $n \times n$ identity matrix be denoted by $IDENT_{ac}$ with elements of i_{ac}. The equations to map from activities QA and PA to commodities QQ and PQS are as follows:

$$QQ_c = \sum_a IDENT_{ac} \cdot QA_a \qquad c \in C \qquad (13.2.5)$$

$$PQS_c = \sum_a IDENT_{ac} \cdot PA_a \qquad c \in C \qquad (13.2.6)$$

The above two equations establish the one-to-one relationship from activity a to the corresponding commodity c.

13.3 Trade and Transport Margins

One advantage to separate production activities and commodities is that we can better study the marketing costs of commodities. These costs include transport, wholesale, retailing and tax costs in the process of commodity supply. These costs raise the prices of the commodities but do not change the quantities. Separating them from the production block would provide convenience and conceptual clarity for data entries in SAM accounts and CGE modeling.

After commodities are produced, additional services are needed for the commodities to pass from the producers to the purchasers. These additional services are called "margin services", or simply "margins". They include services of wholesalers, retailers and transportation. The costs of the services by wholesalers and retailers are called "trade margins" (note the term "trade" here refers only to domestic trade, not "international trade"). The costs of transportation are called "transport margins". Together they may be called "marketing margins" or "transaction margins". In the commodity column of SAM Table 13.1.1, we see that the trade and transport margins are recorded in middle entries. In SAM Table 13.1.2, for instance, the transport margin for the industry commodity (Com2) is 50.

By the SNA convention, marketing margins of a commodity do not change the volume/quantity of the commodity, but they raise the commodity price thus its value because of these additional costs. You can think the marketing margins as additional inputs used in the distributing and delivering processes from the producers to the purchasers. Therefore, the final purchaser's price should reflect all these additional input costs.

Readers may wonder why these service inputs by the wholesalers, retailers and transporters are not included in the intermediate input block. The reason is because we prefer to have the detailed information about the quantity of which particular commodity is purchased by households and the government. Otherwise we would encounter an aggregation problem as described by SNA:

"If all goods handled by wholesalers and retailers were shown as being delivered to the wholesaler or retailer and then supplied by them to the purchaser, then virtually all goods would be used by wholesalers and retailers and almost none would be supplied to other producing units, households or government. The pattern of household consumption would show one large item for purchases from wholesalers and retailers and none from any manufacturing industry or agriculture". (SNA 2008, 14.128).

The purchaser's price is the actual price paid by a purchaser, which includes the producer's price and the marketing margins to have the commodity delivered, plus product taxes. Table 11.4.2 provides the definitions of the basic, producer's and purchaser's prices, which is reprinted here:

Basic price = production cost + some taxes on production such as employment taxes paid by employers
Producer's price = Basic price + product taxes (such as excise tax)
Purchaser's price = Producer's price + transport and trade margins + non-deductible VAT

The term "non-deductible VAT" refers to the VAT that is not deductible by the purchaser. Let the "VAT rate" here refer to only the non-deductible VAT, to summarize in the equation form, the relationship is as follows:

$$PQ_c = PQS_c + \text{product tax rate}$$

$$+ \text{unit trade margin} + \text{unit transport margin} + \text{VAT rate} \qquad (13.3.1)$$

13.4 Marketing Margins in CGE Modeling

In SAM Table 13.1.2, there are three accounts for the marketing margins: transport, wholesale trade and retail trade. We define a set for the marketing services: CTT, which are the trade and transport commodities being used as inputs. The index of CTT is denoted by ct, which includes the three commodity inputs, "transp" for transport, "wholes" for wholesale trade, and "retail" for retail trade, as labeled in the table header.

Let $QCTT_{ct,c}$ be the margin input of ct used in commodity c. This is similar to the input–output relationship in the intermediate input block. We may assume that, in terms of the volumes, the trade and transport service inputs used are proportional to the quantities of commodity QQ_c:

$$QCTT_{ct,c} = ictt_{ct,c} \cdot QQ_c \qquad ct \in CTT, \quad c \in C \qquad (13.4.1)$$

where $ictt_{ct,c}$ are the proportions. $ictt_{ct,c}$ conceptually is just an input–output coefficient. It is the amount of trade and transport input used to serve one unit of commodity c. Equation (13.4.1) would be used in both parameter calibration and modeling.

We assume that the commodity sectors buy margin inputs at the purchasers' prices, just like other intermediate inputs purchased in production activities. In the simple economy with SAM Table 13.1.2, there are only three highly integrated commodity accounts (agriculture, industry and service) and no separate individual commodity accounts for transportation, wholesale trade and retail trade. The three marketing margin inputs are all supposed to be provided by the service sector, the Com3 commodity account. So we assume the price of any trade and transport margin input is the price of service, PQ_3. Further, commodity accounts need to pay the purchaser's price for the trade and transport margin inputs. Hence, to obtain the quantity of $QCTT_{ct,c}$, we need to divide the entry values in the block of trade and transport margins in the SAM table by the purchaser's price PQ_3:

$$QCTT_{ct,c} = \text{SAM}_{ct,c}/PQ_3 \qquad (13.4.2)$$

where $\text{SAM}_{ct,c}$ is the value of entry (ct, c) in the SAM table. For instance, suppose $PQ_3 = 1.083$, then the quantity of transport used in industry commodity is

$$QCTT_{transport,2} = \text{SAM}_{transport,2}/PQ_3 = 50/1.083 = 46.168 \qquad (13.4.3)$$

We can see that when the purchaser's price is not equal to 1, the numbers of quantity and value are different.

Product taxes are tax wedges between the basic and purchasers' prices. The sales tax is *ad valorem*. The sales tax rate is calibrated by

$$tsale_c = (\text{sales tax})/(PQS_c \cdot QQ_c + \sum_{ct} QCTT_{ct,c} \cdot PQ_3) \qquad (13.4.4)$$

Adding the tax and margin costs to supplier's price PQS_c, we have the following price equation for purchaser's price PQ_c:

$$PQ_c \cdot QQ_c = (1 + tsale_c) \cdot (PQS_c \cdot QQ_c + PQ_3 \sum_{ct} ictt_{ct.c} \cdot QQ_c) \qquad (13.4.5)$$

Trade and transport margin services are considered to be additional inputs for commodities to be delivered. By the accounting double entry principle, the SAM table should also record which accounts provide the margin services. SAM Table 13.1.2 shows that these services are provided by the service sector, the Com3 commodity row sector. The grand total amount of the trade and transport margins is $QCTTA$:

$$QCTTA = \sum_{ct}\sum_{c} QCTT_{ct,c} = \sum_{ct}\sum_{c} ictt_{ct} \cdot QQ_c \qquad (13.4.6)$$

They are all purchased at the purchaser's price of the service commodity PQ_3. So, the total value of the margin inputs is $PQ_3 \cdot QCTTA$. Note in the service row account, $QCTTA$ is considered as something similar to an intermediate input, not a final use. Therefore, it is not a part of GDP measured by the final expenditures at purchasers' prices.

13.5 Producer Price Index (PPI) and Basic Prices

Producer Price Index (PPI) is an important economic indicator for study and forecast of the economy, and is published monthly in the U.S. and many other countries. PPI is the average selling prices received by domestic producers before taxes on products. Interestingly and confusingly, PPI by definition corresponds to the concept of basic prices but not "producers' prices" termed in SNA (SNA 14.139). This is because both basic prices and PPI exclude marketing margins, sales taxes, other product taxes and VAT, while "producers' prices" by the SNA definition include the excise tax and other similar product taxes. In our CGE models in this chapter, the activity prices after production PA_a satisfy the definition for the prices for PPI. Hence, PPI can be set as the weighted price of PA_a, whose weights are

$$ppiwt_a = QA_a \left/ \sum_{a' \in A} QA_{a'} \right. \qquad (13.5.1)$$

PPI is

$$PPI = \sum_{a \in A} PA_a \cdot ppiwt_a \qquad (13.5.2)$$

PPI can serve as the numeraire and can be set at 1 in CGE models. CPI can also serve as the numeraire, but we consider PPI has some advantages over CPI in a comprehensive CGE model. CPI is weighted purchasers' prices, while PPI is weighted basic prices. When PPI is set to 1, CPI would equal or be greater than 1. In calculation, it is more convenient to add margins and product taxes on the basic prices to calculate other prices such as purchasers' prices, rather than working backwards. In addition, the weights used for PPI are broader than CPI, thus representing better the overall domestic productions in the economy. If PPI is set to 1, it means PA_a are the base prices and their weighted average is 1 in the model.

13.6 Base Price and Quantity Unit in CGE Modeling

All numbers in the entries of a SAM table are in monetary values which are the products of the prices and quantities $P \times Q$. Given the same monetary value in the entry, in calibration, changing the price for the value would inversely affect the unit of measurement for the quantity implied, and vice versa. In CGE modeling, it is important to know when we are allowed to change or redefine the quantity unit in modeling, and when we cannot change the quantity unit. The basic rule is keeping the consistency of the unit for the same physical

Table 13.6.1. Example of the steel production activity in a SAM table

	Steel production activity Base state	Steel production activity After tax increase
Steel output	1800	2000
Payroll tax	200	400
Labor	1000	1000
Capital	600	600

nature of activities or commodities in the base state and counterfactual states in simulation.

Because inputs and the output in a production activity are normally different in physical nature, in the initial calibration, we are relatively free to choose their measurement units as we prefer. However, once the unit for the particular product is set, in simulation we cannot change the already-defined unit. To illustrate, Table 13.6.1 is the data of the steel production activity from a hypothetical SAM table.

In this economy, steel production needs only factors of labor and capital but no intermediate inputs. The government levies payroll taxes on labor employed by enterprises. Labor, capital and steel are certainly different in physical nature. So in calibration for the base state, we are relatively free to set the measurement units for factors and the steel output. For convenience, we set the factor prices WL and WK to 1. Then the quantities of labor and capital are derived from the SAM table data: $QL = 1000$ and $QK = 600$. This means that we have set the measurement unit for labor or capital, which equals one monetary unit in the base period. Because of a payroll tax the total output value including the payroll tax is $1000 + 600 + 200 = 1800$. In the initial calibration we have freedom to set the measurement unit of steel.

Option 1: $PA = 1$ and $QA = 1800$. Because by convention the base price PB is set to 1, in this case we let PA be the base price, and the base price for steel includes the payroll tax. Then the quantity of steel output QA is calibrated to be 1800. We then calibrate the scale factor α_a in production function $QA_a = \alpha_a[\delta_a QL^\rho + (1 - \delta_a)QK_a^\rho]^{1/\rho}$ to satisfy the relationship between QL, QK and QA.

Option 2: $PA = 1.125$ and $QA = 1600$. Here we prefer to let price PA explicitly reflect the payroll tax impact. In this option, the base price PB is net of the payroll tax, implied in the equation: $PB \cdot QA = 1 \times (1000 + 600) = 1 \times 1600$. The output quantity is calibrated from the value of total costs of labor and capital of 1600. The scale factor α_a would also be calibrated to a different number in the production function. The price including payroll tax is $PA = 1800/1600 = 1.125$. The quantity of steel output is 1600 in Option 2 but is 1800 in Option 1 because they use different measurement units.

Once the steel unit option is chosen and set, it cannot be changed anymore, such as in simulation. Whichever option is used, the simulation results would be the same. To illustrate, suppose the payroll tax rate changes and the enterprises need to pay 200 more in payroll tax for the same amounts of factors employed. This situation is shown in the right column of Table 13.6.1. Because the production function has not changed and neither the amounts of inputs, the real quantity of steel output QA remains unchanged. Yet the total output value has changed to $1000 + 600 + 400 = 2000$. This value change is simply caused by the payroll tax increase, hence it should be reflected only in the steel price but not the quantity. Let us take a look at the percentage changes in steel price in the two optional price-and-quantity-unit settings:

Option 1: $QA = 1800$. The new price PA is $2000/1800 = 1.11$. Compared with the original price $PA = 1$, there is 11% price increase.

Option 2: $QA = 1600$. The new price PA is $2000/1600 = 1.25$. Compared with the original price $PA = 1.125$, it is $1.25/1.125 - 1 = 11\%$ price increase.

Both optional settings give 11% change in the steel output price. That is, regardless of which option we use, the results of percentage changes in variables are the same because we stick to the same measurement unit for the steel product during the simulation process.

In the case of increasing sales taxes, the commodity after tax changes does not change its physical nature; hence, the unit of the quantity of the commodity should be kept the same, and the only change should be its price. In national accounting, in addition to sales taxes, transport and trade margins also insert cost wedges between the basic price and purchaser's price for the same quantity unit of a commodity. In modeling it is important to keep the original quantities of commodities unchanged when we add these costs of margins and taxes to the basic prices to reach purchasers' prices.

13.7 Intermediate Inputs Valued at Purchasers' Prices

By the SNA convention, intermediate inputs in input–output tables are valued at purchasers' prices. It implies that enterprises buy inputs at purchasers' prices which include retailing, wholesale and transport costs, product taxes, and non-deductible VAT taxes. In reality, the purchaser's price of a commodity may vary depending on who the purchaser is. By the SNA definition, purchaser's price includes the VAT and product taxes that are not deductible by the purchaser, but excludes the VAT taxes and similar taxes that are deductible by the purchaser. Let us use examples to illustrate. Suppose an European household bought a bag of wheat flour for the price of 10 euros plus 1 euro of VAT, then the household's purchaser's price is 11 euros for the bag of wheat flour because the VAT is not deductible by the household. Suppose a restaurant bought a bag of wheat flour for 11 euros including 1 euro of VAT, but the VAT is deductible by the restaurant (who can claim tax refund for this 1 euro from the government), then the restaurant's purchaser's price is 10 euros for the bag of wheat flour.

The output prices in the activity accounts are "basic prices" even though the intermediate inputs used in production are paid by purchasers' prices. Input–output tables prepared by statistical authorities such as that of OECD follow this definition. To understand, take a look at the SAM Table 13.1.2, along the activity columns, the definition is:

Value-added (at basic prices) + Intermediate inputs (at purchasers' prices)

= Output (at basic prices) (13.7.1)

In our model economy, along the activity columns, although the intermediate inputs are valued at purchasers' prices PQ, the output prices PA are still basic prices. In other words, basic price of a product is a "bare" price net of direct product taxes and marketing margins charged on the product, but allows those non-deductible taxes and margins included in the intermediate inputs. One simple way to interpret this definition is that: basic price is the production cost paid by the enterprise to produce the commodity.

In most countries with the VAT system, enterprises can claim VAT tax refund/rebate for all intermediate inputs, but final consumers have to pay the full amount of VAT for the commodities they buy. Hence, the purchasers' prices for the same commodity would differ depending on who purchases them. This issue would be further discussed in detail in Chapter 15, but at this moment let us keep the issue simple, assuming that there is no VAT refund/rebate so the enterprises pay the same purchasers' prices PQ for intermediate inputs just like the final consumers. When basic prices are set to 1, purchasers' prices would be *greater* than 1 if product taxes and marketing margins are present. The intermediate input block now is more complicated than the previous models because the real quantities $QINT$ are no longer equal to the value numbers in the SAM table. We need to calibrate the quantity numbers from the values in the intermediate input block. Let $\text{SAM}_{i,j}$ denote the value of entry (i, j) in the SAM table. The quantity of intermediate input c used in activity a is calibrated by

$$QINT_{ca} = \text{SAM}_{ca}/PQ_c \tag{13.7.2}$$

The aggregate intermediate input $QINTA_a$ is the sum of intermediate inputs in quantity:

$$QINTA_a = \sum_c QINT_{ca} \tag{13.7.3}$$

The input–output coefficient ica_{ca} is

$$ica_{ca} = QINT_{ca}/QINTA_a \tag{13.7.4}$$

The price of aggregate intermediate input $PINTA_a$ is

$$PINTA_a = \sum_c PQ_c \cdot ica_{ca} \tag{13.7.5}$$

Because in general the purchaser's price PQ_c does *not* equal 1, the numbers of the commodity quantities purchased by households, the government, enterprises are also different from the numbers of the commodity values in the SAM table. These quantities need to be calibrated by dividing PQ_c in the GAMS program; and other parameters rely on these quantity numbers to calibrate. In previous CGE models, it was easier because the purchasers' prices PQ were set to 1 so calibration for PQ is not needed. With service margins and product taxes, purchasers' prices PQ_c are no longer equal to 1. They need to be first calibrated in the GAMS program so we can in turn calibrate the quantities of intermediate inputs and final uses. To accomplish this job, we use the information from the commodity columns in the SAM table. Suppose we choose activity price as the base price and set $PA_a = 1$, then by mapping, the supplier's price $PQS_c = 1$. The SAM table entries directly provide the values $PQ_c \cdot QQ_c$ and $PQS_c \cdot QQ_c$. Their ratio is PQ_c:

$$(PQ_c \cdot QQ_c)/(PQS_c \cdot QQ_c) = PQ_c/PQS_c = PQ_c/1 = PQ_c \qquad (13.7.6)$$

The above equation can be used to calibrate purchaser's price PQ_c.

As the intermediate input prices PQ now are greater than 1, can we still set the activity output price $PA = 1$? The answer is yes, because the activity output is physically different from the inputs so we can redefine the quantity unit of QA.

Take the example at the top level of a CES production module in the activity accounts of SAM Table 13.1.2. The price of aggregate intermediate input $PINTA_a$ is greater than 1 because all purchasers prices PQ are greater than 1 and $PINTA_a = \sum_c PQ_c \cdot ica_{ca}$. Suppose the aggregate value-added price PVA_a is set to 1. When input prices $PINTA_a$ and PVA_a on average are greater than 1, the output price PA_a can still be set to 1 by redefining the unit of output QA_a as the output is physically different from the two inputs. Suppose for some reasons we need to set $PA_a = 1$, then the output quantity QA_a is calibrated by:

$$QA_a = \text{SAM}_{total,a}/PA_a = \text{SAM}_{total,a}/1 = \text{SAM}_{total,a} \qquad (13.7.7)$$

For instance of activity 3, $QA_3 = 2355/1 = 2355$.

Given the SAM table value, when $PINTA_a > 1$, $QINTA_a$ would be smaller than the sum of intermediate-input-value numbers in the SAM table. For instance, for activity 3, the sum of intermediate-input-value numbers is $270 + 380 + 250 = 900$. If $PINTA_3 = 1.1$, then $QINTA_3$ would be smaller than 900: $QINTA_3 = 900/1.1 = 818$. With this smaller quantity of input $QINTA_3$, how can we still reach the calibrated quantity of output $QA_3 = 2355$? The reason is that the scale factor α_3 would be calibrated to equalize both sides in the CES production function (assuming we set $PVA_3 = 1$ so $QVA_3 = (800 + 655)/1 = 1455$):

$$2355 = \alpha_3[\delta_3 QVA_3^{\rho_3} + (1 - \delta_3^q)QINTA_3^{\rho_3}]^{1/\rho_3}$$

$$= \alpha_3[\delta_3 \cdot 1455^{\rho_3} + (1 - \delta_3^q) \cdot 818^{\rho_3}]^{1/\rho_3} \qquad (13.7.8)$$

It can be verified that price equation $PA_3 \cdot QA_3 = PVA_3 \cdot QVA_3 + PINTA_3 \cdot QINTA_3$ still holds.

This principle also applies to the fixed proportion (Leontief) production case. The aggregate-intermediate-input $QINTA$ is physically different from intermediate inputs $QINT_c$, so we can redefine its quantity unit and set its price $PINTA$ as we prefer. In the previous example Equation (13.7.3) prevents us from freely setting price $PINTA$ because it has fixed the quantity unit of $QINTA$. We need to revise it by adding a scale factor α_α^* so we can adjust input coefficients:

$$QINTA_a = \alpha_\alpha^* \sum_c QINT_{ca} \qquad (13.7.9)$$

Take the intermediate input block in Table 13.1.2 as an example. Suppose we wish to set $PINTA_3^* = 1$, then quantity $QINTA_3^* = 900$ is calibrated from the value in the SAM table. Then we use the following equation to calibrate α_3^*:

$$QINTA_3^* = 900 = \alpha_3^* \sum_c QINT_{c3} \qquad (13.7.10)$$

Then we calibrate the new input coefficients

$$ica^*_{c3} = QINT_{c3}/QINTA^*_3 = QINT_{c3}/900 \qquad (13.7.11)$$

The relationship between the new and old input coefficients is: $ica^*_{ca} = (1/\alpha^*_a) \cdot ica_{ca}$. Because of the scale factor, the new input coefficients do not sum to 1, but this is fine because we have redefined the quantity unit of $QINTA$. The intermediate input module in the CGE model now consists of the following two equations with new input coefficients:

$$QINT_{ca} = ica^*_{ca} \cdot QINTA_a \qquad (13.7.12)$$

$$PINTA_a = \sum_c PQ_c \cdot ica^*_{ca} \qquad (13.7.13)$$

In the multiple-level nested production block, export or import modules, etc., we often encounter the issue of resetting a particular output price and redefining quantity unit for a fixed proportion production function. Then the above technique can be adopted.

13.8 A CGE Model for an Economy with Trade and Transport Margins

We now construct a model for the economy as described by SAM Table 13.1.2. It has service margins: transport, wholesale and retail trade. It also has sales taxes. These costs insert wedges between basic prices and purchasers' prices.

The production block is similar to that in Chapter 12 with a two-level nested structure. The domain of the production block has changed to activity set A with index a. The notations of the parameters are also updated accordingly. The top level is a CES production function module:

$$QA_a = \alpha^a_a[\delta^a_a QVA^{\rho^a_a}_a + (1 - \delta^a_a)QINTA^{\rho^a_a}_a]^{1/\rho^a_a} \qquad a \in A \qquad (13.8.1)$$

$$\frac{PVA_a}{PINTA_a} = \frac{\delta^a_a}{(1 - \delta^a_a)}\left(\frac{QVA_a}{QINTA_a}\right)^{\rho^a_a - 1} \qquad a \in A \qquad (13.8.2)$$

$$PA_a \cdot QA_a = PVA_a \cdot QVA_a + PINTA_a \cdot QINTA_a \qquad a \in A \qquad (13.8.3)$$

At the second level there is a value-added module:

$$QVA_a = \alpha^{va}_a[\delta^{va}_{La} QLD^{\rho^{va}_a}_a + (1 - \delta^{va}_{La})QKD^{\rho^{va}_a}_a]^{1/\rho^{va}_a} \qquad a \in A \qquad (13.8.4)$$

$$\frac{WL}{WK} = \frac{\delta^{va}_a}{(1 - \delta^{va}_a)}\left(\frac{QLD_a}{QKD_a}\right)^{\rho^{va}_a - 1} \qquad a \in A \qquad (13.8.5)$$

$$PVA_a \cdot QVA_a = WL \cdot QLD_a + WK \cdot QKD_a \qquad a \in A \qquad (13.8.6)$$

At the second level, the production function in the intermediate input module is Leontief. Activity a buys commodity c as input, paying the purchasers' prices PQ_c to get it delivered:

$$QINT_{ca} = ica_{ca} \cdot QINTA_a \qquad a \in A, \quad c \in C \qquad (13.8.7)$$

$$PINTA_a = \sum_{c \in C} ica_{ca} \cdot PQ_c \qquad a \in A \qquad (13.8.8)$$

Each activity produces exactly one commodity. $IDENT_{ac}$ is an identity matrix. Mapping from activities to commodities are:

$$QQ_c = \sum_a IDENT_{ac} \cdot QA_a \qquad c \in C \qquad (13.8.9)$$

$$PQS_c = \sum_a IDENT_{ac} \cdot PA_a \qquad c \in C \qquad (13.8.10)$$

In the commodity accounts, we have trade and transport margin inputs $QCTT_{ct,c}$ in order to market the commodities. The set for trade and transport inputs is CTT with index ct:

$$QCTT_{ct,c} = ictt_{ct,c} \cdot QQ_c \qquad ct \in CTT \quad c \in C \qquad (13.8.11)$$

where $ictt_{ct,c}$ are "input coefficients", using margin input ct for marketing one unit of commodity c. All the margin inputs are provided by the service sector Com3, thus their price is PQ_3. The total amount of margin inputs is denoted by $QCTTA$, which is

$$QCTTA = \sum_{ct} \sum_c QCTT_{ct,c} \qquad (13.8.12)$$

There is also a sales tax charged ad valorem on each commodity, with sales tax rate $tsale$. Hence, the purchaser's price includes the supplier's price and these additional costs and taxes. It is represented by the following price equation:

$$PQ_c \cdot QQ_c = (1 + tsale_c) \left(PQS_c \cdot QQ_c + PQ_3 \cdot \sum_{ct} QCTT_{ct,c} \right) \qquad (13.8.13)$$

Households' income is:

$$YH = WL \cdot QLS + shareif_{hk} \cdot WK \cdot QKS + transfer_{h\,gov} \cdot CPI \qquad (13.8.14)$$

where $transfer_{h\,gov}$ is transfer payment from the government to households, automatically adjusted by CPI. $shareif_{hk}$ is the share paid to enterprise owners in enterprises' capital income.

Households' utility function is Cobb–Douglas, so they spend a fixed share on each commodity out of their disposable income:

$$PQ_c \cdot QH_c = shareh_c \cdot mpc \cdot (1 - ti_h) \cdot YH \qquad c \in C \qquad (13.8.15)$$

Because there is no constant term in the consumption function, hence mpc equals the average consumption rate.

Enterprise income includes their retained share in capital income $shareif_{ent\,k}$. In the model economy, enterprises do not receive transfer payments from other institutions. So:

$$YENT = shareif_{ent\,k} \cdot WK \cdot QKS \qquad (13.8.16)$$

Enterprises pay corporate income tax to the government by the rate of ti_{ent}. The enterprise savings is

$$SAVEENT = (1 - ti_{ent})YENT \qquad (13.8.17)$$

Enterprise investment, i.e., capital formation, is $\overline{QINV}_c \cdot INVADJ$, where $\overline{QINV}_c$ is the investment in the base state. The adjustment factor $INVADJ$ is determined either endogenously or exogenously depending on the macroeconomic closure:

$$QINV_c = \overline{QINV}_c \cdot INVADJ \tag{13.8.18}$$

The government tax revenues are from income tax from households, corporate income tax from enterprises with tax rate of ti_{ent}, and sales tax:

$$YG = ti_h \cdot YH_h + ti_{ent} \cdot YENT + \sum_c tsale_c \cdot \left(PQS_c \cdot QQ_c + PQ_3 \cdot \sum_{ct} QCTT_{ct,c} \right) \tag{13.8.19}$$

The total government expenditure is EG and its fiscal budget balance is $SAVEG$:

$$EG = YG - SAVEG \tag{13.8.20}$$

The government's spending on each commodity is a fixed share after it deducts transfer payments:

$$PQ_c \cdot QG_c = shareg_c(EG - transfer_{hg} \cdot CPI) \qquad c \in C \tag{13.8.21}$$

The commodity market clearing equations are based on the balance of the commodity row accounts in the SAM table. For the service sector, commodity account 3, there is a demand for the trade and transport margin product $QCTTA$:

$$QQ_c = \sum_a QINT_{ca} + QCTTA + QH_c + \overline{QINV}_c \cdot INVADJ + QG_c \quad c = 3 \tag{13.8.22}$$

For other commodity sectors, the market clearing equations keep the previous form:

$$QQ_c = \sum_a QINT_{ca} + QH_c + \overline{QINV}_c \cdot INVADJ + QG_c \qquad c \in C \quad c \neq 3 \tag{13.8.22$'$}$$

The factor market clearing equations are as follows:

$$\sum_a QLD_a = QLS \tag{13.8.23}$$

$$\sum_a QKD_a = QKS \tag{13.8.24}$$

The consumer price index (CPI) and producer price index (PPI) are

$$CPI = \sum_{c \in C} PQ_c \cdot cpiwt_c \tag{13.8.25}$$

$$PPI = \sum_{a \in A} PA_a \cdot ppiwt_a \tag{13.8.26}$$

The savings–investment equation has a dummy variable $DUMMYSI$:

$$\sum_c PQ_c \cdot QINV_c = (1 - mpc) \cdot (1 - tih) \cdot YH$$

$$+ SAVEENT + SAVEG + DUMMYSI \tag{13.8.27}$$

Equations (13.8.1)–(13.8.27), a total of 27 equations, form the CGE model for the model economy with marketing margins. The variables are as follows: PA_a, PVA_a, $PINTA_a$, QVA_a, $QINTA_a$, $QINT_{ca}$, QLD_a, QKD_a, QLS, QKS, WL, WK, PQS_c, $PQ_c QQ_c$, $QCTT_{ct,c}$, $QCTTA$, YH, QH_c, $YENT$, $QINV$, $INVADJ$, $SAVEENT$, YG, $QA_a EG$, QG_c, $SAVEG$, CPI, PPI, $DUMMYSI$. In total there are 31 variable groups.

We use the "government spending closure" in the model. It means that the government adjusts its spending thus changing the aggregate expenditure to ensure the full employment output. This closure would add the following constraints:

$$QLS = \overline{QLS} \tag{13.8.28}$$

$$QKS = \overline{QKS} \tag{13.8.29}$$

$$INVADJ = 1 \tag{13.8.30}$$

$$PPI = 1 \tag{13.8.31}$$

where PPI is the numeraire. The constraints reduce the number of variables to 27. The model is square and can be solved.

13.9 GAMS Program

Example 13.9.1. Write a CGE program for the model with trade and transport margins in Section 13.8, based on Table 13.1.2. The values of some parameters are given as follows. GDP is defined as the final uses at the purchasers' prices. Calibrate the parameters and replicate the model. Suppose labor endowment QLS increases by 10%. Compute the resulting changes in GDP in percentage terms.

	Agriculture	Industry	Service
Top level CES ρ	0.2	0.3	0.1
Value-added CES ρ	0.3	0.2	0.5

Solution: The GAMS program is as follows. GDP increases by 5.1% after the increase in labor endowment.

```
$title Example 13.9.1 GAMS program for model with trade and transport margins

*Define sets and subsets

set ac
/act1,act2,act3,com1,com2,com3,transp,wholes,retail,lab,cap,hh,ent,gov,saletx,
tariff,invsav,total/;
set a(ac) /act1,act2,act3/;
set c(ac) /com1,com2,com3/;
set f(ac) /lab,cap/;
*subset ct is for marketing margins
set ct(ac) /transp,wholes,retail/;
set acnt(ac) all accounts excluding total;
```

```
acnt(ac)=YES;
acnt('total')=NO;
*set cns(c) is for all commodities except service
set cns(c);
cns(c)=YES;
cns('com3')=NO;

alias (ac,acp),(a,ap),(c,cp),(f,fp),(ct,ctp),(acnt,acntp);

*If accounts in the table exceed the page width, move the additional one
below, with "+" to continue.

table sam(ac,acp)
```

	act1	act2	act3	com1	com2	com3	transp	wholes	retail
act1				1897					
act2					2900				
act3						2355			
com1	280	420	270						
com2	377	520	380						
com3	220	260	250				130	112	145
transp				60	50	20			
wholes				30	60	22			
retail				40	80	25			
lab	650	700	800						
cap	370	1000	655						
hh									
ent									
gov									
saletx				98	140	128			
invsav									
total	1897	2900	2355	2125	3230	2550	130	112	145

+	lab	cap	hh	ent	gov	saletx	invsav	total
act1								1897
act2								2900
act3								2355
com1			834		178		143	2125
com2			1450		230		273	3230
com3			983		250		200	2550
transp								130
wholes								112

```
retail                                                    145
lab                                                       2150
cap                                                       2025
hh       2150   1725                   293               4168
ent             300                                       300
gov                     515    100            366         981
saletx                                                    366
invsav                  386    200     30                 616
total  2150   2025      4168   300     981    366   616
;

table Identac(a,c)
           com1     com2     com3
act1         1
act2                  1
act3                           1
;

*Check if the SAM table is balanced
parameters

samchk(ac);
samCHK(acnt)=sum(acntp,SAM(acntp,acnt))-sum(acntp,SAM(acnt,acntp));

display samchk,acnt,cns,sam;

*Input parameter values given externally
parameter   rhoAa(a)   /act1 =   0.2,    act2 = 0.3,   act3 = 0.1/
            rhoVA(a)   /act1     0.3,    act2   0.2,   act3   0.5/;

parameters
scaleAa(a)        Scale factor of top level CES function of a
deltaAa(a)        Value-added share parameter in top level CES of a
scaleAVA(a)       Scale factor of value-added CES function of a
deltaVA(a)        Labor share parameter in value-added CES function of a
ica(c,a)          Input coefficient for intermediate inputs
shareh(c          Share of households' income spending on c
shareg(c)         Share of government income spending on c
tih               Households income tax rate
tiEnt             Business income tax rate
transferhg0       Government transfer payment to households
```

shareifhk	Households share of capital income from enterprises
shareifentk	Share of capital income retained by enterprises
mpc	marginal propensity to consume
tsale(c)	Sales tax rate on commodity c
QCTT0(ct,c)	Trade transport ct used in commodity c
ictt(ct,c)	Proportion of trade transport ct used in commodity c
QCTTA0	Grand total of trade and transport margin inputs
PA0(a)	Price of activity a
QA0(a)	Quantity of activity a
PVA0(a)	Price of aggregate value-added
QVA0(a)	Quantity of aggregate value-added
PINTA0(a)	Price of aggregate intermediate input
QINTA0(a)	Quantity of aggregate intermediate input
QINT0(c,a)	Quantity of intermediate input c used in a
QLD0(a)	Labor demand
QKD0(a)	Capital demand
WL0	Labor price
WK0	Capital price
PQ0(c)	Purchaser's price of commodity c
PQS0(c)	Supplier's price of commodity c
QQ0(c)	Total composite commodity supply in the domestic market
QLS0	Total labor supply
QKS0	Total capital supply
YH0	Household income
EH0	Total consumption expenditure of households
QH0(c)	Quantity demanded for c by households
YENT0	Enterprise income
QINV0(c)	Investment (fixed capital consumption) of c by enterprises
INVADJ0	Investment adjust factor
SAVEENT0	Enterprise savings
YG0	Government total revenue
EG0	Government total expenditure
QG0(c)	Government consumption on c
SAVEG0	Government savings, fiscal budget balance
GDP0	GDP
EG0chk	Check if EGO is consistent
cpiwt(c)	Consumer Price Index weight
CPI0	Consumer Price Index
ppiwt(a)	Producer Price Index weight
PPI0	Producer Price Index
;	

```
*Calibrating parameters. Note how purchasers' prices are calibrated
PA0(a)=1;
PQ0(c)=sam('total',c)/(sum(a,sam(a,c)));
QQ0(c)=sam(c,'total')/PQ0(c);
QINT0(c,a)=SAM(c,a)/PQ0(c);
QINTA0(a)=sum(c,QINT0(c,a));
ica(c,a)=QINT0(c,a)/QINTA0(a);
PINTA0(a)=SUM(c,ica(c,a)*PQ0(c));
WK0=1;
WL0=1;
PQS0(c)=1;
QA0(a)=sam('total',a)/PA0(a);
QVA0(a)=sum(f,sam(f,a));
PVA0(a)=sum(f,sam(f,a))/QVA0(a);
QLD0(a)=sam('lab',a)/WL0;
QKD0(a)=sam('cap',a)/WK0;
QLS0=sam('total','lab')/WL0;
QKS0=sam('total','cap')/WK0;
INVADJ0=1;

*Marketing margins and product taxes
tsale(c)=sam('saletx',c)/(sum(a,sam(a,c))+sum(ct,sam(ct,c)));
QCTT0(ct,c)=sam(ct,c)/PQ0('com3');
ictt(ct,c)=QCTT0(ct,c)/(sum(a,sam(a,c)/PA0(a)));
QCTTA0=sum(ct,sum(c,QCTT0(ct,c)));

*Activity production block
deltaAa(a)=PVA0(a)*QVA0(a)**(1-rhoAa(a))/(PVA0(a)*QVA0(a)**(1-
rhoAa(a))+PINTA0(a)*QINTA0(a)**(1-rhoAa(a)));
scaleAa(a)=QA0(a)/(deltaAa(a)*QVA0(a)**rhoAa(a)+(1-
deltaAa(a))*QINTA0(a)**rhoAa(a))**(1/rhoAa(a));
deltaVA(a)=WL0*QLD0(a)**(1-rhoVA(a))/(WL0*QLD0(a)**(1-
rhoVA(a))+WK0*QKD0(a)**(1-rhoVA(a)));
scaleAVA(a)=QVA0(a)/(deltaVA(a)*QLD0(a)**rhoVA(a)+(1-
deltaVA(a))*QKD0(a)**rhoVA(a))**(1/rhoVA(a));

QH0(c)=SAM(c,'hh')/PQ0(c);
cpiwt(c)=QH0(c)/sum(cp,QH0(cp));
CPI0=sum(c,PQ0(c)*cpiwt(c));
transferhg0=sam('hh','gov')/cpi0;
shareifhk=sam('hh','cap')/(WK0*QKS0);
```

```
shareifentk=sam('ent','cap')/(WK0*QKS0);
YH0=WL0*QLS0+shareifhk*WK0*QKS0+transferhg0*cpi0;
tih=sam('gov','hh')/YH0;
mpc=sum(c,sam(c,'hh'))/((1-tih)*YH0);
EH0=mpc*(1-tih)*YH0;
shareh(c)=(PQ0(c)*QH0(c))/EH0;
YENT0=shareifentk*WK0*QKS0;
QINV0(c)=sam(c,'invsav')/PQ0(c)/INVADJ0;
tiEnt=sam('gov','ent')/YEnt0;
SAVEENT0=(1-tiEnt)*YENT0;
YG0=tih*YH0+tiEnt*YENT0+sam('gov','saletx');
QG0(c)=sam(c,'gov')/PQ0(c);
SAVEG0=sam('invsav','gov');
EG0=YG0-SAVEG0;
shareg(c)=PQ0(c)*QG0(c)/(EG0-transferhg0*cpi0);
ppiwt(a)=QA0(a)/sum(ap,QA0(ap));
PPI0=sum(a,PA0(a)*ppiwt(a));
GDP0=sum(c,PQ0(c)*(QH0(c)+QINV0(c)+QG0(c)));

display
deltaAa,scaleAa,deltaVA,scaleAva,PA0,QA0,PQS0,PQ0,QQ0,PINTA0,QINT0,QINTA0,ic
a,PVA0,QVA0,QCTT0,ictt,QCTTA0,EH0,EG0,identac,shareh,shareg,CPI0,PPI0,GDP0;

variable
PA(a),PVA(a),PINTA(a),QA(a),QVA(a),QINTA(a),QINT(c,a),QLD(a),QKD(a),QLS,QKS,
WL,WK,QQ(c),PQS(c),PQ(c),QCTT(ct,c),QCTTA,YH,QH(c),YENT,QINV(c),INVADJ,SAVEE
NT,YG,EG,QG(c),SAVEG,CPI,PPI,GDP,DUMMYSI;

equation
QAfn(a),QAFOCeq(a),PAeq(a),QVAfn(a),QVAFOC(a),PVAeq(a),QINTfn(c,a),PINTAeq(a
),QQQAeq(c),PQSPAeq(c),QCTTeq(ct,c),QCTTAeq,PQSPQeq(c),Yheq,QHeq(c),YENTeq,Q
INVeq(c),SAVEENTeq,YGeq,SAVEGeq,QGeq,ComEqui(c),ComEquiNoQTT(c),Leq,Keq,CPIe
q,PPIeq,GDPeq,SIeq;

*Production block
QAfn(a)..
QA(a)=e=scaleAa(a)*(deltaAa(a)*QVA(a)**rhoAa(a)+(1-
deltaAa(a))*QINTA(a)**rhoAa(a))**(1/rhoAa(a));

QAFOCeq(a)..
PVA(a)/PINTA(a)=e=(deltaAa(a)/(1-deltaAa(a)))*(QVA(a)/QINTA(a))**(rhoAa(a)-1);
```

```
PAeq(a)..
PA(a)*QA(a)=e=(PVA(a)*QVA(a)+PINTA(a)*QINTA(a));


QVAfn(a)..
QVA(a)=e=scaleAVA(a)*(deltaVA(a)*QLD(a)**rhoVA(a)+(1-
deltaVA(a))*QKD(a)**rhoVA(a))**(1/rhoVA(a));


QVAFOC(a)..
WL/WK=e=(deltaVA(a)/(1-deltaVA(a)))*(QLD(a)/QKD(a))**(rhoVA(a)-1);


PVAeq(a)..
PVA(a)*QVA(a)=e=WL*QLD(a)+WK*QKD(a);


QINTfn(c,a)..
QINT(c,a)=e=ica(c,a)*QINTA(a);


PINTAeq(a)..
PINTA(a)=e=SUM(c,ica(c,a)*PQ(c));


*Mapping from activities to commodities
QQQAeq(c)..
QQ(c)=e=sum(a,identac(a,c)*QA(a));


PQSPAeq(c)..
PQS(c)=e=sum(a,identac(a,c)*PA(a));


*trade and transport margins module
QCTTeq(ct,c)..
QCTT(ct,c)=e=ictt(ct,c)*QQ(c);


QCTTAeq..
QCTTA=e=sum(c,sum(ct,QCTT(ct,c)));


PQSPQeq(c)..
PQ(c)*QQ(c)=e=(1+tsale(c))*(PQS(c)*QQ(c)+sum(ct,QCTT(ct,c)*PQ('com3')));


*Households
YHeq..
YH=e=WL*QLS+shareifhk*WK*QKS+transferhg0*CPI;


QHeq(c)..
PQ(c)*QH(c)=e=shareh(c)*mpc*(1-tih)*YH;
```

```
*Enterprises
YENTeq..
YENT=e=shareifentk*WK*QKS;


SAVEENTeq..
SAVEENT=e=(1-tiEnt)*YENT;


QINVeq(c)..
QINV(c)=e=QINV0(c)*INVADJ;


*Government
YGeq..
YG=e=tih*YH+tiEnt*YENT+sum(c,tsale(c)*(PQS(c)*QQ(c)+sum(ct,QCTT(ct,c)*PQ('co
m3'))));


SAVEGeq..
EG=e=YG-SAVEG;


QGeq(c)..
PQ(c)*QG(c)=e=shareg(c)*(EG-transferhg0*CPI);


*Commodity market balance for the service sector
ComEqui('com3')..
QQ('com3')=e=sum(a,QINT('com3',a))+QH('com3')+QINV('com3')+QG('com3')+QCTTA;


*Commodity market balance for sectors other than service
ComEquiNoQTT(cns)..
QQ(cns)=e=sum(a,QINT(cns,a))+QH(cns)+QINV(cns)+QG(cns);


*Factor markets
Leq..
Sum(a,QLD(a))=e=QLS;


Keq..
Sum(a,QKD(a))=e=QKS;


*price indices
CPIeq..
CPI=e=sum(c,PQ(c)*cpiwt(c));
```

```
PPIeq..
PPI=e=sum(a,PA(a)*ppiwt(a));

GDPeq..
GDP=e=sum(c,PQ(c)*(QH(c)+QINV(c)+QG(c)));

SIeq..
sum(c,PQ(c)*QINV(c))=e=(1-mpc)*(1-tih)*YH+SAVEENT+SAVEG+dummysi;

*Assigning initial values
PA.L(a)=PA0(a);
PVA.L(a)=PVA0(a);
PINTA.L(a)=PINTA0(a);
QA.L(a)=QA0(a);
QVA.L(a)=QVA0(a);
QINTA.L(a)=QINTA0(a);
QINT.L(c,a)=QINT0(c,a);
QLD.L(a)=QLD0(a);
QKD.L(a)=QKD0(a);
QLS.L=QLS0;
QKS.L=QKS0;
WL.L=WL0;
WK.L=WK0;
PQS.L(c)=PQS0(c);
PQ.L(c)=PQ0(c);
QQ.L(c)=QQ0(c);
QCTT.L(ct,c)=QCTT0(ct,c);
QCTTA.L=QCTTA0;
YH.L=YH0;
QH.L(c)=QH0(c);
YENT.L=YENT0;
QINV.L(c)=QINV0(c);
INVADJ.L=1;
SAVEENT.L=SAVEENT0;
YG.L=YG0;
EG.L=EG0;
QG.L(c)=QG0(c);
SAVEG.L=SAVEG0;
CPI.L=CPI0;
PPI.L=PPI0;
GDP.L=GDP0;
```

```
*Set constraints
ppi.fx=1;
QLS.fx=QLS0;
QKS.fx=QKS0;
INVADJ.fx=1;

*Executing the model
model cge /all/;
solve cge using mcp;

display QINT.L,QINTA.L,QINT0;

*Simulation for increase in labor endowment
QLS.fx=QLS0*1.1;

model sim /all/;
solve sim using mcp;

Parameter
Multiplier labor multiplier;
Multiplier=GDP.L/GDP0;

display Multiplier;
*END
```

Exercises

13E.1 Copy the GAMS program in Section 13.9, and run it successfully.

13E.2 Revise the GAMS program in Example 13.9.1 by setting the purchasers' prices as the base prices. That is, in calibration, $PQ_c = 1$ for all commodities. In this case, you need to calibrate the activity prices PA_a by using the information on the commodity columns. The commodity units are changed and their quantities are changed accordingly throughout the model. You may use CPI as the numeraire. Compare the results to those in Example 13.9.1. Then verify that the conclusion from the simulation result remains the same.

13E.3 The government of the model economy in Section 13.8 now collects payroll tax from enterprises on their labor employment. The new situation is described by the SAM Table 13E.3.1 The information about the elasticities are the same. The structure of the model is the same, except for the new payroll tax. Write a GAMS program for the economy. Also, simulate the situation when the labor force increases by 10%.

Table 13E.3.1. SAM table for a model economy with payroll taxes.

	Act1	Act2	Act3	Com1	Com2	Com3	Transport	Wholes	Retail	Labor	Capital	Households	Ent	Gov	Payroll tax	Sales tax	Investment	Total
Act1 (agriculture)				1962														1962
Act2 (industry)					2970													2970
Act3 (service)						2435												2435
Com1 (agriculture)	280	420	270									833		178			209	2190
Com2 (industry)	377	520	380									1450		300			273	3300
Com3 (service)	220	260	250				130	112	145			1200		250			63	2630
transport				60	50	20												130
wholesale				30	60	22												112
Retail				40	80	25												145
Labor	650	700	800															2150
Capital	370	1000	655															2025
Households										2150	1725			193				4068
Enterprises											300							300
Government												300	100		215	366		981
Payroll tax	65	70	80															215
Sales tax				98	140	128												366
Savings												285	200	60				545
Total	1962	2970	2435	2190	3300	2630	130	112	145	2150	2025	4068	300	981	215	366	545	

Chapter 14

CGE Models in Open Economies

14.1 Open Economy

In this chapter, we extend our discussion to an open economy which trades goods and services with the rest of the world (ROW). Accordingly, we add an account "ROW" for the external sectors in social accounting matrix (SAM) tables and computable general equilibrium (CGE) models. The new variables include those associated with supplies and demands of imports, exports and domestically produced and consumed commodities. Table 14.1.1 is a descriptive SAM table for the structure of an open economy. The SAM table separates activities and commodities. Table 14.1.2 is an example of a "real" SAM table for a model economy, a country called Openland, with transaction values filled in the entries.

For an open economy, there are three sets of commodities: exports, domestically produced and consumed commodities, and imports. Let us take a look at the descriptive SAM Table 14.1.1. The activity column accounts are basically the same as those in the closed economy of Chapter 13. They record production activities, including value-added, intermediate inputs and production taxes. Production taxes paid by enterprises are included in the value-added part, as defined by system of national accounts (SNA). How to position (value-added tax) VAT in the SAM table is tricky. By the SNA definition, VAT are not production taxes; VAT are costs similar to marketing margins, placed between producers' prices and purchasers' prices, thus VAT should be placed above product taxes in the commodity column accounts. However, when we do CGE modeling, the non-deductible portion of VAT paid by enterprises would affect their input decisions; so, by economics this part of VAT should be modeled in the value-added block in activity accounts. Because of these concerns, in Table 14.1.1, VAT is placed in both activity and commodity accounts. This issue will be further discussed in Section 15.3. What we should be aware of is that, if some VAT are included in the activity prices PA, then PA can no longer be called "basic prices" by the SNA definition. We may just call variable PA "activity output prices" or simply "activity prices". Activity prices PA are basically the production cost of enterprises.

In the activity row accounts, the activity outputs are distributed between the domestic sales and exports. After products are produced, some of them are consumed domestically and others are exported. The SAM table implies the assumption that enterprises receive price PA for their exports at the border before shipping the cargo overseas.

Table 14.1.1.   Descriptive SAM table for an open economy.

	1 Activities	2 Commodities	3 Factors	4 Households	5 Enterprises	6 Government	7 Rest of the World (ROW)	8 Savings–Investment	Total incomes
1 Activities		Domestically marketed outputs QA * PA = QD * PD				Export tax			Output QA * PA
2 Commodities	Intermediate inputs QINT * PQ	Wholesale and retail trade, transport margins		Household consumption QH * PQ		Government expenditure QG * PQ		Investment QINV * PQ	Demand QQ * PQ
3 Factors	Value-added						Factor income from ROW		Factor income
4 Households			Households' factor income	Transfer among households	Enterprise transfer to households	Government transfer to households	Transfer to households from ROW	Household income	
5 Enterprises			Enterprise factor income			Government transfer to enterprises	Transfer to enterprises from ROW		Enterprise income
6 Government	VAT tax*, Employment tax, production tax	VAT tax*, Sales tax, tariffs	Factor taxes as income tax to government	Income tax, direct tax	Enterprise direct tax to government		Transfer to government from ROW		Government income
7 Rest of the World (ROW)		Imports QM * PM	Factor income to ROW		Enterprise surplus to ROW	Government transfers to ROW			Foreign exchange outflow
8 Savings–Investment				Household savings	Enterprise savings	Government savings	Foreign savings		Savings
Total expenditures	Activity QA * PA	Supply QQ * PQ	Factor expenditures	Household expenditures	Enterprises expenditures	Government expenditures	Foreign exchange inflow	Investment	

Note: * See explanation in the text.

Table 14.1.2. SAM table of country Openland.

	Act1	Act2	Act3	Com1	Com2	Com3	Margins	Lab	Cap	HH	Ent	Gov	Employ tax	sales tax	Tariff	ROW	Investment	Total
Act1 (agriculture)				1872												90		1962
Act2 (industry)					2750											260		3010
Act3 (service)						2494										80		2574
Com1 (agriculture)	280	420	240							900		98					209	2147
Com2 (industry)	377	520	380							1381		250					213	3121
Com3 (service)	220	300	540				73			1211		150					143	2637
Transport & trade margins				20	35	18												73
Labor	650	700	690															2040
Capital	370	1000	655															2025
Households								2040	1725			297						4062
Enterprises									300									300
Government										450	100		204	71	30			855
Employment tax	65	70	69															204
Sales tax				18	30	23												71
Tariff				7	16	7												30
Rest of the World				230	290	95												615
Savings										120	200	60				185		565
Total	1962	3010	2574	2147	3121	2637	73	2040	2025	4062	300	855	204	71	30	615	565	

In the commodity column accounts, the commodities supplied to the domestic markets include domestic products and imports. The commodity column accounts also record transport, wholesale and retailing margins, as well as product taxes. The commodity row accounts record the commodities consumed by enterprises as intermediate inputs and investment goods, and by households and government as final goods.

Let us specify the variable notations for the open economy model. For the three sets of commodities, the variables and their definitions are as follows:

QE_a and PE_a: Quantity and price of export from activity a.

QM_c and PM_c: Quantity and price of import c.

QD_a and PD_a: Quantity and price of domestically produced and consumed product from activity a.

QD_c and PD_c: Quantity and price of domestically produced and consumed commodity c.

The quantity and price of activity a and commodity c have the same notation symbols as in Chapter 13, but their definitions/meanings are updated to the new environment:

QA_a and PA_a: Quantity and price of product produced by activity a.

QQ_c: Quantity of composite commodity c supplied in the domestic market, which includes domestic product and import of c.

PQS_c and PQ_c: Supplier's and purchaser's prices of composite commodity c.

Activity output QA_a is distributed between domestic sales QD_a and export QE_a. Commodity QQ_c is a composite commodity that combines both domestically produced and consumed QD_c and imports QM_c. PQS_c is the supplier's price of composite commodity QQ_c. PQ_c is the purchaser's price of composite commodity QQ_c, and it is the most often used price in CGE models. All these variables are important in the open economy CGE models.

14.2 Output Distribution Between Domestic Market and Exports

After a commodity is produced from an activity, enterprises distribute the output between domestic market and foreign market (export) for sale, as recorded in the activity row account of Table 14.1.1. If we believe that the relative sizes of domestic and foreign markets are fairly stable, we can set up fixed shares between the two markets in the CGE model:

$$QE_a = shareea_a \cdot QA_a \tag{14.2.1}$$

$$QD_a = (1 - shareea_a) \cdot QA_a \tag{14.2.2}$$

where $shareea_a$ is the share of export QE_a in the total output of activity QA_a. The above two equations determine the quantities of QE_a and QD_a, as the amount of QA_a is already determined in the production block.

Further, we need to determine the prices by the following price equation:

$$PA_a \cdot QA_a = PD_a \cdot QD_a + PE_a \cdot QE_a \qquad (14.2.3)$$

The above price equation says that PA_a is a weighted price of PE_a and PD_a. PA_a is already determined in the production block. PE_a needs to be determined by a foreign trade closure specification. If we assume this country is a "small country" which takes the world price as given and the exchange rate is fixed, then export price PE_a is fixed. Then by this price equation, PD_a is determined. Note PE_a and PD_a may not be equal because enterprises may differentiate prices between domestic and foreign markets. For instance, if the demand elasticity in the world market is greater than the domestic market, enterprises would set a higher domestic price, $PD_a > PE_a$, to maximize profits.

The fixed proportion relationship may not properly describe the real-world. Domestic and foreign markets can be substitutable, although imperfectly, for enterprises to sell products. Enterprises adjust the sales between the two markets by comparing the relative prices and adjustment costs. The imperfect substitutability of the domestic and foreign markets can be described by a curve similar to the production possibilities frontier for QE and QD (here and in what follows we omit the index subscripts for simplicity when the meaning is clear in the context) as in Figure 14.2.1. A CET (Constant Elasticity of Transformation) function is used for this curve. The mathematical form of a CET function is the same as a constant elasticity of substitution (CES) function, except the value of exponent ρ is restricted to be greater than 1, so the shape of the curve is bowed outwards. Because it is curved, QE and QD are imperfect substitutes.

The CET module to distribute activity output a between exports and domestic consumption consists of three equations. Mathematically, it is similar to the CES production module. The first equation is the CET function for the bowed-out curve:

$$QA_a = \alpha_a^t [\delta_a^t QD_a^{\rho_a^t} + (1 - \delta) QE_a^{\rho_c^t}]^{1/\rho_a^t} \qquad \rho_a^t > 1 \qquad (14.2.4)$$

Note the value of exponent ρ_a^t must be greater than one so as to have the bowed-out shape. Given the output level QA_a, the first-order condition for the optimal distribution

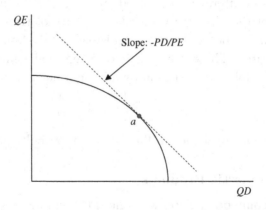

Figure 14.2.1. Distribution between QE and QD by a CET function.

Table 14.2.1.   Elasticity of transformation of CET between domestic sales and exports.

Sectors	Elasticity of transformation of CET between domestic consumption and exports ε_a^t (in absolute values)
Agriculture	3.90
Mining	2.90
Manufacturing	2.90
Services	0.70

Source: de Melo, Jaime and David Tarr (1992), *A General Equilibrium Analysis of US Foreign Trade Policy*, the MIT Press, Cambridge, Massachusetts.

bundle is

$$\frac{PD_a}{PE_a} = \frac{\delta_a^t}{(1 - \delta_a^t)} \left(\frac{QD_a}{QE_a} \right)^{\rho_a^t - 1} \tag{14.2.5}$$

PD, PE and PA are prices of QD, QE and QA, respectively. We need a price equation to regulate the price levels, as follows:

$$PA_a \cdot QA_a = PD_a \cdot QD_a + PE_a \cdot QE_a \tag{14.2.6}$$

The CET module consists of the three above equations and six variables: QA_a, PA_a, QD_a, PD_a, QE_a and PE_a. We need the values of three variables to be determined outside the module, so the remaining three variable values within the module can be determined. QA_a and PA_a are already determined by the production block. If we again assume the country is a "small country" and the exchange rate is fixed, then the exports price PE_a is determined. After these three variable values are determined outside the module, the values of the remaining three variables QD_a, PD_a and QE_a are determined.

Similar to the CES production module, the parameters in the CET module can be calibrated from the SAM table, except for exponent ρ_a^t. Information about the ρ_a^t value is fairly available in existing literature but needs to be carefully interpreted. Normally, it is available in the form of the absolute value of "elasticity of transformation". Let the CET elasticity of transformation be denoted by ε_a^t. Table 14.2.1 shows the published estimates for ε_a^t from the source cited. These values are expressed in absolute values. To convert them to ρ_a^t, we should use the following formula by adding a negative sign for ε_a^t:

$$\rho_a^t = 1 - \frac{1}{-\varepsilon_a^t} = 1 + \frac{1}{\varepsilon_a^t} \tag{14.2.7}$$

For instance, the exponent of the CET function in agriculture is $\rho = 1 - \frac{1}{-3.9} = 1.256$.

14.3 Imports and Domestic Products

Now we examine the commodity supply in the domestic market QQ_c. In the commodity column account in Table 14.1.1, quantity supplied of the composite commodity of QQ_c

includes domestic product QD_c and imports QM_c. If we believe that the share of the imports in the total supply of commodity c in the domestic market is very stable, we can set up a fixed proportion relationship in the CGE model:

$$QM_c = sharemc_c \cdot QQ_c \tag{14.3.1}$$

$$QD_c = (1 - sharemc_c) \cdot QQ_c \tag{14.3.2}$$

where *sharemc* is the share of QM_c in the total domestic supply QQ_c. In addition, we need the price equation to determine the price levels:

$$PQS_c \cdot QQ_c = PD_c \cdot QD_c + PM_c \cdot QM_c \tag{14.3.3}$$

where PQS_c is the supplier's price of QQ_c. QD_c and PD_c are already determined by the CET module after mapping from activities to commodities (as explained previously). PM_c is the after-tariff cif price[1] at the border, which is comparable to the basic price nature of PD_c. Assuming it is a small country with a fixed exchange rate, then import price PM_c is determined. Then, by the above price equation, PQS_c is determined.

The fixed proportion specification may not properly describe the real-world situations. Domestic products and imports usually are substitutes although not perfect substitutes. Domestic demanders including households, enterprises and the government would choose between domestic products and imports by comparing their prices and substitutability. This imperfect substitution between QM and QD can be described by a CES function, which is also referred to as the "Armington function" in CGE models. The Armington module consists of three equations. The composite commodity supplied QQ_c in the domestic market is formed by

$$QQ_c = \alpha_c^q (\delta_c^q QD^{\rho_c^q} + (1 - \delta_c^q) QM^{\rho_c^q})^{1/\rho_c^q} \tag{14.3.4}$$

Because it is a regular CES function type, the isoquant curve is bowed in, thus the exponent ρ_c^q should be less than 1. Further, by common sense, imports and the same domestic product are likely to be substitutes rather than complements, so the range of the exponent ρ_c^q value should be $0 < \rho_c^q < 1$. The first-order condition for the optimal combination is

$$\frac{PD_c}{PM_c} = \frac{\delta_c^q}{(1 - \delta_c^q)} \left(\frac{QD_c}{QM_c} \right)^{\rho_c^q - 1} \tag{14.3.5}$$

The weighted price of the composite commodity c is represented by the price equation:

$$PQS_c \cdot QQ_c = PD_c \cdot QD_c + PM_c \cdot QM_c \tag{14.3.6}$$

The composite commodity QQ_c is viewed as physically similar but not identical to either domestic product QD_c or imports QM_c. Hence, its quantity unit can be redefined but not too differ from QD_c and QM_c. The above Armington module consists of three equations and six variables: QQ_c, PQS_c, QD_c, PD_c, QM_c and PM_c. Three variables need to be determined from outside the module, so the values of the remaining three variables can be determined.

---

[1] "cif" stands for "cost, insurance and freight". "cif price" means that these expenses are already covered by the foreign sellers in the price.

Table 14.3.1.   Elasticity of substitution of CES between domestic products and imports.

Sectors	Elasticity of substitution of CES between domestic products and imports ε_c^q
Agriculture	1.42
Mining	0.50
Manufacturing	3.55
Services	2.00

Source: de Melo, Jaime and David Tarr (1992), *A General Equilibrium Analysis of US Foreign Trade Policy*, the MIT Press, Cambridge, Massachusetts.

Similar to the fixed proportion case, QD_c and PD_c are already determined from the CET module. If we assume a small country case with a fixed exchange rate, then the import price PM_a is determined. Thus, the values of the remaining three variables QQ_c, PQS_c and QM_c are determined by the system of the module.

The parameters of the CES function can be calibrated from the SAM table, except that the value of exponent ρ_c^q. ρ_c^q can be obtained or estimated from external information about the elasticity of substitution between domestic products and imports ε_a^q. Table 14.3.1 lists some published estimates for ε_a^q from the source cited. Because the Armington function is a regular CES function, ρ_c^q is calibrated by the formula of $\rho_c^q = 1 - 1/\varepsilon_c^q$.

14.4 From Activities to Commodities: Mappings and Margins

Above we have discussed equation specification for the relationships among imports, exports, and domestically produced and consumed commodities. The relationships and their positions in the economy are illustrated in a transaction flow chart in Figure 14.4.1.

To write a GAMS program to relate the CET module to the Armington module, we need to deal with some programming issues. In the CET module, the sectoral set is activities A; while in the Armington module, the sectoral set is commodities C. Their domains are different. For domestically produced and consumed goods QD, they appear in both modules but with different domains A and C. To relate them, we need to map from activities to commodities, as discussed in Chapter 13. We need to map from QD_a to QD_c and from PD_a to PD_c. For simplicity, let us assume one activity produces only one commodity, so the prices and quantities of the corresponding a and c are exactly the same:

$$QD_a = QD_c \qquad \forall a = c$$
$$PD_a = PD_c \qquad \forall a = c \tag{14.4.1}$$

The mathematical operation for the mapping relationship uses identity matrix $\mathbf{I}$:

$$\mathbf{QD(c)} = \mathbf{I} \times \mathbf{QD(a)} \qquad \mathbf{PD(c)} = \mathbf{I} \times \mathbf{PD(a)} \tag{14.4.2}$$

where $\mathbf{QD}$ and $\mathbf{PD}$ are the vectors with n elements.

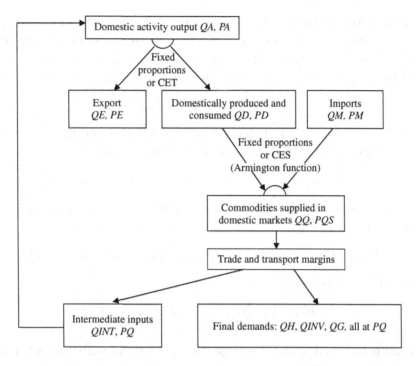

Figure 14.4.1. Flows of activities and commodities.

The GAMS program does not allow using the same variable name for different domain sets. If there is a conflict with different domains for the same variable name, GAMS would take the new defined domain for the variable and discard the old one. To avoid this problem, we change the variable names by adding the letters of their domain sets as follows:

PD_a changes to PDA_a PD_c changes to PDC_c

QD_a changes to QDA_a QD_c changes to QDC_c

Let an $n \times n$ identity matrix be denoted by $IDENT_{ac}$ with elements of i_{ac}. The equations to map from activities to commodities of variables QD and PD are as follows:

$$QDC_c = \sum_a IDENT_{ac} \cdot QDA_a \qquad c \in C \qquad (14.4.3)$$

$$PDC_c = \sum_a IDENT_{ac} \cdot PDA_a \qquad c \in C \qquad (14.4.4)$$

The above two equations establish the one-to-one relationship from activity a to the corresponding commodity c.

For exports, we assume enterprises ship them by bulk transportation to the port. This bulk transport cost is already covered in the activity production. There are no other transport, wholesale and retail margins involved for exports, nor are sales taxes charged on exports. Hence, export prices are directly related to the activity prices.

To supply commodities at home, all marketing margin inputs are needed for delivery to the final consumers. The marketing margins include wholesale and retail trade service, as well as multi-level transport costs to deliver to households and other final users. In Openland, the marketing margins are integrated in the account of transport and trade margins. $QCTT_c$ is the quantity of the aggregate margin input used in commodity c. It is proportional to the composite commodity QQ_c by the coefficient of $ictt_c$:

$$QCTT_c = ictt_c \cdot QQ_c \tag{14.4.5}$$

Openland does not have VAT. It has ad valorem sales tax on the supplier's price PQS_c and unit cost of marketing margins. The sales tax rate is $tsale_c$:

$$tsale_c = (\text{sales tax})/(PQS_c \cdot QQ_c + PQ_3 \cdot ictt_c \cdot QQ_c) \tag{14.4.6}$$

The margin input is provided by the service sector in Openland, thus its price is PQ_3. Including margin costs and sales tax, the purchaser's price PQ_c is

$$PQ_c \cdot QQ_c = (1 + tsale_c) \cdot (PQS_c \cdot QQ_c + PQ_3 \cdot ictt_c \cdot QQ_c) \tag{14.4.7}$$

The total amount of margin inputs is $QCTTA$:

$$QCTTA = \sum_c QCTT_c = \sum_c ictt_c \cdot QQ_c \tag{14.4.8}$$

This amount is provided by the service sector, so the commodity market clearing equation of the service sector ($c = 3$) is

$$QQ_c = \sum_a QINT_{ca} + QCTTA + \sum_h QH_{ch} + \overline{QINV}_c \cdot INVADJ + QG_c \qquad c = 3 \tag{14.4.9}$$

Market clearing equations of other commodities remain the same, without this $QCTTA$ term.

14.5 Exchange Rate and Exchange Rate Regimes

How are the prices of exports and imports determined? In Sections 14.2 and 14.3, we briefly mentioned the case of fixed exchange rate regime and the small country case. In this section, we elaborate on these issues.

When an open economy is engaged in international trade with the ROW, it needs to convert back and forth between the domestic currency and foreign currency by the exchange rate in transactions. The exchange rate is defined as the domestic currency price of one unit of foreign exchange. Suppose the exchange rate between British sterling and U.S. dollar is 0.5 pound for 1 dollar. If the domestic country is the U.S., British sterling is a foreign exchange, then the dollar price of one British pound is 2. That is, the exchange rate for sterling denoted by EXR is 2: $EXR = 2$. If EXR increases, it means that the foreign currency appreciates and the domestic currency depreciates; and vice versa.

In CGE models, however, we normalize the exchange rate to 1 for the base state for convenience. Let $EXR0$ denote the exchange rate value in the base state:

$$EXR0 = 1 \tag{14.5.1}$$

In our above example of British sterling, the normalization implies that the unit of the U.K. currency used now changes to only one half of a British pound. Similar to price normalization, this foreign exchange unit normalization would not change the analysis results because we are only interested in percentage changes in simulation.

In the SAM table, the entries in the account of "rest of the world", abbreviated to ROW, were originally in foreign exchange values but are converted by the exchange rate to the values measured in domestic currency unit. The exchange rate EXR is the price implied in the entry values. In particular, the entry value is value-in-foreign-exchange-unit $\times EXR$. Take an example to illustrate.

Suppose the currency unit of Openland (Table 14.1.2) is peso. The foreign exchange, i.e., foreign currency in ROW is the U.S. dollar. EXR is calibrated to 1. Openland's industry sector exports 260 to ROW. Note all entry values in the SAM table must be in local currency peso. This means Openland earns 260 pesos from ROW. The entry is 260 (peso) = 260 (dollar) $\times EXR$ = 260 (dollar) $\times$ 1. The ROW pays 260 dollars then converts it to 260 pesos. If peso depreciates so 2 pesos are needed for 1 dollar, then EXR = 2. Suppose after depreciation Openland's export quantity in the industry sector remains unchanged. Then the value of export of industry is 520 (peso) = 260 (dollar) $\times EXR$ = 260 (dollar) $\times$ 2.

Suppose in a SAM table there is a transfer from ROW to the government of Openland $transfer_{g\,row}$. It is originally in the foreign exchange unit, the U.S. dollar; but it needs to be converted to local currency peso. The value in the SAM entry should be the product of transfer and exchange rate: $tranfer_{g\,row} \times EXR$.

In summary, all entries in the ROW accounts in the SAM table are foreign exchanges converted to the local currency value. The values are the products of the original values multiplied by exchange rate EXR. Once these values are in local currency unit, they can be added to other entry values in the row and column accounts in the SAM table.

There are two typical exchange rate regimes, fixed and flexible, in CGE models. In the fixed exchange rate regime, EXR is fixed. If exchange rate is fixed, as international economics predicts, the country has no control over its trade balance or current account balance. A country's balance of payments (BOP) consists of current and capital accounts.[2] BOP deficit implies that the country borrows funds from overseas to finance the country's domestic needs. In other words, the country relies on foreign savings to fund its needs. One example is that the U.S. has a large BOP deficit every year, which means that the U.S. relies on foreign savings to finance its domestic savings gap each year. Let $SAVEF$ be foreign savings:

$$SAVEF = \text{deficit in the account of balance of payment}$$

$$= \text{current account deficit} + \text{capital account deficit} \tag{14.5.2}$$

In the simple economy of Openland, because there are no capital account transactions, a trade deficit (surplus) would also be BOP deficit (surplus). Let pwe_a be the world price

---

[2]Here we use the textbook definition for "capital account". By SNA, it is termed "financial account".

of export of activity product a. Let pwm_c be the world price of import commodity c. Both variables are measured in the foreign currency unit. Hence, foreign savings in foreign currency unit is

$$SAVEF = \sum_c pwm_c \cdot QM_c - \sum_a pwe_a \cdot QE_a \qquad (14.5.3)$$

Working in SAM tables, we need to convert these values to be measured in local currency, so they can be added with other entries in local currency unit. Hence:

$$SAVEF \cdot EXR = \sum_c pwm_c \cdot QM_c \cdot EXR - \sum_a pwe_a \cdot QE_a \cdot EXR \qquad (14.5.4)$$

In the flexible exchange rate regime, the exchange rate EXR is flexible, but BOP or $SAVEF$ is balanced.

$$SAVEF = 0 \qquad (14.5.5)$$

In summary, we have two optional closures for the foreign exchange rate regimes in modeling: (1) in the fixed exchange rate regime, EXR is fixed but $SAVEF$ is a variable; and (2) in the flexible exchange rate regime, EXR is a variable but $SAVEF$ needs to be fixed.

14.6 Domestic and World Prices

In international economics, "small country" or "large country" have their special definitions. A small country is a country whose trade volume of a commodity is so small in the world market that changes in its trade volume have no influence over the world market price of that commodity. For instance, India is a large economy in terms of the sizes of population and GDP but is a "small country" in oil exports. A small country has to take the world price as given; and it faces a horizontal demand or supply curve at this price with unlimited quantity demanded or supplied of the commodity from the ROW. For a small country to export activity product a, pwe_a is fixed. Let te_a be the export tax rate, and valorem PE_a (based on the value at PE_a), then we have

$$(1 + te_a)PE_a = pwe_a \cdot EXR \qquad (14.6.1)$$

Or,

$$PE_a = (1/(1 + te_a)) \cdot pwe_a \cdot EXR \qquad (14.6.1')$$

In the case of export subsidy, te_a is negative. Many countries give VAT rebates for exports, which can be treated as export subsidies and calibrated to te_a. If it is a fixed exchange rate regime, EXR is fixed, then export price PE_a is so determined by Equation (14.6.1').

As discussed before, there are no wholesale and retail trade margins involved with exports, but it may involve some bulk transport cost from the producer to the border. An example is the coal export in Canada. In the case that the bulk transport cost needs to be considered in research, we can insert the transport cost between price PE_a and the fob price[3] at the border:

$$PE_a = (1/(1 + te_a)) \cdot pwe_a \cdot EXR - transport_a \tag{14.6.2}$$

In other words, PE_a is the price before shipping to the border. This definition is based on the consideration that PE_a should be comparable to PDA_a, because both PE_a and PDA_a are comparable to the activity price PA_a. The method to handle export taxes and transport margins will be further discussed in detail in Chapter 15.

For a small country to import commodity c, the world price pwm_c is fixed. Let tm_c be the tariff rate for imported commodity c, the import price PM_c is determined by

$$PM_c = pwm_c(1 + tm_c)EXR \tag{14.6.3}$$

PM_c here is defined as the after tariff cif price, which means the price at border plus tariff and all other customs fees paid. We consider this definition of PM_c comparable to the basic price of the domestic product PD_c. Both are net of the same sales taxes and similar marketing margins from the purchaser's price of commodity c. Note the definition for PM_c here is different from that in the IFFRI model (2002), in which PM_c is the price after some marketing margins.

A large country is defined as a country whose changes in volume of import or export would affect the world price of the commodity. For a large exporting country, it faces a downward demand curve by the ROW for its export. The world price of its export pwe_a is a variable which is a function of the country's export volume QE_a.

$$pwe_a = f^a(QE_a) \tag{14.6.4}$$

where $f^a(\cdots)$ is the inverse demand function by ROW for export a.

Suppose we are interested in the impacts of some external shocks on variables of international trade for a large exporting country, in the CGE model we need to specify the relevant ROW demand function(s) $f^a(\cdots)$ and set pwe_a as an endogenous variable. One candidate of the function form $f^a(\cdots)$ is

$$pwe = \lambda QE^{-1/\varepsilon} \tag{14.6.5}$$

where λ is a constant and ε is the price elasticity of demand. This function is called "constant price elasticity of demand function", which will be discussed with a related exercise for the large exporting country case in Chapter 17.

Similarly, for a large importing country, it faces an upward sloping supply curve by ROW for its import. The world price for its import pwm_c is a variable. Let $g^c(\cdots)$ be the inverse supply function of ROW of commodity c:

$$pwm_c = g^c(QM_c) \tag{14.6.6}$$

---

[3]fob stands for "free on board". fob price means that the seller is only responsible for shipping the cargo to the outbound port. The buyers pay the freight and other costs to the destination.

For research on a large importing country in CGE models, we need to first specify and then include function $g^c(\cdots)$ in the models and set pwm_c as an endogenous variable. An example of function $g^c(\cdots)$ is the "constant (price) elasticity of supply function":

$$pwm = \mu QM^{1/\varepsilon} \tag{14.6.7}$$

where μ is a constant and ε is the price elasticity of supply. This issue will be further discussed later and an exercise for the large importing country case will be practiced in Chapter 17.

In theory, it is possible that the ROW supply or demand curves may not have the conventional slope sign, such as in the case of the backward bending supply curve. In CGE empirical studies, the shape of the ROW demand or supply functions would be determined by the specification of the supply or demand function based on empirical estimation and researchers' theoretical judgement.

Because there are many more prices involved in open economy CGE models, we need to set their base levels carefully, to be consistent with the economics theory and the SNA definitions. QA_a, QD_a and QE_a are the same product from activity a. Their prices PA_a, PD_a and PE_a are all net of marketing margins and product taxes, thus are comparable. If PA_a is a base price and set to 1 in the model, then in the base state PE_a is also set to 1. From Equation (14.6.1), the world price for export pwe_a is calibrated by

$$pwe_a = PE_a(1 + te_a)/EXR \tag{14.6.8}$$

In a small country case, pwe_a is a parameter and its value is fixed after calibration. When PE_a equals 1 and the export tax rate is positive, $te_a > 0$, then the calibrated world price pwe_a would be greater than 1. If instead it is a case of an export subsidy or VAT rebate, in which export rate is negative, $te_a < 0$, then the world price is less than 1, lower than the domestic price.

The situation for imports is similar, but in an opposite direction. As said that PM_c is comparable to PD_c and supplier's price PQS_c, because all are net of product taxes and marketing margins from the same purchaser's price. Then in the base state, if PD_c equals 1, PM_c also equals 1. From Equation (14.6.3), the world price for import pwm_c is calibrated by

$$pwm_c = PM_c/((1 + tm_c) \cdot EXR) \tag{14.6.9}$$

In a small country case, pwm_c is a parameter whose value is fixed. When PM_c equals 1 and the tariff rate is positive, $tm_c > 0$, the calibrated world price would be less than 1.

14.7 A CGE Model for an Open Economy

We now set up a CGE model for the open economy of Openland with its SAM Table 14.1.2. The production block has a two-level nested structure. The domain is activity set A with index a. On the top is a CES function:

$$QA_a = \alpha_a^a [\delta_a^a QVA_a^{\rho_a^a} + (1 - \delta_a^a) QINTA_a^{\rho_a^a}]^{1/\rho_a^a} \qquad a \in A \qquad (14.7.1)$$

$$\frac{PVA_a}{PINTA_a} = \frac{\delta_a^a}{(1 - \delta_a^a)} \left(\frac{QVA_a}{QINTA_a} \right)^{\rho_a^a - 1} \qquad a \in A \qquad (14.7.2)$$

$$PA_a \cdot QA_a = PVA_a \cdot QVA_a + PINTA_a \cdot QINTA_a \qquad a \in A \qquad (14.7.3)$$

The following is a value-added module. Enterprises pay employment tax for labor employed. The employment tax rate is *tpayent*. Employment taxes belong to "other production taxes" in SNA, which are included in the basic prices.

$$QVA_a = \alpha_a^{va} [\delta_{La}^{va} QLD_a^{\rho_a^{va}} + (1 - \delta_{La}^{va}) QKD_a^{\rho_a^{va}}]^{1/\rho_a^{va}} \qquad a \in A \qquad (14.7.4)$$

$$\frac{(1 + tpayent) WL}{WK} = \frac{\delta_a^{va}}{(1 - \delta_a^{va})} \left(\frac{QLD_a}{QKD_a} \right)^{\rho_a^{va} - 1} \qquad a \in A \qquad (14.7.5)$$

$$PVA_a \cdot QVA_a = (1 + tpayent) \cdot WL \cdot QLD_a + WK \cdot QKD_a \qquad a \in A \qquad (14.7.6)$$

The production function in the intermediate input module is a Leontief function. Activity a buys commodity c as the input at purchaser's price PQ_c:

$$QINT_{ca} = ica_{c\,a} \cdot QINTA_a \qquad a \in A, \quad c \in C \qquad (14.7.7)$$

$$PINTA_a = \sum_{c \in C} ica_{ca} \cdot PQ_c \qquad a \in A \qquad (14.7.8)$$

QA_a is distributed between export QE_a and domestic sales QDA_a, described in a CET module with the following three equations:

$$QA_a = \alpha_a^t [\delta_a^t QDA_a^{\rho_a^t} + (1 - \delta) QE_a^{\rho_a^t}]^{1/\rho_a^t} \qquad \rho_a^t > 1 \quad a \in A \qquad (14.7.9)$$

$$\frac{PDA_a}{PE_a} = \frac{\delta_a^t}{(1 - \delta_a^t)} \left(\frac{QDA_a}{QE_a} \right)^{\rho_a^t - 1} \qquad a \in A \qquad (14.7.10)$$

$$PA_a \cdot QA_a = PDA_a \cdot QDA_a + PE_a \cdot QE_a \qquad a \in A \qquad (14.7.11)$$

Openland is a small country for its exports and takes the world prices as given. It has a fixed exchange rate regime. It has no export tax in the SAM table, so $te_a = 0$. Hence, the export price is determined by

$$PE_a = pwe_a \cdot EXR \qquad a \in A \qquad (14.7.12)$$

The composite commodity supply QQ_c in the domestic market consists of import QM_c and domestic product QDC_c. Their relationship is described in the Armington module.

$$QQ_c = \alpha_c^q (\delta_c^q QDC_c^{\rho_c^q} + (1 - \delta_c^q) QM_c^{\rho_c^q})^{1/\rho_c^q} \qquad c \in C \qquad (14.7.13)$$

$$\frac{PDC_c}{PM_c} = \frac{\delta_c^q}{(1 - \delta_c^q)} \left(\frac{QDC_c}{QM_c} \right)^{\rho_c^q - 1} \qquad c \in C \qquad (14.7.14)$$

$$PQS_c \cdot QQ_c = PDC_c \cdot QDC_c + PM_c \cdot QM_c \qquad c \in C \qquad (14.7.15)$$

Openland is a small country for imports, too. It levies tariff on imports with tariff rate tm_c. The import price PM_c is determined by

$$PM_c = pwm_c(1 + tm_c)EXR \qquad c \in C \qquad (14.7.16)$$

In Openland, each activity produces exactly one commodity. Mapping from activities to commodities are:

$$QDC_c = \sum_a IDENT_{ac} \cdot QDA_a \qquad c \in C \qquad (14.7.17)$$

$$PDC_c = \sum_a IDENT_{ac} \cdot PDA_a \qquad c \in C \qquad (14.7.18)$$

The integrated trade and transport margin input (marketing margin input) $QCTT_c$ is proportional to QQ_c by "input-coefficient" $ictt_c$:

$$QCTT_c = ictt_c \cdot QQ_c \qquad (14.7.19)$$

The total amount of margin input is $QCTTA$:

$$QCTTA = \sum_c QCTT_c \qquad (14.7.20)$$

The margin inputs are provided by the service sector Com 3, thus their price is PQ_3. Openland also collects sales taxes. In the commodity accounts, the equation from the supplier's price to purchaser's price is

$$PQ_c \cdot QQ_c = (1 + tsale_c)(PQS_c \cdot QQ_c + PQ_3 \cdot QCTT_c) \qquad c \in C \qquad (14.7.21)$$

The above 21 equations complete the relationships from production activities to supplies of commodities.

The major institutions in Openland include households, enterprises, the government and the ROW. Total labor supply from households' endowment is QLS. Households' income is

$$YH = WL \cdot QLS + shareif_{hk} \cdot WK \cdot QKS + transfer_{h\,gov} \cdot CPI \qquad (14.7.22)$$

where $transfer_{h\,gov}$ is the transfer payment from the government to households. Its value is indexed by CPI. $shareif_{hk}$ is the share of enterprise owners in enterprises' capital income.

Households utility function is Cobb–Douglas, and they spend a fixed share on each commodity out of their disposable income:

$$PQ_c \cdot QH_c = shareh_c \cdot mpc \cdot (1 - ti_h) \cdot YH \qquad c \in C \qquad (14.7.23)$$

Because there is no constant term (subsistence consumption level) in the consumption function, here mpc equals the average consumption rate.

Enterprises' income includes their retained share in capital income $shareif_{ent\,k}$, and transfer payments from the government and ROW. Yet in Openland, enterprises do not receive these transfer payments. So enterprises' income is simply:

$$YENT = shareif_{ent\,k} \cdot WK \cdot QKS \qquad (14.7.24)$$

Enterprises pay corporate income tax to the government at the rate of ti_{ent}. The enterprise savings is

$$SAVEENT = (1 - ti_{ent})YENT \qquad (14.7.25)$$

Enterprise investment, i.e., capital formation, is $\overline{QINV}_c \cdot INVADJ$, where $\overline{QINV}_c$ is the investment of c in the base state. The adjustment factor $INVADJ$ is determined exogenously in most closures, except for the automatic investment closure:

$$QINV_c = \overline{QINV}_c \cdot INVADJ \qquad (14.7.26)$$

The government tax revenues are from employment tax, income tax from households, corporate income tax from enterprises, sales tax and tariffs:

$$YG = \sum_a tpayent_a \cdot WL \cdot QLD_a + ti_h \cdot YH_h + ti_{ent} \cdot YENT$$

$$+ \sum_c tsale_c(PQS_c \cdot QQ_c + PQ_3 \cdot QCTT_c)$$

$$+ \sum_c tm_c \cdot pwm_c \cdot QM_c \cdot EXR \qquad (14.7.27)$$

The last term of the above equation is the tariff revenue.

The total government expenditure in Openland is EG and its fiscal budget balance is $SAVEG$:

$$EG = YG - SAVEG \qquad (14.7.28)$$

The government's spending on each commodity is a fixed share in its total expenditure after it deducts transfer payments:

$$PQ_c \cdot QG_c = shareg_c(EG - transfer_{hg} \cdot CPI) \qquad c \in C \qquad (14.7.29)$$

The commodity market clearing equations are based on the balances of the commodity row accounts in the SAM table. The total amount in each sector is the composite commodity available in the domestic market, including import but excluding export. In the service sector, commodity account 3, there is a use of the trade and transport margins $QCTTA$:

$$QQ_c = \sum_a QINT_{ca} + QH_c + \overline{QINV}_c \cdot INVADJ + QG_c + QCTTA \qquad c = 3 \quad (14.7.30)$$

For other commodities, the market clearing equations keep the previous form:

$$QQ_c = \sum_a QINT_{ca} + QH_c + \overline{QINV}_c \cdot INVADJ + QG_c \qquad c \in C \quad \text{and} \quad c \neq 3 \ (14.7.30')$$

The factor market clearing equations are as follows:

$$\sum_a QLD_a = QLS \qquad (14.7.31)$$

$$\sum_a QKD_a = QKS \qquad (14.7.32)$$

The consumer price index (CPI) is

$$CPI = \sum_{c \in C} PQ_c \cdot cpiwt_c \tag{14.7.33}$$

Openland has no VAT. In the activity accounts, the only tax it has is payroll tax paid by enterprises, which is allowed to be included in the basic price. Hence, in Openland, PA_a is still basic price and producer price index (PPI) is the weighted price of PA. (Recall previous discussion: PPI is weighted basic price by the SNA definition)

$$PPI = \sum_{a \in A} PA_a \cdot ppiwt_a \tag{14.7.34}$$

Openland does not have transactions in the capital account with ROW, so its balance-of-payment only includes the current account, i.e., trade balance. Its foreign savings in the domestic currency unit is

$$SAVEF \cdot EXR = \sum_c pwm_c \cdot QM_c \cdot EXR - \sum_a pwe_a \cdot QE_a \cdot EXR \tag{14.7.35}$$

Now the savings–investment equation has one more component, $SAFEF$, as compared with previous closed economy models. As explained in Chapter 12, because the S-I equation is functionally dependent, dummy variable $DUMMYSI$ is added:

$$\sum_c PQ_c \cdot QINV_c = (1 - mpc) \cdot (1 - tih) \cdot YH + SAVEENT + SAVEG$$

$$+ SAVEF \cdot EXR + DUMMYSI \tag{14.7.36}$$

The above 36 equations from (14.7.1) to (14.7.36) form the CGE model for the open economy of Openland. The variables are: PA_a, PVA_a, $PINTA_a$, QA_a, QVA_a, $QINTA_a$, $QINT_{ca}$, QLD_a, QKD_a, QLS, QKS, WL, WK, PDA_a, QDA_a, PDC_c, QDC_c, PE_a, QE_a, EXR, PQS_c, PQ_c, QQ_c, PM_c, QM_c, $QCTT_c$, $QCTTA$, YH, QH_c, $YENT$, $QINV$, $INVADJ$, $SAVEENT$, YG, EG, QG, $SAVEG$, $SAVEF$, CPI, PPI, $DUMMYSI$. In total there are 41 variable groups.

The Openland's government is a Keynesian follower and it automatically adjusts spending EG to ensure full employment of factors. Hence, government spending EG and fiscal budget $SAVEG$ are variables. Investment is exogenous so $INVADJ$ is set at 1 in the base period. Openland has a fixed exchange regime. PPI is used as the price numeraire. Therefore, we have the following constraints:

$$QLS = \overline{QLS} \tag{14.7.37}$$

$$QKS = \overline{QKS} \tag{14.7.38}$$

$$INVADJ = 1 \tag{14.7.39}$$

$$EXR = \overline{EXR} \tag{14.7.40}$$

$$PPI = 1 \tag{14.7.41}$$

The five constraints reduce the number of variable groups to 36. Thus, the model is square and solvable.

Table 14.8.1. Parameter values for Openland.

	Agriculture	Industry	Service
Top activity level CES ρ	0.2	0.3	0.1
Value-added CES ρ	0.3	0.2	0.5
Armington CES ρ	0.4	0.6	0.4
CET function ρ	1.4	1.4	2.0

Table 14.8.2. Changes in imports and exports after currency depreciation.

After currency depreciation	Imports			Exports			BOP deficit (SAVEF)	
	Agri	Indus	Serv	Agri	Indus	Serv	In local currency	In foreign currency
EXR rises 5%	−8.5%	−13.2%	−9.3%	+13.3%	+13.6%	+3.8%	−61.4%	−63.3%

14.8 GAMS Program for an Open Economy

Example 14.8.1. Write a GAMS program for the open economy of Openland described by the model in Section 14.7 and SAM Table 14.1.2. In addition to the data available in the SAM table, we have the information about parameters in Table 14.8.1. After successfully replicating the model, simulate the situation when the exchange rate *EXR* increases by 5% (which means the domestic currency depreciates). Find the changes in imports and exports. Are they consistent with the predictions from the economics theory?

Solution: The GAMS program is provided in what follows. We use basic price as the base prices so activity prices in the base state *PA* are set to 1. The simulation results reported in Table 14.8.2 show that after the domestic currency depreciates by 5%, imports decrease and exports increase. The deficit in BOP shrinks substantially. These simulation results are consistent with the expectations from the economics theory.

```
$title Example 14.8.1 GAMS Program for an open economy Openland

*Define sets
set ac      /act1,act2,act3,com1,com2,com3,margin,lab,cap,hh,ent,gov,emptx,saletx,
tariff,row,invsav,total/;
set a(ac)   /act1,act2,act3/;
set c(ac)   /com1,com2,com3/;
set f(ac)   /lab,cap/;
*The following set acnt is for checking accuracy of SAM
set acnt(ac) all accounts excluding total;
acnt(ac)=YES;
acnt('total')=NO;
*The following set cns is for late selective commodity market balance equations
set cns(c);
cns(c)=YES;
```

```
cns('com3')=NO;
alias (ac,acp),(a,ap),(c,cp),(f,fp),(acnt,acntp);

*If accounts in the table exceed the page width, move down the
additional accounts, with "+" to continue.
table sam(ac,acp)
```

	act1	act2	act3	com1	com2	com3	margin	lab	cap
act1				1872					
act2					2750				
act3						2494			
com1	280	420	240						
com2	377	520	380						
com3	220	300	540				73		
margin				20	35	18			
lab	650	700	690						
cap	370	1000	655						
hh								2040	1725
ent									300
gov									
emptx	65	70	69						
saletx				18	30	23			
tariff				7	16	7			
row				230	290	95			
invsav									
total	1962	3010	2574	2147	3121	2637	73	2040	2025

	+ hh	ent	gov	emptx	saletx	tariff	row	invsav	total
act1							90		1962
act2							260		3010
act3							80		2574
com1	900		98					209	2147
com2	1381		250					213	3121
com3	1211		150					143	2637
margin									73
lab									2040
cap									2025
hh		297							4062
ent									300
gov	450	100		204	71	30			855
emptx									204
saletx									71
tariff									30
row									615
invsav	120	200	60				185		565
total	4062	300	855	204	71	30	615	565	

```
;
```

```
table Identac(a,c)
          com1      com2      com3
act1        1
act2                  1
act3                            1
;

*Check if the SAM table is balanced
parameters
samchk0(ac);
samchk0(acnt)=sum(acntp,SAM(acntp,acnt))-sum(acntp,SAM(acnt,acntp));

display samchk0,acnt,cns,sam;

*Input parameter values given externally
parameter   rhoAa(a)    /act1 =    0.2,    act2 = 0.3,    act3 = 0.1/
            rhoVA(a)    /act1      0.3,    act2   0.2,    act3   0.5/
            rhoCET(a)   /act1      1.4,    act2   1.4,    act3   2.0/
            rhoQq(c)    /com1      0.4,    com2   0.6,    com3   0.4/;

parameters
scaleAa(a)        Scale factor of top level CES function of a
deltaAa(a)        Value-added share parameter in top level CES of a
scaleAVA(a)       Scale factor of value added CES function of a
deltaVA(a)        Labor share parameter in value-added CES function of a
ica(c,a)          Input coefficient for intermediate inputs
scaleCET(a)       Scale factor of CET function
deltaCET(a)       Domestic sales share parameter in CET function
scaleQq(c)        Scale factor of Armington CES function
deltaQq(c)        Domestic product share parameter in Armington CES function
shareh(c)         Share of households' income spending on c
shareg(c)         Share of government income spending on c
tih               Households income tax rate
tiEnt             Business income tax rate
tpayent(a)        Rate of the employment tax paid by enterprises
transferhg0       Base amount of government transfer payment to households
shareifhk         Households share in capital income of enterprises
shareifentk       Share of capital income retained by enterprises
mpc               marginal propensity to consume
tm(c)             import tariff rate
tsale(c)          Sales tax rate on commodity c
QCTT0(c)          Trade and transport margin input used in commodity c
QCTTA0            Sum of trade and transport margin input
ictt(c)           Proportion of trade transport input used in quantity of c
PA0(a)            Price of activity a
QA0(a)            Quantity of activity a
PVA0(a)           Price of aggregate value-added
QVA0(a)           Quantity of aggregate value-added
```

```
PINTA0(a)          Price of aggregate intermediate input
QINTA0(a)          Quantity of aggregate intermediate input
QINT0(c,a)         Quantity of intermediate input c used in production of a
QLD0(a)            Labor demand by a
QKD0(a)            Capital demand by a
WL0                Labor price
WK0                Capital price
PQ0(c)             Purchaser's price of commodity c
PQS0(c)            Supplier's price of commodity c
QQ0(c)             Total composite commodity supplied in domestic market
PM0(c)             Import price of c
QM0(c)             Quantity of import c
PE0(a)             Export price of a
QE0(a)             Quantity of export a
PDA0(a)            Price of activity a produced and supplied domestically
QDA0(a)            Quantity of activity a produced and supplied domestically
PDC0(c)            Price of domestically produced and supplied commodity c
QDC0(c)            Quantity of domestically produced and supplied commodity c
EXR0               Exchange rate
pwm(c)             World price of import c in foreign exchange currency unit
pwe(a)             World price of export a in foreign exchange currency unit
QLS0               Total labor supply
QKS0               Total capital supply
YH0                Household income
EH0                Total consumption expenditure of households
QH0(c)             Quantity demanded for c by households
YENT0              Enterprise income
QINV0(c)           Quantity of investment of c by enterprises
SAVEENT0           Enterprise savings
YG0                Government total revenue
EG0                Government total expenditure
QG0(c)             Quantity of government consumption of c
SAVEG0             Net government savings or fiscal budget balance
SAVEF0             Foreign savings or balance of payment deficit
cpiwt(c)           Consumer Price Index weight
CPI0               Consumer Price Index
ppiwt(a)           Producer Price Index weight
PPI0               Producer Price Index
;


*Assignment and calibration for parameters
PA0(a)=1;
PQ0(c)=sam('total',c)/(sum(a,sam(a,c))+sam('row',c)+sam('tariff',c));
QINT0(c,a)=SAM(c,a)/PQ0(c);
QINTA0(a)=SUM(c, QINT0(c,a));
ica(c,a)=QINT0(c,a)/QINTA0(a) ;
PINTA0(a)=SUM(c,ica(c,a)*PQ0(c));
WK0=1;
```

```
WL0=1;
PE0(a)=1;
PM0(c)=1;
PDA0(a)=1;
PDC0(c)=1;
EXR0=1;
PQS0(c)=1;
QA0(a)=sam('total',a)/PA0(a);
QVA0(a)=SUM(f,sam(f,a));
PVA0(a)=(SUM(f,sam(f,a))+sam('emptx',a))/QVA0(a);
QLD0(a)=sam('lab',a)/WL0;
QKD0(a)=sam('cap',a)/WK0;
QLS0=sam('total','lab')/WL0;
QKS0=sam('total','cap')/WK0;
tpayent(a)=sam('emptx',a)/sam('lab',a);
*Exports and imports
tm(c)=sam('tariff',c)/sam('row',c);
pwm(c)=PM0(c)/((1+tm(c))*EXR0);
QM0(c)=(sam('row',c)+sam('tariff',c))/PM0(c);
pwe(a)=PE0(a)/EXR0;
QE0(a)=sam(a,'row')/PE0(a);
QDA0(a)=sum(c,sam(a,c))/PDA0(a);
QDC0(c)=sum(a,sam(a,c))/PDC0(c);
QQ0(c)=QDC0(c)+QM0(c);

*Marketing margins and sales tax
tsale(c)=sam('saletx',c)/(sum(a,sam(a,c))+sam('row',c)+sam('tariff',c)+sam('margin
',c));
QCTT0(c)=sam('margin',c)/PQ0('com3');
ictt(c)=QCTT0(c)/QQ0(c);
QCTTA0=sum(c,QCTT0(c));

display WL0,WK0,PQ0,PINTA0,PVA0,QQ0,QINTA0,QVA0,QDA0,QDC0,QQ0,pwm,QM0;

deltaAa(a)=PVA0(a)*QVA0(a)**(1-rhoAa(a))/(PVA0(a)*QVA0(a)**(1-
rhoAa(a))+PINTA0(a)*QINTA0(a)**(1-rhoAa(a)));
scaleAa(a)=QA0(a)/(deltaAa(a)*QVA0(a)**rhoAa(a)+(1-
deltaAa(a))*QINTA0(a)**rhoAa(a))**(1/rhoAa(a));
deltaVA(a)=((1+tpayent(a))*WL0)*QLD0(a)**(1-
rhoVA(a))/(((1+tpayent(a))*WL0)*QLD0(a)**(1-rhoVA(a))+WK0*QKD0(a)**(1-rhoVA(a)));
scaleAVA(a)=QVA0(a)/(deltaVA(a)*QLD0(a)**rhoVA(a)+(1-
deltaVA(a))*QKD0(a)**rhoVA(a))**(1/rhoVA(a));
*CET function parameter calibration
deltaCET(a)=PDA0(a)*QDA0(a)**(1-rhoCET(a))/(PDA0(a)*QDA0(a)**(1-
rhoCET(a))+PE0(a)*QE0(a)**(1-rhoCET(a)));
scaleCET(a)=QA0(a)/(deltaCET(a)*QDA0(a)**rhoCET(a)+(1-
deltaCET(a))*QE0(a)**rhoCET(a))**(1/rhoCET(a));
*Arminton function parameter calibration
```

```
deltaQq(c)=PDC0(c)*QDC0(c)**(1-rhoQQ(c))/(PDC0(c)*QDC0(c)**(1-
rhoQq(c))+PM0(c)*QM0(c)**(1-rhoQq(c)));
scaleQQ(c)=QQ0(c)/(deltaQq(c)*QDC0(c)**rhoQq(c)+(1-
deltaQq(c))*QM0(c)**rhoQq(c))**(1/rhoQq(c));
*Calibration of other parameters
QH0(c)=SAM(c,'hh')/PQ0(c);
cpiwt(c)=QH0(c)/sum(cp,QH0(cp));
CPI0=sum(c,PQ0(c)*cpiwt(c));
transferhg0=sam('hh','gov')/cpi0;
shareifhk=sam('hh','cap')/(WK0*QKS0);
shareifentk=sam('ent','cap')/(WK0*QKS0);
YH0=WL0*QLS0+shareifhk*WK0*QKS0+transferhg0*cpi0;
tih=sam('gov','hh')/YH0;
mpc=sum(c,sam(c,'hh'))/((1-tih)*YH0);
EH0=mpc*(1-tih)*YH0;
shareh(c)=(PQ0(c)*QH0(c))/EH0;
YENT0=shareifentk*WK0*QKS0;
QINV0(c)=sam(c,'invsav')/PQ0(c);
tiEnt=sam('gov','ent')/YEnt0;
SAVEENT0=(1-tiEnt)*YENT0;
YG0=tih*YH0+tiEnt*YENT0+sum(a,tpayent(a)*WL0*QLD0(a))+sum(c,sam('saletx',c))+sam('
gov','tariff');
QG0(c)=sam(c,'gov')/PQ0(c);
SAVEG0=sam('invsav','gov');
EG0=YG0-SAVEG0;
shareg(c)=PQ0(c)*QG0(c)/(EG0-transferhg0*cpi0);
SAVEF0=sam('invsav','row');
ppiwt(a)=QA0(a)/sum(ap,QA0(ap));
PPI0=sum(a,PA0(a)*ppiwt(a));

display ica,ictt,tsale,PA0,QA0,PQ0,EG0,identac,shareg;

variable
PA(a),PVA(a),PINTA(a),QA(a),QVA(a),QINTA(a),QINT(c,a),QLD(a),QKD(a),QLS,QKS,WL,WK,
PDA(a),QDA(a),PDC(c),QDC(c),PE(a),QE(a),EXR,QQ(c),PQS(c),PQ(c),PM(c),QM(c),QCTT(c),
QCTTA,YH,QH(c),YENT,QINV(c),INVADJ,SAVEENT,YG,EG,QG(c),SAVEG,SAVEF,CPI,PPI,DUMMYSI;

equation
QAfn(a),QAFOCeq(a),PAeq(a),QVAfn(a),QVAFOC(a),PVAeq(a),QINTfn(c,a),PINTAeq(a),CETf
n(a),CETFOC(a),PCETeq(a),PEeq(a),QQfn(c),QQFOC(c),PQSeq(c),PMeq(c),QDCQDA(c),PDCPD
A(c),QCTTeq,QCTTAeq,PQSPQeq(c),Yheq,QHeq(c),YENTeq,QINVeq(c),SAVEENTeq,Ygeq,QGeq,S
AVEGeq,ComEquiNoQTT(c),Leq,Keq,FEXeq,CPIeq,PPIeq,ComEqui(c),SIeq;

*Production block
QAfn(a)..
QA(a)=e=scaleAa(a)*(deltaAa(a)*QVA(a)**rhoAa(a)+(1-
deltaAa(a))*QINTA(a)**rhoAa(a))**(1/rhoAa(a));
```

```
QAFOCeq(a)..
PVA(a)/PINTA(a)=e=(deltaAa(a)/(1-deltaAa(a)))*(QVA(a)/QINTA(a))**(rhoAa(a)-1);

PAeq(a)..
PA(a)*QA(a)=e=PVA(a)*QVA(a)+PINTA(a)*QINTA(a);

QVAfn(a)..
QVA(a)=e=scaleAVA(a)*(deltaVA(a)*QLD(a)**rhoVA(a)+(1-
deltaVA(a))*QKD(a)**rhoVA(a))**(1/rhoVA(a));

QVAFOC(a)..
((1+tpayent(a))*WL)/WK=e=(deltaVA(a)/(1-deltaVA(a)))*(QLD(a)/QKD(a))**(rhoVA(a)-1);

PVAeq(a)..
PVA(a)*QVA(a)=e=(1+tpayent(a))*WL*QLD(a)+WK*QKD(a);

QINTfn(c,a)..
QINT(c,a)=e=ica(c,a)*QINTA(a);

PINTAeq(a)..
PINTA(a)=e=SUM(c,ica(c,a)*PQ(c));

*CET module
CETfn(a)..
QA(a)=e=scaleCET(a)*(deltaCET(a)*QDA(a)**rhoCET(a)+(1-
deltaCET(a))*QE(a)**rhoCET(a))**(1/rhoCET(a));

CETFOC(a)..
PDA(a)/PE(a)=e=(deltaCET(a)/(1-deltaCET(a)))*(QDA(a)/QE(a))**(rhoCET(a)-1);

PCETeq(a)..
PA(a)*QA(a)=e=PDA(a)*QDA(a)+PE(a)*QE(a);

PEeq(a)..
PE(a)=e=pwe(a)*EXR;

*Armington function module
QQfn(c)..
QQ(c)=e=scaleQq(c)*(deltaQq(c)*QDC(c)**rhoQq(c)+(1-
deltaQq(c))*QM(c)**rhoQq(c))**(1/rhoQq(c));

QQFOC(c)..
PDC(c)/PM(c)=e=(deltaQq(c)/(1-deltaQq(c)))*(QDC(c)/QM(c))**(rhoQq(c)-1);

PQSeq(c)..
PQS(c)*QQ(c)=e=PDC(c)*QDC(c)+PM(c)*QM(c);
```

```
PMeq(c)..
PM(c)=e=pwm(c)*(1+tm(c))*EXR;

*Mapping from activities to commodities
QDCQDA(c)..
QDC(c)=e=sum(a,identac(a,c)*QDA(a));

PDCPDA(c)..
PDC(c)=e=sum(a,identac(a,c)*PDA(a));

*trade and transport margins module
QCTTeq(c)..
QCTT(c)=e=ictt(c)*QQ(c);

QCTTAeq..
QCTTA=e=sum(c,QCTT(c));

PQSPQeq(c)..
PQ(c)*QQ(c)=e=(1+tsale(c))*(PQS(c)*QQ(c)+QCTT(c)*PQ('com3'));

*Households
YHeq..
YH=e=WL*QLS+shareifhk*WK*QKS+transferhg0*CPI;

QHeq(c)..
PQ(c)*QH(c)=e=shareh(c)*mpc*(1-tih)*YH;

*Enterprises
YENTeq..
YENT=e=shareifentk*WK*QKS;

QINVeq(c)..
QINV(c)=e=QINV0(c)*INVADJ;

SAVEENTeq..
SAVEENT=e=(1-tiEnt)*YENT;

*Government
YGeq..
YG=e=sum(a,tpayent(a)*WL*QLD(a))+tih*YH+tiEnt*YENT+sum(c,tsale(c)*(PQS(c)*QQ(c)+QC
TT(c)*PQ('com3'))+tm(c)*pwm(c)*QM(c)*EXR);

SAVEGeq..
EG=e=YG-SAVEG;

QGeq(c)..
PQ(c)*QG(c)=e=shareg(c)*(EG-transferhg0*CPI);
```

```
*Commodity market clearing equation for the service sector
ComEqui('com3')..
QQ('com3')=e=sum(a,QINT('com3',a))+QH('com3')+QINV('com3')+QG('com3')+QCTTA;

*Commodity market clearing equations for other sectors
ComEquiNoQTT(cns)..

QQ(cns)=e=sum(a,QINT(cns,a))+QH(cns)+QINV(cns)+QG(cns);

*Factor markets
Leq..
Sum(a,QLD(a))=e=QLS;

Keq..
Sum(a,QKD(a))=e=QKS;

*price indices
CPIeq..
CPI=e=sum(c,PQ(c)*cpiwt(c));

PPIeq..
PPI=e=sum(a,PA(a)*ppiwt(a));

*BOP equation
FEXeq..
SAVEF*EXR=e=sum(c,pwm(c)*QM(c)*EXR)-sum(a,pwe(a)*QE(a)*EXR);

SIeq..
sum(c,PQ(c)*QINV(c))=e=(1-mpc)*(1-tih)*YH+SAVEENT+SAVEG+SAVEF*EXR+dummysi;

*Assigning initial values
PA.L(a)=PA0(a);
PVA.L(a)=PVA0(a);
PINTA.L(a)=PINTA0(a);
QA.L(a)=QA0(a);
QVA.L(a)=QVA0(a);
QINTA.L(a)=QINTA0(a);
QINT.L(c,a)=QINT0(c,a);
QLD.L(a)=QLD0(a);
QKD.L(a)=QKD0(a);
QLS.L=QLS0;
QKS.L=QKS0;
WL.L=1;
WK.L=1;
PDA.L(a)=1;
QDA.L(a)=QDA0(a);
PDC.L(c)=1;
QDC.L(c)=QDC0(c);
```

```
PE.L(a)=1;
QE.L(a)=QE0(a);
EXR.L=1;
PQS.L(c)=1;
PQ.L(c)=PQ0(c);
QQ.L(c)=QQ0(c);
PM.L(c)=1;
QM.L(c)=QM0(c);
QCTT.L(c)=QCTT0(c);
QCTTA.L=QCTTA0;
YH.L=YH0;
QH.L(c)=QH0(c);
YENT.L=YENT0;
QINV.L(c)=QINV0(c);
INVADJ.L=1;
SAVEENT.L=SAVEENT0;
YG.L=YG0;
EG.L=EG0;
QG.L(c)=QG0(c);
SAVEG.L=SAVEG0;
SAVEF.L=SAVEF0;
CPI.L=CPI0;
PPI.L=PPI0;
DUMMYSI.L=0;

*Fix five variable values to make the system square.  PPI is numeraire
*Government spending closure so EG is a variable
QLS.fx=QLS0;
QKS.fx=QKS0;
INVADJ.fx=1;
EXR.fx=EXR0;
PPI.fx=1;

*Executing the model
model cge /all/;
solve cge using mcp;

display QINT.L,QINTA.L,QINT0,qda.L,qdc.L,qm.L,qe.L,qq.L,tm,pwm,pwe,tpayent;

*Simulation for currency depreciation - EXR increases by 5%

parameter
QMbase(c),QEbase(a),SAVEFbase;
QMbase(c)=QM.L(c);
QEbase(a)=QE.L(a);
SAVEFbase=SAVEF.L;
EXR.fx=1.05;
```

```
model sim  /all/;
solve sim using mcp;

*Measuring the percentage changes in simulation
Parameter
QMchange(c),QEchange(a),SAVEFcgLCU,SAVEFcgFCU;
QMchange(c)=QM.L(c)/QMbase(c)-1;
QEchange(a)=QE.L(a)/QEbase(a)-1;
SAVEFcgLCU=SAVEF.L*EXR.L/SAVEFbase*EXR0-1;
SAVEFcgFCU=SAVEF.L/SAVEFbase-1;

Display QMchange,QEchange,SAVEFcgLCU,SAVEFcgFCU;

*END
```

Exercises

14E.1 The following table is a portion of the SAM table from a model economy. It is in the base state equilibrium. Prices *PD*, *PM* and *EXR* are all equal to 1. Use Excel or other spreadsheets, or calculate by hand, to calibrate the values of the following parameters and variables in the base state: *QD*, *QE*, *PQ*, *tm* and *pwm*.

	Com1	Com2	Com3
Act1 (agriculture)	1872		
Act2 (industry)		2750	
Act3 (service)			2494
Com1 (agriculture)			
Com2 (industry)			
Com3 (service)			
Transport & trade margins	20	35	18
Sales tax	18	30	23
Tariff	7	16	7
Rest of the World	230	290	95
Total	2147	3121	2637

14E.2 Copy the GAMS program of Example 14.8.1 for Openland. Run it successfully.

14E.3 Openland now adopts a flexible exchange rate regime. In the above program, change the exchange rate regime to the flexible regime. That is, fix *SAVEF* at the level of the base state, allow exchange rate *EXR* to be flexible. Replicate the state. To eliminate the trade deficit, that is, making *SAVEF* to zero, how much adjustment should be made in the exchange rate?

14E.4 Revise the model and the GAMS program of Example 14.8.1, by replacing the CET function module with a fixed proportion form, and replacing the Armington CES function module with a fixed proportion form. After successfully replicating the base state, simulate an increase in the exchange rate by 5%. What are the resulting changes in the imports and exports? Comparing to the changes in Example 14.8.1, explain why they are different.

14E.5 Change the households' demand function to linear expenditure system (LES) in the model of Example 14.8.1.

Chapter 15

Complexities in Data and Modeling

Chapter 14 provides a basic structure of a full-fledged computable general equilibrium (CGE) model for an open economy. It is full-fledged because it contains all core variables, institutions and accounts in most CGE models. It is general and basic, because for a research project, you often need to revise the model by adding details and changing closures to fit the research needs. For instance, in studying energy and environmental issues, you may need to add more levels in the production block. In studying income distribution, you need to separate households into many income groups. In studying fiscal policy and public affairs, you need to add more details in taxes and to disaggregate the government spending to detailed categories. For different economic systems and environments, you may have to change the closures and modify the model structure. In this chapter, we discuss some common issues involved in modeling and practice, and the approaches to handle the problems.

15.1 Inputting Data and Files

In order to keep the model simple for demonstration purposes, the model economy in our previous examples has only three sectors. We can easily expand the basic model to a large one by adding many more sectors. Bureau of Economic Analysis in the U.S. regularly publishes the Input–Output tables with three different sizes: 15, 71 and 405 sectors. In theory, expanding the number of sectors from 3 to 405 or even more in the sets of activities and commodities does not pose a problem. In practice, however, we should keep the number of sectors as small as allowable by the research purpose. To do so, we should combine the uninterested sectors and accounts, so the model and GAMS program is more efficient, more reliable and less diverted.

When the size of the social accounting matrix (SAM) table gets bigger, it is not practical and efficient to input the data in text format in the program directly. Although we can use the "+" format to add more pages to continue the table columns, it is error-prone and the program would get lengthy. A better way is to use a spreadsheet such as Excel or Lotus to prepare the SAM data; then convert the spreadsheet to an independent data file to be read by the GAMS core program.

GAMS package has a nice utility software called XLS2GAMS.exe. You may first prepare the SAM table in an Excel spreadsheet including row and column headers. Suppose you name the Excel file "Openland2SAM.xls". Make sure that the row and column headers are consistent with the account names in the defined set and "table" statement in the GAMS program. Then open XLS2GAMS and the software would pop-out a window, you fill in the file name and folder address, then the software would open the Excel spreadsheet. You then highlight the table including column and row headers in the Excel spreadsheet, and provide the name and folder address of the output file to XLS2GAMS. Suppose you name the output data file "sam.inc". Then the software would generate a text data file with that filename in the folder. This sam.inc conforms to the GAMS file syntax for tables and can be directly read by GAMS. Table 15.1.1 is an example of a data file with filename "sam15-2-1.inc", generated by XLS2GAMS from Excel file "Openland2SAM.xls" for the SAM Table 15.2.1. This data file will be inputted by the GAMS program in Example 15.7.1.

To let the GAMS core program read the data file, we use directive code "$include" followed by the data file name and folder address, then the content of the data file will be inserted at the location of $include. For instance in Example 14.8.1, the data file should be inserted right after the GAMS program sentence "table sam(ac,acp)" where the original SAM table is located. We delete the original SAM table and replace it by

```
$include D:\GAMS programs\SAM15-2-1.inc
```

if the data file sam.inc is saved in the directory of D:\GAMS programs\. The GAMS program would run successfully just as before.

$include can be used for other input files. When a GAMS program gets too long, we may group and separate them to several input files. The main program is the core program. The input files are inserted to the core program at the place of call. For instance, in an energy model the production block may be very lengthy. We can make an input file or several input files for the production block, to be read by the core program. Input files can be nested if needed.

15.2 Missing Data and Zeroes

In CGE modeling and programming, in practice, a frequent problem is data irregularity in SAM tables and CGE models. Based on the real-world situation, some entries in the SAM table have no data, which are interpreted by GAMS as zeros. Some entries have negative values. Both may cause problems in running CGE models. Mathematically, denominators cannot have zero values, and the base of an exponential function or the argument of a log function cannot have zero or negative values. When a CGE model encounters these problems, the program ceases to run. For the base of a power function, 0 and negative numbers can also pose potential problems. When these problems present, some techniques can be used to work around. In what follows, we use examples to illustrate.

Table 15.1.1. GAMS data file of a SAM table generated by XLS2GAMS.

```
* -------------------------------------------------
* XLS2GMS 2.8     Feb 14, 2009 23.0.2 WIN 5776.9411 VIS x86/MS Windows
* Erwin Kalvelagen, GAMS Development Corp.
* -------------------------------------------------
* Application: Microsoft Excel
* Version:     15.0
* Workbook:    D:\CGEbook\Openland2SAM.xls
* Sheet:       Openland2SAM table
* Range:       $A$79:$T$98
* -------------------------------------------------
```

	Act1	Act2	Act3	Com1	Com2	Com3	Margin	Lab	Cap	HH	Ent	Gov	VATL	VATQ	Tariff	Subex	ROW	Invsav	total
Act1				1842												-15	135		1962
Act2					2750											13	247		3010
Act3						2474										10	90		2574
Com1	280	420	240							900		210						199	2249
Com2	377	520	380							1391		420						213	3301
Com3	220	300	540				73			1110		286						143	2672
Margin	20	35	18																73
Lab	650	700	690																2040
Cap	370	1000	655																2025
HH								2040	1725			326							4091
Ent									300										300
Gov										440	100		204	530	23	-8			1289
VATL	65	70	69																204
VATQ				150	200	180													530
Tariff				7	16														23
Subex																			0
ROW				230	300														530
Invsav										250	200	47					58		555
total	1962	3010	2574	2249	3301	2672	73	2040	2025	4091	300	1289	204	530	23	0	530	555	

Table 15.2.1. SAM table of the economy of Openland2.

	Act1	Act2	Act3	Com1	Com2	Com3	Margin	Lab	Cap	HH	Ent	Gov	VATL	VATQ	Tariff	Subex	ROW	Invsav	Total
Act1 (agriculture)				1842												−15	135		1962
Act2 (industry)					2750											13	247		3010
Act3 (service)						2474										10	90		2574
Com1 (agriculture)	280	420	240							900		210						199	2249
Com2 (industry)	377	520	380							1391		420						213	3301
Com3 (service)	220	300	540				73			1110		286						143	2672
Transport & Trade margins				20	35	18													73
Labor	650	700	690																2040
Capital	370	1000	655																2025
Households								2040	1725			326							4091
Enterprises									300										300
Government										440	100		204	530	23	−8			1289
Non-deductible VAT on labor (VATL)	65	70	69																204
VAT paid by consumers (VATQ)				150	200	180													530
Tariff				7	16														23
Export subsidy (Subex)																			0
Rest of the World				230	300														530
Savings (Invsav)										250	200	47					58		555
Total	1962	3010	2574	2249	3301	2672	73	2040	2025	4091	300	1289	204	530	23	0	530	555	

To illustrate, suppose in the second year, the economy of Openland in Example 14.8.1 has changed. It is now described by SAM Table 15.2.1. Let us name this economy "Openland2". It has basically the same model structure of Openland in Chapter 14, but data are somewhat different. In the service sector (Com3), there are no imports so the entry `sam('ROW', 'Com3')` is 0. This is very common in the real-world. Some sectors, especially some services, do not have imports. Yet these missing data cause problems in the GAMS program which we need to deal with.

In calibration, parameter assignment `tm(c)=sam('tariff',c)/sam('row',c)` in sector "Com3" would stop the solving process of the GAMS program because the denominator is zero. To fix the problem, we use the dollar condition operator (dollar control operator is discussed briefly in Section 5.2) in the following parameter assignments to skip this sector:

```
tm(c)$sam('row',c)=sam('tariff',c)/sam('row',c);
```

The dollar control term `$sam('row',c)` in the above assignment equations means that the parameter values of tm(c) are only assigned when the sectors have values in the entries of their imports. In other words, the above assignment equation would skip the sectors in which there are no imports.

In the Armington constant elasticity of substitution (CES) module, we also encounter problems. In the CES function $QQ_c = \alpha_c^q (\delta_c^q QDC_c^{\rho_c^q} + (1 - \delta_c^q) QM_c^{\rho_c^q})^{1/\rho_c^q}$, QM_c is the base of the power function $QM_c^{\rho_c^q}$. When the base of a power function is zero, it may cause problems for some solvers, so it is better to fix this problem. In the first-order condition of Equation (14.7.1), QM_c and PM_c are denominators, so they cannot be zeros. Therefore, we need to skip the CES and first order condition (FOC) equations for sector Com3. We can use the dollar control operator as follows:

```
QQfn(c)$sam('row',c)..
QQ(c)=e=scaleQq(c)*(deltaQq(c)*QDC(c)**rhoQq(c)+(1-
deltaQq(c))*QM(c)**rhoQq(c))**(1/rhoQq(c));
QQFOC(c)$sam('row',c)..
PDC(c)/PM(c)=e=(deltaQq(c)/(1-deltaQq(c)))*(QDC(c)/QM(c))**(rhoQq(c)-1);
```

The above GAMS equations would not be executed when the imports are zeros. The above revisions, however, cause another problem. After the two equations in sector Com3 are skipped/deleted by the dollar control operator, the model has two less equations, thus the squareness condition is violated. To fix the problem, we note that the Armington module determines the relationship among *PQS*, *QQ*, *PDC*, *QDC*, *PM* and *QM*. Because *QM* and *PM* do not have values in Com3, but the module still needs to determine the values of *QQ* and *PQS* given the values of *QDC* and *PDC*, hence the two following equations are added:

```
QQfnNoImport(c)$(sam('row',c)=0)..
QQ(c)=e=QDC(c);
PQPDCNoImportfn(c)$(sam('row',c)=0)..
PQS(c)=e=PDC(c);
```

The above equations mean that, if import of sector Com3 is zero, then $QQ = QDC$ and $PQS = PDC$. After these modification, the model is square and can be solved.

When using the dollar operator to skip some equations and variables, we should not allow any potentially active price, such as PM_3 in the above case, to miss value in the model. This is because GAMS sets the missing value of the price to zero. While a commodity's quantity in a CGE model can be zero, the commodity's price can never be zero. Zero price would cause the demand to go to infinity thus the model becomes unstable. In the above GAMS model, PM_3 still has a positive value because it is related to pwm_3 by the PMed equation, and, the value of pwm_3 is assigned in the parameter section. If in a different situation that the value of pwm_3 is also missing, then we need to assign positive values to the missing prices. For instance, we may set PM to 1 for sectors without imports:

```
PM.fx(c)$(NOT sam('row',c))=1;
```

The dollar operator `$(NOT sam('row',c))` means that the equation only operates when the sector has no imports data. But this constraint has reduced the variables in the model. To make the model square, we use dollar control operator to let the following PMed equation skip sectors without imports, thus reducing the same number of equations:

```
PMeq(c)$sam('row',c)..    PM(c)=e=pwm(c)*(1+tm(c))*EXR;
```

After these modifications, the model is square and can be solved. More details for a case of *pwm*-variables can be seen in Appendix of The Openland2 Model at the end of the book.

The above example is for the case of missing values in imports. If instead the missing values occur in the exports, we can handle the problem by the same method. In some models like energy models, the production block has many CES function modules at multiple levels. Missing sectoral values in various production modules occur frequently, which would cause similar problems. Then we need to work around by similar methods.

An alternative trick to deal with the problem of zero values or missing data is replacing zeros with very small values in the SAM table. This sounds sloppy, but it can be quite practical. Indeed, it is not uncommon to see scholars using this method in CGE modeling. The convenience is that you do not need to revise the original CGE program, thus avoiding possible programming errors. The disadvantage is that the results may not be accurate. If there are only a few entries missing data, and the values replacing zeros are tiny fractions of other data values in the SAM table, the deviation caused by this method is very minimal. An experiment is done for Openland2 by changing the service import from 0 to 0.1 in the SAM table. This number of 0.1 is only in the range of 1/200 to 1/20000 of the other values in the SAM table. The numerical results in the GAMS' replication and simulation by this *small value method* have barely changed from the previous *equation replacement method*. The deviation between the two methods for any variable is less than 0.01%.

However, by the "small value method", the replication results of the model would present values of 0.1 or so for those missing-data variables, which we know are actually 0. Hence, in replication or simulation reports, these values need to be cleared to return to zeros. We can manually delete them, or use a program to round the numbers to integers so these small fraction numbers change to zeros. For instance, after running the GAMS program by using the "small value method", the GAMS output report would show that the import of the service sector Com3 is 0.1. We delete this number so the service import is zero in the final report.

The dollar condition operator is very useful in CGE programs. Recall the commodity market clearing equation in Example 14.8.1 has an extra term for margins only in the service sector ($c = 3$). Our previous method is to make a subset for margin input $QCTTA$, and set up two different equations to handle markets with or without $QCTTA$. The two equations, Equations (14.7.30) and (14.7.30′), are copied as follows:

$$QQ_c = \sum_a QINT_{ca} + QH_c + \overline{QINV}_c \cdot INVADJ + QG_c + QCTTA \qquad c = 3$$

$$QQ_c = \sum_a QINT_{ca} + QH_c + \overline{QINV}_c \cdot INVADJ + QG_c \qquad c \in C \text{ and } c \neq 3$$

Correspondingly, the GAMS program also has the two equations.

When we use dollar condition operator, it can be written in a compact way by using just one equation as follows:

```
ComEqui(c)..
QQ(c)=e=sum(a,QINT(c,a))+QH(c)+QINV(c)+QG(c)+QCTTA$sam(c,'margin'));
```

The last term in the equation has the dollar control operator. It means that the $QCTTA$ term would be only included when the row commodity sector has the margins value of $QCTTA$. This usage of the dollar control operator for terms within an equation is quite handy in programming.

Readers are encouraged to do the exercises in this chapter to revise the GAMS program for a model economy with some values missing in its SAM table, by using the above discussed two methods. Missing data or empty entries without values are common in SAM tables. In research projects, various programming problems can be caused by missing variable values or missing equations in the model. In general, they can be resolved by applying techniques similar to what we have discussed above.

15.3 Value-Added Tax (VAT)

Like the U.S., the example of Openland in Chapter 14 does not have VAT. In Europe and most other countries in the world, however, VAT is a major tax revenue for the governments. How to treat VAT in CGE modeling is tricky because of the tax collection approach, various refunding and exemption rules, and some conflicts between its definition in system of national accounts (SNA) and its functional roles in the CGE models.

VAT is charged by sellers to the buyers upon transaction. In practice, at each stage of the supply chain, from production to the point of sale, a seller charges VAT from the buyer but claims VAT tax refund from what he has paid to previous intermediate input suppliers. The seller pays only a portion of VAT based on the value-added in his production, and this portion is not deductible by the seller. Let us call it "the enterprise-portion VAT".

At the final stage of the sales, the full tax amount of VAT of the commodity is passed to the ultimate consumer. This ultimate consumer shares the remaining portion of VAT, which is net of the non-deductible VAT taxes shared by the upstream suppliers in the entire supply chain. This portion shared by the consumers is called "the consumer-portion VAT". So the total amount of VAT on the commodity is split between the enterprise-portion and the consumer-portion.

According to the SNA's convention, a VAT is a tax placed between the producer's price and the purchaser's price, similar to a transport margin. Hence, it should be placed in the commodity account in the SAM table. This arrangement, however, would causes a problem in CGE modeling. Because changes in the enterprise-portion VAT can affect enterprises' input decision in the production block, this portion of VAT should be placed in the production activity accounts. For instance, China switched from the production-type VAT to the consumption-type VAT in order to encourage capital use and upgrade the industry (Chen *et al.*, 2010). This policy is based on the theory that changing the enterprise-portion VAT would affect input combination in production.

The production-type VAT system equally taxes all factors employed in production. Most countries in the world, however, now adopt the consumption-type VAT system. In our CGE models, because there are only two factor inputs, the consumption-type VAT system means that the enterprise-portion VAT is levied only on labor employment. Let *tvatl* stand for the VAT rate on labor employment. In the value-added module, the first-order condition is revised as follows:

$$\frac{(1 + tvatl) \cdot WL}{WK} = \frac{\delta_a^q}{(1 - \delta_a^q)} \left(\frac{QLD_a}{QKDa}\right)^{\rho_a - 1} \qquad a \in A \qquad (15.3.1)$$

The price equation is

$$PVA_a \cdot QVA_a = (1 + tvatl)\, WL \cdot QLD_a + WK \cdot QKD_a \qquad a \in A \qquad (15.3.2)$$

The above equations reveal that we should place the VAT rate in the activity accounts where the optimal input combination is affected and determined. Figure 15.3.1 shows how a change in the VAT rate would affect the optimal combination of inputs. Suppose the government raises VAT rate *tvatl*, which in turn raises the labor cost paid by enterprises. This increase in labor cost is $\Delta tvatl * WL * QLD$. Enterprises would respond by adjusting the optimal inputs combination between uses of labor QLD and capital QKD. Because $\Delta tvatl * WL * QLD$ also raises the price of aggregate value-added PVA, enterprises would adjust the optimal input combination between aggregate value-added QVA and aggregate intermediate input $QINTA$. All these adjustments occur in the production activity block. Input combinations cannot be adjusted at the post-production stage in the commodity column accounts, so the enterprise-portion of VAT on factors cannot be placed in commodity column accounts in the CGE model.

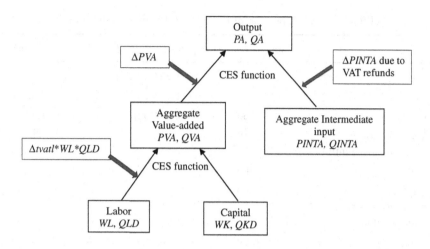

Figure 15.3.1.   Impacts on input combination by changes in the VAT rate.

Under the VAT system, enterprises also claim tax refund for the amount of VAT paid on the intermediate inputs by the suppliers. As the example given in Section 13.7, the purchaser's price of the wheat flour by a restaurant is lower than that by a household, because the former can deduct the VAT on the flour but the latter cannot. Hence, the refunding policy affects the purchaser's price of intermediate inputs, in turn affecting the aggregate intermediate input price *PINTA* (Figure 15.3.1). As a result, it would impact the optimal input use between *QVA* and *QINTA*.

In the form of VAT, an enterprise's refund from intermediate inputs comes from the VAT taxes paid by their suppliers, and they would pass the tax to the downstream buyers. If literally following this form, we would involve too many accounting details in the CGE model. Here we use a clever way to solve the problem. The VAT refund can be thought of as a price subsidy equivalent to the VAT refund rate on intermediate inputs. This subsidy is provided by the government and comes from government's VAT tax revenue from the ultimate consumers. By doing so, we get rid of the individual debit-and-credit details at each stage of the supply chain, so we can focus on the economic functions of the VAT refund in enterprises' behavior and in the government budget balance.

In what follows, we use an example to illustrate. Suppose a model economy has a similar SAM structure as Openland2 but with different data. The activity column account Act1 of the economy is extracted as shown in Table 15.3.1. We have two additional VAT row accounts in the SAM table. One is the enterprise-portion VAT of 80. Another account is the VAT refund on the intermediate inputs of 60. Household purchasers' prices *PQH* in the table are calibrated from the commodity accounts externally. Note the household purchasers' prices include all marketing margins and the full amount of VAT, while the enterprise purchaser's price *PQENT* are different because of the VAT refunds. The figures in the last column are the real quantities which would be explained later.

The consumption-type VAT tax rate on labor input is calibrated to be $tvatl = 80/400 = 0.2$. For convenience, we omit subscript of Act1 here, as there is only one activity account.

Table 15.3.1. A portion of the SAM table of a model economy.

	Act1 (in values)	PQH(PQENT)	Act1 (in quantity)
Com1	250	1.25 (1.0625)	200
Com2	100	1.3 (1.105)	76.92
Com3	50	1.2 (1.02)	41.67
VAT refund on intermediate inputs	−60		
Labor	400		
Capital	200		
enterprise-portion VAT on labor input	80		
Total	1020		

Setting the factor prices WL and WK to 1, we have

$$PVA \cdot QVA = (1 + tvatl) \, WL \cdot QDL + WK \cdot QDK = 1.2 \cdot 1 \cdot 400 + 1 \cdot 1 \cdot 200 = 680 \quad (15.3.3)$$

Because of the enterprise-portion of VAT, the total value of the value-added part increases from 600 to 680. Hence,

$$PVA = 680/600 = 1.133 \qquad QVA = 600 \qquad (15.3.4)$$

A change in *tvatl* in simulation would change the labor cost $1 + tvatl$ and aggregate value-added price PVA, thus affecting the optimal use of factors and QVA in the first-order conditions in the production block:

$$\frac{(1 + tvatl) \, WL}{WK} = \frac{\delta^{va}}{(1 - \delta^{va})} \left(\frac{QLD}{QKD} \right)^{\rho^{va} - 1} \qquad (15.3.5)$$

$$\frac{PVA}{PINTA} = \frac{\delta^{q}}{(1 - \delta^{q})} \left(\frac{QVA}{QINTA} \right)^{\rho - 1} \qquad (15.3.6)$$

Now we examine the intermediate input part. Let $VATRI$ be the total value of VAT refund, assuming the same VAT rate *rvati* applies to all intermediate inputs, *rvati* is calibrated as

$$-rvati = VATRI / \sum_c \text{SAM}_c = -60/(250 + 100 + 50) = -0.15 \qquad (15.3.7)$$

The enterprise purchasers' prices $PQENT$ are derived by deducting the VAT refund,

$$PQENT_c = (1 - rvati) \cdot PQH_c = (1 - 0.15) \cdot PQH_c \qquad (15.3.8)$$

The quantities of intermediate inputs are calibrated by

$$QINT_c = (1 - rvati) \cdot \text{SAM}_c / PQENT_c$$
$$= (1 - rvati) \cdot \text{SAM}_c / ((1 - rvati) PQH_c = \text{SAM}_c / PQH_c \qquad (15.3.9)$$

In the above equation, the numerator is the actual cost of intermediate input c, by subtracting the corresponding refund on c. After canceling the same term $(1 - rvati)$ in the fraction, it is the same equation for $QINT$ by dividing household purchaser's price as we had before. This is not surprising because both the numerator and denominator refer to the situation without VAT refunds by the same proportion. The so derived intermediate input $QINT$ is listed on the last column of Table 15.3.1. The aggregate intermediate input $QINTA$ is the sum of intermediate inputs in quantity and the input–output coefficient ica_c is calibrated accordingly:

$$QINTA = \sum_c QINT_c \qquad ica_c = QINT_c/QINTA \qquad (15.3.10)$$

The price of aggregate intermediate input $PINTA$ is

$$PINTA = \sum_c (1 - rvati) \cdot PQH_c \cdot ica_c = (1 - rvati) \sum_c PQH_c \cdot ica_c \qquad (15.3.11)$$

where the last term $\sum_c PQH_c \cdot ica_c$ is the familiar $PINTA$ without VAT refund. From the equation, we can see that changes in the VAT refunding rate $rvati$ would affect the aggregate-intermediate-input price of $PINTA$. In turn it would affect the optimal use between QVA and $QINTA$, as shown in Figure 15.3.1.

At the top level of the production block, activity output QA is produced by QVA and $QINTA$, and these prices must satisfy the equation:

$$PA \cdot QA = PVA \cdot QVA + PINTA \cdot QINTA \qquad (15.3.12)$$

Because the activity output QA is physically different from QVA and $QINTA$, we can redefine the unit of QA so let $PA = 1$.

Take the example of Table 15.3.1 It can be calculated that $QINTA = 318.6$, $\sum_c PQH_c \cdot ica_c = 1.26$ and $PINTA = 1.07$. Recall $PVA = 1.13$ and $QVA = 600$. Then the price equation at the top level is

$$PA \cdot QA = 1 \times 1020 = PVA \cdot QVA + PINTA \cdot QINTA = 1.13 \times 600 + 1.07 \times 318.6 \quad (15.3.13)$$

The amount VAT refund of 60 should also be recorded in the SAM at the cell address (government, VAT refund) as a subsidy, subtracting from the government's tax revenue. Because the transactions of th,e VAT refunding scheme are treated as independent subsidies by our arrangement, the total VAT amount in the model still consists of only the enterprise-portion and consumer-portion as described before.

To consolidate notations, in the following CGE models we continue to use notation PQ_c for household purchaser's price PQH_c, which is also the purchasers' prices of the government and investment goods. The enterprise purchaser's price, excluding the deductible VAT, $PQENT_c$, is expressed by $(1 - rvati)PQ_c$. Exercise 15E.5 in this chapter provides an exercise for the situation with VAT refunds on intermediate inputs. For simplicity, in the rest of the book we assume the VAT refunds for intermediate inputs use $rvati = 0$, and the models have only one purchaser's price PQ.

By the SNA definition, when the activity price PA includes any VAT such as the enterprise-portion VAT, PA can no longer be called "basic price". Hence, we just call PA "activity price". The price index based on PA will be called "Activity Price Index (API)". If there is a need, we can still derive the "basic price" by deducting all VAT taxes from PA. In the above example, the basic price can be calculated as

$$\text{Basic price} = \frac{PA \cdot QA - VATtax}{PA \cdot QA} = \frac{1020 - 80}{1020} = 0.92 \tag{15.3.14}$$

In general, basic prices are not needed in simulation analyzes in a CGE model. We can construct the CGE model by just using activity prices PA, but keeping in mind that PA includes the enterprise-portion VAT tax.

Under the consumption-type VAT system, in theory, except for the non-deductible VAT on labor employment, sellers pass all other portions of VAT to the buyers. Eventually, all VAT taxes unpaid by the suppliers pass to the final consumers. They form the consumer-portion of VAT. In practice, how the two portions are split depends on the specific VAT refunding scheme.

Let us use the example of Table 15.3.1 to illustrate. Suppose after production, agricultural product QA is directly sold to domestic households as the final consumer. The total output value before any VAT is $250 + 100 + 50 + 400 + 200 = 1000$. In practice, enterprises represent the government to collect VAT from households.

Suppose in one scheme the VAT policy is a 19% rate on the final sales and the enterprise only needs to pay 20% on its labor employment but can claim refunds for all other amounts of VAT. In this case, the enterprise collects $1000 \times 19\% = 190$ of VAT from households and transfers it to the government. The enterprise pays the non-deductible $400 \times 20\% = 80$ on labor employment and claims refund of $190 - 80 = 110$, which includes exemption of capital, intermediate inputs, and any other residuals. The VAT burden of 110 has passed to the final consumers.

In another VAT scheme, while the VAT rate on the final sale is still 19%, the enterprise must specify the allowable items it can claim refunds on. Suppose the only deductible items include 20% of its capital use and the full amount of VAT paid by intermediate input suppliers. The enterprise thus can claim refund of $200 \times 20\% = 40$ on capital uses and refund of 60 from intermediate input uses, so the total allowable refund amounts to $40 + 60 = 100$. In this case, the enterprise pays the VAT tax of $190 - 100 = 90$, and the households bear $40 + 60 = 100$ of VAT. These numbers are different from the previous case because the implied VAT rate for intermediate inputs is different: $60/(250 + 100 + 50 - 60) = 0.176$.

As a remark here, intermediate-input suppliers may share some of the VAT burden of 60 from the final consumers. These shares can be computed in an IO framework. We leave this topic to other publications but focus on the direct VAT impacts in the current analysis.

In most countries with a VAT system, imports are still subject to VAT after the tariff/duty has been paid. In general, this VAT rate for imports is the same VAT rate for the domestic products although it may vary in some special cases. Let *PM* still be the sum of the cif border price and tariff, but net of product taxes and marketing margins. In the Armington module, we combine *PD* and *PM* to derive the composite supplier's price of *PQS*.

$$PM_c = (1 + tm_c) \cdot pwm_c \cdot EXR \tag{15.3.15}$$

$$PQS_c \cdot QQ_c = PM_c \cdot QM_c + PDC_c \cdot QDC_c \tag{15.3.16}$$

The consumer-portion VAT are recorded in the commodity accounts along with marketing margins. The consumer-portion VAT rate, denoted by *tvatq*, is defined by the following equation:

$$PQ_c = (1 + tvatq)(PQS_c + \text{unit cost service margins}_c) \tag{15.3.17}$$

These are the same equations as those in Example 14.8.1 for Openland, except the sales tax rate is replaced by *tvatq*. *tvatq* can be calibrated from the data in the SAM table. For instance, *tvatq* for commodity 1 in Openland2 is $150/2099 = 7.15\%$. In the case that an import has a different VAT rate than the domestic product, and the difference is significant for the research purpose, then we need to specify different VAT rates for imports and domestic products in the Armington module.

15.4 Export Subsidy and Tax

The case of exports is different from that of imports in the real-world. Import taxes, i.e., tariffs or duties, are common for imports in most countries, but export taxes are uncommon. Some countries levy export taxes on primary commodities like mineral and agricultural exports, such as the export tax on palm oil in Indonesia. Export subsidies in practice are more common. Direct subsidies to agricultural exports had been widely adopted among countries in the world until the end of 2018, being stopped by the World Trade Organization (WTO) rule. The fact is that many countries still provide various incentives for exports, mainly of industrial products. These incentives in nature are export subsidies. These issues are hotly debated and disputed in the world trade forum.

In many countries with the VAT system, industrial exports get VAT refunds, such as the export VAT refund practice in Europe, or export VAT rebate programs in South Korea and China. The export refund/rebate rate may vary but with an upper limit that the amount of refund cannot exceed the VAT amount previously paid. A VAT refund in nature is an export subsidy although the SNA system excludes export tax refund from its definition of the term "export subsidy". An export subsidy is a negative export tax. In CGE modeling, an export subsidy or VAT refund can be treated as a negative export tax. However, in CGE modeling you should be careful about the sign difference in the equations for export taxes and subsidies, which can be confusing and error-prone when included in a GAMS program. Let *PE* still be the price received by domestic activity exporters. Recall Equation (14.6.1) for export tax:

$$(1 + te_a) \cdot PE_a = pwe_a \cdot EXR \tag{15.4.1}$$

Rearrange, price PE is determined by

$$PE_a = \frac{1}{1 + te_a} \cdot pwe_a \cdot EXR \qquad (15.4.2)$$

In the IFPRI model, export tax is on the numerator position with a negative sign:

$$PE_a = (1 - te_a^*) \cdot pwe_a \cdot EXR \qquad (15.4.3)$$

Both Equations (15.4.2) and (15.4.3) are correct in the direction that a positive export tax would make the domestic price smaller than the world price, although the magnitudes differ a little by a factor of $1 + te_a$. That is

$$te_a^* = \frac{1}{1 + te_a} \cdot te_a \qquad (15.4.4)$$

Equation (15.4.1) uses the domestic price as the base to apply the export tax rate, which simulates the practice by customs in most countries. Equation (15.4.3) uses the world price as the base to apply the export tax rate, which is not commonly practiced by customs. Yet Equation (15.4.3) can be more intuitive for some purposes. For instance, comparing Equation (15.3.15) to Equation (15.4.3), we see that the signs associated with the tax rates are opposite between the cases of exports and imports. This is because although a commodity tax is a wedge between the prices of buyers and sellers, the role of ROW now switches from sellers to buyers, and the opposite is true for the domestic entities.

If it is an export tax, $te_a > 0$, the exporter's sales revenue is

$$PE_a \cdot QE_a = pwe_a \cdot QE_a \cdot EXR - \frac{te_a}{1 + te_a} \cdot pwe_a \cdot QE_a \cdot EXR \qquad (15.4.5)$$

On right-hand side (RHS), the first term is the value paid by ROW for the exports, the second term is the government's export tax. It carries a negative sign because a positive export tax reduces the seller's price. The following total amount of the tax should be added to the government revenue YG:

$$\text{total-export-tax-value} = \sum_a te_a \cdot PE_a \cdot QE_a \qquad (15.4.6)$$

If it is a case of subsidy, then $te_a < 0$. The negative number of te_a can be directly inputted in the CGE model. For instance, suppose the country gives a VAT rebate equivalent to 10% of export value, then $te_a = -10\%$. In statistical data and CGE modeling, however, people prefer to use the straightforward term of "subsidy" rather than "negative tax". Let $sube$ be the rate of subsidy, which is just the negative export tax rate,

$$sube_a = -te_a \qquad (15.4.7)$$

Then we have the following equation for PE in the CGE model:

$$PE_a = \frac{1}{1 - sube_a} \cdot pwe_a \cdot EXR \qquad (15.4.8)$$

Or equivalently,

$$PE_a \cdot QE_a = pwe_a \cdot QE_a \cdot EXR + \frac{sube_a}{1 - sube_a} \cdot pwe_a \cdot QE_a \cdot EXR \qquad (15.4.9)$$

Equation (15.4.9) says that an export subsidy would raise the domestic price above the world price. You may think it as the case that the government subsidizes foreign buyers to buy our products. The subsidy comes from the government budget so the following amount should be subtracted from the government's revenue YG:

$$\text{total-subsidy-value} = \sum_a sube_a \cdot PE_a \cdot QE_a = \sum_a \frac{sube_a}{1 - sube_a} \cdot pwe_a \cdot QE_a \cdot EXR \quad (15.4.10)$$

In the SAM structure of Openland2, exports are on the activity row accounts, as shown in Table 15.2.1. Unlike commodities, exports have no wholesale and retail margins, nor sales taxes and home delivery costs. Exports are "bare products" after production so they are closer to activity products rather than commodities. Export price PE is comparable to PA and PDA, as all of them are prices after production and before other costs and taxes. If the prices are the same, then the unit of export is the same unit of activity in the same row account. Export subsidies are in the activity row accounts because they raise the sellers' prices of exports PE.

Take the example of the industrial export in Account Act2. For the same quantity of the export, the foreign buyers (ROW) pay 247, the government provides a subsidy of 13 in the name of VAT refund, and the domestic producer receives $247 + 13 = 260$. The subsidy rate is

$$sube_2 = \frac{\text{subsidy value}}{\text{producers' sales revenue}} = \frac{13}{247 + 13} = 5\% \quad (15.4.11)$$

In the GAMS program, let the value of export subsidy be "*subex*", the subsidy rate is calibrated as

```
sube(a)=sam(a,'subex')/(sam(a,'row')+sam(a,'subex'));        (15.4.12)
```

Note the difference between export subsidy rate and import tax rate in calibration. The former is a percentage of the domestic producer's sales revenue, so the subsidy is included in the denominator. The latter, import tax rate, is a percentage of the sales revenue of ROW, so the import tax is not in the denominator.

Because PE is comparable to the base price of PA, we set $PE = 1$ for all sectors, then in Act2, it is calibrated as $QE_2 = 260$. The world price pwe is

$$pwe_a = (1 - sube_a)PE_a/EXR \quad (15.4.13)$$

For Sector Act2, when EXR is set to 1, the world price for industrial product is calibrated as

$$pwe_2 = (1 - 0.05) \cdot PE_2/EXR = 0.95. \quad (15.4.14)$$

The total subsidy in Openland2 is −8, recorded between the government row account and export subsidy column account. The negative value implies the deduction of government's revenue because of the subsidy.

15.5 Negative Values

When we prepare SAM tables, some entry values may be negative, such as price subsidies or institutions' budget deficits. In most cases, the presence of negative values in SAM tables is not a problem. In SAM Table 15.2.1, the number of −8 between the government and export subsidy accounts does not pose any problem in executing the GAMS program. Take another example. In the SAM structure of Openland, if sales taxes are changed to sales subsidies so the current entries for sales taxes are negative numbers, the model and GAMS program would run just fine, although the results of the model would change to reflect the price subsidies.

Sometimes, negative values in SAM can cause problems. Because the argument variable in a logarithmic function cannot be zero or negative, the entropy approach to balance SAM tables cannot allow negative entry values in a SAM table. One method to work around the problem has been discussed in Chapters 4 and 5. Basically, we relocate the negative value from its original entry address $SAM_{i,j}$ to the opposite address $SAM_{j,i}$ and change its sign to positive. After the SAM table has been balanced by the entropy method, we move the post-balancing value back to the original entry and change its sign again. This method can also be used in the CGE modeling but might encounter new problems, as will be discussed later.

Along the activity row accounts, export subsidies carry positive signs because they increase the payment to activities thus raising the sale prices of the activity products. An example is the export subsidy of 13 for industrial Act2 in the SAM table of Openland2. Why is it positive? You may think that the subsidy column account pays the row account of the industrial seller to mark up their sale price, or the government subsidizes foreigners to buy the industrial export. In economics, the two interpretations are equivalent.

On the contrary, if the value in the subsidy column account is negative, it represents a positive export tax. This may sound confusing in the beginning, so one should take caution in interpretation and modeling. Here we replicate the data of the upper-right portion of the SAM table of Openland2 in the following Table 15.5.1.

In the agriculture sector (Act1) of the above table, the value of the export subsidy is −15. This negative number represents a positive export tax of 15 charged by the government

Table 15.5.1.   Export subsidy versus export tax in Openland2.

	Export subsidy	Rest of the World
Activity 1 (agriculture)	−15 (Positive tax)	135
Activity 2 (industry)	13 (Subsidy)	247
Activity 3 (service)	10 (Subsidy)	90

on domestic producers. The export subsidy rate is $-15/(135 - 15) = -15/120 = -12.5\%$, which is actually a positive export tax rate of 12.5%. The export value $PE_1 \cdot QE_1$ is 120, the government adds 12.5% of export tax, so ROW pays 135. The negative value -15 means that the domestic exporter receives less than what the foreign buyer pays because the government charges export tax of 15.

This negative value -15 in this entry should not cause problems in executing the GAMS program. Separately, in CGE modeling no policy is allowed to cause a price to be negative, then the program would crash. If such a case occurs, there must be some errors contained in the SAM table or in the model. Negative commodity prices violate the conditions for the existence of the general equilibrium. A negative price for a "good" would cause the demand to go to infinity, hence no equilibrium exists.

Suppose we prefer to have "standard" signs to record the export taxes as positive numbers and subsidies as negative numbers, or the GAMS program has troubles with the negative values in the original entries. We then transpose these values from the original column account to the row account of "export subsidy" in the lower-left position of the SAM table. Then change the signs of the values and rename the account "export tax". So the values of the column account of "export subsidy" of Table 15.5.1 are transposed to the row account of "export tax" with opposite signs as in Table 15.5.2.

The signs of these values appear intuitively as they are consistent with the standard signs for product taxes and subsidies. Yet this relocation causes other problems. The total values of the activity columns now have changed. It is difficult to interpret the new total activity values and the new price of PA by including the export taxes. At the same time, we need to calibrate the export tax rates by dividing the export taxes in the rows on the lower-left corner by the export values in the columns on the top-right corner of the SAM table, and to calculate the export prices PE between the two opposite corners. That is very inconvenient. Remedies can be done but will involve a lot of additional work in the GAMS program. Hence, it is preferred to have export subsidies/taxes in a "subex" column account as in the SAM structure of Openland2.

Transport margins for exports can also be treated similarly by adding a column account as that for the export subsidy. In general, for simplicity, transport margins for export may be assumed away because the bulk transportation cost is relatively small as compared with the overall export value. Or we may assume that the bulk transport cost to the border is already absorbed in the producer's price PA by arguing that the cost is equivalent to the bulk transport cost to ship cargoes from factories to the warehouses of the wholesalers. Hence, exports QE and domestic supplied products QD are on the same cost ground.

Table 15.5.2. Row account for export tax.

	Act1 (agriculture)	Act2 (industry)	Act3 (service)
Export tax	15 (Positive tax)	-13 (Subsidy)	-10 (Subsidy)

Table 15.5.3.   Transport margins of exports in SAM.

	Transport margin	Export subsidy	Rest of the World
Activity 1 (agriculture)	−9	−15	135
Activity 2 (industry)	−2	13	247
Activity 3 (service)	0	10	90
Activity 4 (Coal)	−10	−5	55

If the domestic transport cost for an export is very significant for the research topic, say, the research is about transporting coal from an inland mine to the port in Canada, we can add a transport margin account in SAM. Table 15.5.3 shows a hypothetical case of transport margins for the SAM structure of Openland2.

The transport margins are recorded in the column account of "transport margin" with negative signs. Similar to a positive export tax, given the amount paid by foreign buyers, transport margins increase the margin cost, thus reducing the seller's price. That is why it carries a negative sign in the column account. The setup for the transport margins for exports in theory is similar to that for the service margin inputs in the commodity accounts, but you need to be cautious about the variable signs in calibration and modeling.

Let PE still be the net price received by the producer, excluding transport margins and export subsidy/tax. Let $iett$ be the proportion of transport margin input to the amount of export in activity a. Assume the transport input is provided by the service sector Com3, so the price equation is

$$(1 - sube_a) \cdot (PE_a \cdot QE_a + PQ_3 \cdot iett_a \cdot QE_a) = pwe_a \cdot EXR \cdot QE_a \qquad (15.5.1)$$

The above equation provides a nice explanation for how the prices and costs add up in the process from the seller to the foreign buyer in sector a. In the entire process, the quantity of export QE_a remains unchanged. The seller's receipt for the product is $PE_a \cdot QE_a$. The shipping cost to the border is $PQ_3 \cdot iett_a \cdot QE_a$. Export subsidy $sube_a$ is given as a percentage of the total cost at the border. So the foreign buyers pay $pwe_a \cdot EXR \cdot QE_a$.

To illustrate how to calibrate the parameters and initial values of the variables from the SAM table data, take the above coal export as an example. Subscript $a = 4$ refers to the coal export. First we calibrate quantity QE_4, by working on the row of the SAM table to obtain the seller's cost:

$$PE_4 \cdot QE_4 = 55 - 5 - 10 = 40 \qquad (15.5.2)$$

Because PE_a is comparable to PA_a, so in the base state we set $PE_4 = 1$, thus calibrate $QE_4 = 40$. After PQ_3 is calibrated in other parts of the GAMS program, the transport margin ratio can be calibrated by

$$iett_4 = 10/(PQ_3 \cdot QE_4) = 10/(PQ_3 \cdot 40) \qquad (15.5.3)$$

The value of export at the border, after transportation but before being taxed (or given subsidy), is $40 + 10 = 50$. The government subsidy rate $sube_4$ is calibrated as

$$sube_4 = \text{subsidy}/(PE_4 \cdot QE_4 + PQ_3 \cdot iett_4 \cdot QE_4) = -5/(40 + 10) = -10\% \qquad (15.5.4)$$

The negative value of $sube_4$ means it is actually a positive export tax.

Exchange rate is set as $EXR = 1$. From the ROW payment $pwe_4 \cdot EXR \cdot QE_4 = 55$, the world price is calibrated by

$$pwe_4 = (pwe_4 \cdot EXR \cdot QE_4)/(EXR \cdot QE_4) = 55/40 = 1.375 \qquad (15.5.5)$$

The following equation shows the relationship from seller's price PE_a to the world price pwe_a:

$$PE_a + PQ_3 \cdot iett_a = \frac{EXR}{1 - sube_a} pwe_a \qquad (15.5.6)$$

The total value of export transport margins in the country of Table 15.5.3 is $-9 - 2 + 0 - 10 = -21$. Suppose transport inputs are provided by the service sector (Com3). By the double-entry bookkeeping principle, in the SAM table, it is also recorded as `SAM('com3', 'export transport margin')=21`, with the sign of the value changed. In the CGE model, the quantity of the total export transport margin is $21/PQ_3$, which is included in the market clearing equation of the service sector.

15.6 CGE Model for Openland2

Now we construct a CGE model for Openland2, as described by SAM Table 15.2.1. The economic structure of Openland2 is similar to Openland in Chapter 14, but its SAM data are more complex and irregular as discussed above. Some data are missing such as the service sector has no imports. It has a consumption-type VAT system. It has an export tax for agricultural export but VAT refunds for other exports. There is an aggregate consumption function. Households' commodity demand function is linear expenditure system (LES). The entire model is provided in what follows. Most of other equations repeat those in the Openland model in Chapter 14. Remarks are made for the differences.

The production block is basically the same as that of Openland, except there is a consumption-type VAT levied by the government. Enterprises pay the enterprise-portion VAT for their labor employment.

$$QA_a = \alpha_a^a [\delta_a^a QVA_a^{\rho_a^a} + (1 - \delta_a^a) QINTA_a^{\rho_a^a}]^{1/\rho_a^a} \qquad a \in A \qquad (15.6.1)$$

$$\frac{PVA_a}{PINTA_a} = \frac{\delta_a^a}{(1 - \delta_a^a)} \left(\frac{QVA_a}{QINTA_a} \right)^{\rho_a^a - 1} \qquad a \in A \qquad (15.6.2)$$

$$PA_a \cdot QA_a = PVA_a \cdot QVA_a + PINTA_a \cdot QINTA_a \qquad a \in A \qquad (15.6.3)$$

$$QVA_a = \alpha_a^{va} [\delta_{La}^{va} QLD_a^{\rho_a^{va}} + (1 - \delta_{La}^{va}) QKD_a^{\rho_a^{va}}]^{1/\rho_a^{va}} \qquad a \in A \qquad (15.6.4)$$

$$\frac{(1 + tvatl) WL}{WK} = \frac{\delta_a^{va}}{(1 - \delta_a^{va})} \left(\frac{QLD_a}{QKD_a} \right)^{\rho_a^{va} - 1} \qquad a \in A \qquad (15.6.5)$$

$$PVA_a \cdot QVA_a = (1 + tvatl) \cdot WL \cdot QLD_a + WK \cdot QKD_a \qquad a \in A \quad (15.6.6)$$

$$QINT_{ca} = ica_{c\,a} \cdot QINTA_a \qquad a \in A, \quad c \in C \qquad (15.6.7)$$

$$PINTA_a = \sum_{c \in C} ica_{c\,a} \cdot PQ_c \qquad a \in A \qquad (15.6.8)$$

In the constant elasticity of transformation (CET) module for exports, the new component is export subsidy. The subsidy rate $sube_a$ is the percentage of the seller's price PE_a. Other equations are the same.

$$QA_a = \alpha_a^t [\delta_a^t QDA_a^{\rho_a^t} + (1 - \delta) QE_a^{\rho_a^t}]^{1/\rho_a^t} \qquad \rho_a^t > 1 \quad a \in A \qquad (15.6.9)$$

$$\frac{PDA_a}{PE_a} = \frac{\delta_a^t}{(1 - \delta_a^t)} \left(\frac{QDA_a}{QE_a} \right)^{\rho_a^t - 1} \qquad a \in A \qquad (15.6.10)$$

$$PA_a \cdot QA_a = PDA_a \cdot QDA_a + PE_a \cdot QE_a \qquad a \in A \qquad (15.6.11)$$

$$PE_a = \frac{1}{1 - sube_a} \cdot pwe_a \cdot EXR \qquad (15.6.12)$$

The equations in the Armington module are the same, except that we need to handle the missing data problem in the GAMS program.

$$QQ_c = \alpha_c^q (\delta_c^q QDC_c^{\rho_c^q} + (1 - \delta_c^q) QM_c^{\rho_c^q})^{1/\rho_c^q} \qquad c \in C \qquad (15.6.13)$$

$$\frac{PDC_c}{PM_c} = \frac{\delta_c^q}{(1 - \delta_c^q)} \left(\frac{QDC_c}{QM_c} \right)^{\rho_c^q - 1} \qquad c \in C \qquad (15.6.14)$$

$$PQS_c \cdot QQ_c = PDC_c \cdot QDC_c + PM_c \cdot QM_c \qquad c \in C \qquad (15.6.15)$$

$$PM_c = pwm_c(1 + tm_c)EXR \qquad c \in C \qquad (15.6.16)$$

Mapping from activities to commodities:

$$QDC_c = \sum_a IDENT_{ac} \cdot QDA_a \qquad c \in C \qquad (15.6.17)$$

$$PDC_c = \sum_a IDENT_{ac} \cdot PDA_a \qquad c \in C \qquad (15.6.18)$$

In the commodity accounts, there are marketing margins. Product tax is VAT rather than sales taxes. Households bear the burden of the consumer-portion VAT:

$$QCTT_c = ictt_c \cdot QQ_c \qquad c \in C \qquad (15.6.19)$$

$$QCTTA = \sum_c QCTT_c \qquad (15.6.20)$$

$$PQ_c \cdot QQ_c = (1 + tvatq_c)(PQS_c \cdot QQ_c + PQ_3 \cdot QCTT_c) \qquad c \in C \qquad (15.6.21)$$

In the household block, except for the household income equation, other equations are new. The variable notations are the same as in Chapter 12.

$$YH = WL \cdot QLS + shareif_{h\,k} \cdot WK \cdot QKS + transfer_{h\,g} \cdot CPI \qquad (15.6.22)$$

A textbook aggregate consumption function is included:

$$EH = eho \cdot CPI + mpc \cdot (1 - ti_h) \cdot YH \qquad (15.6.23)$$

The households' commodity demand function is LES:

$$PQ_c \cdot QH_c = PQ_c \cdot \gamma_c + \beta_c(EH - \sum_{c' \in C} PQ_c \cdot \gamma_{c'}) \qquad c \in C \qquad (15.6.24)$$

The household savings $SAVEH$ is

$$SAVEH = -eho \cdot CPI + (1 - mpc) \cdot (1 - ti_h) \cdot YH \qquad (15.6.25)$$

The enterprise block has the same equations as those in Openland:

$$YENT = shareif_{ent\,k} \cdot WK \cdot QKS \qquad (15.6.26)$$

$$SAVEENT = (1 - ti_{ent})YENT \qquad (15.6.27)$$

$$QINV_c = \overline{QINV_c} \cdot INVADJ \qquad (15.6.28)$$

The government revenue includes a new component "export subsidy". Other equations in the government block are the same.

$$YG = \sum_a tvatl_a \cdot WL \cdot QLD_a + ti_h \cdot YH_h + ti_{ent} \cdot YENT$$

$$+ \sum_c tvatq_c(PQS_c \cdot QQ_c + PQ_3 \cdot QCTT_c)$$

$$+ \sum_c tm_c \cdot pwm_c \cdot QM_c \cdot EXR - \sum_a sube_a \cdot PE_a \cdot QE_a \qquad (15.6.29)$$

$$EG = YG - SAVEG \qquad (15.6.30)$$

$$PQ_c \cdot QG_c = shareg_c(EG - transfer_{h\,g} \cdot CPI) \qquad c \in C \qquad (15.6.31)$$

The commodity and factor market clearing equations are

$$QQ_c = \sum_a QINT_{ca} + QH_c + \overline{QINV_c} \cdot INVADJ + QG_c + QCTTA \qquad c = 3 \qquad (15.6.32)$$

$$QQ_c = \sum_a QINT_{ca} + QH_c + \overline{QINV_c} \cdot INVADJ + QG_c \qquad c \in C \quad \text{and} \quad c \neq 3 \qquad (15.6.32')$$

$$\sum_a QLD_a = QLS \qquad (15.6.33)$$

$$\sum_a QKD_a = QKS \qquad (15.6.34)$$

The price indexes CPI and API are

$$CPI = \sum_{c \in C} PC_c \cdot cpiwt_c \qquad (15.6.35)$$

$$API = \sum_{a \in A} PA_a \cdot apiwt_a \qquad (15.6.36)$$

Note we use activity price index here in case VAT taxes may present in the model. The balance of payments (BOP) equation is

$$SAVEF \cdot EXR = \sum_{c} pwm_c \cdot QM_c \cdot EXR - \sum_{a} pwe_a \cdot QE_a \cdot EXR \qquad (15.6.37)$$

The savings–investment equation with the dummy variable is

$$\sum_{c} PQ_c \cdot QINV_c = SAVEH + SAVEENT + SAVEG + SAVEF \cdot EXR$$

$$+ DUMMYSI \qquad (15.6.38)$$

The above model for Openland2 has a total of 38 group equations. There are total 43 group variables as follows: PA_a, PVA_a, $PINTA_a$, QA_a, QVA_a, $QINTA_a$, $QINT_{ca}$, QLD_a, QKD_a, QLS, QKS, WL, WK, PDA_a, QDA_a, PDC_c, QDC_c, PE_a, QE_a, EXR, PQS_c, PQ_c, QQ_c, PM_c, QM_c, $QCTT_c$, $QCTTA$, YH, EH, $SAVEH$, QH_c, $YENT$, $QINV$, $INVADJ$, $SAVEENT$, YG, EG, QG, $SAVEG$, $SAVEF$, CPI, API, $DUMMYSI$.

We need five constraints to reduce the variables to 38, to meet the squareness condition. Here we assume the government spending closure, so we have the following constraints:

$$QLS = \overline{QLS} \qquad (15.6.39)$$

$$QKS = \overline{QKS} \qquad (15.6.40)$$

$$INVADJ = 1 \qquad (15.6.41)$$

$$EXR = \overline{EXR} \qquad (15.6.42)$$

$$API = 1 \qquad (15.6.43)$$

This completes the model.

15.7 GAMS Program

Example 15.7.1 The SAM table for Openland2 is Table 15.2.1. The parameter values are in Table 15.7.1. Write the GAMS program for Openland2 as specified in Section 15.6. After successfully replicating the base state of the model, simulate the situation if the government eliminates the export tax in agriculture. Report the resulting changes of total activity output, domestic sales and exports in the three sectors.

Solution: The GAMS core program is provided in what follows. The SAM table data is in a separate file "SAM15-2-1.inc" and is called by $include in the program. The simulation results are in the following Table 15.7.2. They are consistent with the expectations: after

Table 15.7.1. Parameter values for Openland2.

	Agriculture	Industry	Service
Top activity level CES ρ	0.2	0.3	0.1
Value-added CES ρ	0.3	0.2	0.5
Armington CES ρ	0.4	0.6	0.4
CET function ρ	1.4	1.4	2.0
LES elasticity	0.5	1.0	1.2
Frisch parameter		-2	

Table 15.7.2. Simulation of eliminating export tax in agriculture.

	Act1 (agriculture)	Act2 (industry)	Act3 (service)
QE	37.6%	-0.5%	-0.6%
QD	0	-0.5%	-0.5%
QA	2.5%	-0.5%	-0.5%

eliminating agricultural export tax, the agricultural export increases by 37.6%. This also stimulates the production in the agricultural sector, but reduces the production in other sectors because of the resource reallocation among the sectors.

```
$title Example 15.7.1 for Openland2
*With irregular data and some structural complexity

*Define sets
set ac
/act1,act2,act3,com1,com2,com3,margin,lab,cap,hh,ent,gov,VATL,VATQ,
tariff,subex,row,invsav,total/;
set a(ac)   /act1,act2,act3/;
set c(ac)   /com1,com2,com3/;
set f(ac)   /lab,cap/;
*The following set acnt is for checking accuracy of SAM
set acnt(ac)  all accounts excluding total;
acnt(ac)=YES;
acnt('total')=NO;

alias (ac,acp),(a,ap),(c,cp),(f,fp),(acnt,acntp);

table sam(ac,acp)
$include D:\GAMS programs\SAM15-2-1.inc
```

```
table Identac(a,c)
          com1      com2     com3
act1        1
act2                 1
act3                          1
;

*Check if the SAM table is balanced
parameters
samchk0(ac);
samchk0(acnt)=sum(acntp,SAM(acntp,acnt))-sum(acntp,SAM(acnt,acntp));

display samchk0,acnt,sam;

*Input parameter values given externally
parameter   rhoAa(a)   /act1 =   0.2,   act2 = 0.3,   act3 = 0.1/
            rhoVA(a)   /act1     0.3,   act2   0.2,   act3   0.5/
            rhoCET(a)  /act1     1.4,   act2   1.4,   act3   2.0/
            rhoQq(c)   /com1     0.4,   com2   0.6,   com3   0.4/
            LESelas(c) /com1     0.5,   com2   1.0,   com3   1.2 /
            Frisch     /-2/;

parameters
scaleAa(a)        Scale factor of top level CES function of a
deltaAa(a)        Value-added share parameter in top level CES of a
scaleAVA(a)       Scale factor of value added CES function of a
deltaVA(a)        Labor share parameter in value-added CES function of a
ica(c,a)          Input coefficient for intermediate inputs
scaleCET(a)       Scale factor of CET function
deltaCET(a)       Domestic sales share parameter in CET function
scaleQq(c)        Scale factor of Armington CES function
deltaQq(c)        Domestic product share parameter in Armington CES function
bgtshare(c)       Average budget share on c in the LES function
bhtsharechk1      Check if average budget share sum is 1
LESbeta(c)        Marginal budget share of LES
Lesbetachk1       Check if the marginal budget share beta sum is 1
LESsub(c)         Subsistence consumption level of c of LES
shareifhk         Households' share in capital income of enterprises
shareifentk       Share of capital income retained by enterprises
shareg(c)         Share of government income spending on c
tih               Households' income tax rate
```

tiEnt	Business income tax rate
tvatl(a)	Rate of VAT on labor paid by enterprises
tvatq(c)	Rate of VAT burden on consumers
transferhg0	Base amount of government transfer payment to households
eho	Consumption function constant
mpc	marginal propensity to consume
QCTT0(c)	Trade and transport margin input used in commodity c
QCTTA0	Sum of trade and transport margin inputs
ictt(c)	Proportion of trade transport input used in quantity of c
PA0(a)	Price of activity a
QA0(a)	Quantity of activity a
PVA0(a)	Price of aggregate value-added
QVA0(a)	Quantity of aggregate value-added
PINTA0(a)	Price of aggregate intermediate input
QINTA0(a)	Quantity of aggregate intermediate input
QINT0(c,a)	Quantity of intermediate input c used in production of a
QLD0(a)	Labor demand by a
QKD0(a)	Capital demand by a
WL0	Labor price
WK0	Capital price
PQ0(c)	Purchaser's price of commodity c
PQS0(c)	Supplier's price of commodity c
QQ0(c)	Total composite commodity supplied in domestic market
PM0(c)	Import price including tariff paid by domestic buyers
QM0(c)	Quantity of import c
PE0(a)	Export price of a
QE0(a)	Quantity of export a
PDA0(a)	Price of activity a produced and supplied domestically
QDA0(a)	Quantity of activity a produced and supplied domestically
PDC0(c)	Price of commodity c produced and supplied domestically
QDC0(c)	Quantity of commodity c produced and supplied domestically
EXR0	Exchange rate
pwm(c)	World price of import c in foreign currency
pwe(a)	World price of export a in foreign currency
tm(c)	Import tariff rate for c
sube(a)	Export subsidy rate for a
QLS0	Total labor supply
QKS0	Total capital supply
YH0	Household income
EH0	Total consumption expenditure of households
QH0(c)	Quantity demanded for c by households

YENT0	Enterprise income
QINV0(c)	Quantity of investment of c by enterprises
SAVEENT0	Enterprise savings
YG0	Government total revenue
EG0	Government total expenditure
QG0(c)	Quantity of government consumption of commodity c
SAVEH0	Household savings
SAVEG0	Net government savings or fiscal budget balance
SAVEF0	Foreign savings or balance of payment
cpiwt(c)	Consumer Price Index weight
CPI0	Consumer Price Index
apiwt(a)	Activity Price Index weight
API0	Activity Price Index
;	

```
*Assignment and calibration of parameters
PA0(a)=1;
PQ0(c)=sam('total',c)/(sum(a,sam(a,c))+sam('row',c)+sam('tariff',c));
QINT0(c,a)=SAM(c,a)/PQ0(c);
QINTA0(a)=SUM(c, QINT0(c,a));
ica(c,a)=QINT0(c,a)/QINTA0(a) ;
PINTA0(a)=SUM(c,ica(c,a)*PQ0(c));
WK0=1;
WL0=1;
PE0(a)=1;
PM0(c)=1;
PDA0(a)=1;
PDC0(c)=1;
EXR0=1;
PQS0(c)=1;
QA0(a)=sam('total',a)/PA0(a);
QVA0(a)=SUM(f,sam(f,a));
PVA0(a)=(SUM(f,sam(f,a))+sam('VATL',a))/QVA0(a);
QLD0(a)=sam('lab',a)/WL0;
QKD0(a)=sam('cap',a)/WK0;
QLS0=sam('total','lab')/WL0;
QKS0=sam('total','cap')/WK0;
tvatl(a)=sam('VATL',a)/sam('lab',a);
*tm(c) is conditional on $sam('row',c), only execute this equation when
import entry has a positive value
*This avoids the problem of denominator equaling 0
```

```
tm(c)$sam('row',c)=sam('tariff',c)/sam('row',c);
pwm(c)=PM0(c)/((1+tm(c))*EXR0);
QM0(c)=(sam('row',c)+sam('tariff',c))/PM0(c);
sube(a)=sam(a,'subex')/(sam(a,'row')+sam(a,'subex'));
pwe(a)=((1-sube(a))*PE0(a))/EXR0;
QE0(a)=(sam(a,'row')+sam(a,'subex'))/PE0(a);
QDA0(a)=sum(c,sam(a,c))/PDA0(a);
QDC0(c)=sum(a,sam(a,c))/PDC0(c);
QQ0(c)=QDC0(c)+QM0(c);
tvatq(c)=sam('VATQ',c)/(sum(a,sam(a,c))+sam('row',c)+sam('tariff',c)+sam
('margin',c));
QCTT0(c)=sam('margin',c)/PQ0('com3');
ictt(c)=QCTT0(c)/QQ0(c);
QCTTA0=sum(c,QCTT0(c));
deltaAa(a)=PVA0(a)*QVA0(a)**(1-rhoAa(a))/(PVA0(a)*QVA0(a)**
(1-rhoAa(a))+PINTA0(a)*QINTA0(a)**(1-rhoAa(a)));
scaleAa(a)=QA0(a)/(deltaAa(a)*QVA0(a)**rhoAa(a)+(1-
deltaAa(a))*QINTA0(a)**rhoAa(a))**(1/rhoAa(a));
deltaVA(a)=((1+tvatl(a))*WL0)*QLD0(a)**(1-rhoVA(a))/
((((1+tvatl(a))*WL0)*QLD0(a)**(1-rhoVA(a))+WK0*QKD0(a)**(1-rhoVA(a))));
scaleAVA(a)=QVA0(a)/(deltaVA(a)*QLD0(a)**rhoVA(a)+
(1-deltaVA(a))*QKD0(a)**rhoVA(a))**(1/rhoVA(a));
*CET function parameter calibration
deltaCET(a)=PDA0(a)*QDA0(a)**(1-rhoCET(a))/(PDA0(a)*QDA0(a)**
(1-rhoCET(a))+PE0(a)*QE0(a)**(1-rhoCET(a)));
scaleCET(a)=QA0(a)/(deltaCET(a)*QDA0(a)**rhoCET(a)+(1-
deltaCET(a))*QE0(a)**rhoCET(a))**(1/rhoCET(a));
*Arminton function parameter calibration
deltaQq(c)=PDC0(c)*QDC0(c)**(1-rhoQQ(c))/(PDC0(c)*QDC0(c)**
(1-rhoQq(c))+PM0(c)*QM0(c)**(1-rhoQq(c)));
scaleQQ(c)=QQ0(c)/(deltaQq(c)*QDC0(c)**rhoQq(c)+(1-
deltaQq(c))*QM0(c)**rhoQq(c))**(1/rhoQq(c));
*Calibration of other parameters
QH0(c)=SAM(c,'hh')/PQ0(c);
cpiwt(c)=QH0(c)/sum(cp,QH0(cp));
CPI0=sum(c,PQ0(c)*cpiwt(c));
transferhg0=sam('hh','gov')/cpi0;
shareifhk=sam('hh','cap')/(WK0*QKS0);
shareifentk=sam('ent','cap')/(WK0*QKS0);
YH0=WL0*QLS0+shareifhk*WK0*QKS0+transferhg0*cpi0;
tih=sam('gov','hh')/YH0;
```

```
SAVEH0=sam('invsav','hh');
YENT0=shareifentk*WK0*QKS0;
QINV0(c)=sam(c,'invsav')/PQ0(c);
tiEnt=sam('gov','ent')/YEnt0;
SAVEENT0=(1-tiEnt)*YENT0;
YG0=tih*YH0+tiEnt*YENT0+sum(a,tvatl(a)*WL0*QLD0(a))+sum(c,sam('VATQ',c))+sam
('gov','tariff')-sum(a,sam(a,'subex'));
QG0(c)=sam(c,'gov')/PQ0(c);
SAVEG0=sam('invsav','gov');
EG0=YG0-SAVEG0;
shareg(c)=PQ0(c)*QG0(c)/(EG0-transferhg0*cpi0);
SAVEF0=sam('invsav','row');
apiwt(a)=QA0(a)/sum(ap,QA0(ap));
API0=sum(a,PA0(a)*apiwt(a));
EH0=sum(c,sam(c,'hh'));
bgtshare(c)=SAM(c,'hh')/EH0;
bhtsharechk1=sum(c,bgtshare(c));
LESbeta(c)=LESelas(c)*bgtshare(c)/(sum(cp,LESelas(cp)*bgtshare(cp)));
LESsub(c)=sam(c,'hh')/PQ0(c)+(LESbeta(c)/PQ0(c))*(EH0/frisch);
LESbetachk1=sum(c,LESbeta(c));
eho=sum(c,PQ0(c)*LESsub(c))/cpi0;
mpc=(EH0-eho*cpi0)/((1-tih)*YH0);

variable
PA(a),PVA(a),PINTA(a),QA(a),QVA(a),QINTA(a),QINT(c,a),QLD(a),QKD(a),QLS,QKS,
WL,WK,PDA(a),QDA(a),
PDC(c),QDC(c),PE(a),QE(a),EXR,QQ(c),PQS(c),PQ(c),PM(c),QM(c),QCTT(c),QCTTA,Y
H,EH,QH(c),SAVEH,YENT,QINV(c),INVADJ,SAVEENT,YG,EG,QG(c),SAVEG,SAVEF,CPI,API
,DUMMYSI;

equation
QAfn(a),QAFOCeq(a),PAeq(a),QVAfn(a),QVAFOC(a),PVAeq(a),QINTfn(c,a),PINTAeq
(a),CETfn(a),CETFOC(a),PCETeq(a),PEeq(a),QQfn(c),QQfnNoImport(c),QQFOC(c),PQSP
DCNoImportfn(c),PQSeq(c),PMeq(c),QDCQDA(c),PDCPDA(c),QCTTeq,QCTTAeq,PQSPQeq
(c),Yheq,EHeq,QHeq(c),SAVEHeq,YENTeq,QINVeq(c),SAVEENTeq,Ygeq,QGeq,SAVEGeq,Co
mEqui(c),Leq,Keq,FEXeq,CPIeq,APIeq,SIeq;

*The following are the system equations. Compact form for equations is used.
QAfn(a)..  QA(a)=e=scaleAa(a)*(deltaAa(a)*QVA(a)**rhoAa(a)+(1-
deltaAa(a))*QINTA(a)**rhoAa(a))**(1/rhoAa(a));
```

```
QAFOCeq(a)..  PVA(a)/PINTA(a)=e=(deltaAa(a)/(1-
deltaAa(a)))*(QVA(a)/QINTA(a))**(rhoAa(a)-1);

PAeq(a)..  PA(a)*QA(a)=e=PVA(a)*QVA(a)+PINTA(a)*QINTA(a);

QVAfn(a)..  QVA(a)=e=scaleAVA(a)*(deltaVA(a)*QLD(a)**rhoVA(a)+(1-
deltaVA(a))*QKD(a)**rhoVA(a))**(1/rhoVA(a));

QVAFOC(a)..  ((1+tvatl(a))*WL)/WK=e=(deltaVA(a)/(1-
deltaVA(a)))*(QLD(a)/QKD(a))**(rhoVA(a)-1);

PVAeq(a)..  PVA(a)*QVA(a)=e=(1+tvatl(a))*WL*QLD(a)+WK*QKD(a);
QINTfn(c,a)..  QINT(c,a)=e=ica(c,a)*QINTA(a);

PINTAeq(a)..  PINTA(a)=e=SUM(c,ica(c,a)*PQ(c));

CETfn(a)..  QA(a)=e=scaleCET(a)*(deltaCET(a)*QDA(a)**rhoCET(a)+(1-
deltaCET(a))*QE(a)**rhoCET(a))**(1/rhoCET(a));

CETFOC(a)..  PDA(a)/PE(a)=e=(deltaCET(a)/(1-
deltaCET(a)))*(QDA(a)/QE(a))**(rhoCET(a)-1);

PCETeq(a)..  PA(a)*QA(a)=e=PDA(a)*QDA(a)+PE(a)*QE(a);

PEeq(a)..  PE(a)=e=(1/(1-sube(a)))*pwe(a)*EXR;

*Using dollar control operator to handle the problem of QM=0
QQfn(c)$sam('row',c)..  QQ(c)=e=scaleQq(c)*(deltaQq(c)*QDC(c)**rhoQq(c)+(1-
deltaQq(c))*QM(c)**rhoQq(c))**(1/rhoQq(c));

QQfnNoImport(c)$(sam('row',c)=0)..  QQ(c)=e=QDC(c);
QQFOC(c)$sam('row',c)..  PDC(c)/PM(c)=e=(deltaQq(c)/(1-
deltaQq(c)))*(QDC(c)/QM(c))**(rhoQq(c)-1);

PQSPDCNoImportfn(c)$(sam('row',c)=0)..  PQS(c)=e=PDC(c);

PQSeq(c)..  PQS(c)*QQ(c)=e=PDC(c)*QDC(c)+PM(c)*QM(c);

PMeq(c)..  PM(c)=e=pwm(c)*(1+tm(c))*EXR;
```

```
QDCQDA(c).. QDC(c)=e=sum(a,identac(a,c)*QDA(a));

PDCPDA(c).. PDC(c)=e=sum(a,identac(a,c)*PDA(a));

QCTTeq(c).. QCTT(c)=e=ictt(c)*QQ(c);

QCTTAeq.. QCTTA=e=sum(c,QCTT(c));

PQSPQeq(c).. PQ(c)*QQ(c)=e=(1+tvatq(c))*(PQS(c)*QQ(c)+QCTT(c)*PQ('com3'));

YHeq.. YH=e=WL*QLS+shareifhk*WK*QKS+transferhg0*CPI;

EHeq.. EH=e=eho*cpi+mpc*(1-tih)*YH;

QHeq(c).. PQ(c)*QH(c)=e=PQ(c)*LESsub(c)+LESbeta(c)*(EH-
sum(cp,PQ(cp)*LESsub(cp)));

SAVEHeq.. SAVEH=e=-eho*cpi+(1-mpc)*(1-tih)*YH;

YENTeq.. YENT=e=shareifentk*WK*QKS;

QINVeq(c).. QINV(c)=e=QINV0(c)*INVADJ;

SAVEENTeq.. SAVEENT=e=(1-tiEnt)*YENT;

YGeq..
YG=e=sum(a,tvatl(a)*WL*QLD(a))+tih*YH+tiEnt*YENT+sum(c,tvatq(c)*(PQS(c)*QQ
(c)+QCTT(c)*PQ('com3'))+tm(c)*pwm(c)*QM(c)*EXR)-sum(a,sube(a)*PE(a)*QE(a));

SAVEGeq.. EG=e=YG-SAVEG;

QGeq(c).. PQ(c)*QG(c)=e=shareg(c)*(EG-transferhg0*CPI);

*The following equation uses dollar operator to handle the optional QCTTA
ComEqui(c)..
QQ(c)=e=sum(a,QINT(c,a))+QH(c)+QINV(c)+QG(c)+QCTTA$sam(c,'margin');

Leq.. Sum(a,QLD(a))=e=QLS;
```

```
Keq..   Sum(a,QKD(a))=e=QKS;

CPIeq..   CPI=e=sum(c,PQ(c)*cpiwt(c));

APIeq..   API=e=sum(a,PA(a)*apiwt(a));

FEXeq..   SAVEF*EXR=e=sum(c,pwm(c)*QM(c)*EXR)-sum(a,pwe(a)*QE(a)*EXR);

SIeq..   sum(c,PQ(c)*QINV(c))=e=SAVEH+SAVEENT+SAVEG+SAVEF*EXR+dummysi;

*Assigning initial values
PA.L(a)=PA0(a);PVA.L(a)=PVA0(a);PINTA.L(a)=PINTA0(a);
QA.L(a)=QA0(a);QVA.L(a)=QVA0(a);QINTA.L(a)=QINTA0(a);QINT.L(c,a)=QINT0(c,a);
QLD.L(a)=QLD0(a);QKD.L(a)=QKD0(a);QLS.L=QLS0;QKS.L=QKS0;WL.L=WL0;WK.L=WK0;
PDA.L(a)=1;QDA.L(a)=QDA0(a); PDC.L(c)=1;QDC.L(c)=QDC0(c);
PE.L(a)=1;QE.L(a)=QE0(a); EXR.L=1;PQS.L(c)=1;PQ.L(c)=PQ0(c);
QQ.L(c)=QQ0(c);PM.L(c)=PM0(c); QM.L(c)=QM0(c);
QCTT.L(c)=QCTT0(c);QCTTA.L=QCTTA0;
YH.L=YH0;EH.L=EH0;QH.L(c)=QH0(c);
YENT.L=YENT0;QINV.L(c)=QINV0(c);INVADJ.L=1; SAVEENT.L=SAVEENT0;
YG.L=YG0;EG.L=EG0; QG.L(c)=QG0(c);SAVEG.L=SAVEG0;SAVEF.L=SAVEF0;
CPI.L=CPI0;API.L=API0; DUMMYSI.L=0;

*Fix five variable values to make the system square.  API is numeraire
*Government spending closure so EG is a variable
QLS.fx=QLS0;
QKS.fx=QKS0;
INVADJ.fx=1;
EXR.fx=EXR0;
API.fx=1;

*Executing the model
model cge  /all/;
solve cge using mcp;

parameter
QAbase(a),QDAbase(a),QEbase(a);
QAbase(a)=QA.L(a);
QDAbase(a)=QDA.L(a);
QEbase(a)=QE.L(a);
```

```
*Simulation for removing export tax in agriculture
sube('act1')=0;
model sim  /all/;
solve sim using mcp;

*Generate the percentage changes
Parameter
QAchange(a),QDAchange(a),QEchange(a);
QAchange(a)=QA.L(a)/QAbase(a)-1;
QDAchange(a)=QDA.L(a)/QDAbase(a)-1;
QEchange(a)=QE.L(a)/QEbase(a)-1;

Display sube,QAchange,QDAchange,QEchange;

*END
```

15.8 GDP and the Keynesian Closure

Example 15.8.1 Suppose Openland2 is currently in economic recession. The government plans to increase spending to stimulate the economy and wants to know the government spending multiplier, which is defined as the increase in GDP because of one monetary unit increase in the government spending *EG*.

Solution: To answer this question, we need to calculate GDP of the economy. There are three approaches to measure GDP: final expenditures, value-added and income. If correctly measured, their outcomes are identical. Remember that taxes on products are parts of GDP.

By the measure of final expenditures:

> GDP = the sum of final expenditures at purchasers' prices
> = consumption by households and government (purchasers' prices)
>   + capital formation (purchasers' prices)
>   + exports (world prices converted to domestic currency)
>   − imports (world prices converted to domestic currency)

Accordingly, in the GAMS program for Openland2, we have the following GAMS sentence:

```
GDP=sum(c,PQ(c)*(QH(c)+QG(c)+QINV(c)))+sum(a,pwe(a)*EXR*QE(a))-
sum(c,pwm(c)*EXR*QM(c))
```

By the measure of value-added:

> GDP = the sum of the gross-value-added at factor costs
>   + all taxes − all subsides on products
>   + all other taxes − all other subsides on production

For Openland2, we need to add the labor and capital costs, all VAT taxes, import and export taxes, and subtract export subsidies. Accordingly, the GAMS sentence is

```
GDP=sum(a,(1+tvatl(a))*WL*QLD(a)+WK*QKD(a))+sum(c,tvatq(c)*(PQS(c)*QQ
(c)+QCTT(c)*PQ('com3'))+sum(c,tm(c)*pwm(c)*EXR*QM(c))-sum(a,sube(a)/(1-
sube(a))*pwe(a)*EXR*QE(a));
```

To have the Keynesian macroeconomic closure, replace the above government spending closure (Equations (15.6.39)–(15.6.43)) with the following five constraints:

```
WL.fx=1; API.fx=1; EG.fx=EG0; INVADJ.fx=1; EXR.fx=EXR0;
```

where labor price and activity prices are fixed, labor and capital employment are endogenous.

Alternatively, we can let labor and capital prices be fixed, so we have these five constraints:

```
WL.fx=1; WK.fx=1; EG.fx=EG0; INVADJ.fx=1; EXR.fx=EXR0;
```

In the Keynesian closure, government expenditure EG is the exogenous variable which determines the economic size. To calculate the multiplier, let EG increase by one monetary unit, then calculate the resulting increase in GDP. Because prices are all fixed, the growth in the simulation for estimating the multiplier is real growth.

The GAMS program for Example 15.8.1 is left as an exercise for the readers. You may verify your answers by checking these results: The GDP figure in the base year is 4814 by both measures. The government expenditure multiplier is 1.464.

Exercises

15E.1 Table 15E.1.1 is the same as Table 15.5.3. It is in the base state equilibrium. Prices *PA*, *PE* and *EXR* all equal 1. Use Excel or other spreadsheets, or calculate by hand, to calibrate the values of the following parameters and variables in the base state for activities 1, 2 and 3: *QE*, *sube*, *iett*, *pwe*, prices at the border after transportation costs but before export tax, the prices paid by the ROW in the foreign currency unit.

Table 15E.1.1. Transport margins of exports in SAM.

	Transport margin	Export subsidy	Rest of the World
Activity 1 (agriculture)	−9	−15	135
Activity 2 (industry)	−2	13	247
Activity 3 (service)	0	10	90
Activity 4 (Coal)	−10	−5	55

Table 15E.5.1. SAM table for Openland3.

	Act1	Act2	Act3	Com1	Com2	Com3	VATR	Margin	Lab	Cap	HH	Ent	Gov	VATL	VATQ	Tariff	Subex	ROW	Invsav	Total
Act1				1819													−15	135		1939
Act2					2696												13	247		2956
Act3						2427											10	90		2527
Com1	280	420	240								916		191						199	2246
Com2	377	520	380								1391		401						213	3282
Com3	220	300	540					146			1094		200						143	2643
VATR	−88	−124	−116																	−328
Margin				40	70	36														146
Lab	650	700	690																	2040
Cap	370	1000	655																	2025
HH									2040	1725			326							4091
Ent										300										300
Gov							−328				440	100		408	530	23	−8			1165
VATL	130	140	138																	408
VATQ				150	200	180														530
Tariff				7	16															23
Subex																				0
ROW				230	300															530
Invsav											250	200	47					58		555
Total	1939	2956	2527	2246	3282	2643	−328	146	2040	2025	4091	300	1165	408	530	23	0	530	555	

15E.2 Copy the GAMS program of Example 15.7.1. Run it successfully.

15E.3 Change the service import of Openland2 from 0 to 0.1 in the SAM table. Let the program read the new data. In this case, because there is a positive value in the service import entry, the dollar control operators in the GAMS program are ignored in the model. Compare the differences in output values between this "small value method" and "equation replacement method".

15E.4 Revise the above GAMS program to the Keynesian closure and answer the questions in Example 15.8.1.

15E.5 The economy of country Openland3 is represented by Table 15E.5.1. It has a VAT system with a refund scheme for intermediate input uses. Revise your GAMS program of Openland2 for Openland3 by using the techniques described in Section 15.3.

Chapter 16

Subaccounts and Subprograms

16.1 Multiple Household Groups

In policy or theoretical research, we often need to investigate economic variables at the disaggregate levels. For instance, to study the alternative energy issue, we need to disaggregate the capital and intermediate inputs in the production block. An example is the global trade analysis project (GTAP-E) model discussed in Section 8.6.

Many computable general equilibrium (CGE) research projects need to investigate behaviors and outcomes of different household groups. To study income distribution, we need to separate households into various income groups. To study urbanization, we split households into rural and urban groups. To study social security policies, we may need to disaggregate the population into various income, age and household size groups. In CGE modeling, to disaggregate households into multiple groups, first we need to set up the corresponding group accounts in the social accounting matrix (SAM) table and in the model. The following is an example.

Suppose we plan to study n regional household groups. Let the set of household groups be $\mathbf{H}$. Each household group is an element of $\mathbf{H}$ indexed by h. That is, $h \in H$. Let total labor supply be $QLSAGG$. The share of group h in labor supply is $sharelh_h$. The income of group h from labor is $WL \cdot sharelh_h \cdot QLSAGG$. Let total capital supply be $QKSAGG$. Enterprises retain part of capital income for themselves and distribute the rest to households. The share of capital income retained by enterprises is still $shareif_{ent\,k}$. The share of group h from capital income is $shareif_{h\,k}$. Note the subscript h is the index for household group h. Hence, $shareif_{ent\,k} + \sum_h shareif_{h\,k} = 1$. Income of group h from capital is $WK \cdot shareif_{h\,k} \cdot QKSAGG$. Transfer payment by the government to group h is $transfer_{h\,gov}$, and it may be consumer price index (CPI) indexed. Transfer payment from enterprises to households is $transfer_{h\,ent}$. This is mostly the write-off of unpaid commodities sold to households. This figure is usually insignificant in national accounts. Transfer payment from rest of the world (ROW) to households is $transfer_{h\,row}$, which can be substantial for some developing countries. Adding together, the income of household group h is

$$YH_h = WL \cdot shareif_{h\,l} \cdot QLSAGG + WK \cdot shareif_{h\,k} \cdot QKSAGG + transfer_{h\,ent}$$
$$+ transfer_{h\,g} \cdot cpi + transfer_{h\,row} \qquad h \in H \qquad (16.1.1)$$

Among the transfer payments, only the government's transfer payment to households is CPI indexed, which is based on the observations in the real world.

If the income tax rate is group-specific, the disposable income of group h is $(1 - ti_h) YH_h$, where ti_h is the income tax rate applied to group h. The marginal propensity to consume is also group-specific, hence, mpc_h. This is extremely important for studies on various income groups, because the marginal propensity to consume can be substantially different between high- and low-income groups. If the household utility functions are Cobb–Douglas, then the demand for commodity c by group h is

$$PQ_c \cdot QH_{ch} = shareh_{ch} \cdot mpc_h \cdot (1 - ti_h) \cdot YH_h \qquad c \in C \quad h \in H \qquad (16.1.2)$$

If the households' utility function is Stone–Geary, the consumption function for group h is

$$EH_h = eho_h \cdot cpi + mpc_h \cdot (1 - ti_h) \cdot YH_h \qquad h \in H \qquad (16.1.3)$$

The demand function of group h is linear expenditure system (LES):

$$PQ_c \cdot QH_{c,h} = PQ_c \cdot \gamma_{c,h} + \beta_{c,h} \left(EH_h - \sum_c PQ_c \cdot \gamma_{c,h} \right) \qquad c \in C \quad h \in H \qquad (16.1.4)$$

These functions are household-group-specific.

16.2 Cross Activities and Commodities in the QX Structure

So far we assume one activity produces only one commodity in our CGE models. For some research topics we need to study the more complex situation when a production activity produces multiple commodities, or a commodity is produced by multiple activities. Examples include: the coal production activity produces chemical, fuel and construction commodities. Commodity cocoa is produced by activities of large-scale farms and small-scale peasants in West Africa. Automobiles are produced by activities from state-owned, private and foreign-owned companies in China. The international food policy research institute (IFPRI) model has the QX structure to handle this multiple cross-production relationship. The IFPRI model is called "standard CGE model", which is said to be the most used CGE model in the world.

In the QX structure, from production activities to commodities, in the middle there is a block of QX as shown in Figure 16.2.1. An activity QA may produce multiple commodities, denoted by $QXAC$. The sum of the same commodity is QX. QX is then distributed between domestic sales and exports in the constant elasticity of transformation (CET) module.

Let us use an example to illustrate the mathematical setup of the QX block. Table 16.2.1 is the corresponding block of the SAM table describing the multiple cross-production relationships in a hypothetical transitional economy. Let us name this economy Transland.

There are five activities, producing three commodities. Among them, the activities of state farms produce both agricultural and industrial commodities. Agricultural commodities

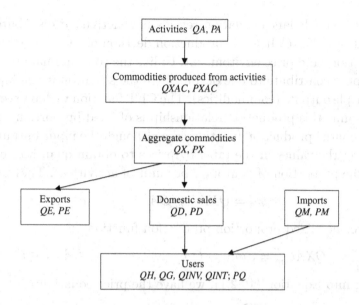

Figure 16.2.1. Flow from activities to commodities in the QX structure.

Table 16.2.1. Activities and commodities in the model economy of Transland ($PA = 1$).

		Commodities			
		Agriculture	Industry	Service	Total activities PA^*QA
Activities	Agriculture (State farms)	850	150		1000
	Agriculture (household farms)	1020			1020
	Industry (State enterprises)		1400		1400
	Industry (private enterprises)		1280		1280
	Service			1930	1930
	Total commodities PX^*QX	1870	2830	1930	

are produced by two activities: state farms and household farms. The industrial commodities are produced by three activities: state farms, state enterprises and private enterprises. In comparative economics literature, it is common to refer to state enterprises as state-owned enterprises, abbreviated to SOE. The service activity produces only its own commodity. Table 16.2.1 represents the base state, in which all activity and commodity prices are set to 1.

Let $QXAC_{ac}$ denote the quantity of c produced by activity a. $PXAC_{ac}$ is the price of $QXAC_{ac}$. $PXAC_{ac} \cdot QXAC_{ac}$ is the value in entry (a, c) in Table 16.2.1. In each row account of Table 16.2.1, we have

$$\sum_c PXAC_{ac} \cdot QXAC_{ac} = PA_a \cdot QA_a \qquad a \in A \qquad (16.2.1)$$

The above account balance equation reveals how activity a distributes its productions among commodities $QXAC$. It is the production decision of the activity, given the available production functions and price environment. Unlike the conventional production function in which many inputs contribute to one output, here the situation is one input (activity) contributes to multiple outputs (commodities). The CET function we have seen is such an example. Here we assume this production relationship is of fixed proportions. It mathematically resembles the Leontief production function case although the input-output story is reversed.

First, dividing the values in the table by prices to obtain quantities of QA and $QXAC$. Let $oxac_{ac}$ be the proportion of "output c per unit of activity a". They are calibrated by:

$$oxac_{a\,c} = QXAC_{ac}/QA_a \qquad\qquad a \in A \qquad\qquad (16.2.2)$$

Now we have the "fixed proportion production functions":

$$QXAC_{ac} = oxac_{a\,c} \cdot QA_a \qquad\qquad a \in A \quad c \in C \qquad\qquad (16.2.3)$$

Substituting into Equation (16.2.1), we have the price equation:

$$PA_a = \sum_c PXAC_{ac} \cdot oxac_{ac} \qquad\qquad a \in A \qquad\qquad (16.2.4)$$

Equations (16.2.3) and (16.2.4) form the module for the fixed proportion relationship from an activity QA_a to multiple commodities $QXAC_{ac}$. Because $QXAC$ are physically different from QA, we have freedom to reset prices $PXAC$, redefine the quantity units of $QXAC$ and calibrate $oxac$ accordingly as discussed in Section 13.7, if needed.

Next we set up the module for multiple activities to contribute to one composite commodity c. In this situation, we work on columns in Table 16.2.1. Take the example of the second column: there are three activities producing the industrial commodity. In the IFPRI model, the relationships from $QXAC$ to QX resemble the case of the Armington module integrating imports and domestic products to a composite good. $QXAC$ produced by different activities are imperfect substitutes and their relationships are represented by a multiple-input constant elasticity of substitution (CES) function. That is, there may be two or more activity products to be integrated into a composite commodity QX.

Let us review the discussion on the CES function for multiple inputs in Section 8.6. The following four equations are duplicated from that section. The CES function with multiple inputs is

$$q = A(\delta_1 x_1^{\rho} + \delta_2 x_2^{\rho} +, \dots\dots, + \delta_n x_n^{\rho})^{1/\rho} \qquad\qquad \sum_i^n \delta_i = 1 \qquad\qquad (16.2.5)$$

Given the exponent ρ, to calibrate parameters of share δ and scale factor A, we use the following formulas:

$$\delta_j = \frac{w_j x_j^{1-\rho}}{w_1 x_1^{1-\rho} + \dots + w_i x_i^{1-\rho} + \cdots + w_n x_n^{1-\rho}} = \frac{w_j x_j^{1-\rho}}{\sum_{i \in X} w_i x_i^{1-\rho}} \qquad (16.2.6)$$

$$A = q/(\delta_1 x_1^{\rho} +, \dots, + \delta_n x_n^{\rho})^{1/\rho} \qquad\qquad (16.2.7)$$

There are four alternative forms of the equation system to determine the optimal use of inputs x and optimal output q, given the prices. The IFPRI model uses the 'marginal-revenue-product form' of Equation (8.6.10):

$$\begin{cases} q = A(\delta_1 x_1^\rho + \delta_2 x_2^\rho +, \ldots\ldots, +\delta_n x_n^\rho)^{1/\rho} & i = 1, \ldots, n \\ w_i = pq(\delta_1 x_1^\rho + \delta_2 x_2^\rho +, \ldots\ldots, +\delta_n x_n^\rho)^{-1} \delta_i x_i^{\rho-1} \end{cases} \quad (16.2.8)$$

Converting the above equations to the CGE model notations, the CES function is

$$QX_c = \alpha_c^{ac} \left(\sum_a \delta_{ac}^{ac} \cdot QXAC_{ac}^{\rho_c^{ac}} \right)^{1/\rho_c^{ac}} \qquad c \in C \qquad (16.2.9)$$

The first-order optimal condition for $QXAC$ and QX, equivalent to Equation (16.2.8), is that "input" price $PXAC$ on LHS equals marginal revenue product of QX on the RHS in the following equation:

$$PXAC_{ac} = PX_c \cdot QX_c \left(\sum_a \delta_{ac}^{ac} \cdot QXAC_{ac}^{\rho_c^{ac}} \right)^{-1} \cdot \delta_{ac}^{ac} \cdot QXAC_{ac}^{\rho_c^{ac}-1} \quad a \in A \quad c \in C \quad (16.2.10)$$

Equations (16.2.9) and (16.2.10) form the system for multiple activity products $QXAC$ to be integrated to a composite output QX. Note the marginal-revenue-product form only needs two equations to complete the module system. Equation (16.2.10) also plays the optimization role of the price function.

This relationship from multiple activities to one composite commodity can also be specified in fixed proportions: the shares contributing to the composite commodity by various activities are fixed. The fixed proportion specification is in general uninteresting to policy studies, because a research project often wants to know how an external shock would change the activity shares in the composite commodity. For instance, how privatization would affect the shares of the state farms in agricultural and industrial outputs in Transland. With fixed proportions, these shares won't change.

In a similar fashion, for Equations (16.2.3) and (16.2.4), the fixed proportion relationship from one activity QA to multiple commodities $QXAC$ can be replaced by a CET function with multiple outputs. Mathematically, the CET system is similar to the above CES function form and the first-order-condition equation, except that the value of exponent ρ should be greater than 1.

16.3 Write and Test a Subprogram

When a CGE model has a big component block with many subaccounts, if possible, it would be more efficient to write and test a subprogram for that component block before integrating the subprogram into the model. Examples can be preparing a subprogram for the production block in the energy models, or for the international trade block in trade models. The idea is similar to modular programming in computer science.

Take the example of the QX block of Transland. We can write a subprogram for this block, test the subprogram by running it independently, to make sure the codes and functions are correct. Doing so needs some planning.

First we need to identify and analyze the equations and the variables in the system of the QX block. The system consists of four equations: (16.2.3) and (16.2.4) determine how an activity QA distributes among the multiple commodity productions. Equations (16.2.9) and (16.2.10) determine how commodities produced by multiple activities form a composite commodity QX. Then we analyze variables, in particular, we need to identify the internal variables and link variables of the block. Among the variables, $QXAC$ and $PXAC$ are internal variables, which means they appear only in equations inside the block but not in the rest of the CGE model. PA, QA, PX, QX are variables interacting between the block system and the rest of the CGE model, which can be called "link variables". The internal variables are always endogenous in the block system and the subprogram. The link variables PA, QA, PX and QX can be either endogenous or exogenous for the block, depending on their specific relationships with the rest of the model, and our concerns over the squareness condition.

To independently run the subprogram by GAMS, the subprogram should be square. The QX block of Table 16.2.1 has five rows (activities) and three columns (commodities). The numbers of rows and columns are not equal. This causes problems in meeting the squareness condition.

Let the number of activity rows be m and the number of commodity columns be n. First, we count the number of equations. Equation (16.2.4) has m equations and Equation (16.2.9) has n equations. Each group of Equations (16.2.3) and (16.2.10) has $m \times n$ equations. So in total there are $m + n + 2(m \times n)$ equations. Next, count the number of variables. Each group of PA and QA has $2m$ variables. Each group of X and QX has $2n$ variables. Each group of $QXAC$ and $PXAC$ has $m \times n$ variables. So in total there are $2(m+n) + 2(m \times n)$ variables. Comparing to the number of equations, there are $m + n$ more variables than equations, thus we need to fix the values of $m + n$ variables, making them exogenous, to reduce the number of variables. $QXAC$ and $PXAC$ are internal variables so they must remain endogenous. The variables whose values are to be fixed must be selected among the link variables of PA, QA, PX and QX with theoretical justification.

To reduce m variables, we can fix either PA or QA. To reduce n variables, we can fix either PX or QX. Together the number of variables in the block is reduced by $m + n$. Thus the subprogram meets the squareness condition and can run independently. Economics justification is also needed to make the decision. Suppose we choose to fix PA and QX. The economics explanation for this choice can be: in the QX block, the activity productions face outside-of-the-block decided prices, while the quantities of commodity are constrained by the outside demands.

When the subprogram is integrated into the CGE model, the constraints of fixing values need to be removed, so all link variables PA, QA, PX and QX return to be endogenous variables in the model. If the link variables and their initial values are specified correctly, the subprogram can immediately work with the rest of the model. Possible errors may occur. One problem is that the link variables are not placed correctly in the model. This kind of errors can be searched and corrected. Another error is that the number of link variables causes the squareness or determination problems in the entire model. These errors need some further modifications of the model.

Suppose the rest of the CGE model is demand-driven, which determines the values of PX and QX outside of the QX block. In this case, the variables in the block are reduced by $2n$. Because $m > n$, this leaves $m + n - 2n = m - n$ excess variables. In Transland, it means $m - n = 5 - 3 = 2$ excess variables. How to set more restrictions to reduce excess variables? We need to add two more constraints with economics justification. For instance, there are 3 activities contributing to the industrial commodity. Suppose that, based on real-world observations, this transitional economy is in a privatization process restricting the expansion of SOEs. Therefore we can add constraints to restrict the outputs of SOEs in agriculture and industry by fixing the capital uses of QKD in these two activities, to meet the squareness condition.

If the rest of the CGE model is production-driven, which determines the values of PA and QA outside the QX block, the variables of the block are reduced by $2m$, thus the number of variables are less than equations by $m - n$. In Transland, it means two excess equations from the activity side. If there are inconsistencies among the equations, the model won't work. If the excess two equations are consistent with others in the system, which means they are linearly dependent with other equations, mathematically the solution of the system can still exist. But the GAMS solver cannot work with the situation when equations and variables are not equal. The trick to solve the problem is adding two dummy variables in equations involving PA or QA in the model. If the two excess equations are consistent, the dummy variables shall converge to zero in replication. Otherwise the model has errors. In general, it would be better to identify the problems in the model which cause the excess equations, then modify the model to fix the problems; rather than relying on adding dummy variables.

The example of Table 16.2.1 has more rows than columns: $m > n$. If instead we have more columns than rows: $m < n$, the approach to solve the squareness condition for the block is the same.

16.4 GAMS Subprogram for the QX Block

Example 16.4.1 The QX block of the economy of Transland is Table 16.2.1. Assume the relationships from one activity producing multiple commodities are in fixed proportions. Assume that relationship for the imperfectly substitutable commodities produced by multiple activities to form the composite commodity is described by a CES function. The elasticity of substitution among them in the CES function is 3. Write a GAMS subprogram for this block, including calibration for the parameters and system equations. Replicate the base state.

Solution: Section 16.2 provides the equations for calibrating parameters of the CES function. The system for the QX block consists of four Equations (16.2.3), (16.2.4), (16.2.9) and (16.2.10), which transform from activities QA, PA to commodities QX, PX. As discussed above, we choose to fix the values of PA and QX to make the subprogram square so it can run independently.

Many entries for $QXAC$ in the QX block have no data. The zero values of these entries would cause errors in running the CES function. We use the same techniques described in

Chapter 15 to fix the missing-data problem. In particular, on the left-hand side (LHS) we use the dollar control operator in the GAMS statements to skip the equations and variables of *PXAC* with missing *OXAC* data:

```
PXACFOC(a,c)$sax(a,c)..
PXAC(a,c)=e=PX(c)*QX(c)*sum(ap,deltaac(ap,c)*QXAC(ap,c)**(rhoac(c)))*
*(-1)*deltaac(a,c)*QXAC(a,c)**(rhoac(c)-1);
IQAQXeq(c)..
QX(c)=e=scaleac(c)*sum(a,deltaac(a,c)$sax(a,c)*QXAC(a,c)**(rhoac(c)))
**(1/rhoac(c));
```

Then, to avoid prices falling to zero in the simulation, add the code:

```
PXAC.fx(a,c)$(NOT sax(a,c))=1;
```

The GAMS subprogram is as follows. This subprogram for the QX block can be integrated into either the Openland model or the Transland model.

```
$title Example 16.4.1 Subprogram for the QX block
*using multiple-input CES function

set a /agrisoe,agrismall,manusoe,manupriv,serv/;
set c  /comagri,commanu,comserv/;

alias (a,ap),(c,cp);

table sax(a,c)
                comagri          commanu         comserv
agrisoe          850              150
agrismall       1020
manusoe                          1400
manupriv                         1280
serv                                             1930
;

Parameter
QA0(a),PA0(a),QX0(c),PX0(c),QXAC0(a,c),PXAC0(a,c),oxac(a,c),
rhoac(c),elasac(c),deltaac(a,c),scaleac(c);

elasac(c)=3;
rhoac(c)=1-1/elasac(c);
PXAC0(a,c)=1;
QXAC0(a,c)=sax(a,c)/PXAC0(a,c);
PA0(a)=1;
QA0(a)=sum(c,sax(a,c))/PA0(a);
```

```
PX0(c)=1;
QX0(c)=sum(a,PXAC0(a,c)*QXAC0(a,c))/PX0(c);
oxac(a,c)=QXAC0(a,c)/QA0(a);
deltaac(a,c)=(PXAC0(a,c)*QXAC0(a,c)**(1-
rhoac(c)))/sum(ap,PXAC0(ap,c)*QXAC0(ap,c)**(1/rhoac(c)));
scaleac(c)=QX0(C)/(sum(a,deltaac(a,c)*QXAC0(a,c)**(rhoac(c))))**(1/rhoac(c));

Display
QA0,PA0,QX0,PX0,QXAC0,PXAC0,oxac;

Variables
QA(a),PA(a),QX(c),PX(c),QXAC(a,c),PXAC(a,c);

Equations
OQAQXeq(a,c),OPAPXeq(a),IQAQXeq(c),PXACFOC(a,c);

OQAQXeq(a,c)..
QXAC(a,c)=e=oxac(a,c)*QA(a);

OPAPXeq(a)..
PA(a)=e=sum(c,PXAC(a,c)*oxac(a,c));

IQAQXeq(c)..
QX(c)=e=scaleac(c)*sum(a,deltaac(a,c)$sax(a,c)*QXAC(a,c)**(rhoac(c)))**(1/rh
oac(c));

PXACFOC(a,c)$sax(a,c)..
PXAC(a,c)=e=PX(c)*QX(c)*sum(ap,deltaac(ap,c)*QXAC(ap,c)**(rhoac(c)))**(-
1)*deltaac(a,c)*QXAC(a,c)**(rhoac(c)-1);

PXAC.fx(a,c)$(NOT sax(a,c))=1;

PXAC.L(a,c)=PXAC0(a,c);
QXAC.L(a,c)=QXAC0(a,c);
QA.L(a)=QA0(a);
PX.L(c)=PX0(c);
*fix the values of m+n variables to meet the squareness condition
PA.fx(a)=PA0(a);
QX.fx(c)=QX0(c);
```

```
model acblock /all/;
solve acblock using mcp;

*end
```

16.5 The IFPRI Model

The IFPRI model is said to be the most used CGE model. Table 16.5.1 is its descriptive SAM table. The account arrangement of the IFPRI model is in the SNA standard but somewhat different from Openland2. Table 16.5.2 is the SAM table of Transland arranged in line with the IFPRI SAM structure, except switching the positions of ROW and the savings–investment accounts.

Table 16.5.1 is self-descriptive. VAT1 refers to the enterprise-portion VAT on labor employment by enterprises. VAT2 refers to the consumer-portion VAT. In our CGE modeling and GAMS program, VAT1 is similar to the employment tax, and VAT2 is similar to the sales tax. The QX block is located in the intersection of activity row accounts and commodity column accounts. The activity accounts in the IFPRI model include a component block for home-consumed outputs. This can be an important part of the economy in low-income countries. Table 16.5.2 does not have this component block, but it can be added as needed.

The major difference between the IFPRI model and the Openland2 is the arrangement of exports and export taxes in the SAM table structure. In the IFPRI structure, exports are positioned in the row commodity accounts. Therefore, the total values of the commodity accounts include imports, exports and domestically produced and consumed commodities. To calculate QQ, i.e., all commodities available on the domestic markets, we need to subtract exports from the total commodity amounts. Further, while most commodities are at purchasers' prices PQ, the exports are not. Exports are at the prices of PE. Therefore, there is no uniform quantity unit throughout the entire commodity row account. The researchers need to be aware of this situation in parameter calibration and modeling.

In parameter calibration of CGE models, purchasers' prices PQ need to be first calibrated because the calibration for other parameters such as the quantities of the intermediate inputs need to use calibrated PQ values. In the Openland structure, because the total commodity values exclude exports, we can simply divide the total commodity values by the sum of the values of QM and QD to obtain PQ. In the IFPRI model, however, the issue is more complicated. We need to first subtract the values of exports from the total amounts. As explained in Equation (13.7.6), we calibrate the purchaser's price in the base state as follows (note the second step in the following equation utilizes the fact that PA, PM and PE all equal 1 in the base state):

$$
\begin{aligned}
PQ0 &= \frac{\text{total commodity value} - \text{export value}}{(\text{domestic production value})/PA + (\text{import value} + \text{tariff})/PM - (\text{export value})/PE} \\[2mm]
&= \frac{\text{total commodity value} - \text{export value}}{\text{domestic production value} + \text{import value} + \text{tariff} - \text{export value}}
\end{aligned}
\tag{16.5.1}
$$

Table 16.5.1. The SAM structure of the IFPRI model.

	1 Activities	2 Commodities	3 Factors	4 Households	5 Enterprises	6 Government	7 Rest of the World (ROW)	8 Savings–Investment	Total incomes
1 Activities		Marketed outputs The QX block		Home consumed outputs					Output
2 Commodities	Intermediate inputs	Trade and transport margins		Household consumption		Government expenditure	Exports	Investment (capital formation)	Demand
3 Factors	Value-added						Factor income from ROW		Factor income
4 Households			Households factor income	Transfer among households	Enterprise transfer to households	Government transfer to households	Transfer to households from ROW		Household income
5 Enterprises			Enterprise factor income			Government transfer to enterprises	Transfer to enterprises from ROW		Enterprise income
6 Government	VAT1, other production taxes	VAT2, Sales tax, tariffs, export taxes/subsidies	Factor taxes as income to government	Income tax, direct tax	Enterprise direct tax to government		Transfer to government from ROW		Government income
7 Rest of the World (ROW)		Imports	Factor income to ROW		Enterprise surplus to ROW	Government transfers to ROW			Foreign exchange outflow
8 Savings–Investment				Household savings	Enterprise savings	Government savings	Foreign savings		Savings
Total expenditures	Activity expenditure	Supply	Factor expenditures	Household expenditures	Enterprises expenditures	Government expenditures	Foreign exchange inflow	Investment	

Note: With some modification from the original IFPRI table such as the arrangement of the VAT and production taxes.
Source: Lofgren H., R. L. Harris, and S. Robinson (2002). *A Standard Computable General Equilibrium (CGE) Model in GAMS.* International Food Policy Research Institute.

Table 16.5.2.   SAM table of Transland.

	Act1	Act2	Act3	Act4	Com1	Com2	Com3	Margin	Lab	Cap	HHR	HHU	Ent	Gov	Employ tax	saletx	Tariff	ROW	Invsav	Total
Act1 (Agriculture)					1750	200														1950
Act2 (SOE industry)						1470														1470
Act3 (Private industry)						1820														1820
Act4 (service)							2480													2480
Com1 (Agriculture)	350	210	250	240							400	450		100				90	100	2190
Com2 (Industry)	300	200	300	410							900	1030		230				290	400	4060
Com3 (Service)	220	220	240	540				310			300	480		210				100	100	2720
Trade transport margin					100	150	60													310
Lab (labor)	650	350	500	670																2170
Cap (Capital)	350	450	470	540																1810
HHR (Rural households)									1000	400				730						2130
HHU (Urban households)									1170	1010				330						2510
Ent (Enterprises)										400										400
Gov (Government)											280	300	100		260	480	30			1450
Employment tax	80	40	60	80																260
Sales taxes					100	200	180													480
Tariff					10	20														30
ROW (Rest of the World)					230	200														430
Invsav (Savings–Investment)											250	250	300	−150				−50		600
Total	1950	1470	1820	2480	2190	4060	2720	310	2170	1810	2130	2510	400	1450	260	480	30	430	600	

In GAMS code, it is as follows:

```
PQ0(c)=(sam('total',c)-sam(c,'row'))/(sum(a,sam(a,c))+sam('row',c)
+ sam('tariff',c)-sam(c,'row'));
```

In the IFPRI SAM table, the export taxes are positioned in rows at the lower-left area, but export values are positioned in columns at the upper-right area. In calibration of export tax rates, we need to calculate values across opposite positions between rows and columns in the SAM table. This can be error-prone. In this aspect, the Openland2 structure is more convenient than the IFPRI structure for trade models. The Transland's SAM Table 16.5.2 follows the IFPRI structure. The following is the CGE model for Transland, which is a simplified version of the IFPRI model and can help readers to understand the original IFPRI model.

Example 16.5.1 The base state of Transland is described by SAM Table 16.5.2. In the base state, factors are fully employed. The government adjusts its spending to ensure full employment of labor and capital. Households are separated into rural and urban groups. The additional information about parameters is provided in the group of three subtables in the following Table 16.5.3. Write a GAMS program for Transland. Suppose Transland is a transitional economy from a command system to a market system. The total factor productivity (TFP) in the private sector is expected to increase by 30% next year. Simulate

Table 16.5.3. Parameter values for Transland.

	Agriculture (Act1)	Industry (SOE) (Act2)	Industry (private) (Act3)	Service (Act4)
Top activity level CES ρ	0.2	0.4	0.5	0.1
Value-added CES ρ	0.3	0.4	0.6	0.5

	Agriculture (Com1)	Industry (Com2)	Service (Com3)
Armington CES ρ	0.4	0.6	0.4
CET function ρ	1.4	1.4	2.0

LES parameters	Households (rural)	Households (urban)
Elasticity Com1	0.5	0.4
Elasticity Com2	1.0	1.1
Elasticity Com3	1.2	1.4
Frisch	−4	−2

Table 16.5.4.   After the productivity increases by 30% in the private sector.

	Private sector	State-owned sector
Industrial output	+67.7%	−31.1%
Labor use	+16.5%	−36.1%
Capital use	+20.8%	−34.5%

the situation and find the changes in the outputs and factors employed by the state-owned and private enterprises in the industry sector.

Solution: The GAMS program is provided as follows. The SAM data is inputted from an external file SAM16-1.inc prepared by using Excel and XLS2GMS. The changes after the shock of a TFP increase in the private and state-owned sectors are exhibited in Table 16.5.4. As expected, the output and input uses of the private sector grow rapidly, but those of the state-owned sector fall.

```
$title Example 16.5.1 for Transland
*dollar control used in the QX block

*Define sets
set ac
/act1,act2,act3,act4,com1,com2,com3,margin,lab,cap,hhr,hhu,ent,gov,emptx,saletx,ta
riff,row,invsav,total/;
set a(ac) /act1,act2,act3,act4/;
set c(ac) /com1,com2,com3/;
set f(ac) /lab,cap/;
set h(ac) /hhr,hhu/;
*The following set acnt will be used for checking accuracy of SAM
set acnt(ac) all accounts excluding total;
acnt(ac)=YES;
acnt('total')=NO;

alias (ac,acp),(a,ap),(c,cp),(f,fp),(acnt,acntp);

*input the SAM data file SAM16-1.inc
table sam(ac,acp)
$include D:\GAMS programs\SAM16-1.inc

parameters
*check if the SAM table is balanced
samchk0(ac);
samchk0(acnt)=sum(acntp,SAM(acntp,acnt))-sum(acntp,SAM(acnt,acntp));
display samchk0,acnt,sam;
```

```
*Input parameter values given externally
parameter rhoAa(a)    /act1    0.2,    act2    0.4,    act3    0.5,    act4  0.1/
          rhoVA(a)    /act1    0.3,    act2    0.4,    act3    0.6,    act4  0.5/
          rhoCET(c)   /com1    1.4,    com2    1.4,    com3    2.0/
          rhoQq(c)    /com1    0.4,    com2    0.6,    com3    0.4/
          rhoac(c)    /com1    0.6,    com2    0.7,    com3    0.6/
          Frisch(h)   /hhr     -4,     hhu     -2/;

table     LESelas(c,h)       LES    elasticities
                         hhr         hhu
               com1      0.5         0.4
               com2      1.0         1.1
               com3      1.2         1.4 ;


parameters
scaleAa(a)      Scale factor of top level CES function of a
deltaAa(a)      Value-added share parameter in top level CES of a
scaleAVA(a)     Scale factor of value-added CES function of a
deltaVA(a)      Labor share parameter in value-added CES function of a
ica(c,a)        Input coefficient for intermediate inputs
oxac(a,c)       Output c per unit of activity a
scaleac(c)      Scale factor CES function from activity to c in QX block
deltaac(a,c)    Share parameter CES function from a to c in QX block
QX0(c)          Quantity of composite commodity c
PX0(c)          Price of of composite commodity c
QXAC0(a,c)      Quantity of commodity c from activity a
PXAC0(a,c)      Price of commodity c from activity a
scaleCET(c)     Scale factor of CET function
deltaCET(c)     Domestic sales share parameter in CET function
scaleQq(c)      Scale factor of Armington CES function
deltaQq(c)      Domestic product share parameter in Armington CES function
bgtshare(c,h)   Average budget share on c in the LES function of group h
bhtsharechk1(h) Check if average budget share sum is unity
LESbeta(c,h)    Marginal budget share of LES of group h
Lesbetachk1(h)  Check if the marginal budget share beta sum is 1
LESsub(c,h)     Subsistence consumption level of c of LES of group h
sharelh(h)      Share household group h in labor endowment
shareifhk(h)    Share household group h in capital income of enterprises
shareifentk     Share of capital income retained by enterprises
shareg(c)       Share of government income spending on c
tih(h)          Households income tax rate
tiEnt           Business income tax rate
tpayent(a)      Rate of the employment tax paid by enterprises
tsale(c)        Rate of sales tax
transferhg0(h)  Base amount of government transfer payment to households
eho(h)          Consumption function constant of group h
mpc(h)          marginal propensity to consume of group h
QCTT0(c)        Trade and transport margin input used in commodity c
```

```
QCTTA0            Sum of trade and transport margin inputs
ictt(c)           Proportion of trade transport input used in quantity of c
PA0(a)            Price of activity a
QA0(a)            Quantity of activity a
PVA0(a)           Price of aggregate value-added
QVA0(a)           Quantity of aggregate value-added
PINTA0(a)         Price of aggregate intermediate input
QINTA0(a)         Quantity of aggregate intermediate input
QINT0(c,a)        Quantity of intermediate input c used in production of a
QLD0(a)           Labor demand by a
QKD0(a)           Capital demand by a
WL0               Labor price
WK0               Capital price
PQ0(c)            Purchaser's price of commodity c
PQS0(c)           Supplier's price of commodity c
QQ0(c)            Total composite commodity supplied in domestic market
PM0(c)            Import price including tariff paid by domestic buyers
QM0(c)            Quantity of import c
PE0(c)            Export price
QE0(c)            Quantity of export c
PDC0(c)           Price of commodity c produced and supplied domestically
QDC0(c)           Quantity of commodity c produced and supplied domestically
EXR0              Exchange rate
pwm(c)            World price of import c in foreign currency
pwe(c)            World price of export c in foreign currency
tm(c)             Import tariff rate for c
QLSAGG0           Total labor supply
QKSAGG0           Total capital supply
QLS0(h)           Labor supply of group h
QKS0(h)           Capital supply of group h
YH0(h)            Household income of group h
EH0(h)            Total consumption expenditure of households of group h
QH0(c,h)          Quantity demanded for c by households of group h
YENT0             Enterprise income
QINV0(c)          Quantity of investment of c by enterprises
SAVEENT0          Enterprise savings
YG0               Government total revenue
EG0               Government total expenditure
QG0(c)            Quantity of government consumption of commodity c
SAVEH0(h)         Household savings of group h
SAVEG0            Net government savings or fiscal budget balance
SAVEF0            Foreign savings or balance of payment
cpiwt(c)          Consumer Price Index weight
CPI0              Consumer Price Index
apiwt(a)          Activity Price Index weight
API0              Activity Price Index
;
```

```
*Assignment and calibration for parameters
PA0(a)=1;
*Note how to calibrate the PQ price
PQ0(c)=(sam('total',c)-
sam(c,'row'))/(sum(a,sam(a,c))+sam('row',c)+sam('tariff',c)-sam(c,'row'));
WK0=1;
WL0=1;
EXR0=1;
QA0(a)=sam('total',a)/PA0(a);
QINT0(c,a)=SAM(c,a)/PQ0(c);
QINTA0(a)=SUM(c, QINT0(c,a));
ica(c,a)=QINT0(c,a)/QINTA0(a) ;
PINTA0(a)=SUM(c,ica(c,a)*PQ0(c));
QVA0(a)=SUM(f,sam(f,a));
PVA0(a)=(SUM(f,sam(f,a))+sam('emptx',a))/QVA0(a);
QLD0(a)=sam('lab',a)/WL0;
QKD0(a)=sam('cap',a)/WK0;
QLSAGG0=sam('total','lab')/WL0;
QKSAGG0=sam('total','cap')/WK0;
QLS0(h)=sam(h,'lab')/WL0;
QKS0(h)=sam(h,'cap')/WK0;
tpayent(a)=sam('emptx',a)/sam('lab',a);
deltaAa(a)=PVA0(a)*QVA0(a)**(1-rhoAa(a))/(PVA0(a)*QVA0(a)**(1-
rhoAa(a))+PINTA0(a)*QINTA0(a)**(1-rhoAa(a)));
scaleAa(a)=QA0(a)/(deltaAa(a)*QVA0(a)**rhoAa(a)+(1-
deltaAa(a))*QINTA0(a)**rhoAa(a))**(1/rhoAa(a));
deltaVA(a)=((1+tpayent(a))*WL0)*QLD0(a)**(1-rhoVA(a))/
(((1+tpayent(a))*WL0)*QLD0(a)**(1-rhoVA(a))+WK0*QKD0(a)**(1-rhoVA(a)));
scaleAVA(a)=QVA0(a)/(deltaVA(a)*QLD0(a)**rhoVA(a)+(1-
deltaVA(a))*QKD0(a)**rhoVA(a))**(1/rhoVA(a));
PXAC0(a,c)=1;
QXAC0(a,c)=sam(a,c)/PXAC0(a,c);
oxac(a,c)=QXAC0(a,c)/QA0(a);
PX0(c)=1;
QX0(c)=sum(a,sam(a,c))/PX0(c);
deltaac(a,c)=(PXAC0(a,c)*QXAC0(a,c)**(1-
rhoac(c)))/sum(ap,PXAC0(ap,c)*QXAC0(ap,c)**(1/rhoac(c)));
scaleac(c)=QX0(C)/(sum(a,deltaac(a,c)*QXAC0(a,c)**(rhoac(c))))**(1/rhoac(c));

PE0(c)=1;
pwe(c)=PE0(c)/EXR0;
QE0(c)=sam(c,'row')/PE0(c);
PM0(c)=1;
tm(c)$sam('row',c)=sam('tariff',c)/sam('row',c);
pwm(c)$sam('row',c)=PM0(c)/((1+tm(c))*EXR0);
QM0(c)=(sam('row',c)+sam('tariff',c))/PM0(c);
PDC0(c)=1;
*QDC is not explicitly shown in IFPRI SAM. It needs to be calibrated:
```

```
QDC0(c)=QX0(c)-QE0(c);
QQ0(c)=QDC0(c)+QM0(c);
PQS0(c)=1;
tsale(c)=sam('saletx',c)/(sum(a,sam(a,c))+sam('row',c)+sam('tariff',c)-
sam(c,'row')+sam('margin',c));
QCTT0(c)=sam('margin',c)/PQ0('com3');
ictt(c)=QCTT0(c)/QQ0(c);
QCTTA0=sum(c,QCTT0(c));
*CET function parameter calibration
deltaCET(c)=PDC0(c)*QDC0(c)**(1-rhoCET(c))/(PDC0(c)*QDC0(c)**(1-
rhoCET(c))+PE0(c)*QE0(c)**(1-rhoCET(c)));
scaleCET(c)=QX0(c)/(deltaCET(c)*QDC0(c)**rhoCET(c)+(1-
deltaCET(c))*QE0(c)**rhoCET(c))**(1/rhoCET(c));
*Arminton function parameter calibration
deltaQq(c)=PDC0(c)*QDC0(c)**(1-rhoQQ(c))/(PDC0(c)*QDC0(c)**(1-
rhoQq(c))+PM0(c)*QM0(c)**(1-rhoQq(c)));
scaleQQ(c)=QQ0(c)/(deltaQq(c)*QDC0(c)**rhoQq(c)+(1-
deltaQq(c))*QM0(c)**rhoQq(c))**(1/rhoQq(c));
*Calibration of other parameters
QH0(c,h)=SAM(c,h)/PQ0(c);
cpiwt(c)=QH0(c,'hhu')/sum(cp,QH0(cp,'hhu'));
CPI0=sum(c,PQ0(c)*cpiwt(c));
transferhg0(h)=sam(h,'gov')/cpi0;
sharelh(h)=(sam(h,'lab')/WL0)/QLSAGG0;
shareifhk(h)=(sam(h,'cap')/WK0)/QKSAGG0;
shareifentk=(sam('ent','cap')/WK0)/QKSAGG0;
YH0(h)=sharelh(h)*WL0*QLSAGG0+shareifhk(h)*WK0*QKSAGG0+transferhg0(h)*cpi0;
tih(h)=sam('gov',h)/YH0(h);
EH0(h)=sum(c,sam(c,h));
bgtshare(c,h)=SAM(c,h)/EH0(h);
bhtsharechk1(h)=sum(c,bgtshare(c,h));
LESbeta(c,h)=LESelas(c,h)*bgtshare(c,h)/(sum(cp,LESelas(cp,h)*bgtshare(cp,h)));
LESsub(c,h)=sam(c,h)/PQ0(c)+(LESbeta(c,h)/PQ0(c))*(EH0(h)/frisch(h));
LESbetachk1(h)=sum(c,LESbeta(c,h));
eho(h)=sum(c,PQ0(c)*LESsub(c,h))/cpi0;
mpc(h)=(EH0(h)-eho(h)*cpi0)/((1-tih(h))*YH0(h));

SAVEH0(h)=sam('invsav',h);
YENT0=shareifentk*WK0*QKSAGG0;
QINV0(c)=sam(c,'invsav')/PQ0(c);
tiEnt=sam('gov','ent')/YEnt0;
SAVEENT0=(1-tiEnt)*YENT0;
YG0=sum(h,tih(h)*YH0(h))+tiEnt*YENT0+sum(a,tpayent(a)*WL0*QLD0(a))+sum(c,sam('sale
tx',c))+sam('gov','tariff');
SAVEG0=sam('invsav','gov');
EG0=YG0-SAVEG0;
QG0(c)=sam(c,'gov')/PQ0(c);
shareg(c)=PQ0(c)*QG0(c)/(EG0-sum(h,transferhg0(h)*cpi0));
```

```
SAVEF0=sam('invsav','row');
apiwt(a)=QA0(a)/sum(ap,QA0(ap));
API0=sum(a,PA0(a)*apiwt(a));

display
ica,ictt,tsale,PA0,QA0,EG0,PX0,QX0,PXAC0,QXAC0,shareg,tpayent,bhtsharechk1,Lesbeta
chk1,YH0,
tih,EH0,eho,mpc,cpi0,WL0,WK0,PQ0,PINTA0,PVA0,QQ0,QINTA0,QVA0,PDC0,QDC0,QQ0,pwm,pwe,
QE0;

variable
PA(a),PVA(a),PINTA(a),QA(a),QVA(a),QINTA(a),QINT(c,a),QLD(a),QKD(a),QLSAGG,QKSAGG,
WL,WK,QX(c),PX(c),QXAC(a,c),PXAC(a,c),
PDC(c),QDC(c),PE(c),QE(c),EXR,QQ(c),PQS(c),PQ(c),PM(c),QM(c),QCTT(c),QCTTA,YH,EH,Q
H(c,h),SAVEH,YENT,
QINV(c),INVADJ,SAVEENT,YG,EG,QG(c),SAVEG,SAVEF,CPI,API,DUMMYSI;

Equation
*List equations by blocks
QAfn(a),QAFOCeq(a),PAeq(a),QVAfn(a),QVAFOC(a),PVAeq(a),QINTfn(c,a),PINTAeq(a),
OQAQXeq(a,c),OPAPXeq(a),IQAQXeq(c),PXACFOC(a,c),
CETfn(c),CETFOC(c),PCETeq(c),PEeq(c),
QQfn(c),QQfnNoImport(c),QQFOC(c),PQSPDCNoImportfn(c),PQSeq(c),PMeq(c),
QCTTeq,QCTTAeq,PQSPQeq(c),
Yheq(h),EHeq(h),QHeq(c,h),SAVEHeq(h),
YENTeq,QINVeq(c),SAVEENTeq,Ygeq,QGeq,SAVEGeq,ComEqui(c),Leq,Keq,FEXeq,CPIeq,APIeq,
SIeq;

*Production block
QAfn(a)..QA(a)=e=scaleAa(a)*(deltaAa(a)*QVA(a)**rhoAa(a)+(1-
deltaAa(a))*QINTA(a)**rhoAa(a))**(1/rhoAa(a));
QAFOCeq(a)..PVA(a)/PINTA(a)=e=(deltaAa(a)/(1-
deltaAa(a)))*(QVA(a)/QINTA(a))**(rhoAa(a)-1);
PAeq(a)..PA(a)*QA(a)=e=PVA(a)*QVA(a)+PINTA(a)*QINTA(a);
QVAfn(a)..QVA(a)=e=scaleAVA(a)*(deltaVA(a)*QLD(a)**rhoVA(a)+(1-
deltaVA(a))*QKD(a)**rhoVA(a))**(1/rhoVA(a));
QVAFOC(a)..((1+tpayent(a))*WL)/WK=e=(deltaVA(a)/(1-
deltaVA(a)))*(QLD(a)/QKD(a))**(rhoVA(a)-1);
PVAeq(a)..PVA(a)*QVA(a)=e=(1+tpayent(a))*WL*QLD(a)+WK*QKD(a);
QINTfn(c,a)..QINT(c,a)=e=ica(c,a)*QINTA(a);
PINTAeq(a)..PINTA(a)=e=SUM(c,ica(c,a)*PQ(c));

*QX block
OQAQXeq(a,c)$sam(a,c)..QXAC(a,c)=e=oxac(a,c)*QA(a);
OPAPXeq(a)..PA(a)=e=sum(c,PXAC(a,c)*oxac(a,c));
IQAQXeq(c)..QX(c)=e=scaleac(c)*sum(a,deltaac(a,c)*QXAC(a,c)**(rhoac(c)))**(1/rhoac
(c));
PXACFOC(a,c)$sam(a,c)..PXAC(a,c)=e=PX(c)*QX(c)*sum(ap,
```

```
deltaac(ap,c)*QXAC(ap,c)**(rhoac(c)))**(-1)*deltaac(a,c)*QXAC(a,c)**(rhoac(c)-1);
PXAC.fx(a,c)$(NOT sam(a,c))=1;

*CET block
CETfn(c)..QX(c)=e=scaleCET(c)*(deltaCET(c)*QDC(c)**rhoCET(c)+(1-
deltaCET(c))*QE(c)**rhoCET(c))**(1/rhoCET(c));
CETFOC(c)..PDC(c)/PE(c)=e=(deltaCET(c)/(1-
deltaCET(c)))*(QDC(c)/QE(c))**(rhoCET(c)-1);
PCETeq(c)..PX(c)*QX(c)=e=PDC(c)*QDC(c)+PE(c)*QE(c);
PEeq(c)..PE(c)=e=pwe(c)*EXR;

*Armington Block
QQfn(c)$sam('row',c)..QQ(c)=e=scaleQq(c)*(deltaQq(c)*QDC(c)**rhoQq(c)+(1-
deltaQq(c))*QM(c)**rhoQq(c))**(1/rhoQq(c));
QQfnNoImport(c)$(NOT sam('row',c))..QQ(c)=e=QDC(c);
QQFOC(c)$sam('row',c)..PDC(c)/PM(c)=e=(deltaQq(c)/(1-
deltaQq(c)))*(QDC(c)/QM(c))**(rhoQq(c)-1);
PQSPDCNoImportfn(c)$(sam('row',c)=0)..PQS(c)=e=PDC(c);
PQSeq(c)..PQS(c)*QQ(c)=e=PDC(c)*QDC(c)+PM(c)*QM(c);
PMeq(c)$sam('row',c)..PM(c)=e=pwm(c)*(1+tm(c))*EXR;
PM.fx(c)$(NOT sam('row',c))=1;

*trade and transport margins module
QCTTeq(c)..QCTT(c)=e=ictt(c)*QQ(c);
QCTTAeq..QCTTA=e=sum(c,QCTT(c));
PQSPQeq(c)..PQ(c)*QQ(c)=e=(1+tsale(c))*(PQS(c)*QQ(c)+QCTT(c)*PQ('com3'));

*Households
YHeq(h)..YH(h)=e=WL*sharelh(h)*QLSAGG+shareifhk(h)*WK*QKSAGG+transferhg0(h)*CPI;
EHeq(h)..EH(h)=e=eho(h)*cpi+mpc(h)*(1-tih(h))*YH(h);
QHeq(c,h)..PQ(c)*QH(c,h)=e=PQ(c)*LESsub(c,h)+LESbeta(c,h)*(EH(h)-
sum(cp,PQ(cp)*LESsub(cp,h)));
SAVEHeq(h)..SAVEH(h)=e=-eho(h)*cpi+(1-mpc(h))*(1-tih(h))*YH(h);

*Enterprises
YENTeq..YENT=e=shareifentk*WK*QKSAGG;
QINVeq(c)..QINV(c)=e=QINV0(c)*INVADJ;
SAVEENTeq..SAVEENT=e=(1-tiEnt)*YENT;

*Government
YGeq..YG=e=sum(a,tpayent(a)*WL*QLD(a))+sum(h,tih(h)*YH(h))+tiEnt*YENT+sum(c,tsale(
c)*(PQS(c)*QQ(c)+QCTT(c)*PQ('com3'))+tm(c)*pwm(c)*QM(c)*EXR);
SAVEGeq..EG=e=YG-SAVEG;
QGeq(c)..PQ(c)*QG(c)=e=shareg(c)*(EG-sum(h,transferhg0(h)*CPI));

*commodity and factor market clear equations
ComEqui(c)..QQ(c)=e=sum(a,QINT(c,a))+sum(h,QH(c,h))+QINV(c)+QG(c)+QCTTA$sam(c,
'margin');
```

```
Leq..Sum(a,QLD(a))=e=QLSAGG;
Keq..Sum(a,QKD(a))=e=QKSAGG;

*price indices
CPIeq..CPI=e=sum(c,PQ(c)*cpiwt(c));
APIeq..API=e=sum(a,PA(a)*apiwt(a));

FEXeq..SAVEF*EXR=e=sum(c,pwm(c)*QM(c)*EXR)-sum(c,pwe(c)*QE(c)*EXR);
SIeq..sum(c,PQ(c)*QINV(c))=e=sum(h,SAVEH(h))+SAVEENT+SAVEG+SAVEF*EXR+dummysi;

*Assigning initial values
PA.L(a)=PA0(a);PVA.L(a)=PVA0(a);PINTA.L(a)=PINTA0(a);QA.L(a)=QA0(a);
QVA.L(a)=QVA0(a);QINTA.L(a)=QINTA0(a);QINT.L(c,a)=QINT0(c,a);
QLD.L(a)=QLD0(a);QKD.L(a)=QKD0(a);QLSAGG.L=QLSAGG0;QKSAGG.L=QKSAGG0;
WL.L=WL0;WK.L=WK0;
PXAC.L(a,c)=PXAC0(a,c);QXAC.L(a,c)=QXAC0(a,c);QA.L(a)=QA0(a);PX.L(c)=PX0(c);
QX.L(c)=QX0(c);PDC.L(c)=1;QDC.L(c)=QDC0(c);PE.L(c)=1;QE.L(c)=QE0(c);EXR.L=1;
PQS.L(c)=1;PQ.L(c)=PQ0(c);QQ.L(c)=QQ0(c);PM.L(c)=PM0(c);QM.L(c)=QM0(c);
QCTT.L(c)=QCTT0(c);QCTTA.L=QCTTA0;
YH.L(h)=YH0(h);EH.L(h)=EH0(h);QH.L(c,h)=QH0(c,h);SAVEH.L(h)=SAVEH0(h);
YENT.L=YENT0;QINV.L(c)=QINV0(c);INVADJ.L=1;SAVEENT.L=SAVEENT0;YG.L=YG0;
EG.L=EG0;QG.L(c)=QG0(c);SAVEG.L=SAVEG0;SAVEF.L=SAVEF0;CPI.L=CPI0;
API.L=API0;DUMMYSI.L=0;

*Fix five variable values to make the system square. API is numeraire
*Using the government spending closure so EG is a variable
QLSAGG.fx=QLSAGG0;
QKSAGG.fx=QKSAGG0;
INVADJ.fx=1;
EXR.fx=EXR0;
API.fx=1;

parameter
scaleaa0(a),QXACchange(a,c),QLDchange(a),QKDchange(a);
scaleaa0(a)=scaleaa(a);

*Executing the model
model cge /all/;
solve cge using mcp;

display scaleaa0;

*Simulation to increase efficiency factor TFP in the private sector
scaleaa('act3')=scaleaa0('act3')*1.3;

model sim /all/;
solve sim using mcp;
```

```
QXACchange(a,c)$(sam(a,c))=QXAC.L(a,c)/QXAC0(a,c)-1;
QLDchange(a)=QLD.L(a)/QLD0(a)-1;
QKDchange(a)=QKD.L(a)/QKD0(a)-1;

Display QXACchange,QLDchange,QKDchange;

*END
```

Exercises

16E.1 Based on the data of Table 16.2.1, revise the subprogram of Example 16.4.1 for the QX block. The relationship from multiple activities to a composite commodity QX is in fixed proportions, rather than in a CES function. The relationships from one activity to multiple commodities are still in fixed proportions as in Example 16.4.1. Test the subprogram.

16E.2 Based on the data of Table 16.2.1, write a subprogram for the QX block, the relationship from an activity QA to multiple commodities $QXAC$ is a CET function with multiple outputs. That is:

$$QA_a = \alpha_a^{axc} \left(\sum_c \delta_{ac}^{axc} \cdot QXAC_{ac}^{\rho_a^{axc}} \right)^{1/\rho_a^{axc}} \qquad a \in A \qquad (16E.2.1)$$

The exponent ρ_a^{axc} is 1.3 for all sectors. You may review Chapter 8.6 to choose an equation system with its first-order condition for the module. The relationship from multiple activities to one composite commodity QX is still a CES function as in Example 16.4.1. Test the subprogram.

16E.3 We need to construct a CGE model for the fossil energy in the economy. The production block has the following flow chart, which is in a three-level nested structure. The corresponding part of the SAM table is Table 16E.3.1. The intermediate input module is of the Leontief functions. All other modules are of the CES functions. The information about parameters is provided in Table 16E.3.2. Write a subprogram for this block and test the subprogram.

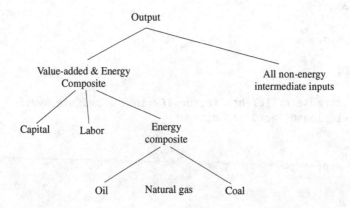

Table 16E.3.1.   The production block of a model economy.

	Act1	Act2	Act3
Com1 (Agriculture)	350	400	250
Com2 (Industry)	300	700	300
Com3 (Service)	220	440	240
Lab (labor)	650	700	500
Cap (Capital)	350	900	470
Oil	60	100	40
Coal	50	120	20
Natural gas (Gas)	50	80	60
Household(HH)			
Ent (Enterprises)			
Gov (Government)			
VAT labor (VATL)	80	100	60
ROW (Rest of the World)			
Invsav (Savings–Investment)			
Total	2110	3540	1940

Table 16E.3.2.   Parameter values.

	Act 1	Act 2	Act 3
Top activity level CES ρ	0.2	0.5	0.1
2nd level value-added CES ρ	0.3	0.6	0.5
3rd level energy-composite ρ	0.8	0.8	0.7

Chapter 17

Assessing Outcomes and Refining the Model

17.1 Refining and Revising CGE Models

After constructing a CGE model and running the GAMS program to simulate external policy shocks, we need to review and analyze the results. If the simulation results are not consistent with our expectations, we need to investigate. In many cases, the inconsistencies are caused by technical errors in the model and GAMS program, then we need to debug and fix the problems. In some cases, the results finally turn out to be legitimate — they initially look counter-intuitive but are theoretically right. These are the surprises which can be academically interesting and have important policy implications. In other cases, the inconsistencies are more serious. They are caused by the problems in the model structure and closures. In these cases, we need to refine, revise or even reconstruct the CGE model.

Take the example of Openland2 in Chapter 15. Suppose the government plans to cut the non-deductible VAT rate on labor employment of enterprises in order to stimulate economy and the labor employment. We simulate this policy shock by cutting VAT rate *tvatl* from 10% to 5% in the GAMS program of Example 15.7.1. Our expectation is activity outputs QA and commodity amount QQ would increase as results. Surprisingly, there are little changes in the real outputs (Table 17.1.1).

A further examination of the model has found that, because labor price WL is flexible, the cut in VAT is entirely offset by an increase in labor price WL. After the VAT rate cut, the new labor price increases from 1 to 1.048. The labor unit cost including VAT actually remains the same. It can be seen as follows. The VAT rate now is 1.05 after the tax cut. The unit labor cost including VAT to the enterprise is $1.048 \times 1.05 = 1.1$. This is exactly the original unit labor cost including the old tax rate $1 \times 1.1 = 1.1$. Hence, the government's tax-cut policy has little impacts on labor employment and activity outputs. The only real effects by this tax-cut policy is that the government revenue has decreased by 6.7% (Table 17.1.2). To conclude, the model is right and the simulation results imply that the policy is not effective in stimulating outputs.

In other cases, we may encounter serious problems. One common problem is caused by changing an endogenous variable to an exogenous variable for research purposes. This seems to be a simple job, but in fact it can involve a substantial work to modify the closure or even to revise the entire model. Take an example. Suppose in the previous CGE models,

Table 17.1.1.   After cutting the VAT rate on labor input from 10% to 5% in Openland2.

	Activity output QA			Total commodity amount QQ		
	Agriculture	Industry	Service	Agriculture	Industry	Service
% changes	-0.2%	0	$+0.2\%$	-0.2%	0	$+0.2\%$

Table 17.1.2.   After cutting VAT rate on labor input from 10% to 5% in Openland2.

	Labor QLS	Capital QKS	Labor price WL	Government revenue YG
Level	2040	2025	1.048	1202
% changes	0	0	$+4.8\%$	-6.7%

the government now plans to control the price of the agricultural commodity, and further, to lower the price ceiling below the base state equilibrium level. To simulate this situation, our first thought is to fix the price of the agricultural commodity. Thus, the number of variables is reduced by one. Then we need to delete one equation in the system in order to meet the squareness requirement. Which equation should be deleted and is it theoretically justified? We may think that we can delete the market clearing equation of the agricultural sector. While mathematically it seems to work, actually the CGE model does not converge to a new equilibrium. The dummy variable reports a number far from zero.

In CGE modeling, one should be very cautious about deleting an equation in the system, unless it is allowable as an option in the predesigned closure. In Section 3.4, we discuss the problem of changing an endogenous price variable to a parameter in an input–output model. Similar difficulties would present in the CGE model if we convert an endogenous price to an exogenous variable. If we fix an endogenous commodity price at an arbitrary level out of the original equilibrium, the model needs to provide a mechanism to address the resulting shortage/surplus in the commodity market and spillover effects in other markets. If we convert a quantity variable to a parameter in a CGE model, we may need to modify the institutional behavior functions, for instance, to derive a commodity demand function of households under quantitative constraints. Consequently, we may have to change the structure of the model with the new behavior functions. The economics theory for this subject is called "general disequilibrium" or "general non-Walrasian equilibrium". Interested readers are referred to Chang (1993) and similar studies in this subject.

17.2 Factor Supply Functions and Flexible Factor Supply Closure

The problem why the cut in the VAT rate in the above Openland2 case has little impact on the activity outputs is due to the flexible factor price and fixed factor supply at full employment. Using the labor supply as a representative factor, Figure 17.2.1 depicts various factor supply functions. The assumption of fixed factor supply at full employment implies that the labor supply curve is L_1, a vertical line at the labor endowment L^*.

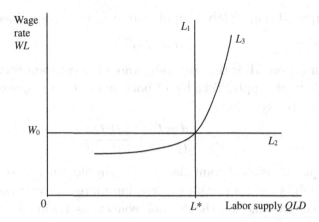

Figure 17.2.1. Different labor supply functions.

Table 17.2.1. Cutting VAT on labor employment in Openland2 with the Keynesian closure.

	Labor quantity QLS	Capital quantity QKS	Activity outputs QA			Gov't YG
			Agriculture	Industry	Service	
% changes	+7.7%	+0.5%	+3.9%	+4.6%	+4%	−5.7%

Suppose we believe the setup of full employment of factors is not a reasonable description for the current economic environment. In particular, we consider that the current economy is in severe economic recession. To simulate this situation, we use the Keynesian closure, in which the labor supply curve is horizontal as L_2 at the current wage rate W_0. Following the instruction in Section 15.8, we change the model of Openland2 to the Keynesian closure and revise the GAMS program of Example 15.7.1 accordingly. In the Keynesian closure, the prices of labor and capital are fixed, but their quantities are variables to be determined endogenously by the aggregate demand. Let the VAT rate on labor employment *tvatl* decreases from 10% to 5%, the simulation results under the Keynesian closure are in Table 17.2.1.

Labor supply increases substantially because the quantity supplied is sensitive to the price change in the case of a horizontal labor supply curve. As a result, the activity outputs also increase noticeably. This reveals that, if the factor supply curves are horizontal, the stimulus policy by cutting the VAT rate is effective, even though the government spending EG remains the same.

So far in our CGE models, the factor supplies either are fixed at the full employment levels, which imply vertical supply curves, or are set at the fixed prices in the Keynesian closure, which imply horizontal supply curves. These are extreme cases. Most of the time, however, the factor supply curves are upward sloping like L_3 in Figure 17.2.1. An increase in the factor price would induce more quantity supplied of that factor, but to some limits.

For instance, the upward sloping labor supply curve L_3 can be specified by a power function

$$L = \lambda W^\varepsilon \qquad (17.2.1)$$

where L is the labor supply, W is the wage rate, and λ is a constant coefficient. The exponent ε is the price elasticity of supply. Take log of both sides of the above equation, differentiate and rearrange, it can be seen that:

$$\varepsilon = \frac{d\ln L}{d\ln W} = \frac{dL/L}{dW/W} \qquad (17.2.2)$$

So the power equation is a constant elasticity of supply function of labor. In general, the supply function exhibits the property of increasing marginal cost; therefore, it is concave. The inverse labor supply function should look convex, as L3 in Figure 17.2.1. This means that elasticity ε becomes increasingly smaller as L approaches the full employment, i.e., raising the wage rate would induce more labor supply from workers but at a diminishing rate.

Using the CGE model notation, the labor supply equation of 17.2.1 is expressed as

$$QLS = LSscale^* \, WL^{**} \, LSelas \qquad (17.2.3)$$

where $LSscale$ and $LSelas$ refer to λ and ε, respectively. To revise the previous CGE models accordingly, we can use the above labor supply function to replace the fixed price or fixed labor supply function. That is, replacing $WL.fx = WL0$ or $QLS = QLS0$ (labor endowment) with $QLS = LSscale^* \, WL^{**} \, LSelas$ in the previous models.

Similarly, let us assume capital supply is also flexible with respect to capital price changes. An increase in capital price WK would attract more capital supply QKS, possibly from foreign direct investment. The capital supply function is

$$QKS = KSscale^* \, WK^{**} \, KSelas \qquad (17.2.4)$$

We can use this capital supply function to replace the constraints of fixed WK price or fixed capital supply in the previous models.

Below are the new codes to be added to the GAMS program to modify the Openland2 model with the flexible supply functions. The values of price elasticities of supply $KSelas$ (=0.4) and $LSeals$ (=0.2) are obtained externally from hypothetical data sources. The GAMS codes for parameter calibration are

```
KSelas=0.4;
KSscale=(sam('cap','total')/WK0)/(WK0**KSelas);
LSelas=0.2;
LSscale=(sam('lab','total')/WL0)/(WL0**LSelas);
```

The GAMS codes for the system equations are

```
Leq.. Sum(a,QLD(a))=e=QLS;
Lsupply.. QLS=e=LSscale*WL**LSelas;
Keq.. Sum(a,QKD(a))=e=QKS;
Ksupply.. QKS=e=KSscale*WK**KSelas;
```

Table 17.2.2. Cutting VAT on labor in Openland 2 with flexible factor supply functions.

	Labor quantity QLS	Capital quantity QKS	Activity outputs QA			Gov't YG
			Agriculture	Industry	Service	
% changes	+0.9%	+0.1%	+0.3%	+0.5%	+0.7%	−6.3%

After the flexible labor and capital supply functions are included in the model, we only need three constraints to meet the squareness condition. Let private investment be exogenously determined, and the government spending EG be a variable, and API serve as the numeraire, together with a fixed exchange rate regime; hence, the three constraints for the model are

```
INVADJ.fx=1;
EXR.fx=EXR0;
API.fx=1;
```

After the model is so modified, we run the model to simulate cutting the VAT rate to 5%. The simulation results are in Table 17.2.2. Comparing the results with those from the full employment closure and Keynesian closure, it can be seen that quantities of total labor and capital supplies, as well as activity outputs, have increased, but the magnitudes of increases are smaller than those in the Keynesian closure.

By replacing the fixed factor supplies or fixed fact prices with the flexible factor supply functions in the production block in CGE models, the new closure is different from either the full employment closure or the Keynesian closure in previous models. We may name the new closure with factor supply functions as "the flexible factor supply closure". The above closure setting with two constraints of private investment and the exchange rate regime can be changed if needed. For instance, we may let the government spending EG or fiscal balance $SAVEG$ be fixed, but private investment $INVADJ$ be variables in the closure setting, if this setup is more suitable for the external economic environment.

17.3 Sensitivity and Robustness Tests

After finding the simulation results are consistent with expectations, we would like to know how reliable these numbers are. In regression models, we run tests from a large size sample data to construct confidence levels for estimates and draw statistical inferences. For CGE models, we do not have the luxury to have enough observations and degrees of freedom to conduct statistical tests for the variables or simulation results. Often, there is only one observation for an entry value in the SAM table. Noises can contaminate the original data and the borrowed elasticity values, errors are likely to occur in balancing the SAM table, etc. In addition, assumptions and function specifications in the model may be inaccurate and subject to uncertainties.

Table 17.3.1. Simulation results of cutting the VAT rate on labor from 10% to 5%.

Percentage changes in	Fixed supply L_1 ($\varepsilon_L = 0$, $\varepsilon_K = 0$), %	Flexible function L_3 ($\varepsilon_L = 0.2$, $\varepsilon_K = 0.4$), %	Fixed labor price L_2 ($\varepsilon_L = \infty$, $\varepsilon_K = \infty$), %
Labor price WL	+4.8	+4.5	0
Capital price WK	0	+0.3	0
Labor supply QLS	0	+0.9	+7.7
Capital supply QKS	0	+0.1	0.5
Activity agriculture QA_1	−0.2	+0.3	+3.9
Activity industry QA_2	0	+0.5	+4.6
Activity service QA_3	+0.2	+0.7	+4.0
Government revenue YG	−6.7	−6.3	−5.7

To deal with these issues, we conduct sensitivity tests for the major simulation results related to the research interests. One simple approach called one-factor-at-a-time (OAT) works as follows. First, perturbing the value of a key parameter while holding other parameters and exogenous variables constant, then check how the simulation results change. Next do the same for another key parameter, and, so on. If the simulation results do not change substantially by perturbing the parameter values, these results are robust. We are more confident about the simulation results and the predictions from the model. If a minor perturbation causes substantial changes in simulation results or even switching their signs, it means the simulation results are very sensitive to the parameter errors. Accordingly, we have less confidence in the simulation results.

Take the example of cutting the VAT rate in Openland2 in Section 17.2. The objectives of the policy are to increase labor employment and outputs. The initial simulation work reveals that the factor price elasticity of supply ε would affect the simulation results. We have tested three cases covering the range of ε: the fixed supply (perfectly inelastic supply) case, the perfectly elastic supply with the fixed labor price case, and a flexible supply case. Table 17.3.1 lists the simulation results in the three cases for easy comparison. Price elasticities of labor supply and capital supply are denoted by ε_L and ε_K, respectively.

After inspecting the simulation results in Table 17.3.1, we conclude the increase in labor employment and the decrease in the government revenue are robust in a large range of possible values for the elasticity parameters. The increases in activity outputs range from −0.2% to 4.6% in various sectors by the VAT cut, which means they are not robust.

The robustness test in Table 17.3.1 is inefficient because the tested elasticity values ε_L and ε_K range from 0 to infinity. Both extreme cases of perfectly elastic and perfectly inelastic supplies of factors are very rare. Usually, we have some information which can be utilized to narrow down the ranges of the possible values of the parameters. For instance, the researchers may have a pretty good knowledge about the current economic environment by examining the macroeconomic indicators and about the shapes of the factor supply curves from other empirical studies. The more efficient method is perturbing the parameter values

Table 17.3.2. Simulation results of cutting the VAT rate on labor from 10% to 5% ($\varepsilon_L = 0.2$).

Percentage changes in	$\varepsilon_K = 0.2$ (%)	$\varepsilon_K = 0.3$ (%)	$\varepsilon_K = 0.4$ (%)	$\varepsilon_K = 0.6$ (%)	$\varepsilon_K = 0.8$ (%)
Labor price WL	+4.5	+4.5	+4.5	+4.5	+4.5
Capital price WK	+0.3	+0.3	+0.3	+0.3	+0.2
Labor supply QLS	+0.9	+0.9	+0.9	+0.9	+0.9
Capital supply QKS	0	0	+0.1	+0.2	+0.2
Activity agriculture QA_1	+0.3	+0.3	+0.3	+0.3	+0.3
Activity industry QA_2	+0.5	+0.5	+0.5	+0.5	+0.5
Activity service QA_3	+0.7	+0.7	+0.7	+0.8	+0.8
Government revenue YG	−6.3	−6.3	−6.3	−6.2	−6.2

Table 17.3.3. Simulation results of cutting the VAT rate on labor from 10% to 5% ($\varepsilon_K = 0.4$).

Percentage changes in	$\varepsilon_L = 0.1$ (%)	$\varepsilon_L = 0.15$ (%)	$\varepsilon_L = 0.2$ (%)	$\varepsilon_L = 0.3$ (%)	$\varepsilon_L = 0.5$ (%)
Labor price WL	+4.6	+4.6	+4.5	+4.4	+4.2
Capital price WK	+0.1	+0.2	+0.3	+0.2	+0.6
Labor supply QLS	+0.5	+0.7	+0.9	+1.3	+2.1
Capital supply QKS	0	0	+0.1	+0.2	+0.3
Activity agriculture QA_1	0	+0.2	+0.3	+0.5	+0.9
Activity industry QA_2	+0.2	+0.4	+0.5	+0.7	+1.2
Activity service QA_3	+0.5	+0.6	+0.7	+1.0	+1.5
Government revenue YG	−6.5	−6.4	−6.3	−6.0	−5.6

in the neighborhood of the initial estimates. Suppose the initial estimates find $\varepsilon_L = 0.2$ and $\varepsilon_K = 0.4$. We start perturbing from these values by using the OAT method.

First, we only perturb ε_K around 0.4 but hold $\varepsilon_L = 0.2$ and other parameters constant. The results are shown in Table 17.3.2. It can be seen that the simulation results are very stable and insensitive to the elasticity of capital supply ε_K.

Next, we hold $\varepsilon_K = 0.4$ constant but perturb ε_L around 0.2. The results are shown in Table 17.3.3. It can be seen that the simulation results are more sensitive to the price elasticity of labor supply ε_L, although the directions of changes are consistent.

By looking at the initial simulation results, suppose we are satisfied with the range of perturbation of the parameter values, we can draw the conclusion as follows: Summarizing the above simulation results from the robustness and sensitivity tests, the policy of cutting the VAT rate to 5% would stimulate the labor employment and product outputs. The effectiveness of the policy mainly depends on the elasticity of labor supply, while other parameters have limited or moderate influences. It is predicted that the labor employment would increase by 0.5–2.1%, the activity outputs increase by 0.5–1.5%, 0.2–1.2%, and 0–0.9% in agriculture, industry and service sectors, respectively. The government revenue would fall by 5.6–6.5%.

The above OAT method is simple and straightforward. Other more sophisticated and systematic techniques such as Monte Carlo filtering are used to test sensitivity and robustness of the CGE model parameters and outcomes. Readers can search google to find the literature on these techniques. Readers who are interested in the Monte Carlo technique may find a list of references and some reviews in Sebastien *et al.* (2013).

17.4 Policy Evaluation: Impacts on Household Welfare

The robustness and sensitivity tests assess the reliability of the simulation results in a technical perspective. Researchers would like to further evaluate the simulation results in the perspective of their merits. What are the benefits and costs of the policy change we can conclude from the simulation results? There are no perfect policies in the real world. A policy change is often mixed with positive and negative effects on various institutions in the economy and the society. For instance, in the example of cutting the VAT rate in the previous section, while the labor employment and activity outputs have increased, the government revenue and fiscal balance have deteriorated. The net benefit or cost of a policy often depends on the preferences and weights assigned by the decision makers. For a research project, what is important is to objectively present and analyze impacts of alternative policies on the economy and society, by quantifiable indicators if possible, to the final decision making body.

To evaluate a public policy, one important indicator often used is the resulting changes in social welfare. Will this policy improve or deteriorate welfare? And, by how much? Because households are the major and fundamentally important institution of the economy, the welfare impact on households is mostly important. In CGE models, we can evaluate the welfare changes of households by estimating the changes in the household utility. Suppose the household utility function is $u(\mathbf{QH})$, where $\mathbf{QH}$ is the vector of the household consumption. Let the initial consumption bundle be $\mathbf{QH0}$, the consumption bundle after the policy change be $\mathbf{QH1}$, then the change in the household welfare is $u(\mathbf{QH1})$-$u(\mathbf{QH0})$.

The unit of the utility function $u(..)$ is util, which lacks a physically measurable standard. In practice, economists use a monetary unit such as dollar to measure the change in utility. The corresponding utility function is called the "money metric utility function". The household utility change of $u(\mathbf{QH1}) - u(\mathbf{QH0})$ can be measured as the implicit change in the monetary income. That is, after the policy change, how much monetary income should the government compensate to or take away from households, so the welfare level of households is restored to the pre-policy-change level?

This idea leads to two important indicators in welfare economics: equivalent variation (EV) and compensating variation (CV). The concepts are illustrated in Figure 17.4.1.

There are two commodities in the economy: q1 and q2. Initially before the policy change, household income is YH0, the commodity price vector is $\mathbf{P0}$, and the consumption bundle is $\mathbf{QH0}$. The utility/welfare level reached by households is represented by the indifference

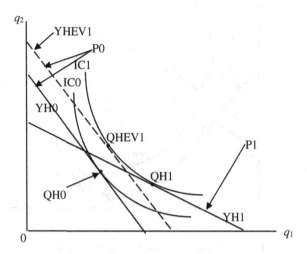

Figure 17.4.1. Equivalent variation (EV).

curve IC0. After the policy change, the price vector is **P1**, household income is YH1, and the consumption bundle is **QH1**. The utility/welfare level reached by households is IC1. In the post-policy-change state, suppose the price is still **P0**, in order to maintain utility level **QH1**, the consumption bundle should be at **QHEV1**. The minimum expenditure to reach **QHEV1** at price vector **P0** is the dashed line YHEV1. The income change from YH0 to YHEV1 measures the utility/welfare change of the households in monetary unit or in dollars. The income change is called "equivalent variation (EV)". The mathematical expression is

$$EV = e(\mathbf{P0}, u(\mathbf{QH1})) - e(\mathbf{P0}, u(\mathbf{QH0})) \tag{17.4.1}$$

where $e(\mathbf{P}, u)$ is the expenditure function in microeconomics.

Similarly, if money metric utility change is measured by the post-policy-change price **P1**, it is called "compensating variation (CV)". The mathematical expression is

$$CV = e(\mathbf{P1}, u(\mathbf{QH1})) - e(\mathbf{P1}, u(\mathbf{QH0})) \tag{17.4.2}$$

Intuitively, CV says that at the new price vector, how much income should be compensated to (or taken away from) the consumers so they are just as well as before. Figure 17.4.2 illustrates the concept of CV.

In Figure 17.4.2, at the post-policy-change price **P1**, to reach the initial utility level IC0, the consumption bundle chosen is **QHCV**. The corresponding minimum income is the dashed line YHCV0. The income difference between YH1 and YHCV0 is compensating variation.

If the household utility function is Cobb–Douglas, EV and CV can be calibrated as follows. First, we calibrate the share spending on commodity c in the budget of household group h, denoted by $shareh(c, h)$. $shareh(c, h)$ is the exponent for commodity c in the Cobb–Douglas utility function for household group h. That is,

$$UHH_{c,h} = \prod_c QH_{c,h}^{shareh_{c,h}} \qquad \sum_c shareh(c, h) = 1 \tag{17.4.3}$$

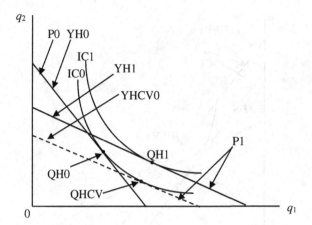

Figure 17.4.2.   Compensating variation (CV).

Take the example of SAM Table 16.5.2. It can be calibrated that the spending shares in budget EH by rural households' are 0.25, 0.5625 and 0.1875, respectively. Hence, the utility function of rural households is

$$UHH_{hhr} = QH_1^{0.25} \cdot QH_2^{0.5625} \cdot QH_3^{0.1875} \tag{17.4.4}$$

Similarly, the utility function of urban households is

$$UHH_{hhu} = QH_1^{0.2296} \cdot QH_2^{0.5255} \cdot QH_3^{0.2449} \tag{17.4.5}$$

For simplicity, we omit the group index h below. From the technique explained in Chapter 9, the expenditure function of a Cobb–Douglas utility function is

$$e(\mathbf{p}, u(\mathbf{QH})) = u(\mathbf{QH}) \cdot \prod_c \left(\frac{p_c}{shareh_c} \right)^{shareh_c} \tag{17.4.6}$$

When the utility level is $u(\mathbf{QH})$, the above function is the money metric utility function. EV is calculated at the initial price level, $\mathbf{p} = \mathbf{P0}$:

$$EV = e(\mathbf{P0}, u(\mathbf{QH1})) - e(\mathbf{P0}, u(\mathbf{QH0}))$$

$$= u(\mathbf{QH1}) \cdot \prod_c \left(\frac{p_c^0}{shareh_c} \right)^{shareh_c} - u(\mathbf{QH0}) \cdot \prod_c \left(\frac{p_c^0}{shareh_c} \right)^{shareh_c}$$

$$= [u(\mathbf{QH1}) - u(\mathbf{QH0})] \cdot \prod_c \left(\frac{p_c^0}{shareh_c} \right)^{shareh_c} \tag{17.4.7}$$

CV is calculated by using the post-policy-change price $\mathbf{p} = \mathbf{P1}$:

$$CV = e(\mathbf{P1}, u(\mathbf{QH1})) - e(\mathbf{P1}, u(\mathbf{QH0}))$$

$$= [u(\mathbf{QH1}) - u(\mathbf{QH0})] \cdot \prod_c \left(\frac{p_c^1}{shareh_c} \right)^{shareh_c} \tag{17.4.8}$$

Example 17.4.1 In the economy of Openland in Chapter 14, the households have a Cobb–Douglas utility function. Modify the GAMS program of Example 14.8.1 by changing the fixed factor supplies to the flexible factor supply functions with elasticities of supply $\varepsilon_L = 0.2$ and $\varepsilon_K = 0.4$. Private investment is variable, but the government expenditure EG is fixed. Suppose the government cuts the payroll tax rate from 10% to 5%. Evaluate the welfare impacts on households by the indicators of EV and CV. What is the cost side of this payroll tax cut?

Solution: The model in Chapter 14 has a Cobb–Douglas utility function for households. The GAMS program is revised to the flexible factor supply closure similar to that in Section 17.2. According to the requirements of the question, the three constraints are `EXR.fx=EXR0`, `PPI.fx=PPI0`, and `EG.fx=EG0`. The policy change is to cut the payroll tax rate from 10% to 5% instead of cutting the VAT tax rate in the example in Section 17.2. The following GAMS codes for estimating EV and CV can be pasted after the statement for executing the simulation model `"solve sim using mcp"` in the GAMS program of Example 14.8.1:

```
parameter
utility0,utility1,EV,CV;
utility0= PROD(c,QH0(c)**shareh(c));
utility1= PROD(c,QH.L(c)**shareh(c));
EV=(utility1-utility0)*PROD(c,(PQ0(c)/shareh(c))**(shareh(c)));
CV=(utility1-utility0)*PROD(c,(PQ.L(c)/shareh(c))**(shareh(c)));
```

The report generated from the GAMS program is duplicated here and is self-explaining. The welfare gain measured by EV and CV for households are 114.921 and 114.922 (in the currency unit of the SAM table), respectively. These are the income gains by households from the tax cut. Labor supply increases by 1.7%, which contributes to the increase of the total activity outputs.

The cost side to the economy and society is the fall in the government revenue YG by 9.3%. Because the government's monetary spending EG is held constant, QG has no changes. The fiscal budget deficit has increased by 79.454 (in the currency unit). The private investment falls substantially by 12.8% in all sectors. We can conclude that the increases in household income has crowed out the private investment and government revenue. This may adversely impact on the future economic growth. The net gain would be determined by the weights assigned to the gains and costs.

```
------      470 PARAMETER QAchange
act1 0.006,     act2 0.009,     act3 0.013
------      470 PARAMETER QQchange
com1 0.006,     com2 0.009,     com3 0.013
------      470 PARAMETER QHchange
com1 0.034,     com2 0.032,     com3 0.033
------      470 PARAMETER QINVchange
com1 −0.128,    com2 −0.128,    com3 −0.128
```

```
——        470 PARAMETER QLSchange              =          0.017
              PARAMETER QKSchange              =          0.001
              PARAMETER YGchange               =         -0.093
              PARAMETER SAVEGchange            =        -79.454
              VARIABLE WL.L                    =          1.042
              VARIABLE WK.L                    =          1.006
              PARAMETER utility0               =       1160.139
              PARAMETER utility1               =       1198.319
              PARAMETER EV                     =        114.921
              PARAMETER CV                     =        114.922
```

Example 17.4.2 In the IFPRI model for Transland in Chapter 16.5, there are two household groups. Each has an LES demand function, which implies the household group has a Stone–Geary utility function. Revise the CGE model of Example 16.5.1 by changing fixed factor supplies to the flexible factor supply functions with elasticities of supply $\varepsilon_L = 0.2$ and $\varepsilon_K = 0.4$. *EG* is fixed and private investment is variable. Suppose that the government cuts the employment tax rate to one half. Estimate the resulting welfare changes of urban and rural household groups by the CV and EV indicators. Also evaluate the cost side.

Solution: The original form of the Stone–Geary utility function is

$$u(\mathbf{q}) = \prod_{i=1}^{n} (q_i - \gamma_i)^{\beta_i} \qquad \sum_{i=1}^{n} \beta_i = 1 \qquad (17.4.9)$$

The expenditure function is

$$e(\mathbf{p}, u) = \sum_{i}^{n} p_i \gamma_i + u \prod_{j=1}^{n} \left(\frac{p_j}{\beta_j} \right)^{\beta_j} \qquad \sum_{i=1}^{n} \beta_i = 1 \qquad (17.4.10)$$

The EV and CV are as follows:

$$EV = e(\mathbf{P0}, u(\mathbf{QH1})) - e(\mathbf{P0}, u(\mathbf{QH0}))$$

$$= \sum_{i}^{n} p_i^0 \gamma_i + u(\mathbf{QH1}) \prod_{j=1}^{n} \left(\frac{p_j^0}{\beta_j} \right)^{\beta_j} - \sum_{i}^{n} p_i^0 \gamma_i - u(\mathbf{QH0}) \prod_{j=1}^{n} \left(\frac{p_j^0}{\beta_j} \right)^{\beta_j}$$

$$= [u(\mathbf{QH1}) - u(\mathbf{QH0})] \cdot \prod_{j=1}^{n} \left(\frac{p_j^0}{\beta_j} \right)^{\beta_j} \qquad (17.4.11)$$

$$CV = e(\mathbf{P1}, u(\mathbf{QH1})) - e(\mathbf{P1}, u(\mathbf{QH0}))$$

$$= [u(\mathbf{QH1}) - u(\mathbf{QH0})] \cdot \prod_{j=1}^{n} \left(\frac{p_j^1}{\beta_j} \right)^{\beta_j} \qquad (17.4.12)$$

The GAMS codes for calculating EV and CV of the Stone–Geary utility function are as follows. The codes can be pasted directly after the command for executing the simulation model. Differing from the previous example, the codes are for multiple household groups and are for the Stone–Geary utility and LES demand functions.

```
utility0(h)= PROD(c,(QH0(c,h)-LESsub(c,h))**LESbeta(c,h));
utility1(h)= PROD(c,(QH.L(c,h)-LESsub(c,h))**LESbeta(c,h));
EV(h)=(utility1(h)-
utility0(h))*PROD(c,(PQ0(c)/LESbeta(c,h))**(LESbeta(c,h)));
CV(h)=(utility1(h)-
utility0(h))*PROD(c,(PQ.L(c)/LESbeta(c,h))**(LESbeta(c,h)));
```

The report generated by the GAMS program is duplicated here and is self-explaining. The estimated welfare improvement measured by EV and CV for rural households are 12.611 and 12.613 while that for urban households are 31.533 and 31.540 (in the currency unit of the SAM table), respectively. These are the income gains by households from the tax cut. The cost side to the economy and society is the fall in the government revenue YG by 6.8%. As the government's monetary spending EG is held constant, the fiscal budget deficit increases by 99.0 (in the currency unit). The private investment falls by 2.2%. The increase in consumption by households from the tax cut are offset by the decreases in private investment and government revenue, which implies negative impacts on public goods and long-run economic growth. The net gain or loss would depend on the weights assigned to these benefits and costs.

```
——      522 PARAMETER QQchange
      com1 0.005,     com2 0.007,    com3 0.009
——      522 PARAMETER QHchange
                  hhr          hhu
      com1        0.004        0.007
      com2        0.009        0.017
      com3        0.010        0.022
——      522 PARAMETER QINVchange
      com1 −0.022,     com2 −0.022,    com3 −0.022
——      522 PARAMETER utility0
      hhr 145.218,     hhu 359.936
——      522 PARAMETER utility1
      hhr 149.796,     hhu 371.518
——      522 PARAMETER EV
      hhr 12.611,      hhu 31.533
——      522 PARAMETER CV
      hhr 12.613,      hhu 31.540
——      522 PARAMETER QLSchange            =         0.011
            PARAMETER QKSchange             =         0.001
            PARAMETER YGchange              =        −0.068
            PARAMETER SAVEGchange           =       −99.009
            VARIABLE WL.L                   =         1.054
            VARIABLE WK.L                   =         1.003
```

17.5 Implicit Expenditure Function Cases

When a utility function is more complicated than the Cobb–Douglas or Stone–Geary functions, sometimes it may not have an explicit expenditure function. In these cases, we can use a GAMS program to solve the minimum expenditure of the money metric utility function instead of writing an explicit expenditure function. Suppose the utility function is $u(\mathbf{QH})$. Given the household consumption vector $\mathbf{QH}1$, the utility level is $u(\mathbf{QH}1)$. The expenditure function $e(\mathbf{P}, u(\mathbf{QH}1)$ is implied in the following minimization problem:

$$\min e = \mathbf{P} \cdot \mathbf{QH} \qquad s.t. \quad u(\mathbf{QH}) \geq u(\mathbf{QH}1) \tag{17.5.1}$$

where e is expenditure in the monetary term.

Let the vectors of price and consumption of commodities before and after the policy changes be $(\mathbf{P}0, \mathbf{QH}0)$ and $(\mathbf{P}1, \mathbf{QH}1)$, the GAMS program is to solve the following equation system:

$$\begin{cases} \min_{QH} EXPEN = \mathbf{P}0 \cdot \mathbf{QH} \\ u(\mathbf{QH}) \geq u(\mathbf{QH}1) \end{cases} \tag{17.5.2}$$

The solutions of the GAMS program for *EXPEN* from the above system, denoted by *EXPEN*1, is the minimum expenditure at $\mathbf{P}0$ to reach the utility level $\mathbf{QH}1$. It is represented by YHEV1 in Figure 17.4.1. Subtracting the initial expenditure $\mathbf{P}0 \cdot \mathbf{QH}0$, we obtain equivalent variation *EV*:

$$EV = EXPEN1 - \mathbf{P}0 \cdot \mathbf{QH}0 \tag{17.5.3}$$

This implicit expenditure solution method applies to any utility functions, regardless of how complicated the original utility function form is, including those in the intertemporal dynamic CGE models.

Example 17.5.1 Suppose in a country, the household demand function is LES, thus they have a Stone–Geary utility function $u(\mathbf{QH}) = \sum_c \beta_c \ln(QH_c - LESSUB_c)$, where $LESSUB_c$ is the subsistence consumption level on commodity c. The government recently changed its tax policy. From their CGE model and simulation results, we have Tables 17.5.1–17.5.3 providing the information about relevant parameters and variables. Estimate the household welfare changes by the policy shock by using the measure of equivalent variation EV.

Solution: It can be seen that the directions of changes in the commodity prices and consumption amounts are mixed by the policy shock. Therefore, it is not obvious whether household welfare has improved or not by the policy change. We would evaluate the welfare change by using EV. The log form of the Stone–Geary utility function

Table 17.5.1.   Known values about the parameters of the LES utility function.

	Commodity 1 (com1)	Commodity 2 (com2)	Commodity 3 (com3)
LESSUB	20	15	10
Beta	0.3	0.32	0.38

Table 17.5.2.   The initial prices and households' consumption before the policy shock.

	Commodity 1 (com1)	Commodity 2 (com2)	Commodity 3 (com3)
P0	1	1	1
QH0	36.5	32.6	30.9

Table 17.5.3.   Prices and households' consumption after the policy shock.

	Commodity 1 (com1)	Commodity 2 (com2)	Commodity 3 (com3)
P1	1.2	0.8	1.3
QH1	34.0	37.4	26.37

$u(\mathbf{QH}) = \sum_c \beta_c \ln(QH_c - LESSUB_c)$ has no explicit expenditure function. Hence, we use the implicit expenditure function method to calculate EV in this case. Following is the GAMS program. Note the codes using /`utility,expenditure`/ instead of /`all`/ to define the equations in the model. It means that the to-be-solved model consists of only the named two equations: utility and expenditure. This usage is helpful in CGE modeling when we only need a subset of equations in the model to solve the problem.

The calculated EV is -3.459, which means that the welfare of households has deteriorated by this policy.

```
$title Example 17.5.1 Implicitly calculating EV


set c          /com1,com2,com3/;
parameter      LESbeta(c) / com1 = 0.3,   com2 = 0.32,   com3 = 0.38/
               LESSub(c)  / com1    20,   com2    15,    com3    10/
               P0(c)      / com1     1,   com2     1,    com3     1/
               QH0(c)     / com1  36.5,   com2  32.6,    com3  30.9/
               P1(c)      / com1   1.2,   com2   0.8,    com3   1.3/
               QH1(c)     / com1    34,   com2  37.4,    com3 26.37/;

variables
QH(c)    Households consumption, choice variable in this mini program
Expen    Monetary expenditure, objective to minimize

equations
utility
Expenditure;
```

```
*Note "=g=" is inequality ">"
utility..
sum(c,LESbeta(c)*log(QH(c)-LESSub(c)))=g=sum(c,LESbeta(c)*log(QH1(c)-
LESSub(c)));
expenditure..
expen=e=sum(c,P0(c)*QH(c));


QH.L(c)=QH1(c);


*Note we can choose several equations to form a model system to solve.
model EVsolve /utility,expenditure/;
solve EVsolve using nlp minimizing expen;


parameter
expen1
EV;


expen1=expen.L;
EV=expen1-sum(c,P0(c)*QH0(c));


display EV,expen1;


*end
```

Exercises

17E.1 You are asked to replicate the results in Section 17.2. First, copy the GAMS program for Openland2 in Example 15.7.1, then change the closure in the GAMS program to the Keynesian one as instructed in Section 15.8. The policy shock is reducing the VAT rate *tvatl* to 0.05. Check if the simulation results are the same as Table 17.2.1.

17E.2 You are asked to practice the flexible factor supply closure. Change the factor supply setup in the above GAMS program for Openland2 to the supply functions as Equations (17.2.3) and (17.2.4), adjusting the set of constraints for the closure as described in Section 17.2. Using the same values for the elasticities, replicate the simulation results in Section 17.2.

17E.3 After this chapter, now you are familiar with the constant elasticity of supply function of Equation (17.2.1) and its properties. This function form is very useful and its variants can be applied to other areas. Suppose Openland2 is a "large country" for imports of commodities 1 and 2. That is, changes of its imports would impact on the world prices of the two commodities. Let the supply function of the commodities by ROW be as follows:

$$QM_c = QMscale_c {}^* pwm_c {}^{**} QMelas_c \qquad (17E.3.1)$$

where *QMscale* and *QMelas* are the scale factor and the price elasticity of supply, respectively. Suppose the supply is elastic and elasticities *QMelas* equal 2 for all imports. Revise the CGE model with this import supply functions. You need to change pwm_c to variables and make other necessary changes in the parameter calibration and equation blocks of the CGE program. Do the following exercises:

(a) Replicate the base state.
(b) Suppose that the government cuts the employment tax rate *tvatl* to one half. Simulate the external shock and report the changes in factor supplies, activity outputs, quantities of imports, and the world prices of the imports. Estimate the welfare changes of households by EV and CV indicators. (The answer to 17E.3 can be found in Appendix.)

17E.4 A variant of the above power function form is the constant elasticity of demand function. In this case, the exponent has a negative sign. Suppose Openland2 is a "large country" for the exports, so changes in its exports would impact the world prices of *pwe*. The ROW's demand function for Openland2's export of *a* is

$$QE_a = QEscale_a {}^* pwe_a {}^{**} (-QEelas_a) \qquad (17E.4.1)$$

where *QEscale* and *QEelas* are the scale factor and the price elasticity of demand, respectively. Note the function has a negative sign for the exponent. Suppose elasticities *QEelas* equal 2 for all exports. Revise the GAMS program accordingly and

(a) Replicate the base state.
(b) Suppose the domestic private investment increases by 30%, that is, INVADJ=1.3. Simulate the external shock and report the changes in quantities and world prices of exports. (Note pwe_a should be changed to variables in the GAMS program.)

17E.5 You will practice the OAT method to test the sensitivity and robustness of the model with respect to elasticities of capital supply. In the GAMS program of 17E.2, use OAT to perturb the elasticity values of factor supplies to replicate the results of Section 17.3. Then, perturb the values of the elasticity of substitution between capital and labor, which is represented by exponent rhoVA(a) in the GAMS program, and test the sensitivities of the model to the deviations from the original exponent values.

17E.6 Revise the GAMS program of minimization to estimate EV and CV implicitly for a Cobb–Douglas utility function. Using the same information of P0, QH0, P1, and QH1 in Section 17.5, calculate EV and CV.

Chapter 18

Limitations and Extensions of the Standard CGE Model

The computable general equilibrium (CGE) models presented in Chapters 14–16 are called the "standard CGE model" in the literature (Lofgren *et al.*, 2002). The standard model is intuitive and constructed directly on the foundations of microeconomics and macroeconomics. Its structure is full-fledged and flexible to serve as the basis for building more complex models. It can be used for most research purposes, whether for economic issues or for public policies.

The standard model, however, has limitations. It is static for a single period. It models a single country. It overlooks the utilities provided by savings, leisure and public goods to the households and society. It does not have financial and capital markets for trading financial goods. In the past three decades, many efforts have been made to extend the standard model to more complicated structures in order to overcome these limitations and address special issues. In this final chapter, we briefly discuss the limitations of the standard CGE model and the major extensions made in literature.

18.1 Savings and Future Consumption

The standard CGE model follows conventional macroeconomics by treating savings as a function of disposable income, without explaining why households save. In neoclassical economics, savings are explained as the households' demand for commodities in the future periods, derived from their intertemporal utility maximization. The simplified treatment for savings in a standard CGE model may lead to biases in policy evaluation of simulation results. For instance, if using EV and CV to measure the households' welfare changes relies only on the current commodity consumption as in Chapter 17, it would overlook the possible households' utility gain or loss from savings. If future consumption is not a component in utility, then a utility-maximizing household would simply reduce savings to zero and exhaust all his income in the current period.

In general, fortunately, we can justify savings within the original version of the CGE model as a result derived from households' utility maximization. For instance, the fixed savings-to-disposable-income ratio in a CGE model can be derived from households'

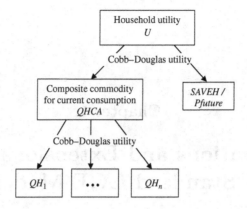

Figure 18.1.1.   Nested utility function to justify the saving-to-income ratio.

maximizing a nested Cobb–Douglas utility function as Figure 18.1.1. At the top level, a Cobb–Douglas utility function includes current consumption and future consumption. $QHCA$ and $PHCA$ are the quantity and price of the composite commodity for all commodities consumed in the current period. Q_{future} and P_{future} are the quantity and price of the composite commodity for all commodities consumed in the future period. If needed, the future price can be set as a function of the interest rate, and the time preference can be included in the utility function, but they won't change the nature of the following discussion and conclusions.

Households' savings is to be spent on future commodities. So we have

$$QH_{future} = SAVEH/P_{future} \qquad (18.1.1)$$

The utility function at the top level is the Cobb–Douglas utility function including Q_{future} and $QHCA$ with the exponent aps.:

$$U(QHCA, SAVEH/P_{future}) = QHCA^{(1-aps)} \cdot (SAVEH/P_{future})^{aps} \qquad (18.1.2)$$

Disposable income is $YDISH$. The budget constraint is

$$PHCA \cdot QHCA + SAVEH = YDISH \qquad (18.1.3)$$

Derived from utility maximization, the spending on the future commodity, $SAVEH$, thus is

$$SAVEH = aps \cdot YDISH \qquad (18.1.4)$$

Hence, savings is a percentage of disposable income by the saving rate aps (average propensity to save). Spending on the current commodities is $PHCA \cdot QHCA = (1 - aps)\,YDISH$. Hence, the fixed share of savings in disposable income in the standard CGE model is theoretically explained as a result of households' utility maximization for future consumption.

At the bottom level of the nested utility function is another Cobb–Douglas function. It is to maximize

$$QHCA = \prod_{c=1}^{n} QH_c^{shareh_c} \qquad \sum_c shareh_c = 1 \qquad (18.1.5)$$

Subject to the constraint:

$$\sum_{c} PQ_c \cdot QH_c = PHCA \cdot QHCA = (1 - aps) \cdot YDISH \qquad (18.1.6)$$

This is the familiar part of deriving the commodity demands in the standard CGE model.

In the CGE model with a linear saving function like Equation (12.1.5), $S = -C_0 + mps \cdot YDISH$, the Stone–Geary utility function may be used to justify the saving behavior and the linear expenditure system (LES) demand for commodities. Let $LESsub_{future}$ denote the subsistence consumption for the future commodity. The utility function is

$$U(QH_1, \ldots, QH_n, SAVEH/P_{future}) = \beta_s \ln(SAVEH/P_{future} - LESsub_{future})$$

$$+ \sum_{c=1}^{n-1} \beta_c \ln(QH_c - LESsub_c) \qquad (18.1.7)$$

and $\sum_{c}^{n} \beta_c + \beta_s = 1$. The derived saving function is the spending on future commodity in the LES function form:

$$SAVEH = P_{future} \cdot LESsub_{future} + \beta_s \left(YDISH - \sum_{c=1}^{n} PQ_c \cdot LESsub_c \right.$$

$$\left. - P_{future} \cdot LESsub_{future} \right) \qquad (18.1.8)$$

This is a standard saving function with a constant and an income-induced-savings term by the rate of marginal propensity to save mps, which is the beta value β_s. The "constant" term of the saving function is

$$(1 - \beta_s) P_{future} \cdot LESsub_{future} - \beta_s \sum_{c=1}^{n} PQ_c \cdot LESsub_c \qquad (18.1.9)$$

This "constant" term would be affected by changes in commodity prices. This property is reflected in a standard CGE model: the subsistence consumption term of the saving function of Equation (12.5.11) is price indexed. The demand for commodity c is

$$PQ_c \cdot QH_c = PQ_c \cdot LESsub_c + \beta_c \left(YDISH - \sum_{c=1}^{n} PQ_c \cdot LESsub_c \right.$$

$$\left. - P_{future} \cdot LESsub_{future} \right) \qquad (18.1.10)$$

Therefore, a linear saving function in the standard CGE model can still be explained as a result derived from households' maximizing a Stone–Geary utility function for future consumption.

As a note here, for the Stony–Geary utility function to be well defined, the following constraints should be satisfied:

$$QH_c > LESsub_c \qquad c \in C$$

$$SAVEH/P_{future} > LESsub_{future} \qquad (18.1.11)$$

This implies that the disposable income must be greater than the total expenditure on the subsistence consumption:

$$YDISH > \sum_{c=1}^{n} PQ_c \cdot LESsub_c + P_{future} \cdot LESsub_{future} \qquad (18.1.12)$$

To sum up, in general, the saving behavior can still be implicitly explained by households' utility maximization in the standard CGE model. In policy evaluation, even though we take into consideration households' future consumption, the simulation results from a policy shock are still acceptable without a need to revise the original model. What is important is that, if a policy shock substantially affects savings, the effects on future consumption in households' overall welfare should be taken into account in the utility function of the model and the policy assessment.

If the CGE research project plans to build a neoclassical model, then the model structure needs to be revised accordingly. In the neoclassical framework, savings are derived from households' utility maximization in their intertemporal consideration. In the financial capital market, households supply financial capital from their savings, enterprises demand financial capital for investment from their consideration of intertemporal profit maximization. Other institutions including the government and the rest of the world may also participate in supplies and demands in the future markets. The price of the financial capital is related to the interest rate. Readers who are interested in this topic can find many CGE works on the subject in the literature.

18.2 Leisure

In the CGE model in Chapter 17, we have a labor supply function, although the function is not derived within the model. In a typical neoclassical model, as discussed in Chapter 6, the labor supply function is derived from households' utility maximization over the trade-off between consumption and leisure. In general, an increase in the wage rate would induce households to supply more labor and reduce leisure, or vice versa. Hence, the labor supply function is upward sloping. It is not difficult to modify a standard CGE model so the labor supply function is derived from households' utility maximization in the system, which is done by some CGE models. Yet such a modification is more of theoretical interest than of practical usefulness. This is because a CGE model normally uses the labor supply function directly, and the parameter value needed for the labor supply function is easier to obtain from external sources. It seems that such a modification in the utility function is justified only if there is a need to study the welfare effects from leisure.

To modify a CGE model accordingly, a nested structure of utility functions with three levels may be constructed (Figure 18.2.1). At the top level, a utility function includes leisure $QLEI$ and a composite consumption good QHA is:

$$U(QHA, QLEI) \qquad (18.2.1)$$

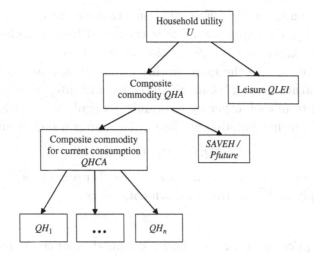

Figure 18.2.1. Nested utility function including leisure.

The corresponding budget constraint is

$$PHA \cdot QHA + WL \cdot QLEI \leq WL \cdot \overline{L} + YEXTRA - TAX \qquad QLS = \overline{L} - QLEI \qquad (18.2.2)$$

where $\overline{L}$ is labor endowment, $YEXTRA$ is households' monetary income other than those from labor supply. TAX is tax.

The second and third levels resemble the nested structure in the previous section. The utility function at the second level includes savings and the composite commodity of all currently consumed commodities. The utility function at the bottom level includes all commodities consumed in the current period.

The utility function at the top level typically is a constant elasticity of substitution (CES) utility function. Its parameters can be calibrated from external data about time endowment and the elasticity of substitution between leisure and consumption. We can find the data from publications in labor economics and other relevant sources, although additional data work and assumptions may be needed to process the data. For instance, time endowment is not directly available but can be inferred from the time distribution between work and leisure. One rough assumption used in modeling is that a typical individual spends 8 hours each on work, leisure and sleeping in a day. Better estimates from some multi-year survey data on households' time spent on leisure can be found in Aguiar and Hurst (2006). Fox (2002) estimates the ratio of time spent on leisure to that spent on working is 1:4. Suppose we use this estimate by Fox and let prices of labor and the composite commodity all be normalized to 1. From the social accounting matrix (SAM) table we do have the data of labor supply QLS. Then the households' time endowment $\overline{L}$ can be calibrated by

$$\overline{L} = ((1 + 4)/4) \cdot QLS \qquad (18.2.3)$$

Leisure is $\overline{L} - QLS$.

The value of exponent of the CES utility function should also be obtained from external sources. Normally, the exponent value is converted from the elasticity of substitution between leisure and labor. If the information about the elasticity of substitution is not directly available, we can use the more readily available data about the elasticity of labor supply in the literature (e.g., MaCurdy, 1981) to calibrate. The two elasticities can be mutually converted from each other by a formula, as explained in what follows.

Suppose the CES utility function at the top level after a monotonic transformation is

$$U(Q, l) = \delta_1 \cdot Q^\rho + \delta_2 \cdot l^\rho \tag{18.2.4}$$

where Q is the composite commodity and l is leisure. If using Fox's ratio estimate, $\delta_1 = 4\delta_2$. Let n be labor supply and $\bar{L}$ be time endowment, we have

$$n + l = \bar{L} \tag{18.2.5}$$

Let w be labor price, p be the composite commodity price, Y be the non-labor extra income. Normalize the composite commodity price so $p = 1$. The budget constraint is

$$pQ = Q = wn + Y = w(\bar{L} - l) + Y \tag{18.2.6}$$

Denote the price elasticity of labor supply by e_n, as follows:

$$e_n = \frac{dn}{dw} \cdot \frac{w}{n} \tag{18.2.7}$$

The price elasticity of demand for leisure is denoted by e_l. Its definition and its relationship with e_n is

$$e_l \equiv \frac{dl}{dw} \cdot \frac{w}{l} = \frac{d(\bar{L} - n)}{dw} \cdot \frac{w}{l} = -\frac{dn}{dw} \cdot \frac{w}{l} \frac{n}{n} = -e_n \cdot \frac{n}{l} \tag{18.2.8}$$

The elasticity of substitution between leisure and commodity in the CES function ε is defined as

$$\varepsilon \equiv \frac{d(Q/l)}{d(w/p)} \cdot \frac{wl}{pQ} \tag{18.2.9}$$

Because $p = 1$, simplify and rearrange

$$\varepsilon \equiv \frac{d(Q/l)}{dw} \cdot \frac{wl}{Q} = \frac{ldQ - Qdl}{l^2 dw} \frac{wl}{Q} = \frac{dQ}{dw} \frac{w}{Q} - \frac{wdl}{ldw} = \frac{w}{Q} \frac{dQ}{dw} - e_l \tag{18.2.10}$$

Totally differentiate the budget constraint (18.2.6),

$$dQ = dw(\bar{L} - l) - wdl = ndw - wdl \tag{18.2.11}$$

Substitute (18.2.6) and (18.2.11) into (18.2.10), simplify:

$$\varepsilon = \frac{w}{Q} \frac{dQ}{dw} - e_l = \frac{w}{dw} \frac{(ndw - wdl)}{(wn + Y)} - e_l = \frac{wn}{wn + Y} - \frac{w^2 dl}{(wn + Y)dw} - e_l$$

$$= \frac{1}{1 + Y/(wn)} - \frac{w \cdot dl}{(n + Y/w)dw} \frac{l}{l} - e_l = \frac{1}{1 + Y/(wn)} - e_l \frac{l}{(n + Y/w)} - e_l$$

$$= \frac{1}{1 + Y/(wn)} - e_l \left(\frac{\bar{L} + Y/w}{n + Y/w} \right) \tag{18.2.12}$$

Substitute price elasticity of labor supply e_n into the above equation,

$$\varepsilon = \frac{1}{1 + Y/(wn)} + e_n \cdot \frac{n}{(\bar{L} - n)} \left(\frac{w\bar{L} + Y}{wn + Y} \right) \tag{18.2.13}$$

If households have no extra non-labor income, Y is zero; and taking Fox's above estimate, the above equation becomes a simple formula as follows:

$$\varepsilon = 1 + e_n \cdot \bar{L}/(\bar{L} - n) = 1 + e_n \cdot \bar{L}/l = 1 + 5e_n \tag{18.2.14}$$

Equations (18.2.13) or (18.2.14) provides a convenient formula to convert from e_n to ε, or vice versa. Variable values including n and Y can be calibrated from the SAM table. Time endowment $\bar{L}$ can be obtained by Equation (18.2.3) or by other estimates. To be more precise, w should be considered as the ratio of labor cost to the commodity price p because we have normalized p to 1. In the base state, labor price is normally set to 1 and commodity purchaser's price is calibrated, hence w would be WL/PQ in our CGE models. The exponent of the CES utility function ρ can be derived from $\rho = 1 - 1/\varepsilon$.

Admittedly, a standard CGE model with a labor supply function is in general sufficient for research purposes. Adding the neoclassical setup for the consumption-leisure tradeoff in a CGE model is often over-engineered, unless there is a need to study the welfare effect from leisure by a policy shock. Many empirical studies in labor economics find the overall labor supply in a country to be quite inelastic in the wage rate. In this case, even a fixed labor supply closure can be a good approximation for the state of the labor market in the CGE model.

18.3 Public Goods and Government Expenditure

In a standard CGE model, one overlooked aspect of the households' welfare is their consumption of public goods from government expenditure. The government makes transfer payments and purchases commodities. Government spending is not all wasted — it provides households with public goods including national defense, infrastructure, environmental protection, social security, education, health service, etc. These public goods raise the welfare and utility of the households. If we totally ignore the utility provided by the public goods provided by the government in a CGE model, a simulation for the tax policy would lead to zero tax rate and zero government spending, so that the households' utility derived only from private goods can be maximized. If we include the additional utility provided by the public goods, the simulation results would be different.

Differing from private goods, public goods are non-rival. A given amount of public good can be shared by many households. An individual household's consumption of a public good is only affected by the total amount of the public good, but would not be reduced by other households sharing the consumption of the same public good. For instance, Household A's consumption of national defense would not reduce Household B's consumption of national defense. To include the households' consumption of public goods, we may refine a CGE model as follows.

Let QG_g be the government's purchase of non-rival public goods (commodities) such as national defense or weather forecast. Suppose the economy has n households. Because of the non-rivalry property, the consumption by the entire population of households is n times greater, $n \cdot QG_g$. Another part of the government's purchase is rival goods, such as providing food to low-income families. Let QG_r be the government consumption on rival goods. Subscript g denotes "non-rival public good" and subscript "r" denotes "rival". We also assume that the government is not as efficient as private enterprises, so there is an efficiency loss in operation. Let the government's efficiency factor be $EFFIG$. Because of the inefficiency in the government's operation, $EFFIG < 1$, the households' utility function including the consumption goods provided by the government is

$$U(QH_1, \ldots, QH_n, QG_r \cdot EFFIG_r, n \cdot QG_g \cdot EFFIG_g, SAVEH/P_{future}) \tag{18.3.1}$$

A Stone–Geary utility form for the above utility function can be

$$U(QH_1, \ldots, QH_n, QG_r, QG_g, SAVEH/P_{future})$$

$$= \sum_c \beta_c \ln(QH_c - LESSUB_c) + \sum_r \beta_r \ln(QG_r \cdot EFFIG_r - LESSUB_r)$$

$$+ \sum_g \beta_g \ln(n \cdot QG_g \cdot EFFIG_g - n \cdot LESSUB_g)$$

$$+ \beta_s \ln(SAVEH/P_{future} - LESSUB_{future}) \tag{18.3.2}$$

where $\sum_c \beta_c + \sum_r \beta_r + \sum_g \beta_g + \beta_s = 1$. And $\beta_s = aps$, the average saving rate. g is the index for the non-rival public goods, and r is the index for the rival goods. The budget constraint of the households needs to be set up carefully to take account of costs of QG_g and QG_r. Households indirectly pay these commodities through taxes paid to the government. The government's budget has other outlays and the government has its own utility and other objectives. Hence, depending on the research projects and the real-world environment, various setups in the CGE model can be made.

18.4 Multi-Regional Models

The standard CGE model is only for a single economy/country/region. As technology develops and market expands, the world economy becomes more and more integrated, and from time to time, we need to study the economic interdependence of various regions and countries. As a result, multi-regional CGE models have developed rapidly. A multi-regional model includes several interrelated member regions in the model. A region can be a province in a country, or a country in a trade bloc or in the entire world. International trade models are multi-regional models. The Global Trade Analysis Project (GTAP) provides a popular platform for the database and software GEMPACK for research on international trade and environment in the Australian style CGE framework. Other useful data sources for multiple-country models include the OECD database and World Input–output Database (WIOD). The standard CGE models can be extended to multi-regional models or international trade models.

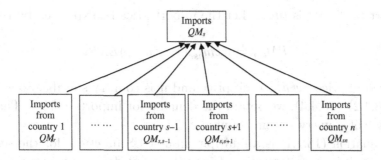

Figure 18.4.1. Imports of country s from multiple foreign countries.

In an international trade CGE model, we need to link imports and exports of the member countries. A member country exports its commodities to other member countries, and also imports from other countries. Suppose we study a trade bloc R with n countries. Country s imports commodities from the other $n-1$ countries (Figure 18.4.1).

In the standard model for country s, instead of having an aggregate import QM, we add a nested structure as Figure 18.4.1. QM is the composite import that consists of imports from various other countries of the same commodity c. The imports from other countries are imperfect substitutes, but with the same elasticity of substitution which can be reasonably assumed. Their relationship can be expressed by a CES function:

$$QM_{cs} = \alpha_{cs}^M \left(\delta_{cs1}^M QM_{cs1}^{\rho_{cs}^M} + \cdots + \delta_{cs,s-1}^M QM_{cs,s-1}^{\rho_{cs}^M} + \delta_{cs,s+1}^M QM_{cs,s+1}^{\rho_{cs}^M} \cdots + \delta_{csn}^M QM_{csn}^{\rho_{cs}^M} \right)^{1/\rho_{cs}^M}$$

$$= \alpha_{cs}^M \left(\sum_r \delta_{csr}^M QM_{csr}^{\rho_{cs}^M} \right)^{1/\rho_{cs}^M} \qquad \sum_{r=1}^{n-1} \delta_{csr}^M = 1 \qquad r \neq s \qquad (18.4.1)$$

In the above equation, QM_{cs} is the total import of c by country s. QM_{csr} and PM_{csr} are the quantity and price of import of commodity c from country r by country s. The parameter notations in the equation follow the convention of other CES functions in the book.

The bottom level of Figure 18.4.1 is sometimes called the second level Armington condition. The setup is as follows. Country s imports commodity c from countries $r = 1, \ldots, n-1$. Its objective is to minimize the total cost $Cost$ at the after-tariff price PM_{csr}, subject to the given total import quantity QM_{cs}:

$$\min_{QM_{csr}} \quad Cost = \sum_r PM_{csr} QM_{csr} \qquad s.t. \quad QM_{cs} = \alpha_{cs}^M \left(\sum_r \delta_{csr}^M QM_{csr}^{\rho_{cs}^M} \right)^{1/\rho_{cs}^M} \qquad (18.4.2)$$

The corresponding price equation is

$$PM_{cs} \cdot QM_{cs} = \sum_r PM_{csr} QM_{csr} \qquad (18.4.3)$$

The import tariff rate is tm_{csr}. Let the import price be expressed by the world price,

$$PM_{csr} = pwm_{csr}(1 + tm_{csr})EXR_s \qquad (18.4.4)$$

Note the world price pwm_{csr} is cif price and it is country-specific. Solving the system of Equations (18.4.2)–(18.4.4), we obtain the demand for imports QM_{csr}. That is, the import of commodity c of country s from country r.

Because Equation (18.4.1) is a multiple-input CES function, for the second level Armington condition, it is more convenient to use the input-demand-function form (as Equation (8.6.8)) for the solutions of the minimization problem of Equation (18.4.2):

$$QM_{csr} = \frac{QM_{cs}}{\alpha_{cs}^M}\left(\frac{\delta_{csr}^M}{PM_{csr}}\right)^{1/(1-\rho_{cs}^M)}\left(\sum_{j}^{n-1}\delta_{csj}^{M/(1-\rho_{cs}^M)}\cdot PM_{csj}^{\rho_{cs}^M/(\rho_{cs}^M-1)}\right)^{-1/\rho_{cs}^M} \qquad (j \neq s) \quad (18.4.5)$$

Adding the price equations, Equations (18.4.3)–(18.4.5) constitute the system equations in the module of the second level Armington condition.

The modification of the export part is similar. If country s exports commodity c to other $n-1$ countries, we can add a level of the constant elasticity of transformation (CET) function in a nested structure for exports. Let the total export of commodity c from country s be QE_{cs}. Let QE_{csr} be the quantity of the export of commodity c from country s to country r. We have the following second level of the CET function:

$$QE_{cs} = \alpha_{cs}^E(\delta_{cs1}^E QE_{cs,1}^{\rho_{cs}^E} + \cdots + \delta_{cs,s-1}^E QE_{cs,s-1}^{\rho_{cs}^E} + \delta_{cs,s+1}^E QE_{cs,s+1}^{\rho_{cs}^E} + \cdots + \delta_{csn}^E QE_{csn}^{\rho_{cs}^E})^{1/\rho_{cs}^E}$$

$$= \alpha_{cs}^E\left(\sum_{r}\delta_{csr}^E QE_{csr}^{\rho_{cs}^E}\right)^{1/\rho_{cs}^E} \qquad \sum_{r=1}^{n-1}\delta_{csr}^E = 1 \qquad r \neq s \qquad (18.4.6)$$

where $\rho_{cs}^E > 1$. The objective of the export of country s is to maximize the export value of $z = \sum_r PE_{csr} QE_{csr}$ subject to the CET condition. PE_{cs} is the price of export c. PE_{csr} is the after-export-tax fob price of commodity c exporting from country s to country r. If the export tax rate is te_{csr}, then we have,

$$(1 + te_{csr})PE_{csr} = pwe_{csr}\cdot EXR_s \qquad (18.4.7)$$

Similar to the Armington condition method, given the quantity and price of the total export QE_{cs} and PE_{csr} of commodity c, the derived conditional supply of export QE_{csr} from optimization is

$$QE_{crs} = \frac{QE_{cs}}{\alpha_{cs}^E}\left(\frac{\delta_{csr}^E}{PE_{csr}}\right)^{1/(1-\rho_{cs}^E)}\left(\sum_{j}^{n-1}\delta_{csj}^{E/(1-\rho_{cs}^E)}\cdot PE_{csj}^{\rho_{cs}^E/(\rho_{cs}^E-1)}\right)^{-1/\rho_{cs}^E} \qquad (j \neq s) \quad (18.4.8)$$

The price condition is

$$PE_{cs} \cdot QE_{cs} = \sum_r PE_{csr} QE_{csr} \qquad (18.4.9)$$

Equations (18.4.7)–(18.4.9) form the modular system for the multi-country exports at the second level of the CET function.

Suppose there are no physical losses during international shipping, then in quantities, export of commodity c from country s to country r should equal the import of the same commodity from country s by country r:

$$QE_{crs} = QM_{csr} \qquad (r, s \in R \quad r \neq s) \qquad (18.4.10)$$

These are the most important linking relationships between countries s and r in the trade model.

The next issue that needs to be addressed is international shipping costs. It adds the transport margin between the fob export prices and cif import prices. The situation resembles the transport margins discussed in Chapter 13. We may assume that the international transport margin $icit_{csr}$ is proportional to the amount of trade flow QE_{csr}. Hence, the cost of international shipping service as an input used in this particular route and commodity csr is $P_{shipping} \cdot icit_{csr} \cdot QE_{csr}$, where $P_{shipping}$ is the international shipping unit cost. Alternatively, many studies simply treat that the international transport margins are ad valorem the fob prices. Let $avit_{csr}$ be the ad valorem transport margin, then, the international shipping cost of commodity c from country r to country s is

$$pwm_{csr} \cdot QM_{csr} = (1 + avit_{crs}) \cdot pwe_{crs} \cdot QE_{crs} \qquad (r, s \in R \quad r \neq s) \qquad (18.4.11)$$

This equation leads to the demand for international shipping of the route/commodity specific in the international currency unit $avit_{crs} \cdot pwe_{crs} \cdot QE_{crs}$. Depending on the other assumptions, they can be aggregated to form the total demand for international shipping.

Who supplies the shipping? Various data about international shipping outputs are available in national accounts for major countries, although the statistics do not provide details about which particular routes/commodity were provided by the country's shipping services. In reality, the shipping service of a particular route can be provided by the exporting country, importing country, or a third country. One solution is aggregating the global shipping supplies and demands, and balancing the aggregate supply and demand of shipping in the international shipping market at the weighted shipping price. Trade flow matrices need to be constructed and SAM tables need to be carefully balanced to ensure consistencies before the CGE modeling and replicating the base state. An example of this multi-country trade model can be found in Robinson, Wang and Martin (2001).

The above multi-country model can also be used for several regions within a country. For example, Jones and Whalley (1988) construct a multi-regional model inside Canada; and Horridge and Wittwer (2008) offer a multi-regional CGE model inside China. Constructing a multi-regional model within a country is more difficult because the data about commodity trade flows and factor migration among regions are often not recorded, and the location of outputs of commodities may not be able to be identified. Hence, some other techniques need to be used to estimate the statistics. Developments in spatial economics have also found applications in refining multi-country CGE models. For instance, the shipping costs, trade routes and trade volumes can be specified as functions of spatial variables such as spatial distance in the multi-country CGE models.

18.5 Dynamic Models

In practice, we often need to study the dynamic path of the economy and forecast the economic states in future periods. A standard CGE model is static and cannot accomplish these tasks. In the standard model, capital formation and capital consumption are two separate variables and their dynamic relationship is not specified. Other overlooked dynamic issues include households' decision on future consumption, enterprises' decision for business expansion, labor force growth, technological progress, etc.

Dynamic CGE models attempt to solve the above problems. Their theoretical foundation is the dynamic and growth theories in economics. The model structures follow the corresponding dynamic models in economics, including recursive models, intertemporal optimization models, overlapping generation models, dynamic stochastic models, and so on. Like standard CGE models, dynamic CGE models study the multi-period dynamic changes of economic variables caused by policy shocks or external environmental changes. Differing from the dynamic or forecasting models in macroeconomics that focus on economic aggregates, dynamic CGE models need to study detailed changes in disaggregated sectors in future periods.

A dynamic CGE model is an extension of a static CGE model. Most of them are discrete time models. Data are collected to build the base-year SAM table, which serves as the base state of the dynamic CGE model. From the base state, the dynamic model is constructed for the future periods. The GAMS program should first successfully replicate the base-year state, then generate forecasts of the economic variables in future periods. These solved dynamic results by the model under the original policy and parameter environment is called the "baseline" scenario. Then we bring external shocks to the model, whether they are changes in policies, parameters or exogenous variables, and execute the model. The simulation results from the changed environment are called the "counterfactual scenario", or just "counterfactuals".

There are several types of discrete-time dynamic CGE models. A simple and practical type is the recursive dynamic model. It extends a static CGE model in the base-period state sequentially to the future periods in a recursive dynamic structure. Inter-period linkages are specified by functions. The dynamic paths for critical determinants of the model are specified, often utilizing the forecasts from external sources as exogenous variables for future periods. The endogenous variables of the next period $t + 1$ along the dynamic paths are solved from the economic states of the current period t. Iteratively, we extend the economic forecasts to future time periods until the terminal period. In what follows, we illustrate a typical type of recursive CGE model, such as Wang (2003).

The first step is to build a standard CGE model in the base-period such as the model of Openland2 in Chapter 15. The next question is, how would this economy evolve in the future?

Because of the full factor employment closure of Openland2, the model is supply-driven. The determinants of the economy from the supply side are the amounts of primary factors. The future economic state in period i depends on factor supplies in period i. Following this principle, we need to specify the growth paths of factor supplies and the inter-period linkages between two consecutive periods. It should be mentioned that, in dynamic models, in addition to labor and capital, technology is another important factor for economic growth and is in general included as a factor in dynamic growth models.

The growth path of the labor supply is determined by the growth of population and labor force, which have their own demographic laws. Research in demography provides better data and forecasts so we can simply borrow these statistics for our needs. For example, the International Labor Organization (ILO) has produced forecasts of the labor force growth in various countries in future periods, so we can use these numbers. Let the projected labor growth rate in period t be $popgw_t$, the total amount of the labor supply be $QLSAGG_t$, we have the following inter-period linkage:

$$QLSAGG_{t+1} = (1 + popgw_t) \cdot QLSAGG_t \qquad (18.5.1)$$

Within each period, if needed, the labor force can be broken down to different types, such as skilled labor and unskilled labor. Each type of the labor force can have its own growth path. In studying urbanization, the rural–urban migration should be considered within each period as a result of changes in endogenous variables. The urban labor and rural labor changes would be affected by both the exogenous change in the total labor force and the endogenous migration due to urbanization.

Capital stock or capital supply is said to be backward-looking, because the capital stock in the current period is related to the investment (capital formation) in the previous periods. Let capital stock in period t be $QKSTOCK_t$, the depreciation rate is $deprate_t$, $QINVAGG_t$ is aggregate capital formation:

$$QKSTOCK_{t+1} = (1 - deprate_t)QKSTOCK_t + QINVAGG_t \qquad (18.5.2)$$

The equation says that the capital stock of the next period is formed by the current capital stock minus depreciation but plus the current capital formation. The statistics of capital stocks and the amount of depreciation in the historical periods can be found in the available database. From these statistics, the depreciation rate can be calibrated by

$$deprate_t = DEP_t/QKSTOCK_t \qquad (18.5.3)$$

This rate may also be calibrated by Equation (18.5.2) if the historical data for capital formation are available. Depreciation rates in future periods are assumed to be fixed at the current rate or at the average rate of the historical data if no other information is available. Capital formation $QINVAGG_t$ is constrained by savings from all institutions and other factors in the economy.

In addition to labor and capital, technology is a major factor driving economic growth. Observing the historical growth data in the United States, Robert Solow concludes that the changes in labor and capital supplies cannot fully explain GDP growth. About two percentage points of the annual growth should be contributed to technology change. Solow's neoclassical growth theory is so influential that almost all growth models nowadays emphasize the role of technology changes. There are three ways to specify the role of technology in raising productivity in the production function: total factor productivity (TFP), capital embodied technology, and labor embodied technology. Among them, TFP is the most popularly used measure for the contribution by technology to productivity growth in empirical studies. In the production block of our CGE models, TFP is represented by the scale factor of α_a^a in the CES production function at the top level, such as that in Equation (15.6.1).

To specify the path of changes in technology and TFP, we wish to obtain the forecasts of the technology change and its contribution to the production from external data sources, but these data, if available, often are not appropriate to apply to the current CGE model. This is because the production functions implied in those models can be quite different from those in the current CGE model. Instead, we can utilize forecasts of the GDP growth rates to calibrate the TFP growth path. The forecasted GDP growth rates can be found in World Economic Outlook by IMF, Oxford Economic Forecasting, etc. Suppose the forecasted GDP growth rate from period t to period $t+1$ is $grategdp_t$. We assume in the same economy the growth rates of GDP and of total output (which also includes the total intermediate output) are the same. We use this rate to compute the activity outputs in period $t+1$: $QA_{a,t+1} = (1 + grategdp_t) \cdot QA_{a,t}$. Then, in the production block, with the forecasted labor and capital inputs for period $t+1$, we use $QA_{a,t+1}$ as the exogenously determined output to calibrate the scale factor $\alpha_{a,t+1}^a$. $\alpha_{a,t+1}^a$ represents TFP in $t+1$. In aggregate, with the calibrated TFP, the GDP figure from the model in period $t+1$ should be quite consistent with (although may not exactly equal) the forecasted GDP figures from the external source. We repeat this process to calibrate TFP of other time periods, thus establishing the baseline of the dynamic CGE model.

Admittedly, assuming the same TFP growth rate for all sectors in the economy is unconvincing. TFP growth rates vary greatly across different sectors. A remedy for the problem is constructing sectoral adjustment factors against the national average based on the historical data of the growth rates in each sector, then using the sectoral adjustment factors to adjust the forecasted activity output in each sector. Finally, the so-computed sectoral outputs are used to calibrate the activity-specific TFP rates in each future period.

After having specified the factor supplies including technology progress on the growth paths, the model has determined the size of the economy and the aggregate output in each future period. To forecast the disaggregated details in sectors and national accounts, which are endogenous variables to be solved in the model, we also need to examine the structural changes from the demand side along the time path. The households' demand function for commodities can be the fixed spending share function derived from the Cobb–Douglas utility function or the LES function. The LES function is preferred in dynamic models because it can capture the Engel curve effects as income increases over time. Similar to the discussion in Section 18.1, households' savings can be either a fixed proportion of disposable income or determined by a linear saving function. The parameter values of the demand functions can be dynamic, adjusting as time evolves. For instance, suppose the dynamic model stretches over many years. During the period, demographic change takes place and the population gets aged. This factor would affect the consumption pattern of households, so the parameters of the households' demand functions would change accordingly.

Capital formation, i.e., private investment, can be set as either following the same growth rate of GDP or as being partially determined by some endogenous factors. Let $QINVAGG_t$ be the quantity of the aggregate investment. Following the economics theory, the investment function is related to the current stock level and the accelerator effect:

$$QINVAGG_t = \gamma_1 \cdot GDP_t + \gamma_2 \cdot (GDP_t - GDP_{t-1}) = \lambda_1 \cdot GDP_t - \gamma_2 \cdot GDP_{t-1} \qquad (18.5.4)$$

where γ_1, γ_2, λ are coefficients and $\lambda_1 = \gamma_1 + \gamma_2$. After rearrangement, capital formation is a function of GDP in the current and previous periods. The values of coefficients γ_1, γ_2, λ_1 may be estimated from the available publications. The exogenous part of the investment can be set at the researchers' discretion based on their considerations of policy options and economics theory. Note investment $QINVAGG_t$ is constrained by the available savings from all institutions in the economy in the same period. It equals the domestic savings plus forecasted foreign savings.

The specification for the government spending along the time path also depends on the research project. A simple version is that the government spending keeps the same pattern as that in the base-period. For instance, in Openland 2, the government spending on each item is a fixed share of the total spending. However, there is a difference between a static situation and a dynamic situation for the government spending. A static model refers to a short-run case, in which the government can run a budget deficit or surplus, possibly by a huge amount. A dynamic model covers the long run, during which a chronic budget deficit or surplus is not sustainable. The intertemporal government saving, $SAVEG$, in a dynamic model should be zero or be limited to a moderate level along the time path. The functions of the government spending and revenue need to be modified from the static model to satisfy the constraint of intertemporal-budget-balance in the long run.

Regarding foreign trade balance or foreign savings $SAVEF$, the system constraints in the dynamic model over time periods covering the long run are also different from those in the static models. Suppose the country is a small country in imports and exports. Given the world prices, a country like Openland2 can import and export any amounts as it wishes. Hence, the country may run trade surplus or deficit, and its $SAVEF$ may be negative or in surplus. In the short run, this is fine. In the long run, however, a country cannot run trade deficits forever (in our simple model without capital account, trade deficit equals balance-of-payment deficit), because it would exhaust all its foreign exchange reserve, hence is not sustainable.[1] Hence, in a dynamic model, a corresponding constraint in the model structure

---

[1] The U.S. is an exception as it has had chronic trade deficits for many decades. A major reason is that the dollar is used as the international reserve.

needs to be made so intertemporal $SAVEF$ is close to zero or is limited within a small range in the long run.

In the literature, there are many multi-country dynamic models to study and simulate the long run inter-country economic relationships, for instance, the LINKAGE model maintained by the World Bank. In some other dynamic models, the households make the intertemporal optimization decision to form the demand and saving functions. Overlapping generation models are used to study the social security issues. Stochastic dynamic models are also developed. Many of these models, however, only have aggregate variables but not the sectoral details provided by standard CGE models. The Monash CGE model by Dixon and Rimmer (2002) is a true dynamic CGE model with sectoral details, although it is in the Australian style.

18.6 Developments in Other Directions

Over the past four decades, many efforts have been made to integrate developments in economics theories into CGE modeling. Some models consider the cases of imperfect competition such as the existence of monopoly and oligopoly in some sectors, some integrate econometric techniques for the parameters and model estimates, others consider the factor of externalities, and so on. Interested readers can find comprehensive reference lists of various developments in CGE modeling in Dixon and Jorgenson (2013).

The production functions in the standard model are characterized by constant-returns-to-scale (CRS), because of the reasons we have discussed. If the observed output data appears to exhibit increasing-returns-to-scale (IRS) in the data sample, we can add some factors to convert the production function to CRS. For instance, in Openland2, if the time-series data shows that doubling labor and capital inputs would more than double the output, we may add a third factor, technology, represented by TFP, in the production function. By calibrating the changing values of the TFP parameter, we can make the production function constant-returns-to-scale in labor, capital and technology.

If the production function is decreasing-returns-to-scale (DRS), the model should still be able to reach equilibrium, because the production set is convex. However, the structure of the model would be more complicated. The following changes must be made in the model:

First, the price equation in the production block needs to be revised. Take the example of the first-order condition (FOC) form of Equation (7.4.2) in the production module. In the CRS production case, the price equation $p = w_1 x_1/q + w_2 x_2/q$ implies the first-order condition of profit maximization "commodity price = marginal cost", because right-hand side (RHS) is marginal cost. In the case of DRS, it is no longer true. The first-order condition has to take the direct form of $p = \frac{\partial c(w_1, w_2, q)}{\partial q}$, which is the commodity supply function. $c(w_1, w_2, q)$ is the cost function and its partial derivative $\frac{\partial c(w_1, w_2, q)}{\partial q}$ can have a complicated function form. Secondly, in the case of DRS, the enterprise revenue does not equal cost. Enterprise has the equation of $pq = c(\mathbf{w}, q) + \pi$ and would earn a positive profit π. Thirdly, the model needs to specify how the enterprises distribute the profits to the owners. After adding these details, a CGE model with the DRS technology is operatable.

Many efforts have been devoted to apply CGE models in developing countries, in which the economic environment is different from mature industrial countries. The IFPRI model has a component block for nonmarket activities in developing countries, and has been applied to the economy of Zimbabwe. The dual-dual CGE model is suggested by Stifel and Thorbecke (2003) for developing economies, which has double duals: urban versus rural areas, and formal versus informal sectors. In the dual-dual model, labor is broken down into skilled and unskilled groups. Capital is broken down into agricultural and non-agricultural capitals. Households have nine groups, including rural unskilled workers, landlords, urban workers in the informal sector, urban skilled workers in the formal sector, urban unskilled workers in the formal sector, capitalists, etc. They argued this dual-dual CGE model can better simulate the real situation in developing countries. While this model is theoretically sound, it has not been applied to a real economy case yet.

Many more issues may be investigated within the CGE framework, including impacts of the money supply and interest rate, trading in the financial market, intertemporal borrowing, etc. A number of scholars are working in these areas.[2] While the standard CGE model has its limitations, it provides the foundation for future development in CGE models in various directions.

Exercise

18E.1 Suppose in the base state of Openland2, the ratio of labor supply to leisure is 2:1. The price elasticity of labor supply is 0.2. Other data needed are available in SAM Table 15.2.1. Using Equation (18.2.13), write a GAMS program to calibrate the value of exponent ρ of the CES utility function of leisure and the composite commodity.

---

[2]Naastepad (2002) discusses "real" financial CGE models.

GAMS Program Codes Used in CGE Models

Key Commands

set
alias
table
parameter
variable
equation
model
solve

Codes Used Often in Programs of This Book

For remarks: Starting with $ontext and ending with $offtext
For remarks: starting with * in the sentence
Suffix .L for variables
Suffix .fx for fixing values

Variables and Parameters in Mathematical Expression, Chapters 8–17

The names of variables and parameters in this book follow the convention in economics textbooks and the computable general equilibrium (CGE) literature such as the international food policy research institute (IFPRI) model. Variables are denoted by upper-case Latin letters. Parameters are denoted by lower-case Latin or Greek letters. The first letter of a variable name or a parameter name follows this convention: Q for quantity, P for price, W for factor price, E for monetary expenditure (except EXR is for the exchange rate), Y for monetary income, and t for tax. Many other names can be read directly: *share*, *transfer*, and *SAVE*. The names for institutions are shortened to: H for households, ENT for enterprises, G for the government, ROW for the rest of the world. The definition of some parameters and variables may change somewhat as needed in a special context.

Sets

A	set of all activities, with index a
C	set of all commodities, with index c
F	set of all factors, with index f
CT	set for trade and transport margin inputs, with index ct
H	set for household groups, with index h

Parameters (Greek letters)

α^q	scale parameter of CES production function of q
α_c^q	scale parameter of CES production function for c (Chapters 8–12)
α_c^q	scale parameter of the Armington CES function for c (Chapters 14–17)
α_a^a	scale parameter of CES production function for a
α_a^t	scale parameter of the CET function of a
α^{va}	scale parameter of the value-added CES function
α_c^{ac}	scale parameter the CES function in the QX block for c
β_c	LES system, marginal budget share spending on commodity c
γ_c	LES subsistence consumption on c

δ^q	share parameter of the output CES production function of q
δ_c^q	share parameter of the output CES production function of c (Chapters 8–12)
δ_c^q	share parameter of the Armington CES function of c (Chapters 14–17)
δ_a^a	share parameter of the output CES production function of a
δ_a^t	share parameter of the CET function of a
δ^{va}	share parameter of the value-added CES function
δ_{ac}^{ac}	share parameter of the CES production in the QX block for c
ε	elasticity of substitution (definition may vary depending on the context)
ρ	exponent of the CES production function of q
ρ_c	exponent of the CES production function of c (Chapters 8–12)
ρ_c^q	exponent of the Armington CES function for c (Chapters 14–17)
ρ_a^a	exponent of the CES production function of a
ρ_a^t	exponent of the CET function in trade models
ρ^{va}	exponent of the value-added CES function
ρ_c^{ac}	exponent of the CES function for c in the QX block

Parameters (Latin letters)

$apiwt$	activity price index weights
$cpiwt$	CPI weights
eho	constant term of the consumption function
ia'_{cc}	input coefficient of using c to produce c'
ica_{ca}	input coefficient of using a to produce c
$ictt_{ct,c}$	trade and transport margin input ct used to produce one unit of c
$iett$	proportion of transport margin to the amount of export
mpc	marginal propensity to consume
mps	marginal propensity to save
$oxac_{ac}$	output c per unit of activity a in the QX block
pwe_c	world price of export of commodity c
pwe_a	world price of export of activity product a
$ppiwt$	PPI weights
pwm_c	world price of import of commodity c
$rvati$	VAT refund on intermediate inputs
$shareg_c$	share of government's consumption expenditure on commodity c
$shareh_c$	share of households' consumption expenditure on commodity c
$shareif_{entk}$	share of the capital income kept internally in enterprises
$shareif_{hk}$	share of the capital income paid to households (or to group h)
$shareif_{hl}$	share of the labor income paid to household group h
$sube_a$	subsidy rate for export of activity product a
$transfer_{h\,ent}$	enterprises' transfer payments to households (or group h)
$transfer_{h\,g}$	government's transfer payments to households (or group h)
$transfer_{h\,row}$	rest-of-the-world's transfer payments to households (or group h)

$transfer_{ent\,g}$	government's transfer payments to enterprises
te_a	export tax rate of activity product a
te_c	export tax rate of commodity c
ti	income tax rate of households
$tibus$	tax rate on the business capital income
ti_{ent}	business income tax rate, corporate income tax rate
tm_c	Import tariff rate for c
$tpayent$	employers' payroll tax rate
$tpayhh$	households' payroll tax rate
$tsale_c$	sales' tax rate
$tvat$	VAT tax rate
$tvatl$	VAT tax rate on employment (consumption-type VAT rate)
$tvatk$	VAT tax rate on capital
$tvatq_c$	VAT tax rate, tax burden on consumers

Variables

API	Activity Price Index
CPI	Consumer Price Index
$DUMMYSI$	Dummy variable for the dependency of the Savings–Investment function
EG	Government total expenditure
EH	Total consumption expenditure of households
EXR	Exchange rate
GDP	GDP
$INVADJ$	Investment adjust factor
PA_a	Price of activity a
PC_c	Price of the commodity c (definition varies in different chapters)
PDA_a	Price of activity a produced and supplied domestically
PDC_c	Price of commodity c produced and supplied domestically
PE_a	Export price of a including subsidy
PE_c	Export price of c including subsidy
$PINTA_a$	Price of aggregate intermediate input a
PM_c	Import price of c including tariff paid by domestic buyers
PP_c	Producer's price of commodity c
PPI	Producer Price Index (Note PPI is not weighted PP_c, as explained in 13-5)
PQ_c	Purchaser's price of commodity c
$PQENT_c$	Enterprises' purchaser's price of commodity c
PQH_c	Household purchaser's price of commodity c
PQS_c	Supplier's price of commodity c
PVA_a	Price of aggregate value-added input for activity a
PX_c	Price of composite commodity c
$PXAC_{a,c}$	Price of commodity c from activity a

QA_a	Quantity of activity a
QC_c	Quantity of the commodity c
$QCTT_c$	Trade and transport margin input used in commodity c
$QCTT_{ct,c}$	Trade and transport margins of ct used in commodity c
$QCTTA$	Sum of trade and transport margin input
QDA_a	Quantity of activity a produced and supplied domestically
QDC_c	Quantity of commodity c produced and supplied domestically
QE_a	Quantity of export a
QE_c	Quantity of export c
QG_c	Quantity of government consumption of commodity c
QH_c	Quantity demanded for c by households
$QH_{c,h}$	Quantity demanded for c by households of group h
$QINT_{c,a}$	Quantity of intermediate input c used in production of a
$QINTA_a$	Quantity of aggregate intermediate input of a
$QINV_c$	Quantity of investment of c by enterprises
QKD_a	Capital demand by activity a
QKS	Total capital supply
QKS_h	Capital supply of group h
$QKSAGG$	Total capital supply
QLD_a	Labor demand by activity a
QLS	Total labor supply
QLS_h	Labor supply of group h
$QLSAGG$	Total labor supply
QM_c	Quantity of import c
QQ_c	Total composite commodity supplied in domestic market
QVA_a	Quantity of aggregate value-added input for activity a
QX_c	Quantity of composite commodity c
$QXAC_{a,c}$	Quantity of commodity c from activity a
$SAVEENT$	Enterprise savings
$SAVEF$	Foreign savings or balance of payment
$SAVEG$	Net government savings or fiscal budget balance
$SAVEH$	Household savings
$SAVEH_h$	Household savings of group h
WK	Capital price
WL	Labor price
$YDISH$	Disposable income of households
$YENT$	Enterprise income
YG	Government total revenue
YH	Household income
$WALRAS$	Dummy variable for the dependency due to Walras' law

Variables and Parameters in GAMS Programs

API	Activity Price Index
apiwt(a)	Activity Price Index weight
bgtshare(c)	Average budget share on c in the LES function
bgtshare$_{c,h}$	Average budget share on c in the LES function of group h
bhtsharechk1	Check if average budget share sum is 1
bhtsharechk1(h)	Check if average budget share sum of group h is 1
CPI	Consumer Price Index
cpiwt(c)	Consumer Price Index weight
CV(h)	Compensating variation of household group h
deltaAa(a)	Share of value-added in the top level CES prod function
deltaac$_{a,c}$	Share parameter in the CES function from a to c in QX block
deltaCET(a)	Domestic sales share parameter in CET function of a
deltaCET(c)	Domestic sales share parameter in CET function of c
deltaQq(c)	Domestic product share parameter in Armington CES function
deltaVA(a)	Labor share parameter in value-added CES function of a
DUMMYSI	Dummy variable for dependency of Savings-Investment function
EG	Government total expenditure
EG0chk	Check if EGO is consistent
EH	Total consumption expenditure of households
EH(h)	Total consumption expenditure of households of group h
eho	Constant term of the consumption function
eho(h)	Constant term of consumption function of group h
EV(h)	Equivalent variation of household group h
Expen	Monetary spending on commodities by households
EXR	Exchange rate
Frisch	Frisch parameter
GDP	GDP
ica(c,a)	Input coefficient for intermediate inputs
ictt(c)	Proportion of trade transport input used in commodity c
ictt(ct,c)	Proportion of trade transport input ct used in commodity c

INVADJ	Investment adjustment factor
KSelas	Price elasticity of capital supply
KSscale	Scale factor of the capital supply function
LESbeta(c)	Marginal budget share of LES
LESbeta(c,h)	Marginal budget share of LES of group h
Lesbetachk1	Check if the marginal budget share beta sum to 1
Lesbetachk1(h)	Check if the marginal budget share beta sum of group h is 1
LESsub(c)	Subsistence consumption level of c of LES
LESsub(c,h)	Subsistence consumption level of c of LES of group h
LSelas	Price elasticity of labor supply
LSscale	Scale factor of the labor supply function
mpc	marginal propensity to consume
mpc(h)	marginal propensity to consume of group h
oxaca,c	output c per unit of activity a
PA(a)	Price of activity a
PDA(a)	Price of activity a produced and supplied domestically
PDC(c)	Price of commodity c produced and supplied domestically
PE(a)	Export price including subsidy of activity output a
PE(c)	Export price including subsidy of commodity c
PINTA(a)	Price of aggregate intermediate input a
PM(c)	Import price of c including tariff paid by domestic buyers
PPI	Producer Price Index
ppiwt(a)	Producer Price Index weight
PQ(c)	Purchaser's price of commodity c
PQS(c)	Supplier's price of commodity c
PVA(a)	Price of aggregate value-added input a
PVA(c)	Price of aggregate value-added input c
pwe(a)	World price of export a in foreign currency unit
pwe(c)	World price of export a in foreign currency unit
pwm(c)	World price of import c in foreign currency unit
PX(c)	Price of composite commodity c
PXAC(a,c)	Price of commodity c from activity a
QA(a)	Quantity of activity a
QCTT(c)	Trade and transport margin input used in commodity c
QCTT(ct,c)	trade and transport margin of ct used in commodity c
QCTTA	Sum of trade and transport margin input
QDA(a)	Quantity of activity a produced and supplied domestically
QDC(c)	Quantity of commodity c produced and supplied domestically
QE(a)	Quantity of export a
QE(c)	Quantity of export c
QG(c)	Quantity of government consumption of commodity c

QH(c)	Quantity demanded for c by households
QH(c,h)	Quantity demanded for c by households of group h
QINT(c,a)	Quantity of intermediate input c used in production of a
QINTA(a)	Quantity of aggregate intermediate input
QINV(c)	Quantity of investment of c by enterprises
QKD(a)	Capital demand by activity a
QKS	Total capital supply
QKS(h)	Capital supply of group h
QKSAGG	Total capital supply
QLD(a)	Labor demand by activity a
QLS	Total labor supply
QLS(h)	Labor supply of group h
QLSAGG	Total labor supply
QM(c)	Quantity of import c
QQ(c)	Total composite commodity c supplied in domestic market
QVA(a)	Quantity of aggregate value-added of activity a
QVA(c)	Quantity of aggregate value-added of commodity c
QX(c)	Quantity of composite commodity c supplied in the QX block
QXAC(a,c)	Quantity of commodity c from activity a
SAVEENT	Enterprise savings
SAVEF	Foreign savings or balance of payment
SAVEG	Net government savings or fiscal budget balance
SAVEH	Household savings
SAVEH(h)	Household savings of group h
scaleAa(a)	Scale factor of top level CES function of a
scaleac(c)	Scale factor CES function from activity to c in QX block
scaleAVA(a)	Scale factor of value-added CES function of a
scaleCET(c)	Scale factor of CET function
scaleQq(c)	Scale factor of Armington CES function
shareg(c)	Share of government income spending on c
shareh(c)	Share of households' income spending on c
shareifentk	Share of capital income retained by enterprises
shareifhk	Households' share in capital income of enterprises
shareifhk(h)	Share household group h in capital income of enterprises
sharelh(h)	Share household group h in labor endowment
sube(a)	Export subsidy rate for a
tiEnt	Business income tax rate
tih	Households income tax rate
tih(h)	Income tax rate of household group h
tm(c)	Import tariff rate for c
tpayent(a)	Rate of the payroll tax paid by enterprises

transferhg0	Base amount of government transfer payment to households
transferhg0(h)	Base amount of government transfer to household group h
tsale(c)	Sales tax rate on commodity c
tvatl(a)	Rate of VAT on labor paid by enterprises
tvatq(c)	Rate of VAT burden on consumers
utility0(h)	Initial utility level of household group h
utility1(h)	Utility level of household group h after policy change
WK	Capital price
WL	Labor price
YENT	Enterprise income
YG	Government total revenue
YH	Household income
YH(h)	Household income of group h
WALRAS	Dummy variable for the system dependency due to Walras' law

Appendix

The Openland2 Model

Note: The model of Openland2 is a full-fledged standard CGE model offered in this book. The basic structure of the Openland2 model is explained in Chapter 15. A major difference from the IFPRI model is the arrangement of the export section, which has advantages as discussed. The SAM table is Table 15.2.1 and the included SAM data file is Table 15.1.1 with the file name Openland2SAM.inc. The following GAMS program is the solution to Exercise 17E.3 at the end of Chapter 17. The closures are set as required by the exercise: It has flexible factor supply functions. It is a "large country" in imports of agricultural and industrial commodities: therefore, it faces upward sloping supply curves from the rest of the world. The output file of the GAMS program attached at the end provides the answers to questions of Exercise 17E.3.

1.1 GAMS Program

```
$title Exercise 17E-3 for Openland2
*Labor and Capital flexible supply curve, test cut tvatl
*A large country closure for imports

*Define sets
set ac       /act1,act2,act3,com1,com2,com3,margin,lab,cap,hh,ent,gov,VATL,VATQ,
tariff,subex,row,invsav,total/;
set a(ac)    /act1,act2,act3/;
set c(ac)    /com1,com2,com3/;
set f(ac)    /lab,cap/;
*The following set acnt is for checking accuracy of SAM
set acnt(ac)  all accounts excluding total;
acnt(ac)=YES;
acnt('total')=NO;

alias (ac,acp),(a,ap),(c,cp),(f,fp),(acnt,acntp);

table sam(ac,acp)
$include D:\GAMS programs\Openland2SAM.inc
```

```
table Identac(a,c)
          com1     com2     com3
act1         1
act2                  1
act3                           1
;


*Check if the SAM table is balanced
parameters
samchk0(ac);
samchk0(acnt)=sum(acntp,SAM(acntp,acnt))-sum(acntp,SAM(acnt,acntp));

display samchk0,acnt,sam;

*Input parameter values given externally
parameter   rhoAa(a)   /act1 =   0.2,   act2 = 0.3,   act3 = 0.1/
            rhoVA(a)   /act1     0.3,   act2   0.2,   act3   0.5/
            rhoCET(a)  /act1     1.4,   act2   1.4,   act3   2.0/
            rhoQq(c)   /com1     0.4,   com2   0.6,   com3   0.4/
            LESelas(c) /com1     0.5,   com2   1.0,   com3   1.2 /
            Frisch     /-2/;

parameters
KSelas           Price elasticity of capital supply
KSscale          Scale factor of the capital supply function
LSelas           Price elasticity of labor supply
LSscale          Scale factor of the labor supply function
QMelas(c)        Price elasticity of import supply
QMscale(c)       Scale factor of import supply
scaleAa(a)       Scale factor of top level CES function of a
deltaAa(a)       Value-added share parameter in top level CES of a
scaleAVA(a)      Scale factor of value-added CES function of a
deltaVA(a)       Labor share parameter in value-added CES function of a
ica(c,a)         Input coefficient for intermediate inputs
scaleCET(a)      Scale factor of CET function
deltaCET(a)      Domestic sales share parameter in CET function
scaleQq(c)       Scale factor of Armington CES function
deltaQq(c)       Domestic product share parameter in Armington CES function
bgtshare(c)      Average budget share on c in the LES function
bhtsharechk1     Check if average budget share sum is 1
LESbeta(c)       Marginal budget share of LES
Lesbetachk1      Check if the marginal budget share beta sum is 1
LESsub(c)        Subsistence consumption level of c of LES
shareifhk        Households share in capital income of enterprises
shareifentk      Share of capital income retained by enterprises
shareg(c)        Share of government income spending on c
tih              Households income tax rate
tiEnt            Business income tax rate
tvatl(a)         Rate of VAT on labor paid by enterprises
```

tvatq(c)	Rate of VAT burden on consumers
transferhg0	Base amount of government transfer payment to households
eho	Consumption function constant
mpc	marginal propensity to consume
QCTT0(c)	Trade and transport margin input used in commodity c
QCTTA0	Sum of trade and transport margin inputs
ictt(c)	Proportion of trade transport input used in quantity of c
PA0(a)	Price of activity a
QA0(a)	Quantity of activity a
PVA0(a)	Price of aggregate value-added
QVA0(a)	Quantity of aggregate value-added
PINTA0(a)	Price of aggregate intermediate input
QINTA0(a)	Quantity of aggregate intermediate input
QINT0(c,a)	Quantity of intermediate input c used in production of a
QLD0(a)	Labor demand by a
QKD0(a)	Capital demand by a
WL0	Labor price
WK0	Capital price
PQ0(c)	Purchaser's price of commodity c
PQS0(c)	Supplier's price of commodity c
QQ0(c)	Total composite commodity supplied in domestic market
PM0(c)	Import price including tariff paid by domestic buyers
QM0(c)	Quantity of import c
PE0(a)	Export price including subsidy of domestic producers
QE0(a)	Quantity of export a
PDA0(a)	Price of activity a produced and supplied domestically
QDA0(a)	Quantity of activity a produced and supplied domestically
PDC0(c)	Price of commodity c produced and supplied domestically
QDC0(c)	Quantity of commodity c produced and supplied domestically
EXR0	Exchange rate
pwm0(c)	World price of import c in foreign currency
pwe(a)	World price of export a in foreign currency
tm(c)	Import tariff rate for c
sube(a)	Export subsidy rate for a
QLS0	Total labor supply
QKS0	Total capital supply
YH0	Household income
EH0	Total consumption expenditure of households
QH0(c)	Quantity demanded for c by households
YENT0	Enterprise income
QINV0(c)	Quantity of investment of c by enterprises
SAVEENT0	Enterprise savings
YG0	Government total revenue
EG0	Government total expenditure
QG0(c)	Quantity of government consumption of commodity c
SAVEH0	Household savings
SAVEG0	Net government savings or fiscal budget balance
SAVEF0	Foreign savings or balance of payment

```
cpiwt(c)            Consumer Price Index weight
CPI0                Consumer Price Index
apiwt(a)            Activity Price Index weight
API0                Activity Price Index
;

*Assignment and calibration for parameters
PA0(a)=1;
PQ0(c)=sam('total',c)/(sum(a,sam(a,c))+sam('row',c)+sam('tariff',c));
QINT0(c,a)=SAM(c,a)/PQ0(c);
QINTA0(a)=SUM(c, QINT0(c,a));
ica(c,a)=QINT0(c,a)/QINTA0(a) ;
PINTA0(a)=SUM(c,ica(c,a)*PQ0(c));
WK0=1;
WL0=1;
PE0(a)=1;
PM0(c)=1;
PDA0(a)=1;
PDC0(c)=1;
EXR0=1;
PQS0(c)=1;
QA0(a)=sam('total',a)/PA0(a);
QVA0(a)=SUM(f,sam(f,a));
PVA0(a)=(SUM(f,sam(f,a))+sam('VATL',a))/QVA0(a);
QLD0(a)=sam('lab',a)/WL0;
QKD0(a)=sam('cap',a)/WK0;
QLS0=sam('total','lab')/WL0;
QKS0=sam('total','cap')/WK0;
tvatl(a)=sam('VATL',a)/sam('lab',a);
*tm(c)conditional on $sam('row',c), means only execute this equation when import
entry is positive.
*This avoids the problem of denominator equaling 0
tm(c)$sam('row',c)=sam('tariff',c)/sam('row',c);
pwm0(c)=PM0(c)/((1+tm(c))*EXR0);
QM0(c)=(sam('row',c)+sam('tariff',c))/PM0(c);
sube(a)=sam(a,'subex')/(sam(a,'row')+sam(a,'subex'));
pwe(a)=((1-sube(a))*PE0(a))/EXR0;
QE0(a)=(sam(a,'row')+sam(a,'subex'))/PE0(a);
QDA0(a)=sum(c,sam(a,c))/PDA0(a);
QDC0(c)=sum(a,sam(a,c))/PDC0(c);
QQ0(c)=QDC0(c)+QM0(c);
*The following are for marketing margins and consumer's burden part of VAT
tvatq(c)=sam('VATQ',c)/(sum(a,sam(a,c))+sam('row',c)+sam('tariff',c)+sam('margin',
c));
QCTT0(c)=sam('margin',c)/PQ0('com3');
ictt(c)=QCTT0(c)/QQ0(c);
QCTTA0=sum(c,QCTT0(c));
deltaAa(a)=PVA0(a)*QVA0(a)**(1-rhoAa(a))/(PVA0(a)*QVA0(a)**(1-
```

```
rhoAa(a))+PINTA0(a)*QINTA0(a)**(1-rhoAa(a)));
scaleAa(a)=QA0(a)/(deltaAa(a)*QVA0(a)**rhoAa(a)+(1-
deltaAa(a))*QINTA0(a)**rhoAa(a))**(1/rhoAa(a));
deltaVA(a)=((1+tvatl(a))*WL0)*QLD0(a)**(1-rhoVA(a))/
(((1+tvatl(a))*WL0)*QLD0(a)**(1-rhoVA(a))+WK0*QKD0(a)**(1-rhoVA(a)));
scaleAVA(a)=QVA0(a)/(deltaVA(a)*QLD0(a)**rhoVA(a)+(1-
deltaVA(a))*QKD0(a)**rhoVA(a))**(1/rhoVA(a));
*CET function parameter calibration
deltaCET(a)=PDA0(a)*QDA0(a)**(1-rhoCET(a))/(PDA0(a)*QDA0(a)**(1-
rhoCET(a))+PE0(a)*QE0(a)**(1-rhoCET(a)));
scaleCET(a)=QA0(a)/(deltaCET(a)*QDA0(a)**rhoCET(a)+(1-
deltaCET(a))*QE0(a)**rhoCET(a))**(1/rhoCET(a));
*Arminton function parameter calibration
deltaQq(c)=PDC0(c)*QDC0(c)**(1-rhoQQ(c))/(PDC0(c)*QDC0(c)**(1-
rhoQq(c))+PM0(c)*QM0(c)**(1-rhoQq(c)));
scaleQQ(c)=QQ0(c)/(deltaQq(c)*QDC0(c)**rhoQq(c)+(1-
deltaQq(c))*QM0(c)**rhoQq(c))**(1/rhoQq(c));
*Calibration of other parameters
QH0(c)=SAM(c,'hh')/PQ0(c);
cpiwt(c)=QH0(c)/sum(cp,QH0(cp));
CPI0=sum(c,PQ0(c)*cpiwt(c));
transferhg0=sam('hh','gov')/cpi0;
shareifhk=sam('hh','cap')/(WK0*QKS0);
shareifentk=sam('ent','cap')/(WK0*QKS0);
YH0=WL0*QLS0+shareifhk*WK0*QKS0+transferhg0*cpi0;
tih=sam('gov','hh')/YH0;
SAVEH0=sam('invsav','hh');
YENT0=shareifentk*WK0*QKS0;
QINV0(c)=sam(c,'invsav')/PQ0(c);
tiEnt=sam('gov','ent')/YEnt0;
SAVEENT0=(1-tiEnt)*YENT0;
YG0=tih*YH0+tiEnt*YENT0+sum(a,tvatl(a)*WL0*QLD0(a))+sum(c,sam('VATQ',c))+sam('gov'
,'tariff')-sum(a,sam(a,'subex'));
QG0(c)=sam(c,'gov')/PQ0(c);
SAVEG0=sam('invsav','gov');
EG0=YG0-SAVEG0;
shareg(c)=PQ0(c)*QG0(c)/(EG0-transferhg0*cpi0);
SAVEF0=sam('invsav','row');
apiwt(a)=QA0(a)/sum(ap,QA0(ap));
API0=sum(a,PA0(a)*apiwt(a));
EH0=sum(c,sam(c,'hh'));
bgtshare(c)=SAM(c,'hh')/EH0;
bhtsharechk1=sum(c,bgtshare(c));
LESbeta(c)=LESelas(c)*bgtshare(c)/(sum(cp,LESelas(cp)*bgtshare(cp)));
LESsub(c)=sam(c,'hh')/PQ0(c)+(LESbeta(c)/PQ0(c))*(EH0/frisch);
LESbetachk1=sum(c,LESbeta(c));
eho=sum(c,PQ0(c)*LESsub(c))/cpi0;
mpc=(EH0-eho*cpi0)/((1-tih)*YH0);
```

```
*parameters for the capital and labor supply functions
KSelas=0.4;
KSscale=sam('cap','total')/(WK0**KSelas);
LSelas=0.2;
LSscale=sam('lab','total')/(WL0**LSelas);
QMelas(c)=2;
QMscale(c)$sam('row',c)=QM0(c)/(pwm0(c)**QMelas(c));

display
ica,ictt,PA0,QA0,EG0,identac,shareg,tvatq,tvatl,bhtsharechk1,Lesbetachk1,YH0,
tih,EH0,eho,mpc,cpi0,WL0,WK0,PQ0,PINTA0,PVA0,QQ0,QINTA0,QVA0,QDA0,QDC0,QQ0,pwm0,pw
e,sube,QE0;

variable
PA(a),PVA(a),PINTA(a),QA(a),QVA(a),QINTA(a),QINT(c,a),QLD(a),QKD(a),QLS,QKS,WL,WK,
PDA(a),QDA(a),
PDC(c),QDC(c),PE(a),QE(a),EXR,QQ(c),PQS(c),PQ(c),PM(c),QM(c),QCTT(c),QCTTA,YH,EH,Q
H(c),SAVEH,YENT,
QINV(c),INVADJ,SAVEENT,YG,EG,QG(c),SAVEG,SAVEF,CPI,API,pwm(c),DUMMYSI;

equation
QAfn(a),QAFOCeq(a),PAeq(a),QVAfn(a),QVAFOC(a),PVAeq(a),QINTfn(c,a),PINTAeq(a),CETfn
(a),
CETFOC(a),PCETeq(a),PEeq(a),QQfn(c),QQfnNoImport(c),QQFOC(c),PQSPDCNoImportfn(c),
PQSeq(c),PMeq(c),QDCQDA(c),PDCPDA(c),QCTTeq,QCTTAeq,PQSPQeq(c),Yheq,EHeq,QHeq(c),S
AVEHeq,YENTeq,
QINVeq(c),SAVEENTeq,Ygeq,QGeq,SAVEGeq,ComEqui(c),Leq,Keq,FEXeq,CPIeq,APIeq,SIeq,Ls
upply,Ksupply,QMsupply(c);

*Production block
QAfn(a)..
QA(a)=e=scaleAa(a)*(deltaAa(a)*QVA(a)**rhoAa(a)+(1-
deltaAa(a))*QINTA(a)**rhoAa(a))**(1/rhoAa(a));

QAFOCeq(a)..
PVA(a)/PINTA(a)=e=(deltaAa(a)/(1-deltaAa(a)))*(QVA(a)/QINTA(a))**(rhoAa(a)-1);

PAeq(a)..
PA(a)*QA(a)=e=PVA(a)*QVA(a)+PINTA(a)*QINTA(a);

QVAfn(a)..
QVA(a)=e=scaleAVA(a)*(deltaVA(a)*QLD(a)**rhoVA(a)+(1-
deltaVA(a))*QKD(a)**rhoVA(a))**(1/rhoVA(a));

QVAFOC(a)..
((1+tvatl(a))*WL)/WK=e=(deltaVA(a)/(1-deltaVA(a)))*(QLD(a)/QKD(a))**(rhoVA(a)-1);

PVAeq(a)..
PVA(a)*QVA(a)=e=(1+tvatl(a))*WL*QLD(a)+WK*QKD(a);
```

```
QINTfn(c,a)..
QINT(c,a)=e=ica(c,a)*QINTA(a);

PINTAeq(a)..
PINTA(a)=e=SUM(c,ica(c,a)*PQ(c));

*CET module
CETfn(a)..
QA(a)=e=scaleCET(a)*(deltaCET(a)*QDA(a)**rhoCET(a)+(1-
deltaCET(a))*QE(a)**rhoCET(a))**(1/rhoCET(a));

CETFOC(a)..
PDA(a)/PE(a)=e=(deltaCET(a)/(1-deltaCET(a)))*(QDA(a)/QE(a))**(rhoCET(a)-1);

PCETeq(a)..
PA(a)*QA(a)=e=PDA(a)*QDA(a)+PE(a)*QE(a);

PEeq(a)..
PE(a)=e=(1/(1-sube(a)))*pwe(a)*EXR;

*Using dollar control operator to handle the problem of QM=0
QQfn(c)$sam('row',c)..
QQ(c)=e=scaleQq(c)*(deltaQq(c)*QDC(c)**rhoQq(c)+(1-
deltaQq(c))*QM(c)**rhoQq(c))**(1/rhoQq(c));

QQfnNoImport(c)$(NOT sam('row',c))..
QQ(c)=e=QDC(c);

QQFOC(c)$sam('row',c)..
PDC(c)/PM(c)=e=(deltaQq(c)/(1-deltaQq(c)))*(QDC(c)/QM(c))**(rhoQq(c)-1);

PQSPDCNoImportfn(c)$(sam('row',c)=0)..
PQS(c)=e=PDC(c);

PQSeq(c)..
PQS(c)*QQ(c)=e=PDC(c)*QDC(c)+PM(c)*QM(c);

PMeq(c)$sam('row',c)..
PM(c)=e=pwm(c)*(1+tm(c))*EXR;

*The following two equations assign fixed prices for sector 3 without imports
PM.fx(c)$(NOT sam('row',c))=1;
pwm.fx(c)$(NOT sam('row',c))=PM0(c)/((1+tm(c))*EXR0);

*Mapping from activities to commodities
QDCQDA(c)..
QDC(c)=e=sum(a,identac(a,c)*QDA(a));
```

```
PDCPDA(c)..
PDC(c)=e=sum(a,identac(a,c)*PDA(a));

*trade and transport margins module
QCTTeq(c)..
QCTT(c)=e=ictt(c)*QQ(c);

QCTTAeq..
QCTTA=e=sum(c,QCTT(c));

PQSPQeq(c)..
PQ(c)*QQ(c)=e=(1+tvatq(c))*(PQS(c)*QQ(c)+QCTT(c)*PQ('com3'));

*Households
YHeq..
YH=e=WL*QLS+shareifhk*WK*QKS+transferhg0*CPI;

EHeq..
EH=e=eho*cpi+mpc*(1-tih)*YH;

QHeq(c)..
PQ(c)*QH(c)=e=PQ(c)*LESsub(c)+LESbeta(c)*(EH-sum(cp,PQ(cp)*LESsub(cp)));

SAVEHeq..
SAVEH=e=-eho*cpi+(1-mpc)*(1-tih)*YH;

*Enterprises
YENTeq..
YENT=e=shareifentk*WK*QKS;

QINVeq(c)..
QINV(c)=e=QINV0(c)*INVADJ;

SAVEENTeq..
SAVEENT=e=(1-tiEnt)*YENT;

*Government
YGeq..
YG=e=sum(a,tvatl(a)*WL*QLD(a))+tih*YH+tiEnt*YENT+sum(c,tvatq(c)*(PQS(c)*QQ(c)+QCTT
(c)*PQ('com3'))+tm(c)*pwm(c)*QM(c)*EXR)-sum(a,sube(a)*PE(a)*QE(a));

SAVEGeq..
EG=e=YG-SAVEG;

QGeq(c)..
PQ(c)*QG(c)=e=shareg(c)*(EG-transferhg0*CPI);
```

```
*The following equation handles the optional QCTTA component
ComEqui(c)..
QQ(c)=e=sum(a,QINT(c,a))+QH(c)+QINV(c)+QG(c)+QCTTA$sam(c,'margin');

*Factor markets
Leq..
Sum(a,QLD(a))=e=QLS;

Lsupply..
QLS=e=LSscale*WL**LSelas;

Keq..
Sum(a,QKD(a))=e=QKS;

Ksupply..
QKS=e=KSscale*WK**KSelas;

QMsupply(c)$sam('row',c)..
QM(c)=e=QMscale(c)*pwm(c)**QMelas(c);

*price indices
CPIeq..
CPI=e=sum(c,PQ(c)*cpiwt(c));

APIeq..
API=e=sum(a,PA(a)*apiwt(a));

*BOP equation
FEXeq..
SAVEF*EXR=e=sum(c,pwm(c)*QM(c)*EXR)-sum(a,pwe(a)*QE(a)*EXR);

SIeq..
sum(c,PQ(c)*QINV(c))=e=SAVEH+SAVEENT+SAVEG+SAVEF*EXR+dummysi;

*Assigning initial values
PA.L(a)=PA0(a);
PVA.L(a)=PVA0(a);
PINTA.L(a)=PINTA0(a);
QA.L(a)=QA0(a);
QVA.L(a)=QVA0(a);
QINTA.L(a)=QINTA0(a);
QINT.L(c,a)=QINT0(c,a);
QLD.L(a)=QLD0(a);
QKD.L(a)=QKD0(a);
QLS.L=QLS0;
QKS.L=QKS0;
WL.L=WL0;
WK.L=WK0;
```

```
PDA.L(a)=1;
QDA.L(a)=QDA0(a);
PDC.L(c)=1;
QDC.L(c)=QDC0(c);
PE.L(a)=1;
QE.L(a)=QE0(a);
EXR.L=1;
PQS.L(c)=1;
PQ.L(c)=PQ0(c);
QQ.L(c)=QQ0(c);
PM.L(c)=PM0(c);
QM.L(c)=QM0(c);
QCTT.L(c)=QCTT0(c);
QCTTA.L=QCTTA0;
YH.L=YH0;
EH.L=EH0;
QH.L(c)=QH0(c);
YENT.L=YENT0;
QINV.L(c)=QINV0(c);
INVADJ.L=1;
SAVEENT.L=SAVEENT0;
YG.L=YG0;
EG.L=EG0;
QG.L(c)=QG0(c);
SAVEG.L=SAVEG0;
SAVEF.L=SAVEF0;
CPI.L=CPI0;
API.L=API0;
DUMMYSI.L=0;
QKS.L=QKS0;
QLS.L=QLS0;
pwm.L(c)=pwm0(c);

*Fix three variable values to make the system square.   API is numeraire
*Government spending closure so EG is a variable
INVADJ.fx=1;
EXR.fx=EXR0;
API.fx=1;

*Executing the model
model cge   /all/;
solve cge using mcp;

parameter
tvatl0(a);
```

```
*Simulation for cutting VAT tax rate by 50%
tvatl0(a)=tvatl(a);
tvatl(a)=tvatl0(a)*0.5;

model sim  /all/;
solve sim using mcp;

parameter
utility0,utility1,EV,CV,QAchange(a),QQchange(c),QINVchange(c),QHchange(c),QLSchang
e,QKSchange,YGchange,
SAVEGchange,QEchange(a),QMchange(c),pwmchange(c),QGchange(c),PQchange(c);

*QH.L and PQ.L are the post-policy-change values.  Calculating EV and CV:
utility0= PROD(c,(QH0(c)-LESsub(c))**LESbeta(c));
utility1= PROD(c,(QH.L(c)-LESsub(c))**LESbeta(c));
EV=(utility1-utility0)*PROD(c,(PQ0(c)/LESbeta(c))**(LESbeta(c)));
CV=(utility1-utility0)*PROD(c,(PQ.L(c)/LESbeta(c))**(LESbeta(c)));

*Report the percentage changes in interested variables:
QAchange(a)=QA.L(a)/QA0(a)-1;
QQchange(c)=QQ.L(c)/QQ0(c)-1;
QEchange(a)=QE.L(a)/QE0(a)-1;
QMchange(c)$sam('row',c)=QM.L(c)/QM0(c)-1;
pwmchange(c)=pwm.L(c)/pwm0(c)-1;
QHchange(c)=QH.L(c)/QH0(c)-1;
QINVchange(c)=QINV.L(c)/QINV0(c)-1;
QGchange(c)=QG.L(c)/QG0(c)-1;
QLSchange=QLS.L/QLS0-1;
QKSchange=QKS.L/QKS0-1;
YGchange=YG.L/YG0-1;
SAVEGchange=SAVEG.L/SAVEG0-1;

Display EV,CV,INVADJ.L,QAchange,QQchange,QEchange,QMchange,pwmchange,QHchange,
QINVchange,QGchange,QLSchange,QKSchange,SAVEGchange,YGchange;

*END
```

1.2 Report from the GAMS Program Output File for Questions of Exercise 17E.3

```
----      494 PARAMETER EV                     =      48.569
              PARAMETER CV                     =      48.574
              VARIABLE INVADJ.L                =       1.000

----      494 PARAMETER QAchange

act1 0.003,    act2 0.005,    act3 0.007
```

——— 494 PARAMETER QQchange

com1 0.003,   com2 0.005,   com3 0.007

——— 494 PARAMETER QEchange

act1 0.004,   act2 0.004,   act3 0.007

——— 494 PARAMETER QMchange

com1 0.001,   com2 0.003

——— 494 PARAMETER pwmchange

com1 5.703644E−4,   com2   0.001

——— 494 PARAMETER QHchange

com1 0.008,   com2 0.015,   com3 0.018

——— 494 PARAMETER QINVchange

(ALL   0.000)

——— 494 PARAMETER QGchange

com1 −0.027,   com2 −0.028,   com3 −0.027

——— 494 PARAMETER QLSchange   =   0.009
        PARAMETER QKSchange   =   0.001
        PARAMETER SAVEGchange   =   −1.188
        PARAMETER YGchange   =   −0.063

Bibliography

Aguiar, M. and E. Hurst (2006). Measuring Trends in Leisure: The Allocation of Time over Five Decades, *Working Papers*, Federal Reserve Bank of Boston, January.

Arndt, C., B. Byiers, S. Robinson, and F. Tarp (2009). VAT and Economy-wide Modelling, In *Taxation in a Low-Income Economy: The Case of Mozambique*, Routledge Studies in Development Economics, Eds. Tarp, F. and C. Arndt, New York: Routledge, pp. 328–340.

Ballard, C. L., D. Fullerton, J. B. Shoven, and J. Whalley (1985). *A General Equilibrium Model for Tax Policy Evaluation*, Chicago: University of Chicago Press.

Bergman, L. and M. Henrekson (2003). CGE Modeling of Environmental Policy and Resource Management, In *Handbook of Environmental Economics*, Eds. M. Karl-Goran and J. Vincent, *Handbook of Environmental Economics*, Vol. 3, Amsterdam: North-Holland Publishing Co., pp. 1274–1302.

Brooke, A., D. Kendrick, and A. Meeraus (1988). *GAMS. A User's Guide*, Redwood City, Ca: Scientific Press.

Bureau of Economic Analysis (BEA) (2020). *Input-Output Accounts Data*, https://www.bea.gov/industry/input-output-accounts-data, December 20.

Burniaux, J.-M. and T. P. Truong (2002). GTAP-E: An Energy-Environmental Version of the GTAP Model, *GTAP Technical Paper No. 16*, Purdue University, West Lafayette, IN.

Bchir, M. H., Y. Decreux, J.-L. Guérin, and S. Jean (2002). MIRAGE, Computable General Equilibrium Model for Trade Policy Analysis, *CEPII Paper*, No. 2002-7, Centre d'Etudes Prospectives et d'Informations Internationales, Munich, Germany.

Chang, G. H. (1993). The Inconsistencies Among Disequilibrium Aggregates, *Journal of Comparative Economics*, 17(1), 70–91.

Chen, Y., G. Chang, E. Kou, and M. Liu (2010). VAT Tax Reform and Its Negative Impact on Employment in China: A CGE Analysis, *Economic Research Journal*, 2010(9), 29–42.

Dervis, K., J. de Melo, and S. Robinson (1982). *General Equilibrium Models for Development Policy*, Cambridge: Cambridge University Press.

Devarajan, S., D. S. Go, J. D. Lewis, S. Robinson, and P. Sinko (1997). *Simple General Equilibrium Modeling, in Applied Methods for Trade Policy Analysis: A Handbook*, Eds. Francois, J. F. and K. A. Reinert, Cambridge: Cambridge University Press, pp. 156–185.

de Melo, J. and David Tarr (1992). *A General Equilibrium Analysis of US Foreign Trade Policy*. Cambridge, Massachusetts: The MIT Press.

Dixon, P., R. Koopman, and M. Rimmer (2013). The MONASH Style of Computable General Equilibrium Modeling: A Framework for Practical Policy Analysis, In *Handbook of Computable General Equilibrium Modeling, Volumes 1A and 1B*, Eds. Dixon, P. and D. Jorgenson, Waltham, MA: North-Holland Publishing Co., pp. 23–103.

Dixon, P. and D. Jorgenson (2013). *Handbook of Computable General Equilibrium Modeling, Volumes 1A and 1B,* Waltham, MA: North-Holland Publishing Co.

Dixon, P. and M. Rimmer (2002). *Dynamic General Equilibrium Modelling for Forecasting and Policy: A Practical Guide and Documentation of MONASH*, Amsterdam: North-Holland Publishing Co.

Dixon, P. B., B. R. Parmenter, J. Sutton, and D. P. Vincent (1982). *ORANI: A Multisectoral Model of the Australian Economy*, Amsterdam: North-Holland Publishing Co.

Environmental Protection Agency (EPA) (2019). The *SAGE CGE Model*, https://www.epa.gov/environmental-economics/cge-modeling-regulatory-analysis, retrieved from January 15, 2020.

Fox, A. (2002). Incorporating Labor-Leisure Choice into a Static General Equilibrium Model, *GTAP Working Paper*, Purdue University, West Lafayette, IN, https://gtap.agecon.purdue.edu/resources/download/3620.pdf, retrieved from January 15, 2020.

Frisch, R. A. (1959). Complete Scheme for Computing All Direct and Cross Demand Elasticities in a Model with Many Sectors, *Econometrica*, 27(2), 177–196.

GAMS (2020). GAMS Release 33.2.0, https://www.gams.com/download/, December 1.

Gilbert, J. and T. Wahl (2002). Applied General Equilibrium Assessment of Trade Liberalization in China, *The World Economy*, 25(6), 697–731.

Ginsburgh, V. and M. Keyzer (2002). *The Structure of Applied General Equilibrium Models*, Cambridge, MA: The MIT Press.

GTAP (2020). *The Global Trade Analysis Project (GTAP)*, Center for Global Trade Analysis, housed in the Department of Agricultural Economics, Purdue University West Lafayette, IN, https://www.gtap.agecon.purdue.edu/default.asp.

Harrison, G. *et al.* eds. (2000). *Using Dynamic General Equilibrium Models for Policy Analysis*, North-Holland: Elsevier, Chapter 1, Introduction, pp. 1–12.

Horridge, M. and G. Wittwer (2008). SinoTerm, a Multi-Regional CGE Model of China, *China Economic Review*, No. 19, pp. 628–634.

The IFPRI model (2002). *A Standard Computable General Equilibrium (CGE) Model in GAMS*, by Lofgren H., R. L. Harris, and S. Robinson, International Food Policy Research Institute: Washington, D.C.

Johansen, L. (1960) *A Multisectoral Study of Economic Growth*, Amsterdam: North-Holland Publishing Company.

Jones, R. and J. Whalley (1988). Regional Effects of Taxes in Canada: An Applied General Equilibrium Approach, *Journal of Public Economics*, 37(1), 1–28.

Jorgenson, D. W. (1998). *Growth. Volume 1: Econometric General Equilibrium Modeling*, Cambridge: The MIT Press.

Kehoe, T. J., P. Noyola, A. Manyesa, C. Polo, and F. Sancho (1988). A General Equilibrium Analysis of the 1986 Tax Reform in Spain, *European Economic Review*, 32, 334–342.

Kohlhaas, M. and K. R. Pearson (2002). Introduction to GEMPACK for GAMS Users, *Preliminary Working Paper No. IP-79*, Monash University, The Centre of Policy Studies, Monash University, http://www.copsmodels.com/ftp/workpapr/ip-79.pdf.

Lofgren, H., R. L. Harris, and S. Robinson (2002). *A Standard Computable General Equilibrium (CGE) Model in GAMS*, International Food Policy Research Institute, Washington, D.C.

de Melo, J. (1988). Computable General Equilibrium Models for Trade Policy Analysis in Developing Countries: A Survey, *Journal of Policy Modeling*, 10(3), 469–503.

MaCurdy, T. (1981) An Empirical Model of Labor Supply in a Life-Cycle Setting, *Journal of Political Economy*, 89, 1059–1085.

McDonald, S. and K. Thierfelder (2004). Deriving a Global Social Accounting Matrix from GTAP Versions 5 and 6 Data, *GTAP Technical Paper No. 22*, Purdue University, https://www.gtap.agecon.purdue.edu/resources/tech_papers.asp.

Mas-Colell, A., M. D. Whinston, and J. R. Green (1995). *Microeconomic Theory*, New York: Oxford University Press, Inc.

Naastepad, C. W. M. (2002). Trade-offs in Stabilization: A Real-Financial CGE Analysis with Reference to India, *Economic Modelling*, 19(2), 221–244, March.

Pereira, A. M. and J. B. Shoven (1988). A Survey of Dynamic Computational General Equilibrium Models for Tax Evaluation, *Journal of Policy Modeling*, 10(3), 401–436.

Piggott, J. and J. Whalley (1985). *U.K. Tax Policy and Applied General Equilibrium Analysis*, NY: Cambridge University Press.

Pollack, R. A. and T. J. Wales (1992). *Demand System Specification and Estimation*, New York: Oxford University Press.

Pyatt, G. (1988). A SAM Approach to Modeling, *Journal of Policy Modeling*, 10(3), 327–352.

Robinson, S. and M. El-Said (2000). GAMS Code for Estimating a Social Accounting Matrix (SAM) using Cross Entropy (CE) Method, *TMD Discussion Paper No.64*, International Food Policy Research Institute, Washington, DC, December 2000, https://www.ifpri.org/publication/gams-code-estimating-social-accounting-matrix-sam-using-cross-entropy-methods-ce, retrieved Oct 10, 2021.

Robinson, S., Z. Wang, and W. Martin (2001). Capturing the Implications of Services Trade Liberalization, *Economic Systems Research*, 14(1), 3–33.

Robinson, S., A. Cattaneo, and M. El Said (2001). Updating and Estimating a Social Accounting Matrix Using Cross Entropy Methods, *Economic Systems Research*, 13(1), 47–64.

Robinson S., A. Y. Naude, R. H. Ojeda, J. D. Lewis, and S. Devarajan (1999). From Stylized Models: Building Multisector CGE Models for Policy Analysis, *North American Journal of Economics and Finance*, 10, 5–38.

Rosenthal, R. (2007). *GAMS — A User's Guide*, Washington, DC, USA: GAMS Development Corporation, accessed on December 2020 at https://www.un.org/en/development/desa/policy/mdg_workshops/training_material/gams_users_guide.pdf.

Scarf, H. E. and T. Hansen (1973). *The Computation of Economic Equilibria*, New Haven: Yale University Press.

Shoven, J. and J. Whalley (1992). *Journal of Economic Literature Applying General Equilibrium*, Cambridge University Press.

Shoven, J. B. and J. Whalley (1984). Applied General Equilibrium Models of Taxation and International Trade, *Journal of Economic Literature*, 22, 1007–1051.

Shoven, J. B. and J. Whalley (1973). General Equilibrium with Taxes: A Computational Procedure and an Existence Proof, *Review of Economic Studies*, 60, 281–321, October.

Stifel, D. C. and E. Thorbecke (2003). A Dual–Dual CGE Model of an Archetype African Economy: Trade Reform, Migration and Poverty, *Journal of Policy Modeling*, 25, 207–235.

Touze, V. *et al.* (2004). A World OLG-CGE Model with Imperfect Financial Markets, Exchange Rates and Stochastic Lifetime, EcoMod2004, No. 330600142, https://ecomod.net/sites/default/files/document-conference/ecomod2004/243.pdf.

United Nations (2008). *System of National Accounts* (SNA), https://unstats.un.org/unsd/nationalaccount/docs/sna2008.pdf, New York.

Varian, H. (1992). *Microeconomic Analysis*, New York: W. W. Norton & Company.

Wang Y., D. Xu, Z. Wang, and F. Zhai (2004). Options and Impact of China's Pension Reform: A Computable General Equilibrium Analysis, *Journal of Comparative Economics*, 32, 105–127.

Wang, Z. (2003). The Impact of China's WTO Accession on Pattern of World Trade, *Journal of Policy Modeling*, 25, 1–41.

World Bank (2005). *The LINKAGE Model*, Washington, DC: The World Bank, http://econ.worldbank.org/WBSITE/EXTERNAL/EXTDEC/EXTDECPROSPECTS/0,,contentMDK:20357492~menuPK:476941~pagePK:64165401~piPK:64165026~theSitePK:476883,00.html.

World Input–Output Database (WIOD) (2020). Brussels: European Commission, www.wiod.org.

Xu, D. and G. Chang (2000). Impact of Trade Liberalization on Structural Employment in China: A Computable General Equilibrium Analysis, *Pacific Economic Review*, 5(2), 157–167.

Index